ISBN: 9781313977876

Published by:
HardPress Publishing
8345 NW 66TH ST #2561
MIAMI FL 33166-2626

Email: info@hardpress.net
Web: http://www.hardpress.net

ELEMENTS

OF

MECHANICAL PHILOSOPHY,

BEING THE SUBSTANCE OF

A COURSE OF LECTURES

ON THAT

SCIENCE.

By JOHN ROBISON, LL.D.

PROFESSOR OF NATURAL PHILOSOPHY IN THE
UNIVERSITY OF EDINBURGH,
FELLOW OF THE ROYAL SOCIETY OF EDINBURGH,
OF THE IMPERIAL ACADEMY OF SCIENCES AT ST. PETERSBURGH,
AND OF THE PHILOSOPHICAL SOCIETIES OF MANCHESTER
AND NEW YORK, &c. &c.

VOLUME FIRST,

INCLUDING

DYNAMICS AND ASTRONOMY.

EDINBURGH:
Printed for
ARCHIBALD CONSTABLE & CO. EDINBURGH;
T. CADELL & W. DAVIES, AND
LONGMAN HURST REES & ORME,
LONDON.

1804.

D. Willison, Printer,
Craig's Close, Edinburgh.

ADVERTISEMENT.

THE following pages contain the fubftance of a Courfe of Lectures, which have been read by me during the annual feffions of the Colleges, ever fince the year 1774. Any perfon, well acquainted with Natural Philofophy muft be fenfible that, in the fhort fpace of a fix months feffion, juftice cannot be done to the various branches of this extenfive fcience. I found that I muft either treat in a loofe manner fubjects which require and admit of ftrict reafoning, or muft omit fome articles ufually taught in this clafs; and I was induced to prefer the latter method, becaufe I was of opinion that a loofer manner of proceeding is neither fuitable to the Inftitution in this Univerfity, nor calculated to convey ufeful knowledge. In one feffion I omitted the confideration of Magnetifm and Electricity, and in the next feffion thefe were treated of, and Optics was omitted.

a   But

But this plan was not always acceptable. I was therefore induced to print thefe Elements, in the hopes of being able to fhorten the lecture, and thus to include all the articles of the courfe. I fhall now think myfelf at liberty to lecture in a more popular manner, as the ftudent, by confulting the text-book, will find the demonftration of what was only fketched in the lecture of the day.

Such being the intention in this publication, the reader will fee in what refpects, and for what reafons, it may differ a little from a formal fyftem of Natural Philofophy. It is intended that it fhall contain a fyftem. But all the articles will not be treated with the fame minutenefs. The experience of thirty years has enabled me to judge what articles are more abftrufe or intricate, and require a more detailed difcuffion.

The general doctrines of Dynamics are the bafis of Mechanical Philofophy, diftinguifhing it from every other department of fcience. They are nearly abftract truths, containing the laws of human judgement concerning all thofe phenomena which we call mechanical. We fhall find thefe laws nearly as fimple and precife as the propofitions in geometry, and that they carry with them

a

a fimilar accuracy, wherever they can be properly applied. We fhall have the pleafure of feeing the complete fuccefs of this application, to very extenfive and important articles of the fcience.

Thefe doctrines being fo important, and fo fufceptible of accurate treatment, nothing is omitted here that is neceffary for their full eftablifhment; and hence this occafions the firft part of the courfe to be very minute and particular. But, afterwards, a more familiar mode of difcuffion may be admitted. If the ftudent make himfelf familiarly acquainted with the principles of Dynamics, it is hoped that he will find little difficulty afterwards, in the application of thefe abftract doctrines to the inveftigation of the laws of mechanical nature, or to the explanation of fubordinate phenomena. For this reafon, it is not intended to annex the mathematical demonftration to every propofition in the fubfequent parts of the courfe. This will not be omitted, however, when either the difficulty or importance of the fubject feems to require it.

The ftudent muft be mindful that this book will not fuperfede the neceffity of carefully attending to the lecture. Many things, illuftrative and interefting, will be heard in the clafs, which

have

have no place here. It will alfo contribute to his improvement, if he accuftom himfelf to take notes in the clafs ; and he is advifed to take particular notice of fuch formulæ, or other fymbols of mathematical reafoning, as occur in the lecture. Thefe will frequently give a compendious expreffion of a procefs of reafoning which he may otherwife find very difficult to remember with diftinctnefs.

In applying the abftract doctrine of Dynamics to the mechanical hiftory of nature, fome arrangement muft be adopted which may facilitate the tafk. It is propofed, in this courfe of lectures, to arrange the mechanical appearances as much as poffible in the order of their generality or extent. It will be found that this is, in fact, arranging them by the great diftinguifhing powers of natural fubftances, by which this generality of event is effected.

All the mechanical phenomena that we obferve are effected,

 1. By gravity.
 2. By cohefion.
 3. By magnetifm.
 4. By electricity.
 5. By the affections of light.

Hence

Hence is fuggefted the following arrangement of the articles which will be treated of in this courfe of lectures.

I. GRAVITY.

1. As it is feen in the celeftial motions—its law of action difcovered by Sir Ifaac Newton—applied by him, with great fuccefs, to the explanation of all the phenomena—univerfal gravitation.
2. As it is obferved on this globe—motion of falling bodies—of projectiles—theory of gunnery.

II. COHESION.

Corpufcular forces—Theory of Bofcovich.
Mechanical qualities of tangible matter—bodies are folid—or fluid—and thefe differ exceedingly in their mechanifm.

Mechanism of Solid Bodies.

Laws of the excitement of corpufcular forces.
1. Motion in free fpace—impulfion—direct —oblique—preceffion of the equinoxes— force of moving bodies.
2. Motion in conftrained paths.

3. Rotation—centrifugal force.
4. Solidity combined with gravity—ſtability —theory of arches and domes.
5. Motion on inclined planes.
6. Motion of pendulums—meaſure of gravity —meaſure of time.
7. Theory of machines—or MECHANICS commonly ſo called—mechanic powers—compound machines—maxims of conſtruction.
   Of friction.
   Of the action of ſprings.

Mechanism of Fluid Bodies.

1. Coherent fluids—HYDROSTATICS, treating of the preſſure and equilibrium of fluids— HYDRAULICS, treating of the motion, impulſe, and reſiſtance of fluids.
   Hydraulic machines.
   Conſtruction and working of ſhips.
2. Expanſive fluids—PNEUMATICS, treating of the preſſure of the air—its elaſticity—its motion, impulſe, and reſiſtance—Pneumatic machines—ſound—theory of muſic—action of gunpowder—theory of artillery, and of mines—account of the ſteam engine.

III.

III. Magnetism.

> General laws of the phenomena—theory of Æpinus—Gilbert's terreſtrial magnetiſm—mariner's compaſs—variation—dip of the needle—artificial magnetiſm.

IV. Electricity.

> General laws.
> Theory of Æpinus.
> Thunder—aurora borealis, &c.
> Galvanic phenomena.

V. Optics.

> Mathematical laws—catoptrics—dioptrics.
> Viſion—optical inſtruments.
> Newtonian diſcoveries concerning colours.
> Phyſical optics—further diſcoveries of Newton—mechanical nature of light—mutual action of bodies and light.
> Province, and hiſtory of natural philoſophy.

Edinburgh, *October* 31. 1804.

Page.	Line.			Page	Line.		
6	12	*c'*	C'	231	1	( )	(345)
	13	*c'*	C'	239	19	caculation	calculatio
9	8	AFB,*Fb*	AFB, *aFb*	326	10	*p n*	*p v n*
35	17	LKIH	LIH	333	17	to	of
	18	KICB, KHDB	LICB,LHDB	384	9	confidering	confider
	23	KC	IC	385	27	retre ts	retreat
47	11	*dg*	*e g*	394	26	*pollente*	*pollente*
	12	*v'*	*v*	395	9	are	is
	20	' P	AC	398	28	MP	MR
53	14	to *m*	from E to *m*	418	4	clotted	dotted
	15	*o*	*m*	449	12	PI	GI
63	14	ADV	ADO		13	PF—PG	PH—PI
64	17	AK	BK		16	PF'—PG'	PH'—PI'
73	23	ultimate	alternate	452	26	Fig 64.	Fig 64. N
75	2	*deflecting forces*	*deflections*	458	28	after P	(Fig.64.N
79	12	particel	particle	471	18	I *e* Q *q*	E *e* Q *q*
82	12	di ding	dividing	476	19	BDF	PDF
149	4	S	C		Note.	Boffuet	Boffut
153	28	equal,	equally	591	26	S	*s*
188	11	ACI	AEI	592	3	Cof.² 2 *x*	Cof 2 *x*
189	20	AEM	ACM	647	19	corrofponds	correfpor
190	12	MI	M*i*				

CORRECTIONS FOR THE FIGURES.

Figure.

9   Draw EQ.

37   Draw ED. The line ES was drawn (295.) perpendicular to IC. In fect. it is fuppofed to be perpendicular to *i* C. The two perpendiculars w not be diftinguifhable.

44   *e* fhould be *a*

46   Produce BS to M

52   Draw SN perpendicular to PN

64   D fhould be in the croffing of I *i* and *e q*

65   Draw A *p*

71   The upper S fhould be *s*

73   Infert G at the croffing of EQ and N *d* S

76   Write *f* to the left of F, on the outfide of all.

EXPLANATION OF SYMBOLS

USED IN THE FOLLOWING PAGES.

———

(a) THE fymbol $a \cdot : b$ expreffes the ratio or propor=
tion of a magnitude a to another magnitude b of the fame
kind, fuch as two lines, two furfaces, two weights, velocities, times, &c.

(b) $a : b = c : d.$ The ratio of a to b is equal to, or
is the fame with, that of c to $d.$—This is ufually read,
a *is to* b *as* c *to* d.

(c) $a\, b$ is the product of two numbers, or the rectangle of two lines, a and $b.$

(d) $a \doteqdot b$ is a fymbol made up of the fymbol : of
proportion, and the fymbol = of equality. It means that
a increafes or decreafes at the fame rate with b, fo that if b
become double or triple, &c. of its primitive value, the
contemporaneous a is alfo double, triple, &c. of its firft
value.

This

This is a fhort way of writing $A : a = B : b$, in which A and a are fucceffive values of one changeable magnitude, and B, b, the correfponding or fimultaneous values of the other. In this fymbol, a and b may be magnitudes of different kinds, which cannot hold with refpect to the fymbol $a : b$, becaufe there is no proportion between magnitudes of different kinds, as between a yard and a pound, an hour and a force, &c. This may be called the fymbol of a PROPORTIONAL EQUATION.

(*e*) $a\,b : c\,d$ expreffes the ratio compounded of the ratio of a to c and that of b to d. It therefore expreffes the ratio of the product of the numbers a and b to that of the numbers c and d. In like manner, it reprefents the proportion of two rectangles, a and b being the fides of the firft, and c and d the fides of the fecond. In the fame manner $a\,b\,c : d\,e\,f$ is the ratio compounded of thofe of a to d, of b to e, and of c to f; and fo on, of any number of ratios compounded together. (See Euclid, VI. 23.)

(*f*) $a : b = \frac{1}{c} : \frac{1}{d}$ means that a is to b in the inverfe proportion of c to d, or, that $a : b = d : c$. It is plain that if c be doubled or trebled, the fraction $\frac{1}{c}$ is reduced to one half or one third, &c. fo that $\frac{1}{c}$ or $\frac{1}{d}$ are increafed in the fame proportion that c or d are diminifhed.

(*g*)

(g) $a : b = \frac{c}{e} : \frac{d}{f}$ means that the ratio of a to b is the same with that of the fraction $\frac{c}{e}$ to the fraction $\frac{d}{f}$, or that the ratio of a to b is compounded of the direct ratio of c to d and the inverse or reciprocal ratio of e to f. It is the same with $a : b = cf : de$.

(h) $x \doteq \frac{1}{y}$ means that x increases at the same ratio that y diminishes, and is equivalent to $X : x = \frac{1}{Y} : \frac{1}{y}$, or equivalent to $X : x = y : Y$.

(i) $x \doteq \frac{y}{z}$ means that x varies in the ratio compounded of the direct ratio of y and the inverse ratio of z.

(k) $x' : y'$ expresses the proportion between the *difference* of two successive values of x and the *difference* of the two corresponding values of y. It is equivalent to the ratio of $X - x$ to $Y - y$.

(l)   Suppose that, in the continual variation of x and y, these simultaneous and corresponding differences are always in the same ratio; then $x' : y'$ is a constant ratio. Thus, Let A D and A F (fig. A) be two right lines diverging from A, and let B C, B c, B D, be successive values of x, and the parallel ordinates C E, c e, D F be corresponding values of y. Draw E G and e g parallel to A D, and consequently equal to C D and c D, then C D and G F are corresponding differences of the successive ceffive values of x and y. So are c D and g F. Now it is plain that $C D : G F = c D : g F$, and $x' : y'$ is a conftant ratio.

(m) But it more frequently happens that the ratio $x' : y'$ is not conftant. Thus, if the line E e F (fig. B) be an arch of a curve, fuch as a hyperbola, of which A is the centre, we know that C D has not the fame ratio to G F that c D has to g F, and that the ratio of x' to y' continually increafes as the point C or c approaches to D. We know that while C is above D, the ratio of C D to G F, or c D to g F is lefs than that of the fubtangent T D to the ordinate D F. But when c' gets below D, the ratio of E' G', or c' D, to G' F is greater than that of T D to D F ; and the difference of thefe ratios increafes, as c feparates from D on either fide. The ratio of x' to y', therefore, approximates to that of T D to D F as c approaches to D from either fide. For this reafon, the ratio of T D to D F has been called the *ultimate* ratio of the *evanefcent* magnitudes x' and y', as the magnitudes x' and y' are continually diminifhed, till both *vanifh* together, when c coalefces with D. If, again, we conceive the point C to fet out, either upward or downward, from D, the ratio T D : D F is called the *prime* ratio of the *nafcent* magnitudes x' and y'.

We know alfo that the ratio of the fubtangent t c to the ordinate c e is lefs than that of T D to D F, and that the ratio of the fubtangent to the ordinate increafes continually, as D is taken further from the vertex V of

the

the hyperbola. But we know alfo that it never is fo great as the ratio of A D to Df (the ordinate produced to the affymptote) but approaches nearer to it than by any difference that can be affigned. For this reafon, A D : Df has been called the *ultimate* ratio of the fubtangent and ordinate—in the fame manner, the ultimate ratio of D F to Df has been faid to be the ratio of e-quality.

(n) But, in thefe two cafes, the employment of the term *ultimate* is rather improper, becaufe this ratio is never attained. Perhaps the term *limiting* ratio, alfo given it by Sir Ifaac Newton, is more proper in both thefe cafes. T D : D F is the limiting ratio of x' : y', or the limit, to which the variable ratio of the nafcent, or, evanefcent magnitudes x' and y' continually approaches.

(o) Sir Ifaac Newton, the author of this way of confidering the variations of magnitude, has expreffed by a particular fymbol this limiting ratio of the variations x' and y'. He expreffes it by $\dot{x}$: $\dot{y}$. It is not the ratio of any x' to any y', however fmall, but the limit to which their ratio continually approaches. When we chance to employ the terms *ultimate* or *prime*, we defire to be underftood always to mean this limiting ratio. The foreign mathematicians employ the fymbol dx : dy, in which d means the infinitely or incomparably fmall difference between two fucceeding values of x or y.

We

We have been thus particular in defcribing this view of the variations of quantity, becaufe without a knowledge of fome of thofe limiting ratios, it is fcarcely poffible to advance in mechanical philofophy.

(p) The cafe already mentioned, namely $TD : DF = x' : y'$, occurs very frequently in our inveftigations.

And, in like manner, if the arch BF be reprefented by the fymbol z, we have $\dot{x} : \dot{z} = TD : TF$, and $\dot{y} : \dot{z} = DF : TF$.

Alfo, if Eϵ be drawn parallel to the tangent te, we have Ee to Eϵ ultimately in the ratio of equality. For, becaufe the triangles tce and E$d\epsilon$ are fimilar, we have $Ed : E\epsilon = tc : te$, that is, $= \dot{x} : \dot{\epsilon}$, that is, $= Cc : Ee$, or $Ed : Ee$, and therefore, ultimately, $E\epsilon = Ee$.

(q) Such limiting ratios may alfo be obtained in curves that are referred to a pole or focus, inftead of an abfciffa. Thus, let BFG (fig. C) be an ellipfe, whofe centre is C, and focus D. Let Fe be a very fmall arch of the curve. Draw DF and De, and about the pole D, with the diftance De, defcribe the circular arch Eeg, cutting FD in g. Draw the tangent FT, and DT perpendicular to DF. Now, reprefenting FD by x, FB by z, and the circular arch eE by y, it is plain that $\dot{x} : \dot{z} = FD : FT$, and $\dot{x} : \dot{y} = FD : DT$. All this is very evident, being demonftrated by the fame reafoning as in the cafe of the hyperbola referred to its axis or abfciffa (m).

(r)

(r) Another limiting ratio, of very frequent occurrence, is the following. Suppose two curves A B and ab (fig. D) round the same pole F, from which are drawn two right lines F A, F B, cutting both lines in A, a, B, and b. Let F B, by revolving round F, continually approach to F A. Let it come, for example, into the situation F c C very near to F A a. Let S and s represent the mixtilineal spaces A F B u F b. Then S' and s' may express the spaces A F C and a F c. It is plain that the limiting ratio of A F C to a F c is that of F A^2 to F a^2, and we may say that $S : s = F A^2 : F a^2$.

(s) The last example which shall be mentioned is of almost continual occurrence in our investigations.— Let F H K and fhk (fig. E) be two curves, having the abscissæ A E and $a e$. Let these abscissæ be divided into an equal number of small equal parts, such as A B, B C, D E and ab, bc, de; and let ordinates be drawn through the points of division. And on these ordinates, as bases, let parallelograms, such as A B L F, B C N G, &c. and $ablf$, $bcng$, &c. be inscribed, and others, such as A B G M, A C H O, and $abgm$, $acho$, &c. be circumscribed.—It is affirmed, $1st$, that if the subdivision be carried on without end, the mixtilineal areas A E K F and $aekf$ are, ultimately, in the ratio of equality to the sum of all the inscribed, or of all the circumscribed parallelograms ; and, $2dly$, that the ratio of the space A E K F to the space $aekf$ is the limiting ratio of the

B   sum

fum of all the parallelograms (infcribed or circumfcribed)
in A E K F to the fum of thofe in *a e k f.*

1*ſt*, Make D S and *d s* equal to A F and *af*, and
draw S R, *s r*, parallel to A E, *a e*. It is evident that
the parallelogram S R K Q is equal to the excefs of all
the circumfcribed over all the infcribed parallelograms.
Therefore, by continuing the fubdivifion of A E without end, this parallelogram may be made fmaller than
any fpace that can be affigned. Therefore the infcribed
and circumfcribed parallelograms are ultimately in the
ratio of equality—or equality is their limiting ratio. The
fpace A E K F is greater than all the infcribed, and lefs
than all the circumfcribed parallelograms, and is nearly
the half fum of both. Therefore, much more accurately
is equality the limiting or ultimate ratio of A E K F to
either fum. The fame muft be true of the other figure.

2*dly*, Since each mixtilineal figure is ultimately equal
to its parallelograms, it is plain that both have the fame
ratio with the fums of the parallelograms.

(*t*) *Cor.* If the ordinates which are drawn through
fimilarly fituated points of the two abfciffæ, be in a conftant ratio, the areas are in the ratio compounded of the
ratio of A E to *a e*, and that of A F to *af*, or are as
A E × A F to *a e* × *af*. This is evident. For, by the
fuppofition, C N : *c n* = A F : *af*. And, fince the number
of parallelograms is the fame in both figures, B C and
b c are fimilar parts of A E and *a e* ; that is, B C : *b c* =
A E : *a e*. Therefore B C N G : *b c n g* = A E × A F : *a e*
                                                   × *af*.

$\times af$. Since this is true of every correfponding pair of parallelograms, it is true of their fums, and of the mixtilineal fpaces A E K F and $aekf$, which are ultimately equal to thofe fums.

(u) It may be thought that in thefe cafes where the limiting ratio is not an ultimate ratio actually attained, there remains fome fmall error. The foreign mathematicians feem to acquiefce in this, and content themfelves with affuming dx or dy as infinitely fmall; inferring from thence that the remaining error is infinitely fmall, fo that it will not amount to a fenfible quantity, though multiplied by any number, however great. But this conceffion leads them *neceffarily* into the fuppofition of quantities infinitely fmaller than quantities already affumed as infinitely fmall; a fuppofition plainly abfurd or unintelligible. But no error whatever lurks in this method of limiting ratios. For it is all founded on the following unqueftionable axiom.

(v) If the ratio of a to b be greater than *any ratio whatever* that is lefs than the ratio of c to d, but lefs than *any ratio whatever* which is greater than that of c to d, then a is to b as c is to d.

For if a be not to b as c to d, let a be to b as m to n. Then if $m:n$ be greater than $c:d$, $a:b$ is lefs than $m:n$. If $m:n$ be lefs than $c:d$, then $a:b$ is greater than $m:n$, both which confequences are contrary to the conditions affumed. Therefore $a:b$ *muft* be $c:d$.

The

The propofition (s) may be demonſtrated in this way. The ſpace A E K F is to a e k f in a greater ratio than that of the parallelograms infcribed in the firſt to thofe circumfcribed on the fecond, but in a lefs ratio than that of the parallelograms circumfcribed on the firſt to thofe infcribed in the fecond. We perceive, by continuing the ſubdiviſion of the two abfciffæ, that this holds true with regard to *every* ratio that is either greater or lefs than that of A E K F to a e k f. Thus, the propofition is demonſtrated without the fmalleſt room for error.

(w) This doctrine of limiting ratios is of the greateſt fervice in the phyfico-mathematical fciences. Nature prefents magnitudes in a continual change. The velocity of a falling body, and the line of its fall, are increafing together.—As a piece of iron approaches a magnet, its diftance, its velocity, and the force by which it is urged, all vary together, and there is an indiffoluble relation between their refpective fimultaneous variations. Thefe variations alfo are the immediate meafures of their *rates* of variation. Hence it is plain that, by knowing thefe rates, we can learn the whole change, and by obferving the whole change we can infer the rate of variation ; juft as the navigator learns his day's progrefs by heaving the log every hour, in order to difcover the fhip's *rate* of failing, and converfely.

(x) The letters F, V, T, &c. will be ufed to exprefs Force, Velocity, Time, and other magnitudes. Thus, F, A

F, A expreſſes the force acting in the point A. F, A B is the force acting along the line A B.

(y) A proper notation, and arrangement of the ſymbols, greatly aſſiſt our conceptions in mathematical reaſoning. When ratios are compounded (a thing perpetually occurring in our diſquiſitions) it is extremely convenient to recollect that the ratio, which is compounded of many numerical ratios, is the ſame with that of the product of all the antecedents to the product of all the conſequents.

Thus, if $\qquad a : b = c : d$

and $\qquad e : f = g : h$

and $\qquad i : k = l : m$

and $\qquad n : o = p : q$

then $a\, e\, i\, n : b\, f\, k\, o = c\, g\, l\, p : d\, h\, m\, q.$

If we uſe lines, we can go no farther without ſubſtitutions than three ſuch compoſitions, becauſe ſpace has but three dimenſions. All our practical uſes of the doctrines muſt be proſecuted by means of arithmetical calculations, although ſome linear ratios, ſuch as that of the diameter of a circle to its circumference, or that of the diagonal of a ſquare to its ſide, cannot be accurately expreſſed by numbers. But, as we know perfectly what ſubſtitutions may be made in every caſe where more than three ratios are compounded, ſo as to obtain accurate ratios, no mathematician objects to this method of merely expreſſing the compoſition.

M E.

MECHANICAL PHILOSOPHY.

INTRODUCTION.

1. MAN is induced by an inftinctive principle, im-
planted in his mind by the Author of Nature, to confider
every change obferved in the condition of things as an
EFFECT, indicating the agency, characterifing the kind,
and meafuring the degree of its CAUSE.

2. The kind and degree of the caufe are, therefore,
inferred from the *obferved* kind and degree of the change
which we confider as its effect.

3. The appearances in the material world, exhibited
in the *changes of motion* which we obferve, are called
MECHANICAL APPEARANCES, or PHENONEMA, and the
caufes, to the agency of which we afcribe them, are called MECHANICAL CAUSES.

4. MECHANICAL PHILOSOPHY is the ftudy of the
mechanical phenomena of the univerfe, in order to difcover their caufes, and by their means to explain fubordinate

dinate phenomena, and to improve arts, and thus increafe man's power over nature.

This definition of the ftudy points out Motion, with all its affections and varieties, as the objects of our firft attention, a knowledge of thefe being indifpenfably neceffary for perceiving and appreciating its changes, from which alone we are to derive all our knowledge of their caufes, the mechanical powers of nature.

OF MOTION.

5. In motion we obferve the *fucceffive* appearance of the thing moved in *different* parts of fpace. Therefore, in our idea of Motion are involved the ideas or conceptions of SPACE and of TIME.

6. Space is conceived by us as a quantity, that is, it may be conceived as great or little. It is one of that fmall clafs of quantities of which we have the cleareft and moft diftinct conceptions. We conceive them as magnitudes made up of their own diftinguifhable parts, and meafurable by one of thefe as a unit. We cannot conceive fo clearly of heat, or preffure, or many other things which are magnitudes, capable of increafe and diminution, but not diftinguifhable into feparate parts.

7. In our fimpleft conception of fpace, it is mere extenfion ; we think of nothing but a diftance between two places. This is the moft ufual conception of it in mechanical

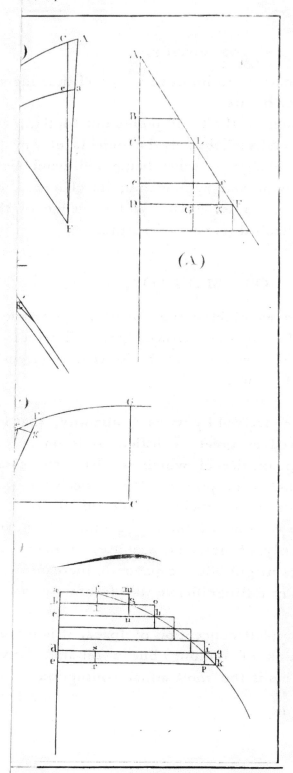

(A)

Pl. 6.

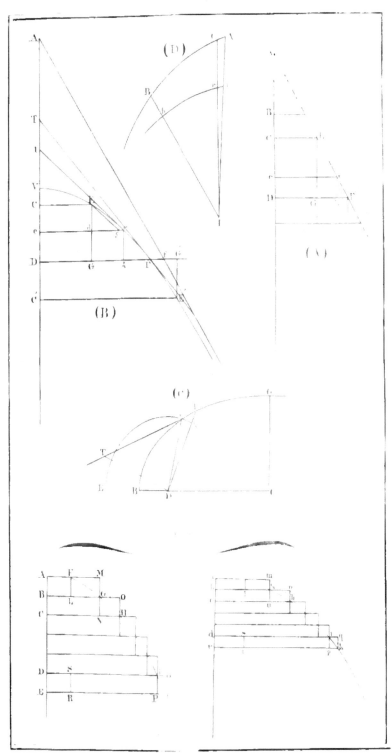

mechanical difquifitions—the path along which a thing moves; and we fay, figuratively, that the thing *defcribes* this path.

But the geometer confiders fpace as having not only length, but alfo breadth, and he then calls it a *furface*; and, in order to have a complete notion of the capacioufnefs of a portion of fpace, he confiders not only its length and breadth, but alfo its thicknefs—and fuch fpace he calls a *folid fpace*. But, by folid, he means nothing but the fufceptibility of meafure in three ways. He calls it extenfion of three dimenfions.

But, in pure mechanics, we feldom have occafion to confider more than one dimenfion of fpace.—In our inveftigations, however, we make ufe of geometrical reafonings, which include both furfaces and folids—but our reafoning always terminates in a mechanical theorem, of which diftance alone is the fubject.

8. The adjoining parts or portions of fpace are diftinguifhed or feparated from one another by their mutual boundaries. Contiguous portions of a line are feparated by points—contiguous portions of a furface are feparated by lines—and contiguous portions of a folid are feparated by furfaces.

9. Thefe boundaries are not parts of the contiguous portions of fpace, but are common to both. They are the places where the one portion of fpace ends, and the other begins. It is of importance to have very clear

C

notions

notions of this diftinction, for great miftakes have arifen in mechanical difcuffions by not attending to it.

10. We cannot conceive fpace as having any bounds, and it is therefore faid to be infinite, or unbounded.

11. A portion of fpace may be confidered in relation to its fituation among other portions. This may be called the RELATIVE PLACE of the Body which occupies this portion of fpace. It may alfo be called its SITUATION.

Or it may be confidered as a determinate portion of infinite fpace, the individuality or identity of which confifts entirely in its being *there*. This is called the ABSOLUTE PLACE of the body which occupies this portion of infinite fpace.—It is plain that in this fenfe, fpace is immoveable—that is, we cannot conceive this identical portion of fpace as removed from where it is, to another place—for whatever be taken from thence, fpace remains. Yet we always proceed on the contrary fuppofition in our actual meafurements. If we find that three applications of a foot rule to one line completely exhauft it, and that fix applications are required for another line, we affirm that the laft is double of the firft. But this really proceeds on another fuppofition, viz. *that the rule, though it do not always occupy the fame fpace, yet, in every fituation, it occupies an equal fpace.* Granting this, the conclufion is juft. It will afterwards appear that this remark on the immobility of fpace is of importance in mechanical difcuffions.

12. We do not perceive the abfolute place of any ob-ject.—A perfon in the cabin of a fhip does not confider the table as changing its place while it remains faftened to the fame plank of the deck. Few perfons think that a mountain changes its place while it is obferved to re-tain the fame fituation among other objects. On the other hand, moft men think that the ftars are continually changing their places, although we have no proof of it, and the contrary is almoft certain.

13. We acquire our notions of time by our faculty of memory, in obferving the fucceffions of events.

14. Time is conceived by us as unbounded, conti-nuous, homogeneous, unchangeable in the order of its parts, and divifible without end.

15. The boundaries between fucceffive portions of time may be called INSTANTS, and minute portions of it may be called *moments.*

16. Time is conceived as a proper quantity, made up of, and meafured by, its own parts. In our actual mea-furements, we employ fome event, which we imagine always to require an equal time for its accomplifhment; and this time is employed as a unit of time or duration, in the fame manner as we employ a foot rule as a unit of extenfion. As often as this event is accomplifhed du-ring fome obferved operation, fo often do we imagine

that

that the time of the operation contains this unit. It is thus that we affirm that the time of a heavy body falling 144 feet, is thrice as great as the time of falling 16 feet ; becaufe a pendulum 39¼ inches long makes three vibrations in the firft cafe, and one in the laft.

17. There is an analogy between the affections of fpace and time fo obvious, that, in moft languages, the fame words are ufed to exprefs the affections of both.— Hence it is that time may be reprefented by lines, and meafured by motion ; for uniform motion is the fimpleft fucceffion of events that can be conceived.

18. All things are placed in fpace, in the order of fituation.—All events happen in time, in the order of fucceffion.

19. No motion can be conceived as inftantaneous. For, fince a moveable, in paffing from the beginning to the end of its path, paffes through the intermediate points ; to fuppofe the motion along the moft minute portion of the path inftantaneous, is to fuppofe the moveable in every intervening point at the fame inftant.— This is inconceivable, or abfurd.

20. ABSOLUTE MOTION is the change of abfolute place. RELATIVE MOTION is the change of fituation among other objects. Thefe may be different, and even contrary

21. The relative motions of things are the differences of their abfolute motions, and cannot, of themfelves, tell us what the abfolute motions are. The detection and determination of the abfolute motions, by means of obfervations of the relative motions, are often tafks of great difficulty.

22. Mathematical knowledge is indifpenfably requifite for the fuccefsful ftudy of mechanical philofophy. On the other hand, the confideration of motion, in all its varieties of fpace, direction, and time, is purely mathematical, and carries with it, into all fubjects, the moft incontrovertible evidence.

23. Motion is fufceptible of varieties in refpect of *quantity* and of *direction.*

24. That affection of motion which determines its quantity, is called VELOCITY. Its moft proper meafure is the length of the line uniformly defcribed during fome given unit of time. Thus, the velocity of a fhip is afcertained, when we fay that fhe fails at the rate of fix miles per hour.

25. The DIRECTION of a motion is the pofition of the ftraight line along which it is performed. A motion is faid to be in the direction A B (fig. 1.) when the thing moved paffes along that line *from* A *towards* B. In common difcourfe we frequently exprefs the direction otherwife.

wife. Thus we fay a wefterly wind, although it moves eaftward.

26. In rectilineal motion, the direction remains the fame, during the whole time of the motion.

27. But if the motion be performed along two contiguous ftraight lines A B, B C (fig. 2.) in fucceffion, the direction is changed in the point B. From B *c*, the prolongation of A B, it is changed to B C.

This change may be called DEFLECTION; and this deflection may be meafured, either by the angle *c* B C, or by a line *c* C drawn from the point *c*, to which the moveable would have arrived, had its motion remained unchanged, to the point C, at which it actually arrives in the fame time.

When a moveable defcribes the fides of a polygon, there are repeated deflections, with undeflected motions intervening.

28. But if the motion be performed along a curve line, fuch as A D B E C (fig. 3.) the direction is *continually* changing. The direction in the point B is that of the tangent B T, that direction alone lying between *any* pair of polygonal directions, fuch as B C and B *c*, or B D and B E, however near we take the points A and C, or D and E, to the point B.

29. A curvilineal motion fuppofes the deviation and

deflection

deflection to be continual, and a continual deflection conſtitutes a curvilineal motion.

1. *Of Uniform Motions.*

30. In our general conceptions of motion, in which we do not attend to its alterations, the motion is ſuppoſed to be equable and rectilineal ; and it is only by the deviations from ſuch motion that we are to obtain the marks and meaſures of all changes, and therefore of all changing cauſes, that is, of the mechanical powers of nature. Let us therefore fix the characters of uniform or unchanged motion.

31. *In uniform motions, the velocities are in the proportions of the ſpaces deſcribed in the ſame, or in equal times.*

For theſe ſpaces are the meaſures of the velocities, and things are in the proportion of their meaſures.

Let S and *s* repreſent the ſpaces deſcribed in the time T, and let V and *v* repreſent the velocities. We have the analogy $V : v = S : s$. This may be expreſſed by the proportional equation $v \doteq s$.

32. *In uniform motions with equal velocities, the times are in the proportion of the ſpaces deſcribed. during their currency.*

For, in uniform motions, equal ſpaces are deſcribed in equal times. Therefore the ſucceſſive portions of time

are

are equal, in which equal fpaces are fucceffively defcribed, and the fums of the equal times muft have the fame
proportion as the correfponding fums of equal fpaces.
Therefore, in all cafes that can be reprefented by numbers, the propofition is evident. This may be extended
to all other cafes, in the fame way that Euclid demonftrates that triangles of equal altitude are in the proportion of their bafes.

33. Thefe propofitions are often expreffed thus :
" *The velocities are proportional to the fpaces defcribed in*
" *equal times.—The times are proportional to the fpaces de-*
" *fcribed with equal velocities.* " Proportion fubfifts only
between quantities of the fame kind.—But nothing more
is meant by thefe inaccurate expreffions, than that the
proportions of the velocities and times are the fame with
the proportions of the fpaces.

34. It is on this authority that uniform motion is
univerfally employed as a meafure of time.—But it is
not eafy to difcover whether a motion which may be propofed for the meafure is really uniform—fandglafs—
clepfydra—fundial—clock—revolution of the ftarry heavens.

35. *In uniform motions, the fpaces defcribed are in the*
ratio compounded of the ratio of the velocities and the ratio
of the times.
Let the fpace S be defcribed with the velocity V, in
the time T, and let the fpace s be defcribed with the velocity

locity *v*, in the time *t*.   Let another fpace Z be defcribed
in the time T with the velocity *v*.

Then, by art. 31, we have S : Z = V : *v*

And, by art. 32,   Z : *s* = T : *t*

Therefore, by compofition of ratios (or by VI. 23. Eucl.)
we have = V × T : *v* × *t* = S × Z : *s* × Z ;   that is,
= S : *s*.

36.   This is frequently exprefled thus :   " *The fpaces*
" *defcribed with a uniform motion are proportional to the*
" *products of the times and the velocities.* "——Or thus :

37.   " *The fpaces defcribed with a uniform motion are*
" *proportional to the rectangles of the times and the veloci-*
" *ties.*"

Thefe are all equivalent expreffions, demonftrated by
the fame compofition of ratios.   By products or rectangles of the times and velocities, is meant the products
of numbers, which are as the times, multiplied by numbers, which are as the velocities ; or the rectangle, whofe
bafes are as the times, and whofe heights are as the velocities.——There are feveral other modes of expreffing
thefe propofitions.

58.   *Cor.* 1.   *If the fpaces defcribed in two uniform mo-*
tions be equal, the velocities are in the reciprocal proportion
of the times.

For, in this cafe, the products V T and *v t* are equal,
and therefore V : *v* = *t* : T, or V : *v* = $\frac{1}{T} : \frac{1}{t}$.   Or, be-

D   caufe

caufe the rectangles A C, D F (fig. 4.) are in this cafe equal, we have (by Eucl. VI. 14.) A B : B F = B D : B C, that is $V : v = t : T$.

39. *In uniform motions, the times are as the fpaces, directly, and as the velocities, inverfely.*

For, by art. 35, $\quad S : s = V T : v t$

therefore $\qquad\qquad S v t = s V T$

and $\qquad\qquad\qquad T : t = S v : s V$

or $\qquad\qquad\qquad\quad T : t = \dfrac{S}{V} : \dfrac{s}{v}$

and $\qquad\qquad\qquad\quad t \,\dot{=}\, \dfrac{s}{v}$

40. *In uniform motions, the velocities are as the fpaces, directly, and as the times, inverfely.*

For, as before, $\quad S v t = s V T$

therefore $\qquad\qquad V : v = S t : s T$

or $\qquad\qquad\qquad\quad V : v = \dfrac{S}{T} : \dfrac{s}{t}$

and $\qquad\qquad\qquad\quad v \,\dot{=}\, \dfrac{s}{t}$

41. It is evident that the abfolute magnitudes of the fpace and time do not change the values of the refults of thefe propofitions, provided both are changed in the fame ratio. The value of $\dfrac{20 \text{ feet}}{40''}$, or of $\dfrac{6 \text{ feet}}{12''}$, is the fame with $\frac{1}{2}$ of a foot per fecond. Therefore, if s' be taken to exprefs an extremely minute portion of fpace defcribed with this velocity in the minute portion of time t',

t', we ftill have the velocity v accurately expreffed by $\frac{s'}{t'}$. Alfo $\frac{s'}{v}$ is the accurate expreffion of the time t'.

2. *Of Variable Motions.*

42. It rarely happens that the phenomena of nature prefent to our obfervation motions perfectly uniform. Yet we diftinctly conceive them, with all their properties ; and the deviations from thefe are the only marks and meafures of the variations, and, therefore, of the changing caufes. Therefore it is plain, that it is of the firft importance that all thefe deviations be thoroughly underftood.

43. If a body continue to move uniformly in the fame direction, its motion, or condition in refpect to motion, is unchanged. Its condition, therefore, muft be allowed to be the fame in any two portions of its path, however diftant they may be. The difference of place does not imply any change, becaufe a change of place is involved in the very conception of motion. If, therefore, two bodies be moving with the fame velocity in this path, or in two lines parallel to it, their condition in refpect of motion muft be allowed to be the fame. They have the fame direction, and move at the fame rate. No circumftance, therefore, feems to enter into our conception of the ftate of a body, in refpect of motion, except its velocity and its direction. Changes in one

or

or both of thefe circumftances conftitute all the changes
of which this condition is fufceptible. We fhall firft
confider changes of velocity.

Of Accelerated and Retarded Motions.

44. Every one is fenfible that a falling ftone is carried downward with greater rapidity in every fucceffive
moment of its fall. During the firft fecond of its fall,
we know that it falls 16 feet; during the next, it falls
48; during the third, it falls 80; during the fourth,
112; and fo on : falling, during every fecond, 32 feet
more than during the preceding.

Such a motion is, with propriety, called an ACCE-
LERATED MOTION. On the contrary, an arrow fhot perpendicularly upward is obferved to rife with a motion
continually RETARDED. Thefe bodies are therefore conceived to be in *different* ftates of motion in every fucceeding inftant. The velocity of the falling body is conceived to be greater in a certain inftant than in any preceding inftant. Mechanicians fay that when it has fallen
144 feet, its velocity is thrice as great as when it has
fallen only 16 feet. But it is plain that this inference
cannot be made *directly*, from a comparifon of the fpaces
defcribed in the following moments; for in thefe, it
falls 112 and 48 feet : nor from the fpaces defcribed in
the moments immediately preceding; for in thefe, the
body fell 80 and 16 feet. The affertion however fuppofes that this variable condition, called Velocity, is fuf-
                                                    ceptible

ceptible of an accurate meafure in every inftant, although
in no moment, however fhort, does the body defcribe
uniformly a fpace which may be taken as the meafure of
its velocity at the beginning of that moment. The fpace
defcribed in any moment is too great for meafuring the
velocity at the beginning of the moment, and too fmall
for the meafure of the velocity at the end of it. Yet
its mechanical condition is not known till we obtain fuch
a meafure.

In a motion, like this, *continually* accelerated, there
can be no fuch meafure. In an inftant, no fpace is defcribed, for this requires time. But the body has, in
that inftant, what may be called a POTENTIAL VELOCITY,
a certain DETERMINATION, however imperfectly conceived by us, which, if not changed, would caufe it to
defcribe, and would be indicated by its actually defcribing, a certain fpace uniformly, during a certain affignable portion of time. At another inftant, it has another
determination, by which, if not changed, another fpace
would be uniformly defcribed in the fame, or an equal
portion of time. It is in the difference of thofe two
determinations that its difference of mechanical ftate confifts. The fpaces which would thus be uniformly defcribed, are the marks and meafures of thofe determinations, and muft therefore be fought for with the moft
fcrupulous care, as the meafures of thofe velocities ; and
the proportions of thofe fpaces muft be taken as the proportions of the velocities. This refearch is effected by
the following propofition.

45.

45. Let the ftraight line A B D (fig. 5.) be defcribed with a motion any how *continually* varied, and let it be required to determine the proportion of the velocity in the point A to the velocity in any other point C.

Let the right line *a b d* reprefent the time of this motion along the path A D, fo that the points *a*, *b*, *c*, *d*, may mark the inftants of the moveable's being in A, B, C, D, and the portions *a b*, *b c*, *c d*, may exprefs the times of defcribing A B, B C, C D, that is, may be in the proportion of thofe times. Moreover, let *a e*, perpendicular to *a d*, exprefs the velocity of the moveable at the inftant *a*, or in the point A.

Let *e g h* be a line, fo related to the axis *a d*, that the areas *a b f e*, *b c g f*, *c d h g*, comprehended between the ordinates *a e*, *b f*, *c g*, *d h*, all perpendicular to *a d*, may be proportional to the fpaces A B, B C, C D, defcribed in the times *a b*, *b c*, *c d*, and let this relation obtain in every part of the figure.

It is then affirmed that the velocity in A is to the velocity in B, or C, or D, as *a e* to *b f*, or *c g*, or *d h*, &c. In other words,

If the abfciffa a d *of a curve* e g h *be proportional to the time of any motion, and the areas interrupted by parallel ordinates be proportional to the fpaces defcribed, the velocities are proportional to thofe ordinates.*

Make *b c* and *c d* equal, fo as to reprefent very fmall and equal moments of time, and make *p a* equal to one of them, and complete the rectancle *p a e q*. This will reprefent the fpace uniformly defcribed in the moment

p a,

p a, with the velocity *a e* (35.) Let P A be the portion of the fpace thus uniformly defcribed in the moment *p a*. Let the lines *i m*, *k n*, parallel to *a d*, make the rectangles *b c m i* and *c d n k*, refpectively equal to the areas *b c g f* and *c d h g*.

If the motions along the fpaces P A and B C had been uniform, their velocities would have been proportional to the fpaces defcribed (31.), becaufe the times *p a* and *b c* are equal. That is, the velocity in A would be to the velocity in C, as the rectangle *p a e q* to the area *b c g f*, that is, as *p a e q* to *b c m i*, that is, as the bafe *a e* to the bafe *c m*, becaufe the altitudes *p a* and *b c* are equal.

But the motion along B C is not reprefented here as uniform. For the line *f g h* diverges from the axis *b d*, the ordinate *c g* being greater than *b f*. Therefore the fpaces, which are meafured by thofe areas, increafe fafter than the times, and the figure reprefents an accelerated motion. Therefore the velocity with which B C would be uniformly defcribed during the moment *b c*, is lefs than the velocity at the end of that moment, that is, at the inftant *c*, or in the point C of the path. It muft therefore be reprefented and meafured by a line greater than *c m*.

We prove, in the fame manner that *c k* reprefents and meafures the velocity with which C D would be uniformly defcribed during the moment *c d*. Therefore, fince the motion along C D is alfo accelerated, the velocity at the beginning of that moment is lefs than the velocity with which it would be uniformly defcribed in the

fame

fame time, and muſt be reprefented by a line leſs than
c k.

Therefore the velocity in A is to that in C in a leſs
ratio than that of *a e* to *c m*, but in a greater ratio
than that of *a e* to *c k*. But, in this example, as long
as the inſtant *b* is prior and *d* poſterior, to the inſtant *c*,
c m is leſs, and *c k* is greater, than *c g*. Therefore the
velocity in A is to that in C in a ratio that is greater
than any ratio leſs than that of *a e* to *c g*, but leſs than
any ratio greater than that of *a e* to *c g*. And, confequently, the velocity in A is to that in C as *a e* to *c g*.
(Symb. (*v*)

Since this can be proved in the fame manner with
refpect to the velocity in any other point D, the propoſition is demonſtrated.

It is plain that the reaſoning would have been preciſely the fame, had the motion along B C D been retarded.

46. *Cor.* 1. *The velocities in different points of the*
path A D *are in the ultimate ratio of the fpaces deſcribed*
in equal fmall moments of time. For, drawing *g o* parallel
to *a d*, the velocity in the inſtant *a* is to that in the inſtant *c* as *a e* to *c g*, that is, as the rectangle *p e* to the
rectangle *c o*, that is, as *p a e q* to *c d h g* very nearly.
As the moments are diminiſhed, the difference *g o h* between the rectangle *c g o d* and *c g h d*, diminiſhes, nearly in the duplicate ratio of the moment; fo that if the
moment be taken $\frac{1}{2}$, $\frac{1}{3}$, or $\frac{1}{4}$ of *c d*, the error *g o h* is reduced.

duced to $\frac{1}{4}$, or $\frac{1}{9}$, or $\frac{1}{16}$. The ultimate ratio of $c\ g\ o\ d$ to $c\ g\ h\ d$ is plainly the ratio of equality, and the corollary is manifeft. That is, the velocity in A is to that in C in the ultimate ratio of P A to B C defcribed in equal fmall moments.

47. It often happens that we cannot afcertain this ultimate ratio, although we can meafure the fpaces defcribed in very fmall moments. We are then obliged to take thefe as meafures of the velocity. The error is reduced almoft to nothing, if we take the half fum of the fpaces B C and C D for the meafure of the velocity in the point C; or, which is the fame thing, if we take B C for the meafure of the velocity in the middle of the moment $b\ c$. For the fpaces B C and C D are meafured by the areas $b\ f\ g\ c$ and $c\ g\ h\ d$, which is very nearly equal to the rectangle $b\ t\ o\ d$. Now $b\ c\ g\ t$, or $c\ d\ o\ g$, is the half of it; and it is evident by this propofition, that the velocity in A is to that in C, as the rectangle $p\ a\ e\ q$ to the rectangle $b\ c\ g\ t$, or $c\ d\ o\ g$.

48. *Cor.* 2. *The momentary increments of the fpaces defcribed are in the ratio compounded of the ratio of the velocities and the ultimate ratio of the moments.*

For the increments P A, C D, are as the rectangles $p\ e$ and $c\ o$ ultimately (35.); and thefe are in the ratio compounded of the ratio of the bafe $a\ e$ to the bafe $d\ o$, and the ultimate ratio of the altitude $p\ a$ to the altitude $c\ d$. This may be exprefled by the proportional equation; $\dot{s} = v\ \dot{t}$.

E

49. Confequently $v \doteq \frac{\dot{s}}{\dot{t}}$, and $\dot{t} \doteq \frac{\dot{s}}{v}$. The equation $\dot{s} \doteq v \, \dot{t}$, $v \doteq \frac{\dot{s}}{\dot{t}}$, and $\dot{t} \doteq \frac{\dot{s}}{v}$ feem to be the fame
with thofe in art. 41. But, in art. 41, the fmall fpace s'
was defcribed uniformly, and the equations were abfolute. In the articles 48. and 49. $\dot{s}$ does not reprefent a
fpace uniformly defcribed. But $\dot{s} : \dot{s}$ expreffes the ultimate ratio of S' to s', when they are diminifhed continually, and vanifh together. The meaning of the equa-
tion $\dot{s} \doteq v \, \dot{t}$ therefore is, that the ultimate ratio of S' to
s' is the fame with that of V T' to $v \, t'$.

50. The converfe of this propofition may be thus expreffed :

If the abfciffa a d *of the line* e f h *reprefent the time
of a motion along the line* A B D, *and if the ordinates* a c,
b f, c g, *&c. be as the velocities in the points* A, B, C,
&c. then the areas are as the fpaces defcribed. This is
moft expeditioufly demonftrated, indirectly, thus :

If the fpaces A B, A D be not proportional to the
areas $a \, b \, f \, e$, $a \, d \, h \, e$, they muft be proportional to fome
other areas $a \, b \, f' \, e$, $a \, d \, h' \, e$, of another line $e \, f' \, h'$, paffing through e. But, if fo, then, by art. 45, the velocity
in A is to that in B as $a \, e$ to $b \, f'$. But the velocity in
A was ftated to that in B as $a \, e$ to $b \, f$. Therefore $a \, e :$
$b \, f = a \, e : b \, f'$, which is abfurd. Therefore, &c.

51. The only immediate obfervation that we can
make on thefe variable motions is the relation between
the

the space defcribed and the time which elapfes. The preceding propofitions teach us how to infer from this relation the mechanical condition of the body, to which condition we have given the name Velocity, which, however, more properly denominates the effect and meafure of this condition or determination.

The fame inference may be made in another way. Inftead of taking the uniform motion along a line to reprefent the uniform lapfe of time, Sir Ifaac Newton often reprefents it by the uniform increafe of an area during the motion along the line taken for the abfciffa. The velocities, or determinations to motion in the different points of this line, will be found inverfely proportional to the ordinates of the curve which bounds this area.

Thus, let a point move along the ftraight line A D (fig. 6.) with a motion any how continually changed, and let the curve L K I H be fo related to A D that the area K I C B is to the area K H D B as the time of moving along B C to that of moving along B D; and let this be true in every point of the line A D. Let C c, D d be two very fmall fpaces defcribed in equal times, draw the ordinates i c, h d, and draw i k, h l perpendicular to K C, H D.

It is evident that the areas I C c i and H D d h are equal, becaufe they reprefent equal moments of time. It is alfo plain that as the fpaces C c and D d are continually diminifhed, the ratio of I C c i and H D d h to the rectangles k C c i and l D d h continually approaches to that of equality, and that the ratio of equality is the limiting or

E 2   ultimate

ultimate ratio. Therefore, fince the areas I C c i and H D d h are equal, the rectangles k C c i and l D d h are ultimately in the ratio of equality. Therefore their bafes i c and h d are inverfely as their altitudes C c and D d, that is, i c : h d = D d : C c. But C c and D d being defcribed in equal times, are ultimately as the velocities in e and d (46). Therefore i c and h d are inverfely as the velocities in c and d. Becaufe this may be fimilarly demonftrated in refpect of every point of the abfciffa, the propofition is demonftrated.

52. It now appears that in all cafes in which we can difcover by obfervation the relation between the fpaces defcribed and the times elapfed during the defcription, we difcover the velocities and the mechanical condition of the moveable. To make any practical application of our conclufions, we muft always have recourfe to arithmetical calculations. Thefe are indicated by the algebraic fymbols of our geometrical reafonings. We reprefent any ordinate c g of fig. 5. by v, and the portion c d of the abfciffa by i, and the area c d h g, or rather, its equal, the rectangle c d o g, by v i. And fince this rectangle is as the correfponding portion C D of the line of motion, and C D is reprefented by i, we have the equation $i = v\, i$.

We may now affume as true, all the mathematical confequences of thefe reprefentations. Therefore $i = \frac{i}{v}$, as in art. 41. For the algebraic fymbols are the reprefentations of arithmetical operations, and they reprefent

the

the operations of geometry more remotely, and only becaufe the area of a rectangle is analogous to the product
of numbers which are proportioned to its fides. If we
ufe the fymbol $\int v \, i$ to reprefent the fum of all thefe
rectangles, it will exprefs the whole area $a\,d\,h\,e$, and
will alfo exprefs the whole line of motion A D, and we
may ftate the equation $s = \int v \, i$. In like manner $\int \frac{i}{v}$
will be equivalent to $\int i$, that is, to t, and will exprefs the whole time $a\,d$. It is alfo eafy to fee that $\frac{s}{v}$
reprefents the ordinate D H of the line L K I H of fig. 6,
becaufe any portion D d of its abfciffa is properly reprefented by i, and the ordinates are reciprocally proportional to the velocities, that is, are proportional to the
quotients of fome conftant number divided by the velocities, and therefore, to $\frac{1}{v}$. Now i being reprefented by
the rectangle $k\,C\,c\,i$, which is alfo reprefented by $s \times \frac{1}{v}$,
we have $i = \frac{s}{v}$, and $t = \int \frac{s}{v}$, as before.

Such fymbolical reprefentations will frequently be
employed in our future difcuffions, and will enable us
greatly to fhorten our manner of proceeding.

53. There is one cafe of varied motion, which has
very particular and ufeful characters, namely, when the
line $e\,f\,g\,h$ of fig. 5. is a ftraight line. Let fig. 7. reprefent this cafe of motion along the line A D, and let
$p\,a$, $b\,c$, $c\,d$ reprefent equal moments of time, in which
the

the moveable defcribes P A, B C, C D; draw $f\,m$, $g\,n$, $e\,s$ parallel to the abfcifs $a\,d$.

It is evident that $m\,g$ and $n\,h$ are equal, or that equal increments of velocity are acquired in equal times. Alfo $e\,q$, $e\,r$, $e\,s$ are proportional to $q\,f$, $r\,g$, $s\,h$, and therefore the increments $q\,f$, $r\,g$, $s\,h$, of velocity, are proportional to the times $a\,b$, $a\,c$, $a\,d$, in which they are acquired.

This motion, may with great propriety be called UNI-FORMLY ACCELERATED, in which the velocity increafes at the fame rate with the times, and equal increments are gained in equal times.

If the line $e\,h$ cut the abfciffa in fome point v, it will reprefent a motion uniformly accelerated from reft, during the time $v\,d$, and will give us the relations between the fpaces, velocities and times in fuch motions.

From this manner of expreffing thefe relations, it follows that, *in motions uniformly accelerated from a ftate of reft, the acquired velocities are proportional to the times from the beginning of the motion.* For $a\,e$, $b\,f$, $c\,g$, $d\,h$, reprefent the velocities acquired during the times $v\,a$, $v\,b$, $v\,c$, $v\,d$, and are in the fame proportion with thofe lines.

54. Alfo, *the momentary increments of velocity are as the moments in which they are acquired ;* or *the increments of velocity are as the increments of time.*

55. Alfo, *the fpaces defcribed from the beginning of the motion are as the fquares of the times.* For the fpaces are reprefented

reprefented by the triangles $v\,a\,e$, $v\,b\,f$, $v\,c\,g$, &c. and
$v\,a\,e : v\,b\,f = v\,a^2 : v\,b^2$ &c.

REMARK.

This gives us the oftenfible character of an uniformly accelerated motion. For all that we can immediately obferve in a motion, is a fpace defcribed, and a time elapfed. Velocity is not an obfervation, but the name of an obferved relation between the increafe of the fpace and that of the time. The fpace defcribed in the time $v\,b$ is obferved to be to that in the time $v\,d$, as $v\,b^2$ to $v\,d^2$. We can reprefent the proportion of $v\,b^2$ and $v\,d^2$ by the triangles $v\,b\,f$ and $v\,d\,h$, which have the fame proportion. We then fee that the points v, f, h are in a ftraight line, and therefore $b\,f$ and $d\,h$ are as $v\,b$ and $v\,d$, that is, when we obferve a motion fuch that the fpaces defcribed are proportional to the fquares of the times, we are certain that the velocities are as the times from the beginning of the motion, and that the increments of velocity are as the increments of the times, and therefore the motion is uniformly accelerated.

56. Alfo, *the increments of the fpaces are as the increments of the fquares of the times* (counted from the beginning of the motion), that is, $v\,b\,f - v\,a\,e : v\,d\,h - v\,c\,g = v\,b^2 - v\,a^2 : v\,d^2 - v\,c^2$.

57. Alfo, *the fpaces defcribed from the beginning of the motion are as the fquares of the acquired velocities.* For $v\,a\,e : v\,b\,f = a\,e^2 : b\,f^2$.

58.

58. Alfo, *the momentary increments of the spaces are as the momentary increments of the squares of the velocities.* For $b c g f : c d h g = c g^2 - b f^2 : d h^2 - c g^2$ &c. This laft is a corollary of frequent ufe, as it often happens that we can only obferve momentary changes.

59. Alfo, *the space defcribed during any portion of time, by a motion uniformly accelerated from reft, is one half of the space uniformly defcribed in the fame time with the final velocity of the accelerated motion.* For the triangle $v d h$ meafures the fpace defcribed in the time $v d$ by the accelerated motion, and the rectangle $v d h$ H meafures the fpace uniformly defcribed in the time $v d$ with the velocity $d h$.

Here it is to be remarked, that $c g h d$ is only half of the difference between the rectangles $v d h$ H and $v c g$ G. If we make $d h = v d$, then $v d h$ H and $v c g$ G will be the fquares of the velocities $d h$ and $c g$. In this cafe, $n h$, the increment of velocity, is alfo equal to $g n$, and $d n \times n h$ is $= c g \times n h$. Employing v and $\dot{v}$ to exprefs velocity and its momentary increment, $v \dot{v}$ will be the expreffion of the rectangle $c g \times n h$. Now $2 v \dot{v}$ is the ufual expreffion of the increment of the fquare of velocity. As halves are proportional to their wholes, $v \dot{v}$ is always proportional to $2 v \dot{v}$, and is generally ufed to exprefs the variation of v^2. But we muft keep in mind that it is only the half of it.

60. *And the space defcribed during any portion of the time of the accelerated motion, is equal to that which would*

b 2

be defcribed in the fame time with the mean between the velocities at the beginning and end of this portion of time. For b d h f = b d × c g.

Thefe properties of uniformly accelerated motion will be found of very great fervice in the invefligation of all other varied motions, particularly in cafes where an approximation is all that can be effected without very tedious and complicated proceffes.

61. Acceleration may be confidered as a meafureable quantity. A ftone falling in the vertical line, much fooner acquires a great velocity, than when rolling down a flope, and all are fenfible that the acceleration is lefs as the declivity is more gentle.

If we fuppofe the acceleration to be always the fame, the conception that we have of this conftancy is, furely, that in equal times equal increments of velocity are acquired ; and, confequently, that the augmentations of velocity are proportional to the times of acquiring them. This being fuppofed, that acceleration muft furely be accounted double or triple, &c. in which a double or triple velocity is acquired ; and, in general, the augmentation of velocity uniformly acquired in a given time, muft be taken for the meafure of the acceleration.

62. *Cor.* Therefore *accelerations are proportional to the fpaces defcribed in equal times with motions uniformly accelerated from a flate of reft,* (in which the velocities gradually increafe from nothing). For, in this cafe the fpaces are the halves of what would be uniformly defcribed in

F

the

the fame time with the acquired final velocities, and are therefore proportional to thefe velocities (31), that is, to the accelerations, feeing that thefe velocities were uniformly acquired in equal times.

On the other hand, that acceleration muft be reckoned double or triple of another, in which a given augmentation of velocity is uniformly acquired in one half or one third of the time. For, if a given augmentation of velocity be acquired in half of the time, then, if the fame acceleration be continued during the remaining half of the given time, another equal augmentation will be acquired, the acceleration being conftant. The whole augmentation acquired in the fame time will be double, and therefore the acceleration is double. The fame thing muft be granted for any other proportion.

63. Therefore, we muft fay that *accelerations are proportional to the increments of velocity uniformly acquired, directly, and to the times in which they are acquired, inverfely.*

$$A : a = \frac{V}{T} : \frac{v}{t}.$$

Or, we may exprefs it by the proportional equation

$$a \doteq \frac{v}{t}.$$

It is to be remarked here, that this relation between the Acceleration, Velocity, and Time, is not confined to the cafe of a motion paffing through all degrees of velocity from nothing to the final magnitude v, but is equally true (in uniformly accelerated motions) with refpect to

any

any momentary change of velocity. For, fince the velocity increafes at the fame rate with the time, we have $v : v' = t : t'$ (v' and t' expreffing the fimultaneous increments of velocity and time). Therefore the fymbols $\frac{v}{t}$ and $\frac{v'}{t'}$ have the fame value, and therefore $a = \frac{v'}{t'}$.

64. On the other hand, fince the augmentation of velocity is the meafure of the acceleration, and is therefore proportional to it, and fince in uniformly accelerated motions, the velocity increafes at the fame rate with the times, it follows that the augmentations of velocity are as the accelerations and as the times, jointly. This gives the proportional equation $v = a t$,

and $v' = a t'$.

65. Since all that we can obferve in a motion is a fpace defcribed, and a time elapfed during the defcription, it is defireable to have a meafure of acceleration expreffed in thefe terms only.

This is eafily obtained. We have feen in art. 62. that, when the velocity has uniformly increafed from nothing, the fpaces defcribed in equal times are very proper meafures of acceleration. And, in uniformly accelerated motions, the fpaces are as the fquares of the times (56). Therefore, when the acceleration remains the fame, the fraction $\frac{s}{t^2}$ muft remain of the fame value, and a is proportional to $\frac{s}{t^2}$.

Therefore,

Therefore, *accelerations are proportional to the spaces described with a motion uniformly accelerated from rest, directly, and to the squares of the times, inversely.*

66. Farther, since $a \doteq \dfrac{v}{t}$ (64) we have $a \doteq \dfrac{v\,v}{v\,t}$; but $v\,t \doteq s$, therefore $a \doteq \dfrac{v^2}{s}$. This gives us another measure of acceleration, *viz. Accelerations are directly as the squares of the velocities, and inversely as the spaces along which the velocities are uniformly augmented.*

67. On the other hand, since, when the spaces are equal, we have $a \doteq v^2$; and, in uniformly accelerated motions, that is, when a remains constant, if the space is increased in any proportion, v^2 increases in the same proportion ; it follows that v^2 increases in the proportion, both of the acceleration and of the space. Therefore we have, in general, $v^2 \doteq a\,s$.

Again (as in art. 64, 65) we shall have $v^2 \doteq a\,S$, and $V^2 - v^2 \doteq a\,S - a\,s$, or $\doteq S - s$, which we may express in this manner $\overline{v\,v'} \doteq a\,s'$. That is, *the momentary change of the square of the velocity, in a motion uniformly accelerated, is proportional to the acceleration and to the space, jointly.* This will be found a most important theorem.

Thus we see that the acceleration continued during a given time t, or t', produces a certain augmentation of the simple velocity ; but the acceleration continued along a given space s, or $'S$, produces a certain augmentation

of

of the fquare of the velocity. This obfervation will be found of very great importance in mechanical philofophy.

68. Hitherto the acceleration has been confidered as conftant—that is, we have been confidering only fuch motions as are *uniformly* accelerated ; but thefe are very rare in the phenomena of nature. Accelerations are as variable as velocities, fo that it is equally difficult to find an actual meafure of them.

Yet it is only by changes of velocity that we get any information of the changing caufe, or the mechanical power of nature. It is only from the continual acceleration of a falling body, that we learn that the power which makes it prefs on our hand, alfo preffes the body downward, while it is falling through the air ; and it is from our obferving that it acquires equal increments of velocity in equal times, that we learn that the downward preffure of gravity on it is the fame, whatever be the rapidity of its defcent. No rapidity withdraws it in the fmalleft degree from the action of its gravity or weight. This is valuable information ; for it is very unlike all our more familiar notions of preffures. We feel that all fuch preffures as we employ, have their accelerating power diminifhed as the body yields to them. A ftream of water or of wind becomes lefs and lefs effective as the impelled bodies move more rapidly away, and, although they are ftill in the ftream, there is a limiting velocity which they cannot pafs, nor ever fully attain. It is of the greateft confequence therefore to ob-

tain

tain accurate meafures of acceleration, even when con‑
tinually varying.

We may obtain this in the very fame way that we
get meafures of a velocity which varies continually. We
can conceive a line to increafe along with our velocity,
and to increafe precifely at the fame rate. It is evident
that this rate of increafe of the velocity is the very thing
that we call Acceleration, juft as the rate at which the
line now mentioned increafes is the very thing that we
call Velocity. We have only therefore to confider the
areas of fig. 5. or the line A D of that figure, as repre‑
fenting a velocity; then it is plain that the ordinates to
the line *e g h*, which we demonftrated to be proportional
to the rate of variation of this area, will reprefent, or be
proportional to the variation of this velocity, that is, to
the acceleration. Hence the following propofition.

69. *If the abfciffa* a d *of a curve line* e g h *reprefent
the time of a motion, and if tho areas* a b f e, a c g e,
a d h e, &c. *are proportioned to the velocities at the in‑
ftants* b, c, d, &c. *then the ordinates* a e, b f, c g, d h,
&c. *are proportional to the accelerations at the inftants*
a, b, c, d, &c.

This is demonftrated precifely in the fame manner as
in art. 45. and we need not repeat the procefs. We
have only to fubftitute the word *acceleration* for the word
velocity.

From this propofition, we may deduce fome corol‑
laries which are of continual ufe in every mechanical
difcuffion.

70.

70. *The momentary increments of velocity are as the accelerations, and as the moments, jointly.*

For, the increment of velocity in the moment *c d* (for example) is accurately reprefented by the area *c d h g*, or by the rectangle *c d n k*; and *c d* accurately reprefents the moment. Alfo, the ultimate ratio of *c k* to fuch another ordinate *b i*, is the ratio of *c g* to *b f* (45); that is, the ratio of the acceleration in the inftant *c* to the acceleration in the inftant *b*. Therefore the increment of velocity during the moment *p a* is to that during the moment *c d* as *p a* × *a e* to *c d* × *d g*.—We may exprefs this by the proportional equation $v \doteq a t$.

71. Converfely. The acceleration *a* is proportional to $\frac{v}{t}$, agreeably to what was fhown when the motion is uniformly accelerated (63).

When, from the circumftances of the cafe, we can meafure the area of this figure, as it is analogous to the fum of all the infcribed rectangles, we may exprefs it by $\int a t$; and thus we obtain the whole velocity acquired during the time A P, and we fay $v \doteq \int a t$.

It frequently happens that we know the intenfities (or at leaft their proportions) of the accelerating powers of nature in the different points of the path, and we want to learn the velocities in thofe points. This is obtained by means of the following propofition :

72. *If the abfciffa* A E *of a line* a c c (fig. 8.) *be the fpace along which a body is moving with a motion continually varied,*

varied, and if the ordinates A *a*, B *b*, C *c*, &c. *be propor-*
tional to the accelerations in the points A, B, C, &c. *then,*
the areas A B *b a*, A D *d a*, A E *e a*, &c. *are proportional*
to the augmentations of the square of the velocity in A *at the*
points B, D, E, &c.

Let B C, C D, be two very fmall portions of the line
A E, and draw *b f*, *c g*, parallel to A E. Then, if we
fuppofe that the acceleration B *b* continues through the
fpace B C, the rectangle B *b f* C will exprefs the augmentation made on the fquare of the velocity in B (67). In
like manner, C *c g* D will exprefs the increment of the
fquare of the velocity in C; and, in like manner, the
rectangles infcribed in the remainder of the figure will
feverally exprefs the increments of the fquares of the
velocity acquired in moving over the correfponding portions of the abfciffa. The whole augmentation therefore of the fquare of the velocity in A (if there be any
velocity in that point) during the paffage from A to B,
is the aggregate of thefe partial augmentations. The
fame muft be affirmed of the motion from B to E.
Now, when the fubdivifion of A E is carried on without
end, it is evident that the ultimate ratio of the area
A E *e a* to the aggregate of infcribed rectangles, is that
of equality; that is, when the acceleration varies, not
by ftarts, but continually, the area A B *b a* will exprefs
the augmentation made on the fquare of the initial velocity in A, during the motion along A B. The fame
muft be affirmed of the motion along B E.——Therefore
the intercepted areas A B *b a*, B D *d b*, D E *e d*, are proportional

Pl. 1.

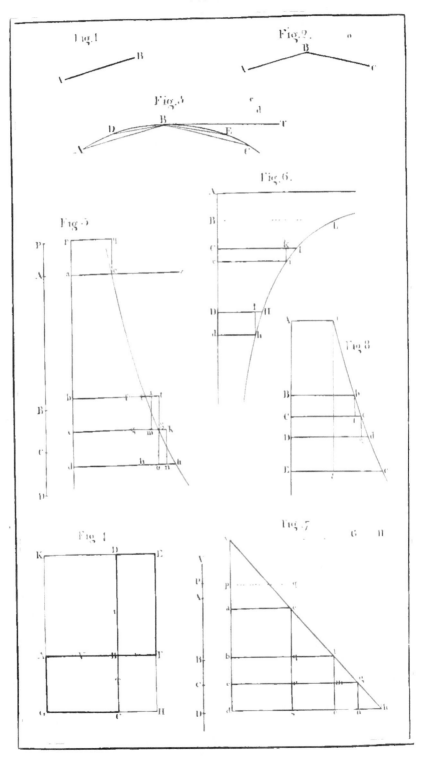

portional to the changes made on the fquares of the velocity in A, B, and D.

73. *Cor.* 1. If the moveable had no velocity in A,
the areas A B *b a*, A D *d a*, &c. are proportional to the
fquares of velocity acquired in B, D, &c.

74. *Cor.* 2. The momentary change on the fquare
of the velocity is as the acceleration and increment of
the fpace jointly, or, we have $v \dot{v} = a \dot{s}$; and thus we find
that what we demonftrated ftrictly in uniformly accelerated motions (67) is equally true when the acceleration
continually changes.

75. *Cor.* 3. Since we found $v \dot{v}$ equal to half the
increment of the fquare of the velocity (59), it follows
that the area A E *e a*, or the fluent $\int a \dot{s}$ is only equal to
$\dfrac{V^2 - v^2}{2}$, fuppofing v and V to be the velocities in $\dot{A}$
and E.

76. All that has been faid of the acceleration of
motion is equally applicable to motions that are retarded,
whether uniformly or unequably; the momentary variations being decrements of velocity inftead of increments.
A moveable, uniformly retarded till it is brought to reft,
will continue in motion during a time proportional to the
initial velocity; and it will defcribe a fpace proportional
to the fquare of this velocity; and the fpace fo defcribed

G   is

is one half of what it would have defcribed in the fame time with the initial velocity undiminifhed, &c. &c. &c.

Having now obtained proper marks and meafures of all variations of velocity, it remains to obtain the fame for all changes of direction. Thus we fhall obtain a knowledge of the greateft part of thofe motions which the fpontaneous phenomena of nature exhibit to our view. It is very doubtful whether we have ever feen a motion ftrictly rectilineal.

3. *Of Compound Motions.*

79. In our endeavours to obtain a general mark or characteriftic of any change of motion, it is evident that when the change is fuppofed to be the fame in any two or more inftances, the oftenfible marks muft be the fame, whatever have been the previous conditions of the two moveables. There muft be obferved, in all the cafes of change, fome circumftance in the difference between the former motions and the new motions, which is precifely the fame, both in refpect of kind and of quantity, that is, in refpect of direction and of velocity. We may there-fore fuppofe one of the bodies to have been previoufly at reft. In this cafe, the whole change produced on it is unqueftionably the very motion which we fee it ac-quire, or the determination to this motion.

Therefore, in the firft place, *a change of motion is, itfelf, a motion, or determination to motion.* In the cafe now mentioned, it is the new motion, and that only.
But

But it is by no means the new motion in every other cafe. For, if the *previous* condition of the body has been different from that of a body at reft, and if the *fame* change has been produced on it, the *new* condition muft alfo be different from the new condition of the other, and therefore the *new condition* cannot be the *change*, becaufe this is fuppofed to be the fame in both cafes. But, farther, when the fame change is made in any previous motion, we muft fee, in the difference between the former motion and the new motion, fomething that is equivalent to, or the fame with, this motion produced in the body that was previoufly at reft, and which has received the fame change. And alfo, the difference between the new motions of thefe two bodies muft be fuch as fhall indicate the difference between thefe previous conditions of each.

Affuming therefore as a principle, that the change of motion is itfelf a motion, let us endeavour to find out a motion, which alone fhall produce that difference from the former motion which is really obferved in the new motion, in all cafes whatever. This, undoubtedly, is the proper mark and meafure of the change.

Something very analogous to thefe indifpenfable conditions may be obferved in the following motions. Suppofe the ftraight line E I (fig. 9.) lying eaft and weft, croffed by the line E K from north to fouth. Let the line E K (which we fuppofe to be material, fuch as a rod or wire) be carried along the line E I in a minute, keeping always parallel to its firft pofition, that is, al-

ways

ways lying north and fouth. At the end of 20″ it will have the pofition G g γ, its end E having moved uniformly along $\frac{1}{3}$ of E I; at the end of 40″ it will have the pofition H h χ, E having defcribed $\frac{2}{3}$ of E I; and at the end of the minute it will have the pofition I i.

In the mean time, let the line E I (alfo fuppofed material) move uniformly from north to fouth, keeping always parallel to its firft pofition E I. At the end of 20″ it will have the pofition m g n, its end E having moved along $\frac{1}{3}$ of E K. At the end of 40″ it has the pofition o h p, and E o is $\frac{2}{3}$ of E K. And at the end of the minute, it has the pofition K γ χ i.

It is plain that the common interfection of thefe two lines will always be found in the diagonal E i of the parallelogram E K i I; for E m g G is a parallelogram fimilar to E K i I, becaufe E G : E I = E m : E K. In like manner E o h H is a parallelogram fimilar to E K i I. Thefe parallelograms are therefore about a common diameter E i.

Further, the motion of the point of interfection of thefe lines is uniform; becaufe E G : E I = E g : E i, and E H : E I = E h : E i, &c.; and therefore the fpaces E g, E h, E i are proportional to the times.

And thus it appears that the interfection of two lines, each of which moves uniformly in the direction of the other, moves uniformly in the direction of the diagonal of the parallelogram formed by the lines in their firft or laft pofition, and that the velocity of the interfection is to the velocity of each of the motions of the lines as the diagonal

diagonal is to the fide in whofe direction the motions are performed.

This motion of the interfection may, with great propriety of language, be faid to be conftituted by, or *compounded* of, the two motions in the direction of the fides. For the point *g* of the line G *γ* is, at the inftant, moving eaftward, and the fame point *g* of the line *m g n* is moving fouthward. Therefore, if the point *g* be confidered as a point of both lines (as if it were a ring embracing both) it partakes, in every inftant, of both motions.

It is alfo evident that the point *g* feparates from G in the fame direction, and with the fame velocity, as if E K had remained at reft, and the ring had moved to *m*. Alfo it feparates from the point *o* at the fame rate, and in the fame direction as if it had moved from E to G. The motion along E *i* therefore contains both of the motions along E I and along E K, and is really identical with a motion compounded of thofe motions, plainly indicating both, or the determination to both. Accordingly, we fay that in every fituation of the point of interfection, its velocity is compounded of the velocity E I and the velocity E K. If therefore E I has been a previous motion, that is, if a body was moving fo that, had its motion continued unchanged, it would have defcribed E I uniformly in a minute, but we obferve that after coming to E, it turns afide, and defcribes E *i* uniformly in a minute, we fhould fay that the change which it fuftains in the point E, is a motion E K. For, if the

body

body had been previoufly at reft in E, and we obferve it
defcribe E K in a minute, then the motion E K is, unqueftionably, the change which it has fuftained. The
motion E *i* is not the change ; for had E L been the
primitive motion, the fame motion E *i* would have refulted from compounding the motion E M with it.
Now, fince E L is different from E I, it is impoffible that
the *fame* change can make the new conditions the fame.

Moreover, there is no other motion, which, by compounding it with E I, will produce the motion E *i*.

And laftly, the motion E K is the only circumftance
of famenefs between changing the motion E I into the
motion E *i*, and giving the motion E K to a body previoufly at reft.

After a mature confideration of all thefe conditions,
we may fay, that

A change of motion is that motion which, by compofi-
tion with the former ftate of motion, produces the new
motion.

80. This compofition of motion is ufually prefented
to the mind in a way fomewhat different. A body is
fuppofed to move uniformly in the direction E I, while
the fpace in which this motion is performed is carried
uniformly in the direction E K. But we *cannot conceive*
a portion of fpace to be moved out of its place. We
can conceive the compofition very diftinctly by fuppofing a man walking along a line E I drawn on a field of
ice, while the ice is floating in the direction E K. This
will produce the very motion E *i*, and affords the cleareft
notion

notion of the compofition. If one man ftands ftill, and another walks in the direction and with the velocity E I, and a third in the direction and with the velocity E L, while the ice floats in the direction and with the velocity E K, then the new condition of the firft man will be the motion E K, that of the fecond will be E i, and that of the third will be E Q. There can be no doubt of thefe three men having fuftained the very fame change of motion. Now, the only circumftance of famenefs in thefe three new conditions is the compofition of their former condition with a motion E K.

The reflecting reader will perceive, however, that this way of illuftrating the fubject, by the motion on moving ice, is not precifely a compofition of two *determinations to motion*. This is completed in the firft inftant. As foon as the motion in the direction and with the velocity E i begins, there is no need of further exertion ; the motion will continue, and E i will be defcribed. But it ferves very well to exhibit to the mind the *mathematical* compofition of *two motions*, which is all we want at prefent. We have fhewn that, in the refult of this combination, all the characteriftics of the two determinations are to be found, becaufe the point of interfection, whether we confider it as a material exiftence, or as a mere mathematical conception, partakes of both motions. There is a phyfical queftion which will come under confideration afterwards, that is very different from the prefent, namely, Whether two natural powers, which are known to be productive, feparately,

of

of two determinations of a body to two diftinct motions, will, by their joint action, produce a determination to that motion which is compounded of thofe which they would produce feparately ?—This is a queftion of very difficult folution ; but we truft that the notions already acquired will enable us to give an anfwer with confidence.

81. Thus then have we obtained a general mark or characteriftic of a change of motion, perfectly confonant with our mark and meafure of every moving caufe, namely, the very motion which we conceive it to produce. Nay, perhaps what we have juft now eftablifhed is the foundation even of our former meafures. For every acceleration, or retardation, or deflection, may be confidered as a new motion, compounded with the former. This is not a mere fubftitution, to aid the imagination ; for it is, almoft always, the very fact. For what we take for the beginning of motion, in all our actions on bodies, and all our obfervations of the bodies which furround us, is in fact only a change induced on a motion already exifting, and exceedingly rapid. This refults from the motion of rotation, by which we are carried round the axis of the earth, and even this is compounded with the motion of revolution round the fun. What we confider as changes of motion, and therefore as the proper meafures and marks of the changing caufes, the powers of mechanical nature, are indeed changes, and the very changes that we imagine. But they are by no means changes of the motions that we imagine.

We

We fhall foon learn, that if we meafure or eftimate the changes of motion in the way now propofed, all our deductions will be perfectly conformable to the appearances of nature, and the inferences of their caufes perfectly confiftent and legitimate, giving us accurate knowledge of thofe caufes. And we fhall find that *no other way of eftimating and meafuring the changes of motion* will have thefe qualities. Thus we demonftrate the juftnefs of our principle, and that it gives a fufficient ground for mechanical fcience.

82. Since the actual compofition of motion is fo general in the phenomena of the univerfe, that it obtains in every motion and change of motion that we can produce or obferve, and fince the characteriftic which we have affumed of a change of motion is the fame, whatever the previous motion may have been, and therefore is equally applicable to motions which are really fimple, and fuch as we obferve them, it is plain that a knowledge of the *general* refults of this compofition of motion muft greatly promote our knowledge of mechanical nature. We fhall therefore confider them in order.

83. The general theorem, to which all others may be reduced, is the following.

Two uniform motions, having the directions and velocities reprefented by the fides E I, E K, *of a parallelogram, compofe a uniform motion in the diagonal.* This is already demonftrated. For the motion of the point of interfec-

H

tion

tion of thefe two lines, while each moves uniformly in
all its points, in the direction of the other, is, in every
inftant, compofed of thefe two motions, and is the fame
as if a point defcribed E I uniformly, while E I is uniformly carried in the direction E K. And this motion,
is along the diagonal E *i*, and is uniform, as has been already fhewn. Alfo, becaufe E I and E *i* are defcribed
in the fame time, the velocities of the motions along
E I, E K, and E *i*, are proportional to thofe lines.

84. *Cor.* 1. The COMPOUND MOTION E *i* is in the
fame plane with the two CONSTITUENT or SIMPLE MO-
TIONS E I and E K. For a parallelogram lies all in one
plane.

85. *Cor.* 2. The motion E *i* may arife from the
compofition of any two uniform motions, which have the
direction and velocities reprefented by the fides of any
parallelogram E L *i* M, or E I *i* K, of which E *i* is the
diagonal.

Cafes frequently occur, where we know the directions of the two fimple motions which compofe an obferved motion, but do not know the proportion of their
velocities. The velocity is afcertained by this propofition, becaufe the direction of the three motions, viz. the
two fimple and the compound motions, determines the
fpecies of parallelogram, and the ratio of the fides.

Sometimes we have the direction and the velocity of
one of the fimple motions, and therefore its proportion

to

to that of the obferved compound motion. The direction and velocity of the other is alfo found by this propofition, becaufe thefe data alfo determine the parallelogram.

The motion in the diagonal is evidently equivalent to
the motions in the fides combined. Thus, if the moveable firft defcribe E I, and then I *i* (or E K), it will be
in the fame point *i* as if it had defcribed E *i*. Therefore E *i* is frequently called the EQUIVALENT motion, the
RESULTING motion.

It frequently gives great affiftance in our inveftigations, if we fubftitute for an obferved motion fuch motions as will produce it by compofition. This is called
the RESOLUTION OF MOTIONS. It is in this way that
the navigator generally computes the fhip's change of
fituation at the end of a day, in which fhe has perhaps
failed in many different courfes. He confiders how
much he has gone to the eaftward, or weftward, and
how much to the northward or fouthward, on each
courfe ; and he then adds together all his eaftings, and
all his fouthings, and then fuppofes that the fhip has
failed for the whole day on that unvaried courfe which
would be produced by the fame eafting and fouthing
combined.

In like manner, it is very uleful for the mechanician
to confider how much his obferved motion has advanced
the body in fome particular direction, E F, for example.
(fig. 10). To do this, he confiders the motion A B as
compofed of a motion A C parallel to the given line E F,

and

and another motion A D perpendicular to E F, A B forming the diagonal of a parallelogram A C B D, of which
one fide A C is parallel, and the other A D is perpendicular to E F. It is plain that the motion A D neither
promotes nor obftructs the progrefs in the direction E F,
and that the body has advanced in the direction of E F,
juft as much as if it had moved from *a* to *b*, inftead of
moving from A to B.

This proceeding is called ESTIMATING a motion in a
given direction, or REDUCING it to that direction.

In like manner, the mechanician is faid to eftimate
a motion A B (fig. 11.) in a given plane E F G H, when
he confiders it as compofed of a motion A D perpendicular to that plane, and A C parallel to it. The lines
D A, B C being drawn perpendicular to the plane, cut
it in two points *a* and *b*, and A C is parallel to *a b*.

86.   Any number of motions A B, A C, A D, A E
(fig. 12.) may be thus compounded, forming a motion
A F. The method for afcertaining the motion refulting
from this compofition is as follows. A B, compounded
with A C, produces the motion A G. This, compounded with A D, produces A H ; and this, compounded
with A E, produces A F.

The fame final fituation F will be found by fuppofing
all the motions A B, A C, A D, A E, to be performed
in fucceffion. Thus the moveable defcribes A B ; then
B G, equal and parallel to A C ; then G H, equal and
parallel to A D ; and then, H F, equal and parallel to A E.

NOTE.

NOTE.—It is not neceſſary that all theſe motions be in one plane.

87. Three motions A B, A C, A D (fig. 13.) which have the direction and proportions of the ſides of a parallelopiped, compoſe a motion in the diagonal A F of that parallelopiped ; for A B and A C compoſe A E, and A E and A D compoſe A F.

The mine-ſurveyor proceeds in this way. Like the navigator, he ſets down any gallery of the mine, not directly by its real poſition, but enters his table with its eaſting or weſting, and with its northing or ſouthing. But he alſo keeps an account of its riſe or dip. He refers all his meaſures to three lines, one running eaſt and weſt, one running north and ſouth, and one running perpendicularly up and down. Theſe three lines are evidently like the three angular boundaries A B, A C and A D of a rectangular box.

This is now the conſtant procedure of the mechanician, in his more elaborate inveſtigations. It was firſt practiſed (we think) by M'Laurin, in the excellent phyſico-mathematical ſpeculations which are to be found in his Treatiſe on Fluxions. The mechanician refers all motions to three *co-ordinate* lines A B, A C, A D, which are perpendicular to each other, and his ultimate reſult is the diagonal A F of ſome parallelopiped.

88. Hitherto we have conſidered the compoſition of uniform motions only. But *any* motions may be compounded,

pounded, as we may eafily conceive, by fuppofing a man to walk on a field of ice along any crooked path, while the ice floats down a crooked ftream.

Thus, a uniform motion in the direction A B (fig. 14.) may be compounded with a uniformly accelerated motion in the direction A C. Such a motion is obferved when we fee a ftone fall from the maft-head of a fhip failing fteadily forward in the direction A B; for this ftone will be obferved to fall down parallel to a plummet hung from the maft-head. The real motion of the ftone will therefore be a parabolic arch A *b f g*, which A B touches in A; for while the maft-head defcribes the equal lines A B, B F, F G, the ftone has fallen to β and φ and γ, and the line A C A' has got into the pofitions B B', F F', G G', fo that A φ is four times A β; and A γ is nine times A β. Therefore A β, A φ, A γ, are as the fquares of β *b*, φ *f*, and γ *g*, and the line A *b f g* is a parabola.

It is in this way that a nail in the fole of a cart-wheel defcribes a cycloid, while the cart moves along a fmooth plane. This is the compofition of a progreffive motion with an equal circular motion. The geometrical lectures of Dr Barrow contain many beautiful examples of fuch compofitions of motion; and it was by introducing this procefs into mathematical reafoning, that this celebrated geometer gave a new department to the fcience, which quickly extended it far beyond the pale of the ancient geometry of the Greeks, and fuggefted to Sir Ifaac Newton his doctrine of Fluxions.

89.

89. When two motions, however variable, are compounded, we difcover the direction and velocity of the compound motions in any inftant, if we know the direction and velocities of each of the fimple motions *at that inftant.* For we may fuppofe, that, at that inftant, each motion proceeds unchanged. Then we conftruct a parallelogram, the fides of which have the directions and proportions of the velocities of the fimple motions. The diagonal of this parallelogram will exprefs the direction and velocity of the compound motion.

90. On the other hand, knowing the direction and velocity of the compound motion, and the directions of each of the fimple motions, we difcover their velocities.

91. When a curvilineal motion A D V (fig. 15.) refults from the compofition of two motions, whofe directions we know to be A C and A F, we learn the velocities of the three motions in any point D, by drawing the tangent D I, and the ordinate D *b* parallel to one of the fimple motions, and from any point L in that ordinate, drawing L I parallel to the other motion, cutting the tangent in I. The three velocities are in the proportion of the three lines I L, L D, and I D. This is of very frequent ufe.

Since the phenomena are our only marks and meafures of their fuppofed caufes, it is plain that every miftake with refpect to a change of motion, is accompanied by a miftake in our inference of its caufe. Such miftakes

takes are avoided with great difficulty, becaufe the motions which we obferve are, at all times, extremely different from what we take them to be. A book lying on
the table feems to be at reft ; but it is really moving
with a prodigious fpeed, and is defcribing a figure very
like the figure defcribed by a nail in the nave of a coach-
wheel while the carriage is going over the fummit of a
gentle rifing. We imagine that we are at reft, and we
judge of the motion of another body merely by its change
of diftance and direction from ourfelves.

Thus, if a fhip is becalmed at B (fig. 16.) in a part
of the ocean where there is an unknown current in the
direction B D ; and if the light of another fhip is feen
at A, and if A really fails to C while B floats to D,
A will not appear to have failed along A C, but along
A K ; for when B is at D, and A at C, A appears at C,
having the bearing and diftance D C. Therefore, if A K
be made equal and parallel to D C, it will have the fame
bearing by the compafs, and the fame diftance from B
that C has from D ; and therefore the fpectator in B,
not knowing that he has moved from B to D, but believing himfelf ftill at B, muft form this opinion of the
motion of A.—In the fame manner it muft follow, that
our notions of the planetary motions muft be extremely
different from the motions themfelves, if it be true that
this earth is moving to the eaftward at the rate of nearly
twenty miles in every fecond. It would feem a defpe-
rate attempt therefore for us to fpeculate concerning the
powers of nature by which thefe motions are regulated.
                                                    And,

And, accordingly, nothing can be conceived more fantaſtical and incongruous than the opinions formerly entertained on this ſubject. But Mathematics affords a clue by which we are conducted through this labyrinth.

92. *The motion of a body* A *relative to, or as ſeen from, another body* B, *which is alſo in motion, is compounded of the real motion of* A, *and the oppoſite to the real motion of* B. (Fig. 16.)

Join A B, and draw A E equal and parallel to B D, and complete the parallelogram A C F E, and join E D and D C. Alſo produce E A till A L is equal to A E or B D, and complete the parallelogram L A C K, and draw A K and B K. Had A moved along A E while B moves along B D, they would have been at E and D at the ſame time, and would have the ſame bearing and diſtance as before. If the ſpectator in B is inſenſible of his own motion, A will appear not to have changed its place. It is well known that two ſhips, becalmed in an unknown current, appear to the crews to remain at reſt. It is plain, therefore, that the real poſition and diſtance D C are the ſame with B K, and that if the ſpectator in B imagines himſelf at reſt, the line A K will be conſidered as the motion of A. This is evidently compoſed of the motion A C, which is the real motion of A, and the motion A L, which is equal and oppoſite to the motion B D.

93. In like manner, if B H be drawn equal and oppoſite to A C, and the parallelogram B H G D be completed,

I

pleted,

pleted, and B G and A G be drawn, the diagonal B G will be the motion of B relative to A. (92.) Now, it is plain that K A G B is a parallelogram. The relative pofition and diftances of A and B at the end of the motion are the fame as in the former cafe. B appears to have moved along B G, which is equal and oppofite to A K. Therefore, *the apparent or relative motions of two bodies are equal and oppofite, whatever the real motions of both may be*, and therefore give no immediate information concerning the real motions.

94. It needs no farther difcuffion to prove the fame propofitions concerning every *change* of motion, viz. that the relative *change* of motion in A is compofed of the real change in A, and of the oppofite to the motion, or change of motion in B.

Suppofe the motion B D to be changed into B δ. This has arifen from a compofition of the motion B D with another D δ; draw C x equal and oppofite to D δ, and complete the parallelogram E C x ϵ. The diagonal E x is the apparent or relative change of motion. For the bearing and diftance δ C is evidently the fame with D x, becaufe the lines δ C and D x which join equal and parallel lines are equal and parallel.

95. Therefore, if no change happen to A, but if the motion of B be changed, the motion of A will *appear* to be equally changed in the oppofite direction.

Hence we draw a very fortunate conclufion, that the obferved or relative changes of motion are equal to the

real

real changes. But we remain ignorant of its direction, becaufe we may not know in which body the change has happened. E *ε* is the apparent *change* of motion of the body A, becaufe E C was the apparent motion before the change into E *κ*. Complete the parallelogram A C *κ α*. The diagonal A *κ* would have been the motion of A, had its motion A C fuftained the compofition or change A *α*. It is plain that either the motion D *ठ*, compounded with B D, or the motion A *α* compounded with AC, will produce the fame apparent or relative change of motion. Still, however, it is important to learn that the apparent and real changes are the fame in magnitude ; becaufe they give the fame indication of the magnitude of the changing caufe.

96. It is evident that if we know the real motion of B, we can difcover the real motion of A, by confidering its apparent motion E C as the diagonal of a parallelogram of which one fide E A is equal and oppofite to the known motion B D. It muft therefore be A C.

97. In like manner, if any other circumftances have affured the fpectator in B, that A C is the true motion of A, which had appeared to him to move along A K, he muft confider A K as the diagonal of a parallelogram A L K C, and then he learns that B has moved over a line B D, equal and oppofite to A L. It was in this manner that Kepler, by obfervations on the planet Mars, difcovered the true form of the earth's orbit round the Sun.

98. If equal and parallel motions be compounded with all and each of the motions of any number of bodies, moving in any manner of way, their relative motions are not changed by this fuperindu&ion. For, by compounding it with the motion of any one of the bodies, which we may call A, the *real* motion of A is indeed changed. But its motion relative to another body B, or its apparent motion as feen from B, is compounded of the real change (94.), and of the oppofite to the real change in B, that is, oppofite to the real change in A, and therefore deftroys that change, and the relative motion of A remains the fame as before.—In this manner, the motions and evolutions of a fleet of fhips in a current which equally affe&s them all, are not changed, or are the fame as if made in ftill water. The motions in the cabin of a fhip are not affe&ed by the fhip's progreffive motion ; nor are the relative motions on the furface of this globe fenfibly affe&ed by its revolution round the fun. We fhould remain for ever ignorant of all fuch common motions, if we did not fee other bodies which are not affe&ed by them. To thefe we refer, as to fo many fixed points.

4.   *Of Motions continually Defle&ed.*

99. A curvilineal motion is a cafe of continual defle&ion. It is fufceptible of infinite varieties, and its modifications and chief properties are of difficult inveftigation.

The

The fimpleft cafe of curvilineal motion is that of uniform motion in a circular arch. Here, the deflections in equal times from rectilineal motion are equal. But, fhould the velocity be augmented, it is plain that the momentary deflection is alfo augmented, becaufe a greater arch will be defcribed, and the end of this greater arch deviates farther from the tangent; but it is not eafy to afcertain in what proportion it is increafed. When one uniform rectilineal motion A B (fig. 17.) is deflected into another B C, we afcertain the linear deflection by drawing a line from the point *c*, at which the body would have arrived without deflection, to the point C, to which it really does arrive. And it is the fame thing whether we draw *d* D, or *c* C, in this manner, becaufe thefe lines, being proportional to B *d*, B *c*, will always give the fame meafure of the velocities (41.), and the lines of deflection are all parallel, and therefore affure us of the direction of the deflection in the point B. But it is otherwife in any curvilineal motion. We never have *d* D : *c* C = B *d* : B *c* ; moreover, it is very rarely that *d* D, *c* C, &c. are parallel. We know not therefore which of thefe lines to felect for an indication of the direction of the deflection at B, or for a meafure of its magnitude.

Not only does a greater velocity in the fame curve caufe a greater deflection, but alfo, if the path be more incurvated, an arch of the fame length defcribed with the fame velocity, deviates farther from the tangent. Therefore, if a body move uniformly in a curve of variable curvature, the deflection will be greater where the curvature is greater.

We

We may learn from thefe general remarks, that the
directions and the meafures of the deflections by which
a body deviates *continually* into a curvilineal path, can
be afcertained, only by inveftigating the ultimate pofitions and ratios of the lines which join the points of
the curve with the fimultaneous points of the tangent, as the points δ and C are taken nearer and nearer
to B. Some rare, but important cafes occur, in which
the lines joining the fimultaneous points c and C, d and δ,
&c. are parallel. In fuch cafes, the deflection in B
is certainly parallel to them, and they are cafes of the
compofition of a motion in the direction of the tan-
gent with a motion in the direction of the lines c C, d δ,
&c. But, in moft cafes, we muft difcover the direction
of the deflection in B, by obferving what direction the
lines d δ, c C, &c. taken on both fides of B, continually
approximate to. The following general propofition, difcovered by the illuftrious Newton, will greatly facilitate
this refearch.

100. *If a body defcribe a curve line* A B C D E F
(fig. 18.) *which is all in one plane, and if there be a point*
S *in this plane, fo fituated, that the lines* S A, S B, S C,
&c. *drawn to the curve, cut off areas* A S B, A S C, A S D,
&c. *proportional to the times of defcribing the arches* A B,
A C, A D, &c. *then are the deflections always directed
to this point* S.

Let us firft fuppofe that the body defcribes the polygon A B C D E F, formed of the chords of this curve,
and that it defcribes each chord uniformly, and is deflected

flected only in the angles B, C, D, &c. Let us alfo (for the greater fimplicity of argument) fuppofe that the fides of this polygon are defcribed in equal times, fo that (by the hypothefis) the triangles A S B, B S C, C S D, &c. are all equal.

Continue the chords A B, B C, &c. beyond the arches, making B c equal to A B, and C d equal to B C, and fo on. Join c C, d D, &c. and draw c S, d S, &c.; alfo draw C b parallel to c B or B A, cutting B S in b, and join b A, and draw C A, cutting B b in o. Laftly, make a fimilar conftruction at E.

Then, becaufe c B is equal to B A, the triangles A S B and B S c, are equal, and therefore B S c is equal to B S C; but they are on the fame bafe S B. Therefore they are between the fame parallels; that is, c C is parallel to B S, and B C is the diagonal of a parallelogram B b C c. The motion B C therefore is compounded of the motions B c and B b, and B b is the deflection, by which the motion B c is changed into the motion B C; therefore the deflection in B is directed to S.—By fimilar reafoning f F, or E i, is the deflection at E, and is likewife directed to S; and the fame may be proved concerning every angle of the polygon.

Let the fides of this polygon be diminifhed, and their number increafed without end. The demonftration remains the fame, and continues, when the polygon exhaufts or coalefces with the curvilineal area, and its fides with the curvilineal arch.

Now, when the whole areas are proportional to the times, equal areas are defcribed in equal times; and therefore,

therefore, in fuch motion, the defleCtions are always direCted to S.

This point S may be called the *centre of defleCtion.*

101. *If the defleCtion by which a curve line* A D F *is
defcribed, be continually direCted to a fixed point, the figure
will be in one plane, and areas will be defcribed round that
point proportional to the times.* For B C is the diagonal
of a parallelogram, and is in the plane of S B and B *c*
(84.) ; and *c* C is parallel to B S, and the triangles S B C,
S B *c*, and S B A, are equal. Equal areas are defcribed
in equal times ; and therefore areas are defcribed proportional to the times, &c. &c.

102. *Cor.* 1. *The velocities in different points of the
curve are inverfely proportional to the perpendiculars* S r
and S t (fig. 19.) *drawn from* S *on the tangents* A r, E t
in thofe points of the curve. For, becaufe the elementary
triangles A S B, E S F, are equal, their bafes A B, E F,
are inverfely as their altitudes S *r*, S *t*. Thefe bafes,
being defcribed in equal times, are as the velocities, and
they ultimately coincide with the tangents at A and E.
Therefore the velocity in A is to that in E as S *t* to S *r*.

103. *Cor.* 2. *The angular velocities round* S *are inverfely as the fquares of the diftances.* For, if we defcribe
round the centre S the fmall arches B *α*, F *δ*, they may
be confidered as perpendiculars on S A and S E ; alfo
with the diftance S F defcribe the arch *g h*. It is evident
that

Pl 2.

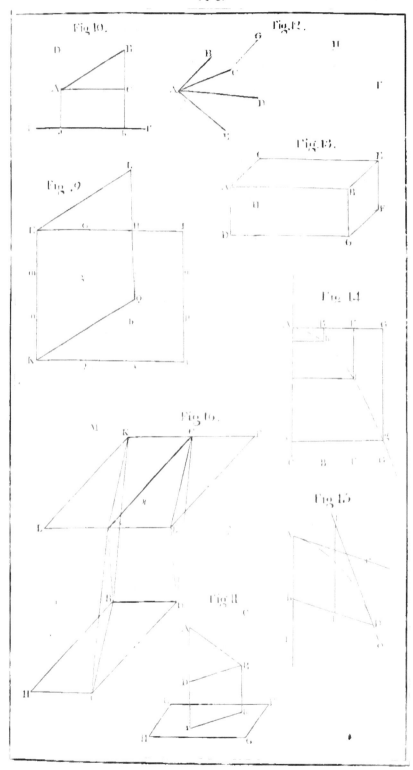

Fig 10.

Fig 12.

Fig 13.

Fig 9

Fig 14

Fig 16.

Fig 15

Fig 11

that $g\,h$ is to $F\,\delta$ as the angle $A\,S\,B$ to the angle $E\,S\,F$. Now, fince the areas $A\,S\,B$, $E\,S\,F$, are equal, we have $B\,\alpha : F\,\delta = S\,E : S\,A$.

But $\qquad g\,h : B\,\alpha = S\,E : S\,A$

therefore $\qquad g\,h : F\,\delta = S\,E^2 : S\,A^2$

and $\qquad A\,S\,B : E\,S\,F = S\,E^2 : S\,A^2$

104. We now proceed to determine the magnitude of the deflection, or, at leaft, to compare its magnitude in B, for example, with its magnitude in E. In the polygonal motion (fig. 18.) the deflection in B is to that in E as the line $B\,b$ to the line $E\,i$; for $B\,b$ and $E\,i$ are the motions, which, by compofition with the motions $B\,c$ and $E\,f$, make the body defcribe $B\,C$ and $E\,F$. Therefore, when the fides of the polygon are diminifhed without end, the ultimate ratio of $B\,b$ to $E\,i$ is the ratio of the deflection at B to the deflection at E.

In order to obtain a convenient expreffion of this ultimate ratio, let $A\,B\,C\,X\,Z\,Y$ be a circle paffing through the points A, B, C, and draw $B\,S\,Z$ through the point S, and draw $C\,Z$, $A\,Z$.

The triangles $B\,C\,b$ and $A\,Z\,C$ are fimilar; for $C\,b$ was drawn parallel to $c\,B$ or $B\,A$. Therefore the angle $C\,b\,B$ is equal to the ultimate angle $b\,B\,A$ or $Z\,B\,A$, which is equal to the angle $Z\,C\,A$, being fubtended by the fame chord $Z\,A$; alfo $C\,B\,b$, or $C\,B\,Z$, is equal to $C\,A\,Z$, ftanding on the fame chord $C\,Z$. Therefore, the remaining angles $b\,C\,B$ and $C\,Z\,A$ are equal, and the triangles are fimilar; therefore $B\,b : C\,A = B\,C : A\,Z$.

K $\qquad\qquad\qquad\qquad\qquad$ Now,

K

Now,

Now, fince, by continually diminifhing the fides of the polygon, the points A and C continually approach to B, and C A continually approaches to c A or to $2\,c$ B, or 2 C B, and is ultimately equal to it ; alfo A Z is ultimately equal to B Z. Therefore, ultimately, B b : 2 B C $=$ B C : B Z, and B $b \times$ B Z $= 2$ B C^2, and B $b = \dfrac{2\,\mathrm{B\,C}^2}{\mathrm{B\,Z}}$.

In like manner, at the point E, we fhall have E i ultimately equal to $\dfrac{2\,\mathrm{E\,F}^2}{\mathrm{E}\,z}$, E z being that chord of the circle through D, E, and F, which paffes through i.

Therefore B b : E $i = \dfrac{2\,\mathrm{B\,C}^2}{\mathrm{B\,Z}} : \dfrac{2\,\mathrm{E\,F}^2}{\mathrm{E}\,z}$.

The ultimate circle, when the three points A, B, C, coalefce, is called the CIRCLE OF EQUAL CURVATURE, or the EQUICURVE CIRCLE, coalefcing with the curve in B in the moſt clofe manner. The chord B Z of this circle, which has the direction of the deflection in B, may be called its DEFLECTIVE CHORD.

Since B C and E F are defcribed in equal times, they are proportional to the velocities in B and E. Therefore, we may exprefs this propofition in the following words :

In curvilineal motions, the deflections in different points of the curve are proportional to the fquare of the velocities in thofe points, directly, and to the deflective chords of the equicurve circles in thofe points, inverfely.

It muſt be here remarked, that this theorem is not limited to curvilineal motions, in which the deflections are always directed to one fixed point, but extends to

all

all curvilineal motions whatever. For it may evidently be expreſſed in this manner ; *The deflecting forces are ultimately proportional to the ſquares of the arches deſcribed in equal times, directly, and to the deflective chords of the equicurve circle, inverſely.*

The equable deſcription of areas only enabled us to ſee that the lines B C and E F were deſcribed in equal times, and therefore are as the velocities.

It will be convenient to have a ſymbolical expreſſion of this theorem. Therefore, let the deflective chord of the equicurve circle be repreſented by c, and the deflection by d, the theorem may be expreſſed by

$$d \doteq \frac{v^2}{c}, \text{ or } d = \frac{2 \text{ arch}^2}{c}$$

105. REMARK.—The line B b is the linear deflection, by which the uniform motion in the chord A B is changed into a uniform motion in the chord B C, or it is the deviation c C from the point where the moveable would have arrived, had it not been deflected at B. But, in the preſent caſe of curvilineal motion, the lines B b and B c expreſs the meaſures of the velocities of theſe motions, or the meaſures of the determinations to them. B c is to B b as the velocity of the progreſſive motion is to the velocity of the deflection, generated during the deſcription of the arch B C. But, becauſe the deflection in the arch has been continual, and becauſe it is to be meaſured, like acceleration, by the velocity which is generated uniformly during a given moment of time, it

K 2   may

may be meafured by the velocity generated during the defcription of the arch B C. Its meafure therefore will be double of the fpace through which the body is *actually* deflected in that time from the tangent in B. The fpace defcribed will be only one half of B *b*, or it will be B ̇O. Now, this is really the cafe ; for the tangent is ultimately parallel to O C, and bifects *c* C ; fo that although the deflection from the tangent to the curve is only half of the deflection from the produced chord to the curve ; yet the velocity gradually generated is that which will produce the deflection from the produced chord, or is that which conftitutes the polygonal motion in the chords.

It is perfectly legitimate, therefore, to reafon from the fubfultory deflections of a polygonal motion to the continual deflections in a curvilineal motion ; for the deflections in the angles of the polygon have the fame ratio to one another with the deflections in the fame points of the curve. But we muft be careful not to confound the deflections from the tangent with thofe from the chords. This has been done by eminent mathematicians. For the employment of algebraical expreffions of the increments of the abfciffæ and ordinates of curves, always gives the true expreffion of the deflections in a polygonal motion. But, when we turn our thoughts to the figures, and to the curvilineal motions themfelves, we naturally think of the deflections (fuch as we fee them) from the tangent to the curve. We then make geometrical inferences, which are true only when affirmed of the curvilineal

vilineal motions. We are apt to mix and confound thefe inferences with the refults of the fluxionary calculus, which always refer to the polygon. By thus mixing quantities that are incongruous, fome celebrated mathematicians have committed very grofs miftakes.

It is, in general, moft convenient, and furely moft natural, to ufe the ultimate ratio of the actual deflections from the tangent, or $\dfrac{B\,C^2}{B\,Z}$; and this even gives us its meafure in feet or inches, when we know the dimenfions of the figure defcribed. Thus we know that, in one minute, the Moon, when at her mean diftance, deflects 193 inches from the tangent to her orbit round the Earth, and that the earth deviates 424 inches in the fame time from the tangent of her orbit round the Sun.

106. The velocity in any point of a curvilineal motion is that which would be generated by the deflection in that point, if continued through $\frac{1}{4}$ of the deflective chord of the equicurve circle. Let x be the fpace along which the body muft be accelerated in order to acquire the velocity $B\,C$.

We have $B\,b^2$, or $4\,B\,O^2 : B\,C^2 = B\,O : x$ (57) and therefore $x = \dfrac{B\,C^2 \times B\,O}{4\,B\,O^2}$, $= \dfrac{B\,C^2}{4\,B\,O}$, and $4\,x = \dfrac{B\,C^2}{B\,O}$, or $B\,O : B\,C = B\,C : 4\,x$. But $B\,O : B\,C = B\,C : B\,Z$. Therefore $x = \frac{1}{4}\,B\,Z$.

RECAPITU-

RECAPITULATION.

Thus have we obtained marks and meafures of all the principal affections of motion.

The acceleration a is $\dfrac{\dot{v}}{t}$ (71) or $\dfrac{v\,\dot{v}}{s}$ (72) or $\dfrac{\dot{s}}{t^2}$ (65)

The momentary variation of velocity $\dot{v} = a\,t$ (71)

The momentary variation of the fquare of velocity

$$2\,v\,\dot{v} = 2\,a\,\dot{s} \quad (72)$$

The momentary deflection $\quad\quad d = \dfrac{\text{arc.}^2}{\text{chord}}$ (105)

The deflective velocity $\quad\quad\quad = \dfrac{2\,v^2}{c}$ (104)

But, in order to apply the doctrines already eftablifhed with the accuracy of which phyfico-mathematical fubjects are fufceptible, it is neceffary to felect fome point in any body of fenfible magnitude, or in any fyftem of bodies, by the pofition or motion of which we may form a juft notion of the pofition and motion of the body or fyftem. It is evident that the condition which afcertains the propriety of our choice, is, that *the pofition, diftance, or motion of this point fhall be a medium or average of the pofitions, diftances, and motions of every particle of matter in the affemblage.*

107. This will be the cafe, if the point be fo fituated that, if a plane be made to pafs through it in any direction *whatever*, and if perpendiculars be drawn to this plane from every particle of matter in this affemblage, the fum of all the perpendiculars on one fide of this

plane

plane is equal to the fum of all the perpendiculars on the other.

That there may be found in every body fuch a point, is demonftrated (after Bofcovich) in the *Encycl. Britan.* Art. *Pofition (Centre of)*.

Let P (fig. 20.) be a point fo fituated, and let QR be a plane (or rather the fection of a plane, perpendicular to the plane of the paper) at any diftance from the body. The diftance Pp of P from this plane, is the average of all the diftances of each particle. For, let the plane APB pafs through this point, parallel to the plane QR. The diftance CS of a parallel C from this plane is $DS - DC$, or $Pp - DC$; and the diftance GT of a particle G is $HT + GH$, or $Pp + GH$. Let n be the number of particles between QR and AP; and let • be the number on the other fide of AP; and let m be the number of particles in the whole body, that is, let $m = n + o$. It is evident that the fum of all the diftances, fuch as CS is $n \times Pp$ *minus* the fum of all the diftances, fuch as CD. Alfo $o \times Pp$, *plus* the fum of the diftances GH, is the fum of all the diftances GT. Now, the fum of the lines CD is equal to that of all the lines GH, and therefore $\overline{n + o} \times Pp$, or $m \times Pp$, is equal to the fum of all the lines CS and GT, and Pp is the mth part of this fum, or the average diftance.

Now, fuppofe the body to have approached to the plane QR (fig. 21), and that P is now at π. It is plain that the diftance πp is again the average diftance, and $m \times \pi p$ is the fum of all the new diftances. The difference from

the

the former fum is $m \times P \pi$, and confequently $m \times P \pi$ is the fum of the approaches of every particle; and $P \pi$ is the mth part of this fum, or is the average of them all. The diftance, pofition, and motion of this point is therefore the average pofition, diftance, and motion of the whole body. The fame demonftration will apply to any fyftem of bodies. The point P is therefore properly chofen.

108. Since the point P is the fame, in whatever direction the plane A P B is made to pafs through it, it follows that the laft propofition is true, although the body may have turned round fome centre or axis, or though the bodies of which the fyftem confifts may have changed their mutual pofitions.

109. The point P, thus felected, may, with great propriety, be called the CENTRE OF POSITION of the body or fyftem.

110. If A and B (fig. 22.) be the centres of pofition of two bodies A and B, and if a and b exprefs the numbers of equal particles in A and B, or their quantities of matter, the common centre C of this fyftem of two bodies lies in the ftraight line A B joining their refpective centres, and $A C : C B = b : a$. This is evident.

111. If a third body D, whofe quantity of matter is d, be added, the common centre of pofition of this fyftem

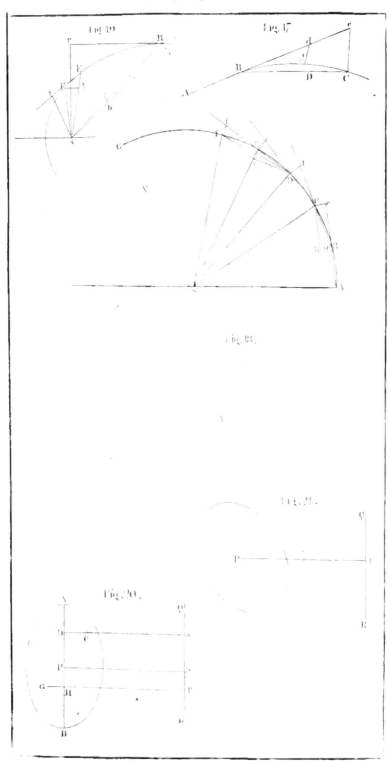

Fig. 19

Fig. 17

Fig. 18.

Fig. 21.

Fig. 20.

fyftem of thefe three bodies lies in the ftraight line D C, joining D with the centre of the other two, and D E : E C $= a + b : d.$

In like manner, if a fourth body be added, the common centre of pofition is in the line joining it with the centre of the other three, and the diftance of the fourth from this common centre, is to the diftance of that from the common centre of the three, as the matter of all the three to the matter of the fourth——And the fame thing is true for every addition.

112. If the particles or bodies of any fyftem be moving uniformly in ftraight lines, with any velocities and directions whatever, the centre of the fyftem is either at reft, or it moves uniformly in a ftraight line.

For, let one of the bodies D move uniformly from D to F. Join F with the centre C of the remaining bodies, and make $C f$ to $F f$ as the matter in F is to that in the remaining bodies. It is plain that $E f$ is parallel to D F, and that $D F : E f = A + B : D.$ In like manner, may the motion of the centre be found that is produced by that of each of the other bodies.

But thefe motions of the centre F are all uniform and rectilineal. Therefore, the motion compounded of them all is uniform and rectilineal.

It may happen that the motion refulting from this compofition may be nothing, by reafon of the contrariety of fome individual motions. In this cafe, the centre will remain in the fame point.

This obtains alfo, if the centres of any number of

L

þodies

bodies

bodies move uniformly in right lines, whatever may have been the motion of each body, by rotation or otherwife. The motion of the common centre will ftill be uniform and rectilineal.

113. *Cor.* 1. The quantity of motion of fuch a fyftem, is the fum of the quantities of motion of each body reduced (85.) to the direction of the centre's motion, and it is had by multiplying the quantity of matter in the whole fyftem by the velocity of the centre.

114. *Cor.* 2. This velocity of the centre is had by reducing the motion of each particle to the direction of the centre motion, and divefting the fum of the reduced motions by the quantity of matter in the fyftem.

115. If equal and oppofite quantities of motion be any how impreffed on any two bodies of fuch an affemblage, the motion of the centre of the whole is not affected by it. For the motion of the centre, arifing from the motion of one of the bodies, being compounded with the equal and oppofite motion of the other, the diagonal of the parallelogram becomes a point, or thefe motions deftroy one another, and no change is induced thereby in the motion of the centre. The fame thing muft be faid of equal and oppofite quantities of motion being impreffed on any other pair of the bodies, and, in fhort, on every pair that can be formed in the affemblage. Therefore the propofition is ftill true.

MECHA-

MECHANICAL PHILOSOPHY.

PART I. Section I.

OF MATTER.

116. The term MATTER expresses that substance of which all things which we perceive by means of our senses are conceived to consist. It is almost synonymous, in our language, with BODY. MATERIAL and CORPOREAL seem also synonymous epithets.

117. Sensible bodies are usually conceived as consisting of a number of equal PARTICLES or ATOMS of this substance. These atoms may also be supposed similar in all their qualities, each possessing such qualities as distinguish them from every thing not material.

118. But we are entirely ignorant of the essential qualities of matter, and cannot affirm any thing concerning it, except what we have learned from observation. To us, matter is a mere phenomenon. But we must as-

L 2

certain

certain with precifion the properties which we felect as diftinctive of matter from all other things.

119. All men feem agreed in calling that alone matter, which excludes all other fubftances of the fame kind, or prevents them from occupying the fame place, and which requires the exertion of what we call force to remove it from its place, or anyhow change its motion. Thefe two properties have been generally called SOLIDITY or IMPENETRABILITY, and INERTIA or MOBILITY. Mere mobility, however, is not, perhaps, peculiar to matter ; for the mind accompanies the body in all its changes of fituation. When mobility is afcribed to matter, as a diftinguifhing quality, we always conceive force to be required. We are confcious of exerting force in moving even our own limbs. In like manner, extenfion, and figure, and divifibility, although primary qualities of matter, are common to it with empty fpace.

120. Mobility in confequence of the exertion of force may be ufed as a characteriftic of matter, or of an atom of matter. All poffefs it—and probably all poffefs it alike, their fenfible differences being the confequence of a difference in the combinations of atoms to form a particle.

121. A particle of matter under the influence of a moving force, is the object of purely mechanical contemplation, and the confideration of the changes of motion

tion which refult from its condition as thus defcribed may be called the MECHANISM of the phenomenon.

122. Perhaps all changes of material nature are cafes of local motion (though unperceived by us) by the influence of moving forces. Perhaps they cannot be faid to be *completely* underftood, till it can be fhewn how the atoms of matter have changed their fituations. Perhaps the folution of a bit of filver in aqua fortis is not *complete-ly* explained, till we fhew, as the mechanician can fhew with refpect to the fatellites of Jupiter, how an individual atom of filver is made to quit its connexion with the reft, and by what path, and with what velocity in every inftant of its motion, it gets to its final ftate of reft, in a diftant part of the veffel. But thefe motions are not confidered by the judicious chemift. He confiders the phenomenon as fully explained, when he has difcovered all the cafes in which the folution takes place, and has defcribed, with accurate fidelity, all the circumftances of the operation.

123. We have derived our notions of SOLIDITY or IMPENETRABILITY chiefly from our fenfe of touch. The fenfations got in this way feem to have induced all men to afcribe this property of tangible matter to the mutual contact of the particles—and to fuppofe that no diftance is interpofed between them.

124. But the compreffibility and elafticity of all known bodies, their contraction by cold, and many ex-

amples of chemical union, in which the ingredients occupy lefs room when mixed, than one of them did before mixture, feem incompatible with this conftitution of tangible matter. Did air confift of particles, elaftic in the fame manner that blown bladders are, it would not be fluid when compreffed into half of its ufual bulk, becaufe, in this cafe, each fpherule would be compreffed into a cube, touching the adjoining fix particles in the whole of its furfaces. No liquid, in a ftate of fenfible compreffion, could be fluid ; yet the water at the bottom of the deepeft fea is as fluid as at the furface. Some optical phenomena alfo fhew incontrovertibly that very ftrong preffure may be exerted by two bodies in *phyfical* or *fenfible* contact, although a meafurable diftance is ftill interpofed between them. On the whole, it feems more probable that the ultimate atoms of tangible matter are not in mathematical contact.

125. Bodies are penetrated by other matter in confequence of their porofity. Therefore the fame bulk may contain different quantities of matter.

126. DENSITY is a term, which, in ftrict language, expreffes vicinity of particles. But, when ufed by the mechanician as a term of comparifon, it expreffes the proportion of the number of equal particles, or the quantity of matter, in one body, to the number of *equal* particles in the fame bulk of another body.

127.

127. Therefore the quantity of matter (frequently called the MASS) is properly expreſſed by the product of numbers expreſſing the bulk B and the denſity D. If M be the quantity of matter,

then
$$M \doteqdot B\,D$$

$$B \doteqdot \frac{M}{D}$$

$$D \doteqdot \frac{M}{B}$$

MECHA-

MECHANICAL PHILOSOPHY.

PART I. SECTION II.

DYNAMICS.

128. DYNAMICS is that department of phyſico-mathematical ſcience which contains the *abſtract* doctrines of moving forces ; that is, the neceſſary reſults of the relations of *our* thoughts concerning motion and the cauſes of its production and changes.

129. Changes of motion are the only indications of the agency, the only marks of the kind, and the only meaſures of the intenſity of thoſe cauſes.

130. We cannot think of motion, *in abſtracto*, as a *thing*, properly ſo called, that can ſubſiſt ſeparately, but as a *quality*, or rather as a *condition*, of ſome other thing. Therefore we conſider this condition as permanent, like the ſituation, figure or colour of the thing, unleſs ſome cauſe of change exert its influence on it.

131.

131. Looking round us, we cannot fail of *observing* that the changes in the state or condition of a body in respect of motion, have a distinct and constant relation to the situation and distance of some other bodies. Thus, the motions of the Moon, or of a stone projected through the air, have an evident and invariable relation to the Earth. A magnet has the same to iron——an electrified body to any body near it——a billiard ball to another billiard ball, &c. &c. Such seeming dependences may be called the *mechanical relations* of bodies. They are, unquestionably, indications of *properties*, that is, of distinguishing qualities. These accompany the bodies wherever they are, and are commonly conceived as *inherent* in them ; and they certainly ascertain and determine what we call their mechanical nature. The mechanician will describe a magnet, by saying that it attracts iron. The chemist will describe it, by saying that it contains the martial oxyd in a particular proportion of metal and oxygen.

132. Philosophers are not uniform, however, in their reference of the qualities indicated by those observed relations. Magnetism is a term expressing a certain class of phenomena, which are relations subsisting between magnets and iron ; but many reckon it a property of the magnet, by which it attracts iron ; others imagine it a property of the iron, by which it tends to the magnet. This difference generally arises from the interest we take in the phenomenon ; both bodies are probably affected alike, and the property is distinctive of both : For, in all

M

cafes that have yet been obferved, we find that the indicating phenomenon is obferved in both bodies ;—the
magnet approaches the iron, and the electrified body approaches the other. The property therefore is equally
inherent in both, or perhaps in neither ; for there are
fome philofophers, who maintain that there are no fuch
mutual tendencies, and that the obferved approaches, or,
in many cafes, mutual feparations, are effected by the
extraneous impulfion of an æthereal fluid, or of certain
miniftering fpirits, intrinfic or extrinfic.

133. Thefe mechanical affections of matter have
been very generally called POWERS or FORCES ; and the
body conceived to poffefs them is faid to ACT on the related body. This is figurative or metaphorical language.
Power, and force, and action, cannot be predicated, in
their original ftrict fenfe, of any thing but the exertions
of animated beings ; nay, it is perhaps only the exerted
influence of the mind on the body which we ought to
call action. But language began among fimple men ;
they gave thefe denominations to their own exertions
with the utmoft propriety. To move a body, they found
themfelves obliged to exert their *ftrength*, or *force*, or
power, and to *act*. When fpeculative men afterwards
attended to the changes of motion obferved in the meetings or vicinity of bodies, and remarked that the phenomena very much refembled the refults of exerting
their own ftrength or force ; and when they would exprefs this occurrence of nature, it was eafier to make ufe
. of

of an old term, than to make a new one for things which fo much refembled; becaufe there are always fuch differences in other circumftances of the cafe, that there is little danger of confounding them. We are not to imagine that they thought that inanimate bodies exerted ftrength, as they themfelves did. This was referved for much later times of refinement.—In the progrefs of this refinement, the word power or force was employed to exprefs *any efficiency whatever;* and we now fay, the power of aqua fortis to diffolve filver—the force of argument—the action of motives, &c. &c.

To this notion of conveniency we muft afcribe, not only the employment of the words *power* and *force*, to exprefs *efficiency* in general, but alfo of the terms *attraction, repulfion, impulfion, preffure,* &c. all of which are metaphorical, unlefs when applied to the actions of animals. But they are ufed as terms of diftinction, on account of the refemblance between the phenomena and thofe which we obferve when we pull a thing toward us, pufh it from us, kick it away, or forcibly comprefs it.

134. Much confufion has arifen from the unguarded ufe of this figurative language. Very flight analogies have made fome animate all matter with a fort of mind, a ὅσπερ ψυχὴ, while other refemblances have made other fpeculatifts materialize intellect itfelf.

The very names which we give to thofe powers which we fancy to be inherent in bodies, fhew that we

M 2

know

know nothing about them. Thefe names either, like magnetifm, exprefs a relation to the particular fubftances which we imagine poffefs the power, or they exprefs fomething of the effect which fuggefted their exiftence. Of this laft kind are *cohefion*, *gravity*, &c. They are almoft all verbal derivatives, and fhould be confidered by us merely as abbreviated defcriptions or hints of the phenomena, or as abbreviated references to certain bodies, but by no means as any explanation of their nature. The terms are the worfe by having fome meaning. For this has frequently mifled us into falfe notions of the manner of acting. Perhaps the only ftrict application of the term ACTION is to the effect produced by our exertions in moving our own limbs. But we think that we move other bodies, becaufe our own body, which is the immediate inftrument of the mind, is overlooked, like the plane in the hand of the carpenter, attending to the plank which he dreffes.

135. Forces have been divided into IMPULSIONS and PRESSURES. Impulfions are thofe which produce the changes of motion by the collifion of moving bodies. Preffure is a very familiar idea, and perhaps enters into every clear conception that we can form of a moving force, when we endeavour to fix our attention on it. We know that preffure is a moving force; for, by preffing round the handle of a kitchen jack, we can urge the fly into any rapidity of motion. Even when one ball puts another in motion by hitting it, we think that fome-

thing

thing precifely like our own preffure is the *immediate* producer of the motion ; for if the ball is compreffible, we fee it dimpled by the blow. Gravity, or elafticity, and the like, are called preffing powers ; becaufe a ball, lying on a mafs of foft clay, makes a pit in it, and, if lying on our hand, it excites the fame feeling that another man would do by preffing on our hand. There are fome indeed who call fuch powers, as gravity, magnetifm, and electricity, SOLICITATIONS to motion. We fhall foon fee that this claffification of forces is of no ufe.

136. Preffure and impulfion are thought to be effentially diftinguifhed by this circumftance, that, in order to produce a finite velocity in a body by preffure, it muft be continued for fome time—as when we urge the fly of a jack into fwift motion by preffing on the handle ; whereas impulfion produces it in an inftant.—They are alfo diftinguifhed by another circumftance. The impelling body lofes as much motion as the impelled body has gained ; fo that there feems fomething like the transfufion of motion from the one to the other. Accordingly, it is called the COMMUNICATION of motion. But we fhall find that neither the inftantaneous production of motion by impulfe, nor the transfufion of it into the body, are true.

137. Some again think that impulfion is the only caufe of motion, faying, ' *Nihil movetur nifi a contiguo*

' *et*

' *et moto* ; ' and they have fuppofed ftreams of æther, which urge heavy bodies downward—which impel the iron and magnet toward each other, &c.

138. But a third fect of mechanicians fay that forces, acting at a diftance, as we fee in the phenomena of gravitation, magnetifm, and electricity, are the fole caufes of motion ; and they affert that fuch forces are exhibited, even in the phenomena of fenfible contact, preffure, and impulfion.

139. The only fafe procedure is to confider all the forces which we obferve in action as mere phenomena. The conftitution of our mind makes us infer the agency of a caufe, whenever we obferve a change. But, whether the exertion of force fhall produce motion or heat, we know not, except by experience, that is, by obferva- tion of the phenomena. Nor will fpeculations about the intimate nature of thefe forces, and their manner of act- ing, contribute much to our *ufeful* knowledge of mecha- nical nature. We gain all that is poffible concerning the nature of thofe faculties which accompany matter, or are fuppofed to be its inherent properties, by noticing the LAWS according to which their exertions proceed. With- out a knowledge of thefe laws, the other knowledge is of no value.

140. It is alfo from the change of motion alone that we learn the *direction* of any force. Thus, by obferving that

that an arrow is retarded during its afcent through the air, but accelerated during its fall, we infer, or learn, that the force of gravity acts downwards.

141. When a force is known to be in action, and yet its characteriftic motion does not follow, we fuppofe that it is oppofed by a force acting in the oppofite direction. Thus the agency of that other force is detected, and its intenfity may be meafured. Thus, the force with which the parts of a ftring cohere, or with which a fpringey body unbends, are detected by their fupporting a weight—and the magnitude of the weight is the meafure of the cohefion of the ftring, or of the elafticity of the fpring.

142. But the body in which this oppofing force is thus detected, is alfo faid to *refift* the force to which it is oppofed. This is figurative language, and, as ufed in mechanical philofophy, it is generally improper. In wreftling, when my antagonift exerts his ftrength, to prevent his being thrown down, I am fenfible of his exertion, and I thus learn that he refifts. But fhould I feel no more exertion neceffary than if he were a mafs of lifelefs matter, I fhould not think that he refifted. In the mechanical operations of nature, a force of any kind always produces its full effect, agreeably to the circumftances of the cafe, and can do no more. The force is indeed expended in producing its effect, becaufe matter is not moved without force. The weight lying on a fpring,

spring, and keeping it in a state of tension, is as completely measured by the degree of tension which supports it, as this tension is measured by the supported weight ;—neither can, with propriety, be said to resist. Silver is said to resist the dissolving power of aqua regia, but not that of aqua fortis ; yet the dissolving power of aqua fortis is expended, and that of aqua regia is not. All this is very inaccurate employment of words, and this inaccuracy has done much harm in natural philosophy. The word INERTIA, which had been employed by Kepler and Newton, to express the indifference of matter as to motion or rest, or its tendency to retain its present state, has got other notions annexed to it by subsequent writers, and has been called a force, *vis inertiæ.* Mr Rutherfurth, in his System of Natural Philosophy, lectures which he read in the University of Cambridge with great applause, is at pains to shew that matter is not merely indifferent, but RESISTS every change of motion, by exerting what he calls the *force of inactivity,* by which it preserves its condition unchanged. But, surely, this is as incongruous as to speak of a square circle. Yet is inertia considered as a real existence, and is said to be proportional to the quantity of matter in a body. When we find that we must employ twice as much force to move A with a certain velocity as to move B, we say that A contains twice as much matter, because we see that it has twice as much inertia. Is it not enough to say that we judge A to have twice as much matter, because all matter requires force to move it ?—this is its characteristic. Should

we

we find that we can move a thing by a very wifh, or a command, we fhould not think it matter. Inertia, taken in this fenfe, as expreffing the neceffity of what we call force, in order to change the motion of matter, is juft one of thofe general phenomena by which it is known to us. Whether this force be, in every cafe, external to the material atom, or whether fome of the obferved powers of body may not be inherent in it, is a queftion of Metaphyfics, and is probably beyond the reach of our faculties. But naturalifts have generally fuppofed that the atom is purely paffive and indifferent, and that all its powers are fuperadded to the mere material atom.

Thefe doubts and difficulties in the ftudy have all arifen from the introduction of the notion of *refiftance*, or force exerted by matter, in order to remain as it is. It would have been infinitely better to have employed the term REACTION, becaufe this is the expreffion of the very fact; for, in all the phenomena of changed motion, there is obferved an equal change in oppofite directions in the two acting bodies. Iron approaches to the magnet— the magnet to the iron. In the collifion of bodies, the impelling and impelled are obferved to fuftain equal and oppofite changes. But in moft, and probably in all, we difcover that thofe changes are brought about by forces familiarly known to us in other ways; and no method has been difcovered, by which we may learn whether the *whole* of the change is owing to thofe mutual forces, or whether fome part is to be afcribed to inertia.

N

143. When the body B is always obferved to approach to A, and no intermediate caufe can be affigned, A is faid to attract B. Thus a magnet is faid to attract a piece of common iron. But if B is always obferved to fhun A, or to feparate from it, A is faid to repel B. Thus one electrified body repels another.

144. Mechanical forces are confidered as meafurable magnitudes. But, fince they are not objects of our perception, but only inferences from the phenomena, it is plain that we can neither meafure nor compare their magnitudes directly. Having no knowledge of their agency, nor any mark of their kind, except the change of motion which we confider as their effect, it is only in this change of motion that we muft look for any meafure of their magnitude or intenfity ;—this is alfo the only mean of comparifon. Now, change of motion, involving no ideas but of fpace and time, affords the moft perfect meafurement. We cannot find a better meafure ; nay, it is improper to employ any other ; and the moft eminent philofophers, by employing other meafures, founded on their fancied knowledge of the intimate nature of mechanical force, have advanced moft incongruous opinions, which have fpoiled the beauty of the fcience. We fhall therefore adhere ftrictly to the meafure fuggefted by this reafoning, and fhall call that a double or triple force, which, by its fimilar action, during the fame time, produces a double or triple change of motion, whether it accelerates, or retards, or deflects a

motion

motion already going on. We exprefs this notion in the moft fimple manner by faying, that we confider force merely as fomething that is proportional to the change of velocity.

Of the Laws of Motion.

145. Such being our notions of motion, and of the caufes of its production and changes, there are certain refults, which, by the conftitution of our minds, necef-farily arife from the relations of thefe ideas. Thefe are laws of human judgement, independent of all experience of external nature, juft as it refults from the laws of judgement that the three angles of a right lined triangle are equal to two right angles, although there fhould not be a triangle in the univerfe.

Some of thefe laws may be intuitive, and may be called axioms; others, equally neceffary truths, may not be fo obvious, and may require fteps of argument.

There are three fuch laws, firft propofed in precife terms by Sir Ifaac Newton, which feem to give a fuffi-cient foundation for all the doctrines of Dynamics, and to which, as to firft principles, we may appeal for the ex-planation of every mechanical phenomenon of nature.

Firft Law of Motion.

146. *Every body continues at reft, or in uniform rec-tilineal motion, unlefs affected by fome mechanical force.*

If

If we adhere to our inference of the agency of force only from an obferved change of motion, and to this inference from every fuch change, and if we grant that we have no notion of a force independent of a change of motion, this law feems little more than a tautological propofition. For, unlefs we fuppofe the agency of a mechanical force, we do not fuppofe a change of motion, that is, the abfence of mechanical agency is the abfence of a change of motion, and the body continues in its former ftate of reft or motion. But philofophers have attempted to demonftrate this law in various ways.

147. Some confider it as a neceffary truth, in the nature of the thing. A body, they fay, can neither accelerate, nor retard, nor deflect, becaufe the event is but one, and there is no caufe of determination whether it fhall accelerate, or retard, or deflect, nor whether to the right or to the left, or which determines any one degree of any of thofe changes. This fort of proof is obfcure and unfatisfactory.

148. Others choofe to confider it as a phyfical law, as an univerfal fact, for which, perhaps, we can give no reafon. They offer numerous proofs by induction. Thus, a coach being fuddenly accelerated, or checked in its progrefs, or turned out of its courfe, the fitters are thrown towards the back, or the front of the coach, or to one fide, fhewing, in all cafes, a tendency to continue in their former condition in refpect of motion. Number-

lefs

lefs examples may be given of the fame marks of this tendency to continue in the former ftate.

149. But it may be objected, that it is very far from being a matter of univerfal experience. Whoever grants the truth of the Copernican defcription of the planetary motions, will alfo grant that we perhaps never faw one inftance, either of reft or of uniform rectili- neal motion. Our moft familiar obfervations fhew an evident tendency to reft, a fort of fluggifhnefs in all matter. For it is a fact, that all motions gradually di- minifh, and, in a fhort time, terminate in reft. No force feems neceffary for maintaining a ftate of reft. But motion, they fay, is a violent ftate, the continual production of an effect, and therefore requiring a con- tinuation of the caufe. Motion therefore requires the continual exertion of the caufe. They fay that a body in motion continues in it, only by the continual agency of a force infufed into it in giving it the motion, and inherent in it while in motion. They call it the *inherent force—vis infita corpori moto.*

150. But this is contrary to our cleareft experience, and to any diftinct notions that we can form of motion as an effect of force. We are not confcious of any ex- ertion, in order to continue our motion in fliding or fkating on. fmooth ice ; and when any obftruction comes in our way, we feel *diftinctly* our natural tendency to continue our fpeed undiminifhed—we feel that we muft

resift

refift a tendency to fall forwards—we feel all obftructions as checks on our fpeed, and think that if the ice were
perfectly fmooth, we fhould go on for ever.   It is equally
contrary to our notions of a moving force.   By its inftantaneous action, it produces motion, that is, a fucceffive change of place, otherwife it produces nothing.
Or if, in any inftant of its action, it .do not produce a
continuing motion, it cannot produce it by continuing
to act.   Continuation of motion is implied in our very
idea of motion.   In any inftant, the body does not
move over any fpace ; but it is in a certain condition
(however imperfectly underftood by us) or has a certain
determination, which we call velocity, by which, if not
hindered, a certain length of path is paffed over in a fecond.   This muft be effected by the inftantaneous action
of the moving caufe, otherwife it is not a caufe of motion.   In fhort, motion is a *ftate* or *condition*, into which
a body may be put, by various caufes, but by no means
a *thing* which can be infufed into a body, or taken out
of it.

Should it be faid that we have full evidence of a
force refiding in a moving body, by obferving its impul-
five power, which is not to be found in the fame body
at reft, we may anfwer, that there *are* forces refiding in
moving bodies, but that they are equally inherent in
them when at reft, but that motion is neceffary, in order that thefe forces may be able to exert their action
on the other body long enough to produce a fenfible effect.   Motion in the impelling body is not the *caufe* of

that

that of the body impelled by it, but only an *occafion* or *opportunity* for the forces to act effectually, and without which the other body would withdraw itfelf from the action. The bow-ftring muft continue preffing the arrow forwards—the hammer muft follow the nail, that it may drive it to the head by one blow. This will be clearly fhewn as we proceed.

The gradual diminution and final ceffation of all motions mentioned above is granted, but is eafily explained by ftating the obftructions. The diminution is obferved to be precifely what fhould arife from thofe obftructions, on the fuppofition that if there were no obftruction, there would be no diminution. For example, where we can fhew that the obftruction is only half, the diminution of motion is only one half. This would not be, if there were any diminution where there is no obftruction. A pendulum is foon brought to reft when vibrating in water; it vibrates much longer in air; and ftill longer in the exhaufted receiver of an air-pump. The planets have continued for many ages without the fmalleft perceptible diminution of their motions.

151. Another fect of philofophers deny this law altogether, and affirm that matter is effentially prone to motion. Every body, when at liberty, begins to move, and continually accelerates this fpontaneous motion. Bodies are fo far from being fluggifh, that they are perpetually active.

152.

152. All thefe differences of opinion may be completely fettled, by adhering to the principle, that ' *every* ' *change is an effect.* ' It is a matter of fact, that the human mind always confiders it as fuch. Therefore, the law is ftrictly deduced from our ideas of motion and its caufes ; for, even if it were effential to matter gradually to diminifh its motion, and, at laft, come to reft, this would not invalidate the law, becaufe our underftanding would confider this diminution as the indication of an effential, or, at leaft, a univerfal property of matter. We fhould afcribe it to a natural retarding force, in the fame way that we give this name to the weight of an arrow difcharged ftraight upwards. The nature of exifting matter would be confidered as the caufe, and we fhould eftimate the law of its action as we have done in the cafe of gravity ; and, as in that cafe, we fhould ftill fuppofe that were it not for this particular property, the material atom would continue its motion for ever undiminifhed.

This is quite fufficient for all the purpofes of mechanical philofophy. Nay, if we affumed any thing elfe in this cafe, we fhould be led into continual blunders. Should we fay that a body maintains its motion undiminifhed folely by the action of an inherent force, we fhould be obliged to adopt the opinion, that when one body in motion impels another, part of this force is transfufed from the impelling into the impelled body, and all the abfurdities which are neceffarily attached to this opinion.

Therefore, to conclude on this fubject, let us confider motion merely as a ftate or condition, into which
matter

matter may be brought by various caufes, and which, like its whitenefs or roundnefs, will remain, till fome ef-ficient caufe fhall change it. This we have called the *mechanical condition of the body*, and have fettled the meaning of the term with fufficient precifion. It con-fifts in its velocity and direction, and in no other cir-cumftance.

In the next place, let us confider the change which may be induced on it as confifting folely in a change in thefe circumftances, and this change as the only indica-tion, the only mark, and the only proper meafure of the changing caufe, that is, of the force (for we are confi-dering mechanical caufes only). It is evident that, as far as this procedure will carry us, we acquire certain knowledge, fufceptible of mathematical treatment. In order to make our tafk ufeful, we muft endeavour to learn whether the deviations from uniform motion follow re-gular laws—what the laws are—and to what bodies they refer.

154. The deviations from uniform motion are dif-coverable only by a comparifon with uniform motions. But we cannot tell whether a propofed motion be uni-form, unlefs we have an accurate meafure of time. For it is to be learned only by obferving the proportions of the fpaces, and thofe of the times, and by obferving that thofe proportions are the fame. To obtain a meafure of time, various contrivances have been employed. They are all to this purpofe—An event is felected, in which

O

we

we have no reafon to think that any variation occurs in
the operation of thofe caufes which effectuate its accomplifhment. It is then prefumed that it will always
be accomplifhed in equal times. The rotation of the
heavens, in twenty-three hours and fifty-fix minutes and
four feconds, has been agreed on as the ftandard to
which all other contrivances are referred or compared,
and their accuracy is eftimated by their agreement with
this ftandard.

Second Law of Motion.

155. *Every change of motion is proportional to the
force impreffed, and is made in the direction of that force.*

This alfo is little more than a tautological propofition. If a force is to be meafured only by the change
which it makes in the motion of a body, the propofition
is only a repetition of this meafure in different terms ;
for, furely, quantities are proportional to their accurate
meafures. Indeed, this would have been a fufficient demonftration, had not philofophers attempted it in another
way, which has given rife to a great fchifm in the eftimation of forces. They have attempted to demonftrate
it as an application of the undoubted maxim, that *effects
are proportional to their caufes.* But it is eafy to fee that
this application *cannot* be made ; for it prefuppofes that
we know the proportion of the forces, and that of their
caufes, and that we perceive thofe proportions to be the
fame.—Now, in moft cafes, this is impoffible ; for the

forces

forces are not objects of our obfervation. We know nothing of their proportions. When Newton fays that gravity at the furface of the earth is 3600 times greater than at the moon, he proves it by fhewing that the deflection caufed by it in a fecond, at the earth's furface, is 3600 times greater than that of the moon. But this is begging the queftion, or affuming this propofition as true, unlefs this law of motion be admitted as an axiom. There are very few cafes indeed, where we can fhew that forces are proportional to the changes of motion produced by them ; yet fuch cafes are not altogether wanting. Thus, a fpring ftilyard can be made, the rod of which is divided by hanging on, in fucceffion, a number of perfectly equal weights. The elafticity of the fpring, in its different ftates of tenfion, is proportional to the preffures of gravity which it balances.—Should we find that, at Quito in Peru, a lump of lead draws out the rod to the mark 312, and that, at Spitzbergen, it draws it to 313, we feem entitled to fay that the preffure of gravity at Quito is to its preffure at Spitzbergen as 312 to 313, on the authority of effects being proportional to their caufes.

But fuch cafes are extremely rare, becaufe it is feldom that a natural power, accurately meafured in fome other way, is *wholly* employed in producing the obferved motion. Part of it is generally expended in fome other way, and therefore we frequently fee that the motions are not in the fame proportion with the fuppofed forces. But even though this could be ftrictly done, this would

O 2 only

only be the proof of a general law or fact, whereas the pretenfions of the philofophers aim at a proof of it *a priori*, of an abftract truth.

156.   Sir Ifaac Newton feems to confider it only as a phyfical law.   In this fenfe, we are not without very good arguments.

I.   A ball moving with a double, triple, or quadruple velocity, generates in another, by impulfe, a double, or triple, or quadruple velocity, or the fame velocity in a double, &c. quantity of matter, and the ball lofes the fame proportions of its own velocity.

II.   Two bodies, meeting with equal quantities of motion, mutually ftop each other.

III.   Two forces, which, by acting fimilarly during equal times, would produce equal velocities in fome third body, will, by acting together during the *fame time*, produce a double velocity.

IV.   If any preffure, acting for a fecond, produce a certain velocity, a double preffure, acting during a fecond, will produce a double velocity in the fame body.

V.   A force, which we know to act equably, produces equal increments of velocity in equal times, whatever thefe velocities may be.

In all thefe examples, we fee the forces in the fame proportion with the change of motion fimilarly produced by them.

157.   But, about the middle of the 17th century, Dr Robert Hooke, Fellow of the Royal Society of London,

don, difcovered a vaft collection of facts, in which the forces feemed to be in a very different proportion.

1. In the production of motion. Four fprings, e-qual in ftrength, and bent to the fame degree, generated only a double velocity in the ball which they impelled; nine fprings produced only a triple velocity, &c.

2. In the extinction of motion. A ball moving with a double velocity will penetrate four times as deep into a uniformly refifting mafs; a triple velocity will make it penetrate nine times as far, &c.

Thefe are but two inftances of an immenfe collection of facts to the fame purpofe, and they are clofely con-nected with the moft important applications of dynami-cal fcience.

158. Mr Leibnitz eagerly availed himfelf of thefe facts, as authority for declaring himfelf the difcoverer of the real nature and meafure of mechanical action and force, which he faid had hitherto been totally miftaken by philofophers; and he affirmed that the inherent force of a body in motion was in the proportion, not of the ve-locity, but of the fquare of the velocity. John Ber-noulli, his zealous champion, warmly fupported him in this argument, adducing a variety of the moft fimple facts, all confirming this relation between the *inherent force* of a body in motion and its velocity. They far-ther fupported it by many metaphyfical confiderations, relating to the procedure of nature in generating this force and velocity, and the way in which it may be ex-tinguifhed. The moft cogent argument offered by Leib-nitz

nitz is, that the force inherent in a moving body is to be estimated by all that it is able to do before its motion is completely extinguished. When, therefore, it penetrates four times as far, it should be considered as having produced a quadruple effect. The mechanicians of Europe were divided in their opinions; the Germans adhering to that of Leibnitz, and the British and French to that of Des Cartes, who first affirmed the relation which we have adopted as a second law of motion. We shall see presently, that, in the Leibnitzian measure, many things are gratuitously assumed, many contradictions are incurred, and, finally, that *it is only because forces are assumed as proportional to the velocities which they generate, that the facts observed by Hooke, and employed by Leibnitz, come to be proportional to the squares of the same velocities.* It shall only be noticed at present, that when Leibnitz assumes the quadruple penetration as the proof of the quadruple force of a body having twice the velocity, he does not consider that a double time is employed in this penetration. Now, a double force acting equably during a double time, should produce a quadruple effect. This circumstance is neglected in one and all of the facts adduced by Mr Leibnitz. It may be added, that his followers, as well as himself, agree with us in every consequence which we draw from the measure adopted by us. They grant that a force which produces a uniformly accelerated motion is a constant force, and they agree with the Cartesians in all the valuations of accelerating and deflecting forces, and have been among the most assidu-

ous

ous and fuccefsful cultivators of the Newtonian philofophy, which proceeds entirely on the meafure of moving
forces by the velocity which they generate.

159. We muft here obferve that we are confidering
nothing but *moving forces*. When a ball has had a certain velocity given it, whether impelled by the air in a
pop-gun, or by a fpring, or ftruck off by a blow, or urged
forward by a ftream of wind or water, or has acquired
it by falling, we conceive that in all thefe cafes it has
fuftained the fame action of moving force. Perhaps
preffure is the only diftinct notion we can form of force ;
but it is experience only that has informed us that preffure produces motion, but does not produce heat or
fweetnefs. Production of motion is a circumftance in
which all mechanical forces may agree, while they may
differ in many others. By, or in, this circumftance of
refemblance, they may be compared, and get a name expreffing this comparifon ; namely, *moving force*. Therefore *this particular faculty* of preffure, elafticity, &c. may
be meafured by the change of motion which preffure produces. And whatever may be the proportions of preffure on the quiefcent body, we may take it for granted
that the preffure *actually exerted* in the production of motion may be meafured by the magnitude of the change of
motion. This is really the only change of mechanical
condition effected by the preffure in the body moved by
it ; therefore it may be meafured by the velocity. Accordingly, we find that when the fame change of velocity

city is produced by preſſure on a ſoft clay ball, the ſame preſſure has *really* been exerted, whether the velocity has been augmented from 99 to 100, or diminiſhed from 4 to 3. For the ſame dimple will be obſerved in both caſes. Nay, all our actions on the ſurface of this globe are proofs of this. A ball ſuſtains the ſame dimple whether we impel it, at noon-day, to the weſtward or to the eaſtward, north or ſouth, or though this ſhould be done at midnight ; yet the real velocities at noon and midnight differ by nearly twice the velocity of a cannon ball battering in breach. This could not be, if the changes of motion were not proportional to the exerted preſſures.

160. The ſame concluſion may be deduced from our notions of a conſtant or invariable force. It is ſurely a force which produces equal effects, or changes of motion, in equal times. Now, equal augmentations of motion are ſurely equal augmentations of velocity. We find this notion of an invariable accelerating force confirmed by what we obſerve in the caſe of a falling body. This receives equal additions of velocity in equal times ; and we have no reaſon to think that this force is variable. We ſhould therefore infer, that whatever force it imparts in one ſecond, it will impart four times as much in four ſeconds. So it does, if we allow a quadruple velocity to indicate a quadruple force ; but in no other eſtimation of force.

To all this may be added, that although four ſprings, applied to an ounce ball, impel it only twice as faſt as

one

one fpring will do, yet they will give the fame velocity to a four ounce ball which one fpring gives to an ounce ball. And we can demonftrate, to the fatisfaction of Mr Leibnitz, that, in this laft cafe, the four fprings act during the fame time with the fingle fpring.

161. *Therefore, finally, a change of motion, in all its circumftances of velocity and direction, is the proper meafure of a changing force.*

But it is alfo the proper meafure of a moving force. For bodies in different ftates of motion may fuftain one and the fame change of motion. Now, fuppofe one of thefe bodies to be previoufly at reft, the change which it fuftains is the fame thing with the motion which it ac- quires. Therefore the force which produces any change of motion in a body already moving, is the fame with the force which produces a motion equivalent to this change, in a body previoufly at reft, in which cafe it is, fimply, a moving force.

It feemed neceffary to be thus particular in the ac- count of this conteft about the meafure of forces, becaufe Mr Leibnitz's opinion has influenced the fentiments of many writers of reputation ; and fome of them, particu- larly Gravefande and Mufchenbroek, have mixed it a good deal with their practical deductions. There could not have been any difpute, had not philofophers allowed themfelves to confider force as fomething exifting in body, whereas the term is never ufed to exprefs any rea- lity except the phenomenon which they conceived to be

P   its

its full effect and adequate meafure. It is quite allowable to meafure *afcenfional*, or *penetrating force*, by the
afcenfion and the *penetration*, and to remark that thefe are
as the fquare of the velocity. But this muft not be confidered as the general, or the beft, meafure of force, and
particularly of *moving force*. This *muft* be meafured by
the fimple change of motion which is produced by it.
And this meafure has the advantage of being equally applicable to the phenomena of afcenfion and penetration,
as we fhall fee very foon. We may now enounce it in a
different form, adapted to the characteriftic and meafure
of a change of motion, which was fhown in art. 79. to
be the moft proper.

Law of the Changes of Motion.

162. *In every change of a motion from* A B (fig. 23.)
to A D, *the new motion* A D *is compounded of the former
motion* A B, *and of the motion* A C, *which the changing
force produces in a body at reft.*

For it was fhewn in art. 79. that the change in any
motion is that motion which, when compounded with
the former motion, produces the new motion ; and, in
art. 81, that the new motion is that compounded of the
former motion and the changing motion. Now, fince
the change of motion is the characteriftic and the meafure of the changing force (161.), determining both its
direction and its intenfity, or the velocity produced by it,
the propofition follows of courfe.

163.

163. It was remarked in art. 80, that the compofition of motions, and the fimilar compofition of forces,
are two very different things. The firft is a truth, purely
mathematical, and as certain as any theorem in geometry. The fecond is a phyfical queftion entirely, depending on the nature of the mechanical forces which exift in
the univerfe. We do not clearly fee that two forces,
each of which will feparately produce motions having
the directions and velocities expreffed by the fides of a
parallelogram, will, by their joint action, produce a motion in the diagonal. The demonftrations given of this
propofition by almoft all the writers of Elements are altogether inconclufive, being all fimilar to the cafe of a man
walking on a field of ice, while the ice floats down a
ftream. This is only the compofition of *motions.* Other
writers, endeavouring to accommodate their reafonings
to phyfical principles, have affumed poftulates that appear gratuitous. The firft legitimate demonftration was
given by Dan. Bernoulli, in the *Comment. Petropol. Vol. I.*
But it employs a feries of many propofitions, fome of
which are very abftrufe. Mr D'Alembert greatly fimplified and improved this demonftration, in a Memoire of
the Acad. des Sciences 1769. But this alfo requires
many propofitions. Fonfenex and Riccati, in vol. III.
of the Memoires of the Academy of Turin, have given
another very ingenious one. D'Alembert has alfo improved this demonftration, and has given another, in the
fame Memoires, and one in his *Dynamique.* The firft is
very refined and obfcure, and the fecond does not feem

P 2   very

very conclufive. An attempt is made in the *Encyclop. Britan. Suppl.* § DYNAMICS, to combine Bernoulli's, D'Alembert's, and one by F. Frifi, which is more expeditious than either of the two firft, and appears legitimate. The demonftration given in this place is undoubtedly complete, if the reafoning be complete that is employed in art. 79, to prove that the motion which, when compounded with the former motion, produces the new motion, is the true change of motion. We apprehend it to be fo.

164. We have moft abundant proof of this law of motion, if we confider it merely as a phyfical law, or univerfal fact.

1. Nothing is more familiar than the joint action of different forces. Thus, we frequently fee a lighter dragged in different directions by two track-ropes, on different fides of the canal, and the lighter moves in an intermediate direction, in the fame manner as if it were dragged by one rope in that direction.

In like manner, we may obferve that if a ball, moving in a particular direction, receive a ftroke athwart this direction, it takes a direction which lies between that of the primitive motion and that of the tranfverfe ftroke.

165. 2. If a point or particle of matter A (fig. 23.) be urged at once by two preffures, in the directions A B and A C, and if A B and A C are proportional to the intenfities of thofe preffures, the joint action of thefe

two

two preffures is equivalent to the action of a third preffure, in the direction of the diagonal A D, having its
intenfity in the proportion of A D. This is completely
proved, by obferving that the point A will be withheld
from moving, by a preffure A E, equal and oppofite to
A D. Now, we know that preffures are moving forces,
and produce velocities (when acting fimilarly during e-
qual times) proportional to their intenfities. Therefore,
the propofition is true with refpect to preffures confidered merely as preffures, and alfo with refpect to the motions produceable by their compofition.

166. 3. A ball fufpended by a thread, and drawn
afide from its quiefcent pofition, is urged downwards by
its weight, and is fupported obliquely by the thread.
We can fay precifely what are the directions and intenfities
of the forces which incite it to motion in any pofition,
and what velocities will refult from them, upon the fuppofition of the truth of this propofition. And we can
tell what number of ofcillations it will make in a day.
It is a fact, that, when every thing is executed with
care, the number of vibrations will not differ from our
computation by one unit in a hundred thoufand.

4. Laftly, the planetary motions, computed on the
fame principles of the compofition of forces, exhibit no
fenfible deviation from our calculations, after thoufands
of years.

There is nothing therefore that we can reft on with
greater confidence, than the perfect agreement between
the

the compofition of motions and the compofition of the forces which would, feparately, produce thofe motions, and are meafured by the velocities which they generate.

It particularly deferves remark, that if we meafure moving forces by the fquares of the velocities which they generate, the compofition is impoffible ; that is, two forces reprefented by the fides of a parallelogram made proportional to the fquares of the velocities, will not compofe a force which can be reprefented by the diagonal. Yet nature fhews the exact compofition of forces, on the fuppofition that they are as the velocities.

Therefore, finally, whether we confider this propofition as an abftract truth, or as a phyfical law, it may be confidered as fully eftablifhed. Its converfe is the following.

167. *The force which changes the motion* A B *into* A D, *is that which would produce in a quiefcent body the motion* A C, *which, when compounded with* A B, *produces the motion obferved* A D.

168. *A force which will produce in a quiefcent body a motion having the direction and velocity reprefented by* A C, *if applied to a body moving with the velocity and in the direction* A B, *will change its motion into the motion* A D, *the diagonal of the parallelogram* A B D C. For the new motion muft be that compounded of A B and A C (80.), that is, muft be A D (83.)

From

From thefe two propofitions combined arifes a third, which is the moft general; viz.

169. *If a body* A *be urged at once by two forces, which would, feparately, caufe it to defcribe* A B *and* A C, *fides of a parallelogram* A B D C, *the body will, by their joint aĉtion, defcribe the diagonal* A D *in the fame time.* For, had the body been already moving with the velocity and in the direĉtion A B, and had it been aĉted on in A by the force A C, it would defcribe A D in the fame time (168.). Now, it is immaterial at what time it got the determination by which it would defcribe A B. Let it therefore be at the inftant that the force A C is applied to it. It muft defcribe A D, becaufe its mechanical condition in A, having the determination to the motion A B, is the fame as in any other point of that line.

170. *Cor.* Two forces, aĉting on a body in the fame, or in oppofite direĉtions, will caufe it to move with a velocity equal to the fum, or to the difference, of the velocities which it would have received from the forces feparately. For, if A C approach continually to A B, by diminifhing the angle B A C, the points C and D will at laft fall on *c* and *d*, and then A D is equal to the fum of A B and A C. But if the angle B A C increafe continually, the points C and D will, at laft, fall on *x* and *ẟ*, and then A *ẟ* becomes equal to the difference of A B and A C.

In the laft cafe, it is evident that if A C be equal to A B, the point D or *ẟ* will coincide with A, and there

will

will be no motion, the two forces being equal, and acting in oppofite directions.

171. In fuch a cafe, the equal and oppofite forces
A C and A B are faid to BALANCE each other, and, in
general, thofe forces which, by their joint operation, produce no change of motion, are faid, in like manner, to
balance each other ; and they are accounted equal and
oppofite, becaufe each produces on the body a change
of motion equal to what it would produce on a body at
reft, and at the fame time equal to the motion produced
by the other force on a body at reft. Thefe two motions are therefore equal and oppofite, and therefore the
forces are fo.

172. We may now apply to the motions produced
by the combined action of forces all that was demonftrated concerning the affections of compound motions, in
the articles 83, 84, 85, 86, 87, 88, 89, & 90.

But, in making this transference, we muft carefully
attend to the effential difference between the compofition
of motions and the compofition of forces. In this laft,
the compofition is complete, as foon as the body has
gotten the determination to move in the diagonal with
the proper velocity, and after this there is no more compofition. The body then moves uniformly, till fome force
change its condition. But, in the compofition of two or
more motions, the two conftituent motions are fuppofed
to continue, and *by their continuance only*, does the compound

pound motion exift. If any force can generate a finite
velocity by its inftantaneous action (which does not appear poffible), two fuch forces generate the determination in the diagonal in an inftant. But if the action muft
continue for fome time, in order to generate the velocities A B or A C, the *joint* action muft continue during
the fame time, in order to produce the velocity A D.
Alfo, it is neceffary that, during the whole time of their
joint action, the moving powers of the two forces muft
retain the fame proportion to each other, although they
may perhaps vary in their intenfity during that time.
From not attending to this circumftance, many experiments, which have been made in order to compare this
doctrine with the phenomena, have exhibited refults
which deviate greatly from it. The experiments made
by the combination of preffures, fuch as weights pulling a
body by means of threads, agree with this doctrine with
the utmoft precifion, it being always found that two
weights pulling in the directions A B, A C, and proportional to thofe lines, are exactly balanced by a third
weight in the proportion of A D, and pulling in the direction A E. By thefe, the compofition of *preffures* is
moft unexceptionably proved ; and, feeing that we have
fcarcely any other clear conception of a moving force,
thefe experiments may be confidered as fufficient. But
we need not ftop here ; for we have the moft diftinct
proof, by experiment, that preffures produce motions in
proportion to their intenfities by their fimilar action during equal times. The planetary motions, in which the

Q   directions

directions and intensities of the compounded forces are
accurately known as moving forces, complete the proof
of the phyfical law, by their exquifite agreement with
the calculations proceeding on the principles of this doctrine.   This perfect agreement muft be received as a full
proof of the propriety of the meafure of a moving force
which we have affumed.   Any other meafure would give
refults widely different from the phenomena.

173.   The force which fingly produces the motion
in the diagonal, may be faid to be EQUIVALENT to the
forces which produce the motions in the fides of the parallelogram.   It may alfo be called the COMPOUND FORCE,
and the RESULTING FORCE ; and the forces which act in
the direction of the fides, may be called the SIMPLE
FORCES, or the CONSTITUENT FORCES.

174.   *The two conftituent forces and their refulting
force act in one plane ; and they are proportional to the three
fides of a triangle having their directions, or of any fimilar
triangle* (84).

175.   *Each force is proportional to the fine of the angle
contained by the directions of the other two.*   For the fides
of any triangle are as the fines of the oppofite angles.

176.   A force acting in the direction parallel to any
line B D does not affect the approach toward that line,
or its recefs from it, occafioned by the action of another
                                                        force

force A C. For, becaufe the motion A D is uniform, the points ∂ and ε, to which the body would have gone by the force A B, are at the fame diftance from B D with the points d and e to which it really goes in the fame time, by the joint action of the forces A B and A C.

177. A body under the influence of any number of forces A B, A C, A D, A E, (fig. 12.) will defcribe the line A F, determined as in article 86.; and A F will exprefs the equivalent or refulting force, both in refpect of direction and intenfity.

178. Any force A B may be conceived as refulting from the joint action of two or more forces having any directions whatever, and their intenfities may be compared as in art. 85.

179. Forces may be *eftimated* in the direction of a given line or plane, or may be *reduced* to that direction, as in art. 35.

180. Any number of forces, acting on a particle of matter, will be balanced by a force equal and oppofite to their refulting or equivalent force.

181. If any number of forces are in equilibrio, and are eftimated in, or reduced to, any one direction, or in one plane, the reduced forces are in equilibrio.

Te

To thefe two laws of motion, which we have attempted to fhew to be neceffary confequences of the relations of thofe conceptions which we form of motion
and of mechanical force, and alfo to be univerfal facts or
phyfical laws, Sir Ifaac Newton has added another, or

Third Law of Motion.

182. *The actions of bodies on one another are always
mutual, equal, and in contrary directions.* It is ufually
expreffed thus—*Reaction is always equal and contrary to
action.*

This is indeed a fact, obferved without exception,
in all the cafes which we can examine with accuracy.
Sir Ifaac Newton, in the general fcholium or remark on
the laws of motion, feems to confider this equality of
action and reaction as an axiom deduced from the relations of ideas. But this feems doubtful. Becaufe a
magnet caufes the iron to approach towards it, it does
not appear that we neceffarily fuppofe that iron alfo attracts the magnet. The fact is, that although many obfervations are to be found in the writings of the ancients
concerning the attractive power of the magnet, not one
of them has mentioned the attractive power of the iron.
It is a modern difcovery, and Dr Gilbert is, I think, the
earlieft writer, in whofe works we meet with it. He
affirms that this *mutual* attraction is obferved between
the magnet and iron, and between all electrical fubftances and the light bodies attracted by them. Kepler
noticed

noticed this mutual influence between the Earth and the Moon. Wallis, Wren, and Huyghens, first diftinctly affirmed the mutual, equal, and contrary action of folid bodies in their collifions; and it has been confirmed by innumerable obfervations. Nay, fince that time, Sir Ifaac Newton himfelf only *prefumed* that, becaufe the Sun attracted the planets, thefe alfo attracted the Sun; and he is at much pains to point out phenomena to aftronomers, by which this may be proved, when the art of obfervation fhall be fufficiently improved. Thefe muft be put on the fame footing with the phenomena by which the mutual actions of the planets are proved. Now, this laft action was *altogether* a prefumption, although the proof was by far the moft eafy. The difcovery and complete demonftration of this, as a phyfical law, is certainly the moft illuftrious fpecimen of Newton's genius and nice judgement.

We muft receive it therefore as a law of motion, with refpect to all bodies on which we can make experiment, or obfervation fit for deciding the queftion.

183. As it is an univerfal law, we cannot rid ourfelves of the perfuafion that it depends on fome general principle, which influences all the matter in the univerfe. It powerfully induces us to believe that the ultimate atoms of matter are all perfectly alike—that a certain collection of properties belong, in the fame degree, to every atom—and that all the fenfible differences of fubftance which we obferve arife from a different combination of

primary

primary atoms in the formation of a particle of thofe fubftances. A very flight confideration may fhew us that this is perfectly poflible. Now, if fuch be the conftitution of every primary atom, there can be no action of any kind of particle, or collection of particles, on another, which will not be accompanied by an equal reaction in the oppofite direction. Nothing can be clearer than this. This therefore is, in all probability, the origin of this Third Law of Motion.

184. The aim of the Newtonian philofophy, which we profefs to follow, is to inveftigate the laws obferved in the production of natural effects, and to comprehend any propofed phenomenon in one or other of thofe laws. We then account it as explained.

Thefe general, but ftill fubordinate, laws are to be eftablifhed only by obfervation and experiment; but when fo eftablifhed as far as obfervation extends, it is only by means of fome obferved analogy that we can ufe them as explanations of many other phenomena. With this we muft reft fatisfied, becaufe it feems impoffible for our faculties to difcover the efficient caufes of thofe general laws, fo as to be able to demonftrate that they *muft* be fuch as we obferve. But in the eftablifhment of them as mere matters of fact, we may obferve them to be of various extent, and that fome are fubdivifions of others. In this fubordination, we can difcern

cern much order, harmony and beauty, and our minds
are left deeply impreffed with admiration of the wifdom
and fkill of the contrivance, by which this magnificent
fabric is fitted for the accomplifhment of a great and
beneficent purpofe.

185. The three axioms, and, indeed, the two firft,
feem to include the whole firft principles of Dynamics,
and enable us, without other help, to accomplifh every
purpofe of the fcience. Some authors of eminence have
thought that there were other principles, which influenced every natural operation, and that thefe operations
could not be fully underftood, nor an explanation properly deduced, without employing thofe principles. Of
this kind is the principle of OECONOMY OF ACTION, or
SMALLEST ACTION, affirmed by Mr Maupertuis to be
purfued in all the operations of nature. This philofopher
fays, that the perfect wifdom of Deity muft caufe him
to accomplifh every change by the fmalleft poffible ex-
penditure of power of every kind ; and he gives a theorem which he fays expreffes this œconomy in all cafes of
mechanical action. He then afferts that, in order to
fhew in what manner fuch and fuch bodies, fo and fo
fituated, fhall change each other's condition, we muft
find what change in each will agree with this value of
the fmalleft action. He applies this to the folution of
many problems, fome of which are intricate, and gives
folutions perfectly agreable to the phenomena.

But the fact is, that the theorem was fuggefted by
the phenomena, and is only an induction of particulars.

It

It is a law, of a certain extent, but by no means a firſt principle ; for the law is comprehended in, and is fubordinate, by many degrees, to the three laws of motion now eſtabliſhed. It is no juſt expreſſion of a minimum of action ; and he has obtained folutions, by its means, of problems, in which its elements are altogether fuppofititious, which is proof fufficient of its nullity and impropriety.

186. Mr D'Alembert and Mr De la Grange have alfo given general theorems, which they call firſt principles, and which they think highly neceffary in dynamical difquifitions. Thefe, too, are nothing but general, but very fubordinate laws, moſt ingeniouſly employed by their authors in the folution of intricate problems, where they are really of immenfe fervice. But ſtill they are not principles ; and a perfon may underſtand the *mechanique analytique* of De la Grange, by ſtudying it with care, and yet be very ignorant of the real natural principles of mechanifm. All thefe theorems are only ingenious combinations of the fecond and third Newtonian Laws of Motion.

187. The application or employment of thefe laws is to a twofold purpofe.

1. To difcover thofe mechanical powers of natural fubſtances which fit them for being parts of a permanent univerfe. We accompliſh this by obferving what changes of motion among the neighbouring bodies always accompany

pany thofe fubftances, wherever they are. Thefe changes
are the only charaƈteriftics of the powers. It is thus
that we difcover and defcribe the power of magnetifm,
gravity, &c.

2. Having obtained the mechanical charaƈter of any
fubftance, we afcertain what will be the refult of its being in the vicinity of the bodies mechanically allied to it,
or we afcertain what change will be induced on the condition of the neighbouring bodies.

To fave us a great labour, which muft be repeated
for every queftion, if we make *immediate* application of
the laws of motion to the phenomenon, it will be extremely convenient to have in readinefs a few general
rules, accommodated to the more frequent cafes of natural operations. The mechanical powers of bodies occafionally accelerate, retard, and defleƈt the motions of
other bodies. Therefore it is proper to premife the principal theorems relating to the aƈtion of accelerating,
retarding, or defleƈting forces. They have got thefe
names, becaufe we know nothing of their nature, or of
the manner in which they are effeƈtive, and therefore
name them, as we meafure them, by the phenomena
which we confider as their effeƈts.

Of Accelerating and Retarding Forces.

188. Since we have adopted the changes of motion
as the marks and meafures of the forces, it is evident
that every thing already faid of accelerations and retarda-

R   tions

tions is equally defcriptive of the effects of accelerating and retarding forces.   Therefore,

If the abfciffa a d (fig. 5.) *reprefent the time of any motion, and if the areas* a b f e, a c g e, &c. *are as the velocities at the inftants* b, c, &c. *the ordinates* a e, b f, c g, &c. *are as the accelerating forces at thofe inftants* (69).

189.   *Cor.* 1.   The momentary change of velocity is as the force f and the time t jointly, which may be thus expreffed (71.)

$$\dot{v}, \text{ or } - \dot{v}, \risingdotseq f\dot{t}.$$

Alfo, the accelerating or retarding force is proportional to the momentary variation of the velocity, directly, and to the moment of time in which it is generated, inverfely (71.)

$$f \risingdotseq \frac{\dot{v}}{t}, \text{ or } \risingdotseq \frac{-\dot{v}}{t}.$$

Indeed, all that we know of force is that it is fomething which is always proportional to $\dfrac{\dot{v}}{t}$.

190.   *Cor.* 2.   *Uniformly accelerated or retarded motion is the indication of a conftant or invariable accelerating force.*   For, in this cafe, the areas *a b f e, a c g e,* &c. increafe at the fame rate with the times *a b, a c,* &c. and therefore the ordinates *a e, b f, c g,* &c. muft all be equal ; therefore the forces reprefented by them are the fame, or the accelerating force does not change its intenfity, or, it is conftant.   If, therefore, the circumftances

ftances mentioned in articles 54, 55, 56, 57, 58, 59, 60, 61, are obferved in any motion, the force is conftant. And if the force is known to be conftant, thofe propofitions are true refpecting the motions.

191. *Cor.* 3. *No finite change of velocity is generated in an inftant by any accelerating or retarding force.* For the increment or decrement of velocity is always expreffed by an area, or by a product $f\dot{t}$, one fide or factor of which is a portion of time. As no finite fpace can be defcribed in an inftant, and the moveable muft pafs in fucceffion through every point of the path, fo it muft acquire all the intermediate degrees of velocity. It muft be *continually* accelerated or retarded.

192. *Cor.* 4. The change of velocity produced in a body in any time, by a force varying in any manner, is the proper meafure of the accumulated or whole action of the force during this time. For, fince the momentary change of velocity is expreffed by $f\dot{t}$, the aggregate of all thefe momentary changes, that is, the whole change of velocity, muft be expreffed by the fum of all the quantities $f\dot{t}$. This is equivalent to the area of the figure employed in art. 188, and may be expreffed by $\int f\dot{t}$.

193. *If the abfciffa* A E (fig. 8.) *of the line* a c e *be the path along which a body is urged by the action of a force,*

varying

varying in any manner, and if the ordinates A *a,* B *b,* C *c,*
&c. *be proportional to the intenfities of the force in the different points of the path, the intercepted areas will be proportional to the changes made on the fquare of the velocity
during the motion along the correfponding portions of the
path.*

For, by art. 72, the areas are in this proportion when
the ordinates are as the accelerations. But the accelerations are the meafures of, and are therefore proportional
to, the accelerating forces. Therefore the propofition is
manifeft.

194. *Cor.* 1. The momentary change on the fquare
of the velocity is as the force, and as the fmall portion
of fpace along which it acts, jointly;

$$v \dot{v} = f \dot{s}$$

and
$$f = \frac{v \dot{v}}{\dot{s}}.$$

195. It deferves remark here, that as the momentary change of the fimple velocity by any force f depends
only on the time of its action, it being $= f t$ (189.), fo
the change on the fquare of the velocity depends on the
fpace, it being $= f s$. It is the fame, whatever is the
velocity thus changed, or even though the body be at
reft when the force begins to act on it. Thus, in every
fecond of the falling of a heavy body, the velocity is augmented 32 feet per fecond, and in every foot of the fall,
the fquare of the velocity increafes by 64.

196.

196. The whole area A E e a, expreffed by $\int \int f \; \dot{s}$, expreffes the whole change made on the fquare of the velocity which the body had in A, whatever this velocity may have been. We may therefore fuppofe the body to have been at reft in A. The area then meafures the fquare of the velocity which the body has acquired in the point E of its path. It is plain that the change on v^2 is quite independent on the time of action, and therefore a body, in paffing through the fpace A E with any initial velocity whatever, fuftains the fame change of the fquare of that velocity, if under the influence of the fame force.

197. This propofition is the fame with the 39th of the Firft Book of Newton's Principia, and is perhaps the moft generally ufeful of all the theorems in Dynamics, in the folution of practical queftions. It is to be found, without demonftration, in his earlieft writings, the Optical Lectures, which he delivered in 1669 and following years.

198. One important ufe may be made of it at prefent. It gives a complete folution of all the facts which were obferved by Dr Hooke, and adduced by Leibnitz with fuch pertinacity in fupport of his meafure of the force of moving bodies. All of them are of precifely the fame nature with the one mentioned in art. 157, or with the fact, " that a ball projected directly upwards " with a double velocity, will rife to a quadruple height,
                                                            " and

" and that a body, moving twice as faft, will penetrate
" four times as far into a uniformly tenacious mafs. "
The uniform force of gravity, or the uniform tenacity
of the penetrated body, makes a uniform oppofition to
the motion, and may therefore be confidered as a uniform retarding force. It will therefore be reprefented,
in fig. 8, by an ordinate always of the fame length, and
the areas which meafure the fquare of the velocity loft
will be portions of a rectangle A E e a. If therefore A E
be the penetration neceffary for extinguifhing the velocity 2, the fpace A B, neceffary for extinguifhing the
velocity 1, muft be $\frac{1}{4}$ of A E, becaufe the fquare of 1
is $\frac{1}{4}$ of the fquare of 2.

199. What particularly deferves remark here, is,
that this propofition is true, *only on the fuppofition that
forces are proportional to the velocities generated by them in
equal times.* For the demonftration of this propofition
proceeds entirely on the previoufly eftablifhed meafure
of acceleration. We had $\dot{v} \doteq f\,t$; therefore $v\,\dot{v} \doteq f\,t\,v$.
But $t\,v \doteq \dot{s}$; therefore $v\,\dot{v} \doteq f\,\dot{s}$, which is precifely
this propofition.

———————

200. Thofe may be called *fimilar* points of fpace,
and *fimilar* inftants of time, which divide given portions
of fpace or time in the fame ratio. Thus, the beginning
of the 5th inch, and of the 2d foot, are fimilar points
of a foot, and of a yard. The beginning of the 21st
                                                    minute,

minute, and of the 9th hour, are fimilar inftants of an hour, and of a day.

Forces may be faid to act *fimilarly* when, in fimilar inftants of time, or fimilar points of the path, their intenfities are in a conftant ratio.

201. *Lemma.* If two bodies be fimilarly accelerated during given times $a c$ and $h k$ (fig. 24.), they are alfo fimilarly accelerated along their refpective paths A C and H K.

Let a, b, c be inftants of the time $a c$, fimilar to the inftants h, i, k of the time $h k$. Then, by the fimilar accelerations, we have the force $a e : h l = b f : i m$. This being the cafe throughout, the area $a f$ is to the area $h m$ as the area $a g$ to the area $h n$ (Symbols (t)). Thefe areas are as the velocities in the two motions (71.) Therefore the velocities in fimilar inftants are in a conftant ratio, that is, the velocity in the inftant b is to that in the inftant i, as the velocity in the inftant c to that in the inftant k.

The figures may now be taken to reprefent the times of the motion by their abfciffæ, and the velocities by their ordinates, as in art. 45. The fpaces defcribed are now reprefented by the areas. Thefe being in a conftant ratio, as already fhewn, we have A, B, C, and H, I, K, fimilar points of the paths. And therefore, in fimilar inftants of time, the bodies are in fimilar points of the paths. But in thefe inftants, they are fimilarly accelerated, that is, the accelerations and the forces are in in a conſtant ratio. They are therefore in a conſtant ratio in ſimilar points of the paths, and the bodies are ſimilarly accelerated along their reſpective paths (200.).

202. *If two particles of matter are ſimilarly urged by accelerating or retarding forces during given times, the whole changes of velocity are as the forces and times jointly ; or* v $\doteq$ f t.

For the abſciſſæ *a c* and *h k* will repreſent the times, and the ordinates *a e* and *h l* will repreſent the forces, and then the areas will repreſent the changes of velocity, by art. 70.   And theſe areas are as *a c* × *a e* to *h k* × *h l*, (by Symbols (*s. Cor.*)

Hence $t \doteq \frac{v}{f}$, and $f \doteq \frac{v}{t}$.

203. *If two particles of matter are ſimilarly impelled or oppoſed through given ſpaces, the changes in the ſquares of velocity are as the forces and ſpaces jointly ; or* $\doteq$ f s.

This follows, by ſimilar reaſoning, from art. 72.

It is evident that this propoſition applies directly to the argument ſo confidently urged for the propriety of the Leibnitzian meaſure of forces, namely, that four ſprings of equal ſtrength, and bent to the ſame degree, generate, or extinguiſh, only a double velocity.

204. *If two particles of matter are ſimilarly impelled through given ſpaces, the ſpaces are as the forces and the ſquares of the times jointly.*

For

For the moveables are fimilarly urged during the times of their motion (converfe of 201.) Therefore $v \doteq f t$, and $v^2 \doteq f^2 t^2$; but (203.) $v^2 \doteq f s$. Therefore $f s \doteq f^2 t^2$, and $s \doteq f t^2$.

Cor. $t^2 \doteq \dfrac{s}{f}$ and $f \doteq \dfrac{s}{t^2}$. That is, the fquares of the times are as the fpaces, directly, and as the forces, inverfely; and the forces are as the fpaces, directly, and as the fquares of the times, inverfely.

205. The quantity of motion in a body is the fum of the motions of all its particles. Therefore, if all are moving in one direction, and with one velocity v, and if m be the number of particles, or quantity of matter, $m v$ will exprefs the quantity of motion q, or $q \doteq m v$.

206. In like manner, we may conceive the accelerating forces f, which have produced this velocity v in each particle, as added into one fum, or as combined on one particle, by article 170. They will thus compofe a force, which, for diftinction's fake, it is convenient to mark by a particular name. We fhall call it the MOTIVE FORCE, and exprefs it by the fymbol p. It will then be confidered as the aggregate of the number m of equal accelerating forces f, each of which produces the velocity v on one particle. It will produce the velocity $m v$, and the fame quantity of motion q.

207. Let there be another body, confifting of n particles, moving with one velocity u. Let the moving

S   force

force be reprefented by π. It is meafured in like manner by $n\,u$. Therefore we have, $p : \pi = m\,v : n\,u$, and $v : u = \dfrac{p}{m} : \dfrac{\pi}{n}$; that is,

The velocities which may be produced by the fimilar action of different motive forces, in the fame time, are directly as thofe forces, and inverfely as the quantities of matter to which they are applied.

In general,

$$\dot{v} \doteq \frac{p}{m}.$$

And f being $= \dfrac{\dot{v}}{t}$,

$$f \doteq \frac{p}{m\,t}.$$

REMARK.

208. In the application of the theorems concerning accelerating or retarding forces, it is neceffary to attend carefully to the diftinction between an accelerative and a motive force. The caution neceffary here has been generally overlooked by the writers of Elements, and this has given occafion to very inadequate and erroneous notions of the action of accelerating powers. Thus, if a leaden ball hangs by a thread, which paffes over a pulley, and is attached to an equal ball, moveable along a horizontal plane, without *the fmalleft* obftruction, it is known that, in one fecond, it will defcend 8 feet, dragging the other 8 feet along the plane, with a uniformly accelerated motion, and will generate in it the velocity 16 feet per fecond. Let the thread be attached to three fuch balls. We know that it will defcend 4 feet in a fecond, and

generate

generate the velocity 8 feet per fecond. Moft readers are difpofed to think that it fhould generate no greater velocity than $5\frac{1}{3}$ feet per fecond, or $\frac{1}{3}$ of 16, becaufe it is applied to three times as much matter (207.) The error lies in confidering the motive force as the fame in both cafes, and in not attending to the quantity of matter to which it is applied. Neither of thefe conjectures is right. The motive force changes as the motion accelerates, and in the firft cafe, it moves two balls, and in the fecond it moves four. The motive force decreafes fimilarly in both motions. When thefe things are confidered, we learn by articles 202 and 207, that the motions will be precifely what we obferve.

Of Deflecting Forces, in general.

209. It was obferved, in art. 99, that a curvilineal motion is a cafe of *continual* deflection. Therefore, when fuch motions are obferved, we know that the body is under the *continual* influence of fome natural force, acting in a direction which crofles that of the motion in every point. We muft infer the magnitude and direction of this deflecting force by the magnitude and direction of the obferved deflection. Therefore, all that is affirmed concerning deflections in the 99th and fubfequent articles of the Introduction, may be affirmed concerning deflecting forces. It follows, from what has been eftablifhed concerning the action of accelerating forces, that no force can produce a finite change of velocity in an inftant.

Now,

Now, a deflection is a compofition of a motion already exifting with a motion accelerated from reft by infenfible degrees. Suppofing the deflecting force of invariable direction and intenfity, the deflection is the compofition of a motion having a finite velocity with a motion uniformly accelerated from reft. Therefore the linear deflection from the rectilineal motion muft increafe by infenfible degrees. The curvilineal path, therefore, muft have the line of undeflected motion for its tangent. To fuppofe any finite angle contained between them would be to fuppofe a polygonal motion, and a fubfultory deflection.

Therefore *no finite change of direction can be produced by a deflecting force in an inftant.*

210. The moft general and ufeful propofition on this fubject is the following, founded on art. 104.

The forces by which bodies are deflected from the tangents in the different points of their curvilineal paths are proportional to the fquares of the velocities in thofe points, directly, and inverfely to the deflective chords of the equicurve circles in the fame points. We may ftill exprefs the propofition by the fame fymbol

$$f \doteqdot \frac{v^2}{c},$$

where f means the intenfity of the deflecting force.

211. We may alfo retain the meaning of the propofition exprefled in article 105, where it is fhewn that the actual

tual

tual linear deflection from the tangent is the third proportional to the deflective chord and the arch defcribed in
a very fmall moment.   For it was demonftrated in that
article (fee fig. 18.) that $BZ : BC = BC : BO$.

We fee alfo that Bb, the double of BO, is the meafure of the velocity, generated by the uniform action of
the deflecting force, during the motion in the arch BC
of the curve.

212. The art. 106. alfo furnifhes a propofition of
frequent and important ufe, viz.

*The velocity in any point of a curvilinear motion is that
which the deflecting force in that point would generate in
the body by uniformly impelling it along the fourth part of
the deflective chord of the equicurve circle.*

REMARK.

213. The propofitions now given proceed on the
fuppofition that, when the points A and C of fig. 18,
after continually approaching to B, at laft coalefce with
it, the laft circle which is defcribed through thefe three
points has the fame curvature which the path has in B.
It is proper to render this mode of folving thefe queftions
more plain and palpable.

If $ABCD$ (fig. 25.) be a material curve or mould,
and a thread be made faft to it at D, this thread may be
lapped on the convexity of this curve, till its extremity
meets it in A.   Let the thread be now unlapped or
EVOLVED from the curve; keeping it always tight.   It is
plain

plain that its extremity A will defcribe another curve line A *b c*. All curves, in which the curvature is neither infinitely great nor infinitely fmall, may be thus defcribed by a thread evolved from a proper curve. The properties of the curve A *b c* being known, Mr Huyghens (the author of this way of generating curve lines) has fhewn how to conftruct the evolved curve A B C which will produce it.

From this genefis of curves we may infer, 1*st*, that the detached portion of the thread is always a tangent to the curve A B C ; 2*dly*, that when this is in any fituation B *b*, it is perpendicular to the tangent of the curve A *b c* in the point *b*, and that it is, at the fame time, defcribing an element of that curve, and an element of a circle *α b x*, whofe momentary centre is B, and which has B *b* for its radius. 3*dly*, That the part *b* A of the curve, being defcribed with radii growing continually fhorter, is *more* incurvated than the circle *b α*, which has B *b* for its conftant radius. For fimilar reafons the arch *b c* of the curve A *b c* is *lefs* incurvated than the circle *α b x*. 4*thly*, That the circle *α b x* has the fame curvature that the curve has in *b*, or is an equicurve circle. B *b* is the radius, and B the centre of curvature in the point *b*.

A B C is the CURVA EVOLUTA or the EVOLUTE. A *b c* is fometimes called the INVOLUTE of A B C, and fometimes its EVOLUTRIX.

214. By this way of defcribing curve lines, we fee clearly that a body, when paffing through the point *b* of the

the curve A bc may be confidered as in the fame ftate, in that inftant, as in paffing through the fame point b of the circle $\alpha\,b\,\varkappa$; and the ultimate ratio of the deflections in both is that of equality, and they may be ufed indifcriminately.

. . The chief difficulty in the application of the preceding theorems´to the curvilineal motions which are obferved in the fpontaneous phenomena of nature, is in afcertaining the direction of the deflection in every point of a curvilineal motion. Fortunately, however, the moft important cafes, namely thofe motions, where the deflecting forces are always directed to a fixed point, afford a very accurate method. Such forces are called by the general name of

Central Forces.

215. *If bodies defcribe circles with a uniform motion, the deflecting forces are always directed to the centres of the circles, and are proportional to the fquare of the velocities, directly, and to their diftances from the centre, inverfely.*

For, fince their motion in the circumference is uniform, the areas formed by lines drawn from the centre are as the times, and therefore (100) the deflections, and the deflecting forces (209) are directed to the centre. Therefore, the deflective chord is, in this cafe, the diameter of the circle, or twice the diftance of the body from the centre. Therefore, if we call the diftance from the centre d, we have $f \doteqdot \dfrac{v^2}{d}$.

216.

216. *These forces are also as the distances, directly, and as the square of the time of a revolution, inversely.*

For the time of a revolution (which may be called the PERIODIC TIME) is as the circumference, and therefore as the distance, directly, and as the velocity, inversely. Therefore $t \doteq \dfrac{d}{v}$, and $v \doteq \dfrac{d}{t}$, and $v^2 \doteq \dfrac{d^2}{t^2}$, and $\dfrac{v^2}{d} \doteq \dfrac{d}{t^2}$.

217. *These forces are also as the distances, and the square of the angular velocity, jointly.*

For, in every uniform circular motion, the angular velocity is inversely as the periodic time. Therefore, calling the angular velocity a, $a^2 \doteq \dfrac{1}{t^2}$, and $\dfrac{d}{t^2} \doteq d\,a^2$, and therefore $f \doteq d\,a^2$.

218. *The periodic time is to the time of falling along half the radius by the uniform action of the centripetal force in the circumference, as the circumference of a circle is to the radius.*

For, in the time of falling through half the radius, the body would describe an arch equal to the radius (59), because the velocity acquired by this fall is equal to the velocity in the circumference (212.) The periodic time is to the time of describing that arch as the circumference to the arch, that is, as the circumference is to the radius.

219. *When a body describes a curve which is all in one plane, and a point is so situated in that plane, that a line*

drawn

Pl 4.

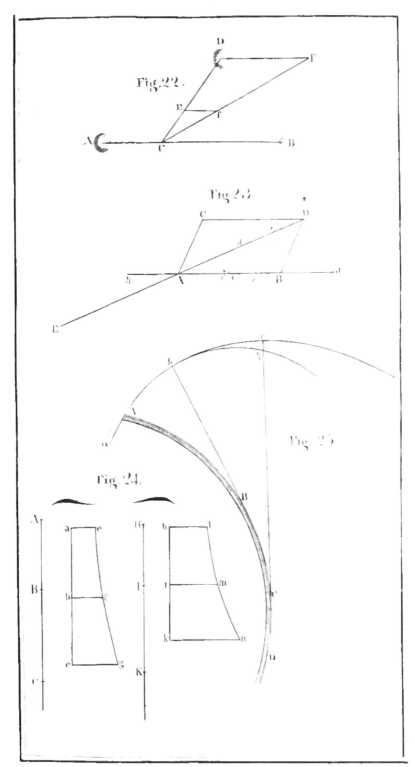

Fig.22.

Fig.23.

Fig.25.

Fig.24.

drawn from it to the body describes round that point areas proportional to the times, the deflecting force is always direct-ed to that point (100.)

220. Conversely. *If a body is deflected by a force al-ways directed to a fixed point, it will describe a curve line lying in one plane which passes through that point, and the line joining it with the centre of forces will describe areas proportional to the times* (101.)

The line joining the body with the centre is called the RADIUS VECTOR. The deflecting force is called CENTRIPETAL, or ATTRACTIVE, if its direction be al-ways *toward* that centre. It is called REPULSIVE, or CENTRIFUGAL, if it be directed outwards *from* the centre. In the firft cafe, the curve will have its *concavity* toward the centre, but, in the fecond cafe, it will be *convex* to-ward the centre. The force which urges a piece of iron towards a magnet is centripetal, and that which caufes two electrical bodies to feparate is centrifugal.

221. *The force by which a body may be made to describe circles round the centre of forces, with the angu-lar velocities which it has in the different points of its curvilineal path, are inversely as the cubes of its distances from the centre of forces.* For the centripetal force in circular motions is proportional to $d a^2$ (217.) But when the deflections (and confequently the forces) are directed to a centre, we have $a \doteqdot \frac{1}{d^2}$ (103.) and $a^2 \doteqdot \frac{1}{d^4}$, there-fore $d a^2 \doteqdot d \times \frac{1}{d^4}$, $\doteqdot \frac{1}{d^3}$, therefore $f \doteqdot \frac{1}{d^3}$.

T   This

This force is often called centrifugal, *the centrifugal force of circular motion*, and it is conceived as always acting in every cafe of curvilineal motion, and to act in oppofition to the centripetal force which produces that motion. But this is inaccurate. We fuppofe this force, merely becaufe we muft employ a centripetal force, juft as we fuppofe a *refifting* vis inertiæ, becaufe we muft employ force to move a body.

222.   *If a body defcribe a curve line* A B C *by means of a centripetal* (fig. 26.) *force directed to* S, *and varying according to fome proportion of the diftances from it, and if another body be impelled toward* S *in the ftraight line* a b S *by the fame force, and if the two bodies have the fame velocity in any points* A *and* a *which are equidiftant from* S, *they will have equal velocities in any other two points* C *and* c, *which are alfo equidiftant from* S.

Defcribe round S, with the diftance S A, the circular arch A a, which will pafs through the equidiftant point a. Defcribe another arch B b, cutting off a fmall arc A B of the curve, and alfo cutting A S in D. Draw D E perpendicular to the curve.

The diftances A S and a S being equal, the centripetal forces are alfo equal, and may be reprefented by the equal lines A D and a b. The velocities at A and a being equal, the times of defcribing A B and a b will be as the fpaces (31). The force a b is wholly employed in accelerating the rectilineal motion along a S. But the force A D, being tranfverfe or oblique to the motion

along

along A B, is not wholly employed in thus accelerating the motion. It is equivalent (173) to the two forces A E and E D, of which E D, being perpendicular to A B, neither promotes nor oppofes it, but incurvates the motion. The accelerating force in A therefore is A E. It was fhewn, in art. 71, that the change of velocity is as the force and as the time jointly, and therefore it is as A E × A B. For the fame reafon, the change of the velocity at a is as $ab \times ab$, or ab^2. But, as the angle A D B is a right angle, as alfo A E D, we have A E : A D = A D : A B, and A E × A B = A D^2, = ab^2. Therefore, the increments of velocity acquired along A B and ab are equal. But the velocities at A and a were equal. Therefore the velocities at B and b are alfo equal. The fame thing may be faid of every fubfequent increafe of velocity, while moving along B C and bc; and therefore the velocities at C and c are equal.

The fame thing holds, when the deflecting force is directed in lines parallel to a S, as if to a point S' infinitely diftant, the one body defcribing the curve line V A' B', while the other defcribes the ftraight line V S.

223. The propofitions in art 102. and 103. are alfo true in curvilineal motions by means of central forces.

When the path of the motion is a line returning into itfelf, like a circle or oval, it is called an ORBIT ; otherwife it is called a TRAJECTORY.

The time of a complete revolution round an orbit is called the PERIODIC TIME.

224. The formula $f \doteq \dfrac{v^2}{c}$ serves for difcovering the law of variation of the central force by which a body defcribes the different portions of its curvilineal path ; and the formula $f \doteq \dfrac{d}{t^2}$ ferves for comparing the forces by which different bodies defcribe their refpective orbits.

225. It muft always be remembered, in conformity to art. 105, that $f = \dfrac{v^2}{c}$ or $f = \dfrac{\text{arc}^2}{c}$ expreffes the linear deflection from the tangent, which may be taken for a meafure of the deflecting force, and that $f = \dfrac{2\,v^2}{c}$ or $f = \dfrac{2\,\text{arc}^2}{c}$ expreffes the velocity generated by this force, during the defcription of the arc, or the velocity which may be compared directly with the velocity of the motion in the arc. The laft is the moft accurate, becaufe the velocity generated is the real change of condition.

226. *A body may defcribe, by the action of a centripetal force, the direction of which paffes through* C *(fig. 27.) a figure* V P S, *which figure revolves (in its own plane) round the centre of forces* C, *in the fame manner as it defcribes the quiefcent figure, provided that the angular motion of the body in the orbit be to that of the orbit itfelf in any conftant ratio, fuch as that of* m *to* n.

For, if the direction of the orbit's motion be the fame with that of the body moving in it, the angular motion

ef

of the body in every point of its motion is increafed in the ratio of m to $n + m$, and it will be in the fame ratio in the different parts of the orbit as before, that is, it will be inverfely as the fquare of the diftance from S (103). Moreover, as the diftances from the centre in the fimultaneous pofitions of the body, in the quiefcent and in the revolving orbit, are the fame, the momentary increments of the area are as the momentary increments of the angle at the centre ; and therefore, in both motions, the areas increafe in the conftant ratio of m to $m + n$ (103). Therefore the areas of the abfolute path, produced by the compofition of the two motions, will ftill be proportional to the times ; and therefore (101) the deflecting force muft be directed to the centre S ; or, a force fo directed will produce this compound motion.

227. *The differences between the forces by which a body may be made to move in the quiefcent and in the moveable orbit are in the inverfe triplicate ratio of the diftances from the centre of forces.*

Let V K S B V (fig. 27.) be the fixed orbit, and $u p k b u$ the fame orbit moved into another pofition ; and let V p n N o N t Q V be the orbit defcribed by the body in abfolute fpace by the compofition of its motion in the orbit with the motion of the orbit itfelf. If the body be fuppofed to defcribe the arch V P of the fixed orbit while the axis V C moves into the fituation u C, and if the arch u p be made equal to V P, then p will be the place of

the

the body in the moveable orbit, and in the compound path $V\,p$. If the angular motion in the fixed orbit be to the motion of the moving orbit as m to n, it is plain that the angle $V\,C\,P$ is to $V\,C\,p$ as m to $m + n$. Let $P\,K$ and $p\,k$ be two equal and very fmall arches of the fixed and moving orbits. $P\,C$ and $p\,c$ are equal, as are alfo $K\,C$ and $k\,C$, and a circle defcribed round C with the radius $C\,K$ will pafs through k. If we now make $V\,C\,K$ to $V\,C\,n$ as m to $m + n$: the point n of the circle $K\,k\,n$ will be the point of the compound path, at which the body in the moving orbit arrives when the body in the fixed orbit arrives at K, and $p\,n$ is the arch of the abfolute path defcribed while $P\,K$ is defcribed in the fixed path.

In order to judge of the difference between the force which produces the motion $P\,K$ in the fixed orbit and that which produces $p\,n$ in the abfolute path, it muft be obferved that, in both cafes, the body is made to ap- proach the centre by the difference between $C\,P$ and $C\,K$. This happens, becaufe the centripetal forces, in both cafes, are greater than what would enable the body to defcribe circles round C, at the diftance $C\,P$, and with the fame angular velocities that obtain in the two paths, viz. the fixed orbit and the abfolute path. We fhall call the one pair of forces the *circular forces*, and the other the *orbital*. Let C and c reprefent the forces which would produce circles, with the angular velocities which obtain in the fixed and moving orbits, and let O and o be the forces which produce the orbital motions in thefe two paths.

Thefe

Thefe things being premifed, it is plain that $o - c$ is equal to $O - C$, becaufe the bodies are equally brought toward the centre by the difference between O and C and by that between o and c. Therefore $o - O$ is equal to $c - C$. * The difference, therefore, of the forces which produce the motions in the fixed and moving orbits is always equal to the difference of the forces which would produce a circular motion at the fame diftances, and with the fame angular velocity. But the forces which produce circular motions, with the angular motion that obtains in an orbit at different diftances from the centre of forces, are as the cubes of the diftances inverfely (221). And the two angular motions at the fame diftance are in the conftant ratio of m to $m + n$. Therefore the forces are in a conftant ratio to each other, and their differences are in a conftant ratio to either of the forces. But the circular force at different diftances is inverfely as the cube of the diftance (221). Therefore the difference of them in the fixed and moveable orbits is in the fame proportion. But the difference of the orbital forces

C O c o

A————•—•————•—•

* For let A o, A O, A c, A C reprefent the four forces o, O, c, and C. By what has been faid, we find that $o c =$ O C. To each of thefe add O c, and then it is plain that o O $= c$ C, that is, that the difference of the circular forces c and C is equal to that of the orbital forces o and O.

forces is equal to that of the circular. Therefore, finally, the difference of the centripetal forces by which a body may be retained in a fixed orbit, and in the fame orbit moving as determined in article 226, is always in the inverfe triplicate ratio of the diſtances from the centre of forces.

In this example, the motion of the body in the orbit is in the fame direction with that of the orbit, and the force to be joined with that in the fixed orbit is always additive. Had the orbit moved in the oppofite direction, the force to be joined would have been fubtractive, unlefs the retrograde motion of the orbit exceeded twice the angular motion of the body. But in all cafes, the reafoning is fimilar.

228. Thus we have confidered the motions of bodies influenced by forces directed to a fixed point. But we cannot conceive a mere mathematical point of fpace as the caufe or occafion of any fuch exertion of forces. Such relations are obferved only between exiſting bodies or maffes of matter. The propofitions which have been demonftrated may be true in relation to bodies placed in thofe fixed points. That continual tendency towards a centre, which produces an equable defcription of areas round it, becomes intelligible, if we fuppofe fome body placed in the centre of forces, attracting the revolving body. Accordingly, we fee very remarkable examples of fuch tendencies towards a central body in the motions of the planets round the Sun, and of the fatellites round the primary planet.

But,

But, fince it is a univerfal fact that all the relations between bodies are mutual, we are obliged to fuppofe that whatever force inclines the revolving body towards the body placed in the centre of forces, an equal force (from whatever fource it is derived) inclines the central body toward the revolving body, and therefore it cannot remain at reft, but muft move towards it. The notion of a fixed centre of forces is thus taken away again, and we feem to have demonftrated propofitions inapplicable to any thing in nature. But more attentive confideration will fhew us that our propofitions are moft ftrictly applicable to the phenomena of nature.

229. For, in the firft place, the motion of the common centre of pofition of two, or of any number of bodies, is not affected by their mutual actions. Thefe, being equal and oppofite, produce equal and oppofite motions, or changes of motion. In this cafe, it follows from art. 115. that the ftate of the common centre is not affected by them.

230. Now, fuppofe two bodies S and P, fituated at the extremities of the line S P (fig. 28.) Their centre of pofition is in a point C, dividing their diftance in fuch a manner that S C is to C P as the number of material atoms in P to the number in S (110.) or $SC : PC = P : S$. Suppofe the mutual forces to be centripetal. Then, being equal, exerted between every atom of the one, and every particle of the other, the vis motrix may be ex-

U   preffed

preſſed by $P \times S$. This muſt produce equal quantities of motion in each of the bodies, and therefore muſt produce velocities inverſely as the quantities of matter (127). In any given portion of time, therefore, the bodies will move towards each other, to s and p, and $S s$ will be to $P p$ as P to S, that is as $S C$ to $P C$. Therefore we ſhall ſtill have $s C : p C = S C : P C$. Their diſtances from C will always be in the ſame proportion. Alſo we ſhall have $S C : S P = P : S + P$, and $s C : p C = P : S + P$; and therefore $S C : S P = s C : s P$. Conſequently, in whatever manner the mutual forces vary by a variation of diſtance from each other, they will vary in the ſame manner by the ſame variation of diſtance from C. And, converſely, in whatever manner the forces vary by a change of diſtance from C, they vary in the ſame manner by the ſame change of diſtance from each other.

Let us now ſuppoſe that when the bodies are at S and P, equal moving forces are applied to each in the oppoſite directions S A and P B. Did they not attract each other at all, they would, at the end of ſome ſmall portion of time, be found in the points A and B of a ſtraight line drawn through C, becauſe they will move with equal quantities of motion, or with velocities S A and P B inverſely as their quantities of matter. Therefore $S A : P B = S C : P C$, and A, C, and B are in a ſtraight line. But let them now attract, when impelled from S and P. Being equally attracted toward each other, they will deſcribe curve lines $S a$ and $P b$, ſo that their deflections $A a$ and $B b$ are as $S C$ and $P C$; and we ſhall

have

have $aC : bC = SC : PC$. As this is true of every part of the curve, it follows that they defcribe fimilar curves round C, which remains in its original place.

Lastly, If the motion of P be confidered by an obferver placed in S, unconfcious of its motion, fince he judges of the motion of P only by its change of direction and of diftance, we may make a figure which will perfectly reprefent this motion. Draw the line E F equal and parallel to P S, and E G equal and parallel to *a b*. Do this for every point of the curve S *a* and P *b*. We fhall then form a curve F G fimilar to the curves S *a* and P *b*, having the homologous lines equal to the fum of the homologous lines of thefe two curves. Thus the bodies will defcribe round each other curve lines which are fimilar and equal (lineally) to the lines which they defcribe round their common centre by the fame forces. They may appear to defcribe areas proportional to the times round each other ; and they really defcribe areas proportional to the times round their common centre of pofition, and the forces, which really relate to the body which *is fuppofed* to be central, have the fame mathematical relation to their common centre.

Thus it appears that the mechanical inferences, drawn from a fuppofed relation to a mere point of fpace, are true in the real relations to the fuppofed central body, although it is not fixed in one place.

231. The time of defcribing any arch F G of the curve defcribed round the other body at reft in a centre

U 2

of

of forces (where we may fuppofe it forcibly withheld from moving) is to the time of defcribing the fimilar arch P b round the common centre of pofition in the fubduplicate ratio of S + P to S, that is, in the ratio of $\sqrt{S + P}$ to $\sqrt{S}$. For the forces being the fame in both motions, the fpaces defcribed by their fimilar actions, that is, their deflections from the tangent are as the fquares of the times T and t (204). That is, H G : B b = $T^2 : t^2$, and
$$T : t = \sqrt{HG} : \sqrt{Bb}, = \sqrt{S + P} : \sqrt{S}.$$

Hence it follows that the two bodies S and P are moved in the fame way as if they did not act on each other, but were both acted upon by a third body, placed in their common centre C, and acting with the fame forces on each ; and the Law of variation of the forces by a change of diftance from each other, and from this third body, is the fame.

232. If a body P (fig. 29.) revolve around another body S, by the action of a central force, while S moves in any path A S B, P will continue to defcribe areas proportional to the times round S, if every particle in P be affected by the fame accelerating force that acts, in that inftant, on every particle in S. For, fuch action will compound the fame motions Pp and Ss with the motions of S and P, whatever they are ; and it was fhown in art. (98.) that fuch compofition does not affect their relative motions. This is another way of making a body defcribe the fame orbit in motion which it defcribes while the orbit is fixed (226).

MECHANICAL PHILOSOPHY.

PART II.

THE MECHANICAL HISTORY OF NATURE.

INTRODUCTION.

233. We have now confidered in fufficient detail thofe general Confequences which refult from the relations of the Ideas that we have of Matter and Motion, and of the Caufes of its changes. Thefe confequences are the metaphyfical or abftract doctrines of Mechanical Philofophy. They are, in reality, defcriptions, not of external nature, but of the proceedings of the human mind in contemplating or ftudying it. Being independent of all experience of any thing beyond our own thoughts, they form a body of demonftrative truths. If this has been made fufficiently complete, that is, if all the poffible mechanical changes are comprehended in the three propofitions which we called the Laws of Motion, we fhould now be in a condition to confider every change of motion, and every changing caufe, which nature prefents to our view, whether in order to inveftigate and

difcover

difcover natural Forces hitherto unknown, and to give
an account of the Laws by which their action is regulated, or to explain complicated phenomena, by referring
them to the operation of fome known forces.

234. Both of thefe purpofes are to be attained by a
careful obfervation of the phenomena. All circumftances
of coincidence or refemblance among them are to be
taken notice of, and confidered as indications of a fimilarity in their Caufes. The more extenfive the obferved
coincidence of appearances is, the more general muft the
affection of matter be which is the caufe of this refemblance. If any fimilarity is univerfally obferved, it muft
be confidered as the indication of a mechanical quality
that is competent to all matter.

235. This confideration points out to us a principle
for arranging the mechanical phenomena of the univerfe.
Thofe fhould be firft confidered that are moft general.
Thus are we made acquainted with the moft general
mechanical properties of Bodies, which extend their influence to phenomena in all the fubordinate claffes, and
modify even that circumftance which forms the particular clafs. Our previous acquaintance with thofe general properties will enable us to free the more particular phenomena from part of that complication which
makes the ftudy of them more difficult ; and then to
confider apart thofe circumftances of the phenomena
which are indications of qualities lefs general.

236.

236. The moſt general phenomenon that we obſerve is the curvilineal motion of bodies in free ſpace. The Globe which we inhabit, the Sun, and all his attending Planets and Comets, are continually moving in curve-lined paths. And theſe curvilineal motions are compounded with all the other motions that are performed on the ſurface of this Globe. When a cannon bullet is diſcharged in a ſoutherly direction with the velocity of 1500 feet in a ſecond, it is at the ſame time carried eaſtward, nearly at the ſame rate, by the rotation of the Earth ; and by its revolution in a year round the Sun, it is moving eaſtward, more than ſixty times as faſt. Such being the condition of the viſible univerſe, it appears that the deflecting forces, by which all theſe bodies are kept in their curvilineal paths, muſt be acknowledged to have the moſt extenſive influence. The phenomena which are the indications of theſe forces, claim the firſt place in the Mechanical hiſtory of Nature. Theſe are obſerved in the celeſtial motions, and Aſtronomy is therefore the firſt department of that hiſtory to which we ſhall turn our attention.

237. This order of ſtudy has other advantages beſides this ſcientific propriety. It is that part of the ſtudy of material nature in which the underſtanding of man has been moſt ſuccefsful. It is perhaps owing to the unexceptionable proofs, which Aſtronomy alone affords of the perfect conformity of our abſtract doctrines with the real ſtate of the world, that thoſe doctrines have been

been admitted as a juft expofition of the elements of Univerfal Mechanics, and thus have given us a groundwork, on which we can proceed with confidence in explaining the mechanical phenomena of this fublunary world.

Aftronomy is alfo the department of natural fcience that is the moft eafily comprehended with the diftinctnefs and accuracy that deferve the name of fcience. Here we have a clear and adequate idea of the fubject, and a diftinct feeling of the validity of the evidence by which any propofition is fupported. In the fimpleft propofition of common Mechanics, or Hydraulics, the fubject under confideration has a degree of complication not to be found in the moft abftrufe propofition in Aftronomy. Accordingly, the knowledge which we can acquire in Aftronomy approaches near to the certainty of firft principles; while in thofe other departments it is only a fuperficial knowledge of fome very general property that we are able to acquire.

Aftronomy is therefore recommended to our firft notice, by the univerfality of the powers of nature that are indicated by the planetary motions,—by the fuccefsfulnefs of the inveftigation,—and by the eafy accefs which it gives us to the elementary principles of all Mechanical fcience.

MECHA-

Pl 5

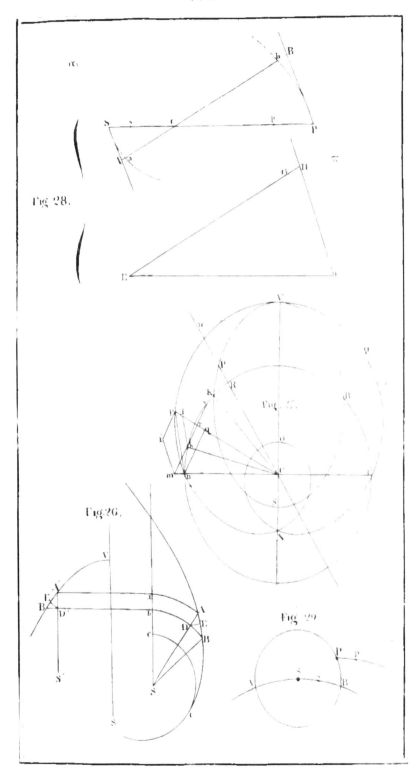

Fig 28.

Fig 26.

Fig 27.

Fig 29

MECHANICAL HISTORY

OF

NATURE.

Sect. I. ASTRONOMY.

238. Astronomy was firſt ſtudied as an art, ſub-ſervient to the purpoſes of ſocial life. Some knowledge of the celeſtial motions was neceſſary, in every ſtate of ſociety, that we might mark the progreſs of the ſeaſons, which regulate the labours of the cultivator, and the migrations of the ſhepherd. It is neceſſary for the re-cord of paſt events, and for the appointment of national meetings.

While the motions of the heavenly bodies afford us the means of attaining theſe uſeful ends, they alſo pre-ſent to the curious philoſopher a ſeries of magnificent phenomena, the operation of the greateſt powers of ma-terial nature ; and thus they powerfully excite his curio-ſity with reſpect to their cauſes. This circumſtance a-lone makes the celeſtial motions the proper objects of attention to a ſtudent of Mechanical Philoſophy, and he has leſs concern in the beautiful regularity and ſubordi-nation which have made them ſo ſubſervient to the pur-poſes of Navigation, of Chronology, and the occupations of rural life.

X

But

MECHANICAL HISTORY

OF

NATURE.

Sect. I. ASTRONOMY.

238. ASTRONOMY was firſt ſtudied as an art, ſub-ſervient to the purpoſes of ſocial life. Some knowledge of the celeſtial motions was neceſſary, in every ſtate of ſociety, that we might mark the progreſs of the ſeaſons, which regulate the labours of the cultivator, and the migrations of the ſhepherd. It is neceſſary for the re-cord of paſt events, and for the appointment of national meetings.

While the motions of the heavenly bodies afford us the means of attaining theſe uſeful ends, they alſo pre-ſent to the curious philoſopher a ſeries of magnificent phenomena, the operation of the greateſt powers of ma-terial nature ; and thus they powerfully excite his curio-ſity with reſpect to their cauſes. This circumſtance a-lone makes the celeſtial motions the proper objects of attention to a ſtudent of Mechanical Philoſophy, and he has leſs concern in the beautiful regularity and ſubordi-nation which have made them ſo ſubſervient to the pur-poſes of Navigation, of Chronology, and the occupations of rural life.

X

But

But the purpofes of the Mechanical philofopher cannot be attained without attending to that beauty, regularity, and fubordination. Thefe features are exhibited in every circumftance of the celeftial motions that renders them fufceptible of fcientific arrangement and inveftigation; and a philofophical view cannot be taken, without the fame accurate knowledge of the motions that is wanted for the arts of life. It muft be added, that fociety never would have derived the benefits which it has received from Aftronomy, without the labours of the philofopher: For, had not Newton, or fome fuch exalted genius as Newton, fpeculated about the deflecting forces which regulate the motions of the Solar fyftem, we never fhould have acquired that exquifite knowledge of the mere phenomena that is abfolutely neceffary for fome of the moft important applications of them to the arts. It was thefe fpeculations alone that have enabled our navigators to proceed with boldnefs through untried feas, and in a few years have almoft completed the furvey of this globe. And thus do we experience the moft beneficial alliance of Philofophy and Art.

Since the motions of bodies are the only indications, characteriftics, and meafures of moving forces, it is plain that the celeftial motions muft be accurately afcertained, that we may obtain the data wanted for the purpofe of philofophical inference. To afcertain thefe is a tafk of great difficulty; and it has required the continual efforts of many ages to acquire juft notions of the

motions

motions exhibited to our view in the heavens. For the fame general appearances may be exhibited, and the fame perceptions obtained, and the fame opinions will be formed, by means of motions very different; and it is frequently very difficult to felect thofe motions which alone can exhibit *every* obferved appearance. If a perfon who is in motion, imagines that he is at reft, and affumes this principle in his reafonings about the effects of the motions which he perceives, he miftakes the conclufions which he draws for real perceptions; and calls that a deception of fenfe, which is really an error in judgement. Errors in our opinions concerning the motions of the heavenly bodies, are neceffarily accompanied by falfe judgements concerning their caufes. Therefore, an accurate examination of the motions which really obtain in the heavens, muft precede every attempt to inveftigate their caufes.

The moft probable plan for acquiring a juft and fatisfactory knowledge of thefe particulars, is to follow the fteps of our predeceffors in this ftudy, and firft to confider the more general and obvious phenomena. From thefe we muft deduce the opinions which moft obvioufly fuggeft themfelves, to be corrected afterwards, by comparing them with other phenomena, which may happen to be irreconcileable with them.

X 2   *Aftronomical*

Aftronomical Phenomena.

239. To an obferver, whofe view on all fides is bounded only by the fea, the heavens appear a concave fphere, of which the eye is the centre, ftudded with a great number of luminous bodies, of which the Sun and Moon are the moft remarkable. This fphere is called the SPHERE OF THE STARRY HEAVENS.

The only diftances in the heavens which are the immediate objects of our obfervation, are arches of great circles paffing through the different points of the ftarry heavens. Therefore, all aftronomical computations and meafurements are performed by the rules of fpherical trigonometry.

240. We fee only the half of the heavens at a time, the other half being hid by the earth, on which we are placed. The great circle H B O D (fig. 30.), which feparates the vifible hemifphere H Z O from the invifible hemifphere H N O, is called the HORIZON. This is marked out on the ftarry heavens by the fartheft edge of the fea. The point Z immediately over the head of the obferver is called the ZENITH ; and the point N, diametrically oppofite to it, is called the NADIR.

241. The zenith and nadir are poles of the horizon.

242.

242. If an obferver looks at the heavens, while a plummet is fufpended before his eye, the plumb line will mark out on the heavens a quadrant of a circle, whofe plane is perpendicular to the horizon, and which therefore paffes through the zenith and nadir, and through two oppofite points of the horizon. Z O N H and Z B N D are fuch circles. They are called VERTICAL CIRCLES and AZIMUTH CIRCLES.

243. The ALTITUDE of any celeftial phenomenon fuch as a ftar A, is the angle A C B, formed in the plane of the vertical circle Z A N, by the horizontal line C B and the line C A. This name is alfo given to the arch A B of the vertical circle which meafures this angle. The arch Z A is called ZENITH DISTANCE of the phenomenon.

244. The AZIMUTH of the phenomenon is the angle O C B, or O Z B, formed between the plane of the vertical circle Z A B paffing through the phenomenon, and the plane of fome other noted vertical Z O N. The arch C B of the horizon, which meafures this angle, is alfo frequently called the Azimuth.

245. The ftarry heavens appear to turn round the earth, which feems pendulous in the centre of the fphere ; and by this motion, the heavenly bodies come into view in the eaft, or RISE ; they attain the greateft altitude, or CULMINATE, and difappear in the weft, or SET. This is called the FIRST MOTION.

246.

246. This motion is performed round an axis N S (fig. 31.), paffing through two points N, S, called the poles of the world. In confequence of this motion, a celeftial object A defcribes a circle A D B F, through the centre C of which the axis N S paffes, perpendicularly to its plane. This motion may be very diftinctly perceived as follows. Let a point, or fight, be fixed in the infide of a fky-light fronting the north, and inclined fouthwards from the perpendicular at an angle equal to the latitude of the place. An eye placed at this point will fee the ftars through the glafs of the window. Let the points of the glafs, through which a ftar appears from time to time be marked. The marks will be found to lie in the circumference of a circle, the centre of which will mark the place of the pole in the heavens.

247. Thofe ftars which are fartheft from the poles will defcribe the greateft circles ; and thofe will defcribe the largeft poffible circles which are in the circumference of the circle Æ W Q E, which is equidiftant from both poles. This circle is called the EQUATOR, and, being a great circle, it cuts the horizon in two points, E, W, diametrically oppofite to each other. They are the eaft and weft points of the horizon.

248. If a great circle A N Q S Æ paffes through the poles perpendicularly to the horizon H W O E, it will cut it in the north and fouth points ; and any ftar A will acquire its greateft elevation when it comes to the

femicircle

femicircle N A S, and its greateft depreffion when it comes to the femicircle N B S; and the arch D A F of its apparition will be bifected in A.

249. If the circle A D B F of revolution be between the equator and that pole N which is above the horizon, the greateft portion of it will be vifible; but if it be on the other fide of the equator, the fmalleft portion will be vifible. One half of the equator is vifible. Some circles of revolution are wholly above the horizon, and fome are wholly below it. A ftar in one of the firft is always feen, and one in the laft is never feen.

250. The diftance A Æ of any point A from the e-quator is called its DECLINATION, and the circle A D B F, being parallel to the equator, is called a PARALLEL OF DECLINATION.

251. The angle Æ C H, contained by the planes of the equator and horizon, is the complement of the angle N C O, which is the elevation of the pole.

252. The revolution of the ftarry heavens is performed in 23ʰ 56′ 4″. It is called the DIURNAL REVOLUTION. No appearance of inequality has been obferved in it; and it is therefore affumed as the moft perfect meafure of time.

253. The time of the diurnal apparition or difpari-·tion of a point of the ftarry heavens is bifected in the

inftant

inftant of its culmination or greateft depreffion. The
fun, therefore, is in the circle N A S Q at noon. For
this reafon the circle N A S Q is called the MERIDIAN.

254. A phenomenon whofe circle of diurnal revolution A D B F is on the fame fide of the equator with
the elevated pole, is longer vifible than it is invifible.
The contrary obtains if it be on the other fide of the
equator.

255. Any great circle N A Æ S, or N B L S (fig. 32.),
paffing through the poles of the world, is called an HOUR
CIRCLE.

256. The angle Æ C L, or Æ N L, contained between the plane of the hour-circle N B L S, paffing
through any phenomenon B, and the plane of the hour
circle N Æ S, paffing through a certain noted point Æ
of the equator, is called the RIGHT ASCENSION of the
phenomenon. The intercepted arch Æ L of the equator, which meafures this angle, is called by the fame
name.

257. In affigning the place of any celeftial phenomenon, we cannot ufe any points of the earth as points of
reference. The ftarry heavens afford a very convenient
means for this purpofe. Moft of the ftars retain their relative fituations, and may therefore be ufed as fo many
points of reference. The application of this to our purpofe
requires

requires a knowledge of the pofitions of the ftars. This may be acquired. The difference between the meridional altitude of a ftar B, and of the equator, gives the arch A Æ, intercepted between the equator and the parallel of declination, or circle of diurnal revolution A B D, defcribed by the ftar. And the time which elapfes between the paffage of this ftar over the meridian, and the paffage of that point Æ of the equator from which the right afcenfions are computed, gives the arch Æ L of the equator which has paffed during this interval. Therefore, an hour circle N L S being drawn through the point L of the equator, and a circle of revolution A B D being drawn at the obferved diftance A Æ from the equator, the place of the ftar will be found in their interfection B.

258. Globes and maps have been made, on which the reprefentations of the ftars have been placed, in pofitions fimilar to their real pofitions ; and catalogues of the ftars have been compofed, in which every ftar is fet down with its declination and right afcenfion, this being the moft convenient arrangement for the practical aftronomer. Their longitudes and latitudes (to be explained afterwards) are alfo fet down, in feparate columns. The moft noted of all thefe is the BRITANNIC CATALOGUE, conftructed by Dr Flamftead, from his own obfervations in the Royal Obfervatory at Greenwich. This catalogue contains the places of 3030 ftars. It is accompanied by a collection of maps, known to all aftronomers by the

Y

title

title of ATLAS CELESTIS. An ufeful abridgement of both has been publifhed by *Bode* in *Berlin*, and by *Fortin* at *Paris*, in fmall quarto. Two planifpheres have alfo been publifhed by *Senex*, in *London*, conftructed from the fame obfervations, and executed with uncommon elegance; as alfo a particular map of that zone of the heavens to which all the planetary motions are limited. This is alfo executed with fuperior elegance and accuracy. The place of any phenomenon may be afcertained in it within 5′ of the truth, by mere infpection, without calculation, fcale, or compaffes. No aftronomer fhould be unprovided with it.

259. All thefe reprefentations and defcriptions of the ftarry heavens become obfolete, in fome meafure, in confequence of a gradual change in the declination and right afcenfion of the ftars. But, as this may be accurately computed, the maps and catalogues retain their original value, requiring only a little trouble in accomodating them to the prefent ftate of the heavens. The Britannic Catalogue and Atlas are adjufted to the ftate of the heavens in 1690; and the planifpheres, &c. by Senex are the fame. The editions of Paris and Berlin are for 1750.

260. In thefe maps and catalogues, it has been found convenient to diftribute the ftars into groups, called CONSTELLATIONS; and figures are drawn, which comprehend all the ftars of a group, and give them a fort of connexion

connexion and a name. Each ſtar is diſtinguiſhed by its number in the conſtellation, and alſo by a letter of the alphabet. Thus, the moſt brilliant ſtar in the heavens, the Dog ſtar, or Sirius, is known to all aſtronomers as Nº 9., or as α, *canis majoris*. The numbers always refer to the Britannic catalogue, it being conſidered as claſſical.

261. Since the publication of that work, however, great additions have been made to our knowldge of the ſtarry heavens, and ſeveral Catalogues and Atlaſes have been publiſhed in different parts of Europe. Of the catalogues, the moſt eſteemed are, 1. a ſmall catalogue of 389 ſtars, the places of which have been determined with the utmoſt care by Dr Bradley, at the Greenwich Obſervatory ; 2. a catalogue of the ſouthern ſtars by Abbé de la Caille ; 3. a catalogue of the zodiacal ſtars by Tobias Mayer at Gottingen ; and, *laſtly*, a new atlas celeſtis, conſiſting of a catalogue and maps of the whole heavens, and containing above 15,000 ſtars, by Mr Bode of Berlin. The Rev. Mr Fr. Wollaſton publiſhed, in 1780, a ſpecimen of a general aſtronomical catalogue of the fixed ſtars, arranged according to their declinations, folio, London, 1780. This is a moſt valuable work, containing the places of many thouſand ſtars, according to the catalogues of Flamſtead, La Caille, Bradley, and Mayer. Theſe being arranged in parallel columns, we ſee the differences between the determinations of thoſe aſtronomers, and are advertiſed of any changes which have occurred in the heavens. The catalogue is accompanied

Y 2   by

by directions for profecuting this method of obtaining a
minute furvey of the whole ftarry heavens.

In the valuable aftronomical tables publifhed in 1776
by the academy of Berlin, Mr Bode has given a fimilar
fynopfis of the catalogues of Flamftead, La Caille, Bradley and Mayer, not indeed fo extenfive, nor fo minute,
as Wollafton's, but of great ufe.

262. Having thus obtained maps of the heavens,
the place of a celeftial phenomenon is afcertained in a
variety of ways.   1. By its obferved diftance from two
known ftars.   2. By its altitude and azimuth.   3. Moft
accurately, by its right afcenfion and declination.

263. This laft being the moft accurate method of
afcertaining the place of any celeftial phenomenon, obfervations of meridional altitude, and of TRANSITS over
the meridian, are the moft important.   For an account of
the manner of conducting thefe obfervations, and a defcription of the inftruments, we may confult Smith's
Optics, Vol. II. ; Mr Vince's Treatife of Practical Aftronomy ; La Lande's Aftronomy, &c.   The MURAL QUAD-
RANT, TRANSIT INSTRUMENT, and CLOCK, are therefore the capital furniture of an obfervatory ; to which,
however, fhould be added an EQUATOREAL INSTRUMENT
for obferving phenomena out of the meridian.   Other inftruments, fuch as the EQUAL ALTITUDE INSTRUMENT,
the RHOMBOIDAL RETICULA, the ZENITH SECTOR, and
one or two more, are fitted for aftronomers on a voyage.

264.

264. The pofition of the meridian, and the latitude of the obfervatory, muft be accurately determined. Various methods of determining the meridian. The moft accurate is to view a circumpolar ftar through a telefcope which has an accurate motion in a vertical plane, and to change the pofition of the telefcope till the times which elapfe between the fucceffive upper and lower tranfits of the ftar are precifely equal. The inftrument is then in the plane of the meridian (fig. 33.)

265. In order to find the declination of a phenomenon more readily, it is convenient to know the inclination of the axis of diurnal revolution N S (fig. 31.) to the horizon, or the elevation of the pole N. The beft method for this purpofe is to obferve the greateft elevation I O, and the leaft elevation K O, of fome circumpolar ftar. The elevation of the pole N is half the fum of thofe elevations.

266. The elevation of the pole is different in different places. An obferver, fituated 69½ ftatute miles due north of another, will find the pole elevated about a degree more above his horizon. From obfervations of this kind, the bulk and fhape of the earth are determined. For it is plain that 360 times 69½ miles muft be the circumference of the globe. It is found to be nearly an elliptical fpheroid, of which the axis is 7904 miles, and the greateft diameter 7940⅔ miles. This deviation from perfect fphericity has been difcovered by meafuring,

in

in the way now mentioned, a degree of the meridian in different latitudes. One was meafured in Lapland, in latitude 66° 20′, and it meafured 122,457 yards, exceeding 69½ miles by 137 yards. Another was meafured at Peru, croffing the very equator. It contained 121,027 yards, falling fhort of 69½ miles by 1293 yards, and wanting 1430 yards, or almoft a mile, of the other. Other degrees have been meafured in intermediate latitudes ; and it is clearly eftablifhed, that the degrees gradually increafe, as we go from the equator towards either pole.

267. The length of a degree is the diftance between two places where the tangents to the furface are inclined to one another one degree, or where two plumb lines, which are perpendicular to the furface of ftanding water, will, when produced downwards, meet one another, intercepting an angle of one degree. The furface of the ftill ocean is therefore lefs incurvated as we approach the poles, or it requires a longer arch to have the fame curvature. It is a degree of a larger circle, and has a longer radius. Perfons who do not confider the thing attentively, are apt to imagine, from this, that the earth is fhaped like an egg ; becaufe, if we draw from its centre lines C N (fig. 33. N° 2.) C O, C P, C Q, equally inclined to one another, the arches N O, O P, P Q, will gradually increafe from N towards Q. If thefe lines make angles of one degree with one another, they will meet the furface in points that are farther and farther afunder,

afunder, and the degree will appear to increafe as we approach the points E and Q, which we fuppofe, at prefent, to be the poles. But let fuch perfons reflect, that if thefe lines from the centre are produced beyond the furface, they cannot be plumb lines, perpendicular to the furface of ftanding water. But if an ellipfe N E S Q (fig. 33. N° 2.) be made to turn round its fhorter axis N S, it will generate a figure flatter round N and S than at E or Q. If we draw two lines a D and b B perpendicular to the curve in a and b, and exceedingly near one another, they will be tangents to a curve A B D F, by the evolution of which the elliptic quadrant E a N is defcribed. A E is the radius of curvature of the equatoreal degree of the meridian E a N. N F is the radius of the polar degree, and a D is the radius of curvature at the intermediate latitude of a, &c. All thefe radii are plumb lines, perpendicular to the elliptical curve of the ocean.

Thefe plumb lines therefore do not meet in the centre of the earth, as is commonly imagined, but meet, in fucceffion, in the circumference of the evolute A B D F. The earth is not a *prolate* fpheroid like an egg, but an *oblate* fpheroid, like a turnip or bias bowl.

268. Since the axis of diurnal revolution paffes through the centre of the earth, it marks on its furface two points, which are the poles of the earth. Thefe are in the extremities of the axis of the terreftrial fpheroid. In like manner, the plane of the celeftial equator

passing

paffing through the centre of the earth, divides it into
two hemifpheres, the northern and fouthern, feparated
by the *terreſtrial* equator.   Alfo the hour circles, paffing
through the earth's centre, mark on its furface the terreſtrial meridians.

269.   The pofition of a place on the furface of the
earth is determined by its LATITUDE, or diſtance from
the terreſtrial equator, and its LONGITUDE, or the angular diſtance of its meridian, from fome noted meridian.

270.   Aſtronomical obfervations are made from a
point on the furface of the earth, but, for the purpofes
of computation, are fuppofed to be made from the centre.   The angular diſtance between the obferved place
A (fig. 34.) of a phenomenon S in the heavens, as feen
from a place D on the Earth's furface, and its place B,
as viewed from the centre, is called the PARALLAX of
the phenomenon.

271.   Befides the motion of diurnal revolution, common to all the heavenly bodies, there are other motions,
which are peculiar to fome of them, and are obferved by
us by means of their change of place in the ſtarry heavens.   Thus, while the ſtarry heavens turn round the
Earth from eaſt to weſt in 23^h 56' 4", the Sun turns
round it in 24^h.   He *muſt*, therefore, change his place
to the eaſtward in the ſtarry heavens.   The Moon has
an evident motion eaſtward among the ſtars, moving her
                                                        own

own breadth in about an hour. There are five ftars which are obferved to change their places remarkably in the heavens, and are therefore called PLANETS, or wanderers ; while thofe which do not change their relative places are called FIXED STARS. The planets are MERCURY, VENUS, MARS, JUPITER, and SATURN. To thefe we muft now add the planet difcovered in 1781 by Dr Herfchel, which he called the Georgian Planet, in honour of his Sovereign, the diftinguifhed patron of Aftronomy. Aftronomers on the continent have not adopted this denomination, and feem generally agreed to call it by the name of the difcoverer. M. Piazzi, at Palermo, has difcovered another, and M. Olbers, at Bremen, a third, which they have named Ceres and Pallas. None of the three are vifible to the naked eye.

272. Planets are diftinguifhable from the fixed ftars by the fteadinefs of their light, while all the fixed ftars are obferved to twinkle. The following fymbols are frequently ufed :

For the Sun	-	-	-	-	☉
the Moon	-	-	-	-	☽
Mercury		-	-	-	☿
Venus	-	-	-	-	♀
the Earth	-	-	-	-	♁
Mars	-	-	-	-	♂
Jupiter	-	-	-	-	♃
Saturn	-	-	-	-	♄
Herfchel		-	-	-	HL

Z

The

The motions of thefe bodies have become interefting on various accounts. In order to acquire a knowledge of their motions more eafily, it is convenient to abftract our attention from the diurnal motion, common to all, and attend only to their proper motions among the fixed ftars.

Of the proper Motions of the Sun.

273. We cannot obferve the motion of the Sun a-mong the fixed ftars immediately, on account of his great fplendour, which hinders us from perceiving the ftars in his neighbourhood. But we can obferve the inftant of his coming to the meridian, and his meridional altitude (257.) The Sun muft be in that point of the heavens which paffes the meridian at that inftant, and with that altitude. Or we can obferve the point of the heavens which comes to the meridian at midnight, with a declination as far on one fide of the equator as the Sun's obferved declination is on the other fide of it. The Sun muft be in the point of the heavens which is diametrically oppofite to this point. By taking either of thefe methods, but particularly the firft, we can afcer-tain a feries of points of the heavens through which the Sun paffes. Thefe are found to be in the circumference of a great circle of the fphere A S V W (fig. 35.), which cuts the celeftial equator in two oppofite points A, V, and is inclined to it at an angle of 23° 28' 10" nearly. This circle, or Sun's path, is called the ECLIPTIC.

274.

274. In confequence of the obliquity of the ecliptic, the Sun's motion in it is accompanied by a change in the Sun's declination and right afcenfion, by a change in the length of the natural day, and by a change of the feafons. Therefore, the revolution of the Sun in the ecliptic is performed in a year.

275. The points V, A, are called EQUINOCTIAL POINTS; becaufe, when the fun is in thefe points, his circle of diurnal revolution is the celeftial equator, and therefore the day and night are equal. The point V, through which he paffes in the month of March, is called the VERNAL EQUINOX, and the point A is called the AUTUMNAL EQUINOX. The points S and W, where he is fartheft from the equator, are called the SOLSTITIAL POINTS, S being the fummer, and W the winter folftice. The parallels of declination paffing through the folftitial points are called TROPICS.

276. Right afcenfion is always computed eaftward on the equator, from the vernal equinox.

277. The ecliptic paffes through the conftellations
Aries, diftinguifhed by the fymbol ♈
Taurus   -   -   -   -   -   ♉
Gemini   -   -   -   -   -   ♊
Cancer   -   -   -   -   -   ♋
Leo   -   -   -   -   -   -   ♌
Virgo   -   -   -   -   -   ♍

Z 2   Libra,

Libra, diftinguifhed by the fymbol   ♎

Scorpio - - - - - ♏

Sagittarius - - - - ♐

Capricornus - - - - ♑

Aquarius - - - - - ♒

Pifces - - - - - ♓

Thefe conftellations are called the SIGNS of the ZODIAC ; and a motion from weft to eaft is faid to be DIRECT, or IN CONSEQUENTIA SIGNORUM, while a contrary motion is called RETROGRADE, IN ANTECEDENTIA SIGNORUM.

278. The changes of the feafons were attributed by the ancients to the influence of the ftars which were feen in the different feafons of the year.

279. The pofition of the ecliptic is invariable, and a complete revolution is performed in 365 days, 6 hours, 9 minutes, and 11 feconds.

280. If fuccefsive obfervations be made of the Sun's crofsing the equator, it will be found that the equinoctial points are not fixed, but move to the weftward about 50″ in a year, fo that they would make a complete revolution in about 25,972 years. This is called the PRECESSION of the EQUINOXES.

281. Sir Ifaac Newton made a very ingenious and important inference from this aftronomical fact. If we

know

know the fituation of the equinoctial points at the time
of any hiftorical event, the date of the event may
be difcovered.   He thinks that this pofition at the
time of the Argonautic expedition may be inferred
from the defcription given by Aratus of the ftarry heavens. The poet defcribes a celeftial fphere by which
Chiron, one of the heroes, directed their motions ; and
from this he deduces data for a chronology of the heroic
or fabulous ages.   But, fince the equinoctial points fhift
only at the rate of a degree in 72 years, and the
Greeks were fo ignorant, for ages after that epoch, that
they did not know that the pofitions of the ftars were
changeable, it does not appear that much reliance can
be had on this datum.   We cannot, from the defcription by Aratus, be certain of the pofition of the vernal
equinox within five or fix degrees.   This makes a difference of 400 years in the epochs.

282.   The axis of diurnal revolution is not always
the fame, and the poles of the heavens defcribe (in 25,972
years) a circle round the pole of the ecliptic, diftant
from it 23° 28′ 10″ nearly.

283.   On account of the wefterly motion of the e-
quinoctial points, the return of the feafons muft be accomplifhed in lefs time than that of the Sun's revolution
round the heavens.   The feafons return after an interval
of 365ᵈ 5ʰ 48′ 45″.   This is called a TROPICAL year, to
diftinguifh it from the interval 365ᵈ 6ʰ 9′ 11″, called a
SYDEREAL year.

284.

284. Aftronomers have chofen to refer the places of the heavenly bodies to the ecliptic, on account of its ftability, rather than to the equator. For this purpofe, great circles, fuch as P V p, PA p, (fig. 36.) are drawn through the poles P, p, of the ecliptic. Thefe are called ECLIPTIC MERIDIANS. The arch A B of one of thefe circles, intercepted between a phenomenon A and the ecliptic, is called the LATITUDE of the phenomenon; and the arch V B, intercepted between the point V of the vernal equinox and the point B, is called the LONGITUDE of the phenomenon. This is fometimes expreffed in degrees and minutes, and fometimes in figns, (each $= 30°$.)

285. The motion of the Sun in the ecliptic is not uniform. On the firft of January his daily motion is nearly 1° 1′ 13″. But on the firft of July, his daily motion is 57′ 13″. The mean daily motion is 59′ 08″. The Sun's place in the ecliptic, calculated on the fuppofition of a daily motion of 59′ 08″, will be behind his obferved place, from the beginning of January to the beginning of July, and will be before it, from the beginning of July to the beginning of January. The greateft difference is about 1° 55′ 32″, which is obferved about the beginning of April and October; at which times, the obferved daily motion is 59′ 08″.

286. This unequable motion of the Sun appeared to the ancient aftronomers to require fome explanation.

It

Pl. 7   P. 182

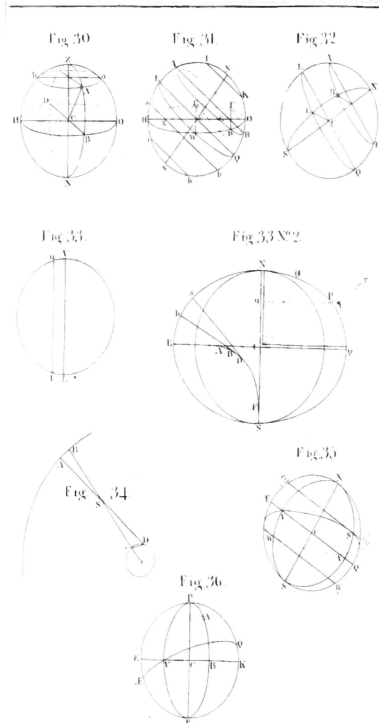

Fig. 30

Fig. 31.

Fig. 32

Fig. 33.

Fig. 33 N°2

Fig. 34

Fig. 35

Fig. 36.

It had been received as a firft principle, that the celeftial motions were of the moft perfect kind—and this perfection was thought to require invariable famenefs. Therefore the Sun muft be carried uniformly in the circumference of a figure perfectly uniform in every part. He muft therefore move uniformly in the circumference of a circle. The aftronomers therefore fuppofed that the Earth is not in the centre of this circle.   Let A *b* P *d* (fig. 37.) reprefent the Sun's orbit, having the Earth in E, at fome diftance from the centre C.   It is plain that if the Sun's motion be uniform in the circumference, defcribing every day 59′ 08″, his angular motion, as feen from the Earth, muft be flower when he is at A, his greateft diftance, than when neareft to the Earth, at P.   It is alfo evident that the point E may be fo chofen, that an arch of 59′ 08″ at A fhall fubtend an angle at E that is only 57′ 13″, and that an arch of 59′ 08″ at P fhall fubtend an angle of 61′ 13″.   This will be accomplifhed, if we make E P to E A as 57′ 13″ to 61′ 13″, or nearly as 14 to 15.   This was accordingly done; and this method of folving the appearances was called the *eccentric hypothefis*.   E C is the ECCENTRICITY, and P E is to P C nearly as 28 to 29.

287.   But although this hypothefis agreed very well with obfervation in thofe points of the orbit where the Sun is moft remote from the Earth, or neareft to it, it was found to differ greatly in other parts of the orbit, and particularly about half way between A and P.   Aftronomers,

It had been received as a firſt principle, that the celeſtial
motions were of the moſt perfect kind—and this perfection was thought to require invariable famenefs.
Therefore the Sun muſt be carried uniformly in the circumference of a figure perfectly uniform in every part.
He muſt therefore move uniformly in the circumference
of a circle. The aſtronomers therefore ſuppoſed that
the Earth is not in the centre of this circle. Let A *b* P *d*
(fig. 37.) repreſent the Sun's orbit, having the Earth in
E, at ſome diſtance from the centre C. It is plain that
if the Sun's motion be uniform in the circumference,
deſcribing every day 59′ 08″, his angular motion, as ſeen
from the Earth, muſt be ſlower when he is at A, his greateſt diſtance, than when neareſt to the Earth, at P. It is
alſo evident that the point E may be ſo choſen, that an
arch of 59′ 08″ at A ſhall ſubtend an angle at E that is
only 57′ 13″, and that an arch of 59′ 08″ at P ſhall
ſubtend an angle of 61′ 13″. This will be accompliſhed,
if we make E P to E A as 57′ 13″ to 61′ 13″, or nearly
as 14 to 15. This was accordingly done ; and this method of ſolving the appearances was called the *eccentric*
hypotheſis.   E C is the ECCENTRICITY, and P E is to
P C nearly as 28 to 29.

287. But although this hypotheſis agreed very well
with obſervation in thoſe points of the orbit where the
Sun is moſt remote from the Earth, or neareſt to it,
it was found to differ greatly in other parts of the orbit,
and particularly about half way between A and P. A-
ſtronomers,

ftronomers, after trying various other hypothefes, were
obliged to content themfelves with reducing the eccentricity confiderably, and alfo to fuppofe that the angular
motion of 59' 08" per day was performed round a point
e on the other fide of the centre, at the fame diftance
with E. This, however, was giving up the principle of
perfect motion, if its perfection confifted in uniformity;
for, in this cafe, the Sun cannot have an uniform motion in the circumference, and alfo an uniform angular
motion round e. Befides, even this amendment of the
eccentric hypothefis by no means agreed with the obfervations in the months of April and October: but
they could not make it any better.

288. Aftronomical computations are made on the
fuppofition of uniform angular motion. The angle proportional to the time is called the MEAN MOTION, and
the place thus computed is called the MEAN PLACE.
The differences between the mean places and the obferved, or TRUE PLACES, are called EQUATIONS. They
are always greateft when the mean and true motions are
equal, and they are nothing when the mean and true
motions differ moft. For, while the true daily angular
motion is lefs than the mean daily motion, the obferved
place falls more and more behind the calculated place
every day; and although, by gradually quickening, it lofes
lefs every day, it ftill lofes, and falls ftill more behind;
and when the true daily motion has at laft become equal
to the mean, it lofes no more indeed, but it is now the
fartheft.

fartheft behind that can be. Next day it gains a little of the loft ground, but is ftill behind. Gaining more and more every day, by its increafe of angular motion, it at laft comes up with the calculated place; but now, its angular motion is the greateft poffible, and differs moft from the equable mean motion.

289. Thefe computations are begun from that point of the orbit where the motion is floweft, and the mean angular diftance from this point is called the MEAN ANO-MALY. A table is made of the equations correfponding to each degree of the mean anomaly. The true anomaly is found by adding to, or fubtracting from the computed mean anomaly, the equations correfponding to it.

In this manner may the fun's longitude, or place in the ecliptic, be found for any time.

290. In confequence of the obliquity of the ecliptic, and the fun's unequal motion in it, the natural days, or the interval between two fucceffive paffages of the fun over the meridian, are unequal; and if a clock, which meafures $365^d\ 5^h\ 48'\ 45''$ in a tropical year, be compared from day to day with an exact fun dial, they will be found to differ, and will agree only four times in the year. This difference is called the EQUATION of TIME, and fometimes amounts to 16 minutes. The time fhewn by the clock is called MEAN SOLAR TIME, and that fhewn by the dial is called TRUE TIME and APPARENT TIME.

A a   291.

291. The change in the fun's motion is accompa-nied by a change in his apparent diameter, which, at the beginning of January, is about 32′ 39″, and at the beginning of July is about 31′ 34″, $\frac{1}{10}$ lefs. This muft be afcribed to a change of diftance, which muft always be fuppofed inverfely proportional to the apparent diameter.

292. By combining the obfervations of the fun's place in the ecliptic with thofe of his diftance, inferred from the apparent diameter, and by other more decifive, but lefs obvicus obfervations, Kepler, a German aftro-nomer, found that his apparent path round the earth is an ellipfe, having the earth in one focus, and having the longer axis to the fhorter axis as 200,000 to 199,972.

The extremities A and P of the longer axis of the fun's orbit A B P D (fig. 37.) are called the APSIDES. The point A, where the fun is fartheft from the earth (placed in E), is called the higher apfis, or APOGEE. P is the lower apfis, or PERIGEE. The diftance E C between the focus and centre is called the ECCENTRI-CITY, and is 1680 parts of a fcale, of which the mean diftance E D is 100,000.

293. Kepler *obferved*, that the fun's angular motion in this orbit was inverfely proportional to the fquare of his diftance from the earth ; for he obferved the fun's daily change of place to be as the fquare of his apparent diameter. Hence, he inferred that the radius vector E B defcribed areas proportional to the times (103.)

294.

294. From this he deduced a method of calculating the fun's place for any given time. Draw a line E F from the focus of the ellipfe, which fhall cut off a fector A E F, having the fame proportion to the whole furface of the ellipfe, which the interval of time between the fun's laft paffage through his apogee, and the time for which the computation is made, has to a fydereal year; F will be the fun's true place for that time. This is called KEPLER'S PROBLEM.

This problem, the moft interefting to aftronomers, has not yet been folved otherwife than by approximation, or by geometrical conftructions which do not admit of accurate computation.

295. Let A B P D (fig. 37.) be the elliptical orbit, having the earth in the focus E. A and P, the extremities of the tranfverfe axis, are the apogee and perigee of the revolving body. B D is the conjugate axis, and C the centre. It is required to draw a line E T which fhall cut off a fector A E T, which has to the whole ellipfe the proportion of m to n; m being taken to n in the proportion of the time elapfed fince the body was in A to the time of a complete revolution.

Kepler, who was an excellent geometer, faw that this would be effected, if he could draw a line E I, which fhould cut off from the circumfcribed circle A b P d the area A E I, which is to the whole circle in the fame proportion of m to n. For, then, drawing the perpendicular ordinate I R, cutting the ellipfe in T, he knew that the area A E T has the fame proportion to the el-

lipfe

lipfe that A E I has to the circle. The proof of this
is eafy, and it feems greatly to fimplify the problem,
Draw I C through the centre, and make E S perpendicular to I C S. The area A E I confifts of the circular
fector A C I, and the triangle C I E. The fector is equal
to half the rectangle of the radius C I and the arch A I,
that is, to $\dfrac{CA \times IA}{2}$. The triangle C I E is equal to
$\dfrac{CI \times ES}{2}$, or $\dfrac{CA \times ES}{2}$. Therefore it is evident
that, if we make the arch I M equal to the ftraight line
E S, the fector A C M will be equal to the circular area
A C I, and the angle A C M will be to 360 degrees, as
m to n.

296. Hence we fee that it will be eafy to find the
time when the revolving body is in any point T. To
find this, draw the ordinate R T I; draw I C S and E S,
and make I M = E S. Then, 360° is to the arch A M
as the time of a revolution to the time in which the body
moves over A T. This is (in the aftronomical language)
finding the mean anomaly when the true anomaly is
given. The angle A C M, proportional to the time, is
called the MEAN ANOMALY, and the angle A E T is the
TRUE ANOMALY. The angle A C I is called the ANO-
MALY OF THE ECCENTRIC, or the ECCENTRIC ANO-
MALY.

297. But the aftronomer wants the true anomaly
correfponding to a given mean anomaly. The procefs
here given cannot be reverfed. We cannot tell how
much

much to cut off from the given mean anomaly A M, fo
as to leave A I of a proper magnitude, becaufe the indifpenfable meafure of M I, namely E S, cannot be had till
I C S be drawn. Kepler faw this, and faid that his
problem could not be folved geometrically. Since the
invention of fluxions, however, and of converging feriefes, very accurate folutions have been obtained. That
given by *Frifius* in his *Cofmographia* is the fame in principle with all the moft approved methods, and the form
in which it is prefented is peculiarly fimple and neat.
But, except for the conftruction of original tables, thefe
methods are rarely employed, on account of the labo-
rious calculation which they require. Of all the direct
approximate folutions, that given by Dr Matthew Stewart at the end of his *Tracts, Phyfical and Mathematical,*
publifhed in 1761, feems the moft accurate and elegant ;
and the calculations founded on it are even fhorter than
the indirect methods generally employed. His conftruction is as follows.

298. Let the angle A E M be the mean anomaly,
join E M, and draw C i parallel to it, and M O perpendicular to C i. If the orbit is not more eccentric than that
of Mars, make the arch i I equal to the excefs of the
arch M i above its fine M O. Then A I is the eccentric anomaly correfponding to the mean anomaly A M,
and the ordinate I R will cut the ellipfe in T, fo that
A E T will be the true anomaly required. The error
will not amount to two feconds in any part of fuch orbits.

bits. But, for orbits of greater eccentricity, another ſtep is neceſſary. Join E i, and draw C Q parallel to E i, meeting the tangent i Q in Q. Let D repreſent the exceſs of the arch M i above its ſine M O *, and inſtitute the following analogy, ſin. M C i : tan. i C Q = D : i I, taking i I from i towards M. The point, I, will be ſo ſituated that the ſector A E I is very nearly equal to the ſector A C M, or A I is the eccentric anomaly correſponding to the mean anomaly A M. The error will not amount to one ſecond, even in the orbit of Mercury.

The demonſtration of this conſtruction is by no means abſtruſe or difficult. Draw I S, and M I. The triangles i C E and i C M are evidently equal, being on one baſe i C, and between the parallels i C and M E. For ſimilar reaſons, the triangles i S I and i E I are equal. Therefore the triangle i C E, together with the ſegment included between the arch M b i and the chord M i, will be equal to the circular ſector i C M.

Now it is plain, from the conſtruction, that S i : C i = S E : i Q, = M O : i Q, = $\overline{\text{M} b i - \text{M O}}$: i I. Therefore S i × i I = C i × M b i — C i × M O. But C i ×
M b i

---

* This exceſs muſt be expreſſed in degrees, minutes, or ſeconds. The radius of a circle is equal to an arch of 206,265 ſeconds. The logarithm of this number is 5.3144251. Therefore we ſhall obtain E S, or the ſeconds in E S, by adding this logarithm to the logarithms of E C (A C being unity), and the logarithm of the ſine of A C I. The ſum is the logarithm of the ſeconds in E S.

M *bi* is equal to twice the fector M C *i*, and C *i* × M O
is equal to twice the triangle M C *i*. Therefore S *i* × *i* I
is equal to twice the fegment contained between M *b i*
and the chord M *i*. Therefore this fegment is equal to
the triangle *i* S I, or to the triangle *i* E I. Therefore the
fpace C *i* I E C is equal to the fector *i* C M, and the
fector A E I to the fector A C M.

The calculation founded on this conftruction is extremely fimple. In the triangle M C E, the fides M C
and C E are given, with the included angle M C E ; and
the angles C E M, C M E are fought. Moreover, A E is
the fum of the given fides, and P E is their difference,
and A C M is the fum of the angles M and E. There-
fore A E : E P = tan. $\dfrac{E + M}{2}$: tan. $\dfrac{E - M}{2}$; and thus E
and M, or their equals, A C *i* and M C *i*, are obtained.
In the next place, in the triangle *i* C E, the fides *i* C,
C E, and the included angle *i* C E, are given, and the
angle E *i* C is fought. We have, in the fame manner as
before, A C *i* equal to the fum of the angles E and *i*,
and therefore A E : E P = tan. $\dfrac{E + i}{2}$: tan. $\dfrac{E - i}{2}$. Thus
the angle E *i* C, or its equal, *i* C Q, is obtained, and then,
the arch *i* I = D × $\dfrac{i\,Q}{M\,O}$, = D × $\dfrac{\text{tan. } i\,C\,Q}{\text{fin. } M\,C\,i}$.

In the very eccentric orbits of the comets, this brings
us vaftly nearer to the truth than any of the indirect methods we know does by the firft ftep. So near indeed, that
the common method, by the *rule of falfe pofition*, may now
be fafely employed. If the point, I, has been accurately
found,

found, it is plain that if to the arch A I we add E S, that is, E C × fin. A C I, we obtain the arch A M with which we began. But if I has not been accurately de-termined, A M will differ from the primitive A M. Therefore, make fome fmall change on A I, and again compute A M. This will probably be again erroneous. Then apply the rule of falfe pofition as ufual. The er-ror remaining after the firft ftep of Dr Stewart's procefs is always fo moderate that the variations of A M are very nearly proportional to the variations of A I; fo that two fteps of the rule will generally bring the calculation within two or three feconds of the truth. The aftrono-mical ftudent will find many beautiful and important propofitions in thefe mathematical tracts. The propofi-tion juft now employed is in page 398, &c.

299. Aftronomers have difcovered, that the line A P moves flowly round E to the eaftward, changing its place about 25′ 56″ in a century. This makes the time of a complete revolution in the orbit to be 365ᵈ 6ʰ 15′ 20″. This time is called the ANOMALISTIC YEAR.

Of the proper Motions of the Moon.

300. Of all the celeftial motions, the moft obvious are thofe of the Moon. We fee her fhift her fituation among the ftars about her own breadth to the eaftward in an hour, and in fomewhat lefs than a month fhe makes a complete tour of the heavens. The gentle beauty of her

her appearance during the quiet hours of a ferene night, has attracted the notice, and we may fay the affections of all mankind ; and fhe is juftly ftyled the Queen of Heaven. The remarkable and diftinct changes of her appearance have afforded to all fimple nations a moft convenient index and meafure of time, both for recording paft events, and for making any future appointments for bufinefs. Accordingly, we find, in the firft hiftories of all nations, that the lunar motions were the firft ftudied, and, in fome degree, underftood. It feems to have been in fubferviency to this ftudy alone that the other appearances of the ftarry heavens were attended to ; and the relative pofitions of the ftars feem to have interefted us, merely as the means of afcertaining the motions of the Moon. For we find all the zodiacs of the ancient oriental nations divided, not into 12 equal portions, correfponding to the Sun's progrefs during the period of feafons, but into 27 parts, correfponding to the Moon's daily progrefs, and thefe are exprefsly called the HOUSES or MANSIONS of the Moon. This is the diftribution of the zodiac of the ancient Hindoos, the Perfians, the Chinefe, and even the Chaldeans. Some have no divifion into 12, and thofe who have, do not give *names* to 12 groups of ftars, but to 27. They firft defcribe the fituation of a planet in one of thefe manfions by name, noting its diftance from fome ftars in that group, and thence infer in what part of which twelfth of the circumference it is placed. The divifion into 12 parts is merely mathematical, for the purpofe of calculation. In all probability, therefore, this

B b   was

was an after-thought, the contrivance of a more cultivated age, well acquainted with the heavens as an object
of fight, and beginning to extend the attention to fpeculations beyond the firft conveniences of life.

301. When the Moon's path through this feries of
manfions is carefully obferved, it is found to be (very
nearly) a great circle of the heavens, and therefore in a
plane paffing through the centre of the earth.

302. She makes a complete revolution of the heavens
in 27^d 7^h $43'$ $12''$, but with fome variations. Her mean
daily motion is therefore $13°$ $10'$ $25''$, and her horary motion is $32'$ $56''$.

303. Her orbit is inclined to the plane of the ecliptic
in an angle of $5°$ $8'$ $45''$, nearly, cutting it in two points
called her NODES, diametrically oppofite to each other;
and that node through which fhe paffes in coming from
the fouth to the north fide of the ecliptic, is called the
ASCENDING NODE.

304. The nodes have a motion which is generally
weftward, but with confiderable irregularities, making a
complete revolution in about 6803^d 2^h $55'$ $18''$, nearly
$18\frac{2}{3}$ years.

305. If we mark on a celeftial globe a feries of
points where the Moon was obferved during three or

four revolutions, and then lap a tape round the globe, covering thofe points, we fhall fee that the tape croffes the ecliptic more·wefterly every turn, and then croffes the laft round very obliquely; and we fee that by continuing this operation, we fhall completely cover with the tape a zone of the heavens, about ten or eleven degrees broad, having the ecliptic running along its middle.

306. The Moon moves unequally in this orbit, her hourly motion increafing from 29′ 34″ to 36′ 48″, and the equation of the orbit fometimes amounts to 6° 18′ 32″; fo that if, fetting out from the point where her horary motion is floweft, we calculate her place, for the eighth day thereafter, at the rate of 32′ 56″ per hour, we fhall find her obferved place fhort of our calculation more than half a day's motion. And we fhould have found her as much before it, had we begun our calculation from the oppofite point of her orbit.

307. Her apparent diameter changes from 29′ 26″ to 33′ 47″, and therefore her diftance from the Earth changes. This diftance may be difcovered in miles by means of her parallax.

She was obferved, in her paffage over the meridian, by two aftronomers, one of whom was at Berlin, and the other at the Cape of Good Hope. Thefe two places are diftant from one another above 5000 miles; fo that the obferver at Berlin faw the Moon every day confiderably more to the fouth than the perfon at the Cape. This difference of apparent declination is the meafure of the angle D S C (fig. 34.) fubtended at the Moon by the line c D of 5443 miles, between the obfervers. The angles S D c and S c D are given by means of the Moon's obferved altitudes. Therefore any of the fides S D or S c may be computed. It is found to be nearly 60 femidiameters of the earth.

308. By combining the obfervations of the Moon's place in the heavens with thofe of her apparent diameter, we difcover that her orbit is nearly an ellipfe, having the Earth in one focus, and having the longer axis to the fhorter axis nearly as 91 to 89. The greateft and leaft diftances are nearly in the proportion of 21 to 19.

309. Her motion in this ellipfe is fuch, that the line joining the Earth and Moon defcribes areas which are nearly proportional to the times. For her angular hourly motion is obferved to be as the fquare of her apparent diameter.

310. The line of the apfides has a flow motion eaftward, completing a revolution in about 3232^d 11^h 14′ 30″, nearly 9 years.

311. While the Moon is thus making a revolution round the heavens, her appearance undergoes great changes. She is fometimes on our meridian at midnight, and, therefore, in the part of the heavens which is oppofite

polite to the Sun. In this lituation, lhe is a complete luminous circle, and is laid to be FULL. As lhe moves
eaftward, lhe becomes deficient on the weft fide, and,
after about 7¼ days, comes to the meridian about fix in
the morning, having the appearance of a femicircle,
with the convex fide next the Sun. In this ftate, her
appearance is called HALF MOON. Moving ftill eaftward,
lhe becomes more deficient on the weft fide, and has now
the form of a crefcent, with the convex fide turned towards the Sun. This crefcent becomes continually more
flender, till, about 14 days after being full, lhe is fo
near the Sun that lhe cannot be feen, on account of his
great fplendour. About four days after this difappearance in the morning before funrife, lhe is feen in the
evening, a little to the eaftward of the Sun, in the form
of a fine crefcent, with the convex fide turned toward
the Sun. Moving ftill to the eaftward, the crefcent becomes more full, and when the Moon comes to the meridian about fix in the evening, lhe has again the appearance of a bright femicircle. Advancing ftill to the eaftward, lhe becomes fuller on the eaft fide, and, at laft,
after about 29½ days, lhe is again oppofite to the Sun,
and again full.

312. It frequently happens that the Moon is ECLIP-
SED when full; and that the Sun is eclipfed fome time
between the difappearance of the Moon in the morning
on the weft fide of the Sun, and her reappearance in the
evening on the eaft fide of the Sun. This eclipfe of the

Sun

Sun happens at the very time that the Moon, in the courfe
of her revolution, paffes that part of the heavens where
the Sun is.

313. From thefe obfervations, we conclude, 1. That
the Moon is an opaque body, vifible only by means of
the Sun's light illuminating her furface; 2. That her orbit round the Earth is nearer than the Sun's.

314. From thefe principles all her PHASES, or appearances, may be explained (fig. 39.)

315. When the Moon comes to the meridian at
mid-day, fhe is faid to be NEW, and to be in CONJUNC-
TION with the Sun. When fhe comes to the meridian
at midnight, fhe is faid to be in OPPOSITION. The line
joining thefe two fituations is called the line of the
SYZIGIES. The points where fhe is half illuminated are
called the QUADRATURES; and that is called the firft
quadrature which happens after new moon.

316. When the Moon is half illuminated, the line
E M (fig. 39.) joining the Earth and Moon, is perpendicular
to the line M S, joining the Moon and Sun. By obferving the angle S E M, the proportion of the diftance of
the Sun to the diftance of the Moon may be afcertained.
This method of afcertaining the Sun's diftance was
propofed by Ariftarchus of Samos, about 264 years before the Chriftian æra. The thought was extremely ingenious,

genious, and ftrictly juft ; and this was the firft obfervation that gave the aftronomers any confident guefs at the
very great diftance of the Sun.   But it is impoffible to
judge of the half illumination of the Moon's difk with
fufficient accuracy for obtaining any tolerable meafure.
Even now, when affifted by telefcopes, we cannot tell
to a few minutes when the boundary between light and
darknefs in the Moon is exactly a ftraight line.   When
this really happens, the elongation S E M wants but 9'
of a right angle, and when it is altogether a right angle,
there is no fenfible change in the appearance of the
Moon.   All that the ancient aftronomers could infer
from their beft eftimation of the bifection of the Moon
was, that the Sun was, for certain, at a much greater
diftance than any perfon had fuppofed before. that time.
Ariftarchus faid, that the angle S E M was not lefs than
87 degrees, and therefore the Sun was at leaft twenty
times farther off than the Moon.   But aftronomers of the
Alexandrian fchool faid, that the angle S E M exceeded
89°, and the Sun was fixty times more remote than the
Moon.   Modern obfervations fhew him to be near four
hundred times more remote.

317. This fucceffion of phafes is completed in a
period of 29^d 12^h 44' 3", called a SYNODICAL MONTH
and a LUNATION.

It may be afked here, how the period of a lunation
comes to differ from that of the Moon's revolution round
the Earth, which is accomplifhed in 27^d 7^h 43' 12" ? This

is

is owing to the Sun's change of place during a revolution of the Moon. Suppofe it new Moon, and therefore the Sun and Moon appearing in the fame place of the heavens. At the end of the lunar period, the Moon is again in that point of the heavens. But the Sun, in the mean time, has advanced above 27 degrees; and fomewhat more than two days muft elapfe before the Moon can overtake the Sun, fo as to be feen by us as new moon.

318. The period of this fucceffion of phafes may be found within a few hours of the truth in a very fhort time. We can tell, within four or five hours, the time of the Moon being half illuminated. Suppofe this obferved in the morning of her laft quarter. We fhall fee this twice repeated in 59 days, which gives 29d 12ʰ for a lunation, wanting about three fourths of an hour of the truth. About 433 years before the Chriftian æra, Meton, a Greek aftronomer, reported to the ftates affembled at the Olympic games, that in nineteen years there happened exactly 235 lunations.

319. The lunar motions are fubject to feveral irregularities, of which the following are the chief:

320. 1. The periodic month is greater when the Sun is in perigee than when in apogee, the greateft difference being about 24 minutes. Tycho Brahé firft remarked this anomaly of the lunar motions, and called

the

the correction, (depending on the Sun's place in his orbit), the ANNUAL EQUATION of the Moon.

321. 2. The mean period is lefs than it was in ancient times.

322. 3. The orbit is larger when the Sun is in perigee than when he is in apogee.

323. 4. The orbit is more eccentric when the Sun is in the line of the lunar apfides; and the equation of the orbit is then increafed nearly 1° 20′ 34″. This change is called the EVECTION. It was difcovered by Ptolemy.

324. 5. The inclination of the orbit changes.

325. 6. The moon's motion is retarded in the firft and third quarters, and accelerated in the fecond and laft. This anomaly was difcovered by Tycho Brahé, who calls it the VARIATION.

326. 7. The motion of the nodes is very unequal.

Of the Calendar.

327. Aftronomy, like all other fciences, was firft practifed as an art. The chief object of this art was to know the feafons, which, as we have feen, depend either

C c   immediately,

immediately, or more remotely, on the Sun's motion in the ecliptic. A ready method for knowing the feafon feems, in all ages, to have been the chief incitement to the ftudy of aftronomy. This muft direct the labours of the field, the migrations of the fhepherd, and the journies of the traveller. It is equally neceffary for appointing all public meetings, and for recording events.

Were the ftars vifible in the day time, it would be eafy to mark all the portions of the year by the Sun's place among them. When he is on the foot of Caftor, it is midfummer; and midwinter, when he is on the bow of Sagittarius. But this cannot be done, becaufe his fplendour eclipfes them all.

328. The beft approximation which a rude people can make to this, is to mark the days in which the ftars of the zodiac come firft in fight in the morning, in the eaftern horizon, immediately before the Sun rife. As he gradually travels eaftward along the ecliptic, the brighter ftars which rife about three quarters of an hour before the Sun, may be feen in fucceffion. The hufbandman and the fhepherd were thus warned of the fucceeding tafks by the appearance of certain ftars before the Sun. Thus, in Egypt, the day was proclaimed in which the Dogftar was firft feen by thofe fet to watch. The inhabitants immediately began to gather home their wandering flocks and herds, and prepare themfelves for the inundation of the Nile in twelve or fourteen days. Hence that ftar was called the *Watch-dog*, THOTH, the Guardian of Egypt.

This

.'This was therefore a natural commencement of the period of feafons in Egypt ; and the interval between the fucceffive apparitions of Thoth, has been called the NA-TURAL year of that country, to diftinguifh it from the civil or artificial year, by which all records were kept, but which had little or no alliance with the feafons. It has alfo been called the *Canicular* year. It evidently depends on the Sun's fituation and diftance from the Dog-ftar, and muft therefore have the fame period with the Sun's revolution from a ftar to the fame ftar again. This requires 365ᵈ 6ʰ 9′ 11″, and differs from our period of feafons. Hence we muft conclude that the rifing of the Dog-ftar is not an infallible prefage of the inundation, but will be found faulty after a long courfe of ages. At prefent it happens about the 12th or 11th of July.

'This obfervation of a ftar's firft appearance in the year, by getting out of the dazzling blaze of the Sun, is called the *heliacal rifing* of the ftar. The ancient alma-nacks for directing the rural labours were obliged to give the detail of thefe in fucceffion, and of the correfponding labours. Hefiod, the oldeft poet of the Greeks, has given a very minute detail of thofe heliacal rifings, or-namented by a pleafing defcription of the fucceffive oc-cupations of rural life. This evidently required a very confiderable knowledge of the ftarry heavens, and of the chief circumftances of diurnal motion, and particularly the number of days intervening between the firft appear-ance of the different conftellations.

C c 2

Such

Such an almanack, however, cannot be expected, except among a fomewhat cultivated people, as it requires
a long continued obfervation of the revolution of the
heavens in order to form it ; and it muft, even among
fuch people, be uncertain. Cloudy, or even hazy weather, may prevent us for a fortnight from feeing the ftars
we want.

329. The Moon comes moft opportunely to the aid
of fimple nations, for giving the inhabitants an eafy divifion and meafure of time. The changes in her appearance are fo remarkable, and fo diftinct, that they cannot
be confounded. Accordingly, we find that all nations
have made ufe of the lunar phafes to reckon by, and for
appointing all public meetings. The feftivals and facred
ceremonies of fimple nations were not all dictated by fuperftition ; but they ferved to fix thofe divifions of time
in the memory, and thus gave a comprehenfive notion of
the year. All thefe feftivals were celebrated at particular phafes of the Moon—generally at new and full Moon.
Men were appointed to watch her firft appearance in the
evening, after having been feen in the morning, rifing
a few minutes before the Sun. This was done in confecrated groves, and in high places ; and her appearance
was *proclaimed.* Fourteen days after, the feftival was generally held *during full Moon.* Hence it is that the firft
day of a Roman month was named KALENDÆ, the day
to be proclaimed. They faid *pridie, tertio, quarto,* &c.
ante calendas neomenias Martias ; the third, fourth, &c.
before

before proclaiming the new Moon of March. And the affemblage of months, with the arrangement of all the feftivals and facrifices, was called a KALENDARIUM.

As fuperftition overran all rude nations, no meeting was held without facrifices and other religious ceremonies—the watching and proclaiming was naturally committed to the priefts—the kalendar became a facred thing, connected with the worfhip of the gods—and, long before any moderate knowledge of the celeftial motions had been acquired, every day of every Moon had its particular fanctity, and its appropriated ceremonies, which could not be transferred to any other.

330. But as yet there feemed no precife diftinction of months, nor of what number of months fhould be affembled into one group. Moft nations feem to have obferved that, after 12 Moons were completed, the feafon was pretty much the fame as at the beginning. This was probably thought exact enough. Accordingly, in moft ancient nations, we find a year of 354 days. But a few returns of the winter's cold, when they expected heat, would fhew that this conjecture was far from being correct ; and now began the embarraffment. There was no difficulty in determining the period of the feafons exactly enough, by means of very obvious obfervations. Almoft any cottager has obferved that, on the approach of winter, the Sun rifes more to the right hand, and fets more to the left every day, the places of his rifing and fetting coming continually nearer to each other ; and

that,

that, after rifing for two or three days from behind the
fame object, the places of rifing and fetting again gradually feparate from each other. By fuch familiar obfervations, the experience of an ordinary life is fufficient
for determining the period of the feafons with abundant
accuracy. The difficulty was to accomplifh the recon-
ciliation of this period with the facred cycle of months,
each day of which was confecrated to a particular deity,
jealous of his honours. Thus the Hierophantic fcience,
and the whole art of kalendar-making, were neceffarily
entrufted to the priefts. We fee this in the hiftory of
all nations, Jews, Pagans, and Chriftians.

331. Various have been the contrivances of different nations. The Egyptians, and fome of the neighbouring Orientals, feem early to have known that the period
of feafons confiderably exceeded 12 months, and contained 365 days. They made the civil year confift of
12 months of 30 days, and added 5 complementary days
without ceremonies ; and when more experience convinced them that the year contained a fraction of a day
more, they made no change, but made the people believe
that it was an improvement on their kalendar that their
great day, the firft of *Thoth*, by falling back one day in
four periods of feafons, would thus occupy in fucceffion
every day of the year, and thus fanctify the whole in
1461 years, as they imagined, but really in 1425 of their
civil years. We have but a very imperfect knowledge of
the arrangement of their feftivals. Indeed they were totally different in almoft every city.

It

It is important to the aftronomer to know this method of reckoning ; becaufe all the obfervations of Hipparchus and Ptolemy, and all thofe which they have
quoted from the Chaldeans, Perfians, &c. are recorded
by it. In An. Dom. 940, the firft day of Thoth fell on
the firft of January, and another Egyptian year commenced on the 31ft of December of that year. From
this datum it is eafy to reckon back by years of 365 days,
and to fay on what day of what month of any of our
years the 1ft day of Thoth falls, and this wandering
year commences.

332. The Greeks have been much more puzzled
with the formation of a lunifolar year than the Egyptians. Solon got an oracle to direct his Athenians (594
years before our æra), θυεῖν κατα τρια, κατα ῾Ηλιον, κατα Σε-
λῆνην, και κατα ἡμερας. The meaning of which feems to
be, to regulate their year by the Sun, or feafons, their
months by the Moon, and their feftivals by the days.
Obferving that 59 days made two months, he made thefe
alternately of 30 and of 29 days, πλειαι, and κοιλαι, full,
and deficient ; and the 30th day of a month, the τριακις,
was called ἑνη και νεα, νεομηνια, as it belonged to both
months.

But this was not fufficiently accurate ; and the Olympic games, celebrated on every fourth year, during the
full Moon neareft to midfummer day, had gone into
great confufion. The Hierophants, whofe proclamation
to all the ftates affembled the chiefs together, had not
fkill

ſkill enough to keep them from gradually falling into the
autumn months.   Injudicious corrections were made
from time to time, by rules for inſerting months to bring
things to rights again.   It deſerves to be remarked here,
that this is the way in which the ancient aſtronomy improved,   before   the   eſtabliſhment   of   the   Alexandrian
ſchool.   It was not by a more accurate obſervation of the
motions,   as   in   modern   times,   but   by   diſcovering   the
errors,   when   they   amounted   to   an   unit   of   the   ſcale   on
which they were meaſured.   The aſtronomers then im-
proved   their   future   computations   by   repeatedly   cutting
off this unit of accumulated error.

333.   All theſe contrivances were publicly propoſed
at the meeting of the States for the Olympic Games.
This   was   an   occaſion   peculiarly   proper,   and   here   the
ſcheme of Meton was received with juſt applauſe.   For
Meton not only gave his countrymen a very exact determination of the lunar month, but accompanied it with a
ſcheme of intercalation, by which all their feſtivals, religious and civil, were arranged ſo as to have very ſmall
diſlocations from the days of new and full Moon.   As
this had hitherto been a matter of inſuperable difficulty,
Meton was declared victor in the firſt department, a ſta-
tue was decreed him, and his arrangement of the feſtivals was inſcribed on a pillar of marble, in letters of gold.
This has occaſioned the number expreſſing the current
year of the cycle of 19 years (called the Metonic cycle)
to be called the Golden Number.   This ſcheme of Me-

ton's was indeed very judicious, though intricate, becaufe he arranged the interpolation of a month fo as never to remove the firft day of the month two days from the time of new Moon, whereas it had often been a week.

The Metonic cycle commenced on 16. July, 433 years before the beginning of the Chriftian æra, at 43 minutes paft 7 in the morning, that being the time of new Moon. The firft year of each cycle is that in which the full Moon of its firft month is the neareft to the fummer folftice.

334. The Roman kalendar was in a much worfe condition than the rudeft of the Greeks. The fuperfti-tious veneration for their ceremonies, or their paffion for public fports, had diverted the attention of the Romans (who never were cultivators or graziers) from the feafons altogether. They were contented with a year of ten months for feveral centuries, and had the moft abfurd contrivances for producing fome conformity with the fea-fons. At laft, that accomplifhed general, Julius Cæfar, having attained the height of his vaft ambition, refolved to reform the Roman kalendar. He was profoundly fkilled in aftronomy, and had written fome differtations on different branches of the fcience, which had great re-putation, but are now loft. He had no fuperftitious or religious qualms to difturb him, and was determined to make every thing yield to the great purpofe of a kalen-dar, its ufe in directing the occupations of the people, and for recording the events of hiftory. He took the

D d   help

help of Sofigenes, an aftronomer of the Alexandrian
fchool, a man perfectly acquainted with all the difcoveries of Hipparchus and others of that celebrated academy.

These eminent fcholars, knowing that the period of
feafons occupied 365 days and a quarter very nearly,
made a fhort cycle of 4 years, containing three years of
365, and one of 366 days; thus cutting off, in the Grecian
manner, the error, when it amounted to a whole day.
Cæfar refolved alfo to change the beginning of the year
from March, where Romulus had placed it in honour
of his patron Mars, to the winter folftice. This is certainly the moft natural way of eftimating the commencement of the year of feafons. What we are moft anxious
to afcertain is the precife day when the Sun, after having withdrawn his cheering beams, and expofed us to
the uncomfortable cold and ftorms of winter, begins to
turn toward us, and to bring back the pleafures of fpring,
and by his genial warmth to give us the hopes of another feafon of productive fertility. *   Cæfar therefore
                                                        chofe

---

* In almoft all nations this feafon is diftinguifhed by fefti-
vities of various kinds. Many of thefe were incorporated with
the religious ceremonies of the Chriftian Church by our eccle-
fiaftics, becaufe they faw that the people were too much wed-
ded to them, to relinquifh them with good humour. Among
ourfelves, there are pretty evident traces of druidical fuperftition. We know that, in ancient times, the chief druid, attended by crowds of the people, went into the woods in the
night of the winter folftice, and with a golden fickle cut a
                                                        branch

chofe for the beginning of his kalendar, a year in which there was a new Moon following clofe upon the winter folftice. This opportunity was afforded him in the fecond year of his dictatorfhip, and the 707th year from the foundation of Rome. He found that there would be a new Moon 6 days after the winter folftice. He made this new Moon the 1ft of January of his firft year. But, to do this, he was obliged to keep the preceding year dragging on 90 days longer than ufual, containing 444

D d 2   days,

---

branch of the mifelto of the oak, called Ghiah in Celtic, and carried it in triumph to the facred grove. The people cut for themfelves, and carried home their prize, confecrated by the druid. At prefent, the pews of our churches, and even the chambers of our cottages, are ornamented with this plant at Chriftmas. In France, till within thefe 150 years, there were ftill more perceptible traces. A man perfonating a prince (*Roi follet*) fet out from the village into the woods, bawling out, *Au Gui menez—le Roi le vent*. The monks followed in the rear with their begging-boxes called *tire-liri*. They rattled them, crying *tire-liri* ; and the people put money into them, under the fiction that it was for a lady in labour. People in difguife (Guifards) forced into the houfes, playing antic tricks, and bullied the indwellers for money, and for choice victuals, crying *tire-liri—tire-liri—maint du blanc, et point du lis*. They made fuch riots, that the Bifhop of Soiffons reprefented the enormities to Louis XIV., and the practice was forbidden. May not the guifearts of Edinburgh, with their cry of " Hog menay, troll lollay ; gie's your white bread, none of your gray, " be derived from this ?

days, inftead of the old number 354. As all thefe days were unprovided with folemnities, the year preceding Cæfar's kalendar was called *the year of confufion*. Cæfar alfo, for a particular reafon, chofe to make his firft year confift of 366 days, and he inferted the intercalary day between the 23d and 24th of February, choofing that particular day, as a feparation of the luftrations and other piaculums to the infernal deities, which ended with the 23d, from the worfhip of the celeftial deities, which took place on the 24th of February. The 24th was the *fextus ante kalendas neomenias Martias*. His inferted day, anfwering civil purpofes alone, had no ceremonies, nor any name appropriated to it, and was to be confidered merely as a fupernumerary *fextus ante kalendas*. Hence the year which had this intercalation was ftyled an *annus biffextilis*, a biffextile year. With refpect to the reft of the year, Cæfar being alfo Pontifex Maximus (an office of vaft political importance), or rather, having all the power of the ftate in his own perfon, ordered that attention fhould be given to the days of the month only, and that the religious feftivals alone fhould be regulated by the facred college. He affigned to each month the number of days which has been continued in them ever fince.

335. Such is the fimple kalendar of Julius Cæfar. Simple however as it was, his inftructions were mifunderftood, or not attended to, during the horrors of the civil wars. Inftead of intercalating every fourth year, the intercalation was thrice made on every fucceeding

third

third year. The miftake was difcovered by Auguftus, and corrected in the beft manner poffible, by omitting three intercalations during the next twelve years. Since that time, the kalendar has been continued without interruption over all Europe till 1582. The years, confifting of 365¼ days, were called *Julian years ;* and it was ordered, by an edict of Auguftus, that this kalendar fhall be ufed through the whole empire, and that the years fhall be reckoned by the reigns of the different emperors. This edict was but imperfectly executed in the diftant provinces, where the native princes were allowed to hold a vaffal fovereignty. In Egypt particularly, although the court obeyed the edict, the people followed their former kalendars and epochs. Ptolemy the aftronomer retains the reckoning of Hipparchus, by Egyptian years, reckoned from the death of Alexander the Great. We muft underftand all thefe modes of computation, in order to make ufe of the ancient aftronomical obfervations. A comparifon of the different epochs will be given as we finifh the fubject.

336. The æra adopted by the Roman Empire when Chriftianity became the religion of the ftate, was not finally fettled till a good while after Conftantine. Dionyfius Exiguus, a French monk, after confulting all proper documents, confiders the 25th of December of the forty-fifth year of Julius Cæfar as the day of our Saviour's nativity. The 1ft of January of the forty-fixth year of Cæfar is therefore the beginning of the æra now

ufed

uſed by the Chriſtian world. Any event happening in this year is dated *anno Domini primo*. As Cæſar had made his firſt year a biſſextile, the year of the nativity was alſo biſſextile ; and the firſt year of our æra begins the ſhort cycle of four years, ſo that the fourth year of our æra is biſſextile.

That we may connect this æra with all the others employed by aſtronomers or hiſtorians, it will be enough to know that this firſt year of the Chriſtian æra is the 4714th of the Julian period.

It coincides with the fourth year of the 194th Olympiad till midſummer.

It coincides with the 753d *ab urbe condita*, till April 21st.

It coincides with the 748th of Nabonaſſar till Auguſt 23d.

It coincides with the 324th civil year of Egypt, reckoned from the death of Alexander the Great.

In the arrangement of epochs in the aſtronomical tables, the years before the Chriſtian æra are counted backwards, calling the year of the nativity 0, the preceding year 1, &c. But chronologiſts more frequently reckon the year of the nativity the firſt before Chriſt. Thus,

Years of Cæſar . . . 41, 42, 43, 44, 45, 46, 47, 48, 49
Aſtronomers 4, 3, 2, 1, 0, 1, 2, 3, 4
Chronologiſts 5, 4, 3, 2, 1, 1, 2, 3, 4

This kalendar of Julius Cæſar has manifeſt advantages in reſpect of ſimplicity, and in a ſhort time ſupplanted

planted all others among the weftern nations. Many other nations had perceived that the year of feafons contained more than 365 days, but had not fallen on eafy methods of making the correction. It is a very remarkable fact, that the Mexicans, when difcovered by the Spaniards, employed a cycle which fuppofed that the year contained 365¼ days. For, at the end of fifty-two years, they add thirteen days, which is equivalent to adding one every fourth year. In their hieroglyphical annals, their years are grouped into parcels of four, each of which has a particular mark.

337. But although the Julian conftruction of the civil year greatly excelled all that had gone before, it was not perfect, becaufe it contained $11' 14\frac{1}{2}''$ more than the period of feafons. This, in 128 years, amounts exactly to a day. In 1582, it amounted to $12^d 7^h$. The equinoxes and folftices no longer happened on thofe days of the month that were intended for them. The celebration of the church feftivals was altogether deranged. For it muft now be remarked, that there occurred the fame embarraffment on account of the lunar months, as formerly in the Pagan world.

The Council of Nice had decreed that the great feftival, Eafter, fhould be celebrated in conformity with the Jewifh paffover, which was regulated by the new moon following the vernal equinox. All the principal feftivals are regulated by Eafter Sunday. But by the deviation of the Julian kalendar from the feafons, and the words

of

of the decree of the Nicene Council, the celebration of Eafter loft all connexion with the Paffover. For the decree did not fay, ' The firft Sunday after the full moon following the vernal equinox, but the firft Sunday after the full moon following the 21ft of March.' It frequently happened that Eafter and the Paffover were fix weeks apart. This was corrected by Pope Gregory the XIII. in 1582, by bringing the 21ft of March to the equinox again. He firft cut off the ten days which had accumulated fince the Council of Nice; and, to prevent this accumulation, he directed the intercalation of a biffextile to be omitted on every centurial year. But the error of a Julian century containing 36525 days, is not a whole day, but 18^h 40'. Therefore the correction introduces an error of 5^h 20'. To prevent this from accumulating, the omiffion of the centurial intercalation is limited to the centuries not divifible by four. Therefore 1600, 2000, 2400, &c. are ftill biffextile years; but 1700, 1800, 1900, 2100, 2200, &c. are common years. There ftill remains an error, amounting to a day in 144 centuries.

The kalendar is now fufficiently accurate for all purpofes of hiftory and record—and even for aftronomy, becaufe the tropical year of feafons is fubject to a periodical inequality.

338. A correction, much more accurate than the Gregorian, occurred to Omar, a Perfian aftronomer at the court of Prince Gelala Eddin Melek Schah. Omar propofed

propofed always to delay to the thirty-third year the intercalation which fhould have been made in the thirty-
fecond. This is equivalent to omitting the Julian intercalation altogether on the 128th year. This method is
extremely fimple, and fcrupuloufly accurate. For the
error of 11′ 15″ of the Julian year amounts precifely
to a day in 128 years. It differs from the truth only
one minute in 120 years. This correction took place in
A° Dⁱ 1079, at the fame time that the Arab Alhazen
was reforming the fcience of aftronomy in Spain.

The Gregorian kalendar, however, has lefs chance of
being forgotten or miftaken. Centurial years are remarkable, and call the attention, even by the unufual
found of the words. The thirty-fecond year has nothing
remarkable, and may be overlooked.

339. It now appears that certain attentions are neceffary for avoiding miftakes, when we would appeal to
very diftant obfervations. We muft know the accurate
interval, however large. Although one hundred Julian
years contain 36525 days, we muft keep in mind that
between 1500 and 1600 ten days are wanting; and that
each of the centuries 1700 and 1800 alfo want a day.
The interval from the beginning of our æra and A. D.
1582 needs no attention; but that between 1505 and
1805 wants twelve days of three Julian centuries.

340. We muft alfo be careful, in ufing the ancient
obfervations, to connect the years of our Lord with the

years

years before Chrift in a proper manner. An eclipfe
mentioned by an aftronomer as having happened on the
1ft of February anno 3tio A. C. muft be confidered as
happening in the forty-fecond year of Julius Cæfar. But
if the fame thing is mentioned by a hiftorian or chrono-
logift, it is much more probable that it was in the forty-
third year of Cæfar. It was chiefly to prevent all am-
biguities of this kind that Scaliger contrived what he
called the *Julian period*. This is a number made by
multiplying together the numbers called the *Lunar or
Metonic cycle*, the *folar cycle*, and the *indiction*. The
lunar cycle is 19, and the firft year of our Lord was
the fecond of this cycle. The folar cycle is 28, being
the number of years in which the days of the month
return to the fame days of the week. As the year contains fifty-two weeks and one day, the firft day of the
year (or any day of any month) falls back in the week
one day every year, till interrupted by the intercalation
in a biffextile year. This makes it fall back two days in
that year ; and therefore it will not return to the fame
day till after four times feven, or twenty-eight years.
The firft year of our Lord was the tenth of this cycle.
The INDICTION is a cycle of fifteen years, at the beginning of which a tax was levied over the Roman Empire.
It took place A. D. 312 ; and if reckoned backward, it
would have begun three years before the Chriftian æra.
The year of this cycle for any year of the Chriftian æra,
will therefore be had by adding three to the year, and
dividing by fifteen. The product of thefe three numbers

bers is 7980; and it is plain that this number of years must elapfe before a year can have the fame place in all the three cycles. If therefore we know the place of thefe cycles belonging to any year, we can tell what year it is of the Julian period.

The firft year of our æra was the fecond of the lunar cycle, the tenth of the folar, and the fourth of indiction, and the 4714th of the Julian period. By this we may arrange all the remarkable æras as follows.

	J. P.	☉	☾	I.	A. C.
Æra of the Olympiads . . .	3938	18	5	8	775,776
Foundation of Rome . . .	3961	13	9	1	752,753
Nabonaffar	3967	19	15	7	746,747
Death of Alexander . . .	4390				323,324
Firft of Julius Cæfar . . .	4669	21	14	4	44, 45
A. Dom. 1	4714	10	2	4	

341. Did the Metonic cycle of the Moon correfpond exactly with our year, it would mark for any year the number of years which have elapfed fince it was new moon on the 1ft of January. But its want of perfect accuracy, the vicinity of an intercalation, and the lunar equations, fometimes caufe an error of two days. It is much ufed, however, for ordinary calculations for the Church holidays. To find the golden number, add one to the year of our Lord, divide the fum by 19, the remainder is the golden number. If there be no remainder, the golden number is 19.

E e 2

342.

342. Another number, called Epact, is also used for facilitating the calculation of new and full moon in a gross way. The epact is nearly the moon's age on the 1st of January. To find it, multiply the golden number by 11, add 19 to the product, and divide by 30. The remainder is the epact.

Knowing, by the epact, the Moon's age on the 1st of January, and the day of the year corresponding to any day of a month, it is easy to find the Moon's age on that day, by dividing the double of the sum of this number and the epact by 59. The half remainder is nearly the Moon's age.

Although these rude computations do not correspond with the motions of the two luminaries, they deserve notice, being the methods employed by the rules of the Church for settling the moveable. Church festivals.

Of the proper Motions of the Planets.

343. The planets are observed to change their situations in the starry heavens, and move among the signs of the zodiac, never receding far from the ecliptic.

Their motions are exceedingly irregular, as may be seen by fig. 65. A, which represents the motion of the planet Jupiter, from the beginning of 1708 to the beginning of 1716. E K represents the ecliptic, and the initial letters of the months are put to those points of the apparent path where the planet was seen on the first day of each month.

It

It appears that, on the 1ſt of January 1708, the planet was moving ſlowly eaſtward, and became ſtationary
about the middle of the month, in the ſecond degree of
Libra.   It then turned weſtward, gradually increaſing its
weſterly motion, till about the middle of March, when
it was in oppoſition to the Sun, at R, all the while deviating farther from the ecliptic toward the north.   It
now ſlackened its weſterly motion every day, · and was a-
gain ſtationary about the 20th of May, in the twenty-ſecond
degree of Virgo, and had come nearer to the ecliptic.
Jupiter now moved eaſtward, nearly parallel to the ecliptic, gradually accelerating in his motion, till the beginning of October, when he was in conjunction with the
Sun at D, about the eleventh degree of Libra.   He now
ſlackened his progreſſive motion every day, till he was a-
gain ſtationary, in the ſecond degree of Scorpio, on the
12th or 13th of February 1709.   He then moved weſtward,
was again in oppoſition, in the twenty-ſeventh degree of
Libra, about the middle of April.   He became ſtationary, about the end of June, in the twenty-firſt degree
of Libra ; and from this place he again proceeded eaſtward ; was in conjunction about the beginning of November, very near the ſtar in the ſouthern ſcale of Libra ;
and, on the 1ſt of January 1710, he was in the twenty-
fourth degree of Scorpio.

This figure will very nearly correſpond with the apparent motions of the planet in the ſame months of 1803
and 1804.   Jupiter will go on in this manner, forming
a loop in his path in every thirteenth month ; and he is
in

in oppofition to the Sun, when in the middle of each
loop. His regrefs in each loop is about 10 degrees, and
his progreffive motion is continued about 40°. He gradually approaches the ecliptic, croffes it, deviates to the
fouthward, then returns towards it ; croffes it, about fix
years after his former croffing, and in about twelve years
comes to where he was at the beginning of thefe obfervations.

344. The other planets, and particularly Venus and
and Mercury, are ftill more irregular in their apparent
motions, and have but few circumftances of general refemblance.

The firft *general* remark which can be made on thefe
intricate motions is, that a planet always appears largeft
when in the points R, R, R, which are in the middle
of its retrograde motions. Its diameter gradually diminifhes, and becomes the leaft of all when in the points
D′, D′, D′, which are in the middle of its direct motions. Hence we infer that the planet is neareft to the
Earth when in the middle of its retrograde motion, and
fartheft from it when in the middle of its direct motion.

It may alfo be remarked, that a planet is always in
conjunction with the Sun, or comes to our meridian at
noon, when in the middle of its direct motions. The
planets Venus and Mercury are alfo in conjunction with
the Sun when in the middle of their retrograde motions.
But the planets Mars, Jupiter, and Saturn, are always
in oppofition to the Sun, or come to our meridian at
                                              midnight,

midnight, when in the middle of their retrograde motions. Their fituations alfo, when ftationary, are always fimilar, relative to the Sun. Thefe appearances in all the planetary motions have therefore an evident relation to the Sun's place.

345. The ancient aftronomers were of opinion that the perfection of nature required all motions to be uniform, as far as the purpofe in view would permit. The planetary motions muft therefore be uniform, in a figure that is uniform; and the aftronomers maintained that the obferved irregularities were only apparent. Their method for reconciling thefe with their principle of perfection is very obvioufly fuggefted by the reprefentation here given of the motion of Jupiter. They taught that the planet moves uniformly in the circumference of a circle *q r s* (fig. 40.) in a year, while the centre Q of this circle is carried uniformly round the Earth T, in the circumference of another circle Q A L. The circle Q A L is called the DEFERENT CIRCLE, and *q r s* is called the EPICYCLE. They explained the deviation from the ecliptic, by faying that the deferent and the epicycle were in planes different from that of the ecliptic. By various trials of different proportions of the deferent and the epicycle, they hit on fuch dimenfions as produced the quantity of retrograde motion that was obferved to be combined with the general progrefs in the order of the figns of the zodiac.—But another inequality was obferved. The arch of the heavens intercepted between two

fucceffive

fucceffive oppofitions of Jupiter, (for example), was obferved to be variable, being always lefs in a certain part
of the zodiac, and gradually increafing to a maximum
ftate in the oppofite part of the zodiac.

In order to correfpond with this SECOND INEQUALITY,
as it was called, and yet not to imply any inequality of
the motion of the epicycle in the circumference of the
deferent circle, the aftronomers placed the Earth not in,
but at a certain diftance from, the centre of the deferent ; fo that an equal arch between two fucceeding oppofitions fhould fubtend a fmaller angle, when it is on
the other fide of that centre. Thus, the unequal motion of the epicycle was explained in the fame way as
the Sun's unequal motion in his annual orbit. The
line drawn through the Earth and the centre of the deferent is called the line of the planet's APSIDES, and its
extremities are called the *apogee* and *perigee* of the deferent as in the cafe of the Sun's orbit (292.) In this
manner, they at laft compofed a fet of motions which
agreed tolerably well with obfervation.

The celebrated geometer Apollonius gave very judicious directions how to proportion the epicycle to the
deferent circle. But they feem not to have been attended to, even by Ptolemy ; and the aftronomers remained
very ignorant of any method of conftruction which a-
greed fufficiently with the phenomena, till about the
thirteenth century, when the doctrine of epicycles was
cultivated with more care and fkill.

A very full and diftinct account is given of all the
ingenious contrivances of the ancient aftronomers for
                                                    explaining

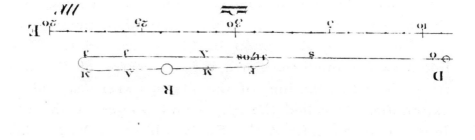

explaining the irregularities of the celeftial motions, in the firft part of Dr Small's Hiftory of the Difcoveries of Kepler, publifhed in 1803.

Of the Motions of Venus and Mercury.

346. Venus has been fometimes feen moving acrofs the Sun's difk from eaft to weft, in the form of a round black fpot, with an apparent diameter of about 59″. A few days after this has been obferved, Venus is feen in the morning, rifing a little before the Sun, in the form of a fine crefcent, with the convexity turned toward the Sun. She moves gradually weftward, feparating from the Sun, with a retarded motion, and the crefcent becomes more full. In about ten weeks, fhe has moved 46° weft of the Sun, and is now a femicircle, and her diameter is 26″. She now feparates no farther from the Sun, but moves eaftward, with a motion gradually accelerated, and fhe gradually diminifhes in apparent diameter. She overtakes the Sun, about 9½ months after having been feen on his difk. Some time after, Venus is feen in the evening, eaft of the Sun, round, but very fmall. She moves eaftward, and increafes in apparent diameter, but lofes of her roundnefs, till fhe gets about 46° eaft of the Sun, when fhe is again a femicircle, having the convexity toward the Sun. She now moves weftward, increafing in diameter, but becoming a crefcent, like the waneing Moon ; and, at laft, after a period of nearly 584 days, comes again into conjunction with the Sun, with an apparent diameter of 59″.

F f

347.

347. From thefe phenomena we conclude that the Sun is included within the orbit of Venus, and is not far from its centre, while the Earth is without this orbit. Therefore, while the Sun revolves round the Earth, Venus revolves round the Sun.

The time of the revolution of Venus round the Sun may be deduced from the interval which elapfes between two or more conjunctions, by help of the following theorem :

348. Let two bodies A and B revolve uniformly in the fame direction, and let a and b be their refpective periods, of which b is the leaft, and t the interval between two fucceffive conjunctions or oppofitions.

Then $b = \dfrac{a\,t}{a + t}$, and $a = \dfrac{b\,t}{t - b}$.

For the angular motions are inverfely proportional to the periodic times. Therefore the angular motions of A and B are as $\dfrac{1}{a}$ and $\dfrac{1}{b}$. And, fince they move in the fame direction, the fynodical or relative motion is the difference of their angular motions. Therefore the fundamental equation is $\dfrac{1}{b} - \dfrac{1}{a} = \dfrac{1}{t}$. Hence $\dfrac{1}{b} = \dfrac{1}{t} + \dfrac{1}{a}$, $= \dfrac{a + t}{a\,t}$, and $b = \dfrac{a\,t}{a + t}$. Alfo $\dfrac{1}{a} = \dfrac{1}{b} - \dfrac{1}{t}$, $= \dfrac{t - b}{t\,b}$, and $a = \dfrac{b\,t}{t - b}$.

We may alfo calculate the fynodical period t, when we know the real periods of each. For $\dfrac{1}{t} = \dfrac{1}{b} - \dfrac{1}{a} = \dfrac{a - b}{a\,b}$, and $t = \dfrac{a\,b}{a - b}$.

This

This gives for the periodic time of Venus round the Sun 224^d 16^h 49' 13".

349. But it is evident that if this angular motion is not uniform, the interval between two fucceffive conjunctions may chance to give a falfe meafure of the period. But, by obferving many conjunctions, in various parts of the heavens, and by dividing the interval between the firft and laft by the number of intervals between each (taking care that the firft and laft fhall be nearly in the fame part of the heavens), it is evident that the inequalities being diftributed among them all, the quotient may be taken as nearly an exact medium. Hence arifes the great value of ancient obfervations. In eight years we have five conjunctions of Venus, and fhe is only 1° 32' fhort of the place of the firft conjunction. The period deduced from the conjunctions in 1761 and 1769, fcarcely differs from that deduced from the conjunctions in 1639 and 1761. But the other planets require more diftant obfervations.

350. Venus does not move uniformly in her orbit. For, if the place of Venus in the heavens be obferved in a great number of fucceffive conjunctions with the Sun (at which time her place in the ecliptic, as feen from the Sun, is either the Sun's place, as feen from the Earth, or the oppofite to it), we find that her changes of place are not proportional to the elapfed times. By obfervations of this kind, we learn the inequality of the angular

F f 2   motion

motion of Venus round the Sun, and hence can find the
equations for every point of the orbit of Venus, and can
thence deduce the position of Venus, as seen from the
Sun, for any given instant.

This however requires more observations of this kind
than we are yet possessed of, because her conjunctions
happen so nearly in the same points of her orbit, that
great part of it is left without observations of this kind.
But we have other observations of almost equal value,
namely, those of her greatest elongations from the Sun.
There is none of the planets, therefore, of which the
equations (which indeed are very small) are more accurately determined.

351. We can now determine the form and position
of the orbit. For we can *observe* the place of the Sun,
or the position of the line E S (fig. 41.), joining the
Earth and Sun. We know the length of this line (291.)
We can *observe* the GEOCENTRIC place of Venus, or the
position of the line E D joining the Earth and Venus.
And we can compute (350.) the HELIOCENTRIC place of
Venus, or the position of the line S C joining Venus
and the Sun. Venus must be in V, the intersection of
these two lines ; and therefore that point of her orbit is
determined.

352. By such observations Kepler discovered that the
orbit of Venus is an ellipse, having the Sun in one focus,
the semitransverse axis being 72333, and the eccentricity

city 510, meafured on a fcale of which the Sun's mean diftance from the Earth is 100000.

353. The upper apfis of the orbit is called the APHELION, and the lower apfis is called the PERIHELION of Venus.

354. The line of the apfides has a flow motion eaftward, at the rate of 2° 44′ 46″ in a century.

355. The orbit of Venus is inclined to the ecliptic at an angle of 3° 20′, and the nodes move weftward about 31″ in a year.

356. Venus moves in this orbit fo as to defcribe round the Sun areas proportional to the times.

357. The planet Mercury refembles Venus in all the circumftances of her apparent motion ; and we make fimilar inferences with refpect to the real motions. His orbit is difcovered to be an ellipfe, having the Sun in one focus. The femitranfverfe axis is 38710, and the eccentricity 7960. The apfides move eaftward 1° 57′ 20″ in a century. The orbit is inclined to the ecliptic 7°. The nodes move weftward 45″ in a year. The periodic time is 87ᵈ 23ʰ 15′ 37″ ; and areas are defcribed proportional to the times.

Of

Of the proper Motions of the Superior Planets.

358. Mars, Jupiter, and Saturn, exhibit phenomena confiderably different from thofe exhibited by Mercury and Venus.

1. They come to our meridian both at noon and at midnight. When they come to our meridian at noon, and are in the ecliptic, they are never feen croffing the Sun's difk. Hence we infer, that their orbits include both the Sun and the Earth.

2. They are always retrograde when in oppofition, and direct when in conjunction.

The planet Jupiter may ferve as an example of the way in which their real motions may be inveftigated.

359. Jupiter is an opaque body, vifible by means of the reflected light of the Sun. For the fhadows of fome of the heavenly bodies are fometimes obferved on his difk, and his fhadow frequently falls on them.

360. His apparent diameter, when in oppofition, is about 46″, and, when in conjunction, it is about 31″, and his difk is always round. Hence we infer, that he is neareft when in oppofition, and that his leaft and greateft diftance are nearly as two to three. The Earth is, therefore, far removed from the centre of his motion ; and, if we endeavour to explain his motion by means of a deferent

circle

circle and an epicycle ( ), the radius of the deferent muſt be about five times the radius of the epicycle.

361. Since Jupiter is always retrograde when in op-poſition, and direct when in conjunction, his poſition, with reſpect to the centre of his epicycle, muſt be ſimi-lar to the poſition of the Sun with reſpect to the Earth. His motion, therefore, in the epicycle, has a dependence on the motion of the Sun ; and his motion, as ſeen from the Sun, muſt be ſimpler than as ſeen from the Earth.

His poſition, as ſeen from the Sun, may be accurately *obſerved* in every oppoſition and conjunction.

It was very natural for the ancient aſtronomers of Greece to infer, from what has been ſaid juſt now, that the poſition of Jupiter, in reſpect of the centre of his epicycle, was the ſame as that of the Sun in reſpect of the Earth, not only in oppoſition and conjunction, but in every other ſituation. For, in twelve years, we ſee it to be ſo in the oppoſitions obſerved in 12 parts of the heavens, and in 83 years we ſee it in 76 parts. It is very improbable, therefore, that it ſhould be otherwiſe in the intervals.

The motion of a ſuperior planet may be explained upon theſe principles in the following manner :

Let T (fig. 40.) be the Earth, and $\alpha \beta \varkappa \delta \epsilon \varphi \gamma \chi \alpha$ be the Sun's orbit. Alſo, let A, B, C, D, E, F, G, H, I, be the places of the centre of the epicycle in the circum-ference of the deferent when the ſun is in α, β, $\varkappa$, δ, ϵ, φ, γ, χ, α, make A a parallel to T α, and B b parallel to

T β,

T β, and C c parallel to T κ, &c., and make thefe lines
of a length that is duly proportioned (by the Apollonian
rule) to the radius T A of the deferent circle.

When the Sun is in α, β, κ, &c. the centre of the
epicycle is in A, B, C, &c. and the planet is in a, b, c,
&c. ; and the dotted curve a b c d e f g h a k is its path
in abfolute fpace between two fucceeding oppofitions to
the Sun, viz. in a, and in k.

362. If we make the radius of Jupiter's deferent
circle to that of the epicycle, as 52 to 10, the epicyclical
motion arifing from this conftruction will very nearly
agree with the obfervation. Only we may obferve that
the oppofitions which fucceed each other near the conftellation Virgo, are lefs diftant from one another than
thofe obferved in the oppofite part of the heavens ; fo
that the centre of the epicycle feems to move flower in
the firft cafe than in the laft. To reconcile this with the
perfect uniformity of the motion of that centre in the
circumference of the deferent circle, the ancient aftronomers faid that the earth was not exactly in the centre of
the deferent, but fo placed that the equable motion of
the centre of the epicycle appeared flower, becaufe it is
then more remote ; and after various trials, they fixed on
a degree of eccentricity for the deferent, which accorded
better than any other with the obfervations, and really
differed very little from them. Copernicus fhews that
their hypothefis for Jupiter never deviates more than half
a degree from obfervation, if it be properly employed.
They found that the epicycle moved round the de-

ferent in 4332¼ days, with an equation gradually increafing to near 6 degrees; fo that if the place of the
epicycle be calculated for a quarter of a revolution from
the apogee, at the mean rate of 5′ per day, it will be
found too far advanced by near ten weeks motion.

363. But the ancient aftronomers had no fuch data
for determining the abfolute magnitude of the deferent
circles and epicycles for the fuperior planets, as Mercury
and Venus afforded them. The rules given them by
Apollonius only taught them what proportion the epicycle
of each planet muft have to its deferent circle, but gave
no information as to the abfolute magnitude of either,
or the proportion between the deferent circles of any two
fuperior planets. Accordingly, no two ancient aftronomers agree in their meafures, farther than in faying that
Saturn is farther off than Jupiter, and Jupiter than
Mars. This they inferred from their longer periods.
All that they had to take care of was to make their fizes
fufficiently different, fo that the epicycles of two neighbouring planets fhould not crofs and juftle each other.
Yet they might eafily have come very near the truth, by
a fmall and very allowable addition to their hypothefis of
epicyclical motion, namely, by fuppofing that the epicycle
of each planet is equal to the Sun's orbit. This was
quite allowable.

364. If we do this, we fhall deduce confequences
that are very remarkable, and which would have put the

G g   ancient

ancient aftronomy on a footing very near to perfection.
For, if C c (fig. 40.) be not only parallel to T x, but
alfo equal to it, then C T $x c$ is a parallelogram, and $x c$
is equal and parallel to T C. The bearing (to exprefs it
as a mariner) and diftance of Jupiter from the Sun, is at
all times the fame with the bearing and diftance of the
centre of his epicycle from the Earth; and Jupiter is always found in an orbit round the Sun, equal and fimilar
to the deferent orbit round the Earth. Thus, αa is e-
qual to T A; βb to T B; $x c$ to T C, &c. with refpect
to all the points of the looped curve. If the Earth be in
the centre of the deferent, the diftance of Jupiter from
the Sun is always the fame, and he may be faid to defcribe a circle round the Sun, while the Sun moves
round the Earth. Nay, it refults from the equality of
A a to T α, of B b to T β, &c., that whatever eccentricity, or whatever form it has been thought neceffary
to affign to the deferent, the diftances αa, βb, $x c$, &c.
will ftill be refpectively equal to T A, T B, T C, &c.
The circle which the aftronomers called the deferent,
becaufe it is fuppofed to carry Jupiter's epicycle round
the Earth, may be fuppofed to accompany the Sun, being carried round by him in a year, the line of its apfides (362.) keeping parallel to itfelf, that is, in our
figure, to T A. And thus, the motion of Jupiter round
the Sun will be incomparably more fimple than the
looped curve round the Earth; for it will be precifely
the motion which was given by the aftronomers to the
centre of Jupiter's epicycle. The motion of Jupiter in
                                                    abfolute

àbfolute fpace is indeed the fame looped curve in both
cafes; but the way of conceiving it is much more fimple.

365. This fuppofition of the equality of Jupiter's
epicycle to the Sun's orbit, and the parallelifm of C *c*
to T *x* in every pofition of Jupiter, are fully verified by
the modern difcoveries of his fatellites. Thefe little planets revolve round him with perfect regularity, and their
fhadows frequently fall on his difk, and they are often
obfcured by his fhadow. This fhews the pofition of Jupiter's fhadow at all times, and, confequently, Jupiter's
pofition in refpect of the Sun. This we find at all times
to be parallel to the fuppofed pofition of the centre of
his epicycle. Thus *x c* is found parallel to T C.

366. We now can tell the precife point in which
Jupiter is found in any moment of time. Having made
the radius T *x* to the radius T A in the due proportion
of 10 to 52, and having placed the Earth at the proper
diftance from the centre of the deferent Q A L, we can
calculate (298.) the pofition and length of the line T *x*
joining the Earth with the Sun. We can draw the line
T C to the fuppofed centre of Jupiter's epicycle, having
learned the law or equation of the fuppofed motion of
that centre by our obfervation of his oppofitions in all
quarters of the ecliptic (362.), and we then draw *x* V
parallel to it. This muft pafs through Jupiter, or Jupiter muft be fomewhere in this line. We obferve Jupiter, however, in the direction T Z. Jupiter muft there-

fore

fore be in the interfection c of the lines x V and T Z. And then we can meafure $c x$, Jupiter's diftance from the Sun.

367. Kepler, by taking this method with a feries of obfervations made by Tycho Brahé, difcovered that Jupiter was always found in the circumference of an ellipfe, having the Sun in its focus. Its femitranfverfe axis is 520098, the mean diftance of the Earth from the Sun being fuppofed 100000. Its eccentricity is 25277. Its inclination to the ecliptic is 1° 20′, and the nodes move eaftward about 1′ in a year.

368. The revolution in this orbit is completed in 4332¼ days, and areas are defcribed proportional to the times.

369. Proceeding in the fame manner, we difcover that the planets Mars, Saturn, and the one difcovered by Dr Herfchel in 1781, are always found in the circumference of ellipfes, with the Sun in one focus, and defcribe round him areas proportional to the times.

The chief circumftances of their motions are ftated as follows :

	Mean Diftance.	Eccentricity.	Period in Days.
Georgian planet	1908584	90738	30456,07
Saturn - - - -	953941	53210	10759,27
Mars - - - - -	152369	14218	686,98

370.

Pl 9

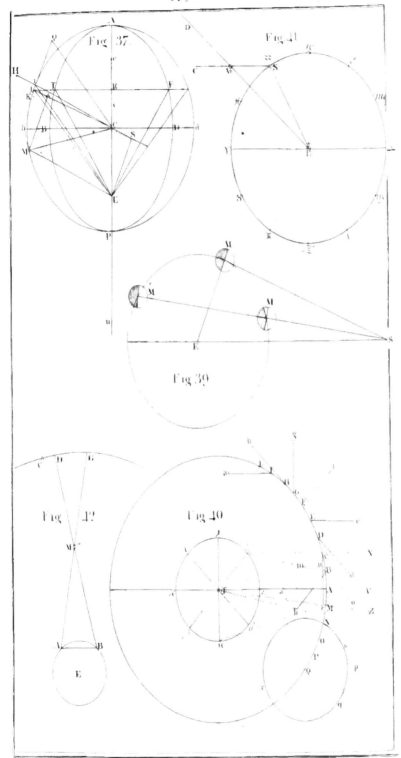

Fig 37.

Fig 41

Fig 39

Fig 42

Fig 40

370.   Two other bodies have been lately detected in the planetary regions, revolving round the Sun in orbits which do not feem very eccentric, and feem placed between thofe of Mars and Jupiter.   The firft was obferved in 1801 by Mr Piazzi of Palermo, and by him named Ceres.   The other was difcovered in 1802 by Mr Olberg of Bremen, who has called it Pallas.   They are exceedingly fmall, and we have feen too little of their motions as yet to enable us to ftate their elements with any precifion.

371.   Thus it has been difcovered, that, while the Sun revolves round the Earth, the fix planets now mentioned are always found in the circumferences of ellipfes, having the Sun in one focus ; and that they defcribe round the Sun areas proportional to the times.

372.   But now, inftead of fuppofing that the centre of a fmall epicycle is carried round the circumference of a greater deferent circle, different for each planet, we may rather confider the Sun's orbit round the Earth as the only deferent circle, and fuppofe that the planets defcribe their great elliptical epicycles round him with different periods, while he moves round the Earth in a year.   The real motions of the planets are ftill the fame looped curves in both cafes.   For, in either cafe, the motion of a planet is compounded of the fame motions.   But the latter fuppofition is much more probable.   We can fcarcely conceive the motion of Jupiter in the epicycle $q\ r\ s$ as

having

having any phyfical relation to its centre, a mere mathematical point of fpace. We cannot confider this point as
having any phyfical properties that fhall influence the
motions of the planet. This point alfo is fuppofed to be
in motion, carrying with it the influence by which the
planet is retained in the circumference of the epicycle.
This is another inconceivable circumftance. This combination of circles, therefore, cannot be confidered as
any thing but a mere mathematical hypothefis, to furnifh
fome means of calculation, or for the delineation of the
looped path of the planet. Accordingly, the firft pro-
pofers of thefe epicycles, fenfible of the mere nothing-
nefs of their centre, and the impoffibility of a nothing
moving in the circumference of a circle, and drawing a
planet along with it, farther fuppofed that the epicycles
were vaft folid tranfparent globes, and that the planet
was a luminous point or ftar, fticking in the furface of
this globe. And, to complete the hypothefis, they fuppofed that the globe turned round its centre, carrying
the planet round with it, and thus produced the direct
and retrograde motions that we obferve. Ariftotle taught
that this motion was effected by the genius of the planet
refiding in the globe, and directing it, as the mind of
man directs his motions. But, further, to account for
the motion of this globe in the circumference of the deferent, the ancient philofophers fuppofed that the deferent was alfo a vaft cryftalline, or, at leaft, tranfparent
material fpherical fhell, turning round the earth, and that
this fhell was of fufficient thicknefs to receive the epi-
cyclic

cyclic globe within its folid fubftance, not adhering, but at liberty to turn round its own centre. This hypothefis, though more like the dream of a feverifh man than the thoughts of one in his fenfes, was received as unqueftionable, from the time of Ariftotle till that of Copernicus. It is fcarcely credible that thinking men fhould admit its truth for a minute, even in its moft admiffible form. But, as the art of obferving improved, it was found neceffary to add another epicycle to the one already admitted, in order to account for an annual inequality in the epicyclical motion. This was a fmall tranfparent globe, placed where Ariftotle placed the planet, and the planet was ftuck on *its* furface. Even this was found infufficient, and another fet of epicycles were added, till, in fhort, the heavens were filled with folid matter. It is needlefs to fay any more of this epicyclical doctrine and machinery.

373. But the other mode of conceiving the planetary motions, while it equally furnifhes the means of caculation or graphical operation, has much more the appearance of reality. The Sun's motion is round the Earth, which we are naturally difpofed to think the centre of the world; and the planets revolve, not round a mathematical point, a nothing, but round the Sun, a real, and very remarkable fubftance.

374. Kepler, to whom we are indebted for this difcovery of the elliptical motions, and the equable defcription

tion of areas, alfo obferved that the fquares of the periodic times in thefe ellipfes are proportional to the cubes
of the mean diftances from the Sun.   He alfo obferved
the fame analogy with refpect to the Sun's period and
diftance from the Earth.

375. The diftances here alluded to, are all taken
from a fcale of equal parts, of which the Sun's mean
diftance from the Earth, contains 100000.   But aftronomers wifh to know the abfolute quantity of thofe diftances in fome known meafures.   This may be learned
by means of the parallax of any one of the planets.
Thus, let Mars be in M (fig. 42.), and let his diftance
from fome fixed ftar C be obferved by two perfons on
the furface of the Earth at A and B.   The difference
G D of the obferved diftances C G, C D, will give the
angle D M G, or its equal A M B.   The angles M A B
and M B A are given by obfervation, and the line A B
is given; and therefore A M, and confequently E M,
may be computed in miles.

The tranfit of Venus acrofs the Sun's difk affords
much better obfervations for this purpofe.   For, at the
time, Venus is much nearer to the Earth than Mars is
when in oppofition, their diftances from us being nearly
as 28 to 52.   Therefore the diftance between the obfervers will fubtend a larger angle at Venus.   This may
be meafured by the diftance between the apparent tracks
of Venus acrofs the Sun's difk.   A fpectator in Lapland, for example, fees Venus move in the line C D

(fig.

(fig. 43.), while one at the Cape of Good Hope fees her move in the line A B.   Alfo, as C D is a fhorter chord than A B, the tranfit will occupy lefs time.   This difference in time, amounting, in fome fortunate cafes, to many minutes, will give a very exact meafure of the interval between thofe two chords:

376.   The tranfits in 1761 and 1769 were employed for this purpofe, at the earneft recommendation of Dr Edmund Halley.   From thofe obfervations, combined with the proportions deduced from Kepler's third law, we may affume the following diftances from the Sun in Englifh ftatute miles, as pretty near the truth.

The Earth   93,726,900
Mercury   36,281,700
Venus   67,795,500
Mars   142,818,000
Jupiter   487,472,000
Saturn   894,162,000
Georgian Planet 1,789,982,000

Of the Secondary Planets.

377.   Jupiter is obferved to be always accompanied by four fmall planets called SATELLITES, which revolve round him, while he revolves round the Sun.

Their diftances from Jupiter are meafured by means of their greateft elongations, and their periods are difcovered by their eclipfes, when they come into his fha-

H h   dow,

dow, and by other methods. They are obferved to defcribe ellipfes, having Jupiter in one focus ; and they defcribe areas round Jupiter, which are proportional to the
times. Alfo the fquares of their periods are in the
proportion of the cubes of their mean diftances from
Jupiter.

378. It has been difcovered by means of the eclipfes
of Jupiter's fatellites, that light is propagated in time,
and employs about 8' 11" in moving along a line equal
to the mean diftance of the Earth from the Sun.

The times of the revolutions of thefe little bodies
had been ftudied with the greateft care, on account of the
eafy and accurate means which their frequent eclipfes gave
us for afcertaining the longitudes of places. But it was
found that, after having calculated the time of an eclipfe
in conformity to the periods, which had been moft accurately determined, the eclipfe happened later than the
calculation, in proportion as Jupiter was farther from
the Earth. If an eclipfe, when Jupiter is in oppofition,
be obferved to happen precifely at the time calculated ;
an eclipfe three months before, or after, when Jupiter
is in quadrature, will be obferved to happen about eight
minutes later than the calculated time. An eclipfe happening about fix weeks before or after oppofition, will
be about four minutes later than the calculation, when
thofe about the time of Jupiter's oppofition happen at the
exact time. In general, this *retardation* of the eclipfes
is obferved to be exactly proportional to the increafe of
Jupiter's

Jupiter's diftance from the Earth. It is the fame with refpect to all the fatellites. This error greatly perplexed the aftronomers, till the connexion of it with Jupiter's change of diftance was remarked by Mr Roemer, a Danifh aftronomer, in 1674. As foon as this gentleman took notice of this connexion, he concluded that the retardation of the eclipfe was owing to the time employed by the light in coming to us. The fatellite, now eclipfed, continued to be feen, till the *laft* reflected light reached us, and, when the ftream of light ceafed, the fatellite difappeared, or was eclipfed. When it has paffed through the fhadow, and is again illuminated, it is not feen at that inftant by a fpectator almoft four hundred millions of miles off—it does not reappear to him, till the *firft* reflected light reaches him. It is not till about forty minutes after being reilluminated by the Sun, that the firft reflected light from the fatellite reaches the Earth when Jupiter is in quadrature, and about thirty-two minutes when he is in oppofition.

This ingenious inference of Mr Roemer was doubted for fome time ; but moft of the eminent philofophers agreed with him. It became more probable, as the motions of the fatellites were more accurately defined ; and it received complete confirmation by Dr Bradley difcovering another, and very different confequence of the progreffive motion of light from the fixed ftars and planets. This will be confidered afterwards ; and, in the mean time, it is evinced that light, or the caufe of vifion, is propagated in time, and requires about 16¼ mi-

H h 2   nutes

nutes to move along the diameter of the Sun's orbit, or about 8′ 11″ to come from the Sun to us, moving about 200,000 miles in a fecond. Some imagine vifion to be produced by the undulation of an elaftic medium, as found is produced by the undulation of air. Others imagine light to be emitted from the luminous body, as a ftream of water from the difperfer of a watering-pan. Whichever of thefe be the cafe, Light now becomes a proper fubject of Mechanical difcuffion; and we may now fpeculate about its motions, and the forces which produce and regulate them.

379. Saturn is alfo obferved to be accompanied by feven fatellites, which circulate round him in ellipfes, having Saturn in the focus. They defcribe areas proportional to the times, and the fquares of the periodic times are proportional to the cubes of their mean diftances.

380. Befides this numerous band of fatellites, Saturn is alfo accompanied by a vaft arch or ring of coherent matter, which furrounds him, at a great diftance. Its diameter is about 208,000 miles, and its breadth about 40,000. It is flat, and extremely thin; and as it fhines only by reflecting the Sun's light, we do not fee it when its edge is turned towards us. Late obfervation has fhewn it to be two rings, in the fame plane, and almoft united. But that they are feparated, is demonftrated by a ftar being feen through the interval between them.

them.   Its plane makes an angle of 29° or 30° with that
of Saturn's orbit ; and when Saturn is in 11ˢ 20°, or
5ˢ 20°, the plane of the ring paffes through the Sun,
and reflects no light to us.

381.   In 1787, Dr Herfchel difcovered two fatellites
attending the Georgian planet ; and in 1798, he difcovered four more.   Their diftances and their periodic
times obferve the laws of Kepler ; but the pofition of
their orbits is peculiarly interefting.   Inftead of revolving
in the order of the figns, in planes not deviating far from
the ecliptic, their orbits are almoft, if not precifely perpendicular to it ; fo that it cannot be faid that they move
either in the order of the figns, or in the oppofite.

382.   Thus do they prefent a new problem in Phyfical Aftronomy, in order to afcertain the Sun's influence
on their motions—the interfection of their nodes, and
the other difturbances of their motions round the planet.

383.   They alfo fhew the miftake of the Cofmogo-
nifts, who would willingly afcribe the general tendency
of the planetary motions from weft to eaft along the
ecliptic to the influence of fome general mechanical impulfion, inftructing us how the world may be made as
we fee it.   Thefe perpendicular orbits are incompatible
with the fuppofed influence.

Of

Of the Rotation of the Heavenly Bodies.

384. In 1611, Scheiner, profeſſor at Ingolſtadt, obſerved ſpots on the diſk of the Sun, which come into
view on the eaſtern limb, move acroſs his diſk in parallel
circles, diſappear on the weſtern limb, and, after ſome
time, again appear on the eaſtern limb, and repeat the
ſame motions. Hence it is inferred that the Sun revolves from weſt to eaſt in the ſpace of 25ᵈ 14ʰ 12′,
round an axis inclined to the plane of the ecliptic 7½ degrees, and having the aſcending node of his equator in
longitude 2ˢ 10°.

Philoſophers have formed various opinions concerning
the nature of theſe ſpots. The moſt probable is, that
the Sun conſiſts of a dark nucleus, ſurrounded by a luminous covering, and that the nucleus is ſometimes laid
bare in particular places. For the general appearance of
a ſpot during its revolution is like fig. 43.

385. A ſeries of moſt intereſting obſervations has
been lately made by Dr Herſchel, by the help of his
great teleſcopes. Theſe obſervations are recorded in the
Philoſophical Tranſactions for the years 1801 and 1802.
They lead to very curious concluſions reſpecting the peculiar conſtitution of the Sun. It would ſeem that the
Sun is immediately ſurrounded by an atmoſphere, heavy
and tranſparent, like our air. This reaches to the height
of ſeveral thouſand miles. On this atmoſphere ſeems to

float

float a ftratum of fhining clouds, alfo fome thoufands of miles in thicknefs. It is not clear however that this cloudy ftratum fhines by its native light. There is above it, at fome diftance, another ftratum of matter, of moft dazzling fplendor. It would feem that it is this alone which illuminates the whole planetary fyftem, and alfo the clouds below it. This refplendent ftratum is not equally fo, but moft luminous in irregular lines or ridges, which cover the whole difk like a very clofe brilliant network. Something of this appearance was noticed by Mr James Short in 1748, while obferving a total eclipfe of the Sun, and is mentioned in the Philofophical Tranf-actions. Some operation of nature in this folar atmo-fphere feems to produce an upward motion in it, like a blaft, which caufes both the clouds and the dazzling ftratum to remove from the fpot, making a fort of hole in the luminous ftrata, fo that we can fee through them, down to the dark nucleus of the Sun. Dr Herfchel has obferved that this change, and this denudation of the nucleus, is much more frequent in fome particular places of the Sun's difk. He has alfo obferved a fmall bit of fhining cloud come in at one fide of an opening, and, in a fhort time, move acrofs it, and difappear on the other fide of the opening; and he thinks that thefe moving clouds are confiderably below the great cloudy ftratum.

386. Dr Herfchel is difpofed to think that the up-per refplendent ftratum never fhines on the nucleus; not even

even when an opening has been made in the ftratum of clouds. For he remarks that the upper ftratum is always much more driven afide by what produces the opening than the clouds are ; fo that even the moft oblique rays from the fplendid ftratum do not go through, being intercepted by the border of clouds which immediately furround the opening.

387. From Dr Herfchel's defcription of this wonderful objeét, we are almoft led to believe that the furface of the Sun may not be fcorched with intolerable and deftruétive heat. It not unfrequently happens that we have very cold weather in fummer, when the fky is overcaft with thick clouds, impenetrable by the direét rays of the Sun. The curious obfervations of Count Rumford of the manner in which heat is moft copioufly communicated through fluid fubftances, concur with what we knew before, to fhew us that even an intenfe heat, communicated by radiation to the upper furface of the fhining clouds by the dazzling ftratum above them, may never reach far down through their thicknefs. With much more confidence may we affirm that it would never warm the tranfparent atmofphere below thofe clouds, nor fcorch the firm furface of the Sun. It is far from being improbable therefore, that the furface may not be uninhabitable, even by creatures like ourfelves. If fo, there is prefented to our view a fcene of habitation 13,000 times bigger than the furface of this Earth, and about 50 times greater than thofe of all the planets added together.

388.

388. Similar obfervations, firft made by Dr Hooke in 1664, on fpots in the difk of Jupiter, fhow that he revolves from weft to eaft in 9ʰ 56′, round an axis inclined to the plane of his orbit 2½°. It is alfo obferved that his equatoreal diameter is to his axis nearly as 14 to 13.

389. There are fome remarkable circumftances in the rotation of this planet. The fpots, by whofe change of place on the difk we judge of the rotation, are not permanent, any more than thofe obferved on the Sun's difk. We muft therefore conclude that, either the furface of the planet is fubject to very confiderable variations of brightnefs, or that Jupiter is furrounded by a cloudy atmofphere. The laft is, of itfelf, the moft probable ; and it becomes ftill more fo from another circumftance. There is a certain part of the planet that is fenfibly brighter than the reft, and fometimes remarkably fo. It is known to be one and the fame part by its fituation. This fpot turns round in fomewhat lefs time than the reft. That is, if a dark fpot remains during feveral revolutions, it is found to have feparated a little from this bright fpot, to the left hand, that is, to the weftward. There is a minute or two of difference between the rotation of Jupiter, as deduced from the fucceffive appearances of the bright fpot, and that deduced from obfervations made on the others.

390. Thefe circumftances lead us to imagine that Jupiter is really covered with a cloudy atmofphere, and

I i

that

that this has a flow motion from eaſt to weſt relative to the ſurface of the planet. The ſtriped appearances, called Belts or Zones, are undoubtedly the effect of a difference of climate. They are diſpoſed with a certain regularity, generally occupying a complete round of his ſurface. Mr Schroeter, who has minutely ſtudied their appearances for a long tract of time, and with excellent glaſſes, ſays that the changes in the atmoſphere are very anomalous, and often very ſudden and extenſive ; in ſhort, there ſeems almoſt the ſame unſettled weather as on this globe. He does not imagine that we ever ſee the real ſurface of Jupiter ; and even the bright ſpot which ſo firmly maintains its ſituation, is thought by Schroeter to be in the atmoſphere. The general current of the clouds is from eaſt to weſt, like our trade winds, but they often move in other directions. The motion is alſo frequently too rapid to be thought the transference of an individual ſubſtance ; it more reſembles the rapid propagation of ſome ſhort-lived change in the ſtate of the atmoſphere, as we often obſerve in a thunder ſtorm. The axis of rotation is almoſt perpendicular to the plane of the orbit, ſo that the days and nights are always equal.

391. The rotation of Mars, firſt obſerved by Hooke and Caſſini in 1666, is ſtill more remarkable than that of Jupiter. The ſurface of the planet is generally of unequal brightneſs, and ſomething like a permanent figure may be obſerved in it, by which we gueſs at the

time

time of the rotation. But the figure is fo ill defined, and fo fubject to confiderable changes, that it was long before aftronomers could be certain of a rotation, fo as to afcertain the time. Dr Herfchel has been at much pains to do this with accuracy, and, by comparing many fucceffive apparitions of the fame objects, he has found that the time of a revolution is 24 hours and 40 minutes, round an axis inclined to the plane of the ecliptic in an angle of nearly 60 degrees, but making an angle of 61° 18' with his own orbit.

392. It is midfummer-day in Mars when he is in long. 11ˢ 19° from our vernal equinox. As the planet is of a very oblate form, and probably hollow, there may be a confiderable preceffion of his equinoctial points, by a change in the direction of his axis.

393. Being fo much inclined to the ecliptic, the poles of Mars come into fight in the courfe of a revolution. When either pole comes firft into view, it is obferved to be remarkably brighter than the reft of the difk. This brightnefs gradually diminifhes, and is generally altogether gone, before this pole goes out of fight by the change of the planet's pofition. The other pole now comes into view, and exhibits fimilar appearances.

394. This appearance of Mars greatly refembles what our own globe will exhibit to a fpectator placed on Venus or Mercury. The fnows in the colder climates

mates

mates diminifh during fummer, and are renewed in the enfuing winter. The appearances in Mars may either be owing to fnows, or to denfe clouds, which condenfe on his circumpolar regions during his winter, and are diffipated in fummer. Dr Herfchel remarks that the atmofphere of Mars extends to a very fenfible diftance from his difk.

395. Obfervers are not agreed as to the time of the rotation of Venus. Some think that fhe turns round her axis in 23^h, and others make it 23 days and 8 hours. The uncertainty is owing to the very fmall time allowed for obfervation, Venus never being feen for more than three hours at a time, fo that the change of appearance that we obferve day after day may either be a *part* of a flow rotation, or more than a complete rotation made in a fhort time. Indeed no diftinct fpots have been obferved in her difk fince the time of the elder Caffini, about the middle of the feventeenth century. Dr Herfchel has always obferved her covered with an impenetrable cloud, as white as fnow, and without any variety of appearance.

396. The Moon turns round her axis in the courfe of a periodic month, fo that one face is always prefented to our view. There is indeed a very fmall LIBRATION, as it is called, by which we occafionally fee a little variation, fo that the fpot which occupies the very centre of the difk, when the Moon is in apogee and in
perigee,

perigee, fhifts a little to one fide and a little up or down.
This arifes from the perfect uniformity of her rotation,
and the unequal motion in her orbit.   As the greateft
equation of her orbital motion amounts to little more
than 5°, this caufes the central fpot to fhift about $\frac{1}{14}$ of
her diameter to one fide, and, returning again to the
centre, to fhift as far to the other fide.   She turns always the fame face to the other focus of her elliptical
orbit round the Earth, becaufe her angular motion round
that point is almoft perfectly equable.

397.   It has been difcovered by Dr Herfchel that
Saturn turns round his axis in 10^h 16', and that his ring
turns round the fame axis in 10^h 32$\frac{1}{4}$'.   This axis is inclined to the ecliptic in an angle of 60° nearly, and the
interfection of the ring and ecliptic is in the line paffing
through long. 5^s 20° and 11^s 20°.   We fee it very open
when Saturn is in long. 2^s 20°, or 8^s 20°; and its length
is then double of its apparent breadth.   It is then midfummer and midwinter on Saturn.   When Saturn is in
the line of its nodes, it difappears, becaufe its plane
paffes through the Sun, and its edge is too thin to be
vifible.   It fhines only by reflecting the Sun's light.   For
we fometimes fee the fhadow of Saturn on it, and fometimes its fhadow on Saturn.   It will be very open in
1811.   Juft now (1803) it is extremely flender, and it
difappeared for a while in the month of June.   Its diameter is above 200,000 miles, almoft half of that of the
Moon's orbit round the Earth.

398.

398. No rotation can be obferved in Mercury, on account of his apparent minutenefs; nor is any obferved in the Georgian planet for the fame reafon.

399. Many philofophers have imagined that the Earth revolves round its axis in 23^h $56'$ $4''$ from weft to eaft : and that this is the caufe of the obferved diurnal motion of the heavens, which is therefore only an appearance. It muft be acknowledged that the appearances will be the fame, and that we muft be infenfible of the motion. There are alfo many circumftances which render this rotation very probable.

400. 1. All the celeftial motions will be rendered incomparably more moderate and fimple. If the heavens really turn round the Earth in 23^h $56'$ $4''$, the motion of the Sun, or of any of the planets, is fwifter than any motion of which we have any meafure ; and this to a degree almoft beyond conception. The motion of the Sun would be 20,000 times fwifter than that of a cannon ball. That of the Georgian planet will be twenty times greater than this. If the Earth turns round its axis, the fwifteft motion neceffary for the appearances is that of the Earth's equator, which does not exceed that of a cannon ball.

The motions alfo become incomparably fimpler. For the combination of diurnal motion with the proper motion of the planets makes it vaftly more complex, and impoffible to account for on any mechanical principles.
This

This diurnal motion muft vary, in all the planets, by their change of declination, being about ⅟ flower when they are near the tropics.   Yet we cannot conceive that any phyfical relation can fubfift between the orbital motion of a planet and the pofition of the Earth's equator, fufficient for producing fuch a change in the planet's motion.   Befides, the axis of diurnal revolution is far from being the fame juft now and in the time of Hipparchus. Juft now, it paffes near the ftar in the extremity of the tail of the little Bear.   When Hipparchus obferved the heavens, it paffed near the fnout of the Camelopard. It is to the laft degree improbable that every object in the univerfe has changed its motion in this manner.   It fnuft be fuppofed that all have changed their motions in different degrees, yet all in a certain precife order, without any connexion or mutual dependence that we can conceive.

401.   2. There is no withholding the belief that the Sun was intended to be a fource of light and genial warmth to the organized beings which occupy the furface of our globe.   How much more fimply, eafily, and beautifully, this is effected by the Earth's rotation, and how much more agreeably to the known œconomy of nature !

402.   3. This rotation would be analogous to what is obferved in the Sun and moft of the planets.

403,

403. 4. We obferve phenomena on our globe that are neceffary confequences of rotation, but cannot be accounted for without it. We know that the equatoreal regions are about twenty miles higher than the circumpolar ; yet the waters of the ocean do not quit this elevation, and retire and inundate the poles. This may be prevented by a proper degree of rotation. It may be fo fwift, that the waters would all flow toward the equator, and inundate the torrid zone ; nay, fo fwift, that every thing loofe would be thrown off, as we fee the water difperfed from a twirled mop. Now, a very fimple calculation will fhew us that a rotation in 23^h 56′ is precifely what will balance the tendency of the waters to flow from the elevated equator towards the poles, and will keep it uniformly fpread over the whole fpheroid. We alfo obferve that a lump of matter of any kind weighs more (by a fpring fteelyard) at Spitzbergen than at Quito, and that the diminution of gravity is precifely what would arife from the fuppofed rotation, viz. $\frac{1}{289}$.

There are arguments which give the moft convincing demonftration of the Earth's rotation.

404. 1. Did the heavens turn round the Earth, as has long been believed, it is almoft certain that no zodiacal fixed ftar could be feen by us. For it is highly probable that light is an emiffion of matter from the luminous body. If this be the cafe, fuch is the diftance of any fixed ftar A (fig. 44.) that, when its velocity A C is compounded with the velocity of light emitted in

any

any direction A B, or A *b*, it would produce a motion in a direction A D, or A *d*, which would never reach the Earth, or which might chance to reach it, but with a velocity infinitely below the known velocity of light; and, in *any* hypothefis concerning the nature of light, the velocity of the light by which we fee the circumpolar ftars muft greatly exceed that by which we fee the equatoreal ftars. All this is contrary to obfervation.

2. The fhadow of Jupiter alfo fhould deviate greatly from the line drawn from the Sun to Jupiter, juft as we fee a fhip's vane deviate from the direction of the wind, when fhe is failing brifkly acrofs that direction. If the diurnal revolution is a real motion, when Jupiter is in oppofition, his firft fatellite muft be feen to come from behind his difk, and, after appearing for about 1^h 10', muft be eclipfed. This is alfo contrary to obfervation; for the fatellites are eclipfed precifely when they come into that line, whereas it fhould happen more than an hour after.

405. We muft therefore conclude that the Earth revolves round its axis from weft to eaft in 23^h 56' 4". We muft further conclude, from the agreement of the ancient and modern latitudes of places, that the axis of the Earth is the fame as formerly; but that it changes its pofition, as we obferve in a top whofe motion is nearly fpent. This change of pofition is feen by the fhifting of the equinoctial points. As thefe make a tour of the ecliptic in 25972 years, the pole of the equator, keeping

K k   always

always perpendicular to its plane, muſt deſcribe a circle round the pole of the ecliptic, diſtant from it 23° 28' 10", the inclination of the equator to the ecliptic. It will be ſeen, in due time, that this motion of the Earth's axis, which appeared a myſtery even to Copernicus, Tycho Brahé and Kepler, is a neceſſary conſequence of the general power of nature by which the whole aſſemblage is held together ; and the detection of this conſequence is the moſt illuſtrious ſpecimen of the ſagacity of the diſcoverer, Sir Iſaac Newton.

Of the Solar Syſtem.

406. We have ſeen (372.) that the planets are always found in the circumferences of ellipſes, which have the Sun in their common focus, while the Sun moves in an ellipſe round the Earth. The motion of any planet is compounded of any motion which it has in reſpect of the Sun, and any motion which the Sun has in reſpect of the Earth. Therefore (92. 93.) the appearances of the planetary motions will be the ſame. as we have deſcribed, if we ſuppoſe the Sun to be at reſt, and give the Earth a motion round the Sun, equal and oppoſite to what the Sun has been thought to have round the Earth.

In the ſecond part of that article concerning relative motion, it was ſhewn that the relative motion, or change of motion, of the body B, as ſeen from A, is equal and oppoſite to that of A ſeen from B. In the preſent caſe, the diſtance of the Sun from the Earth is equal to that
of

of the Earth from the Sun. The pofition or bearing is the oppofite. When the Earth is in Aries or Taurus, the Sun will be feen in Libra or Scorpio. When the Earth is in the tropic of Capricorn, the Sun will appear in that of Cancer, and her north pole will be turned toward the Sun ; fo that the northern hemifphere will have longer days than nights. In fhort, the gradual variation of the feafons will be the fame in both cafes, if the Earth's axis keeps the fame pofition during its revolution round the Sun. It muft do fo, if there be no force to change its pofition ; and we fee that the axes of the other planets retain their pofition.

407. Then, with refpect to the planets, the appearances of direct and retrograde motion, with points of ftation, will alfo be the fame as if the Sun revolved round the Earth. That this may be more evident, it muft be obferved that our judgement of a planet's fituation is precifely fimilar to that of a mariner who fees a fhip's light in a dark night. He fets it by the compafs. If he fees it due north, and a few minutes after, fees it a little to the weftward of north, he imagines that the fhip has really gone a little weftward Yet this might have happened, had both been failing due eaft, provided that the fhip of the fpectator had been failing fafter. It is juft the fame in the planetary motions. If we give the Earth the motion that was afcribed to the Sun, the real velocity of the Earth will be more than double of the velocity of Jupiter. Now fuppofe, according to the

K k 2   old

old hypothefis, the Earth at T (fig. 40.) and the Sun
at α. Suppofe Jupiter in oppofition. Then we muft
place the centre of his epicycle in A, and make A a
equal to T α. Jupiter is in a, and his bearing and diftance from the Earth is T a, nearly $\frac{4}{5}$ of T A. Six
weeks after, the Sun is in β; the centre of Jupiter's epicycle is in B. Draw B b equal and parallel to T β, and
b is now the place of Jupiter, and T b is now his bearing and diftance. He has changed his bearing to the
right hand, or weftward on the ecliptic; and his change
of pofition is had by meafuring the angle a T b. His
longitude on the ecliptic is diminifhed by this number of
degrees.

408. Now let the Sun be at T, according to the
new hypothefis, and let A B E L be Jupiter's orbit round
the Sun. Let Jupiter be in oppofition to the Sun. We
muft place Jupiter in A, and the Earth in ε, fo as to
have the Sun and Jupiter in oppofition. It is evident
that Jupiter's bearing and diftance from the Earth are the
fame as in the former hypothefis. For A a being equal
to ε T, we have ε A, the diftance of Jupiter from the
Earth, equal to T a of the former hypothefis. Six weeks
after, the Earth is at φ, and Jupiter at B. Join φ B,
and draw φ Ṅ parallel to T A. It is evident that the
diftance φ B of Jupiter from the Earth, is equal to the
diftance T b of the former conftruction. Alfo the angle
Ṅ φ B, which is Jupiter's change of bearing, (by the
aftronomer's compafs, the ecliptic), is equal to the angle
a T b

a T *b* of the former conftruction.   Jupiter therefore, inftead of moving to the left hand, has moved to the right,
or weftward, and has diminifhed his ecliptical bearing or
longitude by the degrees in the angle N' φ B.

409.   In the fame manner may the apparent motion
of Jupiter be afcertained for every fituation of the Earth
and Jupiter; and it will be found that, in every cafe,
the line correfponding to φ B is equal and parallel to the
line correfponding to T *b*; thus γ C is equal and parallel
to T *c*; χ D is equal and parallel to T *d*, &c.

The apparent motions of the planets are therefore
precifely the fame in either hypothefis, fo that we are
left to follow either opinion, as it appears beft fupported
by other arguments.

410.   Accordingly, it has been the opinion of fome
philofophers, both in ancient and modern times, that the
Earth is a planet, revolving round the Sun placed in the
focus of its elliptical orbit, and that it is accompanied
by the Moon, in the fame manner as Jupiter and Saturn
are by their fatellites.

The following are the reafons for preferring this opinion to that contained in the 371st and 373d articles,
which equally explains all the phenomena hitherto mentioned, and is more confiftent with our firft judgements.

411.   1. The celeftial motions become incomparably
more fimple, and free of thofe looped contortions which

muft

muft be fuppofed in the other cafe, and which are extremely improbable, and incompatible with what we
know of the laws of motion.

412.   2. This opinion is alfo more reafonable, on
account of the extreme minutenefs of the Earth, when
compared with the immenfe bulk of the Sun, Jupiter,
and Saturn ; and becaufe the Sun is the fource of light
and heat to all the planets.

The reafons adduced in this and the preceding article
were all that could offer themfelves to the philofophers
of antiquity.   They had not the telefcope, and the fatellites were therefore unknown.   They had no knowledge of the powers of nature by which the planetary
motions are produced and regulated ; their knowledge of
dynamical fcience was extremely fcanty.   Yet Pythagoras, Philolaus, Apollonius, Anaxagoras, and others, maintained this opinion.   But they had few followers in an
opinion fo different from our habitual thoughts, and
for which they could only offer fome reafons founded
on certain notions of propriety or fuitablenefs.   But, as
men became more converfant, in modern times, with
the mechanical arts, every thing connected with the
motion of bodies became more familiar, and was better
underftood, and we had lefs hefitation in adopting fentiments unlike the firft and moft familiar fuggeftions of
fenfe.   Other arguments now offered themfelves.

413.   3. If the Earth turns round the Sun, then the
analogy between the fquares of the periodic times and
                                                    the

the cubes of the diſtances, will obtain in all the bodies which circulate round a common centre; whereas this will not be the cafe with refpeſt to the Sun and Moon, if both turn round the Earth.

414. 4. It is thought that the motion of the Sun round the Earth is inconſiſtent with the difcoveries which have been made concerning the forces which operate in the planetary motions.

We have feen, by article 230, combined with the third law of motion, that neither can the Sun revolve round the Earth at reſt, nor the Earth round the Sun at reſt, but that both muſt revolve round their common centre of pofition. It is difcovered that the quantity of matter in the Sun is more than 300,000 times that of the matter in the Earth. Therefore the centre of pofition of thefe two bodies muſt be almoſt in the centre of the Sun. Nay, if all the planets were on one fide of the Sun, the common centre would be very near his centre.

415. But, perhaps, this argument is not of the great weight that is fuppofed. The difcovery of the proportion of thefe quantities of matter feems to depend on its being previouſly eſtabliſhed that the Sun is in, or near, the centre of pofition of the whole affemblage. It muſt be owned, however, that the perfeſt harmony of all the comparative meafures of the quantities of matter of the Sun and planets, deduced from

fources

fources independent of each other, renders their accuracy almoft unqueftionable.

416. 5. It is inconteftably proved by obfervation.
A motion has been difcovered in all the fixed ftars, which
arifes from a combination of the motion of light with
the motion of the Earth in its orbit.

Suppofe a fhower of hail falling during a perfect
calm, and therefore falling perpendicularly. Were it required to hold a long tube in fuch a pofition that a hailftone fhall fall through it without touching either fide,
it is plain that the tube muft be held perpendicular.
Suppofe now that the tube is faftened to the arm of a
gin, fuch as thofe employed in raifing coals from the
pit, and that it is carried round, with a velocity that is
equal to that of the falling hail. It is now evident
that a perpendicular tube will not do. The hailftones
will all ftrike on the hindmoft fide of the tube. The
tube muft be put into the direction of the *relative* motion
of the hailftones. Now, it was demonftrated in § 92,
that this is the diagonal of a parallelogram, one fide of
which is the real motion of the hail, and the other is
equal, but oppofite, to the motion of the tube. Therefore if the tube be inclined *forward*, at an angle of
45°, the experiment will fucceed, becaufe the tangent of this angle is equal to the radius ; and, while the
hailftone falls two feet, the tube advances two, and the
hailftone will pafs along the tube without touching it.

In the very fame manner, if the Earth be at reft,
and

and we would view a ftar near the pole of the ecliptic, the telefcope muft be pointed directly at the ftar. But if the Earth be in motion round the Sun, the telefcope muft be pointed a little forward, that the light may come along the axis of the tube. The proportion of the velocity of light to the fuppofed velocity of the Earth in its orbit is nearly that of 10,000 to 1. Therefore the telefcope muft lean about 20″ forward.

Half a year after this, let the fame ftar be viewed again. The telefcope muft again be pointed 20″ a-head of the true pofition of the ftar : but this is in the oppofite direction to the former deviation of the telefcope, becaufe the Earth, being now in the oppofite part of its orbit, is moving the other way. Therefore the pofition of the ftar muft appear to have changed 40″ in the fix months.

It is eafy to fhew that the confequence of this is, that every ftar muft appear to have 40″ more longitude when it is on our meridian at midnight, than when it is on the meridian at mid-day. The effect of this compofition of motions which is moft fufceptible of accurate examination is the following. Let the declination of fome ftar near the pole of the ecliptic be obferved at the time of the equinoxes. It will be found to have 40″ more declination in the autumnal than in the vernal equinox, if the obferver be in latitude 66° 30′ ; and not much lefs if he be in the latitude of London. Alfo every ftar in the heavens fhould appear to defcribe a little ellipfe, whofe longer axis is 40″.

L l

417.

417. Now this is actually obferved, and was difcovered by Dr Bradley about the year 1726. It is called the ABERRATION OF THE FIXED STARS, and is one of the moft curious, and moft important difcoveries of the eighteenth century. It is important, by furnifhing an incontrovertible proof that the Earth is a planet, revolving, like the others, round the Sun. It is alfo important, by fhewing that the light of the fixed ftars moves with the fame velocity with the light of the Sun, which illuminates our fyftem.

418. This arrangement of the planets is called the COPERNICAN SYSTEM, having been revived and eftablifhed by Copernicus, reprefented in fig. A. The other opinion, mentioned (371.), which equally explains the general phenomena, was maintained by Longomontanus.

419. Account of the PTOLEMAIC, EGYPTIAN, and TYCHONIC fyftems (fig. B, C, D.) *

420. The Copernican fyftem is now univerfally admitted ; and it is fully eftablifhed, 1. That the planets and

---

* In the preceding pages, no notice has been taken of the latitude of the planets, and the obfervations by which it may be afcertained. What is delivered here is not to be confidered as a treatife of the celeftial motions ; nothing was inferted but what was neceffary for enabling the reader to judge of the evidences for the progreffive and other motions of the heavenly bodies,

and the comets defcribe round the Sun areas proportional
to the times ; and that the Moon, and the fatellites of
Jupiter and Saturn, defcribe round the Earth, Jupiter,
and Saturn, areas proportional to the times. 2. That
the orbits defcribed by thofe bodies are ellipfes, having
the Sun, or the primary planet, in one focus. 3. That
the fquares of the periodic times of thofe bodies which
revolve round a common centre are proportional to the
cubes of their mean diftances from that centre. Thefe
three propofitions are called the LAWS OF KEPLER.

421. There is however an objeftion to this account
of the planetary motions, which has been thought for-
midable. Suppofe a telefcope pointed in a direftion
perpendicular to the plane of the Earth's orbit, and carried round the Sun in this pofition. Its axis, produced
to the ftarry firmament, fhould trace out a figure precifely equal and fimilar to the orbit, and we fhould be
able to mark it among the ftars round the pole of the
ecliptic. But, if this be tried, we find that we are always looking at the fame point, which always remains
the centre of the little ellipfe which is the effeft of the
aberration of light.

This objeftion was made, even in the fchools of
Greece, to Ariftarchus of Samos, when he ufed his ut-

L l 2   moft

bodies, from which we are to infer the nature of thofe forces
by which they are continually regulated. The motion of revolution, from which the inference is made, is in one plane,
and is elliptical. This fuffices for the purpofe of philofophy.

moſt endeavours to bring into credit the later opinion of Pythagoras, placing the Sun in the centre of the ſyſtem. And the anſwer given by Ariſtarchus is the only one that we can give at the preſent day.

422. The only anſwer that can be given to this is, that the diſtance of the fixed ſtars is ſo great, that a figure of near 200 millions of miles diameter is not a ſenſible object. This, incredible as it may ſeem, has nothing in it of abſurdity. We know that their diſtance is immenſe. The comet of 1680 goes 150 times farther from the Sun than we are, and we muſt ſuppoſe it much farther from the neareſt ſtar, that it may not be affected by it in its motion round our Sun. Suppoſe it only twice as far, the Earth's orbit traced among the ſtars would appear only half the diameter of the Sun. We have teleſcopes which magnify the diameter of objects 1200 times. Yet a fixed ſtar is not magnified by them in the ſmalleſt degree. That is, though we were only at the 1200dth part of our preſent diſtance from it, it would appear no bigger. The more perfect the teleſcope is, the ſtars appear the ſmaller. We need not be ſurpriſed therefore that obſervation ſhews no parallax of the fixed ſtars, not even 1″. Yet a parallax of 1″ puts the object 206,000 times farther off than the Sun. But ſpace is without bounds, and we have no reaſon to think that our view comprehends the whole creation. On the contrary, it is more probable that we ſee but an inconſiderable part of the ſcene on which the perfections of the Creator and Governor of the univerſe are diſplayed.

Of the Comets.

423. There are fometimes feen in the heavens certain bodies, accompanied by a train of faint light, which
has occafioned them to be called comets. Their appearance and motions are extremely various; and the only
general remarks that can be made on them are, that the
train, or tail, is generally fmall on the firft appearance
of a comet, gradually lengthens as the comet comes into
the neighbourhood of the Sun, and again diminifhes as
it retires to a diftance. Alfo the tail is always extended
in a direction nearly oppofite to the Sun.

424. The opinions of philofophers concerning comets
have been very different. Sir Ifaac Newton firft fhowed
that they are a part of the folar fyftem, revolving round
the Sun in trajectories, nearly parabolical, having the Sun
in the focus. Dr Halley computed the motions of feveral
comets, and, among them, found fome which had precifely
the fame trajectory. He therefore concluded, that thefe
were different appearances of one comet, and that the
path of a comet is a very eccentric ellipfe, having the
Sun in one focus. The apparition of the comet of 1682
in 1759, which was predicted by Halley, has given his
opinion the moft complete confirmation.

425. Comets are therefore planets, refembling the
others in the laws of their motion, revolving round the
Sun in ellipfes, defcribing areas proportional to the times,

and

and having the fquares of their periodic times proportional to the cubes of their mean diftances from the Sun.
They differ from the planets in the great variety in the
pofition of their orbits, and in this, that many of them
have their courfe *in antecedentia fignorum.*

426. Their number is very great; but there are
but few with the elements of whofe motions we are well
acquainted. The comet of 1680 came very near to the
Sun on the 11th of December, its diftance not exceeding
his femidiameter. When in its aphelion, it will be almoft 150 times farther from the Sun than the Earth is.
Our ideas of the extent of the folar fyftem are thus greatly
enlarged.

427. No fatisfactory knowledge has been acquired
concerning the caufe of that train of light which accompanies the comets. Some philofophers imagine that it
is the rarer atmofphere of the comet, impelled by the
Sun's rays. Others imagine, that it is the atmofphere
of the comet, rifing in the folar atmofphere by its fpecific
levity. Others imagine, that it is a phenomenon of the
fame kind with the aurora borealis, and that this Earth
would appear like a comet to a fpectator placed on another planet. Confult Newton's Principia;—a Differtation, by Profeffor Hamilton of Trinity College, Dublin;
—a Differtation, by Mr Winthorpe of New Jerfey, &c.;
both in the Philofophical Tranfactions.

PHYSI-

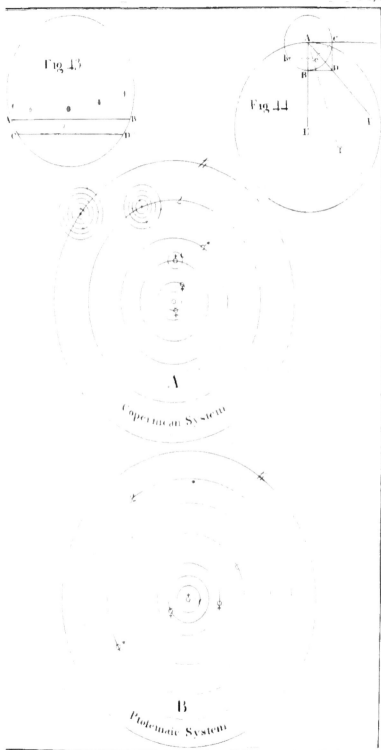

Fig. 43

Fig. 44

A

Copernican System

B

Ptolemaic System

PHYSICAL ASTRONOMY.

428. It is hoped that the preceding account of the celeſtial phenomena has given the attentive ſtudent a diſtinct conception of the nature of that evidence which Kepler had for the truth of the three general facts diſcovered by him in all the motions, and for the truth of thoſe ſeeming deviations from Kepler's laws which were ſo happily reconciled with them by Sir Iſaac Newton, by ſhewing that theſe deviations are examples of mutual deflections of the celeſtial bodies towards one another. Several phenomena were occaſionally noticed, although not immediately ſubſervient to this purpoſe. Theſe are the chief objects of our ſubſequent attempts to explain. The account given of the kind of obſervation by which the different motions were proved to be what has been affirmed of them, has been exceedingly ſhort and ſlight, on the preſumption that the young aſtronomer will ſtudy the celeſtial phenomenology in the detail, as delivered by Gregory, Keill, and other authors of reputation. This ſtudy will terminate in the fulleſt conviction of the validity of the evidence for the truth of the Copernican ſyſtem of the Sun and planets ; and in a minute acquaintance

with

PHYSICAL ASTRONOMY.

428. I⊤ is hoped that the preceding account of the celeſtial phenomena has given the attentive ſtudent a diſtinct conception of the nature of that evidence which Kepler had for the truth of the three general facts diſcovered by him in all the motions, and for the truth of thoſe ſeeming deviations from Kepler's laws which were ſo happily reconciled with them by Sir Iſaac Newton, by ſhewing that theſe deviations are examples of mutual deflections of the celeſtial bodies towards one another. Several phenomena were occaſionally noticed, although not immediately ſubſervient to this purpoſe. Theſe are the chief objects of our ſubſequent attempts to explain. The account given of the kind of obſervation by which the different motions were proved to be what has been affirmed of them, has been exceedingly ſhort and ſlight, on the preſumption that the young aſtronomer will ſtudy the celeſtial phenomenology in the detail, as delivered by Gregory, Keill, and other authors of reputation. This ſtudy will terminate in the fulleſt conviction of the validity of the evidence for the truth of the Copernican ſyſtem of the Sun and planets ; and in a minute acquaintance with

with all thofe peculiarities of motion that diftinguifh the individuals of the magnificent affemblage.

We are now in a condition to inveftigate the particular characters of thofe extenfive powers of nature, thofe mechanical affections of matter, which caufe the obferved deviations from that uniform rectilineal motion which would have been obferved in every body, had it been under no mechanical influence. And we fhall alfo be able to explain or account for the diftinguifhing peculiarities of motion which characterife the individuals of the fyftem, if we fhall fo far fucceed in our firft inveftigation as to fhew that no other force operates in the fyftem, and that thefe peculiarities are only particular and accurately narrated cafes of the three general laws, precifely conformable to their legitimate confequences. *

In

---

* I think it neceffary here to forewarn the well-informed mathematician, if any fuch fhall honour thefe pages with a perufal, that he will be difappointed if he look for any thing profound, or curious, or new, in what follows. My fole aim is to affift the ignorant in the elements of phyfical aftronomy ; and I mean to infert nothing but what feems to me to be elementary in the Newtonian philofophy. This ftudy requires (I think) a few more fteps than are ufually given in the elementary publications of this country. Thefe performances generally leave the ftudent too fcantily prepared for reading the valuable works on this fubject, unlefs by a very obftinate and fatiguing ftudy. They are deterred by the great difficulties

In our firſt inveſtigation, we muſt affirm the forces to be ſuch as are indicated by the motions, in the manner agreed on in the general doctrines of Dynamics. That is, the kind and the intenſity of the force muſt be inferred from the direction and the magnitude of the change which we conſider as its effect.

In all this procefs, it is plain that we conſider the heavenly bodies as conſiſting of matter that has the ſame mechanical properties with the bodies which are daily in our hands. We are not at liberty to imagine that the celeſtial matter has any other properties than what is indicated by the motions, otherwiſe we have no explanation,

---

ties thus occaſioned in the beginning ; and, proceeding no further, they never taſte the great pleaſure afforded by this noble ſcience. I wiſh to render it acceſſible to all who have learned Euclid's Elements, and the leading properties of the three conic ſections. I have preferred the geometrical to the algebraical manner of expreſſing the quantities under conſideration. Frequently both methods are ſymbolical ; but, even in this caſe, the geometrical ſymbol, by preſenting a picture of the thing, gives an object of eaſier recollection, and more expreſſive of its nature, than an algebraical formula ; and in phyſical aſtronomy, the geometrical figure is often not a ſymbol, but the very quantity under examination. It is from the experience of my own ſtudies that I am induced to prefer this method, fully aware, however, that its advantages are reſtricted to mere elementary inſtruction, and that no very great progreſs will be made in the more recondite parts of

M m   phyſical

tion, and may as well reft contented with the fimple narration of the facts. The conftant practice, in all attempts to explain a natural appearance, is to try to find
a clafs of familiar phenomena which refemble it ; and if
we fucceed, we account it to be one of the number, and
we reft fatisfied with this as a fufficient explanation. Accordingly, this is the way that philofophers, both in ancient and modern times, have proceeded in their attempt
to difcover the caufes of the planetary motions.

429. 1. Nothing is more familiar to our experience
than bodies carried round fixed centres by means of folid
matter connecting the bodies with the centre, in one way
or another. This was the firft attempt to explain the
planetary

---

phyfical aftronomy without employing the algebraic along with
the geometrical analyfis..

I fear that I fhall frequently be thought prolix and inele-
gant. But I beg that it may be remembered for whom thefe
pages are written—for mere beginners in the ftudy. I wifh
to leave no difficulty in the way that I can remove. If I have
failed in this—*operam perdidi et oleum.* But I hope that I
may enable an attentive ftudent to read Newton's lunar theory
with fome relifh, and a perception of its beauty. If fo, my
favourite point is gained,—the ftudent will go forward.

The two articles which occupy fo much at the clofe of
this fubject, are not fo far purfued in our elementary books ;
yet what is here inferted are only the elements of the fubject ;
and without this inftruction, we can have no conception of
them that is of any ufe.

planetary motions of which we have any account. Eudoxus and Callippus, many ages before our æra, taught
that all the ftars in the firmament are fo many lucid
points or bodies, adhering to the infide of a vaft material
concave fphere, which turned round the Earth placed in
the centre in twenty-four hours. It was called the CRYS-
TALLINE ORB or Sphere.

But this will not explain the eafterly motion of the
Sun and Moon, unlefs we fuppofe them endowed with
fome felf-moving power, by which they can creep flowly
eaftward along the furface of the cryftalline orb ; far lefs
will it account for the Moon fometimes hiding the Sun
from us. Thefe philofophers were therefore obliged to
fay that there were other fpheres, or rather fpherical
fhells, tranfparent, like vaft glafs globes, one within another, and all having a common centre. The Sun and
the Moon were fuppofed to be attached to the furface of
thofe globes. The fphere which carried the Moon was
the fmalleft, immediately furrounding the Earth. The
fphere of the Sun was much larger, but ftill left a vaft
fpace between it and the fphere of the fixed ftars, which
contained all.

This machinery may make a fhift to carry round the
Moon, the Sun, and the ftars, in a way fomewhat like
what we behold. But the planets gave the philofophers
much trouble, in order to explain their retrograde and
direct motions, and ftationary points, &c. To move Jupiter in a way refembling what we behold, they fuppofed
the fhell of his fphere to be of vaft thicknefs, and in its

M m 2   folid

folid matter they lodged a fmall tranfparent fphere, in the furface of which Jupiter was fixed. This fphere turned round in the hollow made for it in the thick fhell of the deferent fphere, and, as all was tranfparent, exhibited Jupiter moving to the weftward, when his epifphere brought him toward us, and to the eaft, when it carried him round toward the outer furface of the deferent fhell. Meanwhile, the great deferent globe was moving flowly eaftward, or rather was turning more flowly weftward than the fphere of the ftars.

No doubt, this mechanifm will produce round-about motions, and ftations and retrogradations, &c. This, however, is only a very grofs outline of the planetary motions. But the Sun's unequable motion could not be reprefented without fuppofing the Earth out of the centre of rotation of his fphere. This was accordingly fuppofed—and it was an eafy fuppofition. But the motion of Jupiter in relation to the centre of his epicycle muft be fimilar to the Sun's motion in relation to the Earth (361.); but a folid fphere, turning in a hollow which exactly fits it, can only turn round its centre. This is evident. Therefore the inequality of Jupiter's epicyclical motion cannot be reprefented by this mechanifm. The deferent fphere may be eccentric, but the epicycle cannot. This obliged thofe engineers to give Jupiter a fecondary epicycle much fmaller than the epicycle which produced his retrogradations and ftations. It moved in a hollow lodgement made for it in the folid matter of the epicycle, juft as this moved in a hollow in the folid matter of the deferent globe.

Even

Even this would not correfpond with tolerable exactnefs with the obferved tenor of Jupiter's motion ; other
epicycles were added, to tally with every improvement
made on the equation of the apparent motion, till the
whole fpace was almoft crammed full of folid matter ;
and after all thefe efforts, fome mathematicians affirmed
that there are motions in the heavens that are neither
uniform nor circular, nor can be compounded of fuch
motions. If fo, this fpherical machinery is impoffible.
In modern times, Tycho Brahé proved beyond all contradiction that the comet of 1574 paffed through all thofe
fpheres, and therefore their exiftence was a mere fiction.

One fhould think the whole of this contrivance fo
artlefs and rude, that we wonder that it ever obtained
the leaft credit ; yet was it adopted by the prince of ancient philofophers,—by Ariftotle ; and his authority gave
it poffeffion of all the fchools till modern times.

But where, all this while, is the mover of all this
machinery ? Ariftotle taught that each globe was conducted, or turned round its axis, by a peculiar genius
or dæmon. This was worthy of the reft ; and when
fuch affertions are called *explanations*, nothing in nature
need remain unexplained. We muft however do Hipparchus and Ptolemy the juftice to fay that they never
adopted this hypothefis of Eudoxus and Callippus ; they
did not fpeculate about the caufes, but only endeavoured
to afcertain the motions ; and their epicycle and deferent
circles are given by them merely as fteps of mathematical contemplation, and in order to have fome principle

to direct their calculation, juft as we demonftrate the
parabolic path of a cannon ball by compounding a uniform motion in the line of direction with a uniformly
accelerated motion in the vertical line. There is no fuch
compofition, but the motion of the ball is the fame as if
there were.

430. 2. A much more feafible attempt was made
by Cleanthes, another philofopher of Greece, to affign
the caufes of the planetary motions. He obferved that
bodies are eafily carried round in whirlpools or vortices
of water. He taught that the celeftial fpaces are filled
with an ethereal fluid, which is in continual motion
round the Earth, and that it carried the Sun and planets
round with it. But a flight examination of this fpecious
hypothefis fhewed that it was much more difficult to
form a notion of the vortices, fo as to correfpond with
the obferved motions, than to ftudy the motions themfelves. It therefore gave no explanation. Yet this very
hypothefis was revived in modern times, and was maintained by two of the moft eminent mathematicians and
philofophers of Europe, namely, by Des Cartes and Leibnitz ; and, for a long while, it was acquiefced in by all.

We muft conftantly keep in mind that an explanation always means to fhew that the fubject in queftion
is an example of fomething that we clearly underftand.
Whatever is the avowed property of that more familiar
fubject, muft therefore be admitted in the ufe made of
it for explanation. We explain the fplitting of glafs by
heat,

heat, by fhewing that the known and avowed effects of
heat make the glafs fwell on one fide to a certain degree, with a certain known force ; and we fhew that the
tenacity of the other fide of the glafs, which is not
fwelled by the heat, is not able to refift this force which
is pulling it afunder ; it muft therefore give way.   In
fhort, we fhew the fplitting to be one of the ordinary
effects of heat, which operates here as it operates in all
other cafes.

Now, if we take this method, we find that the effects of a vortex or whirl in a fluid are totally unlike
the planetary motions, and that we cannot afcribe them
to the vortical motion of the æther, without giving it
laws of motion unlike every thing obferved in all the
fluids that we know ; nay, in contradiction of all thofe
laws of mechanics which are admitted by the very patrons of the hypothefis.   To give this fluid properties
unknown in all others, is abfurd ; we had better give
thofe properties to the planets themfelves.   The fact is,
that thefe two philofophers had not taken the trouble to
think about the matter, or to inquire what motions of a
vortex of fluid are poffible, and what are not, or what
effects will be produced by fuch vortices as are poffible.
They had not thought of any means of moving the fluid itfelf, or for preferving it in motion ; they contented themfelves (at leaft this was the cafe with Des Cartes) with
merely throwing out the general fact, that bodies *may*
be carried round by a vortex.   It is to Sir Ifaac Newton
that we are indebted for all that we know of vortical
motion.

motion. In examining this hypothefis of Des Cartes, which had fupreme authority among the philofophers at that time, he found it neceffary to inquire into the manner in which a vortex may be produced, and the conftitution of the vortex which refults from the mode of its pro-duction. This led him, by neceffary fteps, to difcover what forms of vortical motion are poffible, what are permanent, and the variations to which the others are fubject. In the fecond book of his Mathematical Prin-ciples of Natural Philofophy, he has given the refult of this examination ; and it contains a beautiful fyftem of mechanical doctrine, concerning the mutual action of the filaments of fluid matter, by which they modify each other's motion. The refult of the whole was a complete refutation of this hypothefis as an explanation of the planetary motions, fhewing that the legitimate confe-quences of a vortical motion are altogether unlike the planetary motions, nay, are incompatible with them. It is quite enough, in this place, for proving the infufficiency of the hypothefis, to obferve that it muft explain the motion of the comets as well as that of the planets. If Mars be carried round the Sun by a fluid vortex, fo is the comet which appeared in 1682 and 1759. This comet came from an immenfe diftance, in the north-ern quarter of the heavens, into our neighbourhood, paff-ing through the vortices of all the planets, defcribing its very eccentric ellipfe with the moft perfect regularity. Now, it is abfolutely impoffible that, in one and the fame place, there can be paffing a ftream of the vortex

of

of a planet, and a ftream of the cometary vortex, having a direction and a velocity fo very different. It is inconceivable that thefe two ftreams of fluid fhall have force enough, one of them to drag a planet along with it, and the other to drag a comet, and yet that the particles of the one ftream fhall not difturb the motion of thofe of the other in the fmalleft degree : even the infinitely rare vapour which formed the tail of the comet was not in the leaft deranged by the motion of the planetary vortices through which it paffed. All this is inconceivable and abfurd.

It is a pity that the account given by Newton of vortical motions appeared on fuch an occafion ; for this limited the attention of his readers to this particular employment of it, which purpofe being completely anfwered in another way, this argument became unneceffary, and was not looked into. But it contains much valuable information, of great fervice in all problems of hydraulics. Many confequences of the mutual action of the fluid filaments produce important changes on the motion of the whole ; fo that till thefe are underftood and taken into the account, we cannot give an anfwer to very fimple, yet important queftions. This is the caufe why this branch of mechanical philofophy is in fo imperfect a ftate, although it is one of the moft important.

431. 3. Many of the ancient philofophers, ftruck with the order, regularity, and harmonious cooperation

of

of the planetary motions, imagined that they were conducted by intelligent minds. Ariftotle's way of conceiving this has been already mentioned. The fame doctrine
has been revived, in fome refpect, in modern times.
Leibnitz animates every particle of matter, when he
gives his *Monads* a perception of their fituation with
refpect to every other monad, and a motion in confequence of this perception. This, and the elemental mind
afcribed by Lord Monboddo to every thing that begins
motion, do not feem to differ much from the ὁσπηρ ψυχη
of Ariftotle ; nor do they differ from what all the world
diftinguifhes by the name of *force.*

This doctrine cannot be called a hypothefis ; it is rather a definition, or a mifnomer, giving the name Mind
to what exhibits none of thofe phenomena by which we
diftinguifh mind. No end beneficial to the agent is
gained by the motion of the planet. It may be beneficial
to its inhabitants—But fhould we think more highly of
the mind of an animal when it is covered with vermin ?—
Nor does this doctrine give the fmalleft explanation of
the planetary motions. We muft explain the motions
by ftudying them, in order to difcover the laws by which
the action of their caufe is regulated : this is juft the
way that we learn the nature of any mechanical force.
Accordingly,

432. 4. Many philofophers, both in ancient and
modern times, imagined that the planets were deflected
from uniform rectilineal motion by forces fimilar to what
we

we obferve in the motions of magnetical and electrical bodies, or in the motion of common heavy bodies, where one body feems to influence the motion of another at a diftance from it, without any intervening impulfion. It is thus that a ftone is bent continually from the line of its direction towards the Earth. In the fame manner, an iron ball, rolling along a level table, will be turned afide toward-a magnet; and, by properly adjufting the diftance and the velocity, the ball may be made to revolve round the pole of the magnet. Many of the ancients faid that the curvilineal motions of the planets were produced by *tendencies* to one another, or to a common centre. Among the moderns, Fermat is the firft who faid in precife terms that the weight of a body is the fum of the tendencies of each particle to every particle of the Earth. Kepler faid ftill more exprefsly, that if there be fuppofed two bodies, placed out of the reach of all external forces, and at perfect liberty to move, they would approach each other, with velocities inverfely proportional to their quantities of matter. The Moon (fays he) and the Earth mutually attract each other, and are prevented from meeting by their revolution round their common centre of attraction. And he fays that the tides of the ocean are the effects of the Moon's attraction, heaping up the waters immediately under her. Then, adopting the opinion of our countryman, Dr Gilbert of Colchefter, that the Earth is a great magnet, he explains how this mutual attraction will produce a deflection into a curvilineal path, and adds, '*Veritatis* '*in me fit amor an gloriæ, loquantur dogmata mea, quæ ple-*

N n 2   '*raque*

' *raque ab aliis accepta fero.* *Totam astronomiam Coper-*
' *nici hypothesibus de mundo, Tychonis vero Brahei observa-*
' *tionibus, denique Gulielmi Gilberti Angli philosophiæ mag-*
' *neticæ inædifico.*' EPIT. ASTR. COPERN.

433. The moſt expreſs ſurmiſe to this purpoſe is
that of Dr Robert Hooke, one of the moſt ardent and
ingenious ſtudents of nature in that buſy period. At a
meeting of the Royal Society, on May 3. 1666, he expreſſed himſelf in the following manner.

" I will explain a ſyſtem of the world very different
" from any yet received ; and it is founded on the three
" following poſitions.

" 1. That all the heavenly bodies have not only a gra-
" vitation of their parts to their own proper centre, but
" that they alſo mutually attract each other within their
" ſpheres of action.

" 2. That all bodies having a ſimple motion, will
" continue to move in a ſtraight line, unleſs continually
" deflected from it by ſome extraneous force, cauſing
" them to deſcribe a circle, an ellipſe, or ſome other curve.

" 3. That this attraction is ſo much the greater as
" the bodies are nearer. As to the proportion in which
" thoſe forces diminiſh by an increaſe of diſtance, I own
" (ſays he) I have not diſcovered it, although I have made
" ſome experiments to this purpoſe. I leave this to others,
" who have time and knowledge ſufficient for the taſk."

This is a very preciſe enunciation of a proper philoſophical theory. The phenomenon, the change of motion,

is

is confidered as the mark and meafure of a changing force, and his audience is referred to experience for the nature of this force. He had before this exhibited to the Society a very pretty experiment contrived on thefe principles. A ball fufpended by a long thread from the ceiling, was made to fwing round another ball laid on a table immediately below the point of fufpenfion. When the pufh given to the pendulum was nicely adjufted to its deviation from the perpendicular, it defcribed a perfect circle round the ball on the table. But when the pufh was very great, or very fmall, it defcribed an ellipfe, having the other ball in its centre. Hooke fhewed that this was the operation of a deflecting force proportional to the diftance from the other ball. He added, that although this illuftrated the planetary motions in fome degree, yet it was not fuitable to their caufe. For the planets defcribe ellipfes having the Sun, not in the centre, but in the focus. Therefore they are not retained by a force proportional to their diftance from the Sun. This was ftrict reafoning, from good pinciples. It is worthy of remark, that in this clear, and candid, and modeft expofition of a rational theory, he anticipated the difcoveries of Newton, as he anticipated, with equal diftinctnefs and precifion, the difcoveries of Lavoifier, a philofopher inferior perhaps only to Newton.

Thus we fee that many had noticed certain points of refemblance between the celeftial motions and the motions of magnets and heavy bodies. But thefe obfervers let the remark remain barren in their hands, becaufe they

had

had neither examined with fufficient attention the celeftial motions, which they attempted to explain, nor had they formed to themfelves any precife notions of the motions from which they hoped to derive an explanation.

· · 434. At laft a genius arofe, fully qualified both by talents and difpofition, for thofe arduous tafks. I fpeak of Sir Ifaac Newton. This ornament, this boaft of our nature, had a moft acute and penetrating mind, accompanied by the foundeft judgment, with a modeft and proper diffidence in his own underftanding. He had a patience in inveftigation, which I believe is yet without an equal, and was convinced that this was the only compenfation attainable for the imperfection of human underftanding, and that when exercifed in profecuting the conjectures of a curious mind, it would not fail of giving him all the information that we are warranted to hope for. Although only 24 years of age, Mr Newton had already given the moft illuftrious fpecimen of his ability to promote the knowledge of nature, in his curious difcoveries concerning light and colours. Thefe were the refult of the moft unwearied patience, in making experiments of the moft delicate kind, and the moft acute penetration in feparating the refulting phenomena from each other, and the cleareft and moft precife logic in reafoning from them ; and they terminated in forming a body of fcience which gave a total change to all the notions of philofophers on this fubject. Yet this body of optical fcience was nothing but a fair narration of the facts

prefented

prefented to his view. Not a fingle fuppofition or conjecture is to be found in it, nor reafoning on any thing
not immediately before the eye ; and all its fcience confifted in the judicious claffification. This had brought to
light certain general laws, which comprehended all the
reft. Young Newton faw that this was fure ground,
and that a theory, fo founded, could never be fhaken.
He was determined therefore to proceed in no other way
in all his future fpeculations, well knowing that the fair
exhibition of a law of nature is a difcovery, and all the
difcovery to which our limited powers will ever admit
us. For he felt in its full force the importance of that
maxim fo warmly inculcated by Lord Bacon, that nothing is to be received as proved in the ftudy of nature
that is not logically inferred from an obferved fact ; that
accurate obfervation of phenomena muft precede all
theory; and that the only admiffible theory is a proof
that the phenomenon under confideration is included in
fome general fact, or law of nature.

435. Retired to his country houfe, to efcape the
plague which then raged at Cambridge where he ftudied,
and one day walking in his garden, his thoughts were
turned to the caufes of the planetary motions. A conjecture to this purpofe occurred to him. Adhering to
the Baconian maxim, he immediately compared it with
the phenomena by calculation. But he was mifled by a
falfe eftimation he had made of the bulk of the Earth.
His calculation fhewed him that his conjecture did not
agree

agree with the phenomenon. Newton gave it up without hefitation; yet the difference was only about a fixth or feventh part; and the conjecture, had it been confirmed by the calculation, was fuch as would have acquired him great celebrity. What youth but Newton could have refifted fuch a temptation? But he thought no more of it.

As he admired Des Cartes as the firft mathematician of Europe, and as his. defire of underftanding the planetary motions never quitted his mind, he fet himfelf to examine, in his own ftrict manner, the Cartefian theory, which at this time was fupreme in the univerfities of Europe. He difcovered its nullity, but would never have publifhed a refutation, hating controverfy above all things, and being already made unhappy by the contefts to which his optical difcoveries had given occafion. His optical difcoveries had recommended him to the Royal Society, and he was now a member. There he learned the accurate meafurement of the Earth by Picard, differing very much from the eftimation by which he had made his calculation in 1666; and he thought his conjecture now more likely to be juft. He went home, took out his old papers, and refumed his calculations. As they drew to a clofe, he was fo much agitated, that he was obliged to defire a friend to finifh them. His former conjecture was now found to agree with the phenomena with the utmoft precifion. No wonder then that his mind was agitated. He faw the revolution he was to make

make in the opinions of men, and that he was to ftand at the head of philofophers.

436. Newton now faw a grand fcene laid open before him ; and he was prepared for exploring it in the completeft manner ; for, ere this time, he had invented a fpecies of geometry that feemed precifely made for this refearch. Dr Hooke's difcourfe to the Society, and his fhewing that the pendulum was not a proper reprefentation of the planetary forces, was a fort of challenge to him to find out that law of deflection which Hooke owned himfelf unable to difcover. He therefore fet himfelf ferioufly to work on the great problem, to " determine the " motion of a body under the continual influence of a de- " flecting force. " There were found among his papers many experiments on the force of magnets ; but this does not feem to have detained him long. He began to confider the motions of terreftrial bodies with an attention that never had been beftowed on them before ; and in a fhort time compofed twelve propofitions, which contained the leading points of celeftial mechanifm. Some years after, viz. in 1683, he communicated them to the Royal Society, and they were entered on record. But fo little was Newton difpofed to court fame, that he never thought of publifhing, till Dr Edmund Halley, the moft eminent mathematician and philofopher in the kingdom, went to vifit him at Cambridge, and never ceafed importuning and entreating him, till he was prevailed on to bring his whole thoughts on the fubject together, digefted into a

O o regular

regular fyftem of univerfal mechanics. Dr Halley was even obliged to correct the manufcript, to get the figures engraved, and, finally, to take charge of the printing and publication. Newton employed but eighteen months to compofe this immortal work. It was publifhed at laft, in 1687, under the title of *Mathematical Principles of Natural Philofophy*, and will be accounted the facred oracles of natural philofophy as long as any knowledge remains in Europe.

437. It is plain, that in this procefs of inveftigation, in order to explain the planetary motions by means of our knowledge of motions that are more familiar, Newton was obliged to fuppofe that the planets confift of common matter, in which we infer the nature of the moving caufe from the motions that we obferve. Newton's firft ftep, therefore, was a fcrupulous obfervation of the celeftial motions, knowing that any miftake with regard to thefe muft bring with it a fimilar miftake with regard to the natural power inferred from it. Every force, and every degree of it, is merely a philofophical interpretation of fome change of motion according to the Copernican fyftem. The Earth is faid to gravitate toward the Sun, becaufe, and only becaufe fhe defcribes a curve line concave toward the Sun, and areas proportional to the times. If this be not true, it is not true that the Earth gravitates to the Sun. For this reafon, a doubt was expreffed (415.), whether the Newtonian difcoveries were ufed with propriety as arguments for the truth of the Copernican fyftem.

Moft

Moſt fortunately for ſcience, the real motions of the heavenly bodies had been at laſt detected; and the ſagacious Kepler had reduced them all to three general facts, known by the name of the laws of Kepler.

438. The firſt of thoſe laws is, that *all the planets move round the Sun in ſuch a manner that the line drawn from a planet to the Sun paſſes over or deſcribes* (verrit, *ſweeps*) *areas proportional to the times of the motion.*

Hence Newton made his firſt and great inference, *that the deflection of each planet is the action of a force always directed toward the Sun* (219.), that is, ſuch, that if the planet were ſtopped, and then let go, it would move toward the Sun in a ſtraight line, with a motion continually accelerated, juſt as we obſerve a ſtone fall toward the Earth. Subſequent obſervation has ſhewn this obſervation to be much more extenſive than Kepler had any notion of; for it comprehends above ninety comets, which have been accurately obſerved. A ſimilar action or force is obſerved to connect the Moon with this Earth, four ſatellites with Jupiter, ſeven with Saturn, and ſix with Herſchel's planet, all of which deſcribe round the central body areas proportional to the times. Newton aſcribed all theſe deflections to the action of a mechanical force, on the very ſame authority with which we aſcribe the deflection of a bombſhell, or of a ſtone, from the line of projection to its *weight*, which all mankind conſider as a *force*. He therefore ſaid that *the primary planets are retained in their paths round the Sun,*

and

*and the satellites in their paths round their respective pri-
maries, by a force tending toward the central body.* But it
must be noticed that this expression afcertains nothing
but the direction of this force, but gives no hint as to its
manner of acting. It may be the impulfe of a ftream
of fluid moving toward that centre ; or it may be the
attraction of the central body. It may be a tendency inherent in the planet—it may be the influence of fome
miniftring fpirit—but, whatever it is, this is the direction of its effect.

439. Having made this great ftep, by which the relation of the planets to the Sun is eftablifhed, and the
Sun proved to be the great regulator of their motions,
Newton proceeded to inquire farther into the nature of
this deflecting force, of which nature he had difcovered
only one circumftance. He now endeavoured to difcover what variation is made in this deflection by a change
of diftance. If this follow any regular law, it will be
a material point afcertained. This can be difcovered
only by comparing the momentary deflections of a planet
in its different diftances from the Sun. The magnitude
or intenfity of the force muft be conceived as precifely
proportional to the magnitude of the deflection which
it produces in the fame time, juft as we meafure the
force of terreftrial gravity by the deflection of fixteen
feet in a fecond, which we obferve, whether it be a
bombfhell flying three miles, or a pebble thrown to the
diftance of a few yards, or a ftone fimply dropped from
the

the hand. Hence we infer that gravity is every where the fame. We muſt reaſon in the fame way concerning the planetary deflections in the different parts of their orbits.

Kepler's ſecond law, with the aſſiſtance of the firſt, enabled Newton to make this compariſon. This ſecond general fact is, that *each planet deſcribes an ellipſe, having the Sun in one focus.* Therefore, to learn the proportion of the momentary deflections in different points of the ellipſe, we have only to know the proportion of the arches deſcribed in equal ſmall, moments of time. This we may learn by drawing a pair of lines from the Sun to different parts of the ellipſe, ſo that each pair of lines ſhall comprehend equal areas. The arches on which theſe areas ſtand muſt be deſcribed in equal times; and the proportion of their linear deflections from the tangents muſt be taken for the proportion of the deflecting forces which produced them. To make thoſe equal areas, we muſt know the preciſe form of the ellipſe, and we muſt know the geometrical properties of this figure, that we may know the proportion of thoſe linear deflections. *

440.

---

* Some of thoſe properties are not to be found among the elementary propoſitions. For this reaſon, a few propoſitions, containing the properties frequently appealed to in aſtronomical diſcuſſions, are put into the hands of the ſtudents, and they are requeſted to read them with care. Without this information,

440. *The force by which a planet defcribes areas pro-*
portional to the times round the focus of its elliptical orbit is
as the fquare of its diftance from the focus, inverfely.

Let F be the deflecting force in the aphelion A (fig.
45.) and f the force in any intermediate point P. Let
V and v be the velocities in A and P, and C and c be
the deflective chords of the equicurve circles in thofe
points.

Then, by the dynamical propofition in art. 210, we
have $F : f = \dfrac{V^2}{C} : \dfrac{v^2}{c}$, or $= V^2 c : v^2 C$. But, when areas
are defcribed proportional to the times, the velocity in
A is to that in P inverfely as the perpendiculars drawn
from F to the tangents in A and P (102.) F A is perpendicular to the tangent in A, and F N is perpendicu-
lar to the tangent P N. Therefore $F : f = \dfrac{c}{F A^2} : \dfrac{C}{F N^2}$
$= F N^2 \times c : F A^2 \times C$.

But it is fhewn (Ellipfe, § 4.) that C, the deflective
chord at A, is equal to L the principal parameter of the
ellipfe. It was alfo fhewn (Ellipfe, § 9.) that P O is
half the deflective chord at P, and (§ 8.) that P R is half
the principal parameter L. Moreover, the triangles F N P
and P Q O and P Q R are fimilar, and therefore F N : FP
$= P Q : P O$. But $P O : P Q = P Q : P R$. Therefore
$P O : P R = P O^2 : P Q^2$. Therefore $F N^2 : FP^2 = P R : P O$,
and

---

formation, no *confident* knowledge can be acquired of that
noble collection of demonftrative truths taught by our illuftrious countryman.

and $FN^2 \times PO = FP^2 \times PR$, and $FN^2 \times 2PO = FP^2 \times 2PR$, that is, $FN^2 \times c = FP^2 \times L$.

Therefore $F : f = FP^2 \times L : FA^2 \times L, = FP^2 : FA^2$, that is, inverfely as the fquare of the diftance from F.

441. This propofition may be demonftrated more briefly, and perhaps more palpably, as follows:

It was fhewn (Ellipfe, § 10. Cor.) that if Pp be a very minute arch, and pr be perpendicular to the radius vector PF, then qp, the linear deflection from the tangent is, ultimately, in the proportion of pr^2. But, becaufe equal areas are defcribed in equal times, the elementary triangle PFp is a conftant quantity, when the moments are fuppofed equal, and therefore pr is inverfely as PF, and pr^2 inverfely as PF^2. Therefore qp is inverfely as PF^2, or the momentary deflection from the tangent is inverfely as the fquare of PF, the diftance from the focus. Now, the momentary deflection is the meafure of the deflecting force, and the force is inverfely as the fquare of the diftance from the focus.

Here then is exhibited all that we know of that property or mechanical affection of the maffes of matter which compofe the folar fyftem. Each is under the continual influence of a force directed toward the Sun, urging the planet in that direction; and this force is variable in its intenfity, being more intenfe as the planet comes nearer to the Sun; and this change is in the inverfe duplicate ratio of its diftance from the Sun. It will free us entirely from many metaphyfical objections

which

which have been made to this inference, if, inftead of
faying that the planets manifeft fuch a variable tendency
toward the Sun, we content ourfelves with fimply affirm-
ing the fact, that the planets are continually deflected toward the Sun, and and that the momentary deflections
are in the inverfe duplicate ratio of the diftances from
him.

442. We muft affirm the fame thing of the forces
which retain the fatellites in their elliptical orbits round
their primary planets. For they alfo defcribe ellipfes
having the primary planet in the focus; and we muft
alfo include the Halleyan comet, which fhewed, by its
reapparition in 1759, that it defcribes an ellipfe having
the Sun in the focus. If the other comets be alfo carried round in eccentric ellipfes, we muft draw the fame
conclufion. Nay, fhould they defcribe parabolas or hy-
perbolas having the Sun in the focus, we fhould ftill
find that they are retained by a force inverfely proportional to the fquare of the diftance. This is demonftrated
in precifely the fame manner as in the cafe of elliptical
motion, namely, by comparing the linear deflections correfponding to equal elementary fectors of the parabola
or hyperbola. Thefe are defcribed in equal times, and
the linear deflections are proper meafures of the deflecting forces. We fhall find in both of thofe curves $q\,p$
proportional to $p\,r^2$. It is the common property of the
conic fections referred to a focus.

It is moft probable that the comets defcribe very eccentric

Pl. II.   P. 296.

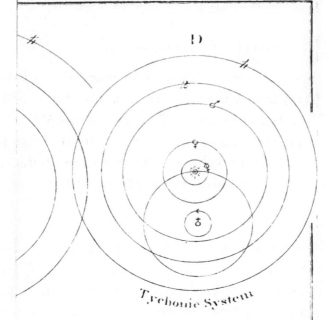

Tychonic System

Fig. 45.

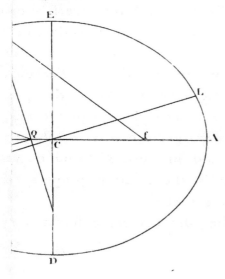

Pl II

P. 296

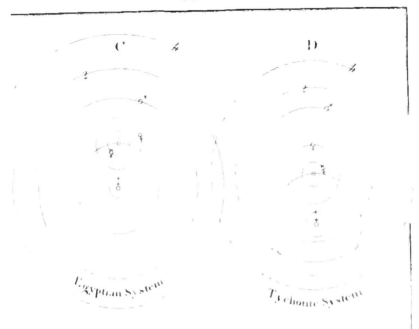

Egyptian System

Tychonic System

Fig. 45

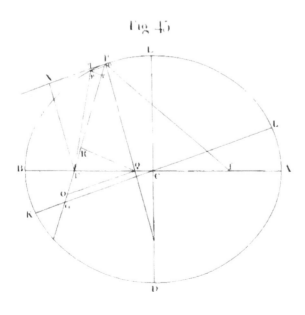

centric ellipfes. But we get fight of them only when they come near to the Sun, within the orbit of Saturn. None has yet been obferved as far off as that planet. The vifible portion of their orbits fenfibly coincides with a parabola or hyperbola having the fame focus ; and their motion, computed on this fuppofition, agrees with obfervation. The computation in the parabola is very eafy, and can then be transferred to an ellipfe by an ingenious theorem of Dr Halley's in his *Aftronomy of Comets*. **M.** Lambert of Berlin has greatly fimplified the whole procefs. The ftudent will find much valuable information on this fubject in M'Laurin's *Treatife of Fluxions*. The chapters on curvature and its variations, are fcarcely diftinguifhable from propofitions on curvilineal motion and deflecting forces. Indeed, fince all that we know of a deflecting force is the deflection which we afcribe to it, the employment of the word *force* in fuch difcuffions is little more than an abbreviation of language.

This propofition being, by its fervices in explaining the phenomena of nature, the moft valuable mechanical theorem ever given to the world, we may believe that much attention has been given to it, and that many methods of demonftrating it have been offered to the choice of mathematicians, the authors claiming fome merit in facilitating or improving the invefligation. Newton's demonftration is very fhort, but is a good deal incumbered with compofition of ratios, and an arithmetical or algebraical turn of expreffion frequently mixed

P p

with

with ideas purely geometrical. Newton was obliged to
comprefs into it fome properties of the conic fections
which were not very familiar at that time, becaufe not
of frequent ufe : they are now familiar to every ftudent,
making part of the treatifes of conic fections. By referring to thefe, the fucceeding authors gave their demonftrations the appearance of greater fimplicity and
elegance. But Newton gives another demonftration in
the fecond and third editions of the *Principia*, employing
the deflective chord of the equicurve circle precifely in
the way employed in our text. This mode of demonftration has been varied a little, by employing the radius
of curvature, inftead of the chord paffing through the
centre of forces. The theorems given by M. De Moivre
were the firft in this way, and are very general, and very
elegant. Thofe of Jo. Bernoulli, Hermann, and Keill,
fcarcely differ from them, and none of them all is preferable to Newton's now mentioned, either for generality,
fimplicity, or elegance.

443. It remains now to inquire whether there be
any analogy between the forces which retain the different planets in their refpective orbits. It is highly probable that there is, feeing they all refpect the Sun. But
it is by no means certain. Different bodies exhibit very
different laws of action. Thofe of magnetifm, electricity, and cohefion, are extremely different ; and the chemical affinities, confidered as the effects of attractive and
repulfive

repulfive forces, are as various as the fubftances themfelves. As we know nothing of the conftitution of the
heavenly bodies, we cannot, *a priori*, fay that it is not fo
here. Perhaps the planets are deflected by the impulfion
of a fluid in motion, or are thruft toward the Sun by
an elaftic æther, denfer and more elaftic as we recede
from the Sun. The Sun may be a magnet, and at the
fame time electrical. The Sun fo conftituted would act
on a magnetical planet both by magnetical and electrical
attraction, while another planet is affected only by his
electricity. A thoufand fuch fuppofitions may be formed, all very poffible. Newton therefore could not leave
this queftion undecided.

Various means of deciding it are offered to us by the
phenomena. The motion of the comets, and particularly
of the Halleyan comet, feems to decide it at once. This
comet came from a diftance, far beyond the remoteft of
the known planets, and came nearer to the Sun than
Venus. Therefore we are entitled to fay, that a force
inverfely as the fquare of the diftance from the Sun, extends without interruption through the whole planetary
fpaces. But farther, if we calculate the deflection actually obferved in the Halleyan comet, when it was at
the fame diftance from the Sun as any of the planets,
we fhall find it to be precifely the fame with the deflection of that planet. There can remain no doubt therefore that it is one and the fame force which deflects
both the comet and the planet.

But

But Newton could not employ this argument. The motions of the comets were altogether unknown, and probably would have remained fo, had he not difcovered the famenefs of the planetary force through its whole fcene of influence. The fact is, that Newton's firft conjectures about the law of the folar force were founded on much eafier obfervations.

Kepler's third law is, that *the fquares of the periodic times of the planets are in the fame proportion with the cubes of their mean diftances from the Sun.* Thus, Mars is nearly four times as far from the Sun as Mercury, and his period is nearly eight times that of Mercury—Now $4^3 = 64, = 8^2$.

The planets defcribe figures which differ very little from circles, whofe radii are thofe mean diftances. If they defcribed circles, it would have been very eafy to afcertain the proportion of the centripetal forces. For, by art. 216, we had $f \doteq \dfrac{d}{t^2}$. Now, in the planetary motions, we have $t^2 \doteq d^3$. Therefore, in this cafe, $f \doteq \dfrac{d}{d^3}$, or $\doteq \dfrac{1}{d^2}$, that is, the forces which regulate the motions of the planets at their mean diftances are inverfely as the fquares of thofe diftances.

It was this notion (by no means precife) of the planetary force, which had firft occupied the thoughts of young Newton, while yet a ftudent at college—and, on no better authority than this, had he fuppofed that a fimilar analogy would be obferved between the deflection

of the Moon and that of a cannon ball. His difappoint-
ment, occafioned by his erroneous eftimation of the bulk
of this Earth, and his horror at the thoughts of any fuch
controverfies as his optical difcoveries had engaged him
in, feem to have made him refolve to keep thefe thoughts
to himfelf. But when Picard's meafure of the Earth
had removed his caufe of miftake, and he faw that the
analogy did really hold with refpect to the force reaching from the Earth to the Moon; he then thought it
worth his while to ftudy the fubject feriouflly, and
to inveftigate the deflection in the arch of an ellipfe.
His ftudy terminated in the propofition demonftrated
above,—doubtlefs, to his great delight. He was no
longer contented with the vague guefs which he had
made as to the proportion of the forces which deflected
the different planets. The orbit of Mars, and ftill more,
the orbit of Mercury, is too eccentric to be confidered
as a circle. Befides, at the mean diftances, the radius
vector is not perpendicular to the curve, as it is in a circle.
He was now in a condition to compare the fimultaneous
deflections of any two planets, in any part of their orbits. This he has done. In the fifteenth propofition of
the firft book of the *Principia*, he demonftrates that if
the forces actuating the different planets are in the inverfe duplicate ratio of the diftances from the Sun, then
the fquares of the periodic times muft be as the cubes
of the mean diftances.—This being a matter of obfervation, it follows, converfely, that the forces are in this
inverfe duplicate ratio of the diftances.

Thus

Thus was his darling object attained. But, as this fifteenth propofition has fome intricacy, it is not fo clear as we fhould wifh in an elementary courfe like ours. The fame truth may be eafily made appear in the following manner.

444. *If a planet, when at its mean diftance from the Sun, be projected in a direction perpendicular to the radius vector, with the fame velocity which it has in that point of its orbit, it will defcribe a circle round the Sun in the fame time that it defcribes the ellipfe.*

Let A B P D (fig. 46.) be the elliptical orbit, having the Sun in the focus S. Let A P, B D, be the two axes, C the centre, A the aphelion, P the perihelion, and B, D, the two fituations of mean diftance. About S defcribe the circle B D M. Let B K and B N be very fmall equal arches of the circle and the ellipfe, and let B E be one half of B S.

B M, the double of B S, is the deflective chord of the circle of curvature in the point B of the orbit (ellipfe, § 9.), and B E is $\frac{1}{4}$ of that chord. Therefore (212.) the velocity in B is that which the force in B would generate by uniformly impelling the planet along B E. But a body projected with this velocity in the direction B K will defcribe the circle B K M D. (106—212.)

The arches B K and B N, being equal, and defcribed with equal velocities, will be defcribed in equal times. The triangles B K S, B N S, having equal bafes B K and
                                                                    B N,

B N, are proportional to their altitudes B S and B C (for the elementary arch B N may be confidered as coinciding with the tangent in B, and B C is perpendicular to this tangent). But, becaufe B S is equal to C A, the area of the circle B M D is to that of the ellipfe A B P D as A C to B C, that is, as B S to B C, that is, as the triangle B K S to the triangle B N S. Thefe triangles are therefore fimilar portions of the whole areas, and therefore, fince they are defcribed in equal times, the circle B M D and the ellipfe A B P D will alfo be defcribed in equal times.

Thus it appears that Newton's firft conjecture was perfectly juft. For if the planets, inftead of defcribing their elliptical orbits, were defcribing circles at the fame diftances, and in the fame times, they would do it by the influence of the fame forces. Therefore fince, in this cafe, we fhould have $t^2 \doteq d^3$, the forces will be proportional to d^2 inverfely.

445. We now fee that the forces which retain the different planets in their orbits are not different forces, but that all are under the influence of one force, which extends from the Sun in every direction, and decreafes in intenfity as the fquare of the diftance from the Sun increafes. The intenfity at any particular diftance is the fame, in whatever direction the diftance is taken. Although the planetary courfes do not depart far from our ecliptic, the influence of the regulating force is by no means confined

fined to that neighbourhood. Comets have been feen which rife almoft perpendicular to the ecliptic; and their orbits or trajectories occupy all quarters of the heavens.

This relation, in which they all ftand to the Sun, may juftly be called a cofmical relation, depending on their mutual conftitution, which appears to be the fame in them all. As this force refpects the Sun, it may be called a SOLAR FORCE, in the fame fenfe as we ufe the term magnetical force. All perfons unaffected by peculiar philofophical notions, conceive magnetifm diftinctly enough by calling it *Attraction*. For, whatever it is, its effects refemble thofe of attraction. If we conceive the magnetical phenomena as effects of a tendency toward the magnet, inherent in the iron, we may conceive the planetary deflections as produced in the fame way; but this alfo indicates a famenefs in the conftitution of all the planets. Or we may afcribe the deflections to the impulfions or preffure of an æther; but this alfo indicates a famenefs of conftitution over the whole fyftem.

Thus, whatever notion we entertain of what we have called a folar or a planetary force (and the obferved law of action limits us to no exclufive manner of conceiving it), we fee a power of nature, whether extrinfic, like the action of a fluid, or intrinfic, like tendencies or attractions, which fit the Sun and planets for a particular purpofe, giving them a cofmical relation, and laws of action.

‘ ———*quas*

' ——quas dum primordia rerum
' Pangeret, omniparens leges violare Creator
' Noluit, eternique operis fundamina fixit.
' Sol folio refidens ad fe jubet omnia prono
' Tendere defcenfu, nec rečto tramite currus
' Sidereos patitur vaſtum per inane moveri,
' Sed rapit; immotis, fe centro, fingula gyris. '

HALLEY.

446. It is ſtill more intereſting to remark that the ſatellites obſerve the ſame law of action. For, in the little fyſtems of a planet and its ſatellites, we obſerve the ſame analogy between the diſtances and periodic times. In ſhort, a centripetal force in the inverſe duplicate ratio of the diſtance ſeems to be the bond by which all is held together.

447. As the analogy obſerved by Kepler between the diſtances of the revolving bodies and the periods of their revolutions, led Newton to the diſcovery of the law of planetary deflection; fo, this law being eſtabliſhed, we are led to the fecond and third fact obſerved by Kepler as its neceſſary conſequences. It appears that the periodic time of a planet under the influence of a force inverſely as the fquare of the diſtance, depends on its mean diſtance alone, and will be the fame, whether the planet deſcribe a circle or an ellipfe having any degree whatever of eccentricity. This, as was already obſerved, is the fifteenth propoſition of the firſt book of Newton's

Q q   Principia.

Principia. Suppofe the fhorter axis B D of the ellipfe A B P D (fig. 47.) to diminifh continually, the longer axis A P remaining the fame. As the extremity B of the invariable line B S moves from B toward C, the extremity S will move toward P, and when B coincides with C, S will coincide with P, and the ellipfe is changed into a ftraight line P A, whofe length is twice the mean diftance S B.

In all the fucceffive ellipfes produced by this gradual diminution of C B, the periodic time remains unchanged. Juft before the perfect coincidence of B with C, the ellipfe may be conceived as undiftinguifhable from the line P A. The revolution in this ellipfe is undiftinguifhable from the afcent of the body from the perihelion P to the aphelion A; and the fubfequent defcent from A to P. Therefore a body under the influence of the central force will defcend from A to P in half the time of the revolution in the ellipfe A D P B A. Therefore the time of defcending from any diftance B S is half the period of a body revolving at half that diftance from the Sun. By fuch means we can tell the time in which any planet would fall to the Sun. Multiply the half of the time of a revolution by the fquare root of the cube of $\frac{1}{2}$, that is, by the fquare root of $\frac{1}{8}$; the product is the time of defcent. Or divide the time of half a revolution by the fquare root of the cube of 2, that is, by the fquare root of 8, that is, by 2,82847 ; or, which is the fhorteft procefs, multiply the time of a revolution by the decimal 0,176776;

Mercury

							d.	h.
Mercury will fall to the Sun in	-		-		-		15	13
Venus	-	-	-	-	-	-	39	17
The Earth	-	-	-	-	-	-	64	10
Mars	-	-	-	-	-	-	121	0
Jupiter	-	-	-	-	-	-	290	0
Saturn	-	-	-	-	-	-	798	0
Georgian planet		-	-	-	-	-	5406	0
The Moon to this Earth		-	-	-	-		4	21

Cor. The fquares of the times of falling to the Sun
are as the cubes of the diftances from him.

448. So far did Newton proceed in his reafonings
from the obfervations of Kepler. But there remained
many important queftions to be decided, in which thofe
obfervations offered no direct help.

It appeared improbable that the folar force fhould
not affect the fecondary planets. It has been demonftrated (252.) that if a body P (fig. 29.) revolve round
another body S, defcribing areas proportional to the times,
while S revolves round fome other body, or is affected
by fome external force, P is not only acted on by a central force directed to S, but is alfo affected by every accelerating force which acts on S.

While, therefore, the Moon defcribes areas proportional to the times round the Earth, it is not only deflected toward the Earth, but it is alfo deflected as much
as the Earth is toward the Sun. For the Moon accom-

Q q 2   panies

panies the Earth in all its motions. The fame thing muſt be affirmed concerning the ſatellites attending the other planets.

And thus has Newton eſtabliſhed a fourth propoſition, namely,

The force by which a ſecondary planet is made to accompany the primary in its orbit round the Sun is continually directed to the Sun, and is inverſely as the ſquare of the diſtance from him. For, as the primary changes its diſtance from the Sun, the force by which it is retained in its orbit varies in this inverſe duplicate ratio of the diſtance. Therefore the force which cauſes the ſecondary planet to accompany its primary *muſt* vary in the ſame proportion, in order to produce the ſame change in its motion that is produced in that of the primary. And, further, ſince the force which retains Jupiter in his orbit is to that which retains the Earth as the ſquare of the Earth's diſtance is to that of Jupiter's diſtance, the forces by which their reſpective ſatellites are made to accompany them muſt vary in the ſame proportion.

Thus, all the bodies of the ſolar ſyſtem are continually urged by a force directed to the Sun, and decreaſing as the ſquare of the diſtance from him increaſes.

449. Newton remarked, that in all the changes of motion obſervable in our ſublunary world, the changes in the acting bodies are equal and oppoſite. In all impulſions, one body is obſerved to loſe as much motion as the other gains. All magnetical and electrical

cal attractions and repulsions are mutual.   Every action
feems to be accompanied by an equal reaction in the
oppofite direction.   He even imagined that it may be
proved, from abftract principles, that it muft be fo.   He
therefore affirmed that this law obtained alfo in the celeftial motions, and that not only were the planets continually impelled toward the Sun, but alfo that the Sun
was impelled toward the planets.   The doubts which
may be entertained concerning the authority of this law
of motion have been noticed already.   At prefent, we
are to notice the facts which the celeftial motions furnifh
in fupport of Sir Ifaac Newton's affertion.

450.   Directions have been given (294.) how to calculate the Sun's place for any given moment.   When
the aftronomers had obtained inftruments of nice conftruction, and had improved the art of obferving, there
was found an irregularity in this calculation, which had
an evident relation to the Moon.   At new Moon, the
obfervations correfponded exactly with the Sun's calculated place ; but feven or eight days after, the Sun is
obferved to be about 8″ or 10″ to the eaftward of his
calculated place, when the Moon is in her firft quadrature, and he is obferved as much to the weftward when
fhe is in the laft quadrature.   In intermediate fituations,
the error is obferved to increafe in the proportion of the
fine of the Moon's diftance from conjunction or oppofition.

Things muft be fo, if it be true that the deflection of
the

the Moon toward the Earth is accompanied with an equal deflection of the Earth toward the Moon. For (230.) the Moon will not revolve round the Earth, but the Earth and Moon will revolve round their common centre of pofition. When the Moon is in her firft quadrature, her pofition may be reprefented by M (fig. 48.) while the Earth is at E, and their common centre is at A. A fpectator in A will fee the Sun S in his calculated place B. But the fpectator in the Earth E fees the Sun in C, to the left hand, or eaftward of B. The interval B C meafures the angle B S C, or A S E, fubtended at the Sun by the diftance E A of the common centre of the Earth and Moon from the centre of the Earth. At new Moon, A, E, and S, are in a ftraight line, fo that B and C coincide. At the laft quadrature, the Moon is at m, the Earth at e, and the common centre at a. Now the Sun is feen at c, 8″ or 10″ to the weftward of his calculated place. This correction has been pointed out by Newton, but it was not obferved at the firft, owing to its being blended with the Sun's horizontal parallax which had not been taken into account. But it was foon recognifed, and it now makes an articie among the various equations ufed in calculating the Sun's place.

Here, then, is a plain proof of a mutual action and reaction of the Earth and Moon. For, fince they revolve round a common centre, the Earth is unqueftionably deflected into the curve line by the action of a force directed towards the Moon. But we have a much better proof.

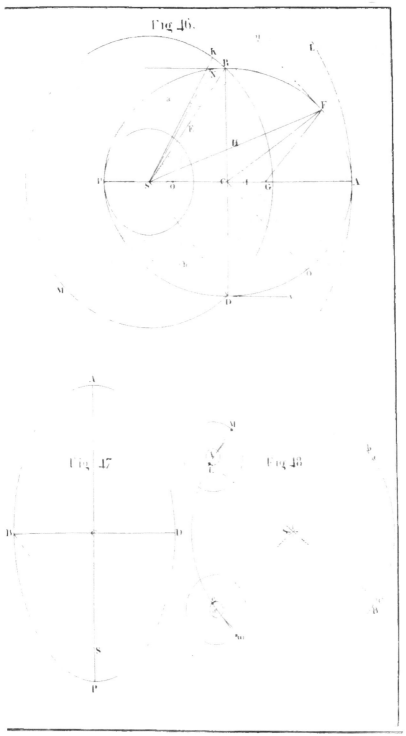

Fig. 16.

Fig. 17

Fig. 18

proof. The waters of the ocean are obferved every day to heap up on that part of our globe which is under the Moon. In this fituation, the weight of the water is diminifhed by the attraction of the Moon, and it requires a greater elevation, or a greater quantity, to compenfate for the diminifhed weight. On the other hand, we fee the waters abftracted from all thofe parts which have the Moon in the horizon. Kepler, after afferting, in very pofitive terms, that the Earth and Moon would run together, and are prevented by a mutual circulation round their common centre, adduces the tides as a proof.

451. As the art of obfervation continued to improve, aftronomers were able to remark abundant proofs of the tendency of the Sun toward the planets. When the great planets Jupiter and Saturn are in quadrature with the Earth, to the right hand of the line drawn from the Earth to the Sun's calculated place, the Sun is then obferved to fhift to the left of that line, keeping always on the oppofite fide of the common centre of pofition. Thefe deviations are indeed very minute, becaufe the Sun is vaftly more maffive than all the planets collected into one lump. But in favourable fituations of thefe planets, they are perfectly fenfible, and have been calculated ; and they *muft* be taken into account in every calculation of the Sun's place, in order to have it with the accuracy that is now attainable. It muft be granted that this accuracy, actually attained by means of thofe corrections, and unattainable without them, is a pofitive proof of

this

this mutual deflection of the Sun toward the planets.
The quantity correfponding to one planet is too fmall, of
itfelf, to be very diftinctly obferved ; but, by occafionally
combining with others of the fame kind, the fum becomes very fenfible, and fufceptible of meafure.   It
fometimes amounts to 38 feconds, and muft never be o-
mitted in the calculations fubfervient to the finding the
longitude of a fhip at fea.   Philofophy, in this inftance,
is greatly indebted to the arts.   And fhe has liberally re-
paid the fervice.

452.   Here it is worthy of remark, that had the Sun
been much fmaller than he is, fo that he would have moved much further from the common centre, and would have
been much more agitated by the tendencies to the different planets, it is probable that we never fhould have acquired any diftinct or ufeful knowledge of the fyftem.
For we now fee that Kepler's laws cannot be ftrictly
true ; yet it was thofe laws alone that fuggefted the
thought, and furnifhed to young Newton the means
of inveftigation.   The analogy of the periodic times and
diftances is accurate, only with refpect to the common
centre, but not with refpect to the Sun.   But the great
mafs of the Sun occafions this common centre to be
generally within his furface, and it is never diftant from
it $\frac{1}{4}$ of his diameter.   Therefore this third law of Kepler
is fo nearly exact in refpect of the Sun, that the art of
obfervation, in Newton's lifetime, could not have found
any errors.   The penetrating eye of Newton however
immediately

immediately perceived his own good fortune, and his error in suppoſing Kepler's laws accurately true. But this was not enough for his philoſophy; he was determined that it ſhould narrate nothing but truth. With great ingenuity, and elegance of method, he demonſtrates that his mechanical inferences from Kepler's laws are ſtill ſtrictly true, and that his own law of planetary force is exact, although the centre of revolution is not the centre of the Sun. All the difference reſpects the abſolute magnitude of the periodic times in relation to the magnitude of the force. This he demonſtrates in a ſeries of propoſitions, of which our § 231. is the chief.

453. Newton proceeds ſtill further in his inveſtigation of the extent of the influence of this planetary force, and ſays that *all the planets mutually tend toward each other*. It does not appear how this opinion aroſe in his mind. There are abundance of phenomena, however, of eaſy obſervation, which make it very evident. It was probably a conjecture, ſuggeſted by obſerving this reciprocal action between the Earth and Moon. But he immediately followed it into its conſequences, and pointed them out to the aſtronomers. They are very important, and explain many phenomena which had hitherto greatly perplexed the aſtronomers.

Suppoſe Jupiter and Mars to be in conjunction, lying in the ſame line from the Sun. As Mars revolves much quicker than Jupiter, he gets before him, but, being attracted by Jupiter, his motion is retarded—and Jupiter,

being

being attracted by Mars, is accelerated. On the contrary, before Mars arrives at conjunction with Jupiter, Mars is accelerated, and Jupiter is retarded. Further, the attraction of Mars by Jupiter must diminish the tendency of Mars to the Sun, or must act in opposition to the attraction of the Sun ; therefore the curvature of Mars's orbit in that place must be diminished. On the contrary, the tendency of Jupiter to Mars, acting in the same direction as his tendency to the Sun, must increase the curvature of that part of Jupiter's orbit. If Jupiter be at this time advancing to his aphelion, this increase of curvature will sooner bend the line of his motion from an obtuse into a right angle with the radius vector. Therefore his aphelion will be sooner attained, and it will appear to have shifted to the westward. For the opposite reasons, the apsides of Mars will seem to shift to the eastward. There are other situations of these planets where the contrary effects will happen. In each revolution, each planet will be alternately accelerated twice, and twice retarded, and the apsides of the exterior planet will continually recede, and that of the interior will advance. It is obvious that this disturbance of the motion of a planet by its deflection to another, though probably very minute, yet being continued for a tract of time, its accumulated result may become very sensible. These changes are all susceptible of accurate calculation, as we shall afterwards explain particularly.

This must be considered as a convincing proof of the mutual action of the heavenly bodies, and it adds fresh

lustre

luftre. to the penetration and genius of Newton, who made thefe affertions independent of obfervation, pointing out to aftronomers the fure means of perfecting their knowledge of the celeftial motions.

454. Here therefore we have eftablifhed a fifth propofition in phyfical aftronomy, namely, that *all the bodies in the folar fyftem tend mutually toward one another, with forces which vary in the inverfe duplicate ratio of the diftances.*

It did not fatisfy Newton that he merely pointed out the grofs effect of this mutual tendency. He gave aftronomers the means of inveftigating and afcertaining its intenfity, and its variation by a variation of diftance. The effect of the Earth's tendency to Jupiter during any length of time, may be computed by means of Newton's dynamical propofitions, contained in the firft book of his Principia, particularly by the 39th. Of thefe we have given a proper felection in the general doctrines of Dynamics.

455. But the inquifitive mind of Newton did not ftop here. He was anxious to learn whether 'this planetary tendency had any refemblance or relation to forces with which we are more familiarly acquainted. Of this kind are magnetifm and gravity. He was the more incited to this inveftigation by the conjectures on this fubject which had arifen in the mind of Kepler. This great aftronomer had been much 'taken with the difco-

very

very juft publifhed by Dr Gilbert of Colchefter, ftating
that this Earth is a great magnet, and he was difpofed to
afcribe the revolution of the Moon to the magnetical influence of the Earth. It appears from Newton's papers,
that he had made a great many experiments for difcovering the law of magnetic action. But he had found
it fo dependant on circumftances of form and fituation,
and fo changeable by time, that it feemed fufceptible
of no comparifon with the folar force; and he foon gave
it up. He was more fuccefsful in tracing the refemblances obfervable in the phenomena of common gravity. It has been already remarked (435.), that, very
early in life, he had conjectured that it was the fame
with the folar force; and that after he had formed the
opinion that the folar force varied in the inverfe duplicate ratio of the diftance, he put his conjecture to the
teft, by comparing the fall of a ftone with the deflection of the Moon. The diftance of the Moon is eftimated to be 60 femidiameters of the Earth. Therefore,
if gravity and the lunar deflecting force be the fame,
the ftone fhould deflect as much in one fecond as the
Moon does in a minute. For we may, without any fenfible error, fuppofe that the lunar force acts uniformly
during one minute. If fo, the linear deflections muft
be as the fquares of the times. The deflection in a minute muft be 60 × 60 times, or 3600 times the deflection in a fecond. But, according to the law of planetary force, the deflection at the Earth's furface muft be
60 × 60, or 3600 times the deflection at the Moon.

Now,

Now, in a fecond, a ftone falls 16 feet and an inch.
Therefore the Moon fhould deflect 16 feet and an inch in
a minute from the tangent of her orbit. Newton calculated the verfed fine of the arch defcribed by the Moon
in a minute, to a radius equal to 60 femidiameters of
the Earth. He found it only about $13\frac{1}{2}$ feet, and he
gave over any farther inquiry. But he had haftily fuppofed a degree to contain 60 miles, not attending to the
difference between a geographical mile, or 60th of a
degree, and an Englifh ftatute mile. A degree contains
$69\frac{1}{2}$ fuch miles; fo that he had made the Moon's orbit,
and confequently her deflection, too fmall in the fame
proportion. If we increafe the calculated deflection in
this proportion, it comes out exactly $16\frac{1}{12}$; and the conjecture is fully eftablifhed.

When Picard's accurate meafure of the Earth had
enabled Newton to confirm his former conjecture concerning the identity of the planetary force and terreftrial
gravity, he again made the calculation and comparifon
in the moft fcrupulous manner. For we now fee that feveral circumftances muft be taken into the account, which
he had omitted in his firft computation from Picard's
meafure of the Earth. The fall in a fecond is not the
exact meafure of terreftrial gravity. A ftone would fall
farther, were it not that its gravity is diminifhed by the
Earth's rotation. It is alfo diminifhed by the action of
the Sun and Moon, and by the weight of the air which
the ftone difplaces. All thefe diminutions of the accelerating force of gravity are fufceptible of exact calculation,

tion, and were accordingly calculated by Newton, and
the amount added to the obferved acceleration of a falling body.   In the next place, the real radius of the
Moon's orbit muft be reckoned only from the common
centre of the Earth and Moon.   And then the force deduced from this deflection muft be increafed in the fubduplicate ratio of the matter in the Earth to the matter
in the Earth and Moon added together (231.)   All this
has been done, and the refult coincides precifely with
obfervation.

This may be demonftrated in another way.   We can
tell in what time a body would revolve round the Earth,
clofe to its furface.   For we muft. have t^2 proportional
to d^3.   It will be found to be 84 minutes and 34 feconds.
Then we know the arch defcribed in one fecond, and
can calculate its deflection from the tangent.   We fhall
find it $16\frac{1}{12}$ feet, the fame with that produced by common gravity.

456. *Terreftrial gravity, therefore, or that force which
caufes bodies to fall, or to prefs on their fupports, is only a
particular example of that univerfal tendency, by which all
the bodies of the folar fyftem are retained in their orbits.*

We muft now extend to thofe bodies the other fymp-
toms of common gravity.   It is by gravity that water ar-
ranges itfelf into a level furface, that is, a furface which
makes a part of the great fphere of the ocean.   The
weight of this water keeps it together, in a round form.
We muft afcribe the globular forms of the Sun and planets

nets to a fimilar operation. A body on their furface will prefs it as a heavy body preffes the ground. Dr Hooke remarks that all the protuberances on the furface of the Moon are of forms confiftent with a gravity toward its centre. They are generally floping, and, though in fome places very rugged and precipitous, yet nowhere overhang, or have any fhape that would not ftand on the ground. The more rugged parts are moft evidently matter which has been thrown up by volcanic explofion, and have fallen down again by their lunar gravity.

457. That property by which bodies are heavy is called GRAVITY, HEAVINESS—the being heavy; and the *fact* that it moves toward the Earth, may be called GRAVITATION. While it falls, or preffes on its fupports, it may be faid to *gravitate*, to give indication of its being *gravis* or heavy. In this fenfe the planets *gravitate* to the Sun, and the fecondary planets to their primaries, and, in fhort, every body in the folar fyftem to every other body. By the verb *to gravitate*, nothing is meant but the fact, that they either actually approach, or manifeft, by a very fenfible preffure, tendencies to approach the body to which they are faid to gravitate. The verb, or the noun, fhould not be confidered as the expreffion of any quality or property, but merely of a phenomenon, a fact or event in nature.

458. But this deviation from uniform rectilineal motion is confidered as an *effect*, and it is of importance to discover

difcover the *caufe*. Now, in the moft familiar inftance, the fall or preffure of a heavy body, we afcribe the fall, or preffure indicating the tendency to fall, to its heavinefs. But we have no other notion of this heavinefs than the very thing which we afcribe to it as an effect. The feeling the heavinefs of the piece of lead that lies in our hand, is *the fum of all that we know about it*. But we confider this heavinefs as a *property* of all terreftrial matter, becaufe all bodies give fome of thofe appearances which we confider as indications of it. All move toward the Earth if not fupported, and all prefs on the fupport. The feeling of preffure which a heavy body excites might be confidered as its characteriftic phenomenon ; for it is this feeling that makes us think it a force—we muft oppofe our force to it ; but we cannot diftinguifh it from the feeling of any other equal preffure. It is moft diftinguifhable as the caufe of motion, as a moving or accelerating force. In fhort, we know nothing of gravity but the phenomena, which we confider, not as gravity, but as its indication. It is, like every other force—an unknown quality.

The *weight* of a body fhould be diftinguifhed from its gravity or heavinefs, and the term fhould be referved for expreffing the meafure of the united gravitation of all the mater in the body. This is indeed the proper fenfe of the term *weight—pondus*. In ordinary bufinefs, we meafure the weights of bodies by means of known units of weight. A piece of lead is faid to be of twenty pounds weight, when it balances twenty pieces of matter, each of which

is

is a pound; but we frequently meafure it by means of other preffures, as when we judge of it by the divifion to which it draws the fcale of a fpring fteelyard.

459. We eftimate the quantity of matter in a body by its weight, and fay that there is nineteen times as much matter in a cubic foot of gold as there is in a cubic foot of water. This evidently prefuppofes that *all matter is heavy, and equally heavy*—that every primitive atom of matter is equally heavy. But this feems to be more than we are entitled to fay, without fome pofitive proof. There is nothing inconceivable or abfurd in fuppofing one atom to be twice or thrice as heavy as another. As gravity is a contingent quality of matter, its abfolute ftrength or force is alfo contingent and arbitrary. We can conceive an atom to have no weight. Nay, we can as clearly conceive an atom of matter to be endowed with a tendency upwards as with a tendency downwards. Accordingly, during the prevalence of the Stahlian doctrine of combuftion, that matter which imparts inflammability to bodies was fuppofed to be not only without weight, but pofitively light, and to diminifh the weight of the other ingredients with which it was combined in a combuftible body. In this way, the abettors of that doctrine accounted for the increafe of weight obfervable when a body is burnt.

There is nothing abfurd or unreafonable in all this; and had we no other indication of gravity but its preffure, we do not fee how this queftion can be decided. But gravity is not only a preffing power, but alfo a

S f   moving

moving or accelerating power. If a body confifted of a
thoufand atoms of gravitating matter, and as many atoms
of matter which does not gravitate, and if the gravity of
each atom exerted the preffure of one grain, this body
would weigh a thoufand grains, either by a balance or a
fpring fteelyard, yet it contains two thoufand atoms of
matter. But take another body of the fame weight, but
confifting wholly of gravitating atoms ; drop thefe two
bodies at once from the hand—the laft mentioned will
fall 16 feet in the firft fecond—the other will fall only
8 feet. For in both there is the fame moving force ;
therefore the fame quantity of motion will be produced
in both bodies ; that is, the products of the quantities of
matter by the velocities generated will be the fame.
Therefore the velocity acquired by the mixed body will
be one half of that acquired in the fame time by the
fimple body. The phenomenon will be what was afferted, one will fall 16 and the other only 8 feet.

This will be ftill more forcibly conceived, if we take
two bodies a and b, each containing 1000 atoms of gravitating matter, and attach a to another body c, containing
1000 atoms which do not gravitate. Now, unlefs we
fuppofe c moveable and arreftable by a thought or a
word, we can have no hefitation in faying that the mafs
$a + c$ will fall with half the velocity of b.

We fee therefore that the *accelerating power* alone of
gravity enables us to decide the queftion, ' whether all
terreftrial matter gravitates,' and gravitates alike. We
have only to try whether all terreftrial bodies fall equally

far

far in the fame time, or receive an equal increment of velocity in the fame time. This teft of the matter did not efcape the penetrating genius of young Newton. He made experiments on every kind of fubftance, metals, ftones, woods, grain, falts, animal fubftances, &c. and made them in a way fufceptible of the utmoft accuracy, as we fhall fee afterwards. The refult was, that all thefe fubftances were equally accelerated; and, on this authority, Newton thought himfelf entitled to fay that ALL TERRESTRIAL MATTER IS EQUALLY HEAVY.

This however may be difputed. For it is plain that if all bodies contain *an equal proportion* of gravitating and nongravitating matter, they will be equally accelerated; nay, the unequal gravitation of different fubftances, and even pofitive levity, may be fo compenfated by the proportion of thofe different kinds of matter, that the total gravitation may ftill be proportional to the whole quantity of matter.

But, till we have fome authority for faying that there is a difference in the gravitation of different atoms, the juft rules of philofophical difcuffion oblige us to believe that all gravitate alike. This is corroborated by the univerfality of the law of mutual and equal reaction. This is next to demonftration that the primitive atoms are alike in every refpect, and therefore in their gravitation.

We are entitled therefore to fay that all terreftrial matter is equally heavy, and that the weight of a body is the meafure of the united gravitation of every atom, and therefore is a meafure of, or is proportional to, the quantity of matter contained in it.

460. Newton naturally, and juftly, extended the af-
firmation to the planets and to the Sun. But here arifes
a queftion, at once nice and important. The law of
gravitation, fo often mentioned, is exhibited in the mutual deflections of great maffes of matter. Thefe deflections are in the inverfe duplicate ratio of the diftances
between the centres of the maffes. Are we warranted
by this obfervation to fay that this is alfo the law of action between every atom of one body and every atom
of another? Can we fay in general that the law of corpufcular action is the fame with that of maffes, refulting from the combined action of each atom on each?
We are affured by experience that it is not. For we
obferve that, in magnets, the law of action (that is, the
relation fubfifting between the diftances and the intenfities of force) is different in almoft every different magnet, and feems to depend in a great meafure on their
form.

Newton was too cautious, and too good a logician,
to advance fuch a propofition without proof; and therefore, confining himfelf to the fingle cafe of fpherical
and fpheroidal bodies, the forms in which we obferve
the planetary maffes to be compacted, he inquired what
fenfible action between the maffes will refult from an
action between their particles inverfely proportional to
the fquare of their diftances.

Let A L B M, $a\ i\ b\ m$ (fig. 49.) be two fpherical furfaces, of which C is the common centre, and let the
fpace between them be filled with gravitating matter,
uniformly

uniformly denfe. Let p be a particle placed any where within this fpherical fhell, to every particle of which it gravitates with a force inverfely as the fquare of its diftance from it. This particle will have no tendency to move in any direction, becaufe its gravitation in any one direction is exactly balanced by an equal gravitation in the oppofite direction.

Draw through p the two ftraight lines $d\,p\,\varepsilon$, $e\,p\,\eth$, making a very'fmall angle at p. This may reprefent the fection of a very flender double cone $d\,p\,e$, $\eth\,p\,\varepsilon$, having p for the common vertex, and $d\,e$, $\eth\,\varepsilon$ for the diameters of the circular bafes. The gravitation of p to the matter in the bafe $d\,e$ is equal to its gravitation to the matter in the bafe $\eth\,\varepsilon$. For the number of particles in $d\,e$ is to the number in $\eth\,\varepsilon$ as the furface of the bafe $d\,e$ to that of the bafe $\eth\,\varepsilon$, that is, as $d\,e^{2}$ to $\eth\,\varepsilon^{2}$, that is, as $p\,d^{2}$ to $p\,\eth^{2}$, that is, as the gravitation to a particle in $\eth\,\varepsilon$ to the gravitation to a particle in $d\,e$. Therefore the whole gravitation to the matter in $d\,e$ is the fame with the whole gravitation to the matter in $\eth\,\varepsilon$—fince it is alfo in the oppofite direction, the particle p is in equilibrio. The fame thing may be demonftrated of the gravitation to the matter in $q\,r$ and in $s\,t$, and, in like manner, of the gravitation to the matter in the fections of the cones $d\,p\,e$, $\eth\,p\,\varepsilon$ by any other concentric furface. Confequently, the gravitation to the whole matter contained in the folid $d\,q\,r\,e$ is equal to the gravitation to the whole matter in the folid $\eth\,t\,s\,\varepsilon$, and the particle p is ftill in equilibrio.

Now,

Now, fince the lines $dp\,e$, $ep\,\delta$ may be drawn in any direction, and thus be made to occupy the whole fphere, it is evident that the gravitation of p is balanced in every direction, and therefore it has no tendency to move in any direction in confequence of this gravitation to the fpherical fhell of matter comprehended between the furfaces A L B M and $a\,l\,b\,m$.

It is alfo evident that this holds true with refpect to all the matter comprehended between A L B M and the concentric furface $p\,n\,v$ paffing through p; in fhort, p is in equilibrio in its gravitation to all the matter more remote than itfelf from the centre of the fphere, and appears as if it did not gravitate at all to any matter more remote from the centre.

461. We have fuppofed the fpherical fhell to be uniformly denfe. But p will ftill be in equilibrio, although the fhell be made up of concentric ftrata of different denfity, provided that each ftratum be uniformly denfe. For, fhould we fuppofe that, in the fpace comprehended between A L B M and $p\,n\,v$, there occurs a furface $a\,l\,b\,m$ of a different denfity from all the reft, the gravitation to the intercepted portions $q\,r$ and $s\,t$ are equal, becaufe thefe portions are of equal denfity, and are proportional to $p\,q^2$ and $p\,s^2$ inverfely. The propofition may therefore be expreffed in the following very general terms. " *A particle placed any where within a fpherical fhell of* " *gravitating matter, of equal denfity at all equal diftances* " *from the centre, will be in equilibrio, and will have no* " *tendency to move in any direction.* "

Remark.

Remark —The equality of the gra·itation to the furface *e d* and to the furface *ε ∂* is affirmed, becaufe the
numbers of particles in the two furfaces are inverfely as
the gravitations towards one in each. For the very fame
reafon, the gravitations to the furfaces *e d*, and *q r*, and
t s, are all equal. Hence may be derived an elementary
propofition, which is of great ufe in all inquiries of this
kind ;—namely,

462. If a cone or pyramid *d p e*, of uniform gravitating matter, be divided by parallel fections *d e*, *q r*, &c.
the gravitation of a particle *p* in the vertex to each of
thofe fections is the fame, and the gravitations to the
folids *p q r*, *p d e*, *q d e r*, &c. are proportional to their
lengths *p q*, *p d*, *q d*, &c. The firft part of this propofition is already demonftrated. Now, conceive the cone
to be thus divided into innumerable flices of equal thicknefs. It is plain that the gravitation to each of thefe is
the fame, and therefore the gravitation to the folid *q p r*
is to the gravitation to the folid *q d e r* as the number of
flices in the firft to the number in the fecond, that is, as
p q, the length of the firft, to *q d*, the length of the fecond.

The cone *d p e* was fuppofed extremely flender. This
was not neceffary for the demonftration of the particular
cafe, where all the fections were parallel. But in this
elementary propofition, the angle at *p* is fuppofed fmaller
than any affigned angle, that the cone or pyramid may
be confidered as one of the elements into which we may

refolve

refolve a body of any form.   In this refolution, the bafes
are fuppofed, if not otherwife exprefsly ftated, to be parallel, and perpendicular to the axes ; indeed they are
fuppofed to be portions *x r*, *y e*, *z s*, &c. of fpherical
furfaces, having their centres in *p*.   The fmall portions
x r q, *y e d*, *z s ꝺ*, &c. are held as infignificant, vanifhing
in the ultimate ratios of the whole folids.

It is eafy alfo to fee that the equilibrium of *p* is not
limited to the cafe of a fpherical fhell, but will hold true
of any body compofed of parallel ftrata, or ftrata fo formed that the lines *p d*, *p ꝺ* are cut in the fame proportion
by the fections *d e*, *q r*, &c.   In a fpheroidal fhell, for
example, whofe inner and outer furfaces are fimilar, and
fimilarly pofited fpheroids, the particle *p* will be in equilibrio any where within it, becaufe in this cafe, the lines
p ꝺ and *n e* are equal ; fo are the lines *p s* and *o d*, the
lines *t ꝺ* and *r e*, the lines *s s* and *q d*, &c.   In moft
cafes, however, there is but one fituation of the particle *p*
that will infure this equilibrium.   But we may, at the
fame time, infer the following very ufeful propofition.

463.   *If there be two folids perfectly fimilar, and of the
fame uniform denfity, the gravitation to each of thefe folids
by a particle fimilarly placed on or in each, is proportional to
any homologous lines of the folids.*

For, the folids being fimilar, they may be refolved
into the fame number of fimilar pyramids fimilarly placed
in the folids.   The gravitations to each of any coref-
ponding pair of pyramids are proportional to the lengths
of

of thofe pyramids. Thefe lengths have the fame proportion in every correfponding pair. Therefore the abfolute gravitations to the whole pyramids of one folid has
the fame ratio to the abfolute gravitation to the whole
pyramids of the other folid. And, fince the folids are
fimilar, and the particles are at the fimilarly placed ver-
texes of all the fimilar and fimilarly placed pyramids, the
gravitation compounded of the abfolute gravitations to
the pyramids of one folid has the fame ratio to the gravitation fimilarly compounded of the abfolute gravitations
to the pyramids of the other.

464. *The gravitation of an external particle to a fpherical furface, fhell, or entire fphere, which is equally denfe
at all equal diflances from the centre, is the fame as if the
whole matter were collected in its centre.*

Let A L B M (fig. 49.) reprefent fuch a fphere, and
let P be the external particle. Draw P A C B through
the centre C of the fphere, and crofs it by L C M at right
angles. Draw two right lines P D, P E, containing a very
fmall angle at P, and cutting the great circle A L B M
in D, E, D', E'. About P as a centre, with the diftance
P C, defcribe the arch C *d m*, cutting D P in *d*, and E P
in *e*. About the fame centre defcribe the arc D O.
Draw *d* F, *e* G parallel to A B, and cutting L C in *f*
and *g*. Draw C K perpendicular to P D, and *d* H, D δ,
and F I φ perpendicular to A B. Join C D and C F.

Now let the figure be fuppofed to turn round the
axis P B. The femicircumference A L B will generate

a complete fpherical furface. The arch C *d m* will generate another fpherical furface, having P for its centre.
The fmall arches D E, *d e*, F G will generate rings or
zones of thofe fpherical furfaces. D O will alfo generate a zone of a furface having P for its centre. *f g* and
F I will generate zones of flat circular furfaces.

It is evident that the zones generated by D E and
D O (which we may call the zones D E and D O), having the fame radius D $\eth$, are to each other as their refpective breadths D E and D O. In like manner, the
zones generated by *d e*, *f g*, F I, F G, being all at the
fame diftance from the axis A B, are alfo as their refpective breadths *d e*, *f g*, F I, F G. But the zone D O is
to the zone *d e* as P D² to P *d*². For D O is to *d e* as
P D to P *d*, and the radius of rotation D $\eth$ is to the radius *d* H, alfo as P D to P *d*. The circumferences defcribed by D O and *d e* are therefore in the fame proportion of P D to P *d*. Therefore the zones, being as
their breadths and as their circumferences jointly, are as
P D² and P *d*².   .

C K and *d* H, being the fines of the fame arch C *d*,
are equal. Therefore K D and *f* F, the halves of chords
equally diftant from the centre, are alfo equal. Therefore the triangles C D K and C F *f* are equal and fimilar.
But C D K is fimilar to E D O. For the right angles
P D O and C D E are equal. Taking away the common
angle C D O, the remainders C D K and E D O are e-
qual. In like manner, C F *f* and G F I are fimilar, and
therefore (fince C D K and C F *f* are fimilar) the ele-

mentary

mentary triangles $E\,D\,O$ and $G\,F\,I$ are fimilar, and $D\,O : D\,E = F\,I : F\,G$.

The abfolute gravitation or tendency of P to the zone $D\,O$ is equal to its abfolute gravitation to the zone $d\,e$, becaufe the number of particles of the firft is to the number in the laft in $P\,D^2$ to $P\,d^2$, that is, inverfely as the gravitation to a particle in the firft to the gravitation to a particle in the laft. Therefore let c exprefs the circumference of a circle whofe radius is 1. The furface of the zone generated by $D\,O$ will be $D\,O \times c \times D\,\delta$, and the gravitation to it will be $\dfrac{D\,O \times c \times D\,\delta}{P\,D^2}$, to which $\dfrac{d\,e \times c \times d\,H}{P\,d^2}$, or $\dfrac{d\,e \times c \times d\,H}{P\,C^2}$ is equal. This expreffes the abfolute gravitation to the zone generated by $D\,O$, this gravitation being exerted in the direction $P\,D$.

But it is evident that the tendency of P, arifing from its gravitation to every particle in the zone, muft be in the direction $P\,C$. The oblique gravitation muft therefore be eftimated in the direction $P\,C$, and muft (178.) be reduced, in the proportion of $P\,d$ to $P\,H$. It is plain that $P\,d : P\,H = d\,e : f\,g$, becaufe $d\,e$ and $f\,g$ are perpendicular to $P\,d$ and $P\,H$. Therefore the reduced or central gravitation of P to the zone generated by $D\,O$ will be expreffed by $\dfrac{f\,g \times c \times d\,H}{P\,C^2}$.

But the gravitation to the zone generated by $D\,O$ is to the gravitation to the zone generated by $D\,E$ as $D\,O$ to $D\,E$, that is, as $F\,I$ (or $f\,g$) to $F\,G$. Therefore the central gravitation to the zone generated by $D\,E$ will be

expreffed

expreſſed by $\dfrac{\mathrm{F\,G} \times c \times d\,\mathrm{H}}{\mathrm{P\,C^2}}$.   Now F G $\times$ c $\times$ d H is
the value of the ſurface of the zone generated by F G.
And if all this matter were collected in C, the gravita-
tion of P to it would be exactly $\dfrac{\mathrm{F\,G} \times c \times d\,\mathrm{H}}{\mathrm{P\,C^2}}$, and it
would be in the direction P C.   Hence it follows that
the central gravitation of P to the zone generated by
D E, is the ſame as its gravitation to all the matter in
the zone generated by F G, if that matter were placed
in C.

What has been demonſtrated reſpecting the arch D E
is true of every portion of the circumference.   Each has a
ſubſtitute F G, which being placed in the centre C, the
gravitation of P is the ſame.   If P T touch the ſphere in
T, every portion of the arch T L B will have its ſubſtitute in the quadrant L B, and every part of the arch A T
has its ſubſtitute in the quadrant A T L, as is eaſily ſeen.
And hence it follows that the gravitation to a particle P
to a ſpherical ſurface A L B M is the ſame as if all the
matter of that ſurface were collected in its centre.

We ſee alſo that the gravitation to the ſurface generated by the rotation of A T round A B is equal to the
gravitation to the ſurface generated by T L B, which is
much larger, but more remote.

What we have now demonſtrated with reſpect to the
ſurface generated by the ſemicircle A L B is equally true
with regard to the ſurface generated by any concentric
ſemicircle, ſuch as $a\,l\,b$.   It is true, therefore, in regard
to the ſhell comprehended between thoſe ſurfaces; for
this

this fhell may be refolved into innumerable concentric
ftrata, and the propofition may be affirmed with refpect
to each of them, and therefore with refpect to the whole.
And this will ftill be true if the whole fphere be thus
occupied.

Laftly, it follows that the propofition is ftill true, although thofe ftrata fhould differ in denfity, provided that
each ftratum is uniformly denfe in every part.

It may therefore be affirmed in the moft general
terms, that a particle P, placed without a fpherical furface, fhell, or entire fphere, equally denfe at equal diftances from the centre, tends to the centre with the fame
force as if the whole matter of the furface, fhell, or
fphere, were collected there.

This will be found to be a very important propofition,
greatly affifting us in the explanation of abftrufe phenomena in other departments of natural philofophy.

465. *The gravitation of an external particle to a
fpherical furface, fhell, or entire fphere, of uniform denfity at equal diftances from the centre, is as the quantity
of matter in that body, directly, and as the fquare of the
diftance from its centre, inverfely.*

For, if all the matter were collected in its centre, the
gravitation would be the fame, and it would then vary in
the inverfe duplicate ratio of the diftance.

466. *Cor.* 1. Particles placed on the furface of fpheres
of equal denfity gravitate to the centres of thofe fpheres
with forces proportional to the radii of the fpheres.

For

For the quantities of matter are as the cubes of the radii. Therefore the gravitation g is as $\dfrac{d^3}{d^2}$, that is, as d. This is a particular cafe of Prop. 463.

467. *Cor.* 2. The fame thing holds true, if the diftance of the external particles from the centres of the fpheres are as the diameters or radii of the fpheres.

468. *Cor.* 3. If a particle be placed within the furface of a fphere of uniform denfity, its gravitation, at different diftances from the centre, will be as thofe diftances. For it will not be affected by any matter of the fphere that is more remote from the centre (463.); and its gravitation to what is lefs remote is as its diftance from the centre, by the laft corollary.

469. *The mutual gravitation of two fpheres of uniform denfity in their concentric ftrata is in the inverfe duplicate ratio of the diftance between their centres.*

For the gravitation of each particle in the fphere A to the fphere B is the fame as if all the matter in B were collected at its centre. Suppofe it fo placed. The gravitation of B to A will be the fame as if all the matter in A were collected in its centre. Therefore it will be as d^2 inverfely. But the gravitation of A to B is equal to that of B to A. Therefore, &c.

470. The abfolute gravitation of two fpheres whofe quantities of matter are a and b, and d the diftance of
their

their centres, is $\frac{a \times b}{d^2}$. For the tendency of one particle of a to b, being the aggregate of its tendencies to every particle of b, is $\frac{b}{d^2}$. Therefore the tendency of the whole of a to b muft be $\frac{a \times b}{d^2}$. And the tendency of b to a is equal to that of a to b.

471. This confequence of a mutual gravitation between particles proportional to $\frac{1}{d^2}$, is agreeable to what is obferved in the folar fyftem. The planets are very nearly fpherical, and they are obferved to gravitate mutually in this proportion of the diftance between their centres. This mutual action of two fpheres could not refult from any other law of action between the particles. Therefore we conclude that the particles of gravitating matter of which the planets are formed gravitate to each other according to this law, and that the obferved gravitation of the planets is the united effect of the gravitation of each particle to each. There is juft one other cafe, in which the law of corpufcular action is the fame with the law of action between the maffes; and this is when the mutual action of the corpufcles is as their diftance directly. But no fuch law is obferved in all the phenomena of nature.

The general inference drawn by Sir Ifaac Newton from the phenomena, may be thus expreffed : *Every particle of matter gravitates to every other particle of matter*

with

*with a force inversely proportional to the square of the dis-
tance from it.* Hence this doctrine has been called THE
DOCTRINE OF UNIVERSAL GRAVITATION.

The description of a conic section round the focus
fully proves that this law of the distances is the law
competent to all the gravitating particles. But, whether
all particles gravitate, and gravitate alike, is not demonstrated. The analogy between the distance of the different planets and their periodic times only proves that
the total gravitation of the different planets is in the
same proportion with their quantity of matter. For the
force observed by us, and found to be in the inverse
duplicate ratio of the distance of the planet, is the *accelerating* force of gravity, being measured by the acceleration which it produces in the different planets.
But if one half of a planet be matter which does not
gravitate, and the other half gravitates twice as much as
the matter of another planet, these two planets will still
have their periods and distances agreeable to Kepler's
third law. But, since no phenomenon indicates any inequality in the gravitation of different substances, it is
proper to admit its perfect equality, and to conclude with
Sir Isaac Newton.

472. The general consequence of this doctrine is,
that any two bodies, at perfect liberty to move, should
approach each other. This may be made the subject of
experiment, in order to see whether the mutual tendencies of the planets arise from that of their particles.

For

For it muft ftill be remembered that although this conftitution of the particles will produce this appearance, it
may arife from fome other caufe.

. Such experiments have accordingly been made. Bodies have been fufpended very nicely, and they have been
obferved to approach each other. But a more careful
examination of all circumftances has fhewn that moft of
thofe mutual approaches have arifen from other caufes.
Several philofophers of reputation have therefore refufed
to admit a mutual gravitation as a phenomenon competent to all matter.

But no fuch approach fhould be obferved in the experiments now alluded to: The mutual approach of two
fpheres A and B, at the diftance D of their centres,
muft be to the approach to the Earth E at the diftance d
of their centres in the proportion of $\dfrac{A \times B}{D^2}$ to $\dfrac{A \times E}{d^2}$,
that is, of $\dfrac{B}{D^2}$ to $\dfrac{E}{d^2}$. Therefore, if a particle be placed
at the furface of a golden fphere one foot in diameter,
its gravitation to the Earth muft be more than ten millions of times greater than its gravitation to the gold.
For the diameter of the Earth is nearly forty millions of
feet, and the denfity of gold is nearly four times the
mean denfity of the Earth. And therefore, in a fecond,
it would approach lefs than the ten millionth part of 16
feet—a quantity altogether infenfible.

If we could employ in thefe experiments bodies of
fufficient magnitude, a fenfible effect might be expected:
Suppofe T (fig. 50.) to be a ball of equal denfity with

U u   rhe

the Earth, and two geographical miles in diameter, and
let the particle B be at its furface.   Its gravity to T will
be to its gravitation to the Earth nearly as 1 to 2300,
and therefore, if fufpended like a plummet, it would certainly deviate 1′ from the perpendicular.   A mountain
two miles high, and hemifpherical, rifing in a level
country, would produce the fame deviation of the
plummet.

474. Accordingly, fuch deviation of a plumb line
has been obferved.   Firft by the French academicians
employed to meafure a degree of the meridian in Peru.
Having placed their obfervatories on the north and fouth
fides of the vaft mountain Chimboracao, they found
that the plummets of their quadrants were deflected toward the mountain.   Of this they could accurately judge,
by means of the ftars which they faw through the telefcope of their quadrant, when they were pointed vertically by means of the plummet.

Thus, if the plummets take the pofitions A B, C D
(fig. 51.), inftead of hanging in the verticals A F and
C H, a ftar I, will feem to have the zenith diftances e I,
g I, inftead of E I, G I, which it ought to have; and the
diftance F H on the Earth's furface will feem the meafure of the difference of latitude $e\,g$, whereas it correfponds to E G.   The meafure of a degree including the
fpace F H, and eftimated by the declination of a ftar I,
will be too fhort, and the meafure of a degree terminating either at F or H will be too long, when the fpace
F H is excluded.

                                          Confiderable

Confiderable doubts remaining as to the inferences drawn from this obfervation, the philofophers were very defirous of having it repeated. For this reafon, our Sovereign, George III., ever zealous to promote true fcience, fent the Royal aftronomer Dr Mafkelyne to Scotland, to make this experiment on the north and fouth fides of Shihallien, a lofty and folid mountain in Perthfhire. The deviation toward the mountain on each fide exceeded 7″; thus confirming, beyond doubt, the noble difcovery of our illuftrious countryman.

Perhaps a very fenfible effect might be obferved at Annapolis-Royal in Nova Scotia, from the vaft addition of matter brought on the coaft twice every day by the tides. The water rifes there above a hundred feet at fpring-tide. If a leaden pipe, a few hundred feet long, were laid on the level beach at right angles with the coaft, and a glafs pipe fet upright at each end, and the whole filled with water; the water will rife at the outer end, and fink at the end next the land, as the tide rifes. Such an alternate change of level would give the moft fatisfactory evidence. Perhaps the effect might be fenfible on a very long plummet, or even a nice fpirit level.

475. A very fine and fatisfactory examination was made in 1788 by Mr H. Cavendifh. Two leaden balls were faftened to the ends of a flender deal rod, which was fufpended horizontally at its middle by a fine wire. This arm, after ofcillating fome time horizontally by the

twifting

twifting and untwifting of the wire, came to reft in a certain pofition. Two great maffes of 'lead were now brought within a proper diftance of the two fufpended balls, and their approach produced a deviation of the arms from the points of reft. By the extent of this deviation, and by the times of the ofcillations when the great maffes were withdrawn, the proportion was difcovered between the elafticity of the wire and the gravitation of the balls to the great maffes; and a medium of all the obfervations was taken.

By thefe experiments, the mutual gravitation of terreftrial matter, even at confiderable diftances, was moft evincingly demonftrated; and it was legitimately deduced from them that the medium denfity of the Earth was more than five times the denfity of water. Thefe curious and valuable experiments are narrated in the Philofophical Tranfactions for 1798.

476. The oblate form of the Earth alfo affords another proof that gravity is directed, not to any fingular point within the Earth, but that its direction is the combined effect of a gravitation to every particle of matter. Were gravity directed to the centre, by any peculiar virtue of that point, then, as the rotation takes away $\frac{1}{189}$ of the gravity at the equator, the equatorial parts of a fluid fphere muft rife one half of this, or $\frac{1}{578}$, before all is in equilibrio.

For, fuppofe C N and C Q (fig. 33.) to be two canals reaching from the pole and from the equator to the centre.

centre. Since the diminution of gravity at Q is obferved to be $\frac{1}{289}$, and the gravitation of every particle in
CQ is diminifhed by rotation in proportion to its diftance from the axis of rotation, the diminution occafioned in the weight of the whole canal will be one half of
the diminution it would fuftain if the weight of every
particle were as much diminifhed as that of the particle
Q is. Therefore the canal preffes lefs on the centre by
$\frac{1}{578}$, and muft be lengthened fo much before it will balance N C, which fuftains no diminution of weight.
Every other canal parallel to C Q fuftains a fimilar lofs
of weight, and muft be fimilarly compenfated. This will
produce an elliptical fpheroidal form.

But the equatoreal parts of our globe are much more
elevated than this ; not lefs than $\frac{1}{312}$. The reafon is
this. When the rotation of the Earth has raifed the
equatoreal points $\frac{1}{578}$, the plummet, which at a (fig. 33.)
would have hung in the direction a D, tangent to the
evolute A B D F, is attracted fidewife by the protuberant
matter toward the equator. But the furface of the ocean
muft ftill be fuch that the plummet is perpendicular to
it. Therefore it cannot retain the elliptical form produced by the rotation alone, but fwells ftill more at the
equator ; and this ftill increafes the deviation of the
plummet. This muft go on, till a new equilibrium is
produced by a new figure. This will be confidered afterwards. No more is mentioned at prefent than what
is neceffary for fhewing that the protuberance produced
by the rotation caufes, by its attraction, the plummet to
deviate

deviate from the pofition which it had acquired in confequence of the fame rotation.

477. By fuch induction, and fuch reafoning, is eftablifhed the doctrine of univerfal gravitation, a doctrine
which is placed beyond the reach of controverfy, and
has immortalized the fame of its illuftrious inventor.

Sir Ifaac Newton has been fuppofed by many to have
affigned this mutual gravitation, or, as he fometimes calls
it, this attraction, as a property inherent in matter, and
as the *caufe* of the celeftial phenomena ; and for this reafon, he has been accufed of introducing the occult qualities of the peripatetics into philofophy. Nay, many ac-
cufe him of introducing into philofophy a manifeft abfurdity, namely, that a body can act where it is not prefent. This, they fay, is equivalent with faying that the
Sun attracts the planets, or that any body acts on another that is at a diftance from it.

Both of thofe accufations are unjuft. Newton, in no
place of that work which contains the doctrine of univerfal gravitation, that is, in his *Mathematical Principles
of Natural Philofophy*, attempts to *explain* the *general* phenomena of the folar fyftem from the principle of univerfal gravitation. On the contrary, it is in thofe general
phenomena that he difcovers it. The only difcovery to
which he profeffes to have any claim is, *1ft*, the matter
of fact, that every body in the folar fyftem is continually
deflected toward every other body in it, and that the
deflection of any individual body A toward any other
                                                    body

body B is *obferved* to be in the proportion of the quantity of matter in B directly, and of the fquare of the diftance A B inverfely ; and, 2*dly*, that the falling of terreftrial bodies is juft a particular example of this univerfal deflection.   He employs this difcovery to explain phenomena that are more particular ; and all the explanation
that he gives of thefe is the fhewing that they are modified cafes of this general phenomenon, of which he knows
no explanation but the mere defcription.   Newton was
not more eminent for mathematical genius, and penetrating judgement, than for logical accuracy.   He ufes
the word gravitation as the expreffion, not of a quality,
but of a fact ; not of a caufe, but of an event.   Having
eftablifhed this fact beyond the power of controverfy,
by an induction fufficiently copious, nay without a fingle
exception, he explains the more particular phenomena, by
fhewing with what modifications, arifing from the circumftances of the cafe, they are included in the general
fact of mutual deflection ;   and, *finally*, as all changes
of motion are conceived by us as the effects of force, he
fays that there is a deflecting force continually acting on
every particle of matter in the folar fyftem, and that this
deflecting force is what we call weight, heavinefs.   Few
perfons think themfelves chargeable with abfurdity, or
with the abetting of occult qualities, when they really
confider the heavinefs of a body as one of its properties.
So far from being occult, it feems one of the moft manifeft.   It is not the heavinefs of this body that is the
occult quality ; it is the caufe of this heavinefs.   In thus
confidering

confidering gravity as competent to all matter, Newton does nothing that is not done by others, when they afcribe impulfivenefs or inertia to matter. Without fcruple, they fay that impulfivenefs is an univerfal property of matter. Impulfivenefs and heavinefs are on precifely the fame footing—mere phenomena ; and the moft general phenomena that we know. We know none more general than impulfivenefs, fo as to include it, and thus enable us to explain it. Nor do we know any that includes the phenomena of univerfal deflection, with all the modifications of the heavinefs of matter. Whether one of thefe can explain the other is a different queftion, and will be confidered on another occafion, when we fhall fee with how little juftice philofophers have refufed all action at a diftance.

But it would feem that there is fome peculiarity in this explanation of the planetary motions which hinders it from giving entire fatisfaction to the mind. If this be the cafe, it is principally owing to miftake ; to carelefsly imputing to Newton views which he did not entertain. His doctrine of univerfal gravitation does not attempt to explain *how* the operating caufe retards the Moon's motion in the firft and third quarters of a lunation ; it merely narrates in what direction, and with what velocity this change is produced ; or rather, it fhews how the Moon's deflection toward the Earth, joined to her deflection toward the Sun, both of which are matters of fact, conftitute this *feeming* irregularity of motion which we confider as a difturbance. But with refpect to the operating caufe

of

of this general deflection, and the manner in which it
produces its effect, fo as to explain that effect, Newton
is altogether filent. He was as anxious as any perfon
not to be thought to afcribe inherent gravity to matter,
or to affert that a body could act on another at a diftance,
without fome mechanical intervention. In a letter to
Dr Bentley he expreffes this anxiety in the ftrongeft
terms. It is difficult to know Newton's precife meaning
by the word *action*. In very ftrict language, it is abfurd
to fay that matter acts at all,—in contact, or at a diftance.
But, if one fhould affert that the condition of a particle *a*
cannot depend on another particle *b* at a diftance from
it, hardly any perfon will fay that he makes this affertion
from a clear perception of the abfurdity of the contrary propofition. Should a perfon fay that the mere
prefence of the particle *b* is a fufficient reafon for *a* approaching it, it will be difficult to prove the affertion to
be abfurd.

478. Such, however, has been the general opinion
of philofophers; and numberlefs attempts have been
made to thruft in fome material agent in all the cafes of
feeming action at a diftance. Hence the hypothefes of
magnetical and electrical atmofpheres; hence the vor-
texes of Des Cartes, and the celeftial machinery of Eudoxus and Callippus.

Of all thofe attempts, perhaps the moft rafh and un-
juftifiable is that of Leibnitz, publifhed in the Leipzig
Acts 1689, two years after the publication of Newton's

X x   Principia.

Principia, and of the review of it in thofe very acts; It may be called rafh, becaufe it trufted too much to the deference which his own countrymen had hitherto fhewn for his opinions. In this attempt to account for the elliptical motion of the planets, Leibnitz pays no regard to the acknowledged laws of motion. He affumes as principles of explanation, motions totally repugnant to thofe laws, and motions and tendencies incongruous and contradictory to each other. And then, by the help of geometrical and analytical errors, which compenfate each other, he makes out a ftrange conclufion, which he calls a demonftration of the law of planetary gravitation ; and fays that he fees that this theorem is known to Mr Newton, but that he cannot tell how he has arrived at the knowledge of it. This is fomething very remarkable. Newton's procefs is fufficiently pointed out in the *Acta Eruditorum*, which M. Leibnitz acknowledges that he had feen. A copy of the *Principia* was fent to him, by order of the Royal Society, in lefs than two months after the publication.—It was foon known over all Europe.

It is without the leaft foundation that the partifans of M. Leibnitz give him any fhare in the difcovery of the law of gravitation. None of them has ventured to quote this differtation as a propofition juftly proved, nor to defend it againft the objections of Dr Gregory and Dr Keill. M. Leibnitz's remarks on Dr Gregory's criticifm were not admitted into the *Acta Eruditorum*, though under the management of his particular friends. In October

tober 1706 they inserted an extract from a letter, containing some of those remarks;—if possible, they are more absurd and incongruous than the original dissertation.

It is worth while, as a piece of amusement, to read the account of this dissertation by Dr Gregory in his Astronomy, and the observations by Dr Keill in the *Journal Literaire de la Haye*, August 1714.

479. Sir Isaac Newton has also shewn some disposition to account for the planetary deflection by the action of an elastic æther. The general notion of the attempt is this. The space occupied by the solar system is supposed to be filled with an elastic fluid, incomparably more subtile and more elastic than our air. It is supposed to be of greater and greater density as we recede from the Sun, and in general, from all bodies. In consequence of this, Newton thinks that a planet placed any where in it will be impelled from a denser into a rarer part of the æther, and in this manner have its course incurvated toward the Sun.

But, without making any remarks on the impossibility of conceiving this operation with any distinctness that can entitle the hypothesis to be called an *explanation*, it need only be observed that it is, in its first conception, quite unfit for answering the very purpose for which it is employed, namely, to avoid the absurdity of bodies acting on others at a distance. For, unless this be allowed, an æther of different density and elasticity in its different strata cannot exist. It must either be uniform-

ly

Iy denfe and elaſtic throughout, or there muſt exiſt a
repulfive force operating between very diſtant particles—
perhaps extending its influence as far as the folar influence extends—nay, elaſticity without an action *e diſtanti*,
even between the adjoining particles, is inconceivable.
What is meant by elaſticity ? Surely fuch a conſtitution
of the affemblage of particles as makes them recede
from each other ; and the abfurdity is as great at the diftance of the millionth part of a hair's breadth as at the
diſtance of a million of leagues. If we attempt to evade
this, by faying that the particles are in contact, and are
elaſtic, we muſt grant that they are compreffible, and
are really compreffed, otherwife they are not exerting
any elaſtic force ; therefore they are dimpled, and can
no more conſtitute a fluid than fo many blown bladders
compreffed in a box.

The laſt attempt of this kind that ſhall be mentioned
is that of M. Le Sage of Geneva, put into a better ſhape
by M. Prevôt, in a Memoir publiſhed by the Academy
of Berlin, under the name of *Lucrece Newtonien*. This
philofopher fuppofes that through every point of fpace
there is continually paffing a ſtream of æther in *every*
direction, with immenfe rapidity. This will produce no
effect on a folitary body ; but if there are two, one of
them intercepts part of the ſtream which would have
acted on the other. Therefore the bodies, being lefs
impelled on that fide which faces the other, will move
toward each other. Le Sage adds fome circumſtances
refpecting the ſtructure of the bodies, which may give a

ſort

sort of progreſſion in the intenſity of the impulſe, which may produce a deflection diminiſhing as the diſtance or its ſquare increaſes. But this hypotheſis alſo requires that we make light of the acknowledged laws of motion. It has other inſuperable difficulties, and, ſo far from affording any *explanation* of the planetary motions, its moſt trifling circumſtance is incomparably more difficult to comprehend, or even to conceive, than the moſt intricate phenomenon in aſtronomy.

481. Indeed this difficulty obtains in every attempt of the kind, it being neceſſary to conſider the combined motion of millions of bodies, in order to explain the motion of one. But ſuch hypotheſes have a worſe fault than their difficulty ; they tranſgreſs a great rule of philoſophical diſquiſition, " never to admit as the cauſe of " a phenomenon any thing of which we do not know " the exiſtence. " For, even if the legitimate conſequences of the hypotheſis were agreeable to the phenomena, this only ſhews the *poſſibility* of the theory, but gives no explanation whatever. The hypotheſis is good, only as far as it agrees with the phenomena ; we therefore underſtand the phenomena as far as we underſtand the explanation. The *obſerved* laws of the phenomena are as extenſive as our explanation, and the hypotheſis is uſeleſs. But, alas, none of thoſe hypotheſes agree, in their legitimate conſequences, with the phenomena ; the laws of motion muſt be thrown aſide, in order to employ them, and new laws muſt be adopted. This is unwiſe ;

it

it were much better to give thofe *pro re nata* laws to
the planets themfelves.

Mr Cotes, a philofopher and geometer of the firft e-
minence, wrote a preface to the fecond edition of the
Principia, which was publifhed in 1713 with many alterations and improvements by the author. In this preface Mr Cotes gives an excellent account of the principles of the Newtonian philofophy, and many very pertinent remarks on the maxim which made philofophers
fo adverfe to the admiffion of attracting and repelling
forces. Whatever may have been Newton's fentiments
in early life about the competency of an elaftic æther
to account for the planetary deflections, he certainly put
little value on it afterwards. For he never made any
ferious ufe of it for the explanation of any phenomenon
fufceptible of mathematical difcuffion. He had certainly
rejected all fuch hypothefes, otherwife he never would
have permitted Mr Pemberton to prefix that preface of
Mr Cotes to an edition carried on under his own eye.
For in this preface the abfurdity of the hypothefis of an
elaftic æther is completely expofed, and it is declared to
be a contrivance altogether unworthy of a philofopher.
Yet, when Mr Cotes died foon after, Sir Ifaac Newton
fpoke of him in terms of the higheft refpect. Alas, faid
he, *we have loft Mr Cotes ; had he lived, we fhould foon
have learned fomething excellent.*

At prefent the moft eminent philofophers and mathematicians in Europe profefs the opinion of Mr Cotes,
and fee no validity in the philofophical maxim that bodies
cannot

cannot act at a diftance.   M. de la Place, the excellent
commentator of Newton, and who has given the finifh-
ing ftroke to the univerfality of the influence of gravitation on the planetary motions, by explaining, by this
principle, the fecular equation of the Moon, which had
refifted the efforts of all the mathematicians, endeavours,
on the contrary, to prove that an action in the inverfe
duplicate ratio of the diftances refults from the very ef-
fence or exiftence of matter.   Some remarks will be
made on this attempt of M. de la Place afterwards.   But
at prefent we fhall find it much more conducive to our
purpofe to avoid altogether this metaphyfical queftion,
and ftrictly to follow the example of our illuftrious In-
ftructor, who clearly faw its abfolute infignificance for
increafing our knowledge of Nature.

Newton faw that any inquiry into the *manner of acting* of the efficient caufe of the planetary deflections was
altogether unneceffary for acquiring a complete knowledge of all the phenomena depending on the law which
he had fo happily difcovered.   Such was its perfect fimplicity, that we wanted nothing but the affurance of its
conftancy—an affurance eftablifhed on the exquifite a-
greement of phenomena with every legitimate deduction
from the law.

Even Newton's perfpicacious mind did not fee the
number of important phenomena that were completely explained by it, and he thought that fome would
be found which required the admiffion of other principles. But the firft mathematicians of Europe have acquired

quired moſt deſerved fame in the cultivation of this philoſophy, and in their progreſs have found that there is
not one appearance in the celeſtial motions that is inconſiſtent with the Newtonian law, and ſcarcely a phenomenon that requires any thing elſe for its complete explanation.

Hitherto we have been employed in the eſtabliſhment
of a general law. We are now to ſhew how the motions actually obſerved in the individual members of the
ſolar ſyſtem reſult from, or are examples of the operation of the power called Gravity, and how its effects
are modified, and made what we behold, by the circumſtances of the caſe.—To do this in detail would occupy
many volumes; we muſt content ourſelves with adducing one or two of the moſt intereſting examples.
The ſtudent in this noble department of mechanical philoſophy will derive great aſſiſtance from *Mr M'Laurin's
Account of Sir Iſaac Newton's Diſcoveries*. *Dr Pemberton's View of the Newtonian Philoſophy* has alſo conſiderable merit, and is peculiarly fitted for thoſe who are leſs
habituated to mathematical diſcuſſion. The *Coſmographia*
of the *Abbé Friſi* is one of the moſt valuable works extant
on this ſubject. This author gives a very compendious,
yet a clear and perſpicuous account of the Newtonian
doctrines, and of all the improvements in the manner
of treating them which have reſulted from the unremit-
ting labour of the great mathematicians in their aſſiduous
cultivation of the Newtonian philoſophy. He follows,
in general, the geometrical method, and his geometry is
elegant,

elegant, and yet he exhibits (alfo with great neatnefs) all the noted analytical proceffes by which this philofophy has been brought into its prefent ftate.

What now follows may be called an outline of

The Theory of the Celeftial Motions.

482. The firft general remark that arifes from the eftablifhment of univerfal and mutual gravitation is that the common centre of the whole fyftem is not affected by it, and is either at reft, or, if in motion, this motion is produced by a force which is external to the fyftem (98.), and acts equally and in the fame direction on every body of the fyftem (229.)

483. A force has been difcovered pervading the whole fyftem, and determining or regulating the motions of every individual body in it. The problem which naturally offers itfelf firft to our difcuffion is, to afcertain *what will be the motion of a body, projected from any given point of the folar fyftem, in any particular direction, and with any particular velocity—what will be the form of its path, how will it move in this path, and where will it be at any inftant we choofe to name.*

Sir Ifaac has given, in the 41ft propofition of his firft book, the folution of this problem, in the moft general terms, not limited to the obferved law of gravitation, but extended to any conceivable relation between the dif-

Y y   tances

tances and the intensity of the force. This is, unquestionably, the most sublime problem that can be proposed in mechanical philosophy, and is well known by the name of the INVERSE PROBLEM OF CENTRIPETAL FORCES.

But, in this extent, it is a problem of pure dynamics, and does not make a part of physical astronomy. Our attention is limited to the centripetal force which connects this part of the creation of God—a force inversely proportional to the square of the distances. It may be stated as follows.

Let a body P, (fig. 52.) which gravitates to the Sun in S, be projected in the direction P N, with the velocity which the gravitation at P to the Sun would generate in it by impelling it along P T, less than P S.

Draw P Q perpendicular to P N. Take P O equal to twice P T, and draw O Q perpendicular to P Q, and Q R perpendicular to P S. Also draw P s, making the angle Q P s equal to Q P S. Join S Q, and produce S Q till it meet P s in s.

The body will describe an ellipsis, which P N touches in P, whose foci are S and s, and whose principal parameter is twice P R.

For, draw S N perpendicular to P N. Make P O' = 2 P O or = 4 P T, and draw O' Q' perpendicular to P O', and describe a circle passing through P, O' and Q'. It will touch P N, because P O' Q' was made a right angle, and therefore P Q' is the diameter of the circle.

We know that an ellipse may be described by a body influenced by gravitation. This ellipse may have S and s

for

for its foci, and P N for a tangent in P, becaufe the angles are equal which P N makes with the two focal lines. This being the cafe, we know that if P Q, O Q, and Q R be drawn as directed in the foregoing conftruction, P O′ Q′ is the circle which has the fame curvature with the ellipfe in P, whofe foci are S and *s*, and tangent P N, and P T is ¼ of the chord of curvature in P, and P R is half the parameter of the ellipfe. Therefore (212.) P T is the fpace along which the body muft be uniformly impelled by the force in P, that it may acquire the velocity with which the body, actually defcribing this ellipfe, paffes through P. If this body, which we fhall call A, thus revolves in an ellipfe, we fhould infer that it is deflected toward S, by a force inverfely proportional to the fquare of its diftance from S, and of fuch magnitude in P, that it would generate the velocity with which the body paffes through P, by uniformly impelling it along P T.

Now, the other body (which we fhall call P) was actually projected in the direction P N, that is, in the direction of A's motion, with the very velocity with which A paffes through P in the fame direction, and it is under the influence of a force precifely the fame that muft have influenced A in the fame place. The two bodies A and P are therefore in precifely the fame mechanical condition ; in the fame place ; moving in the fame direction ; with the fame velocity ; deflected by the fame intenfity of force, acting in the fame direction. Their motions in the next moment cannot be different, and

they

they muft, at the end of the moment, be again in the fame condition ; and this muft continue. A defcribes a certain ellipfe ; P muft defcribe the fame ; for two motions that are different cannot refult from the fame force acting in the fame circumftances.

484. This demonftration is given by Sir Ifaac Newton in four lines, as a corollary from the propofition in which he deduces the law of planetary deflection from the motion in a conic fection. But it feemed neceffary here to expand his procefs of reafoning a little, becaufe the validity of the inference has been denied by Mr John Bernoulli, one of the firft mathematicians of that age. He even hinted that Newton had taken that illogical method, becaufe he could not accommodate his 41ft propofition to the particular law of gravitation obferved in the fyftem. And he claims to himfelf the honour of having the firft demonftrated that a centripetal force, inverfely as the fquare of the diftance, neceffarily produces a motion in a conic fection. The argument by which he fupports this bold claim is very fingular, coming from a confummate mathematician, who could not be ignorant of its nullity ; fo that it was not a ferious argument, but a trick to catch the uninformed. Newton, fays he, might with equal propriety have inferred, from the defcription of the logarithmic fpiral by a body influenced by a force inverfely proportional to the cube of the diftance, that a body fo deflected will defcribe the logarithmic fpiral, whereas we know that it may defcribe the
hyperbolic

hyperbolic fpiral. Not fatisfied with this triumph, he-
attacks Newton's procefs in his 41ft or general propofition of central forces, faying that it is deduced from principles foreign to the queftion; and, after all, does not
exhibit the body in a ftate of continued motion, but
merely informs us where it will be found, and in what
condition, in any affigned moment. He concludes by
vaunting his own procefs as accomplifhing all that can be
wanting in the problem.

Thefe affertions are the moft unfounded and bold
vauntings of this vainglorious mathematician; and his
own folution is a manifeft plagiarifm from the writings
of Newton, except in the method taken by him to demonftrate the lemma which he as well as Newton premifes.
Newton's demonftration of this lemma is by the pureft
principles of free curvilineal motion; and it is, in this
refpect, a beautiful and original propofition. It makes our
§ 222. Bernoulli confiders it as fynonymous with motion on an inclined plane; with which it has no analogy.
The folution of the great problem by Bernoulli is, in every
principle, and in every ftep, the fame with Newton's; and
the only difference is, that Newton employs a geometrical,
and Bernoulli an algebraical expreffion of the proceeding.
Newton exhibits continued motion, whereas Bernoulli
employs the differential calculus, which *effentially* exhibits only a fucceffion of points of the path. It is
worth the ftudent's while to read Dr Keill's Letter to
John Bernoulli, and his examination of this boafted folution of the celebrated problem. But it is ftill more

worth

worth his while to read Newton's folution, and the propofitions in M'Laurin's Fluxions and Hermann's Phoro-
nomia, which are immediately connected with this problem. This reading will greatly conduce to the forming
a good tafte in difquifitions of this kind. *

485. Our occupation at prefent is much more limited. We are chiefly interefted to fhew that gravitation
produces an elliptical motion, when the fpace P T, along
which the body muft be uniformly impelled by the force
as it exifts in P, in order to acquire the velocity of projection, is lefs than P S. But every ftep would have
been the fame, had we made P T equal to P S (as in
fig. 52. N° 2.) But we fhould then have found that
when the angle Q P s is made equal to Q P S, the line
P s will be parallel to S Q, fo that S Q will not interfect
it, and the path will not have another focus. It is a
parabola, of which P R is the principal parameter.

486. We fhall alfo find that if P T be made greater
than P S (as in fig. 52. N° 3.) the line P s (making the
angles Q P S and Q P s equal) will cut S Q on the other
fide of S, fo that S and s are on the fame fide of Q.
The path will be a hyperbola, of which P R is the principal parameter.

487.

---

* The propofitions given by M. de Moivre in No. 352.
of the Philofophical Tranfactions, and thofe by Dr Keill in
No. 317. and 340. are peculiarly fimple and good.

Pl 13

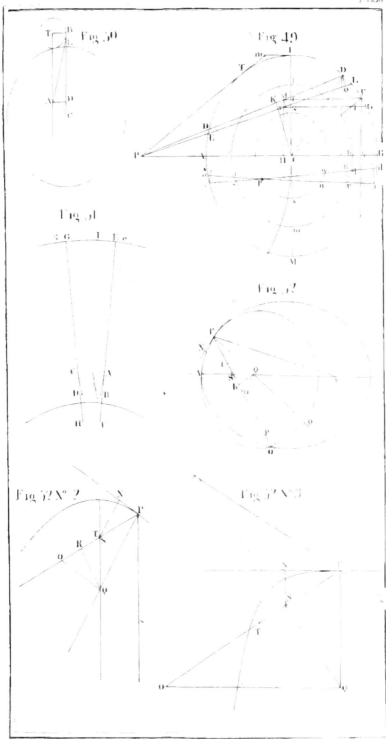

Fig. 50

Fig. 49

Fig. 51

Fig. 52

Fig. 52 Nº 2

Fig. 52 Nº 3

487. This reftriction to the conic fections plainly follows from the line P R, the third proportional to P O and P Q, being the principal parameter, whether the path be an ellipfe, parabola, hyperbola, or circle. *

· It remains to point out the general circumftances of this elliptical motion, and their phyfical connexions. For this purpofe, the following propofition is ufeful.

488. When a body defcribes any curve line B D P A (fig. 53.) by means of a deflecting force directed to a focus S, the angle S P N, which the radius vector makes with the direction of the motion, diminifhes, if the velocity in the point P be lefs than what would enable the body to defcribe a circle round S, and increafes, if the velocity be greater.

If

---

* The only difficulty in the inference of a conic fection as the neceffary path of a projectile influenced by a force in the inverfe duplicate ratio of the diftance from the centre, has arifen from the practice of the algebraic analyfts, of defining all curve lines by the relation of an abfciffa to parallel ordinates. But this is by no means neceffary ; and all curves which enclofe fpace, are as naturally referable to a focus, and definable by the relation between the radii and a circular arch. An equation expreffing the focal chord of curvature is as diftinctive as the ufual equation, and leads us with eafe to the chief properties of the figure. Therefore

Let S P, the *given* diftance, be *a*, and any indeterminate diftance be *x*. Let the perpendicular S N (alfo given by S P

and

487. This reſtriction to the conic ſections plainly follows from the line P R, the third proportional to P O and P Q, being the principal parameter, whether the path be an ellipſe, parabola, hyperbola, or circle. *

· It remains to point out the general circumſtances of this elliptical motion, and their phyſical connexions. For this purpoſe, the following propoſition is uſeful.

. 488. When a body deſcribes any curve line B D P A (fig. 53.) by means of a deflecting force directed to a focus S, the angle S P N, which the radius vector makes with the direction of the motion, diminiſhes, if the velocity in the point P be leſs than what would enable the body to deſcribe a circle round S, and increaſes, if the velocity be greater.

If

---

* The only difficulty in the inference of a conic ſection as the neceſſary path of a projectile influenced by a force in the inverſe duplicate ratio of the diſtance from the centre, has ariſen from the practice of the algebraic analyſts, of defining all curve lines by the relation of an abſciſſa to parallel ordinates. But this is by no means neceſſary ; and all curves which encloſe ſpace, are as naturally referable to a focus, and definable by the relation between the radii and a circular arch. An equation expreſſing the focal chord of curvature is as diſtinctive as the uſual equation, and leads us with eaſe to the chief properties of the figure. Therefore

Let S P, the *given* diſtance, be *a*, and any indeterminate diſtance be *x*. Let the perpendicular S N (alſo given by S P and

If the velocity of the body in P be lefs than that which might produce a circular motion round S, then its path will coalefce with the nafcent arch P *p* of a circle whofe deflective chord of curvature is lefs than 2 P S (212.) Let its half be P O, lefs than P S, and let P *p* be a very minute arch. Draw the tangents P N, *p n,* and the perpendiculars S N, S *n*. P *q* perpendicular to P N will meet *p q* perpendicular to *p n* (P *p* being evanefcent) in *q* the centre of curvature. Draw *p* S and *p* O.

It is evident that the angles P *q p* and P O *p* are ultimately equal, as they ftand on the fame arch P *p* of the equicurve

---

and the given angle S P N) be *b,* and let *p* be the perpendicular and *q* the focal chord of curvature, correfponding to the diftance *x.* Let 4 P T be $= d.$ Then (102. 210.) we have

$$\frac{1}{b^2 d} : \frac{1}{p^2 q} = \frac{1}{a^2} : \frac{1}{x^2}$$

$$b^2 d : p^2 q = a^2 : x^2$$

$$b^2 d x^2 = p^2 q a^2$$

therefore $q = \dfrac{b^2 d x^2}{a^2 p^2}, = \dfrac{b^2}{a^2} d \times \dfrac{x^2}{p^2}$

Let $\dfrac{b^2}{a^2} d = e$ then $q = \dfrac{e x^2}{p^2}$, which is an equation to a conic fection, of which *e* is the parameter, S the focus, and P N a tangent in P. Now *e* is a given magnitude, becaufe *a, b, d,* are all given. Expreffing the angle S P N by φ, we have $e = d \times$ fin.$^2 \varphi$. See alfo for the particular cafe of a force proportional to $\dfrac{1}{x^2}$ the differtations by Dr Jo. Keill in the Philofophical Tranfactions, No. 317. and No. 340.

equicurve circle, and are, refpectively, the doubles of the angles at the circumference. P ς p is evidently equal to N S n. Therefore P O p is equal to N S n, and P S p is lefs than N S n. Therefore P S N is lefs than p S n, and S P N is greater than S p n. Therefore the angle S P N diminifhes when P O is lefs than P S, that is, when the velocity in P is lefs than what would enable the centri-petal force in P to retain the body in a circle round S.

On the other hand, if the velocity in P be greater than what fuits a circular motion round S, it is plain that P O will be greater than P S, and the angle P S p will be greater than N S n, and the angle P S N greater than p S n, and therefore the angle S P N will be lefs than S p n, &c.

489. Applying this obfervation to the cafe of ellip-tical motion, we get a more diftinct notion of its differ-ent affections, and their dependence on their phyfical caufes.

In the half D A B (fig. 46.) of the ellipfe defcribed by a planet round the Sun in its focus S, the middle point of the deflective or focal chord of curvature lies between the planet and the focus. Therefore, during the whole motion from D to B, along the femiellipfe D A B, the angle contained between the radius vector and the line of the planet's motion is continually dimi-nifhing. But during the motion in the femiellipfe, B P D, the angle is continually increafing. It is therefore the greateft poffible in D, and the fmalleft in B.

Z z   Let

Let the planet fet out from its aphelion A, with its due velocity, moving in the direction A F. The velocity in A, being equal to that acquired by a uniform acceleration along $\frac{1}{4}$ of the parameter, is vaftly lefs than what would make it move in the circular arch A L, of which S is the centre, and the planet muft fall within that circle. Therefore its path will no longer be perpendicular to the radius vector, but muft now make with it an angle fomewhat acute. The centripetal force therefore is now refolvable into two forces, one of which accelerates the planet's motion, and the other incurvates its path. Its direction brings it nearer to the Sun. While in the quadrant A F B, the velocity is always lefs than what is required for a circular motion. For, if from any point F in this quadrant, F G be drawn perpendicular to the tangent, meeting the tranfverfe axis in G, and if G H be drawn perpendicular to the normal F G, H F is one half of the focal chord of curvature, and H lies between P and S. Now, it has been fhewn that when this is the cafe, the angle S F n diminifhes, and, with it, the ratio of S n to S F (this ratio is that of C B to the femidiameter C O, the conjugate of C F, ($ 6. Ell.) Confequently, there will be continually more and more of the centripetal force employed in accelerating the motion, and lefs employed in incurvating the path, the firft part being F n and the other S n. When the planet arrives at B, the point H falls upon S, and the velocity is precifely what would fuffice for a circular motion round S, if the direction of the motion were perpendicular to
the

the radius vector. But the direction of the motion brings it ftill nearer to S. A great part of the centripetal force is ftill employed in accelerating the motion; and the moment the planet paffes B, the velocity becomes greater than what might produce a circular motion round S. For H now lies beyond S from B. Therefore the angle S B N, which is now in its fmalleft poffible ftate, begins to open again; and this diminifhes the proportion of the centripetal force which accelerates the motion, and increafes the proportion of the incurvating force. The planet is, however, ftill accelerated, preferving the equable defcription of areas. The angle S B N increafes with the increafing velocity, and becomes a right angle, when the planet arrives at its perihelion P.

It has been fhewn (Ellipfe, § 4.) that the chord P I cut off from any diameter P A by the equicurve circle P a I, is equal to the parameter of that diameter. Therefore the centre o of this circle lies beyond S. The planet, paffing through P, is defcribing a nafcent arch of this circle. Confequently, the curve which it is defcribing paffes without a circle defcribed round S, and the planet is now receding from the Sun. This is ufually accounted for, by faying that its velocity is now too great for defcribing a circle round the Sun. And this is true, when the intenfity of the deflecting force is confidered. But it has been thought difficult to account for the planet now retiring from the Sun, in the perihelion, where the centripetal force is the greateft of all —greater than what has already been able to bring it

Z z 2   continually

continually nearer to the Sun. We are apt to expect that it will come ftill nearer. But the fact is, that the planet, in paffing through P, is really moving fo that, if the Sun were fuddenly transferred to *o*, it would circulate round it for ever. But, in defcribing the fmalleft portion of the circle P *a* I, it goes without the circle which has S for its centre, and its motion now makes an obtufe angle with the radius vector, although it is perpendicular to a radius drawn to *o*. There is now a portion of the centripetal force employed in retarding the motion of the planet, and its velocity is now diminifhed ; and the angle of the radius vector and the path is now increafed, by the fame degrees by which they had been increafed and diminifhed during the approach to the Sun. At D, the planet has the fame diftance from the Sun that it had in B, and the fame velocity. The angle S D *v* is now as much greater than a right angle as S B N was lefs ; and at A, it is reduced to a right angle, and the velocity is again the fame as the firft. In this way the planet will revolve for ever.

It was fhewn in § 223. that in the curvilineal motion of bodies by the action of a central force, the velocities are inverfely as the perpendiculars from the centre of forces on the lines of their directions. In the perihelion, the radius vector is perpendicular to the path. The perihelion diftance may therefore be taken as the unit of the fcale on which all the other velocities are meafured. The other velocities may therefore be confidered as fractions of the perihelion velocity, which is the greateft of all.

In

In elliptical motions, the velocities in every point are as the perpendiculars drawn from the other focus on the tangents in that point. For the perpendiculars on any tangent drawn from the two foci are reciprocal.

490. Hence it appears that if a body fets out from P, with the velocity acquired by uniform acceleration along P S, and defcribes a parabola by means of a centripetal force directed to S, the velocity diminifhes without limit. For the perpendicular drawn from the focus on a tangent to a parabola may be greater than any line that can be affigned, if the point in the parabola be taken fufficiently remote from the vertex.

491. If the body fet out from P with a velocity exceeding what it would acquire by uniform acceleration along P S, it will defcribe a hyperbola, and its velocity will diminifh continually. But it will never be lefs than a certain determinable magnitude, to which it continually approximates. For the perpendicular from the focus on the tangent in the moft remote point of the hyperbola that can be affigned, is ftill lefs than the perpendicular to the affymptote, to which the tangent continually approaches.

But, when the velocity in the perihelion is lefs than that acquired by uniform acceleration along P S, there will always be a limit to its diminution by the recefs from the centre of force. For the velocity being fo moderate, the path is more incurvated by the centripetal force;

force ; fo th·t the body is made to defcribe a curve which has an upper apfis A, as well as a lower apfis P, The body, after paffing through A at right angles to the radius ve·or, is now accelerated, becaufe its path now makes an acute angle with the radius vector ; and thus the velocity is again increafed.

492. The velocity in any point of the ellipfe defcribed by a planet is to the velocity that would enable the fame force to retain it in a circle at the fame diftance, in the fubduplicate ratio of its diftance from the upper focus f to the femitranfverfe axis. That is, calling the elliptic velocity V, and the circular velocity v, we have $V^2 : v^2 = P s : C A$. (fig. 53.)

For (488.) $V^2 : v^2 = P O : P S$.

But (Ellipfe 9.) it was fhewn that $P O \times C A$ was equal to $C K^2$, $= P S \times P s$. Therefore $P O : P S = P s : C A$ and $V^2 : v^2 = P s : C A$.

493. The angular motion in the ellipfe is to the angular motion in a circle at the fame diftance, and by the action of the fame force, in the fubduplicate ratio of half the parameter to the diftance from S.

Take $P p$, a fmall arch of the ellipfe, and, with the centre S, and diftance S P, defcribe the circular arch $P z V$, cutting $S p$ in z. Make $P p$ to $P V$ as the velocity in the ellipfe to that in the circle. Then it is plain that $P z$ is to $P V$ as the angular motion in the ellipfe is to the angular motion in the circle.

The

The angle $z\,\mathrm{P}\,p$ being the complement of N P S (becaufe N P may be confidered as coinciding with $p\,$P) it is equal to N S P. Therefore

$$\mathrm{P}\,z^2 : \mathrm{P}\,p^2 = \mathrm{S}\,\mathrm{N}^2 : \mathrm{S}\,\mathrm{P}^2, = \mathrm{P}\,\mathrm{Q}^2 : \mathrm{P}\,\mathrm{O}^2$$

therefore $\quad \mathrm{P}\,z^2 : \mathrm{P}\,p^2 = \mathrm{P}\,\mathrm{R} : \mathrm{P}\,\mathrm{O}$

but $\quad\quad \mathrm{P}\,p^2 : \mathrm{P}\,\mathrm{V}^2 = \mathrm{P}\,\mathrm{O} : \mathrm{P}\,\mathrm{S}$

therefore $\quad \mathrm{P}\,z^2 : \mathrm{P}\,\mathrm{V}^2 = \mathrm{P}\,\mathrm{R} : \mathrm{P}\,\mathrm{S}.$

Cor. The angular motion in the circle exceeds that in the ellipfe, when the point R lies between P and S, and falls fhort of it when R lies beyond S. They are equal when P S is perpendicular to A C, or when the true anomaly of the planet is 90°. For then R and S coincide. Here the approach to S is moft rapid.

494. In any point of the ellipfe, the gravitation or centripetal force is to that which would produce the fame angular motion in a circle, at the fame diftance from the Sun, as this diftance is to half the parameter, that is, as P S to P R.

For, by the laft propofition, when the forces in the circle and ellipfe are the fame, the angular motion in the circle was to that in the ellipfe as P V to P z, which has been fhewn to be as $\sqrt{\mathrm{PS}}$ to $\sqrt{\mathrm{PR}}$. Therefore, when the angular velocity in the circle, and confequently the real velocity, is changed from P V to P z, in order that it may be the fame with that in the ellipfe, the centripetal force muft be changed in the proportion of P V^2 to P z^2, that is, of P S to P R. Therefore the force which retains the body in the ellipfe is to that which will retain

it

it with the fame angular motion in a circle at that diftance as P S to P R.

Thefe are the chief affections of a motion regulated by a centripetal force in the inverfe duplicate ratio of the diftance from the centre of forces. The comparifon of them with motions in a circle gives us, in moft cafes, eafy means of ftating every change of angular motion, or of approach to or recefs from the centre, by means of any change of centripetal force, or of velocity.

Such changes frequently occur in the planetary fpaces; and the regular elliptical motion of any individual planet, produced by its gravitation to the Sun, is continually difturbed by its gravitation to the other planets. This difturbance is proportional to the fquare of the diftance from the difturbing planet inverfely, and to the quantity of matter in that planet directly. Therefore, before we can afcertain the difturbance of the Earth's motion, for example, by the action of Jupiter, we muft know the proportion of the quantity of matter in Jupiter to that in the Sun. This may feem a queftion beyond the reach of human underftanding. But the Newtonian philofophy furnifhes us with infallible means for deciding it.

Of the Quantity of Matter in the Sun and Planets.

SINCE it appears that the mutual tendency which we have called Gravitation is competent to every particle of

matter,

matter, and therefore the gravitation of a particle of matter to any mass whatever is the sum or aggregate of its gravitation to every atom of matter in that mass, it follows that the gravitation to the Sun or to a planet is proportional to the quantity of matter in the Sun or the planet. As the gravitation may thus be computed, when we know the quantity of matter, so this may be computed when we know the gravitation towards it. Hence it is evident that we can ascertain the proportion of the quantities of matter in any two bodies, if we know the proportion of the gravitations toward them.

495. The tendency toward a body, of which m is the quantity of matter and d the distance, is $\div \dfrac{m}{d^2}$. It is this tendency which produces deflection from a straight line, and it is measured by this deflection. Now this, in the case of the planets, is measured by the distance at which the revolution is performed, and the velocity of that revolution. We found (224.) that this combination is expressed by the proportional equation $g \div \dfrac{d}{p^2}$, where p is the periodic time. Therefore we have $\dfrac{m}{d^2} \div \dfrac{d}{p^2}$, and, consequently, $m \div \dfrac{d^3}{p^2}$.

By this means we can compare the quantity of matter in all such bodies as have others revolving round them. Thus, we may compare the Sun with the Earth, by comparing the Moon's gravitation to the Earth with the Earth's gravitation to the Sun. It will be convenient

3 A

to confider the Earth as the unit in this comparifon with the other bodies of the fyftem.

The Sun's diftance in miles is   -   -   -   93726900

The Moon's diftance -   -   -   -   -   -   240144

The Earth's revolution (fydereal) days   -   365,25

The moon's fydereal revolution (days)   -   27,322

Therefore $\dfrac{93726900^3 \times 27,322^2}{240144^3 \times 365,25^2} = 332669.$

But this muft be increafed by about $\frac{1}{70}$, becaufe the gravitation to the Earth is ftated beyond its real value by the fuppofition that the revolution of the Moon is performed round the centre of the Earth, whereas it is really performed round their common centre (231.) Thus increafed, the Sun's quantity of matter may be eftimated at 337422 times that of this Earth.

It muft be obferved that this computation is not of very great accuracy. It depends on the diftance of the Sun ; and any miftake in this is accompanied by a fimilar miftake, but in a triplicate proportion. Now our eftimation of the Sun's diftance depends entirely on the Sun's horizontal parallax, as meafured by means of the tranfits of Venus. The error of $\frac{1}{10}$ of a fecond in this parallax, (which is only about 8″,7 or 8″,8) will induce an error of $\frac{1}{30}$ of the whole.

In like manner, we compare Jupiter with the Earth, by comparing the gravitation of the firft fatellite with that of the Moon. This makes Jupiter about 313 times more maffive than the Earth.

The quantity of matter in Saturn deduced from the revolution

revolution of his fecond Caffinian fatellite, is about 103 times that of the Earth.

Herfchel's planet contains about 17 times as much matter as our globe, as we learn by the revolution of its firft fatellite.

We have no fuch means for obtaining a knowledge of the quantity of matter in Venus, Mars, or Mercury. Thefe are therefore only guefted at, by means of certain phyfical confiderations which afford fome data for an opinion. Venus is thought to be about $\frac{18}{20}$ of the Earth, Mars about $\frac{1}{4}$, and Mercury about $\frac{1}{16}$. But thefe are very vague guefles. We judge of the Moon's quantity of matter with fome more confidence, by comparing the influence of the Sun and Moon on the tides, and on the preceffion of the equinoxes. The Moon is fuppofed about $\frac{1}{70}$ of the Earth.

From this comparifon it will appear that the Sun con-tains nearly 800 times as much matter as all the planets combined into one mafs. Therefore the gravitation to the Sun fo much exceeds that of any one planet to an-other, that their mutual difturbances are but inconfi-derable.

496. The proportion of the quantities of matter, dif-covered by this procefs of reafoning, is very different from what we fhould have deduced from the obferved bulk of the different bodies. Thus, Saturn's diameter being about ten times that of the Earth, we fhould have inferred that he contained a thoufand times as much

matter,

matter, whereas he contains only about 103 or 104.
We muft therefore conclude that the denfities of the Sun
and planets are very different.   Still taking the Earth as
the unit of the fcale, and combining the ratios of the
bulks and the quantities of matter, we may fay that the

denfity of the Sun is	-	-	-	-	0,25
Venus	-	-	-	-	1,27
Earth	-	-	-	-	1
Mars	-	-	-	-	0,73
Jupiter	-	-	-	-	0,292
Saturn	-	-	-	-	0,184
Georgian Planet	-	-	-	0,212

It appears by this ftatement that the denfity of the
planets is lefs as they are more remote from the centre
of revolution.   Herfchel's planet is an exception ; but a
fmall change on his apparent diameter, not exceeding
half a fecond, will perfectly reconcile them.

497. Knowing the quantity of matter, and the diameter of the bodies of the fyftem, we can eafily tell the
accelerative force of gravity acting on a body at their
furfaces by article 465, that is, what velocity gravity
will generate in a fecond of time, or how far a body
will fall in a fecond.   In like manner, we can tell the
preffure occafioned by the weight or heavinefs of a body,
as this may be meafured by the fcale of a fpring fteelyard, graduated by additions of equal known preffures.
It cannot be meafured by a balance, which only compares
one mafs of equally heavy matter with another.

                                                    Thus,

Thus, the fpace fallen through, and the apparent weight of a lump of matter, by a fpring fteelyard, will be

		Fall in 1″.	Weight.
At the furface of the Sun	-	451 feet.	28,2
Earth	-	16,09	1
Jupiter	-	41,64	2,6
Saturn	-	14,4	0,89
Herfchel		18,7	1,16

Of the Mutual Difturbances of the Planetary Motions.

498. The queftions which occur in this department of the ftudy are generally of the moft delicate nature, and require the moft fcrupulous attention to a variety of circumftances. It is not enough to know the direction and intenfity of the difturbing force in every point of a planet's motion. We muft be able to collect into one aggregate the minute and almoft imperceptible changes that have accumulated through perhaps a long tract of time, during which the forces are continually changing, both in direction and in intenfity, and are frequently combined with other forces. This requires the conftant employment of the inverfe method of fluxions, which is by far the moft difficult department of the higher geometry, and is ftill in an imperfect ftate. Thefe problems have been exclufively the employment of the moft eminent

eminent mathematicians of Europe, the only perfons who
are in a condition to improve the Newtonian philofophy ;
and the refult of their labours has fhewn, in the cleareft
manner, its fupreme excellence, and total diffimilitude to
all the phyfical theories which have occupied the attention of philofophers before the days of the admired inventor. For the feeming anomalies that are obferved in
the folar fyftem are, all of them, the confequences of
the univerfal operation of one fimple force, without the
interference of any other, and are all fufceptible of the
moft precife meafurement and comparifon with obfervation ; fo that what we choofe to call anomalies, irregularities, and difturbances, are as much the refult of the
general pervading principle as the elliptical motions, of
which they are regarded as the difturbances. *

It is in this part of the ftudy alfo in which the penetrating and inventive genius of Newton appear moft con-
fpicuoufly. The firft law of Kepler, the equable defcription of areas, led the way to all the reft, and made
the detection of the law of planetary force a much eafier tafk. But the moft difcriminating attention was neceffary for feparating from each other the deviations from
fimple elliptical motion which refult from the mutual gravitation of the planets, and a confummate knowledge of dynamics for computing and fumming up all thofe deviations.
The fcience was yet to create ; and it is chiefly to this
that the firft book of Newton's great work is dedicated.
He has given the moft beautiful fpecimen of the inveftigation in his theory of the lunar inequalities. To every
one

one who has acquired a juft tafte in mathematical compofition, that theory will be confidered as one of the
moft elegant and *pleafing* performances ever exhibited to
the public. It is true, that it is but a commencement
of a moft delicate and difficult inveftigation, which has
been carried to fucceffive degrees of much greater improvement, by the unceafing labours of the firft mathematicians. But in Newton's work are to be found all the
helps for the profecution of it, and the firft application
of his new geometry, contrived on purpofe ; and all the
fteps of the procefs, and the methods of proceeding, are
pointed out—all of Newton's invention, *fua mathefi facem
præferente.*

It muft be farther remarked that the knowledge of
the anomalies of the planetary motions is of the greateft
importance. Without a very advanced ftate of it, it
would have been impoffible to conftruct accurate tables
of the lunar motions. But, by the application of this
theory, Mayer has conftructed tables fo accurate, that
by obferving the diftance of the Moon from a properly
felected ftar, the longitude may be found at fea with
an exactnefs quite fufficient for navigation. This method
is now univerfally practifed on board of our Eaft India
fhips. This requires fuch accurate theory and tables of
the Moon's motion, that we muft at all times be able to
determine her place within the 30th part of her own
diameter. Yet the Moon is fubject to more anomalies
than any other body in the folar fyftem.

But the ftudy is no lefs valuable to the fpeculative
philofopher.

philofopher. Few things are more pleafing than the being able to trace order and harmony in the midft of feeming confufion and derangement. No where, in the wide range of fpeculation, is order more completely effected. All the feeming diforder terminates in the detection of a clafs of fubordinate motions, which have regular periods of increafe and diminution, never arifing to a magnitude that makes any confiderable change in the fimple elliptical motions ; fo that, finally, the folar fyftem feems calculated for almoft eternal duration, without fuftaining any deviation from its prefent ftate that will be perceived by any befides aftronomers. The difplay of wifdom, in the felection of this law of mutual action, and in accommodating it to the various circumftances which contribute to this duration and conftancy, is furely one of the moft engaging objects that can attract the attention of mankind.

In this elementary courfe of inftruction, we cannot give a detail of the mutual difturbances of the planetary motions. Yet there are points, both in refpect of doctrine and of method, which may be called elementary, in relation to this particular fubject. It is proper to confider thefe with fome attention.

499. The regularity of the motions of a planet A round the Sun would not be difturbed by the gravitation of both to another planet B, if the Sun and the planet A gravitate to B with equal force, and in the fame or in a parallel direction (98.) The difturbance arifes entirely

tirely from the inequality and the obliquity of the gravitations of the Sun and of the planet A to B. The manner in which thefe difturbances may be confidered, and the grounds of computation, will be more clearly underftood by an example.

Let S (fig. 54.) reprefent the Sun, E the Earth, and J the planet Jupiter. Let it be farther fuppofed (which may be done without any great error) that the Earth and Jupiter defcribe concentric circles round the Sun, and that the Sun contains 1000 times as much matter as Jupiter. Make J S to E A as the fquare of E J to the fquare of S J. Then, if we take S J to reprefent the gravitation of the Sun to Jupiter, it is plain that E A will reprefent the gravitation of the Earth, placed in E, to Jupiter. Draw E B, parallel and equal to J S, and complete the parallelogram E B A D. The force with which Jupiter deranges the motion of the Earth round the Sun will be reprefented by E D.

For the force E A is equivalent to the combined forces E B and E D. But if the Sun and Earth were impelled only by the equal and parallel forces S J and E B acting on every particle of each, it is plain that their relative motions would not be affected (98.) It is only by the impulfion arifing from the force E D that their relative fituations will fuftain any derangement.

500. This derangement is of two kinds, affecting either the gravitation of the Earth to the Sun, or her angular motion round him. Let E D be confidered as the

3 B   diagonal

diagonal of a rectangle E F D G, E G lying in the direction of the radius S E, and E F being in the direction of the tangent to the Earth's orbit. It is plain that the force E G affects the Earth's gravitation to the Sun, while E F affects the motion round him. As E G is in the direction of the radius, it has no tendency to accelerate or retard her motion round the Sun. E F, on the other hand, does not affect the gravitation, but the motion in the curve only.

This disturbing force E D varies, both in direction and magnitude, by a variation in the Earth's position in relation to the Sun and Jupiter. Thus, in fig. A, which represents the Earth as almost arrived at the conjunction with Jupiter, having Jupiter near his opposition to the Sun, the force E G greatly diminishes the Earth's gravitation to the Sun, and the force E F accelerates her motion round him in the order of the letters E C P O Q. In fig. B, the force E G still diminishes the Earth's gravitation to the Sun, but E F retards her motion from O to Q. In fig. C, E G increases the Earth's gravitation to the Sun, and E F accelerates her motion round him. It appears very plainly that the motion round the Sun is accelerated in the quadrants Q C and P O, and is retarded in the quadrants C P and O Q. We may also see that the gravitation to the Sun is increased in the neighbourhood of the points P and Q, but is diminished in the neighbourhood of C and O, and that there is an intermediate point in each quadrant where the gravitation suffers no change. The greatest diminution of the

Earth's

Earth's gravitation to the Sun muſt be in C, when Jupiter is neareſt to the Earth, in the time of his oppoſition to the Sun.

We alſo fee very plainly how all theſe diſturbing forces may be preciſely determined, depending on the proportion of E I to E S and to S I. Nor is the conſtruction reſtricted to circular orbits. Each orbit is to be conſidered in its true figure, and the parallelogram E G D F is not always a rectangle, but has the fide E F lying in the direction of the tangent. But we believe that the computation is found to be ſufficiently exact without conſidering the parallelogram E G D F as oblique. The eccentricity of Jupiter's orbit muſt not be neglected becauſe it amounts to a fourth part of the Earth's diſtance from the Sun.

We have taken the Sun's gravitation to Jupiter as the ſcale on which the diſturbing forces are meaſured ; but this was for the greater facility of comparing the diſturbing forces with each other. But they muſt be compared with the Earth's gravitation to the Sun, in order to learn their effect on her motions. It will be exact enough for the preſent purpoſe of merely explaining the method, to ſuppoſe Jupiter's mean diſtance five times the Earth's from the Sun, and that the quantity of matter in the Sun is 1000 times that of Jupiter. Therefore the Earth's gravitation to the Sun muſt be 25000 times greater than to Jupiter, when the Earth is about P or Q. When the Earth is at C, her gravitation to Jupiter is increaſed in the proportion of 4^2 to 5^2, and it is now $\frac{1}{16000}$ of her

gravitation.

gravitation to the Sun. When the Earth is in O, her gravitation to Jupiter is $\frac{1}{10000}$ of her gravitation to the Sun.

But we are not to imagine that when the Earth is at C, her motion relative to the Sun is affected in the same manner as if $\frac{1}{10000}$ of her gravitation were taken away. For we muſt recollect that the Sun alſo gravitates to Jupiter, or is deflected toward him, and therefore toward the Earth at C. The diminution of the relative gravitation of the Earth is not to be meaſured by E A, but by E G. All the diſturbing forces E G and E F, correſponding to every poſition of the Earth and Jupiter, muſt be conſidered as fractions of S J, the meaſure taken for the mean gravitation to Jupiter. This is $\frac{1}{15000}$ of the Earth's gravitation to the Sun.

Meaſuring in this way, we ſhall find that when the Earth is at P or Q her gravitation to the Sun is increaſed by $\frac{1}{125000}$. For P S or Q S will, in this caſe, come in the place of E G in fig. C, and there will be no ſuch force as E F. At C the Earth's gravitation is diminiſhed $\frac{1}{15043}$, and at O, $\frac{1}{81800}$.

To be able to aſcertain the magnitude of the diſturbing force in the different ſituations of the Earth is but a very ſmall part of the taſk. It only gives us the momentary impulſion. We muſt aſcertain the accumulated effect of the action during a certain time, or along a certain portion of the orbit of the diſturbed planet. This is the celebrated *problem of three bodies*, as it is called, which has employed the utmoſt efforts of the great mathematicians ever ſince the time that it firſt appeared in

Newton's

Newton's lunar theory. It can only be solved by approximation ; and even this solution, except in some very particular cafes, is of the utmost difficulty, which shews, by the way, the folly of all who pretend to *explain* the motions of the planets by the impulfions of fluids, when not three, but millions of particles are acting at once.

We have to afcertain, in the firft place, the accumulated effect of the acceleration and retardation of the angular motion of the Earth round the Sun. The general procefs is one of the two following.

1/t, Suppofe it required to determine how far the attraction of Jupiter has made the Earth overpafs the quadrantal arch Q C of her annual orbit. The arch is fuppofed to be unfolded into a ftraight line, and divided into minute portions, defcribed in equal times. At each point of divifion is erected a perpendicular ordinate equal to the accelerating difturbing force E F correfponding to that point. A curve line is drawn through the extremities of thofe ordinates. The unfolded arch being confidered as the reprefentation of the time, and the ordinates as the accelerating forces, it is plain that the area will reprefent the acquired velocity (70.) Now let another figure be conftructed, having an abfciffa to reprefent the time of the motion. But the ordinates muft now be made proportional to the areas of the laft figure. It is plain, from article 50, that the area of this new figure will reprefent, or be proportional to the fpaces defcribed, in confequence of the action of the difturbing force ; and therefore it will exprefs, nearly, the addition

to

to the fpace defcribed by the undifturbed planet, or the diminution, if the accelerations have been exceeded by the retardations.

The *other* method is to make the unfolded arch the fpace defcribed, and the ordinates the accelerations, as before. The area now reprefents the augmentation of the fquare of the velocity (75.) A fecond figure is now conftructed, having the fame abfciffa now reprefenting the time. The ordinates are made proportional to the fquare roots of the areas of the firft figure, and they will therefore reprefent the velocities. The areas of this new figure will reprefent the fpaces, as in the firft procefs, to be added to the arch defcribed by the undifturbed planet, or fubtracted from it.

501. All this being a tafk of the utmoft labour and difficulty, the ingenuity of the mathematicians has been exercifed in facilitating the procefs. The penetrating eye of Newton perceived a path which feemed to lead di-rectly to the defired point. All the lines which reprefent the difturbing forces are lines connected with circular arches, and therefore with the circular motion of the planet. The main difturbing force E D is a function of the angle of commutation C S E, and E F and E G are the fine and cofine of the angle D E G. Newton, in his lunar theory, has given moft elegant examples of the fummation of all the fucceffive lines E F that are drawn to every point of the arch. Sometimes he finds the fums or accumulated actions of the forces expreffed by the

the fine of an arch; fometimes by the tangent; by a fegment of the circular area, &c. &c. &c. Euler, D'Alembert, De la Grange, Simpfon, and other illuftrious cultivators of this philofophy, have immenfely improved the methods pointed out and exemplified by Newton, and, by more convenient reprefentations of the forces than this elementary view will admit, have at laft made the whole procefs tolerably eafy and plain. But it is ftill only fit for adepts in the art of fymbolical analyfis. Their proceffes are in general fo recondite and abftrufe that the analyft lofes all conception, either of motions or of forces, and his mind is altogether occupied with the fymbols of mathematical reafoning.

502. The fecond part of the tafk, the afcertaining the accumulated effect of the force E G, is, in general, much more difficult. It includes both the changes made on the radius vector S E, and the change made in the curvature of the orbit. The department of mathematical fcience immediately fubfervient to this purpofe, is in a more imperfect ftate than the quadrature of curves. The procefs is carried on, almoft entirely by means of converging feriefes. We cannot add any thing here that tends to make it plainer. The lunar theory of Newton, with the commentary of Le Seur and Jacquier, commonly called *the Jefuits' Commentary*, gives very good examples of the methods which muft be followed in this procefs. We muft refer to the works of Euler, Clairaut, Simpfon, and De la Place, on the perturbations of Ju-

piter

piter and Saturn, &c. and content ourselves with merely pointing out some of the more general and obvious confequences of this mutual action of the planets. La Lande has given in his aftronomy a very good fynopfis of the moft approved method. In the *Tracts Phyfical and Mathematical*, by Dr Matthew Stewart, and in his Effay on the Diftance of the Sun, are fome beautiful fpecimens of the geometrical folutions of thefe problems.

503. When we confidering the motion of an inferior planet, difturbed by its gravitation to a fuperior planet, we fee that the inferior planet is retarded in the quadrants C P and O Q, and accelerated in the quadrants P O and Q C of its fynodical period. Its orbit is more incurvated in the vicinity of the points P and Q, and its curvature is diminifhed in the vicinity of the points O and C, and moft of all in the vicinity of C in the line of conjunction with the fuperior planet. Therefore, if the aphelion and perihelion of the inferior planet fhould chance to be near the line J C S O of the fynodical motion, thefe points will feem to fhift forward. For, the gravitation of the inferior planet to the Sun being diminifhed, it will not be able fo foon to bend its path to a right angle with the radius vector. On the other hand, fhould the apfides of the inferior orbit be near the line P S Q, the increafe of the inferior planet's gravitation to the Sun muft fooner produce this effect, and it will arrive fooner at its aphelion or perihelion, or thofe points will feem to come weftward and to meet it. And thus,

Fig.53.

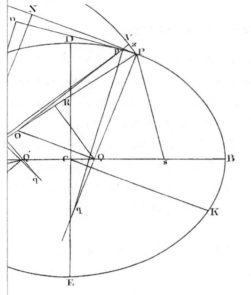

Fig.54.

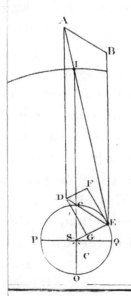

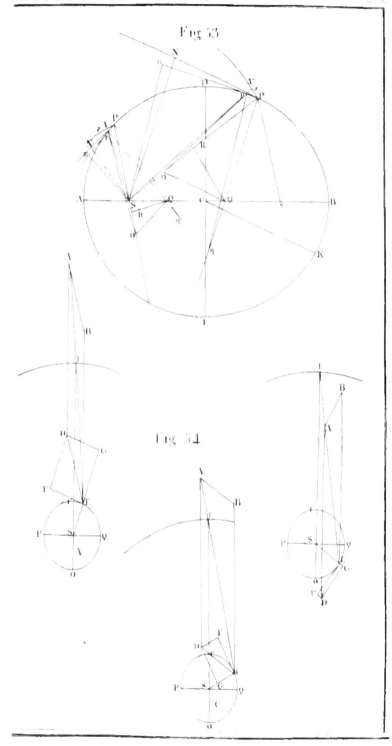

Fig 53

Fig 54

thus, in every fynodical revolution, the apfides of the inferior planet will twice advance and twice retreat, as if the elliptical orbit fhifted a little to the eaftward or weftward. But, as the diminution of the inferior planet's gravitation to the Sun is much greater when it is in the line C S O than the augmentation of it when in the line P S Q, the advances of the apfides, in the courfe of a fynodical period will exceed the retreats, and, on the whole, they will advance.

The perturbations of the motion of a fuperior planet by its gravitation to an inferior, are in general oppofite, both in kind and in direction, to thofe of the inferior planet. Therefore, in general, their apfides retreat.

All thefe derangements, or deviations from the fimple elliptical motion, are diftinctly obferved in the heavens; and the calculated effect on each planet correfponds with what is obferved, with all the precifion that can be wifhed for. It is evident that this calculation muft be extremely complicated, and that the effect depends not only on the refpective pofitions, but alfo on the quantities of matter of the different planets. For thefe reafons, as Jupiter and Saturn are much larger than any of the other planets, thefe anomalies are chiefly owing to thefe two planets. The apfides of all the planets are obferved to advance, except thofe of Saturn, which fenfibly retreat, chiefly by the action of Jupiter. The apfides of the planet difcovered by Dr Herfchel doubtlefs retreats confiderably, by the action of the great planets Jupiter and Saturn. It might be imagined that the vaft number

3 C   of

3 C

of

of comets, which are almoſt conſtantly without the orbits of the planets, would cauſe a general advance of all
the apſides. But theſe bodies are ſo far off, and probably contain ſo little matter, that their action is inſenſible.

504. The alternate accelerations and retardations of
the planets Mercury, Venus, the Earth, and Mars, in
conſequence of their mutual gravitations, and their gravitations to Jupiter, nearly compenſate each other in e-
very revolution; and no effects of them remain after a
long tract of time, except an advance of their apſides.
But there are peculiarities in the orbits of Jupiter and
Saturn, which occaſion very ſenſible accumulations, and
have given conſiderable trouble to the aſtronomers in diſcovering their cauſes. The period of Saturn's revolution
round the Sun increaſes very ſenſibly, each being about
7 hours longer than the preceding. On the contrary,
the period of Jupiter is obſerved to diminiſh about half
as much, that is, about $1\frac{1}{4}$ hours in each revolution.

This is owing to the particular poſition of the aphe-
lions of thoſe two planets. Let A B P C (fig. 55.) be
the elliptical orbit of Jupiter, A being the aphelion and
P the perihelion. Suppoſe the orbit *a b p c* of Saturn to
be a circle, having the Sun S in the centre, and let Saturn be ſuppoſed to be in *a*. Then, becauſe Jupiter employs more time (about 140 days) in moving from A to
C than in moving from C to P, he muſt retard the motion of Saturn more than he accelerates him, and Jupiter
muſt

muſt be more accelerated by Saturn than he is retarded. The contrary muſt happen if Saturn be in the oppoſite part *p* of his orbit. After a tract of ſome revolutions, all muſt be compenſated, becauſe there will be as many oppoſitions of Saturn to the Sun on one ſide of the tranſverſe diameter of Jupiter's orbit as on the other.

But if the orbit of Saturn be an ellipſe, as in fig. 55. B, and if the aphelion *a* be 90 degrees more advanced in the order of the ſigns than the aphelion A of Jupiter, it is plain that there will be more oppoſitions of Saturn while Jupiter is moving over the ſemiellipſe A C P, than while he moves over the ſemiellipſe P B A, for Saturn is about 400 days longer in the portion *b a c* of his orbit; and therefore Saturn will, on the whole, be retarded, and Jupiter accelerated.

Now, it is a fact that the aphelion of Saturn is 70 degrees more advanced on the ecliptic than that of Jupiter. Therefore theſe changes muſt happen, and the retardations of Saturn muſt exceed the accelerations. They do ſo, nearly in the proportion of 353 to 352. This exceſs will continue for about 2000 years, when the angle A S *p* will be 90 degrees complete. It will then begin to decreaſe, and will continue decreaſing for 16000 years, after which Saturn will be accelerated, and Jupiter will be retarded. The preſent retardation of Saturn is about 2', or a day's motion, in a century, and the concomitant acceleration of Jupiter is about half as much. (See *Mem. Acad. Par.* 1746.)

M. de la Place has happily ſucceeded in account-

ing

ing for feveral irregularities in this gradual change of the
mean motions of thefe two planets, which had confiderably
perplexed the aftronomers in their attempts to afcertain
their periods and their maximum by mere obfervation.
Thefe were accompanied by an evident change in the
elliptical equations of the orbit, indicating a change of
eccentricity. M. de la Place has fhewn that all are
precife confequences of univerfal gravitation, and depend
on the *near* equality of five times the angular motion of
Saturn to twice that of Jupiter, while the deviation from
perfect equality of thofe two motions introduces a variation in thefe irregularities, which has a very long period
(about 877 years). He has at laft given an equation,
which expreffes the motions with fuch accuracy, that the
calculated place agrees with the modern obfervations,
and with the moft ancient, without an error exceeding 2'. (See *Mem. Acad. Par.* 1785.)

505. In confequence of the mutual gravitation of
the planets, the node of the difturbed planet retreats on
the orbit of the difturbing planet. Thus, let E K (fig. 56.)
be the plane of the difturbing planet's orbit, and let A B
be the path of the other planet, approaching to the node
N. As the difturbing planet is fomewhere in the plane
E K, its attraction for A tends to make A approach
that plane. We may fuppofe the oblique attraction refolved into two forces, one of which is parallel to E K,
and the other perpendicular to it. Let this laft be fuch
that, in the time that the planet A, if not difturbed,
would

would move from A to B, the perpendicular force would
caufe it to defcribe the fmall fpace A C.   By the combined action of this force A C with the motion A B, the
planet defcribes the diagonal A D, and croffes the plane
E K in the point *n*.   Thus the node has fhifted from N
to *n*, in a direction contrary to that of the planet's motion.   The planet now proceeds in the line *n a*, getting
to the other fide of the plane E K.   The attraction of
the difturbing planet now becomes oblique again to the
plane, and is partly employed in drawing A (now in *a*)
toward the plane.   Let this part of the attraction be a-
gain reprefented by a fmall fpace *a c*.   This, compounded with the progreffive motion *a b*, produces a motion in
the diagonal *a d*, as if the planet had come, not from *n*,
but from N′, a point ftill more to the weftward.   The
node feems again to have fhifted *in antecedentiâ fignorum*.
And thus it appears that, both in approaching the node,
and in quitting the node, the node itfelf fhifts its place,
in a direction contrary to that of the motion of the difturbed planet.

It is farther obfervable that the inclination of the difturbed orbit increafes while the planet approaches the
node, and diminifhes during the fubfequent recefs from
it.   The original inclination A N E becomes A *n* E, which
is greater than A N E.   The angle A *n* E or *a n* K is afterwards changed into *a* N′ K, which is lefs than *a n* K.

In this manner we perceive that when a planet, having croffed the ecliptic, proceeds on the other fide of
it, the node recedes, that is, the planet moves as if it
had

had come from a node fituated farther weft on the ecliptic ; and all the while, the inclination of the orbit to the ecliptic is diminifhing. When the planet has got 90° eaftward from the node which it quitted, it is at the greateft diftance from the ecliptic, and, in its farther progrefs, it approaches the oppofite node. Its path now bends more and more *toward* the ecliptic, and the inclination of its orbit to the ecliptic increafes, and it croffes the ecliptic again, in a point confiderably to the weftward of the point where it croffed it before.

The confequence of this modification of the mutual action of the planets is, that the nodes of all their orbits in the ecliptic recede on the ecliptic, except the node of Jupiter's orbit J J (fig. 57.), which advances on the ecliptic E K, by retreating on the orbit S S of Saturn, from which Jupiter fuffers the greateft difturbance *.

506. We have hitherto confidered the ecliptic as a permanent circle of the heavens. But it now appears that the Earth muft be attracted out of that plane by the other

---

* As this motion of the nodes, and that of the apfides formerly mentioned, become fenfible by continual accumulation, and as they are equally fufceptible of accurate meafure and comparifon as the greater gravitations which retain the revolving bodies in their orbits, Mr Machin, profeffor of aftronomy at Grefham College, propofed them as the fitteft phenomena for informing us of the diftance of the Sun. Dr Matthew

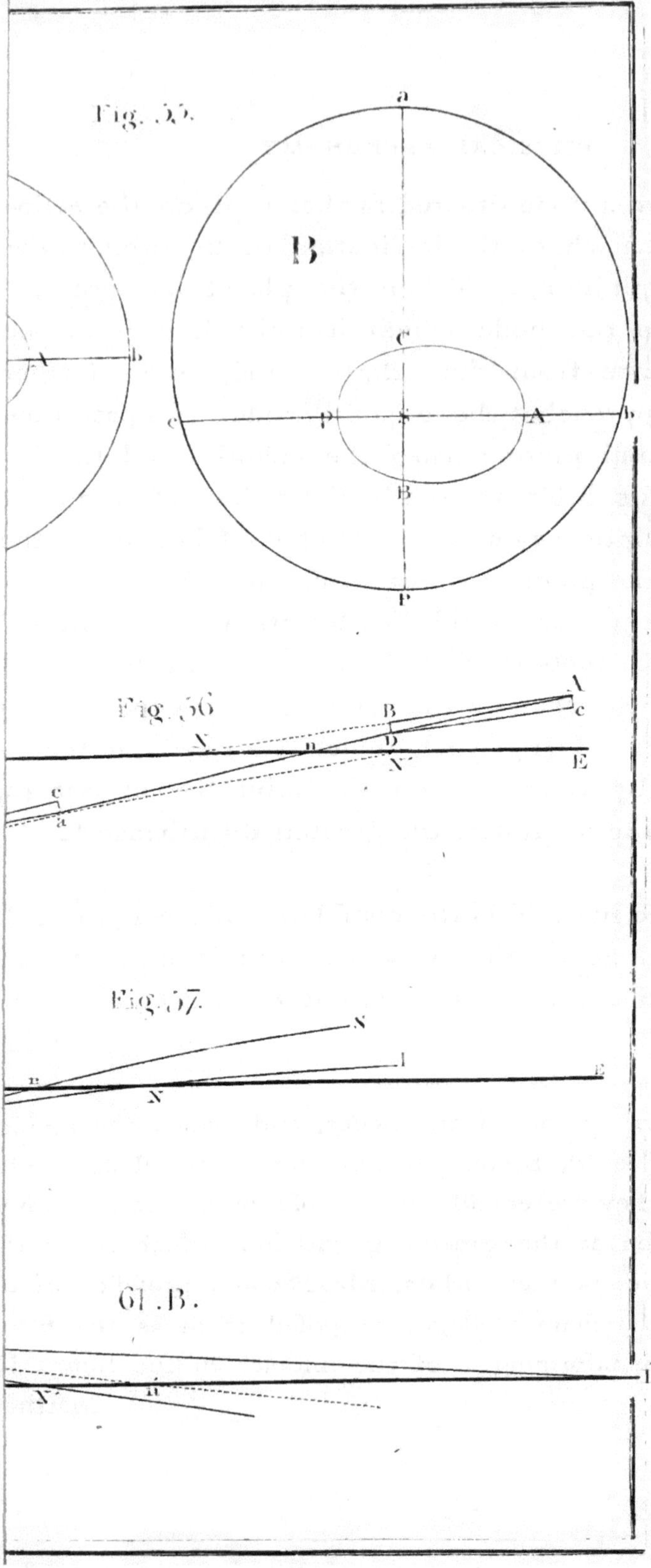

Pl. 10.   P.390.

Fig. 55.

B

A

c

C

P

A

B

P

Fig. 56

A
c
B
N
n
D
N'
E
c
a

Fig. 57.

S
n
l
E
N

61. B.

N'
n
I

Pl. 15

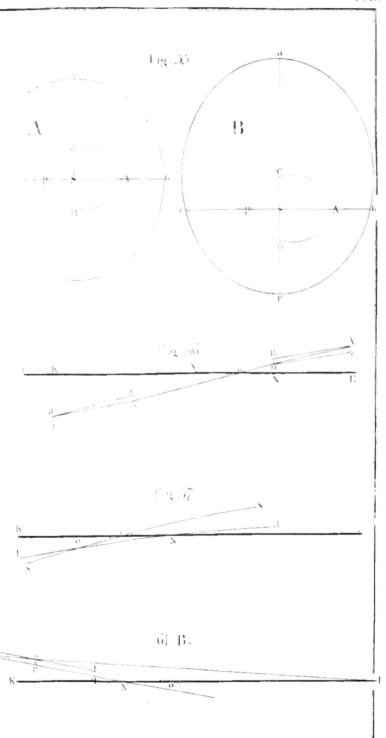

Fig. 55

Fig. 56

Fig. 57

Fig. 58

other planets. As we refer every phenomenon to the e-
cliptic by its latitude and longitude in relation to the apparent path of the Sun, it is plain that this deviation of
the Sun from a fixed plane, muſt change the latitude of
all the ſtars. The change is ſo very ſmall, however, that
it never would have been perceived, had it not been
pointed out to the aſtronomers by Newton, as neceſſarily
following from the univerſal gravitation of matter. The
ecliptic (or rather the Sun's path) has a ſmall irregular
motion round two points ſituated about 7¼ degrees weſtward from our equinoctial points.

507. The comets appear to be very greatly deranged
in their motions by their gravitation to the planets. The
Halleyan comet has been repeatedly ſo diſturbed, by paſſing near to Jupiter, that its periods were very conſiderably altered by this action. A comet, obſerved in 1770
by Lexel, Proſperin, and other accurate aſtronomers, has
been ſo much deranged in its motions, that its orbit has
been totally changed. Its mean diſtance, period, and perihelion diſtance, calculated from good obſervations,
which

Matthew Stewart made a trial of this method, employing
chiefly the motion of the lunar apogee, and has deduced a
much greater diſtance than what can be fairly deduced from
the tranſit of Venus. Notwithſtanding ſome overſights in the
ſummations there given of the diſturbing forces, the concluſion ſeems unexceptionable, and the Sun's diſtance is, in all
probability, not leſs than 110 or 115 millions of miles.

35

ha
tic
ec
ea
gr
pr
be
cli
cr
w

ac
in
Ju
cli
fr

pe
th

fo
tic
an
re
tr
pl

which had been continued during three months, agreed
with all the obfervations within 1' of a degree. In its
aphelion, it is a fmall matter more remote than Jupiter,
and muft have been fo near him in 1767 (about $\frac{1}{60}$ of
its diftance from the Sun) that its gravitation to Jupiter
muft have been thrice as great as that to the Sun. Moreover, in its revolution following this appearance in 1770,
namely on the 23d of Auguft 1777, it muft have come
vaftly nearer to Jupiter, and its gravitation to Jupiter
muft have exceeded its gravitation to the Sun more than
200 times. No wonder then that it has been diverted
into quite a different path, and that aftronomers cannot
tell what is become of it. And this, by the way, fuggefts fome fingular and momentous reflections. The
number of the comets is certainly great, and their courfes
are unknown. They may frequently come near the planets. The comet of 1764 has one of its nodes very clofe
to the Earth's orbit, and it is very poffible that the Earth
and it may chance to be in that part of their refpective
orbits at the fame time. The effect of fuch vicinity muft
be very remarkable, probably producing fuch tides as
would deftroy moft of the habitable furface. But, as its
continuance in that great proximity muft be very momentary, by reafon of its great velocity, the effect may not be
fo great. When the comet of 1770 was fo near to Jupiter, it was *in aphelio*, moving flowly, and therefore
may have continued fome confiderable time there. Yet
it does not appear that it produced any derangement in
the motion of his fatellites. We muft therefore conclude

clude that either the comet did not continue in the path
that was fuppofed, or that it contained only a very fmall
quantity of matter, being perhaps little more than a
denfe vapour. Many circumftances in the appearance
of comets countenance this opinion of their nature. As
they retire to very great diftances from the Sun, and in
that remote fituation move very flowly, they may greatly
difturb each other's motion. It is therefore a reafonable
conjecture of Sir Ifaac Newton that the comet of 1680,
at its next approach to the Sun, may really fall into him
altogether.

Of the Lunar Inequalities.

508. Of all the heavenly bodies, the Moon has attracted the greateft notice, and her motions have been
the moft fcrupuloufly examined : and it may be added,
that of them all fhe has been the moft refractory. It is
but within thefe few years paft that we have been able
to afcertain her motions with the precifion attained in
the cafes of the other planets. Not that her apparent
path is contorted, like thofe of Mercury and Venus, running into loops and knots, but becaufe the orbit is continually fhifting its place and changing its form; and her real
motions in it are accelerated, retarded, and deflected, in
a great variety of ways. While the afcertaining the
place of Jupiter or Saturn requires the employment of
five or fix equations, the Moon requires at leaft forty to

3 D

attain the *fame* exactnefs. The corrections introduced by thofe equations are fo various, both in their magnitude and in their periods, and have, of confequence, been fo blended and complicated together, that it furpaffed the power of obfervation to difcover the greateft part of them, becaufe we did not know the occafions which made them neceffary, or the phyfical connexion which they had with the afpects of the other bodies of the folar fyftem. Only fuch as arofe to a confpicuous magnitude, and had an evident relation to the fituation of the Sun, were fifhed out from among the reft.

509. From all this complication and embarraffment the difcovery of univerfal gravitation has freed us. We have only to follow this into its confequences, as modified by the particular fituation of the Moon, and we get an equation, which *muft* be made, in order to determine a deviation from fimple elliptical motion that *muft* refult from the action of the Sun. This alone, followed regularly into all its confequences, gives, all the great equations which the fagacity of obfervers had difcovered, and a multitude of other corrections, which no fagacity could ever have detected.

> *Difcimus hinc tandem quâ cauſâ argentea Phœbe*
> *Paſſibus haud æquis eat, cur ſubdita nulli*
> *Hactenus aſtronomo, numerorum fræna recuſat*
> *Obvia conſpicimus, nubem pollente mathefi.*

We have feen (232.) that fince the Moon accompanies the Earth in its revolution round the Sun, we muft

conclude

conclude that fhe is under the influence of that force which deflects the Earth into that revolution. If, in every inftant, the Moon were impelled by precifely the fame force which then impels the Earth, and if this force were alfo in the fame direction, the Moon's motion relative to the Earth would not fuftain any change (98.) She would defcribe an accurate ellipfe having the Earth in the focus, and would defcribe areas proportional to the times. But neither of thefe conditions are agreeable to the real ftate of things. The Moon is fometimes nearer to the Sun, and fometimes more remote from him than the Earth is, and is therefore more or lefs attracted by him ; and though the diftances of both from the Sun are fometimes equal (as when the Moon is in quadrature) the direction of her gravitation to the Sun is then confiderably different from that of the Earth's gravitation to him.

Thefe circumftances change confiderably all her motions relative to the Earth. But, fince the planetary force follows the precife inverfe duplicate ratio of the diftances, we can tell what its intenfity is in every pofition of the Moon, in what direction it acts, and what deviation it will produce during any interval of time. We may proceed in the following manner.

510. Let S (fig. 59.) reprefent the Sun, E the Earth, moving in the arch A E B. Let the Moon be fuppofed to defcribe round the Earth the circle C B O A. Join E S and M S, and let S M cut the Earth's orbit in N.

3 D 2　　　　　　　　Laftly,

Laftly, Let E S be taken as the meafure of the Earth's gravitation to the Sun, and as the fcale on which we eftimate the difturbing forces.

To learn the magnitude and direction of the force which difturbs the Moon's motion when fhe is in any point M of her orbit, gravitating to the Sun in the direction M S, we muft inftitute the following. analogy M S² : E S² = E S : M G. Then it is evident that if the Moon's gravitation to the Sun be reprefented by E S when fhe is in the points A or B, equally diftant with the Earth, M G will reprefent her gravitation to the Sun when fhe is in M ; for it is to E S in the inverfe duplicate ratio of the diftances from him.

Now this force M G, being neither equal to E S, nor in the fame direction, muft change or difturb the Moon's motion relative to the Earth. We may fuppofe M G to refult from the combined action of two forces M F and M H (that is, M G may be the diagonal of a parallelogram M F G H), of which one, M F, is parallel and equal to E S. Were the Earth and Moon urged by the forces E S and M F only, their relative motions would not be affected (98.) Therefore M H alone difturbs this relative motion, and may be taken for its indication and meafure.

The difturbing force may be otherwife reprefented, by varying the conditions on which the parallelogram M F G H is formed. It may be formed on the fuppofition that one fide of the parallelogram fhall have the direction M E. And this is perhaps the beft way of refolving

folving M G for the purpofes of calculation, and accordingly has been moft generally employed by the great geometers who have cultivated this theory. But the method followed in this outline was thought more elementary, and moft illuftrative of the effeects.

The magnitude and direction of this difturbing force depends on the form of the parallelogram M F G H, and confequently on the proportion of M F and M G, and on their relative pofitions. We may obtain an eafy expreffion of the force M H by the confideration that the rate of increafe of MS^2 is double of the rate of increafe of M S. When a line increafes by a very fmall addition, the ratio of the increment of the line to the line is but the half of that of the fquare to the fquare. Thus, let the line M S be fuppofed 100, and E S 101, differing by one part in a hundred. We have $MS^2 = 10000$, and $ES^2 = 10201$, differing by very nearly two parts in a hundred; the error of this fuppofition being only one part in ten thoufand. Suppofe M S = 1000, and E S = 1001, differing by one part in a thoufand. Then $MS^2 = 1000000$, and $ES^2 = 1002001$, differing from MS^2 by two parts in a thoufand very nearly, the error of the fuppofition being only one part in a million, &c. &c.

Now the greateft difference that can occur between E S and M S is at new and full Moon, when the Moon is in C or O. In this cafe E C is nearly the 390th part of E S, and we have $ES^2 : OS^2 = 390^2 : 391^2$, or $= 390 : 392,026$; and therefore, in fuppofing ES^2 to OS^2

as 390 to 392, we commit an error of no more than
$\frac{1}{40}$ of $\frac{1}{392}$, that is $\frac{1}{15680}$, viz. lefs than one part in
fifteen thoufand, in the moft unfavourable circumftances.
Therefore the difference between N S (or E S) and M G
may be fuppofed equal to M D, without any fenfible
error, that is, to the double of N M, the difference of
N S and M S. Therefore M G — N S = 2 M N very
nearly, and M G — M S, that is, S G = 3 M N very
nearly. We may alfo take M I for M H without any
fenfible error, and may fuppofe E I = 3 M N. For the
lines M F, I P, H G, being equal and parallel, and S P
nearly coinciding with S G, from which it never deviates
more than 9′, E I will nearly coincide with E H, = S G,
= 3 M N nearly.

511. Thefe confiderations will give us a very fimple
manner of reprefenting and meafuring the difturbing
force in every pofition of the Moon, which will have no
error that can be of any fignificance. Moreover, any
error that inheres in it, is completely compenfated by an
equal error of an oppofite kind in another point of the
orbit. Therefore

Let us fuppofe that the portion of the Earth's path
round the Sun fenfibly coincides with the ftraight line
A B (fig. 60.) perpendicular to the line O C S, paffing
through the Sun, and called the line of the SYZIGIES, as
A B is called the line of the QUADRATURES. Let M D
crofs A B at right angles, and produce it to R fo that
M P = 3 M N. Join R E, and draw M I parallel to it.

M I

M I will, in all cafes, have the pofition and magnitude correfponding to the difturbing force.

Or, more fimply, make $EI = 3 MN$, taking the point I on the fame fide of A B with M, and draw M I. M I is the difturbing force.

512. This force M I may be refolved into two, viz. M L, having the direction of the Moon's motion, and M K, perpendicular to her motion, that is, M K lying in the direction of the radius vector M E, and M L having the direction of the tangent. The force M L affects the Moon's angular motion round the Earth, either accelerating or retarding it, while the force M K either augments or diminifhes her gravitation to the Earth.

The difturbing force M I may alfo be refolved into $MR' = 3 MN$, and R' I, or M E; that is, into a force always proportional to M N, and in that direction, and another force in the direction of the Moon's gravitation to the Earth. This is ufeful on another occafion.

513. When the Moon is in quadrature, the point I coincides with E, becaufe there is no M N. In this cafe, therefore, the force M L does not exift, and M K coincides with M E. The difturbing force M I is now wholly employed in augmenting the Moon's gravitation to the Earth. The gravitations of the Earth and Moon to the Sun are equal, but not parallel. If E S exprefles the magnitude of the Moon's gravitation to the Sun, then M E will exprefs (on the fame fcale) the augmentation

in

in quadratures of the Moon's gravitation to the Earth,
occafioned by the obliquity of the Sun's action. It is
convenient to take this quadrature augment of the Moon's
gravitation to the Earth as the unit of the fcale on which
all the difturbing forces are meafured, and to calculate
what fraction of her whole gravitation it amounts to.

514. Let G exprefs the Moon's gravitation to the
Sun, g her gravitation to the Earth, and g' the increafe
of this gravitation. Alfo let y and m be the length of a
fydereal year and of a fydereal month. In order to learn
in what proportion the Moon's gravitation to the Earth
is affected by the difturbing force, it will be convenient
to know what proportion its increment in quadrature has
to the whole gravitation. We may therefore inftitute
the following proportions.

$$G : g = \frac{D}{P^2} : \frac{d}{p^2} = \frac{ES}{y^2} : \frac{EB}{m^2} \quad *$$

$$g' : G = \qquad\qquad EB : ES. \quad \text{Therefore}$$

$$g' : g = \qquad \frac{ES \times EB}{y^2} : \frac{EB \times ES}{m^2}, = m^2 : y^2.$$

$$\qquad\qquad\qquad\qquad\qquad\qquad\qquad\qquad\qquad\qquad\text{The}$$

$* \dfrac{ES}{y^2} : \dfrac{EB}{m^2} = \dfrac{390}{365,256^2} : \dfrac{1}{27,322^2}, = 2,1833 : 1$

very nearly. Thus we fee that the Moon's gravitation to the
Sun is more than twice her gravitation to the Earth. The
confequence of this is, that even when the Moon is in conjunction, at new Moon, between the Earth and the Sun, her
path in abfolute fpace is concave toward the Sun, and convex
toward

The Moon's mean gravitation to the Earth is there-fore to its increment in the quadratures by the action of the Sun, in the duplicate ratio of the Earth's period round the Sun to the lunar period round the Earth. This is very nearly in the proportion of 179 to 1. Her gravi-tation is increased, when in quadrature, about $\frac{1}{179}$. This will diminish the chord of curvature and increase the curvature in the same proportion.

515. In order to fee what change it fuftains in any other pofition of the Moon, fuch as M, join E D, and draw

---

toward the Earth. Even there fhe is deflected, not toward the Earth, but toward the Sun. This is a very curious, and feemingly paradoxical affertion. But nothing is better efta-blifhed. The tracing the Moon's motion in abfolute fpace is the completeft demonftration of it. It is not a looped curve, as one, at firft thinking, would imagine, but a line always concave toward the Sun. Indeed fcarcely any things can be more unlike than the real motions of the Moon are to what we firft imagine them to be. At new Moon, fhe appears to be moving to the left, and we fee her gradually paffing the ftars, leaving them to the right; and, calculating from the diftance 240000 miles, and the angular motion, about half a degree in an hour, we fhould fay that fhe is moving to the left at the rate of 38 miles in a minute. But the fact is that fhe is then moving to the right at the rate of 1100 miles in a minute. But as the Earth, from whence we view her, is moving at the rate of 1140 miles in a minute, the Moon is left behind.

3 F.

draw D Q perpendicular to E M. It is plain that D Q
is the fine of the angle D E Q, which is twice the angle
O E Q or C E M, that is, twice the Moon's diftance
from the neareft fyzigy. Q E is the cofine of the fame
angle. The triangles M D Q and E I K are fimilar.
E I is equal to $1\frac{1}{2}$ M D. Therefore E K = $1\frac{1}{2}$ M Q,
= $1\frac{1}{2}$ M E + $1\frac{1}{2}$ E Q, ufing the fign + when D E m is
lefs than 90°, or C E M is lefs than 45°, and the fign —
when C E M is greater than 45°. Therefore M K =
$\frac{2}{3}$ M E + $1\frac{1}{2}$ E Q. Therefore, if $\frac{1}{2}$ M E be equal to
$1\frac{1}{2}$ E Q, that is, if M E be = 3 E Q, M K is reduced
to nothing, or the force M I is then perpendicular to the
radius vector, or is a tangent to the circle. The angle
C E M, or the arch C M, has then its fecant E I equal
to thrice its cofine M N. This arch is 54° 44'. There
are therefore four points in the circular orbit diftant
54° 44' from the line of the fyzigies, where the Moon's
gravitation to the Earth is not affected by the action of
the Sun. If the arch C M exceed this, the point K
will lie within the orbit, as in fig. 60. 2. indicating an
augmentation of the Moon's gravitation to the Earth.

At B, $1\frac{1}{2}$ E Q = $1\frac{1}{2}$ E M, and therefore $1\frac{1}{2}$ E Q —
$\frac{1}{2}$ E M = E M, as before.

516. At O and at C, $1\frac{1}{2}$ E Q + $\frac{1}{2}$ E M = 2 E M.
Therefore, in the fyzigies, the diminution of the Moon's
gravitation to the Earth is double of the augmentation
of it in quadratures, or it is $\dfrac{1}{89\frac{1}{2}}$ of her gravitation to
the Earth.

517.

517. With refpect to the force M L, it is evidently = 1½ D Q or 1½ of the fine of twice the Moon's diftance from oppofition or conjunction. It augments from the fyzigy to the octant, where it is a maximum, and from thence it diminifhes to nothing in the quadrature. In its maximum ftate, it is about $\frac{1}{170}$ of the Moon's gravitation to the Earth.

518. It appears, by conftructing the figure for the different pofitions of the Moon in the courfe of a lunation, that this force M L retards the Moon's motion round the Earth in the firft and third quarters C A and O B, but accelerates her motion in the fecond and laft quarters A O and B C. Thus, in fig. 60, M L leads from M in a direction oppofite to that of the Moon's motion eaftward from her conjunction at C to her firft quadrature in A. In fig. 60. 3. M L lies in the direction of her motion ; and it is plain that M L will be firmilarly fituated in the quadrants C A and O B, as alfo in the quadrants A O and B C.

All thefe difturbing forces depend on the proportion of E B to E S. Therefore, while E S remains the fame, the difturbing forces will change in the fame proportion with the Moon's diftance from the Earth.

519. But let us fuppofe that E S changes in the courfe of the Earth's motion in her elliptical orbit. Then, did the Sun continue to act with the fame force as before, ftill the difturbing force would change in the pro-

portion

portion of E S, becoming fmaller as E S becomes greater, becaufe the proportion of E B to E S becomes fmaller. But, when E S increafes, the gravitation to the Sun diminifhes in the duplicate ratio of E S. Therefore the difturbing force varies in the inverfe proportion of ES^3, and, in general, is $\dot{=} \dfrac{EB}{ES^3}$. Therefore, as the Earth is nearer to the Sun about $\frac{1}{60}$ in January than in July, it follows that in January all the difturbing forces will be nearly $\frac{1}{20}$ greater than in July.

What has now been faid muft fuffice for an account of the forces which difturb the Moon's motion in the different parts of a circular orbit round the Earth. The fame forces operate on the Moon revolving in her true elliptical orbit, but varying, with the Moon's diftance from the Earth. They operate in the fame manner, producing, not the fame motions, but the fame changes of motion.

520. It would feem now that it is not a very difficult matter to compute the motion and the place of the Moon for any particular moment. But it is one of the moft difficult problems that have employed the talents of the firft mathematicians of Europe. Sir Ifaac Newton has treated this fubject with his ufual fuperiority, in his Principles of Natural Philofophy, and in the feparate Effay on the Lunar Theory. But he only began the fubject, and contented himfelf with marking the principal topics of inveftigation, pointing out the roads that were

to be held in each, and furnishing us with the mathematics and the methods which were to be followed. In all these particulars, great improvements have been made by Euler, D'Alembert, Clairaut, and Mayer of Gottingen. This last gentleman, by a most sagacious examination and comparison of the *data* furnished by observation, and a judicious employment of the physical principles of Sir Isaac Newton, has constructed equations so exactly fitted to the various circumstances of the case, that he has made his lunar tables correspond with observation, both the most ancient and the most recent, to a degree of exactness that is not exceeded in any tables of the primary planets, and far surpassing any other tables of the lunar motions.

We can, with propriety, only make some very general observations on the effects of the continued action of the disturbing forces.

521. In the syzigies and quadrature, the combined force, arising from the Moon's natural gravitation to the Earth and the Sun's disturbing force, is directed to the Earth. Therefore the Moon will, notwithstanding the disturbing force, continue to describe areas proportional to the times. But as soon as the Moon quits those stations, the tangential force M L begins to operate, and the combined force is no longer directed precisely to the Earth. In the octants, where the tangential force is at its maximum, it causes the combined force to deviate

about

about half a degree from the radius vector, and therefore
confiderably affects the angular motion.

Let the Moon fet out from the fecond or fourth octant, with her mean angular velocity. Therefore M L,
then at its maximum, increafes continually this velocity,
which augments, till the Moon comes to a fyzigy. Here
the accelerating force ends, and a retarding force begins
to act, and the motion is now retarded by the fame degrees by which it was accelerated juft before. At the
next octant, the fum of the retardations from the fyzigy
is juft equal to the fum of the accelerations from the
preceding octant. The velocity of the Moon is now
reduced to its mean ftate. But her place is more advanced by 37′ than it would have been, had the Moon
not been affected by the Sun, but had moved from the
fyzigy with her mean velocity. Proceeding in her courfe
from this octant, the retardation continues, and in the
quadrature the velocity is reduced to its loweft ftate ;
but here the accelerating force begins again, and reftores
the velocity to its mean ftate in the next octant.

Thus, it appears that in the octants, the velocity is
always in its medium ftate, attains a maximum in paffing through a fyzigy, and is the leaft poffible in quadrature. In the firft and third octant, the Moon is 37′
eaft, or a-head, of her mean place ; and in the fecond
and fourth, is as much to the weftward of it ; and in the
fyzigies and quadratures her mean and true places are
the fame. Thus, when her velocity differs. moft from
its medium ftate, her calculated and obferved places

are

are the fame, and where her velocity has attained its mean ftate, her calculated and obferved places differ moft widely. This is the cafe with all aftronomical equations. The motions are computed firft in their mean ftate ; and when the changing caufes increafe to a maximum, and then diminifh to nothing, the effect, which is a change of place, has attained its maximum by continual addition or deduction.

522. This alternate increafe and diminution of the Moon's angular motion in the courfe of a lunation was firft difcovered, or at leaft diftinguifhed from the other irregularities of her motion, by Tycho Brahé, and by him called the Equation of VARIATION. The deduction of it from the principle of univerfal gravitation by Sir Ifaac Newton is the moft elegant and perfpicuous fpecimen of mechanical inveftigation that is to be feen. The addrefs which he has fhewn in giving fenfible reprefentations and meafures of the momentary actions, and of their accumulated refults, in all parts of the orbit, are peculiarly pleafing to all perfons of a mathematical tafte, and are fo appofite and plain, that the inveftigation becomes highly inftructive to a beginner in this part of the higher mathematics. The late Dr Mathew Stewart, in his *Tracts Phyfical and Mathematical*, following Newton's example, has given fome very beautiful examples of the fame method.

523. We have hitherto confidered the Moon's orbit as circular, and muft now inquire whether its form will

suffer

fuffer any change. We may expect that it will, fince
we fee a very great diiturbing force diminifhing its ter-
reitrial gravity in the fyzigies, and increafing it in the
quadratures. Let us fuppofe the Moon to fet out from
a point 35° 16' fhort of a quadrature. The force M K,
which we may call a centripetal force, begins to act, increafing the deflecting force. This muft render the orbit more incurvated in that part, and this change will
be continued through the whole of the arch extending
35° 16' on each fide of the quadrature. At 35° 16' caft
of a quadrature, the gravity recovers its mean ftate; but
the path at this point now makes an acute angle with the
radius vector, which brings the Moon nearer to the
Earth in paffing through the point of conjunction or oppofition. Through the whole of the arch V v, extending 54° 44' on each fide of the fyzigies, the Moon's gravitation is greatly diminifhed; and therefore her orbit in
this place is flattened, or made lefs curve than the circle.
till at v, 54° 44' caft of the fyzigy, the Moon's gravity
recovers its mean ftate, and the orbit its mean curvature.

524. In this manner, the orbit, from being circular,
becomes of an oval form, moft incurvated at A and B,
and leaft fo at O and C, and having its longeft diameter
lying in the quadratures; not exactly however in thofe
points, on account of the variation of velocity which we
have fhewn to be greateft in the fecond and fourth quadrants. The longeft diameter lies a fmall matter fhort

of

of the points A and B, that is, to the weſtward of them. Sir Iſaac Newton has determined the proportion of the two diameters of this oval, viz. A B = 70 and O C = 69. It may ſeem ſtrange that the Moon comes neareſt to the Earth when her gravity is moſt diminiſhed; but this is owing to the incurvation of the orbit in the neighbourhood of the quadratures.

525. The Moon's orbit is not a circle, but an ellipſis, having the Earth in one of the foci. Still, however, the above aſſertions will apply, by always conceiving a circle deſcribed through the Moon's place in the real orbit. But we muſt now inquire whether this orbit alſo ſuffers any change of form by the action of the Sun.

Let us ſuppoſe that the line of the apſides coincides with the line of ſyzigies, and that the Moon is in apogee. Her gravitation to the Earth is diminiſhed in conjunction and oppoſition, ſo that, when her gravitation in perigee is compared with her gravitation in apogee, the gravitations differ more than in the inverſe duplicate ratio of the diſtance. The natural forces in perigee and apogee are inverſely as the ſquares of the diſtance. If the diminutions by the Sun's action were alſo inverſely as the ſquare of the diſtance, the remaining gravitations would be in the ſame proportion ſtill. But this is far from being the caſe here; for the diminutions are directly as the diſtance, and the greateſt quantity is taken from the ſmalleſt force. Therefore the forces thus diminiſhed muſt differ in a greater proportion than before, that is,

3 F

in

in a greater ratio than the inverfe of the fquare of the
diftances. *

Let the Moon come from the apogee of this difturbed orbit. Did her gravity increafe in the due proportion,
fhe would come to the proper perigee. But it increafes in
a greater proportion, and will bring the Moon nearer to
the focus ; that is, the orbit will become more eccentric,
and its elliptical equation will increafe along with the
eccentricity. Similar effects will refult in the Moon's
motion from perigee to apogee. Her apogean gravity
being too much diminifhed, fhe will go farther off, and
thus the eccentricity and the equation of the orbit will
be increafed. Suppofe the Moon to change when in
apogee, and that we calculate her place feven days after,
when fhe fhould be in the vicinity of the quadrature.
We apply her elliptical equation (about 6° 20') to her
mean motion. If we compare this calculation with her
real

---

* Thus, let the following perigee and apogee diftances be
compared, and the correfponding gravitations with their diminutions and remainders.

	Perigee.	Mean.	Apogee.
Diftances - - - - -	8	10	12
Gravitations - - - -	144	100	64
Diminutions - - - -	2	$2\frac{1}{2}$	3
Remaining gravities - -	142	$97\frac{1}{2}$	61

Now $12^2 : 8^2 = 142 : 63,11$. Therefore 142 is to 61 in a much
greater ratio than the inverfe of the fquare of the diftance.

real place, we shall find the true place almost 2° behind
the calculation. We should find, in like manner, that
in the last quadrature, her calculated place, by means of
the ordinary equation of the orbit, is more than 2° behind the true or obferved place. The orbit has become
more eccentric, and the motion in it more unequable,
and requires a greater equation. This may rife to 7° 40',
inftead of 6° 20', which correfponds to the mean form of
the orbit.

But let us next fuppofe that the apfides of the orbit
lie in the quadratures, where the Moon's gravitation to
the Earth is increafed by the action of the Sun. Were
it increafed in the inverfe duplicate ratio of the diftances,
the new gravities would ftill be in this duplicate proportion. But, in the prefent cafe, the greateft addition
will be made to the fmalleft force. The apogee and
perigee gravities therefore will not differ fufficiently; and
the Moon, fetting out from the apogee in one quadrature, will not, on her arrival at the oppofite quadrature,
come fo near the Earth as fhe otherwife would have
done. Or, fhould fhe fet out from her perigee in one
quadrature, fhe will not go far enough from the Earth
in the oppofite quadrature; that is, the eccentricity of
the orbit will, in both cafes, be diminifhed, and, along
with it, the equation correfponding. Our calculations
for her place in the adjacent oppofition or conjunction,
made with the ordinary orbital equation, will be faulty,
and the errors will be of the oppofite kind to the former.

3 F 2   The

The equation neceſſary in the preſent caſe will not exceed 5° 3'.

In all intermediate poſitions of the apſides, ſimilar anomalies will be obſerved, verging to the one or the other extreme, according to the poſition of the line of the apſides. The equation *pro expediendo calculo*, by Dr Halley, contains the corrections which muſt be made on the equation of the orbit, in order to bring it into the ſtate which correſponds with the preſent eccentricity of the orbit, depending on the Sun's poſition in relation to its tranſverſe axis.

526. All theſe anomalies are diſtinctly obſerved, agreeing with the deductions from the effects of univerſal gravitation with the utmoſt preciſion. The anomaly itſelf was diſcovered by Ptolemy, and the diſcovery is the greateſt mark of his penetration and ſagacity, becauſe it is extremely difficult to find the periods and the changes of this correction, and it had eſcaped the obſervation of Hipparchus and the other eminent aſtronomers at Alexandria during three hundred years of continued obſervation. Ptolemy called it the Equation of EVECTION, becauſe he explained it by a certain ſhifting of the orbit. His explanation, or rather his hypotheſis for directing his calculation, is moſt ingenious and refined, but is the leaſt compatible with other phenomena of any of Ptolemy's contrivances.

527. The deduction of this anomaly from its phyſical principles was a far more intricate and difficult taſk than

than the variation which equation had furnished. It is
however accomplished by Newton in the completeft
manner.

It is an interefting cafe of the great *problem of three
bodies*, which has employed, and continues to employ,
the talents and beft efforts of the great mathematicians.
In   , Mr Machin gave a pretty theorem, which feemed to promife great affiftance in the folution of this problem. Newton had demonftrated that a body, deflected
by a centripetal force directed to a fixed point, moved
fo that the radius vector defcribed areas proportional to
the times. Mr Machin demonftrated that if deflected by
forces directed to two fixed points, the triangle connecting it with them (which may be called the *plana vectrix*)
alfo defcribed folids proportional to the times. Little
help has been gotten from it. The equations founded
on it, or to which it leads, are of inextricable com-
plexity.

528. Not only the form, but alfo the pofition of the
lunar orbit, muft fuffer a change by the action of the
Sun. It was demonftrated (226.) that if gravity de-
creafed fafter than in the proportion of $\frac{1}{d^2}$, the apfides of
an orbit will advance, but will retreat, if the gravitation
decreafe at a flower rate. Now, we have feen that
while the Moon is within 54° 44' of the fyzigies, the
gravity is diminifhed in a greater proportion than that of
$\frac{1}{d^2}$. Therefore the apfides which lie in this part of the
fynodical

fynodical revolution muft advance. For the oppofite
reafons, while they lie within 35° 16′ of the quadratures, they muft recede. But, fince the diminution in
fyzigy is double of the augmentation in quadrature, and
is continued through a much greater portion of the orbit, the apfides muft, in the courfe of a complete lunation, advance more than they recede, or, on the whole,
they muft advance. They muft advance moft, and recede leaft, when near the fyzigies; becaufe at this time
the diminution of gravity by the difturbing force bears
the greateft proportion to the natural diminution of gravity correfponding to the elliptical motion, and becaufe
the augmentation in quadrature will then bear the fmalleft proportion to it, becaufe the conjugate axis of the
ellipfe is in the line of quadrature.

The contrary muft happen when the apfides are near
the quadratures, and it will be found that in this cafe
the recefs will exceed the progrefs. In the octants, the
motion of the *apfides in confequentia* is equal to their
mean motion; but their place is moft diftant from their
true place, the difference being the accumulated fum of
the variations.

. But, fince in the courfe of a complete revolution of
the Earth and Moon round the Sun, the apfides take
every pofition with refpect to the line of the fyzigies,
they will, on the whole, advance. Their mean progrefs
is about three degrees in each revolution.

. 529. It has been obferved, already, that the inveftigation of the effects of the force M K is much more
                                                    difficult

difficult than that of the effects of the force M L. This laft, only treating of acceleration and retardation, rarely employs more than the direct method of fluxions, and the finding of the fimpler fluents which are expreffed by circular arches and their concomitant lines. But the very elementary part of this fecond inveftigation engages us at once in the ftudy of curvature and the variation of curvature ; and its fimpleft procefs requires infinite fe- riefes, and the higher orders of fluxions. Sir Ifaac New- ton has not confidered this queftion in the fame fyftema- tic manner that he has treated the other, but has gene- rally arrived at his conclufions by more circuitous helps, fuggefted by circumftances peculiar to the cafe, and not fo capable of a general application. He has not even given us the fteps by which he arrived at fome of his conclufions. His excellent commentators Le Seur and Jaquier have, with much addrefs, fupplied us with this in- formation. But all that they have done has been very par- ticular and limited. The determination of the motion of the lunar apogee by the theory of gravity is found to be only one half of what is really obferved. This was very foon remarked by Mr Machin, but without being able to amend it ; and it remained, for many years, a fort of blot on the doctrine of univerfal gravitation.

530. As the Newtonian mathematics continued to improve by the united labours of the firft geniufes of Europe, this inveftigation received fucceffive improve- ments alfo. At laft, M. Clairaut, about the year 1743, confidered

confidered the problem of thefe bodies, mutually gravitating, in general terms. But, finding it beyond the
reach of our attainments in geometry, unlefs confiderably limited, he confined his attention to a cafe which
fuited the interefting cafe of the lunar motions. He fuppofed one of the three bodies immenfely larger than the
other two, and at a very great diftance from them ; and
the fmalleft of the others revolving round the third in
an ellipfe little different from a circle ; and limited his
attention to the *difturbances only* of this motion.—With
this limitation, he folved the problem of the lunar theory,
and conftructed tables of the Moon's motion. But he
too found the motion of the apogee only one half of
what is obferved.—Euler, and D'Alembert, and Simpfon,
had the fame refult ; and mathematicians began to fuf-
pect that fome other force, befides that of a gravitation
inverfely as the fquare of the diftance, had fome fhare
in thefe motions.

At laft, M. Clairaut difcovered the fource of all their
miftakes and their trouble. A term had been omitted,
which had a great influence in this particular circumftance, but depended on fome of the other anomalies of
the Moon, with which he had not fufpected any connexion. He found that the difturbances, which he was
confidering as relating to the Moon's motion in the
fimple ellipfe, fhould have been confidered as relating
to the orbit already affected by the other inequalities.
When this was done, he found that the motion of the
apogee, deduced from the action of the Sun, was precifely

cifely what is obferved to obtain. Euler and D'Alembert, who were employed in the fame inveftigation, acceded without fcruple' to M. Clairaut's improvement of his analyfis ; and all are now fatisfied with refpect to the competency of the principle of univerfal gravitation to the explanation of all thefe phenomena of the lunar motions.

531. In the whole of the preceding inveftigation, we have confidered the difturbing force of the Sun as acting in the plane of the Moon's orbit, or we have confidered that orbit as coinciding with the plane of the ecliptic. But the Moon's orbit is inclined to the plane of the ecliptic nearly 5°, and therefore the Sun is feldom in its plane. His action muft generally have a tendency to draw the Moon out of the plane in which fhe is then moving, and thus to change the inclination of the Moon's orbit to the ecliptic.

But this oblique force may always be refolved into two others, one of which fhall be in the plane of the orbit, and the other perpendicular to it. The firft will be the difturbing force already confidered in all its modifications. We muft now confider the effect of the other. *

532.

---

* It is very difficult to give fuch a reprefentation of the lunar orbit, inclined to the plane of the ecliptic, that the lines which reprefent the different affections of the difturbing force

3 G   may

532. Let A C B O (fig. 61.) be the moon's orbit cutting the ecliptic in the line N N' of the nodes, the half N M A N', being raifed above the ecliptic, and the other half N B O N' being below it. The clotted circle is the orbit, turned on the line N N' till it coincide with the plane of the ecliptic. C, O, A and B are, as formerly, the points of fyzigy and quadrature. Let the Moon be in M. Let A E B be the interfection of a plane perpendicular to the ecliptic. Draw M n perpendicular to the plane A E B, and therefore parallel to the ecliptic, and to O C. Take E I equal to 3 M n, and join M I. M I is the Sun's difturbing force (511.), and E M meafures the augmentation of the Moon's gravitation when in quadrature. It is plain that M I is in a plane paffing through E S, and interfecting the lunar orbit in the line M E, and the ecliptic in the line E I. M I therefore does not lie in the plane of the lunar orbit, nor in that of the ecliptic, but is between them both. The force M I may therefore be conceived as refolvable into two forces, one of which lies in the Moon's orbit, and the other is perpendicular to it. This refolution will be effected, if we draw I i upward from the ecliptic, till it meet the plane of the lunar orbit perpendicularly in i.

Now

may appear detached from the planes of the orbit and ecliptic, and thus enable us to perceive the efficiency of them, and the nature of the effect produced. The moft attentive confideration by the reader is neceffary for giving him a diftinct notion of thefe circumftances.

Now join M i, and complete the parallelogram M i I m, having M I for its diagonal. The force M I is equivalent to M i lying in the plane of the Moon's orbit, and M m perpendicular to it. By the force M i the Moon is accelerated or retarded, and has her gravitation to the Earth augmented or diminished, while the force M m draws the Moon out of the plane N C M ; or that plane is made to fhift its pofition, fo that its interfection N N' fhifts its place a little. The inclination of the orbit to the ecliptic alfo is affected. Let a plane I i G be drawn through I i perpendicular to the line N N' of the nodes. The line E G is perpendicular to this plane, and therefore to the lines G I and G i. Alfo I i G is a right angle, becaufe I i was drawn perpendicular to the plane M i G E.

Now, if E M be confidered as the radius of the tables, M n is the fine of the Moon's diftance from quadrature. Call this q. Then E I = 3 q. Alfo making E I radius, I G is the fine of the node's diftance from the line of fyzigy. Call this s. Alfo, I G being made radius, I i or M m is the fine of the inclination of the orbit to the ecliptic. Call this i.

Therefore we have $\quad$ E M : E I = R : 3 q

$$E I : I G = R : s$$

$$I G : M m = R : i$$

Therefore $\quad$ E M : M m = R^3 : 3 $q s i$

and $\qquad$ M m = 3 E M $\times \dfrac{q s i}{R^3}$.

Thus we have obtained an expreffion of the force M m, which tends to change the pofition and inclination of the orbit.   From this expreſſion we may draw ſeveral concluſions which indicate its different effects.

Cor. 1.   This force vaniſhes, that is, there is no ſuch force when the Moon is in quadrature.   For then q, or the line **M** n, is nothing.   Now q being one of the numerical factors of the numerator of the fraction $\frac{q\,s\,i}{R^5}$, the fraction itſelf has no value.   We eaſily perceive the phyſical cauſe of the evaneſcence of the force **M** m when M comes into the line of quadrature.   When this happens, the whole diſturbing force has the direction A E, the then radius vector, and is in the plane of the orbit. There is no ſuch force as **M** m in this ſituation of things, the diſturbing force being wholly employed in augmenting the Moon's gravitation to the Earth.

2.   The force **M** m vaniſhes alſo when the nodes are in the ſyzigy.   For there, the factor s in the numerator vaniſhes.   We perceive the phyſical reaſon of this alſo. For, when the nodes are in the ſyzigies, the Sun is in the plane of the orbit ; or this plane, if produced, paſſes through the Sun.   In ſuch caſe, the diſturbing force is in the plane of the orbit, and can have no part, **M** m acting out of that plane.

3.   The chief varieties of the force **M** m depend however on s, the ſine of the node's diſtance from ſyzigy. For in every revolution, q goes through the ſame ſeries of ſucceſſive values, and i remains nearly the ſame in all revolutions.   Therefore the circumſtance which will moſt diſtinguiſh the different lunations is the ſituation of the node.

534. This force bends the Moon's path *toward* the ecliptic, when the points M and I are on the same fide of the line of the nodes, but bends it away *from* the ecliptic when N lies between I and M. This circumftance kept firmly in mind, and confidered with care, will explain all the deviations occafioned by the force M *m*. Thus, in the fituation of the nodes reprefented in the figure, let the Moon fet out from conjunction in C, moving in the arch C M A O. All the way from C to A, the difturbing force M I is below the elevated half N M N' of the Moon's orbit between it and the ecliptic, and therefore the force M *m* pulls the Moon out of the plane of her orbit toward the ecliptic. The fame thing happens during the Moon's motion from N to C. This will appear by conftructing the fame kind of parallelogram on the diagonal M I drawn from any point between N and C.

When the Moon has paffed the quadrature A, and is in M', the force M' I' is both above the ecliptic, and above the elevated half of the Moon's orbit. This will appear by drawing M' *g* perpendicular to E N', and joining *g* I'. The line M' *g* is in the orbit, and *g* I' is in the ecliptic, and the triangle M' *g* I' ftands elevated, and nearly perpendicular on both planes, fo that M' I' is above them both. In this cafe, the force M' *m'* in pulling the Moon out of the plane of her orbit, feparates her from it on that fide which is moft remote from the ecliptic ; that is, caufes the path to approach more obliquely to the ecliptic. The figure 61. B will illuftrate this.

N' I'

N' I' is the ecliptic, and M' N' is the orbit, both feen edge-
wife, as they would appear to an eye placed in *t*, (fig. 61.)
in the line N N' produced beyond the orbit. The difturbing force, acting in the direction M' I', may be refolved
into M' *p* in the direction of the orbit plane, and M' *m'*
perpendicular to it. The part M' *m'*, being compounded
with the fimultaneous motion M' *q*, compofes a motion
M' *r*, which interfects the ecliptic in *n*. When M' in
fig. 61. gets to M'', the path is again bent toward the
ecliptic, and continues fo all the way from N' to B, where
it begins to act in the fame manner as in M' between A
and N'.

535. By the action of this lateral force, the orbit
muft be continually fhifting its pofition, and its interfection with the ecliptic ; or, to fpeak more accurately, the
Moon is made to move in a line which does not lie all in
one plane. In imagination, we conceive an orbital material
line, fomewhat like a hoop, of an elliptical fhape, all in one
plane, paffing through the Earth, and, inftead of conceiving
the Moon to quit this hoop, we fuppofe the hoop itfelf
to fhift its pofition, fo that the arch in which the Moon
is in any moment takes the direction of the Moon's motion in that moment. Its interfection with the ecliptic
(perhaps at a confiderable diftance from the point occupied by the Moon) fhifts accordingly. This hoop may
be conceived as having an axis, perpendicular to its plane,
paffing through the Earth. This axis will incline to one
fide from the pole of the ecliptic about five degrees,
                                                    and,

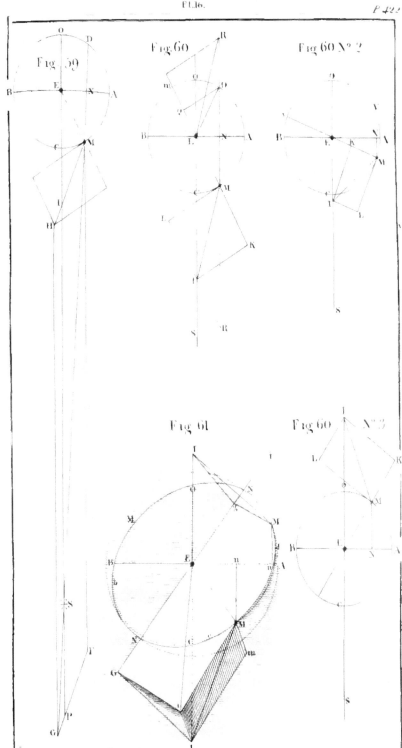

Fig. 59

Fig. 60

Fig. 60 N.º 2

Fig. 61

Fig. 60 N.º 3

and, as the line N N' of the nodes fhifts round the ecliptic, the extremity of this axis will defcribe a circle round
the pole of the ecliptic, diftant from it about 5° all
round, juft as the axis of the Earth defcribes a circle
round the pole of the ecliptic, diftant from it about 23½
degrees.

536. When the Moon's path is bent toward the
ecliptic, fhe muft crofs it fooner than fhe would otherwife have done. The node will appear to meet the
Moon, that is, to fhift to the weftward, *in antecedenti.t
fignorum*, or to recede. But if her path be bent more
away from the ecliptic, fhe muft proceed farther before
fhe crofs it, and the nodes will fhift *in confequentia*, that
is, will advance.

Cor. 1. Therefore, if the nodes have the fituation
reprefented in the figure, in the fecond and fourth quadrant, the nodes muft retreat while the Moon defcribes
the arch N C A, or the arch N' O B, that is, while fhe
paffes from a node to the next quadrature. But, while
the Moon defcribes the arch A N', or the arch B N, the
force which pulls the Moon from the plane of the orbit,
caufes her to pafs the points N' or N before fhe reach
the ecliptic, and the node therefore advances, while the
Moon moves from quadrature to a node.

It is plain that the contrary muft happen when the
nodes are fituated in the firft and third quadrants. They
will advance while the Moon proceeds from a node to
the next quadrature, and recede while fhe proceeds from
a quadrature to the next node.

Cor.

and, as the line N N′ of the nodes shifts round the ecliptic, the extremity of this axis will describe a circle round
the pole of the ecliptic, distant from it about 5° all
round, just as the axis of the Earth describes a circle
round the pole of the ecliptic, distant from it about 23½
degrees.

536. When the Moon's path is bent toward the
ecliptic, she must cross it sooner than she would other-
wise have done. The node will appear to meet the
Moon, that is, to shift to the westward, *in antecedentia
signorum*, or to recede. But if her path be bent more
away from the ecliptic, she must proceed farther before
she cross it, and the nodes will shift *in consequentia*, that
is, will advance.

Cor. 1. Therefore, if the nodes have the situation
reprefented in the figure, in the fecond and fourth quadrant, the nodes must retreat while the Moon defcribes
the arch N C A, or the arch N′ O B, that is, while she
passes from a node to the next quadrature. But, while
the Moon defcribes the arch A N′, or the arch B N, the
force which pulls the Moon from the plane of the orbit,
causes her to pass the points N′ or N before she reach
the ecliptic, and the node therefore advances, while the
Moon moves from quadrature to a node.

It is plain that the contrary must happen when the
nodes are situated in the first and third quadrants. They
will advance while the Moon proceeds from a node to
the next quadrature, and recede while she proceeds from
a quadrature to the next node.

Cor.

Cor. 2. In each fynodical revolution of the Moon, the nodes, on the whole, retreat. For, to take the example reprefented in the figure, all the while that the Moon moves from N to A, the line M 1 lies between the orbit and ecliptic, and the path is continually inclining more and more towards it, and, confequently, the nodes are all this while receding. They advance while the Moon moves from A to N′. They retreat while fhe moves from N′ to B, and advance while fhe proceeds from B′ to N. The time therefore during which the nodes recede exceeds that during which they advance. There will be the fame difference or excefs of the regrefs of the nodes when they are fituated in the angle C E A.

It is evident that the excefs of the arch N C A above the arch B N or A N′, is double of the diftance N C of the node from fyzigy. Therefore the retreat or wefter-ly motion of the nodes will gradually increafe as they pafs from fyzigy to quadrature, and again decreafe as the node paffes from quadrature to the fyzigy.

Cor. 3. When the nodes are in the quadratures, the lateral force M *m* is the greateft poffible through the whole revolution, becaufe the factor *s* in the formula $\frac{q\,s\,i}{r^3}$ is then equal to radius. In the fyzigies it is nothing.

The nodes make a complete revolution in 6803^d 2^h 55′ 18″, but with great inequality, as appears from what has been faid in the preceding paragraphs. The exact determination of their motions is to be feen in Newton's Principia, L. III. Prop. 32.; and it is a very beautiful example

ample of dynamical analyfis. The principal equation a-
mounts to 1° 37′ 45″ at its maximum, and in other fituations, it is proportional to the fine of twice the arch N C.
The annual regrefs, computed according to the principles
of the theory, does not differ two minutes of a degree
from what is actually obferved in the heavens. This
wonderful coincidence is the great boaft of the doctrine
of univerfal gravitation. At the fame time, the perufal
of Newton's inveftigation will fhew that fuch agreement
is not the *obvious* refult of the happy fimplicity of the
great regulating power; we fhall there fee many abftrufe and delicate circumftances, which muft be confidered and taken into the account before we can obtain a
true ftatement.

This motion of the nodes is accompanied by a variation of the inclination of the orbit to the ecliptic. The
inclination increafes, when the Moon is drawn from the
ecliptic while leaving a node, or toward it in approaching a node. It is diminifhed, when the Moon is drawn
toward the ecliptic when leaving a node, or from it in
approaching a node. Therefore, when the nodes are
fituated in the firft and third quadrants, the inclination
increafes while the Moon paffes from a node to the next
quadrature, but it diminifhes till fhe is 90° from the
node, and then increafes till fhe reaches the other node.
Therefore, in each revolution, the inclination is increafed, and becomes continually greater, while the node recedes from the quadrature to the fyzigy; and it is the
greateft poffible when the nodes are in the line of the

3 H   fyzigies,

fyzigies, and it is then nearly 5° 18′ 30″. When the nodes are fituated in the fecond and fourth quadrants, the inclination of the orbit diminifhes while the Moon paffes from the node to the 90th degree ; it is increafed from thence to the quadrature, and then diminifhes till the Moon reaches the other node. While the nodes are thus fituated, the inclination diminifhes in every revolution, and is the leaft of all when the node is in quadrature, and the Moon in fyzigy, being then nearly 4° 58′, and it gradually increafes again till the nodes reach the line of fyzigy. While the nodes are in the quadratures, or in the fyzigies, the inclination is not fenfibly changed during that revolution.

Such are the general effects of the lateral force M m, that appear on a flight confideration of the circumftances of the cafe. A more particular account of them cannot be given in this outline of the fcience. We may juft add, that the deductions from the general principle agree precifely with obfervation. The mathematical inveftigation not only points out the periods of the different inequalities, and their relation to the refpective pofitions of the Sun and Moon, but alfo determines the abfolute magnitude to which each of them rifes. The only quantity deduced from mere obfervation is the mean inclination of the Moon's orbit. The time of the complete revolution of the nodes, and the magnitude and law of variation of this motion, and the change of inclination, with all its varieties, are deduced from the theory of univerfal gravitation.

539. There is another cafe of this problem which is confiderably different, namely, the fatellites of Dr Herfchel's planet, the planes of whofe orbits are nearly perpendicular to the orbit of the planet. This problem offers fome curious cafes, which deferve the attention of the mechanician ; but as they intereft us merely as ob-jects of curiofity, they have not yet been confidered.

540. There is ftill another confiderable derangement of the lunar motions by the action of the fun. We have feen that, in quadrature, the Moon's gravitation to the Earth is augmented $\frac{4}{79}$, and that in fyzigy it is dimi-nifhed $\frac{2}{179}$. Taking the whole fynodical revolution to-gether, this is equivalent, nearly, to a diminution of $\frac{\frac{1}{2}}{179}$, or $\frac{1}{358}$. That is to fay, in confequence of the Sun's action, the general gravitation of the Moon to the Earth is $\frac{1}{358}$ lefs than if the Sun were away. If the Sun were away, therefore, the Moon's gravitation would be $\frac{1}{358}$ greater than her prefent mean gravitation. The confequence would be, that the Moon would come nearer to the Earth. As this would be done without any change on her velocity, and as fhe now will be retained in a fmaller orbit, fhe will defcribe it in a proportionally lefs time ; and we can compute exactly how near fhe would come before this increafed gravitation will be balanced by the velocity (224.) We muft conclude from this, that the mean diftance and the mean period of the Moon which we obferve, are greater than her natural diftance and pe-riod.

From

From this it is plain that if any thing fhall increafe or diminifh the action of the Sun, it muft equally increafe or diminifh the diftance which the Moon affumes from the Earth, and the time of her revolution at that diftance.

Now there actually is fuch a change in the Sun's action. When the Earth is *in perihelio*, in the beginning of January, fhe is nearer the Sun than in July by 1 part in 30 ; confequently the ratio of E M to E S is increafed by $\frac{1}{30}$, or in the ratio of 30 to 31. But her gravitation (and confequently the Moon's) to the Sun is increafed $\frac{1}{15}$, or in the ratio of 30 to 32. Therefore the difturbing force is increafed by 1 part in 10 nearly. The Moon muft therefore retire farther from the Earth 1 part in 1790. She muft defcribe a larger orbit, and employ a greater time.

We can compute exactly what is the extent of this change. The fydereal period of the Moon is 27^d 7^h 43′, or 39343′. This muft be increafed $\frac{1}{1790}$, becaufe the Moon retains the fame velocity in the enlarged orbit. This will make the period 39365′, which exceeds the other 22′. The obferved difference between a lunation in January and one in July fomewhat exceeds 25′. This, when reduced in the proportion of the fynodical to the periodical revolution, agrees with this mechanical conclufion with great exactnefs, when the computation is made with due attention to every circumftance that can affect the conclufion. For it muft be remarked that the computation here given proceeds on the legitimacy of affuming a general diminution of $\frac{1}{178}$ of the Moon's gravitation as equivalent to the variable change of gravity that really takes

takes place. In the particular circumftances of the cafe, this is very nearly exact. The true method is to take the average of all the difturbing forces M K through the quadrant, multiplying each by the time of its action. And, here, Euler makes a fagacious remark, that, if the diameter of the Moon's orbit had exceeded its prefent magnitude in a very confiderable proportion, it would fcarcely have been poffible to affign the period in which fhe would have revolved round the Earth ; and the greateft part of the methods by which the problem has been folved could not have been employed.

541. There ftill remains an anomaly of the lunar motions that has greatly puzzled the cultivators of phyfical aftronomy. Dr Halley, when comparing the ancient Chaldean obfervations with thofe of modern times, in order to obtain an accurate meafure of the period of the Moon's revolution, found that fome obfervations made by the Arabian aftronomers, in the eighth and ninth centuries, did not agree with this meafure. When the lunar period was deduced from a comparifon of the Chaldean obfervations with the Arabian, the period was fenfibly greater than what was deduced from a comparifon of the Arabian and the modern obfervations ; fo that the Moon's mean motion feems to have accelerated a little. This conclufion was confirmed by breaking each of thefe long intervals into parts. When the Chaldean and Alexandrian obfervations were compared, they gave a longer period than the Alexandrian compared with the Arabian of the eighth century ;

century ; and this laft period exceeded what is deduced
from a comparifon of the Arabian with the modern obfervations ; and even the comparifon of the modern obfervations with each other fhews a continued diminution.
This conjecture was received by the mechanical philofophers with hefitation, becaufe no reafon could be affigned
for the acceleration ; and the more that the Newtonian
philofophy has been cultivated, the more confidently did
it appear that the mean diftances and periods could fuftain no change from the mutual action of the planets.
Nay, M. de la Grange has at laft demonftrated that, in
the folar fyftem as it exifts, this is ftrictly true, as to any
change that will be permanent : all is periodical and com-
penfatory. Yet, as obfervation alfo improved, this acceleration of the Moon's mean motion became undeniable
and confpicuous, and it is now admitted by every aftronomer, at the rate of about 11″ in a century, and her
change of longitude increafes in the duplicate ratio of the
times.

Various attempts have been made to account for this
acceleration. It was imagined by feveral that it was owing to the refiftance of the celeftial fpaces, which, by de-
minifhing the progreffive velocity of the Moon, caufed
her to fall within her preceding orbit, approaching the
Earth continually in a fort of elliptical fpiral. But the
free motion of the tails of comets, the rare matter of
which feems to meet with no fenfible refiftance, rendered
this explanation unfatisfactory. Others were difpofed to
think that gravity did not operate inftantaneoufly through
the

the whole extent of its influence. The application of this principle did not feem to be obvious, nor its effects to be very clear or definite.

At laft, M. de la Place difcovered the caufe of this perplexing fact ; and in a differtation read to the Royal Academy of Sciences in 1785, he fhews that the acceleration of the Moon's mean motion neceffarily arifes from a fmall change in the eccentricity of the Earth's orbit round the Sun, which is now diminifhing, and will continue to diminifh for many centuries, by the mutual gravitation of the planets. He was led to the difcovery by obferving in the feries which exprefies the increafe of the lunar period by the difturbing force of the Sun (a feries formed of fines and cofines of the Moon's angular motion and their multiples) a term equal to $\frac{1}{179}$ of her angular motion multiplied by the fquare of the eccentricity of the Earth's orbit. Confequently, when this eccentricity becomes fmaller, the natural period of the Moon is lefs enlarged by the Sun's action, and therefore, if the Earth's eccentricity continue to diminifh, fo will the lunar period, and this in a duplicate proportion. Without entering into the difcuffion of this analyfis, which is abundantly complicated, we may fee the general effect of a diminution of the Earth's eccentricity in this manner. The ratio of the cube of the mean diftance of the Earth from the Sun to the cube of her perihelion diftance is greater than the ratio of the cube of her aphelion diftance to that of the mean diftance. Hence it follows that the increafe of the mean lunar period, during the fmaller

diftances

diſtances of the Earth from the Sun, is greater than its
diminution, during her greater diſtances; and the ſum of
all the lunations, during a complete revolution of the
Earth, exceeds the ſum of the lunations that would have
happened in the ſame time, had the Earth remained at her
mean diſtance from the Sun. Therefore, as the Earth's
eccentricity diminiſhes, the lunar period alſo diminiſhes,
approximating more and more to her period, undiſturbed
by the change in the Sun's action. M. de la Place finds
the diminution in a century $= 11'',135$, which differs
little from that aſſumed by Mayer from a compariſon of
obſervations. This centurial change of angular velocity
muſt produce a change in the ſpace deſcribed, that is, in
the Moon's longitude, in the duplicate proportion of the
time, as in any uniformly accelerated motion. Therefore $11'',135$ multiplied by the ſquare of the number of
centuries forward or backward, will give the correction
of the Moon's longitude computed by the preſent tables.
La Place finds that, in going back to the Chaldean obſervations, we muſt employ another term (nearly $\frac{1}{2^1 7}$ of a
ſecond) multiplied by the cube of the number of centuries. With theſe corrections, the computation of the
Moon's place agrees with all obſervations, ancient and
modern, with moſt wonderful accuracy; ſo that there
no longer remains any phenomenon in the ſyſtem which
is not deducible from the Newtonian gravitation.

542. We ſhould, before concluding this account of
the perturbations of the planetary motions, pay ſome attention

tention to the motions of the other fecondary planets, and particularly of Jupiter's fatellites, feeing that the exact knowledge of their motions is almoft as conducive to the improvement of navigation and geography as that of the lunar motions. But there is no room for this difcuffion, and we muft refer to the differtations of Wargentin, Profperin, La Place, and others, who have ftudied the operation of phyfical caufes on thofe little planets with great affiduity and judgement, and with the greateft fuccefs. The little fyftem of Jupiter and his fatellites has been of immenfe fervice to the philofophical ftudy of the whole folar fyftem. Their motions are fo rapid, that, in the courfe of a few years, many fynodical periods are accomplifhed, in which the perturbations arifing from their mutual actions return again in the fame order. Nay, fuch fynodical periods have been obferved as bring the whole fyftem again into the fame relative fituation of its different bodies. And, in cafes where this is not *accurately* accomplifhed, the deficiency introduces a fmall difference between the perturbations of any period and the correfponding perturbations of the preceding one; by which means another and much longer period is indicated, in which this difference goes through all its varieties, fwelling to a maximum and again diminifhing to nothing. Thus the fyftem of Jupiter and his fatellites, as a fort of epitome of the great folar fyftem, has fuggefted to the fagacious philofopher the proper way of ftudying the great fyftem, namely, by *looking out* for fimilar periods in *its* anomalies, and by boldly afferting

the

the reality of fuch correfponding equations as can be fhewn to refult from the operation of univerfal gravitation. The fact is, that we have now the moft demonftrative knowledge of many fuch periods and equations, which could not be deduced from the obfervations of many thoufand years.

In the courfe of this inveftigation, M. de la Grange has made an important obfervation, which he has demonftrated in the moft incontrovertible manner, namely, that it *neceffarily* refults from the fmall eccentricity of the planetary orbits—their fmall inclination to each other—the immenfe bulk of the Sun—and from the planets all moving in one direction—that all the perturbations that are obferved, nay *all that can exift* in this fyftem, are periodical, and are compenfated in oppofite points of every period. He fhews alfo that the greateft perturbations are fo moderate, that none but an aftronomer will obferve any difference between this perturbed ftate and the mean ftate of the fyftem. The mean diftances and the mean periods remain for ever the fame. In fhort, the whole affemblage will continue, almoft to eternity, in a ftate fit for its prefent purpofes, and not diftinguifhable from its prefent ftate, except by the prying eye of an aftronomer.

Cold, we think, muft be the heart that is not affected by this mark of beneficent wifdom in the Contriver of the magnificent fabric, fo manifeft in felecting for its connecting principle a power fo admirably fitted for continuing to anfwer the purpofes of its firft formation. And he muft be little fufceptible of moral impreffion who does

does not feel himself highly obliged to the Being who has made him capable of perceiving this display of wisdom, and has attached to this perception sentiments so pleasing and delightful. The extreme simplicity of the constitution of the solar system is perhaps the most remarkable feature of its beauty. To this circumstance are we indebted for the pleasure afforded by the contemplation. For it is this alone that has allowed our limited understanding to acquire such a comprehensive body of well-founded knowledge, far exceeding, both in extent and in accuracy, any thing attained in other paths of philosophical research. But we have not yet seen all the capabilities of this wonderful power of nature. Let us therefore still follow our excellent leader in a new path of investigation.

Of the Figures of the Planets.

544. Sir Isaac Newton, having so happily explained all the phenomena of *progressive* motion exhibited by the heavenly bodies, by shewing that they are all, without exception, modified examples of deflection towards one another, in the inverse duplicate ratio of the distances, was induced to examine the other motions observed in some of those bodies, to see what modification these motions received by the influence of universal gravitation. The Sun, and several planets turn round their axes. The study of celestial mechanism is not complete, till we see

whether

whether this kind of motion is in any way influenced by gravitation.

It does not appear, at firſt conſideration, that there can be any great myſtery in the mere rotation of a body round its axis. It ſeems to be one of the ſimpleſt mechanical queſtions. But the faƈt is juſt the oppoſite. Before the rotative motion that we obſerve in our Earth can be ſecured, in the way in which we ſee it aƈtually performed, adjuſtments are neceſſary, which are very abſtruſe, and required all the ſagacity of Newton to diſcover and appreciate ; and it is acknowledged that this is the department of phyſical aſtronomy where his acuteneſs of diſcernment appears the moſt remarkable. It is alſo the claſs of phenomena in which the effeƈts of univerſal gravitation are moſt convincingly ſeen. For this reaſon, ſome more notice will be taken of the rotation of the planets, and of its conſequences, than is uſually done in our elementary treatiſes. But, as in the other departments, ſo here, it is only the more ſimple and general faƈts that can be conſidered. To go a very ſmall ſtep beyond theſe, engages us at once in the moſt difficult problems, which have occupied and ſtill occupy the firſt mathematicians of Europe, and require all the reſources of their ſcience. Such diſcuſſion, however, would be unſuitable here. But without ſome attempt of this kind, we muſt remain ignorant of the mechaniſm of ſome phenomena, more familiar and important than many of thoſe which we have already diſcuſſed.

When a body turns round an axis, each particle deſcribes

scribes a circle, to which this axis is perpendicular. Now we know that a particle of matter cannot describe a circle, unless some deflecting force retain it in the periphery. In coherent masses, this retaining force is supplied by the cohesion. But even this is a limited thing. A stone may be so briskly whirled about in a sling that the cord will break. Grindstones are sometimes whirled about in our manufactures with such rapidity that they split, and the pieces fly off with prodigious force. If matters be lying loose on the surface of a revolving planet, their gravitation may be insufficient to retain them in that velocity of rotation. In every case, the force which actually retains such loose bodies on the surface can be found only in their weight; and part of it is thus expended, and they continue to press the ground only with the remainder. If the velocity of rotation be increased to a certain degree, it may require the whole weight of the body for its supply. If the velocity still increase, the body is not retained, but thrown off. If this Earth turned round in 84 minutes, things lying on the equator might remain there; but they would not press the ground, nor stretch the thread of a plummet. For this is precisely the time in which a planet would circulate round the Earth, close to the surface, moving about 17 times faster than a cannon ball. The weight of the body, deflecting it 16 feet in a second, just keeps it in the circumference of a circle close to the surface of the Earth. The Earth, turning as fast, will have the planet always immediately above the same point of its surface; and the planet will

not

not appear to have any weight, becaufe it will not defcend, but keep hovering over the fame fpot. If the rotation were ftill fwifter, every thing would be thrown off, as we fee water flirted from a mop brifkly whirled round.

545. As things are really adjufted, this does not happen. But yet there is a certain meafurable part of the weight of any body expended in keeping it at reft, in the place where it lies loofe. At the equator, a body lying on the ground defcribes, in one fecond, an arch of 1528 feet nearly. This deviates from the tangent nearly $\frac{67}{100}$ of an inch. This is very nearly $\frac{1}{288}$ part of $16\frac{1}{12}$ feet, the fpace through which gravity, or its heavinefs, would caufe a ftone to fall in that time. Hence we muft infer that the centrifugal tendency arifing from rotation is $\frac{1}{288}$ of the fenfible weight of a body on the equator, and $\frac{1}{289}$ of its real weight. Were this body therefore taken to the pole, it would manifeft a greater heavinefs. If, at the equator, it drew out the fcale of a fpring fteelyard to the divifion 288, it would draw it to 289 at the pole.

546. M. Richer, a French mathematician, going to Cayenne in 1672, was directed to make fome aftronomical obfervations there, and was provided with a pendulum clock for this purpofe. He found that his clock, which had been carefully adjufted to mean time at Paris, loft above two minutes every day, and he was obliged to

fhorten

shorten the pendulum $\frac{1}{10}$ of an inch before it kept right time. Hence he concluded that a heavy body dropped at Cayenne would not fall 193 inches in a second. It would fall only about 192$\frac{1}{4}$. Richer immediately wrote an account of this very singular diminution of gravity. It was scouted by almost all the philosophers of Europe, but has been confirmed by many repetitions of the experiment. Here then is a direct proof that the heaviness of a body, whether confidered as a mere pressure, or as an accelerating force, is employed, and in part expended, in keeping bodies united to a whirling planet.

547. These confiderations are not new. Even in ancient times, men of reflection entertained such thoughts. The celebrated Roman general Polybius, one of the most intelligent philosophers of antiquity, is quoted by Strabo, as faying that in confequence of the Earth's rotation, every body was made lighter, and that the globe itself swelled out in the middle. Were it not so, says he, the waters of the ocean would all run to the shores of the torrid zone, and leave the polar regions dry. Dr Hooke is the first modern philosopher who professed this opinion. Mr Huyghens, however, is the first who gave it the proper attention. Occupied at the time of Richer's remark with his pendulum clocks, he took great interest in this obfervation at Cayenne, and instantly perceived the true caufe of the retardation of Richer's clock. He perceived that pendulums must vibrate more flowly, in proportion as their fituation removes them farther from the

the axis of the Earth ; and he affigned the proportion of the retardation in different places.

548. Refuming this fubject fome time after, it occurred to him, that unlefs the Earth be protuberant all around the equator, the ocean muft overflow the lands, increafing in depth till the height of the water compenfated for its diminifhed gravity. He confiders the condition of the water in a canal reaching from the furface of the equator to the centre of the Earth (fuppofe the canal C Q, fig. 33.) and there communicating with a canal C N reaching from the centre to the pole. The water in the laft muft retain all its natural gravity, becaufe its particles do not defcribe circles round the axis. But every particle in the column C Q reaching to the furface of the equator muft have its weight diminifhed in proportion to its diftance from the centre of the globe. Therefore the whole diminution will be the fame as if each particle loft half as much as the outermoft particle lofes. This is very plain. Therefore thefe two columns cannot balance each other at the centre, unlefs the equatoreal column be longer than the polar column by $\frac{1}{577}$ (for the extremity of this column lofes $\frac{1}{289}$ of its weight by the centrifugal force employed in the rotation).

Being an excellent and zealous geometer, this fubject feemed to merit his ferious ftudy, and he inveftigated the form that the ocean muft acquire fo as to be *in equilibrio*. This he did by inquiring what will be the pofition of a plummet in any latitude. This he knew muft be
perpendicular

perpendicular to the furface of ftill water. On the fuppofition of gravity directed to the centre of the Earth,
and equal at all diftances from that centre, he conftructed the meridional curve, which fhould in every point have
the tangent perpendicular to the direction of a plummet
determined by him on thefe principles.

549. At this very time, another circumftance gave a
peculiar intereft to this queftion of the figure of the Earth.
The magnificent project of meafuring the whole arch of
the meridian which paffes through France was then carrying on. (See § 267.) It feemed to refult from the comparifon of the lengths of the different portions of this arch,
that the degrees increafed as they were more foutherly.
This made the academicians employed in the meafurement conclude that the Earth was of an egg-like fhape.
This was quite incompatible with the reafoning of Mr
Huyghens. The conteft was carried on for a long while
with great pertinacity, and fome of the firft mathematicians of the age abetted the opinion of thofe aftronomers, and the honour of France was made a party in the
difpute. The opinion of Mr Huyghens, the greateft ornament of their academy, could not prevail ; indeed his
inferences were fuch, in fome refpects, that even the
impartial mathematicians were diffatisfied with them.
The form which he affigned to the meridian was very remarkable, confifting of two paraboloidal curves, which
had their vertex in the poles, and their branches inter-
fected each other at the equator, there forming an angu-

3 K   lar

lar ridge, elevated about feven miles above the infcribed fphere. No fuch ridge had been obferved by the navigators of that age, who had often croffed the equator. Nor had any perfon on fhore at the line obferved that two plummets near each other were not parallel, but fenfibly approached each other. All this was unlike the ordinary gradations of nature, in which we obferve nothing abrupt.

550. While this queftion was fo keenly agitated in France, Mr Newton was engaged in the fpeculations which have immortalized his name, and it was to him an interefting thing to know what form of a whirling planet was compatible with an equilibrium of all the forces which act on its parts. He therefore took the queftion up in its moft fimple form. He fuppofed the planet completely fluid, and therefore every particle is at liberty to change its place, if it be not in perfect equilibrium. The particles all, attract one another with a force in the inverfe duplicate ratio of the diftance, and they are at the fame time actuated by a centrifugal tendency, in confequence of the rotation ; or, to exprefs it more accurately, part of thofe mutual attractions is employed in keeping the particles in their different circles of rotation. He demonftrated that this was poffible, if the globe have the form of an elliptical fpheroid, compreffed at the poles, and protuberant at the equator $\frac{1}{2 3 0}$ part of the axis. He alfo pointed out the phenomena by which this may be afcertained, namely, the variation of gravity as we recede

cede from the equator to the poles, shewing that the increments of sensible gravity are as the squares of the fines of the latitude. This can easily be decided by experiments with nice pendulum clocks. He shewed also that the remaining gravity, on different parts of the Earth's surface, is inversely proportional to the distance from the centre, when estimated in the direction of the centre, &c. &c. His demonstration of the precise elliptical form consists in proving two things : 1st, That on this suppofition, gravity is always perpendicular to the surface of the spheroid : 2d, That all rectilineal canals leading from the centre to the surface will balance one another. Therefore the ocean will maintain its form.

It was some time before the philosophy of Newton could prevail in France over the hypothesis of the French philosopher Des Cartes; and the great mathematician Bernoulli endeavoured to shew that the oblong form of the Earth which had been demonstrated (he says) by the meafurement of the degrees, was the effect of the preffure of the vortices in which the Earth was carried about.

551. Mr Hermann, a mathematician of most refpectable talents, took another view of the question of the figure of the Earth. Newton had demonstrated in the most convincing manner that particles gravitated to the centre of similar solids, or portions of a solid, with forces proportional to their distances from the centre. Hermann availed himself of this, and of another theorem

3 K 2

of

of Newton founded on it, viz. that fuperficial gravity in different latitudes is inverfely as the diftance from the centre. *   But he obferved that Newton had by no means demonftrated the elliptical form, but had merely affumed it, or, as it were, gueffed at it.   This is indeed true, and his application is made by means of the vulgar rule of falfe pofition.   Hermann therefore fet himfelf to in-quire what form a fluid will affume when turning round an axis, its particles fituated in the fame diameter gravi-tating to the centre proportionally to their diftance, yet exhibiting a fuperficial gravity in different parts inverfely as the diftance from the centre.   He found it to be an ellipfe, with fuch a protuberancy, that the r..lius of the equator is to the femiaxis in the fubduplicate ratio of the primitive equatoreal gravity to the remaining equatoreal gravity.   This gives the fame proportion of the axes which had been affigned by Huyghens, though accom-panied by a very different form.   He then inverted his procefs, and demonftrated the perpendicularity of gravity to the furface, the equilibrium of canals, and fome other conditions that appeared indifpenfable ;   and he found all right.   This confirmed him in his theory, and he found fault with Dr D. Gregory, the commentator of Newton, for adhering to Newton's form of the ellipfe.   He defied them to point out any fault in his own demonftration of

the

---

*   * Both of thefe propofitions are eafily inferred from Art. 463, and need not be particularly infifted on in this place, for reafons which will foon appear.

the elliptical figure, and confidered this as fufficient for proving the inaccuracy of the Newtonian conjecture, for it could get no higher name.

552. By very flow degrees, the French academicians began to acknowledge the compreffed form of the Earth, and to reexamine their obfervations, by which it had feemed that the degrees increafed to the fouthward. They now affected to find that their meafurement had been good, but that fome circumftances had been over-looked in the calculations, which fhould have been taken into the account. But they were not aware that they were now vindicating the goodnefs of their inftruments and of their eyefight at the expence of their judgement.

All thefe things made the problem of the figure of the Earth extremely interefting to the great mathematical philofophers. Newton took no part in the further difcuffion, being fatisfied with the evidence which he had for his own determination of the precife fpecies of the terraqueous fpheroid. His philofophy gradually acquired the afcendancy ; but the comparifon made of the degrees of the meridian argued a fmaller ellipticity than he had affigned to the Earth, on the fuppofition of uniform denfity and primitive fluidity. He had however fufficiently pointed out the varieties of ellipticity which might arife from a difference of denfity in the interior parts. Thefe were acquiefced in, and the mathematicians fpeculated on the ways by which the obfervations

and

and the theory of univerfal gravitation might be adapted
to each other. But, all this while, the original problem
was confidered as too difficult to be treated in any cafe
remarkably deviating from a fphere, and even this cafe
was folved by Newton and his followers only in an indirect manner.

553. The firft perfon who attempted a direct general folution was Mr James Stirling. In 1735 he communicated to the Royal Society of London two elegant propofitions (but without demonftration), which determine
the form of a homogeneous fpheroid turning round its
axis, and which, when applied to the particular cafe of
the Earth, perfectly coincided with Newton's determination. In 1737 Mr Clairaut communicated to our Royal
Society, and alfo to the Royal Academy at Paris, very
elaborate and elegant performances on the fame fubject,
which he afterwards enlarged in a feparate publication.
This is the completeft work on the fubject, and is full
of the moft curious and valuable refearch, in which are
difcuffed all the circumftances which can affect the queftion. It is alfo remarkable for an example of candour
very rare among rivals in literary fame. The author, in
extending his memoire to a more complete work, quits
his own method of inveftigation, though remarkable for
its perfpicuity and neatnefs, for that of another mathematician, becaufe it was fuperior ; and this with unaffected acknowledgement of its fuperiority. The refults
of Clairaut's theory perfectly coincide with the Newtonian

nian theory, making the equatoreal diameter to the polar diameter as 231 to 230, though it is agreed by all the mathematicians that Newton's method had a chance of being inaccurate. So true is the saying of Daniel Bernoulli, when treating this subject in his theory of the the tides, " *The sagacity of that great man (Newton) saw* " *clearly through a mist what others can scarcely discover* " *through a microscope.* "

Mr Stirling had said that the revolving figure was not an accurate elliptical spheroid, but approached infinitely near to it. Mr Clairaut's solutions, in most cases, suppose the spheroid very nearly a sphere, or suppose lines and angles equal which are only very nearly so. Without this allowance, the treatment of the problem seemed impracticable. This made Mr Stirling's assertion more credited ; and we apprehend that it became the general opinion that the solutions obtainable in our present state of mathematical knowledge were only approximations, exact indeed, to any degree that we please, in the cases exhibited in the figures of the planets, but still they were but approximations.

554. But in 1740, Mr M'Laurin, in a dissertation on the tides, which shared the prize given by the Academy of Paris, demonstrated, in all the rigour and elegance of ancient geometry, that an homogeneous elliptical spheroid, of *any eccentricity whatever,* if turning in a proper time round its axis, will for ever preserve its form. He gave the rule for investigating this form, and
the

the ratio of its axes. His final propofitions to this purpofe are the fame that Mr Stirling had communicated
without demonftration. This performance was much admired, and fettled all doubts about the figure of a homogeneous fpheroid turning round its axis. It is indeed
equally remarkable for its fimplicity, its perfpicuity and
its elegance. Mr M'Laurin had no occafion to profecute
the fubject beyond this fimple cafe. Proceeding on his
fundamental propofitions, the mathematical philofophers
have made many important additions to the theory. But
it ftill prefents many queftions of moft difficult folution,
yet intimately connected with the phenomena of the folar
fyftem.

In this elementary outline of phyfical aftronomy, we
cannot difcufs thofe things in detail. But it would be
a capital defect not to include the *general* theory of the
figure of planets which turn round their axes. No more,
however, will be attempted than to fhew that a homogeneous elliptical fpheroid will anfwer all the conditions that are required, and to give a *general* notion of
the change which a variable denfity will produce in this
figure. *

The

---

* The ftudent will confult, with advantage, the original
differtations of Mr Clairaut and Mr M'Laurin, and the great
additions made by the laft in his valuable work on Fluxions.
The *Cofmographia* of *Frifius* alfo contains a very excellent epitome of all that has been done before his time ; and the *Mechanique*

The following lemma from Mr M'Laurin muſt be premiſed.

555. Let A E B Q and *a e b q* (fig. 64. No. 1.) be two concentric and ſimilar ellipſes, having their ſhorter axes A B and *a b* coinciding. Let P *a* L touch the interior ellipſe in the extremity *a* of the ſhorter axis, to which let P K, a chord of the exterior ellipſe be parallel, and therefore equal. Let the chords *a f* and *a g* of the interior ellipſe make equal angles with the axis, and join their extremities by the chord *f g* perpendicular to it in *i*. Draw P F and P G parallel to *a f* and *a g*, and draw F H and P I perpendicular to P K.

Then, P F together with P G are equal to twice *a i*, when P F and P G lie on different ſides of P K. But if they are on the ſame ſide (as P F′ and P G′) then 2 *a i* is equal to the difference of P F′ and P G′.

Draw K *k* parallel to P G or *a g*, and therefore equal to P F, being equally inclined to K P. Draw the diameter M C *z*, biſecting the ordinates K *k*, P G, and *a g*, in *m*, *s*, and *z*, and cutting P K in *n*.

By ſimilarity of triangles, we have

$$K \, m : K \, n = P \, s : P \, n, = a \, z : a \, C, = a \, g : a \, b.$$

Therefore

---

chanique Celeſte of *La Place* contains ſome very curious and recondite additions. A work of *F. Boſcovich* on the Figure of the Earth has peculiar merit. This author, by employing geometrical expreſſions of the acting forces, wherever it can be done, gives us very clear ideas of the ſubject.

Therefore $K m + P s : K n + P n = a g : a b$,

and $\quad$ $K k$ (or P F) $+ P G : 2 P K = 2 a g : 2 a b$,

and $\quad$ $P F + P G : 2 a g = 2 P K : 2 a b$;

and, by fimilarity of triangles, we have

$$P H + P I : 2 a i = 2 P K : 2 a b.$$

But $2 P K = 2 a b$. Therefore $P H + P I = 2 a i$, and $P I' - P H' = 2 a i'$.

556. Let the two planes A G g B (fig. 63.) A E e B, interfecting in the line A B, and containing a very fmall angle G A E, be fuppofed to comprehend a thin elementary wedge or flice of a folid confifting of gravitating matter. If two planes G P E, F P D, ftanding perpendicularly on the plane A D d B, contain a very fmall angle E P D, they will comprehend a flender, or elementary pyramid of this flice, having its vertex in P, and a quadrilateral bafe G E D F. If two other planes g p e, f p d, be drawn from another point p, refpectively parallel to the planes G P E, f p d, they will comprehend another pyramid, having its fides parallel to thofe of the other, and containing equal angles, and the elementary pyramids F P E, f p e, may therefore be confidered as fimilar. The bafe g e d f is not indeed always parallel and fimilar to G E D F. But for each of them may be fubftituted fpherical furfaces, having their centres in P and in p, and then they will be fimilar.

The gravitation of a particle P to the pyramid G P D is to the gravitation of p to the pyramid g p d as any

fide

fide P D of the one to the homologous fide $p\, d$ of the other. This is evident, by what was fhewn in § 462.

The fame proportion will hold when the abfolute gravitation in the direction of the axis of the pyramid is eftimated in any other direction, fuch as P m. For, drawing $p\, n$ parallel to P m, and the perpendiculars D m, $d\, n$, it is plain that the ratio P D : $p\, d$ = P m : $p\, n$, = D m : $d\, n$.

This propofition is of moft extenfive ufe. For we thus eftimate the gravitation of a particle to any folid, by refolving it into elementary pyramids ; and having found the gravitation to each, and reduced them all to one direction, the aggregate of the reduced forces is the whole gravitation of the particle eftimated in that direction. The application of this is greatly expedited by the following theorem.

558. Two particles fimilarly fituated in refpect of fimilar folids, that is to fay, fituated in fimilar points of homologous lines, have their whole gravitations proportional to any homologous lines of the folids.

For, we can draw through the two particles ftraight lines fimilarly pofited in refpect of the folids, and then draw planes paffing through thofe lines, and through fimilar points of the folids. The fections of the folids made by thofe two planes muft be fimilar, for they are fimilarly placed in fimilar folids. We can then draw other planes through the fame two ftraight lines, containing with the former planes very fmall equal angles. The

3 L 2   fections

fections of thefe two planes will alfo be fimilar, and there will be comprehended between them and the two former planes fimilar flices of the two folids.

We can now divide the flices into two feriefes of fimilar pyramids, by drawing planes fuch as G P E, $g\,p\,e$, and F P D, $f\,p\,d$, of fig. 63. the points P and p being fuppofed in different lines, related to each of the two folids. By the reafonings employed in the laft propofition, it appears that when the whole of each flice is occupied by fuch pyramids, the gravitations to the correfponding pyramids are all in one proportion. Therefore the gravitation compounded of them all is in the fame proportion. As the whole of each of the two fimilar flices may be thus occupied by feriefes of fimilar and fimilarly fituated pyramids, fo the whole of each of the two fimilar folids may be occupied by fimilar flices, confifting of fuch pyramids. And as the compound gravitations to thofe flices are fimilarly formed, they are not only in the proportion of the homologous lines of the folids, but they are alfo in fimilar directions. Therefore, finally, the gravitations compounded of thefe compound gravitations are fimilarly compounded, and are in the fame proportion as any homologous lines of the folids.

Thefe things being premifed, we proceed to confider the particular cafe of elliptical fpheroids.

559. Let A E B Q, $a\,e\,b\,q$ (fig. 64.) be concentric and fimilar ellipfes, which, by rotation round their fhorter axis

axis A *a b* B, generate fimilar concentric fpheroids.   We may notice the following particulars..

560.   (*a*)   A particle *r*, on the furface of the interior fpheroid, has no tendency to move in any direction in confequence of its gravitation to the matter contained between the furfaces of the exterior and interior fpheroids.   For, drawing through *r* the ftraight line P *r t* G, it is an ordinate to fome diameter C M, which bifects it in *s*.   The part *r t* comprehended by the interior fpheroid is alfo an ordinate to the fame diameter and is bifected in *s*.   Therefore P *r* is equal to *t* G.   Now *r* may be conceived as at the vertex of two fimilar cones or pyramids, on the common axis P *r* G.   By what was demonftrated in art. 462. & 557, it appears that the gravitation of *r* to the matter of the cone or pyramid whofe axis is *r* P is equal and oppofite to the gravitation to the matter contained in the *fruftum* of the fimilar cone or pyramid, whofe axis is *t* G.   As this is true, in whatever direction P *r* G be drawn through *r*, it follows that *r* is *in equilibrio* in every direction, or, it has no tendency to move in any direction.

561.   (*b*)   The gravitations of two particles P and *p* (fig. 64. No. 2.) fituated in one diameter P C, are proportional to their diftances P C, *p* C, from the centre. For the gravitation of *p* is the fame as if all the matter between the furfaces A E B Q and *a e b q* were away (by the laft article), and thus P and *p* are fimilarly fituated

ated on fimilar folids ; and P C and *p* C are homologous lines of thofe folids ; and the propofition is true, by
§ 558.

562. (*c*) All particles equally diftant from the plane
of the equator gravitate towards that plane with equal
forces.

Let P be the particle (fig. 64. No. 1.) and P *a* a line
perpendicular to the axis, and parallel to the equator
E Q. Let P *d* be perpendicular to the equator. Let
a e b q be the fection of a concentric and fimilar fpheroid, having its axis *a b* coinciding with A B. Drawing
any ordinate *f g* to the diameter *a b* of the interior ellipfe, join *a f* and *a g*, and draw P F and P G parallel
to *a f* and *a g*, and therefore making equal angles with
P *d* K. Let *f g* cut *a b* in *i*, and draw F H, G I, perpendicular to P I.

The lines P F and P G may be confidered as the
axes of two very flender pyramids, comprehended between the plane of the figure and another plane interfecting it in the line P *a* L and making with it a very minute angle. Thefe pyramids are conftituted according
to the conditions defcribed in art. 556. The lines *a f*,
a g are, in like manner, the axes of two pyramids, whofe
fides are parallel to thofe of P F and P G. The gravitation of P to the matter contained in the pyramids P F
and P G, and the gravitation of *a* to the pyramids *a f*
and *a g*, are as the lines P F, P G, *a f*, and *a g*, refpectively. Thefe gravitations, eftimated in the direction
P *d*,

P d, a C, perpendicular to the equator, are as the lines P H, P I, $a i$, $a i$, refpectively. Now it has been fhewn (555.) that P H + P I are equal to $a i + a i$. Therefore the gravitations of P to this pair of pyramids, when eftimated perpendicularly to the equator, is equal to the gravitation of a to the correfponding pyramids lying on the interior ellipfe $a e b q$.

It is evident that by carrying the ordinate $f g$ along the whole diameter from b to a, the lines $a f$, $a g$, will diverge more and more (always equally) from $a b$ and the pyramids of which thefe lines are the axes, will thus occupy the whole furface of the interior ellipfe. And the pyramids on the axes P F and P G, will, in like manner, occupy the whole of the exterior ellipfe. It is alfo evident that the whole gravitation of P, eftimated in the direction P d, arifing from the combined gravitations to every pair of pyramids eftimated in the fame direction, is equal to the whole gravitation of a, arifing from the combined gravitation to every correfponding pair of pyramids. That is, the gravitation of P in the direction P d to the whole of the matter contained in the elementary flice of the fpheroid comprehended between the two planes which interfect in the line P a L, is equal to the gravitation of a to the matter contained in that part of the fame flice which lies within the interior fpheroid.

But this is not confined to that flice which has the ellipfe A E B Q for one of its bounding planes. Let the fpheroid be cut by any other plane paffing through the line P a L. It is known that this fection alfo is an ellipfe.

lipfe, and that it is concentric with and fimilar to the
ellipfe formed by the interfection of this plane with the
interior fpheroid *a e b q*.   They are concentric fimilar ellipfes, although not fimilar to the generating ellipfes
A E B Q and *a e b q*.   Upon this fection may another
flice be formed by means of another fection through
P *a* L, a little more oblique to the generating ellipfe
A E B Q.   And the folidity of this fection may, in like
manner, be occupied by pyramids conftituted according
to the conditions mentioned in art. 558.

From what has been demonftrated, it appears that the
gravitation of P to the whole matter of this flice, eftimated in the direction perpendicular to P *a* L, is equal
to the gravitation of *a* to the matter in the portion of
this flice contained in the interior fpheroid.

Hence it follows that when thefe flices are taken in
every direction through the line P *a* L, they will occupy
the whole fpheroid, and that the gravitation of P to the
matter in the whole folid, eftimated perpendicularly to
P *a* L, is equal to the gravitation of *a* to the matter that
is contained in the interior fpheroid, eftimated in the
fame manner.

This gravitation will certainly be in the direction perpendicular to the plane of the equator of the two fpheroids.   For the flices which compofe the folid, all paffing
through the generating ellipfe A E B Q, may be taken in
pairs, each pair confifting of equal and fimilar flices,
equally inclined to the plane of the generating ellipfe.
The gravitations to each flice of a pair are equal, and
equally

equally inclined to the plane A E B Q. Therefore they compose a gravitation in the direction which bisects the angle contained by the slices, that is, in the direction of the plane A E B Q, and parallel to its axis A B, or perpendicular to the equator.

From all this it follows, that the gravitation of P to the whole spheroid, when estimated in the direction P *d* perpendicular to the plane of its equator, is equal to the gravitation of *a* to the interior spheroid *a e b q*, which is evidently in the same direction, being directed to the centre C.

In like manner, the gravitation of another particle P' (in the line P *a* L), in a direction perpendicular to the equator of the spheroid, is equal to the gravitation of *a* to the interior spheroid *a e b q* ; for P' may be conceived as on the surface of a concentric and similar spheroid. When thus situated, it is not affected by the matter in the spheroidal stratum without it, and therefore its gravitation is to be estimated in the same way with that of the particle P. Consequently the gravitation of P and of P', estimated in a direction perpendicular to the equator, are equal, each being equal to the central gravitation of *a* to the spheroid *a e b q*. Therefore all particles equidistant from the equator gravitate equally toward it.

563. (*d*) By reasoning in the same manner, we prove that the gravitation of a particle P in the direction P *a*, perpendicular to the axis A B, is equal to the

3 M   gravitation

gravitation of the particle d to the concentric similar spheroid $d \alpha q \beta$; and therefore all particles equidistant from the axis gravitate equally in a direction perpendicular to it.

564. (e) The gravitation of a particle to the spheroid, estimated in a direction perpendicular to the equator, or perpendicular to the axis, is proportional to its distance from the equator, or from the axis. For the gravitation of P in the direction P d is equal to the gravitation of a to the spheroid $a e b q$. But the gravitation of a to the spheroid $a e b q$, is to the gravitation of A to A E B Q as a C to A C (558.) Therefore the gravitation of P in the direction P d is to the gravitation of A to the spheroid A E B Q as a C to A C, or as P d to A C; and the same may be proved of any other particle. The gravitation of A is to the gravitation of any particle as the distance A C is to the distance of that particle. All particles therefore gravitate towards the equator proportionally to their distances from it.

In the same manner, it is demonstrated that the gravitation of E to the spheroid in the direction E C perpendicular to the axis, is to the gravitation of any particle P in the same direction as E C to P a, the distance of that particle from the axis.

Therefore, &c.

565. (f) We are now able to ascertain the direction and intensity of the compound or absolute gravitation of any particle P.

For

For this purpofe let A reprefent the gravitation of the particle A in the pole, and E the gravitation of a particle E on the furface of the equator; alfo let the force with which P is urged in the direction P d be expreffed by the fymbol f, P d, and let f, P a exprefs its tendency in the direction P a. We have

$$f, \text{P } d : \text{A} = \text{P } d : \text{A C}$$

and $\qquad$ A : E = A : E

and $\qquad$ E : f, P a = E C : P a. Therefore

$$f, \text{P } d : f, \text{P } a = \text{P } d \times \text{A} \times \text{E C} : \text{A C} \times \text{E} \times \text{P } a.$$

Now make $d\text{C} : d v = \text{A} \times \text{E C} : \text{E} \times \text{A C}$, and draw P v. We have now f, P d : f, P $a = \text{P } d \times d \text{C} : \text{P } a \times d v$, $= \text{P } d \times \text{P } a : \text{P } a \times d v$, $= \text{P } d : d v$. P is therefore urged by two forces, in the directions P d and P a, and thefe forces are in the proportion of Pd and $d v$. Therefore the compound force has the direction P v.

Moreover, this compound force is to the gravity at the pole, or the gravitation of the particle A, as P v to A C. For the force P v is to the force P d as P v to P d; and the force P d is to A as P d to A C. Therefore the force P v is to A as P v to A C.

In like manner, it may be compared with the force at E. Make $a \text{C} : a u = \text{E} \times \text{C A} : \text{A} \times \text{C E}$. We fhall then have f, P a : f, P $d = \text{P } a : a u$; and the force in the direction P a, when compounded with that in the direction P d, form a force in the direction P u, and having to the force at E the proportion of P u to E C.

Thus have we obtained the direction of gravitation for any individual particle on the furface, and its magni-

tude

tude when compared with the forces at A and at E, which are fuppofed known.

566. (g) But it is neceffary to have the meafure of the accumulated force or preffure occafioned by the gravitation of a column or row of particles.

Draw the tangent E T, and take any portion of it, fuch as E T, to reprefent the gravitation of the particle E. Join C T, cutting the perpendicular $d\delta$ in δ. Since the gravitations of particles in one diameter are as their diftances from the centre (561.) $d\delta$ will exprefs the gravitation of a particle d. Thus, the gravitation of the whole column E C will be reprefented by the area of the triangle C E T, and the gravitation of the part E d, or the preffure exerted by it at d, is reprefented by the area E T δd. We may alfo conveniently exprefs the preffure of the column E C at C by $\dfrac{E \times E C}{2}$, and, in like manner, $\dfrac{A \times A C}{2}$ expreffes the weight of the column A C, or the preffure exerted by it at C.

Should we exprefs the gravitation of E by a line E T equal to E C, the weight of the whole column E C would be expreffed by $\dfrac{E C^2}{2}$, and that of the portion E d by $\dfrac{E C^2 - d C^2}{2}$, or by its equal $\dfrac{E d \times d Q}{2}$. We fee alfo that whatever value we affign to the force E, the gravitations or preffures of the columns E C and E d are proportional to E C^2, and E C^2 — d C^2, or to E C^2 and E $d \times d$ Q. This remark will be frequently referred to.

567.

567. From thefe obfervations it appears that the two columns A C and E C will exert equal or unequal preffures at the centre C, according to the adjuftment of the forces in the direction of the axis, and perpendicular to the axis. If the ellipfe do not turn round an axis, then, in order that the fluid in the columns A C and E C may prefs equally at C, we muft have A × A C = E × E C, or A C : E C = E : A. The gravitation at the pole muft be to that at the equator as the radius of the equator to the femiaxis. But we fhall find, on examination, that fuch a proportion of the gravitations at A and E cannot refult folely from the mutual gravitation of the particles of a homogeneous fpheroid, and that this fpheroid, if fluid, and at reft, cannot preferve its form.

568. The fix preceding articles afcertain the mechanical ftate of a particle placed any where in a homogeneous fpheroid, inafmuch as it is affected folely by the mutual gravitation to all the other particles. We are now to inquire what conditions of form and gravitating force will produce an exact equilibrium in every particle of an elliptical fpheroid of gravitating fluid when turning round its axis. For this purpofe, it is neceffary, in the firft place, that the direction of gravity, affected by the centrifugal force of rotation, be every where perpendicular to the furface of the fpheroid, otherwife the waters would flow off toward that quarter to which gravity inclines. Secondly, all canals reaching from the centre to the furface muft balance at the centre, otherwife the preponderating

preponderating column will fubfide, and prefs up the other, and the form of the furface will change. And, laftly, any particle of the whole mafs muft be *in equili-brio*, being equally preffed in *every* direction. Thefe three conditions feem fufficient for infuring the equilibrium of the whole.

569. Thefe conditions will be fecured in an elliptical fluid fpheroid of uniform denfity turning round its axis, *if the gravity at the pole be to the equatoreal gravity, diminiſhed by the centrifugal force ariſing from the rotation, as the radius of the equator to the ſemiaxis.*

We fhall firft demonftrate that in this cafe gravity will be every where perpendicular to the fpheroidal furface.

Let *p* exprefs the polar gravity, *e* the primitive equatoreal gravity, and *c* the centrifugal force at the furface of the equator, and let $e - c, = s$, be the fenfible gravity remaining at the equator. Then, by hypothefis, we have $p : s = CE : CA$. Confidering the ftate of any individual particle P on the furface of the fpheroid, we perceive that that part of its compound gravitation which is in a direction perpendicular to the plane of the equator is not affected by the rotation. It ftill is therefore to the force *p* at the pole as P *d* to A C (564.) But the other conftituent of the whole gravitation of P, which is eftimated perpendicular to the axis, is diminiſhed by the centrifugal force of rotation, and this diminution is in proportion to its diftance from the axis, that is, in proportion

portion to this primitive conftituent of its whole gravitation. Therefore its remaining gravity in a direction perpendicular to the axis is ftill in the proportion of its diftance from it. And this is the cafe with every individual particle. Each particle therefore may ftill be confidered as urged only by two forces, one of which is perpendicular to the equator and proportional to its diftance from it, and the other is perpendicular to the axis and proportional to its diftance from it. Therefore, if we draw a line $P v u$, fo that $d C$ may be to $d v$ as $p \times E C$ to $s \times A C$, $P v$ will be the direction of the compound force of gravity at P, as affected by the rotation.

But, by hypothefis $p : s = E C : A C$; therefore $p \times E C : s \times A C = E C^2 : A C^2$, and $E C^2 : A C^2 = d C : d v$, $= P u : P v$. But (Ellipfe 7.) if $P u$ be to $P v$ as $E C^2$ to $A C^2$, the line $P v u$ is perpendicular to the tangent to the ellipfe in the point P, and therefore to the fpheroidal furface, or to the furface of the ftill ocean.

Thus, then, the firft condition is fecured, and the fuperficial waters of the ocean will have no tendency to move in any direction. Having therefore afcertained a fuitable *direction* of the affected gravitation of P, we may next inquire into its intenfity.

570. The fenfible gravity of any fuperficial particle P is every where to the polar gravity as the line $P u$ (the normal terminating in the axis) to the radius of meridional curvature at the pole ; and it is to the fenfible gravity at the equator as the portion $P v$ of the fame normal terminating

terminating in the equator is to the radius of meridional curvature at the equator. For it was fhewn (565.) to be to the force at E as P u to E C. If, therefore, the radius of the equator be taken as the meafure of the gravitation there, P u will meafure the fenfible gravitation at P. And fince the ultimate fituation of the point u, when P is at the pole, is the centre of curvature of the ellipfe at A, the radius of curvature there will meafure the polar gravity. That is, the fenfible gravity at the equator is to the gravity at the pole, as the radius of the equator to the radius of polar curvature. By a perfectly fimilar procefs of reafoning, it is proved that if the gravity at the pole be meafured by A C, the gravity at P is meafured by P v, and at the equator by the radius of curvature of the ellipfe in E.

571. *Cor.* 1. The fenfible gravity in every point P of the furface is reciprocally as the perpendicular C t from the centre on the tangent in that point. For every where in the ellipfe, C t × P u = C E^2, and C t × P v = C A^2, as is well known.

572. *Cor.* 2. The central gravity of every fuperficial particle P, that is, its abfolute gravity P u or P v eftimated in the direction P C, is inverfely proportional to its diftance from the centre, that is, the central gravity at P is to the central gravity at E as E C to P C, and to the polar gravity as A C to P C. For, if the gravity P v be reduced to the direction P C by drawing $v o$ perpendicular to C P, P o will meafure this central gravity.

vity. Now, it is well known that P o × P C is every where = A C^2; and, in like manner, P ω × P C = E C^2. Therefore P o, or P ω, are every where reciprocally as P C.

Hence it follows that the fenfible increment of gravity in proceeding from the equator to the pole is very nearly as the fquare of the fine of the latitude ; for, without entering on a more curious inveftigation, it is plain that the increments of gravity, when fo minute in comparifon with the whole gravity, are very nearly as the decrements of the diftance. Now, in a fpheroid very little compreffed, thefe decrements are in that proportion. It may be demonftrated that in the latitude where fin.^{2} = $\frac{1}{3}$, namely, lat. 35° 16′, the gravity is the fame as to a perfect fphere of the fame capacity, having for its radius the femidiameter of the ellipfe in that point. It is alfo a diftinguifhing property of this latitude that, if this femidiameter be produced, the gravitation of a particle, at any diftance in this direction, is the fame as to a perfect fphere of the fame capacity. This is not the cafe in any other direction.

573. *Cor*. 3. Laftly, the force eftimated in the direction P d is to the force in the direction P a as E C^2 × P d to A C^2 × P a. For we had (564.) f, P d : f, P a = A × E C × P d : E × A C × P a, which, by fubftituting p and s for A and E, it becomes p × E C × P d : s × A C × P a, = E C^2 × P d : A C^2 × P a.

Hitherto we have confidered only the particles on the

3 N   furface

furface of the fpheroid. But we muſt know the condition of a particle any where within it.

574. A particle p, in any internal point of a diameter, has its fenfible gravity in the direction perpendicular to the furface of a concentric and fimilar fpheroid
paſſing through the particle. For the gravity at p is compounded of forces perpendicular to the axis and to the
equator, and proportional to the diſtances from them,
and therefore proportional to the fimilar forces acting on
the particle P (558.) Therefore the compound force of
p will be parallel, and in the fame proportion, to the
compound force $P v$ of P, and muſt therefore be perpendicular to the tangent of the furface in p. It is as
$p v'$.

575. Cor. Hence we muſt infer that if there were
a cavern at p, containing water, the furface of this ſtill
water would be a part of the fpheroidal furface $a e b q$.
Should this cavern extend all the way to e or a, the water ſhould arrange itſelf according to this furface ; or, if
$e r p$ be a pipe or conduit, the water in it ſhould be ſtill,
except fo far as it is affected by the preſſures of the columns A a and P p and E e (thefe preſſures will be
proved to be equal).

It would feem, from thefe premifes, that if the elliptical fpheroid conſiſt of different fluids, which do not
mix, and which differ in denfity, they will be difpofed
in concentric fimilar elliptical ſtrata, fo that their bounding

ing furfaces fhall be fimilar. The proof of this feems
the fame with what is received for a demonftration of the
horizontal furface of the boundary between water and
oil contained in a veffel. Accordingly, this has been fuppofed by many refpectable writers, as a thing that needed
no other proof. But this is by no means the cafe. It
can be ftrictly demonftrated that the denfer fluids occupy
the loweft place, and that the ftrata become lefs and lefs
eccentric as we approach the centre, where the ultimate
evanefcent figure may be denominated a fpherical point.
It may be feen, even at prefent, that they cannot be fimilar, unlefs homogeneous. For, without this condition,
it cannot be generally demonftrated that the gravitation
of a particle p to the equator, and to the axis, is as the
diftance from them, which is the foundation of all the
fubfequent demonftrations.

576. In the next place, all rectilineal columns, extending from the centre to the furface, will balance in
the centre. For, drawing $v\,o$, $v'\,o'$ perpendicular to P C,
it is plain that P o and $p\,o'$ reprefent the gravities of P
and p eftimated in the direction P C. Now P $c:p\,o' =$
P C $:p$ C. Therefore the gravitation of the whole co-
lumn, or the preffure on C, is reprefented by $\dfrac{\text{P}\,o \times \text{P C}}{2}$
(566.) Now, in the ellipfe P $o \times$ P C $=$ C A', a con-
ftant quantity. Therefore the preffure of every column
at C is the fame. In like manner, the preffure of the
columns, C p and C a are equal, and therefore alfo the

3 N 2   preffures

preffures of P p, E e, and A a, at p, e, and a, are all equal.

577. Laftly, any particle of the fluid is equally preffed in every direction, and if the whole were fluid, would be *in equilibrio*, and remain at reft.

To prove this, let P p (fig. 64. 3.) be a column reaching from P to the furface, and taken in any direction, but, firft, in one of the meridional planes, of which A B is the axis, and E Q the interfection by the equatoreal plane. In the tangent A a take A a equal to E C, and A α equal to A C. Draw a C e and α C ϵ to the tangent E ϵ at the equator. It is evident that E e = A C, and E ϵ = E C. Through p and P draw the lines p L l, N P z, parallel to E C, and the lines p N φ, I P δ parallel to A B. Draw alfo I K k parallel to E C.

Since, by hypothefis, the whole forces at A and E are inverfely as A C and E C, A a and E e are as the forces acting at A and E. Confequently, the weights of the columns F D, L Z, and K L, will be reprefented by the areas F f d D, L l z Z, and K k l L (566.)

All the preffures or forces which act on the particles of the column p P may be refolved into forces acting parallel to A C, and forces acting parallel to E C, and the force acting on each particle is as its diftance from the axis to which it is directed (564.) Therefore the whole force with which the column p P is preffed in the direction A C is to the force with which the column O P is preffed in the fame direction, as the number of particles

in

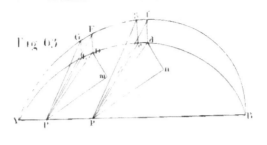

Fig 63

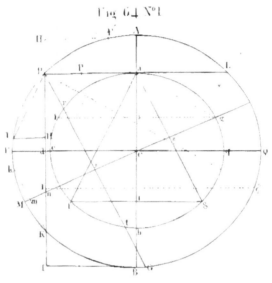

Fig 64 N°1

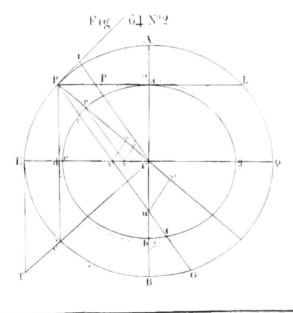

Fig 64 N°2

in $p\,P$ to the number in $O\,P$, that is, as $p\,P$ to $O\,P$. But there is only a part of this force employed in preffing the particles in the direction of the canal. Another part merely preffes the fluid to the fide of the canal $p\,P$. Draw $O\,g$ perpendicular to $p\,P$. The force acting in the direction $A\,C$ on any particle in $p\,P$ is to its efficacy in the direction $p\,P$ as $O\,P$ to $g\,P$, that is, as $p\,P$ to $O\,P$ Therefore, the preffure which the particle P fuftains in the direction $p\,P$, from the action of all the particles in $p\,P$ in the direction $A\,C$, is precifely equal to the preffure it fuftains from the action of the column $O\,P$, acting in the fame direction $A\,C$. But it has been fhewn (566.) that the preffure of $O\,P$ in the direction $A\,C$ is precifely the fame with the weight of the column $L\,Z$, which weight is reprefented by the area $L\,l\,z\,Z$.

In the very fame manner, the whole preffure on P in the direction $p\,P$ arifing from the preffure of each of the particles in $p\,P$ in the direction $E\,C$, is precifely the fame with the preffure on P, arifing from the preffure of the column $N\,P$ in this direction $E\,C$, that is, it is equal to the weight of the column $F\,D$, which is reprefented by the area $F\,f\,d\,D$.

Becaufe $E\,s$ is equal to $E\,C$, we have $F\,\varphi\,\partial\,D = \dfrac{C\,F^2 - C\,D^2}{2}, = \dfrac{L\,p^2 - L\,O^2}{2}, = \dfrac{p\,O \times O\,m}{2}$. And in like manner, $K\,\varkappa\,\lambda\,L = \dfrac{I\,O \times O\,i}{2}$. But $p\,O \times O\,m : I\,O \times O\,i = E\,C^2 : A\,C^2$, and therefore

$$F\,\varphi\,\partial\,D : K\,\varkappa\,\lambda\,L = E\,C^2 : A\,C^2$$

but $K\,\varkappa\,\lambda\,L : K\,k\,l\,L = A\,C : E\,C$

and

in p P to the number in O P, that is, as p P to O P. But there is only a part of this force employed in pressing the particles in the direction of the canal. Another part merely presses the fluid to the side of the canal p P. Draw O g perpendicular to p P. The force acting in the direction A C on any particle in p P is to its efficacy in the direction p P as O P to g P, that is, as p P to O P Therefore, the pressure which the particle P sustains in the direction p P, from the action of all the particles in p P in the direction A C, is precisely equal to the pressure it sustains from the action of the column O P, acting in the same direction A C. But it has been shewn (566.) that the pressure of O P in the direction A C is precisely the same with the weight of the column L Z, which weight is represented by the area L l z Z.

In the very same manner, the whole pressure on P in the direction p P arising from the pressure of each of the particles in p P in the direction E C, is precisely the same with the pressure on P, arising from the pressure of the column N P in this direction E C, that is, it is equal to the weight of the column F D, which is represented by the area F$f$$d$ D.

Because E s is equal to E C, we have $F \varphi \partial D = \dfrac{C F^2 - C D^2}{2}, = \dfrac{L p^2 - L O^2}{2}, = \dfrac{p O \times O m}{2}$. And in like manner, $K \varkappa \lambda L = \dfrac{I O \times O i}{2}$. But $p O \times O m$: $I O \times O i = E C^2 : A C^2$, and therefore

$$F \varphi \partial D : K \varkappa \lambda L = E C^2 : A C^2$$

but $K \varkappa \lambda L : K k l L = A C : E C$

and

and $F f d D : F \phi \partial D = A C : E C$, therefore

$$F f d D : K k l L = E C^2 \times A C^2 : A C^2 \times E C^2,$$

that is, in the ratio of equality. Now the area $K k l L$ reprefents the weight of the column $K L$, or the preffure exerted in the direction $A C$ by the column $I O$.

Thus it appears that when the forces acting on the particles in the column $p P$ are eftimated in the direction of the canal, the preffure exerted on the particle P is equal to the united preffures of the columns $O P$ and $I O$ acting in the direction $A C$, that is, to the preffure of the fluids in the canal $I P$ in its own direction. * Therefore the fluid in the canal $I P$ will balance the fluid in the canal $p P$, and the particle P will have no tendency to move in either direction. And, fince this is equally true, whatever may be the direction of the canal $P p$, or $P \pi$, it follows that the particle P is equally preffed in every direction in the plane of the figure, and would remain at reft, if the whole fpheroid were fluid.

But now let the canal $P p$ be in a plane different from a meridional plane (as in fig. 64. 4.) In whatever direction

---

* The ftudent muft not confound this with a compofition of two preffures or forces $N P$ and $O P$, compofing a preffure or force $p P$. There is no fuch compofition in the prefent cafe. It is only meant that the preffure in the direction $p P$ arifing from the gravitation of the particles in the canal, is the fame, in refpect of magnitude, with the preffure in the direction $I P$, arifing from the gravitation of the fluid in $I P$.

tion P p is difpofed, a plane may be made to pafs through
it, perpendicular to the plane E e Q q of the equator of
the fpheroid.   Let p I q i e be this plane.   Its fection
with the fpheroid will be an ellipfe, fimilar to the generating ellipfe A E B Q, as is well known.   Let the meridional fection A E B Q pafs through the point P of the
canal p P.   It will cut the fection e I q i in a line I P i
perpendicular to its interfection e q with the equator of
the fpheroid, and therefore parallel to the axis a c b of
the fection, if it do not coincide with this axis.   Let
C D E be the femidiameter of the generating ellipfe
which paffes through the interfection D of I i and e q;
and draw P Z parallel to D C, and P z parallel to e q
cutting a c b in z, and join z Z and c C.   It is plain
that the plane paffing through the axis A B of the fpheroid and the axis a b of the fection e I q i is perpendicular to that fection (for it bifects e q, which is a chord
of the equatoreal circle L e Q q), and that the planes
D c C and P z Z are parallel, and the angles at c and z
right angles.

Let us now confider the forces which act on the particles of fluid in the canal p P.   They are, as before, all
refolvable into two, one of them parallel to A C, and
the other perpendicular to· it.   Thus, the particle P is
urged by a force in the direction P D parallel to A C,
and proportional to its diftance P D from the equator of
the fpheroid.   It is alfo urged by a force in the direction
P Z perpendicular to A C, and proportional to its diftance
P Z.   This force P Z may be refolved into P z and z Z.
The

The force $z Z$ remains the same, for all the particles in the canal $p P$, $z Z$ being equal to $c C$. But the force $P z$ is always proportional to the diſtance of the particle in the canal $p P$ from the axis $a c b$ of the ſection $e I q i$. It is alſo to the axipetal force in the direction $P Z$ as $P z$ to $P Z$.

Moreover, it has been ſhewn (573.) that the force in the direction $P Z$ is to the force in the direction $P D$ in the ratio of $A C^2 \times P Z$ to $E C^2 \times P D$, that is (on account of the ſimilarity of the ſections $A E B Q$ and $a e b q$), as $a c^2 \times P Z$ to $e c^2 \times P D$. Therefore the force in the direction $P z$ is to the force in the direction $P D$ as $a c^2 \times P z$ to $e c^2 \times P D$. Wherefore, ſince from theſe elements it has been proved already that the whole preſſure on P in the canal $p P$, lying in the plane $A E B Q$, is equal to the preſſure of the canal $I P$, it follows that the preſſure of the canal $p P$, lying in the plane $a e b q$ is alſo equal to the preſſure of the canal $I P$.

Thus it now appears that the particle P is urged in every direction with the ſame force by the fluid in any rectilineal canal whatever reaching to the ſurface. It is therefore *in equilibrio;* and, as it is taken at random, in any part of the ſpheroid, the whole fluid ſpheroid is *in equilibrio.*

We alſo ſee that the whole force with which any particle P is preſſed in any direction whatever is to the preſſure at the centre C as the rectangle $I P i$ to $A C^2$. For that is the proportion of the preſſure of the canal $I P$

to

to that of the canal A C ; and all canals terminating in the centre exert equal preſſures.

578. It is now demonſtrated that a maſs of uniformly denſe matter, influenced in every particle by gravitation, and ſo conſtituted that an equilibrium of force on every particle is neceſſary for the maintenance of its form, may exiſt, with a motion of rotation, in the form of an elliptical ſpheroid, if there be a proper adjuſtment between the proportion of the two axes and the time of the rotation. Whatever may be the proportion of the axes of an oblate ſpheroid, there is a rapidity of rotation which will induce that proportion between the undiminiſhed gravity at the pole and the diminiſhed gravity on the ſurface of the equator, which is required for the preſervation of that form. But it has not been proved that a fluid ſphere, when ſet in motion round its axis, muſt aſſume the form of an elliptical ſpheroid, but only that this is a poſſible form. This was all that Newton aimed at, and his proof is not free from reaſonable objeĉtions. The great mathematicians ſince the days of Newton have done little more. They have not determined the figure that a fluid ſphere, or a nucleus covered with a fluid, *muſt* aſſume when ſet in motion round its axis. * But they have added to the number of conditions that muſt be implemented, in order to produce *another kind* of aſſurance that an elliptical ſpheroid

---

* Montucla ſays (Vol. IV.) that M. le Gendre has demonſtrated that an elliptical ſpheroid is the only poſſible form for a homogeneous fluid turning round its axis.

fpheroid will anfwer the purpofe, and by this limitation
have greatly increafed the difficulty of the queftion.   M.
Clairaut, who has carried his fcruples farther than the
reft, requires, befides the three conditions which have
been fhewn to confift with the permanence of the elliptical form, that it alfo be demonftrated, 1*mo*, That a canal of any form whatever muft every where be *in equilibrio* : 2*do,* That a canal of any fhape, reaching from one
part of the furface, through the mafs, or along the furface, to any other part, fhall exert no force at its extremities : 3*tio,* That a canal of any form, returning into
itfelf, fhall be *in equilibrio* through its whole extent.

579.   I apprehend that in the cafe of uniform denfity,
all thefe conditions are involved in the propofition in art.
(577.)   For we can fuppofe the canal *p* P of fig. 64.
N° 4. to communicate with the canal P δ.   It has been
fhewn that they are *in equilibrio* in P.   The canal 4 β
may branch off from P δ.   Thefe are *in equilibrio* in
the point 4.   The canal 3 α may branch off at 3, and
they will be ftill *in equilibrio ;* and the canal 2 1 will
be *in equilibrio* with all the foregoing.   Now thefe
points of derivation may be multiplied, till the polygonal
canal *p* P 4 3 2 1 becomes a canal of continual curvature
of any form.   In the next place, this canal exerts no force
at either end.   For the *equilibrium* is proved in every
ftate of the canal *p* P—it may be as fhort as we pleafe—
it may be evanefcent, and actually ceafe to have any
length, without any interruption of the *equilibrium.*
                                Therefore,

"Therefore, there is no force exerted at its extremity to
diſturb the form of the ſurface. It may be obſerved that
this very circumſtance proves that the direction of gravity is perpendicular to the ſurface.   And it muſt be obſerved that the perpendicularity of gravity to the ſurface
is not employed in demonſtrating this propoſition.   The
whole reſts on the propoſitions in art. 562. 563. and 564,
both of which we owe to Mr M'Laurin.

580. Having now demonſtrated the competency of the
elliptical ſpheroid for the rotation of a planet, we proceed
to inveſtigate the preciſe proportion of diameters which is
required for any propoſed rotation.   For example, What
protuberancy of the equator will diffuſe the ocean of this
Earth uniformly, conſiſtently with a rotation in 23^h
56′ 04″, the planet being uniformly denſe ?

Let p and e expreſs the primitive gravity of a particle
placed at the pole and at the ſurface of the equator, ariſing
ſolely from the gravitation to every particle in the ſpheroid, and let c repreſent the centrifugal tendency at the
ſurface of the equator, ariſing from the rotation.   We
ſhall have an elliptical ſpheroid of a permanent form, if
A C be to E C as $e - c$ is to p (569.) We muſt therefore find, firſt of all, what is the proportion of p to e reſulting from any proportion of A C to E C.

To accompliſh this in general terms with preciſion, appeared ſo difficult a taſk, even to Newton, that he avoided it, and took an indirect method, which his ſagacity

3 O 2   ſhewed

fhewed him to be perfectly fafe ; and even this was difficult.   It is in the complete folution of this problem that
the genius of M'Laurin has fhewn itfelf moft remarkable
both for acutenefs and for geometrical elegance.   It is not
exceeded (in the opinion of the firft mathematicians) *
by any thing of Archimedes or Apollonius.   For this
reafon, it is to be regreted that we have not room for the
feries of beautiful propofitions that are neceffary in his
method.   We muft take a fhorter courfe, limited indeed to fpheroids of very fmall eccentricity (whereas
the method of M'Laurin extends to any degree of eccentricity), but, with this limitation, perfectly exact, and
abundantly eafy and fimple.   It is, in its chief fteps, the
method followed by M. Bofcovich.   •

580.   Let A E B Q (fig. 65.) reprefent the terreftrial
fpheroid, nearly fpherical, and let A e B q and E a Q b
reprefent the infcribed and circumfcribed fpheres.   With
the axis and parameter A B defcribe the parabola A F G,
drawing the ordinates B D F, E C H, &c.   Defcribe
alfo the curve line A I L G, fuch, that we have, in every
point of it, A B : A D = D F : D I ; A B : A C = C H :
C L, &c.
Our firft aim fhall be to find an expreffion and value
of the polar gravity.   We may conceive the fpheroid as
a fphere, on which there is fpread the redundant matter
contained between the fpherical and the fpheroidal furfaces,

---

* See Boffuet *Hift. des Mathematiques,*

faces. We know the gravitation of the polar particle A to the fphere, and now want to have the meafure of its gravitation to this redundant matter. Suppofe the figure to turn round the axis A B. The femiellipfis A E B will generate a fpheroidal furface ; the femicircle A *e* B will generate a fpherical furface, and the intercepted portions P *p*, E *e*, &c. of the ordinates will generate flat rings of the redundant matter. As the deviation from a fphere is fuppofed very fmall (E *e* not exceeding the 500dth part of E Q), we may fuppofe, without any fenfible error, that A *p* is the diftance of A from the whole of the ring generated by P *p*.

Proceeding on this affumption, we fay that the gravitation of A to the rings generated by P *p*, E *e*, &c. is proportional to the portions F I, H L, &c. of the correfponding ordinates D F, C H, &c., and that the gravitation of A to the whole redundant matter may be expreffed by the furface A F H G L I A comprehended between the lines A F H G and A I L G.

For, the abfolute gravitation of A to the ring P *p* is directly as the furface of the ring, and inverfely as the fquare of its diftance from A. Now, the furface of the ring is as its breadth, and its circumference jointly. Its breadth P *p*, and alfo its circumference, being proportional to D *p*, the furface is proportional to D p^2. The abfolute gravitation is therefore proportional to $\dfrac{D p^2}{A p^2}$. This may be refolved into forces in the directions A D and D *p*. The force in the direction D *p* is balanced

by

by an equal force on the other fide of the axis. Therefore, to have the gravitation in the direction of the axis,
the value of the abfolute gravitation in the direction Ap
muft be reduced in the proportion of Ap to AD. It
therefore becomes $\dfrac{Dp^2 \times AD}{Ap^2 \times Ap}, = \dfrac{Dp^2 \times AD}{Ap^3}$, or,
which is the fame thing, $\dfrac{Dp^2 \times AD \times Ap}{Ap^4}$. But
$Ap^2 = AB \times AD$, and $Ap^4 = AB^2 \times AD^2$. Alfo
$Dp^2 = AD \times DB$. Therefore the value laft found be-
comes $\dfrac{AD \times DB \times AD \times Ap}{AB^2 \times AD^2}$, which is equal to,
or the fame thing with $\dfrac{DB \times Ap}{AB^2}$. Since AB^2 is a
conftant quantity, the gravitation in the direction AC
to the ring generated by Pp is proportional to $DB \times Ap$.

It is very obvious that DF, CH, BG, &c. are refpectively equal to Ap, Ae, AB, &c. Therefore the
gravitation to the matter in the ring generated by Pp
is proportional to $DB \times DF$.

Now, by the conftruction of the curve line ALG,
we have $\qquad AB : AD = DF : DI$
$\quad$ therefore $\quad AB : DB = DF : IF$
$\quad$ and $\qquad AB \times IF = DB \times DF$
Therefore, fince AB is conftant, IF is proportional to
$DB \times DF$, that is, to the gravitation to the ring generated by Pp. Therefore the gravitation to the whole
redundant matter may be reprefented by the fpace
$AHGLA$.

$\hspace{11cm}$ Let

Let π be the periphery of a circle of which the radius is 1. The circumference of that generated by Ee will be $\pi \times Ce$, and its surface $= \pi \times Ce \times Ee$, and the absolute gravitation to it is $\dfrac{\pi \times Ce \times Ee}{Ae^2}$, or $\dfrac{\pi \times Ce \times Ee}{2\,AC^2}$, that is, $\dfrac{\pi \times Ee}{2\,AC}$. This, when reduced to the direction AC, becomes $\dfrac{\pi \times Ee \times AC}{2\,Ae \times AC}$, that is, $\dfrac{\pi \times Ee}{2\,Ae}$, or $\dfrac{\pi \times Ee \times Ae}{2\,Ae^2}$. And becaufe $Ae^2 = 2\,AC^2$, and $LH = \frac{1}{2}CH, = \frac{1}{2}Ae$, the reduced gravitation becomes $\dfrac{\pi \times Ee}{2\,AC^2} \times LH$.

This being the meafure or reprefentative of the gravitation to the material furface or ring generated by Ee, the gravitation to the whole redundant matter contained between the fpheroid and the infcribed fphere will be reprefented by $\dfrac{\pi \times Ee}{2\,AC^2}$ multiplied by the fpace comprehended between the curve lines AFG and ALG. We muft find the value of this fpace.

The parabolic fpace AHGBA is known to be $= \frac{2}{3}AB \times BG, = \frac{2}{3}AB^2$. The fquare of DI is proportional to the cube of BD. For, by the conftruction of the curve $AB^2 : AD^2 = DF^2 : DI^2$, and $DI^2 = \dfrac{AD^2 \times DF^2}{AB^2}, = \dfrac{AD^2}{AB} \times \dfrac{DF^2}{AB}, = \dfrac{AD^2}{AB}AD, = \dfrac{AD^3}{AB}$. Therefore DI is proportional to $AD^{\frac{3}{2}}$, and the area ABGLA is $= \frac{2}{5}AB \times BG, = \frac{2}{5}AB^2$. Take this from the parabolic area $\frac{2}{3}AB^2$, and there remains $\frac{4}{15}AB^2$

$\frac{4}{15}$ A B² for the value of A L G H A. This is equal to $\frac{16}{15}$ A C².

Now, the gravitation of A to the redundant matter was fhewn to be $= A L G H A \times \frac{\pi \times E e}{2 A C^3}$. This now becomes $\frac{16}{15} A C^2 \times \frac{\pi \times E e}{2 A C^2}$, or $\frac{8}{15} \pi \times E e$. Such is the gravitation of a particle in the pole of the fpheroid to the redundant matter fpread over the infcribed fphere.

The gravitation of a particle fituated on the furface of the equator to the fame redundant matter is not quite fo obvious as the polar gravity, but may be had with the fame accuracy, by means of the following confiderations.

581. Let A B a b (fig. 66.) reprefent an oblate fpheroid, formed by rotation round the fhorter axis B b of the generating ellipfe, and viewed by an eye fituated in the plane of its equator. Let A E a e be the circumfcribed fphere. This fpheroid is deficient from the fphere by two menifcufes or cups, generated by the rotation of the lunulæ A E a B A and A e a b A.

Now fuppofe the fame generating ellipfe A B a b A to turn round its longer axis A a. It will generate an oblong fpheroid, touching the oblate fpheroid in the whole circumference of one elliptical meridian, viz. the meridian A B a b A which paffes through the poles A and a of this oblong fpheroid. It touches the equator of the oblate fpheroid only in the points A and a, and has the diameter

diameter A *a* for its axis. This oblong fpheroid is otherwife wholly within the oblate fpheroid, leaving between
their furfaces two menifcufes of an oblong form. This
may be better conceived by firft fuppofing that both the
fpheroids and alfo the circumfcribed fphere are cut by a
plane P G *g p*, perpendicular to the axis A *a* of the oblong fpheroid, and to the plane of the equator of the oblate fpheroid. Now fuppofe that the whole figure makes
the quarter of a turn round the axis B *b* of the oblate
fpheroid, fo that the pole *a* of the oblong fpheroid comes
quite in front, and is at C, the eye of the fpectator being in the axis produced. The equator of the oblong
fpheroid will now appear a circle O B *o b* O, touching the
oblate fpheroid in its poles B and *b*. The fection of the
plane P *p* with the circumfcribed fphere will now appear
as a circle P' R *p' r*. Its fection with the oblate fpheroid
will appear an ellipfe R G' *r g'* fimilar to the generating
ellipfe A B *a b*, as is well known. And its fection with
the oblong fpheroid will now appear a circle I G' *i g'* parallel to its equator O B *o b*. P *p* is equal to P'*p'*, and
G *g* to G'*g'*. Thus it appears that as every fection of
the oblate fpheroid is deficient from the concomitant fection of the circumfcribed fphere by the want of two lunulæ R P' *r* G' and R *p' r g'*, fo it exceeds the concomitant fection of the oblong fpheroid by two lunulæ
G' R *g'* I and G' *r g' i*. It is alfo plain that if thefe
fpheroids differ very little from perfect fpheres, as when
E B does not exceed $\frac{1}{100}$ of E *e*, the deficiency of each
fection G *g* from the concomitant fection of the circum-

3 P   fcribed

fcribed fphere is very nearly equal to its excefs above the concomitant fection of the infcribed oblong fpheroid. It may fafely be confidered as equal to one half of the fpace contained between the circles on the diameters P'p and, G'g', * in the fame way that we confidered the lunula A P E B e p A of fig. 65. as one half of the fpace contained between the femicircles A e B and a E b.

From this view of the figure, it appears that the gravitation of a particle a in the equator of the oblate fpheroid to the two cups or menifcufes R P' r G' and R p' r g', by which the oblate fpheroid is lefs than the circumfcribed fphere, may be computed by the very fame method that we employed in the laft propofition. But, inftead of computing (as in laft propofition) the gravitation of a to the ring generated by the revolution of P G (fig. 66.), that is, to the furface contained between the two circles R P' r p' and I G' i g', we muft employ only the two lunulæ R P' r G' R and R p' r g' R. In this way, we may account the gravitation to the deficient matter (or the deficiency of gravitation) to be one half of the quantity determined by that propofition, and therefore $= \frac{4}{15} \pi \times$ E e of fig. 65. The laft propofition gave us the gravitation to all the matter by which the fpheroid exceeded the infcribed fphere. The prefent propofition

gives

---

* For the circumfcribed circle is to the ellipfe as the ellipfe to the infcribed circle. When the extremes differ fo little, the geometrical and arithmetical mean will differ but infenfibly.

gives the gravitation to all the matter by which it falls
short of the circumfcribed fphere.

582. We can now afcertain the primitive gravitation at the pole and at the equator, by adding or fubtracting the quantities now found to or from the gravitation to the fpheres. Let r be the radius of the fphere,
and πr the circumference of a great circle. The diameter is $2\ r$. The area of a great circle is $\frac{\pi\ r^2}{2}$, and
the whole furface of the fphere is $2\ \pi\ r^2$, and its folid
contents is $\frac{2}{3}\ \pi\ r^3$. Therefore, fince the gravitation to a
fphere of uniform denfity is the fame as if all its matter
were collected in its centre, and is as the quantity of
matter directly, and as the fquare of the diftance r inverfely, the gravitation to a fphere will be proportional
to $\frac{2}{3}\ \frac{\pi\ r^3}{r^2}$, that is, to $\frac{2}{3}\ \pi\ r.$ *

Now

---

* I beg leave to mention here a circumftance which fhould
have been taken notice of in art. 464, when the firft principles
of fpherical attractions were eftablifhed.   It was fhewn that
the gravitation of the particle P to the fpherical furface generated by the rotation of the arch A D′ T is equal to its gravitation to the furface generated by the rotation of B D T.
Therefore if P be infinitely near to A, fo that the furface
generated by A D′ T may be confidered as a point or fingle
particle, the gravitation to that particle is equal to the gravitation to all the reft of the furface ; that is, it is one half of

the

Now let A E B Q (fig. 65.) be an oblate fpheroid, whofe poles are A and B. The gravity of a particle A to the fphere whofe radius is A C is $\frac{2}{3}\pi \times$ A C, $= \frac{2}{3}\pi \times$ E C $- \frac{2}{3}\pi \times$ E e, or $\frac{2}{3}\pi \times$ E C $- \frac{10}{15}\pi \times$ E e. Add to this its gravitation $\frac{8}{15}\pi \times$ E e, to the redundant matter. The fum is evidently $\frac{2}{3}\pi \times$ E C $- \frac{2}{15}\pi \times$ E e.

The gravitation of the particle E on the furface of the equator to a fphere whofe radius is E C is $\frac{2}{3}\pi \times$ E C. From this fubtract its deficiency of gravitation, viz. $\frac{4}{15}\pi \times$ E e, and there remains the equatoreal primitive gravity $= \frac{2}{3}\pi \times$ E C $- \frac{4}{15}\pi \times$ E e.

Therefore, in this fpheroid, the polar gravity is to the equatoreal gravity as $\frac{2}{3}\pi \times$ E C $- \frac{2}{15}\pi \times$ E e to $\frac{2}{3}\pi \times$ E C $- \frac{4}{15}\pi \times$ E e, or (dividing all by $\frac{2}{3}\pi$) as E C $- \frac{1}{5}$ E e to E C $- \frac{2}{5}$ E e, or (becaufe E e is fuppofed to be very fmall in comparifon with E C) as E C to E C $- \frac{1}{5}$ E e. In general terms, let g reprefent the mean gravity, p the polar, and e the equatoreal gravity, r the radius of the infcribed fphere, and x the elevation E e of the equator above the infcribed fphere. We have, for a general expreffion of this proportion of the primi-

tive

---

the whole gravitation. If we fuppofe P and A to coincide, that is, make P one of the particles of the furface, its gravitation to the fpherical furface will be only one half of what it was when it was without the furface ; and if we fuppofe P adjoining to A internally, it will exhibit no gravitation at all.

tive gravitations, $p : e = r + \frac{1}{7} x : r$, or (becaufe x is very fmall in comparifon with r), $p : e = r : r - \frac{1}{7} x$. This laſt is generally the moſt convenient, and it is exact, if r be taken for the equatoreal radius.

583. Had the fpheroid been prolate (oblong) the fame reafoning would have given us $p : e = r : r + \frac{1}{7} x$.

I may add here that the gravitation at the pole of an oblong fpheroid, the gravitation at the equator of an oblate fpheroid (having the fame axes) and the gravitation to the circumfcribed fphere, on any point of its furface, are proportional, refpectively, to $\frac{1}{3} r + \frac{1}{15} x$; $\frac{1}{3} r + \frac{1}{7} x$; and $\frac{1}{3} r + \frac{1}{7} x$. *

584. It now appears, as was formerly hinted (567.) that we cannot have an elliptical fpheroid of uniform denfity,

in

---

* Many queſtions occur, in which we want the gravitation of a particle P′ fituated in the direction of any diameter C P (fig. 65.) Draw the conjugate diameter C M, and fuppofe the fpheroid cut by a plane paſſing through C M perpendicular to the plane of the figure. This fection will be an ellipfe, of which the femiaxes are C M and C E $(= r + x)$. A circle whofe radius is the mean proportional between C M and C E has the fame area with this fection, and the gravitation to this circle will be the fame (from a particle placed in the axis) with the gravitation to this fection. Therefore, as the angle P C M is very nearly a right angle, the gravitation of

P′

in which the gravitation at the pole is to that at the e-
quator as the equatoreal radius to the polar radius. This
would make $p : e = r : r - x$, a ratio five times greater
than that which results from a gravitation proportional
to $\frac{1}{d^2}$.

Thus have we obtained, with sufficient accuracy, the
ratio of polar and equatoreal gravity, unaffected by any
external force, and we are now in a condition to tell
what velocity of rotation will so diminish the equatoreal
gravitation that the remaining gravity there shall be to the
polar gravity as A C to E C.

585. Let c be taken to represent the centrifugal
tendency generated at the surface of the equator by the
rotation of the planet round its axis, and let the other
symbols be retained. The sensible gravity at the equator
is $e - c$, the polar gravity p, and the excess of the equatoreal radius above the semiaxis r is x.

We have shewn (582.) that the primitive gravities at
the pole and the equator are in the ratio of r to $r - \frac{1}{5}x$,

or,

P to the spheroid will be the same with its polar (or axicular)
gravitation to another spheroid, whose polar semiaxis is P C,
and whose equatoreal radius is the mean proportional between
C M and C E. This is easily computed. If the arch P E
be 35° 16', a sphere having the radius P C has the same capacity with the spheroid A E B Q (when E e is very small).
Hence follows what was said in the note on art. 572.

or, (becaufe x is a very fmall part of r), in the ratio of $r + \frac{1}{5}x$ to r. That is, $r : r + \frac{1}{5}x = e : p$. This gives $p = e + \frac{e x}{5 r}$. Therefore the ratio of the *fenfible* equatoreal gravity to the gravity at the pole is $e - c : e + \frac{e x}{5 r}$, or, very nearly, $e : e + \frac{e x}{5 r} + c$. Therefore we muft have, for a revolving fphere of fmall eccentricity,

$$e : e + \frac{e x}{5 r} + c = r : r + x$$

and

$$e : \frac{e x}{5 r} + c = r : x$$

confequently

$$e x = \frac{e x}{5} + r c$$

and

$$e x - \frac{e x}{5} \text{ or } \frac{4 e x}{5} = r c$$

and

$$4 e x = 5 r c, \text{ and } x = \frac{5 r c}{4 e}$$

and the ellipticity $\frac{x}{r} = \frac{5 c}{4 e}$, that is,

Four times the primitive gravity at the equator is to five times the centrifugal force of rotation as the femiaxis to the elevation of the equator above the infcribed fphere.

586. It is a matter of obfervation that the diminution of equatoreal gravity by the Earth's rotation in $23^h 56' 4''$ is nearly $\frac{1}{289}$. Therefore $4 \times 289 : 5 = r : x = 231\frac{1}{5} : 1$, very nearly. This is the ratio deduced by Newton in his indirect, and feemingly incurious, method. That method has been much criticifed by his fcholars, as if it could be fuppofed that Newton was ignorant that the proportionality

proportionality employed by him, in a rough way, was not *neceſſarily* involved in the nature of the thing. But Newton knew that, in the preſent caſe, the error, if any, muſt be altogether inſignificant. He did not demonſtrate, but aſſumed as granted, that the form is elliptical, or that an elliptical form is competent to the purpoſe. His juſt-neſs of thought has been ſo repeatedly verified in many caſes as abſtruſe as this, that it is unreaſonable to aſcribe it to conjecture, and it ſhould rather, as by Dan. Ber-noulli, be aſcribed to his penetration and ſagacity. He had ſo many new wonders to communicate, that he had not time for all the lemmas that were requiſite for enab-ling inferior minds to trace his ſteps of inveſtigation.

587. When conſidering the aſtronomical phenomena, ſome notice was taken of the attempts which have been made to decide this matter by obſervation alone, by mea-ſuring degrees of the meridian in different latitudes.

But ſuch irregularity is to be ſeen among the mea-ſures of a degree, that the queſtion is ſtill undecided by this method. All that can be made evident by the com-pariſon is that the Earth is oblate, and much more oblate than the ellipſe of Mr Hermann ; and that the medium de-duction approaches much nearer to the Newtonian form. When we recollect that the error of one ſecond in the eſtimation of the latitude induces an error of more than thirty yards in the meaſure of the degree, and that the form of this globe is to be learned, not from the lengths of the degrees, but from the differences of thoſe lengths,

it

Pl.18.

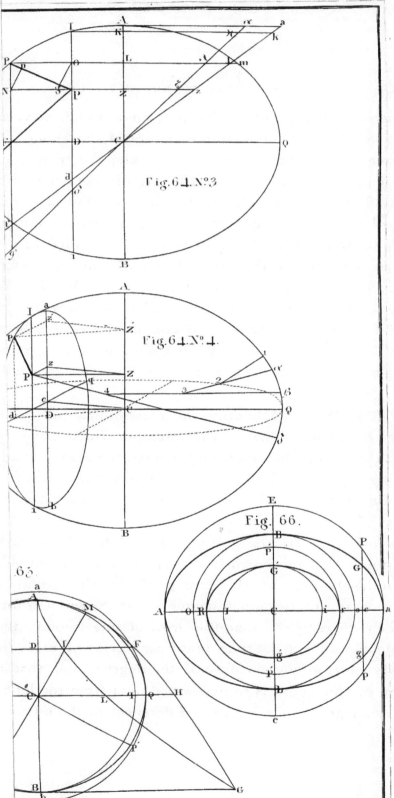

Fig. 64. N.º 3.

Fig. 64. N.º 4.

Fig. 66.

65.

Pl. 18

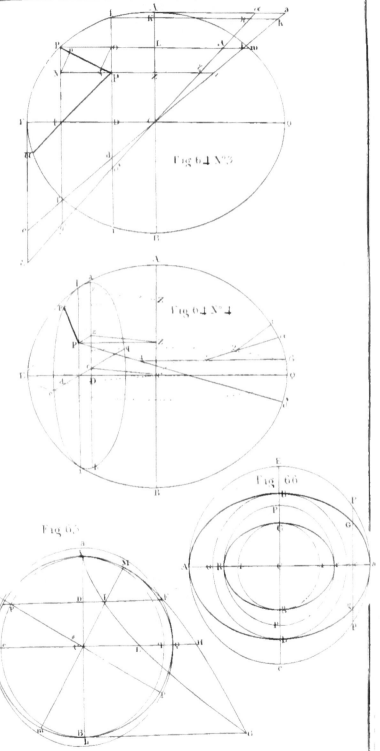

Fig. 64 N° 3.

Fig. 64 N° 4.

Fig. 66

Fig. 65

it muſt be clear that, unleſs the lengths, and the celeſtial arc correſponding, can be aſcertained with great preciſion indeed, our inference of the variation of curvature muſt be very vague and uncertain. The peruſal of any page of the daily obſervations in the obſervatory of Paris will ſhew that errors of 5″ in declination are not uncommon, and errors of 2″ are very frequent indeed. * So many circumſtances may alſo affect the meaſure of the terreſtrial arc, that there is too much left to the judgement and *choice* of the obſerver, in drawing his concluſions. The hiſtory of the firſt meaſurement of the French meridian by Caſſini and La Hire is a proof of this. The degrees ſeemed to increaſe to the ſouthward—the obſervations were affirmed to be excellent—and for ſome time the Earth was held to be an oblong ſpheroid. Philoſophy prevailed, and this was allowed to be impoſſible ;—yet the obſervations were ſtill held to be faultleſs, and the blame was laid on the neglect of circumſtances which ſhould have been conſidered. It was afterwards found that the deduced meaſures

---

* I mention particularly the daily obſervations of the Pariſian Obſervatory, becauſe the French aſtronomers are diſpoſed to reſt the queſtion on the obſervations of their own academicians, who have certainly ſurpaſſed all the aſtronomers of Europe in the extent of their meaſurement of degrees. I ſee no reaſon for giving their obſervations made in diſtant places a greater accuracy than what is to be found in the Royal Obſervatory, with capital inſtruments, fixed up in the moſt ſolid manner.

3 Q

it muft be clear that, unlefs the lengths, and the celeftial arc correfponding, can be afcertained with great precifion indeed, our inference of the variation of curvature muft be very vague and uncertain. The perufal of any page of the daily obfervations in the obfervatory of Paris will fhew that errors of 5″ in declination are not uncommon, and errors of 2″ are very frequent indeed. * So many circumftances may alfo affect the meafure of the terreftrial arc, that there is too much left to the judgement and *choice* of the obferver, in drawing his conclufions. The hiftory of the firft meafurement of the French meridian by Caffini and La Hire is a proof of this. The degrees feemed to increafe to the fouthward—the obfervations were affirmed to be excellent—and for fome time the Earth was held to be an oblong fpheroid. Philofophy prevailed, and this was allowed to be impoffible ;—yet the obfervations were ftill held to be faultlefs, and the blame was laid on the neglect of circumftances which fhould have been confidered. It was afterwards found that the deduced meafures

---

* I mention particularly the daily obfervations of the Parifian Obfervatory, becaufe the French aftronomers are difpofed to reft the queftion on the obfervations of their own academicians, who have certainly furpaffed all the aftronomers of Europe in the extent of their meafurement of degrees. I fee no reafon for giving their obfervations made in diftant places a greater accuracy than what is to be found in the Royal Obfervatory, with capital inftruments, fixed up in the moft folid manner.

3 Q

fures did not agree with fome others of unqueftionable authority, but would agree with them if the corrections were left out;—they were left out, and the obfervations declared excellent, becaufe agreeable to the doctrine of gravitation. *

588. The theory of univerfal gravitation affords another means of determining the form of the terraqueous globe directly from obfervation. Mr Stirling fays, very juftly, that the diminution of gravity deducible from the remark of M. Richer, and confirmed by many fimilar obfervations, gives an inconteftible proof, both of the rotation of the Earth, and of its oblate figure. It could not be of an oblate figure, and have the ocean uniformly diftributed,

---

* They were reconciled with the doctrine of gravitation by attributing the enlargement of the fouthern degrees to the action of the Pyrenean mountains, and thofe in the fouth of France, upon the plummets. But it appears clearly, by the examination of thefe obfervations by Profeffor Celfius, that the obfervations were very incorrect, and fome of them very injudicioufly contrived (See Phil. Tranf. N° 457. and 386.) The palpable inaccuracies gave fuch latitude for adjuftment that it was eafy for the ingenious Mr Mairan to combine them in fuch a manner as to deduce from them inferences in fupport of opinions altogether contradictory of thofe of the academy. Have we not a remarkable example of the doubtfulnefs of fuch meafures, in the meafurement of the Lapland degree? It is found to be almoft 200 fathoms too long.

diftributed, without turning round its axis ; and it could not turn round its axis without inundating the equator, unlefs it have an oblate form, accompanied with diminifhed equatoreal gravity. By the Newtonian theory, the increments of gravity as we approach the poles are in the duplicate ratio of the fines of the latitude. The increments of the length of a feconds pendulum will have the fame proportion. Nothing can be afcertained by obfervation with greater accuracy than this. For the London artifts can make clocks which do not vary one fecond from mean motion in three or four days. We need not meafure the change in the length of the pendulum, a very delicate tafk—but the change of its rate of vibration by a change of place, which is eafily done ; and we can thus afcertain the force of gravity without an error of one part in 86400. This furpaffes all that can be done in the meafurement of an angle. Accordingly, the ellipticities deduced from the experiments with pendulums are vaftly more confiftent with each other, and it were to be wifhed that thefe-experiments were more repeated. We have but very few of them.

589. Yet even thefe experiments are not without anomalies. Since, from the nature of the experiment, we cannot afcribe thefe to errors of obfervation, and the doctrine of univerfal gravitation is eftablifhed on too broad a foundation to be called in queftion for thefe anomalies, philofophers think it more reafonable to attribute the anomalies to local irregularity in terreftrial gravity.

If,

If, in one place, the pendulum is above a great mafs of
folid and denfe rock, perhaps abounding in metals, and,
in another place, has below it a deep ocean, or a deep
and extenfive ftratum of light fand or earth, we fhould
certainly look for a retardation of the pendulum in the
latter fituation.   The French academicians compared the
vibrations of the fame pendulum on the fea-fhore in
Peru, and near the top of a very lofty mountain, and
they obferved that the retardation of its motion in the latter fituation was not fo great as the removal from the
centre required, according to the Newtonian theory, viz.
in the proportion of the diftance (the gravity being in the
inverfe duplicate proportion). *   But it fhould not be fo
much retarded.   The pendulum was not raifed aloft in
the air, but was on the top of a great mountain, to which,
as well as to the reft of the globe, its gravitation was directed.   Some obfervations were reported to have been
made in Switzerland, which fhewed a greater gravitation
on the fummit of a mountain than in the adjacent vallies ; and much was built on this by the partizans of vortices.

---

* The length of a pendulum vibrating feconds was found
to be 439,21 French lines on the fea-fhore at Lima ; when
reduced to time at Quito, 1466 fathoms higher, it was 438,88 ;
and on Pichinka, elevated 2434 fathoms, it was 438,69. Had
gravity diminifhed in the inverfe duplicate ratio of the diftances,
the pendulum at Quito fhould have been 438,80, and at Pichinka it fhould have been 438,55.

tices. But, after due inquiry, the obfervations were found to be altogether fictitious. It may juft be noticed here, that fome of the anomalies in the experiments with pendulums may have proceeded from magnetifm. The clocks employed on thofe occafions probably had gridiron pendulums, having five or feven iron rods, of no inconfiderable weight. We know, for certain, that the lower end of fuch rods acquires a very diftinct magnetifm by mere upright pofition. This may be confiderable enough, efpecially in the circumpolar regions, to affect the vibration, and it is therefore advifeable to employ a pendulum having no iron in its compofition.

Although the deduction of the form of this globe from obfervations on the variations of gravity is expofed to the fame caufe of error which affects the pofition of the plummet, occafioning errors in the meafure of a degree, yet the errors in the variations of gravity are incomparably lefs. What would caufe an error of a whole mile in the meafure of a degree will not produce the $\frac{1}{100}$ part of this error in the difference of gravity.

590. Thefe obfervations naturally lead to other reflections. Newton's determination of the form of the terraqueous globe, is really the form of a homogeneous and fluid or perfectly flexible fpheroid. But will this be the form of a globe, conftituted as ours in all probability is, of beds or layers of different fubftances, whofe denfity probably increafes as they are farther down?

This is a very pertinent and momentous queftion. But

But this outline of mechanical philofophy will not admit of a difcuffion of the many cafes which may reafonably be propofed for folution. All that can, with propriety, be attempted here is to give a *general* notion of the change of form that will be induced by a varying den-fity. And even in this, our attention muft be confined to fome fimple and probable cafe. We fhall therefore fuppofe the denfity to increafe as we penetrate deeper, and this in fuch fort, that at any one depth the denfity is uniform. It is highly improbable that the internal conftitution of this globe is altogether irregular.

591. We fhall therefore fuppofe a fphere of folid matter, equally denfe at equal diftances from the centre, and covered with a lefs denfe fluid ; and we fhall fup-pofe that the whole has a form fuitable to the velocity of its rotation. It is this form that we are to find out. With this view, let us fuppofe that all the matter, by which the folid globe or nucleus is denfer than the fluid, is collected in the centre. We have feen that this will make no change in the gravitation of any particle of the incumbent fluid. Thus, we have a folid globe, covered with a fluid of the fame denfity, and, befides the mutual gravitation of the particles of the fluid, we have a force of the fame nature acting on every one of them, direct-ed to the central redundant matter. Now, let the globe liquefy or diffolve. This can induce no change of force on any particle of the fluid. Let us then deter-mine the form of the now fluid fpheroid, which will

maintain

maintain itfelf in rotation. This being determined, let the globe again become folid. The remaining fluid will not change its form, becaufe no change is induced on the force acting on any particle of the fluid. Call this Hypothefis A.

592. In order to determine this ftate of *equilibrium*, or the form which infures it, which is the chief diffi-culty, let us form another hypothefis B, differing from A only in this circumftance, that the matter collected in the centre, inftead of attracting the particles of the incumbent fluid with a force decreafing in the inverfe duplicate ratio of their diftances, attracts them with a force increafing in the direct ratio of their diftances, keeping the fame inten-fity at the diftance of the pole as in hypothefis A. This fictitious hypothefis, fimilar to Hermann's, is chofen, be-caufe a mafs fo conftituted will maintain the form of an accurate elliptical fpheroid, by a proper adjuftment of the proportion of its axis to the velocity of its rotation. This will eafily appear. For we have already feen that the mutual gravitation of the particles of the elliptical fluid fpheroid produces, in each particle, a force which may be refolved into two forces, one of them perpendi-cular to the axis, and proportional to the diftance from it, and the other perpendicular to the equator, and pro-portional to the diftance from its plane. There is now by hypothefis B fuperadded, on each particle, a force proportional to its diftance from the centre, and directed to the centre. This may alfo be refolved into a force

perpendicular

perpendicular to the axis, and another perpendicular to the equator, and proportional to the diftances from them. Therefore the whole combined forces acting on each particle may be thus refolved into two forces in thofe directions and in thofe proportions. Therefore a mafs fo conftituted will maintain its elliptical form, provided that the velocity of its rotation be fuch that the whole forces at the pole and the equator are inverfely as the axes of the generating ellipfe. We are to afcertain this form, or this required magnitude of the centrifugal force. Having done this, we fhall reftore to the accumulated central matter its natural gravitation, or its action on the fluid in the inverfe duplicate ratio of the diftances, and then fee what change muft be made on the form of the fpheroid in order to reftore the *equilibrium*.

593. Let B A *b a* (fig. 67.) be the fictitious elliptical fpheroid of hypothefis B. Let B E *b e* be the infcribed fphere. Take E G, perpendicular to C E, to reprefent the force of gravitation of a particle in E to the central matter, correfponding to the diftance C E or C B. Draw C G. Draw alfo A I perpendicular to C A, meeting C G in I. Defcribe the curve G L R, whofe ordinates G E, L A, R M, &c. are proportional to $\frac{1}{CE^2}$, $\frac{1}{CA^2}$, $\frac{1}{CM^2}$, &c. Thefe ordinates will exprefs the gravitations of the particles E, A, M, &c. to the central matter by hypothefis A.

In hypothefis A, the gravitation of A is reprefented by

by A L, but in hypothefis B it is reprefented by A I.
For in hypothefis B the gravitations to this matter are as
the diftances.   E G is the gravitation of E in both hypothefes.   Now, $E G : A L = C A^2 : C E^2$, but $E G : A I$
$= C E : C A$.—In hypothefis A the weight of the column
A E is reprefented by the fpace A L G E, but by A I G E
in hypothefis B.   If therefore the fpheroid of hypothefis
B was *in equilibrio*, while turning round its axis, the
equilibrium is deftroyed by merely changing the force
acting on the column E A.   There is a lofs of preffure
or weight fuftained by the column E A.   This may be
expreffed by the fpace L G I, the difference between the
two areas E G I A and E G L A.   But the *equilibrium*
may be reftored by adding a column of fluid A M,
whofe weight A L R M fhall be equal to L G I, which
is very nearly $= \dfrac{L I \times A E}{2}$.

   In order to find the height of this column, produce
G E on the other fide of E, and make E F to E G as
the denfity of the fluid to the denfity by which the nucleus exceeded it.   E F will be to E G as the gravitation
of a particle in E to the globe (now of the fame denfity
with the fluid) is to its gravitation to the redundant matter collected in the centre.   Now, take D E to reprefent the gravitation of E to the fluid contained in the
concentric fpheroid E β e β, which is fomewhat lefs
than its gravitation to the fphere E B e b.   Draw C D N.
Then A N reprefents the gravitation of A to the whole
fluid fpheroid, by § 558.   In like manner, N I is the u-

nited gravitation of A to both the fluid and the central
matter, in the fame hypothefis. But in hypothefis A,
this gravitation is reprefented by N L.

Let N O reprefent the centrifugal force affecting the
particle A, taken in due proportion to N A or N L, its
whole gravitation in hypothefis A. Draw C K O. D K
will be the centrifugal force at E. The fpace O K G I
will exprefs the whole fenfible weight of the fluid in
A E, according to hypothefis B, and O K G L will ex-
cxprefs the fame, according to hypothefis A. L G I is
the difference, to be compenfated by means of a due
addition A M.

This addition may be defined by the quadrature of
the fpaces G E A L and G L I. But it will be abundantly exact to fuppofe that G L R fenfibly coincides with
a ftraight line, and then to proceed in this manner. We
have, by the nature of the curve G L R,

$$A L : E G = E C^2 : A C^2$$

Alfo   A H, or E G : A I = E C : A C

Therefore   A L : A I = E C^3 : A C^3.

Now, when a line changes by a very fmall quantity, the variation of a line proportional to its cube is
thrice as great as that of the line proportional to the
root. H I is the quantity proportional to E A the increment of the root E C. I L is proportional to the variation of the cube, and is therefore very nearly equal to
thrice H I.

                                        Therefore

Therefore fince $EG : HI = EC : AE$, we may
ftate $EG : LI = EC : 3AE$,
or $3EG : LI = EC : AE$.

Now, $QOLR$ may be confidered as equal to $QR \times AM$, or as equal to $KG \times AM$, and LGI may be confidered as equal to $LI \times \frac{1}{4}AE$, and $2KG \times AM = LI \times AE$.

Therefore $2KG : AE = LI : AM$
but $EC : AE = 3EG : LI$
therefore $2KG \times EC : AE^2 = 3EG : AM$
and $2KG : \dfrac{AE^2}{EC} = 3EG : AM$
and $2KG : 3EG = \dfrac{AE^2}{EC} : AM$

That is, twice the fenfible gravity at the equator is to thrice the gravitation to the central matter as a third proportional to radius and the elevation of the equator is to the addition neceffary for producing the *equilibrium* required in hypothefis A.

This addition may be more readily conceived by means of a conftruction. Make $AE : Ee = 2KG : 3EG$. Draw ea parallel to EA, and draw Cem, cutting AN in m. Then am is the addition that muft be made to the column AC. A fimilar addition muft be made to every diameter CT, making $2KG : 3EG = \dfrac{TV^2}{CV} : Tt$, and the whole will be *in equilibrio.*

594. This determination of the ellipticity will equally fuit thofe cafes where the fluid is fuppofed denfer than

the folid nucleus, or where there is a central hollow. For E G may be taken negatively, as if a quantity of matter were placed in the centre acting with a repelling or centrifugal force on the fluid. This is reprefented on the other fide of the axis B b. The fpace g i l in this cafe is negative, and indicates a diminution of the column a c, in order to reftore the *equilibrium*.

595. It is evident that the figure refulting from this conftruction is not an accurate ellipfe. For, in the ellipfe, T t would be in a conftant ratio to V T, whereas it is as VT^2 by our conftruction. But it is alfo evident that in the cafes of fmall deviation from perfect fphericity, the change of figure from the accurate ellipfe of hypothefis B is very fmall. The greateft deviation happens when E e is a maximum. It can never be fenfibly greater in proportion to A E than $\frac{1}{4}$ of A E is in proportion to E C, unlefs the centrifugal force F D be very great in comparifon of the gravity D E. In the cafe of the Earth, where E A is nearly $\frac{1}{230}$ of E C, if we fuppofe the mean denfity of the Earth to be five times that of fea water, a m will not exceed $\frac{1}{111111}$ of E C, or $\frac{1}{724}$ of E A.

596. We are not to imagine that, fince central matter requires an addition A M to the fpheroid, a greater denfity in the interior parts of this globe requires a greater equatoreal protuberancy than if all were homogeneous ; for it is juft the contrary. The fpheroid to which

the

the addition muſt be made is not the figure ſuited to a homogeneous maſs, but a fictitious figure employed as a ſtep to facilitate inveſtigation. We muſt therefore define its ellipticity, that we may know the ſhape reſulting from the final adjuſtment.

Let f be the denſity of the fluid, and n the denſity of the nucleus, and let $n - f$ be $= q$, ſo that q correſponds with E G of our conſtruction, and expreſſes the redundant central matter (or the central deficiency of matter, when the fluid is denſer than the nucleus). Let B C or E C be r, A E be x, and let g be the mean gravity (primitive), and c the centrifugal force at A. Laſtly, let π be the circumference when the radius of the circle is 1.

The gravitation of B to the fluid ſpheroid is $\frac{2}{3} \pi f r$ (582.), and its gravitation to the central matter is $\frac{2}{3} \pi q r$. The ſum of theſe, or the whole gravitation of B, is $\frac{2}{3} \pi n r$. This may be taken for the mean gravitation on every point of the ſpheroidal ſurface.

But the whole gravitation of B differs conſiderably from that of A.

1*mo*. C A, or C E, is to $\frac{1}{5}$ A E as the primitive gravity of B to the ſpheroid is to its exceſs above the gravitation (primitive) of A to the ſame, (582.) That is, $r : \frac{1}{5} x = \frac{2}{3} \pi f r : \frac{2}{15} \pi f x$, and $\frac{2}{15} \pi f x$ expreſſes this exceſs.

2*do*. In hypotheſis B, we have C E to C A as the gravitation of B or E to the central matter is to the gravitation of A to the ſame. Therefore C E is to E A as the gravitation of E to this matter is to the exceſs of A's
gravitation

gravitation to the fame. This excefs of A's gravitation is expreffed by $\frac{2}{3} \pi q x$, for $r : x = \frac{2}{3} \pi q r : \frac{2}{3} \pi q x$.

3*tio.* Without any fenfible error, we may ftate the ratio of g to c as the ratio of the whole gravitation of A to the centrifugal tendency excited in A by the rotation. Therefore $g : c = \frac{2}{3} \pi n r : \dfrac{2 \pi n r c}{3 g}$, and this centrifugal tendency of the particle A is $\dfrac{2 \pi n r c}{3 g}$. This is what is expreffed by N O in our conftruction.

The whole difference between the gravitations of B and A is therefore $\frac{2}{15} \pi f x - \frac{2}{3} \pi q x + \dfrac{2 \pi n r c}{3 g}$. The gravitation of B is to this difference as $\frac{2}{3} \pi n r$ to $\frac{2}{15} \pi f x - \frac{2}{3} \pi q x + \dfrac{2 \pi n r c}{3 g}$ or (dividing all by $\frac{2}{3} \pi n$) as r to $\dfrac{f x}{5 n} - \dfrac{q x}{n} + \dfrac{c r}{g}$.

Now the equilibrium of rotation requires that the whole polar force be to the fenfible gravitation at the equator as the radius of the equator to the femiaxis (569.) Therefore we muft make the radius of the equator to its excefs above the femiaxis as the polar gravitation to its excefs above the fenfible equatoreal gravitation. That is $r : x = r : \dfrac{f x}{5 n} - \dfrac{q x}{n} + \dfrac{c r}{g}$, and therefore $x = \dfrac{f x}{5 n} - \dfrac{q x}{n} + \dfrac{c r}{g}$. Hence we have $\dfrac{c r}{g} = x + \dfrac{q x}{n} - \dfrac{f x}{5 n}$. But $q = n - f$. Therefore $\dfrac{c r}{g} = x + \dfrac{n x}{n} - \dfrac{f x}{n} - \dfrac{f x}{5 n}$, $= x + x - \dfrac{6 f x}{5 n}$, $= 2 x - \dfrac{6 f x}{5 n} = x \times \left(2 - \dfrac{6 f}{5 n} \cdot \right)$

Wherefore

Wherefore $x = \dfrac{c\,r}{g \times \left(2 - \dfrac{6f}{5\,n}\right)}, = \dfrac{5\,n\,c\,r}{g \times 10\,n - 6f}$, which

is more conveniently expreſſed in this form $x = \dfrac{5\,c\,r}{2\,g} \times$

$\dfrac{n}{5\,n - 3f}$. The ſpecies, or ellipticity of the ſpheroid is

$\dfrac{x}{r}, = \dfrac{5\,c}{2\,g} \times \dfrac{n}{5\,n - 3f}$.

Such then is the elliptical ſpheroid of hypotheſis B ; and we ſaw that, in reſpect of form, it is ſcarcely diſtinguiſhable from the figure which the maſs will have when the fictitious force of the central matter gives place to the natural force of the denſe ſpherical nucleus. This is true at leaſt in all the caſes where the centrifugal force is very ſmall in compariſon with the mean gravitation.

We muſt therefore take ſome notice of the influence which the variations of denſity may have on the form of this ſpheroid. We may learn this by attending to the formula

$$\dfrac{x}{r} = \dfrac{5\,c}{2\,g} \times \dfrac{n}{5\,n - 3f}.$$

The value of this formula depends chiefly on the fraction

$\dfrac{n}{5\,n - 3f}$.

597. If the denſity of the interior parts be immenſely greater than that of the ſurrounding fluid, the value of this fraction becomes nearly $\frac{1}{5}$, and $\frac{x}{r}$ becomes nearly $= \dfrac{c}{2\,g}$, and the ellipſe nearly the ſame with what Hermann aſſigned to a homogeneous fluid ſpheroid.

If

If $n = 5f$; then $\dfrac{n}{5\,n - 3f} = \dfrac{5}{22}$; and, in the cafe of the Earth, $\dfrac{x}{r}$ would be nearly $= \dfrac{1}{508,6}$, making an equatoreal elevation of nearly 7 miles.

598.   If $n = f$, the fraction $\dfrac{n}{5\,n - 3f}$ becomes $\frac{1}{2}$, and $\dfrac{x}{r} = \dfrac{5}{4}\dfrac{c}{g}$, which we have already fhewn to be fuitable to a homogeneous fpheroid, with which this is equivalent. The protuberance or ellipticity in this cafe is to that when the nucleus is incomparably denfer than the fluid in the proportion of 5 to 2. This is the greateft ellipticity that can obtain when the fluid is not denfer than the nucleus.

Between thefe two extremes, all other values of the formula are competent to homogeneous fpheroids of gravitating fluids, covering a fpherical nucleus of greater denfity, either uniformly denfe or confifting of concentric fpherical ftrata, each of which is uniformly denfe.

From this view of the extreme cafes, we may infer in general, that as the incumbent fluid becomes rarer in proportion to the nucleus, the ellipticity diminifhes.   M. Bernoulli (Daniel), mifled by a gratuitous affumption, fays in his theory of the tides that the ellipticity produced in the aëreal fluid which furrounds this globe will be 800 times greater than that of the folid nucleus ; but this is a miftake, which a jufter affumption of *data* would have prevented. The aëreal fpheroid will be fenfibly lefs oblate than the nucleus.

It

It was faid that the value of the formula depended chiefly on the fraction $\dfrac{n}{5\,n - 3f}$. But it depends alfo on the fraction $\dfrac{5\,c}{2\,g}$, increafing or diminifhing as c increafes or diminifhes, or as g diminifhes or increafes. It muft alfo be remarked that the theorem $\dfrac{x}{r} = \dfrac{5\,c}{4\,g}$ for a homogeneous fpheroid was deduced from the fuppofition that the eccentricity is very fmall (See § 580. 585.) When the rotation is very rapid, there is another form of an elliptical fpheroid, which is in that kind of *equilibrium*, which, if it be difturbed, will not be recovered, but the eccentricity will increafe with great rapidity, till the whole diffipates in a round flat fheet. But within this limit, there is a kind of ftability in the *equilibrium*, by which it is recovered when it is difturbed. If the rotation be too rapid, the fpheroid becomes more oblate, and the fluids which accumulate about the equator, having lefs velocity than that circle, retard the motion. This goes on however fome time, till the true fhape is overpaffed, and then the accumulation relaxes. The motion is now too flow for this accumulation, and the waters flow back again toward the poles. Thus an ofcillation is produced by the difturbance, and this is gradually diminifhed by the mutual adhefion of the waters, and by friction, and things foon terminate in the refumption of the proper form.

599. When the denfity of the nucleus is lefs than that of the fluid, the varieties which refult in the form

3 S

from

from a variation in the denfity of the fluid are much greater, and more remarkable. Some of them are even paradoxical. Cafes, for example, may be put, (when the ratio of n to f differs but very little from that of 3 to 5), where a very fmall centrifugal force, or very flow rotation, fhall produce a very great protuberance, and, on the contrary, a very rapid rotation may confift with an oblong form like an egg. But thefe are very fingular cafes, and of little ufe in the explanation of the phenomena actually exhibited in the folar fyftem. The *equilibrium* which obtains in fuch cafes may be called a *tottering equilibrium*, which, when once difturbed, will not be again recovered, but the diffipation of the fluid will immediately follow with accelerated fpeed. Some cafes will be confidered, on another occafion, where there is a deficiency of matter in the centre, or even a hollow.

600. The chief diftinction between the cafes of a nucleus covered with an equally denfe fluid, and a denfe nucleus covered with a rarer fluid, confifts in the difference between the polar and equatoreal gravities; for we fee that the difference in fhape is inconfiderable. It has been fhewn already that, in the homogenous fpheroid of fmall eccentricity, the excefs of the polar gravity above the fenfible equatoreal gravity is nearly equal to $\frac{g \, x}{5 \, r}$ (for $r : \frac{1}{5} x = g : \frac{g \, x}{5 \, r}$). When, in addition to this, we take into account the diminution c, produced by rotation, we have $\frac{g \, x}{5 \, r} + c$ for the whole difference between the po-

lar and the fenfible equatoreal gravity. But, in a homo-geneous fpheroid, we have $x = \frac{5\,c\,r}{4\,g}$. Therefore the ex-cefs of polar gravity in a homogeneous revolving fphe-roid is $\frac{c}{4} + c$ or $\frac{5\,c}{4}$. We may diftinguifh this excefs in the homogeneous fpheroid by the fymbol E.

601. But, in hypothefis B, the equilibrium of rota-tion requires that r be to x as g to $\frac{g\,x}{r}$, and the excefs of polar gravity in this hypothefis is $\frac{g\,x}{r}$. But we have alfo feen that in this hypothefis, $\frac{x}{r} = \frac{5\,c}{2\,g} \times \frac{n}{5\,n - 3\,f}$. Therefore the excefs of polar gravity in this hypothefis is $\frac{5\,c}{2} \times \frac{n}{5\,n - 3\,f}$. Let this excefs be diftinguifhed by the fymbol s.

602. The excefs of polar gravity muft be greater than this in hypothefis A. For, in that hypothefis the equatoreal gravity to the fluid part of the fpheroid is al-ready fmaller. And this fmaller gravity is not fo much increafed by the natural gravitation to the central matter, in the inverfe duplicate ratio of the diftance, as it was in-creafed by the fictitious gravity to the fame matter, in the direct ratio of the diftances. The fecond of the three diftinctions noticed in § 596. between the gravi-tations of B and A was $-\frac{q\,x}{n}$. This muft now be changed into $+\frac{2\,q\,x}{n}$, as may eafily be deduced from

3 S 2

§ 593,

§ 593, where $-\dfrac{q\,x}{n}$ is reprefented by H I in fig. 67, and the excefs, forming the compenfation for hypothefis A is reprefented by H L, nearly double of H I, and in the oppofite direction, diminifhing the gravitation of A. The difference of thefe two ftates is $\dfrac{3\,q\,x}{n}$, by which the tendency of A to the central matter in hypothefis A falls fhort of what it was in hypothefis B. Therefore, as $\dfrac{f\,x}{5\,n} - \dfrac{q\,x}{n} + \dfrac{c\,r}{g}$ is to $\dfrac{3\,q\,x}{n}$, fo is the excefs ε to a quantity ε', which muft be added to ε, in order to produce the difference of gravities e, conformable to the ftatement of hypothefis A. Now, in hypothefis B, we had $x = \dfrac{f\,x}{5\,n} - \dfrac{q\,x}{n} + \dfrac{c\,r}{g}$, and we may, without fcruple, fuppofe x the fame in hypothefis A. Therefore $\varepsilon : \varepsilon' = x : \dfrac{3\,q\,x}{n}$, $= 1 : \dfrac{3\,q}{n}$, and $\varepsilon' = \varepsilon \times \dfrac{3\,q}{n} = \varepsilon \times \dfrac{3\,n - 3\,f}{n}$,

$= \dfrac{5\,c}{2} \times \dfrac{n}{5\,n - 3\,f} \times \dfrac{3\,n - 3\,f}{n}, = \dfrac{5\,c}{2} \times \dfrac{3\,n - 3\,f}{5\,n - 3\,f}.$

Add to this ε, which is $\dfrac{5\,c}{2} \times \dfrac{n}{5\,n - 3\,f}$, and we obtain for the excefs e of polar gravity in hypothefis A $= \dfrac{5\,c}{2} \times \dfrac{4\,n - 3\,f}{5\,n - 3\,f}.$

603. Let us now compare this excefs of polar gravity above the fenfible equatoreal gravity in the three hypothefes : 1ft, A, fuited to the fluid furrounding a fpherical nucleus of greater denfity : 2d, B, fuited to the fame fluid, furrounding a central nucleus which attracts with a force proportional to the diftance : and, 3d,

C 2

C, fuited to a homogeneous fluid fpheroid, or enclofing a fpherical nucleus of equal denfity. Thefe exceffes are

$$\text{A} \qquad \frac{5\,c}{2} \times \frac{4\,n - 3\,f}{5\,n - 3\,f}$$

$$\text{B} \qquad \frac{5\,c}{2} \times \frac{n}{5\,n - 3\,f}$$

$$\text{C} \quad \frac{5\,c}{4}, \text{ or } \frac{5\,c}{4} \times \frac{5\,n - 3\,f}{5\,n - 3\,f}.$$

It is evident that the fum of A and B is $\frac{5\,c}{2} \times$ $\frac{5\,n - 3\,f}{5\,n - 3\,f}$, which is double of C, or $\frac{5\,c}{4} \times \frac{5\,n - 3\,f}{5\,n - 3\,f}$, and therefore C is the arithmetical mean between them.

Now we have feen that $\frac{5\,c}{2\,g} \times \frac{4\,n - 3\,f}{5\,n - 3\,f}$ expreffes the ratio of the excefs of polar gravity to the mean gravity in the hypothefis A. We have alfo feen that $\frac{5\,c}{2\,g}$ $\times \frac{n}{5\,n - 3\,f}$ may fafely be taken as the value of the ellipticity in the fame hypothefis. It is not perfectly exact, but the deviation is altogether infenfible in a cafe like that of the Earth, where the rotation and the eccentricity are fo moderate. And, laftly, we have feen that the fame fraction that expreffes the ratio of the excefs of polar gravity to mean gravity, in a homogeneous fpheroid, alfo expreffes its ellipticity, and that twice this fraction is equal to the fum of the other two.

604. Hence may be derived a beautiful theorem, firft given by M. Clairaut, that *the fraction expreffing twice the ellipticity of a homogeneous revolving fpheroid is the*

fum

fum of two fractions, one of which expreffes the ratio of the excefs of polar gravity to mean gravity, and the other expreffes the ellipticity of any fpheroid of fmall eccentricity, which confifts of a fluid covering a denfer fpherical nucleus.

If therefore any other phenomena give us, in the cafe of a revolving fpheroid, the proportion of polar and equatoreal gravities, we can find its ellipticity, by fubtracting the fraction expreffing the ratio of the excefs of polar gravity to the mean gravity from twice the ellipticity of a homogeneous fpheroid. Thus, in the cafe of the Earth, twice the ellipticity of the homogeneous fpheroid is $\frac{1}{115}$. A medium of feven comparifons of the rate of pendulums gives the proportion of the excefs of polar gravity above the mean gravity $= \frac{1}{180}$. If this fraction be fubtracted from $\frac{1}{115}$, it leaves $\frac{1}{319}$ for the medium ellipticity of the Earth. Of thefe feven experiments, five are fcarcely different in the refult. Of the other two, one gives an ellipticity not exceeding $\frac{1}{355}$. The agreement in general is incomparably greater than in the forms deduced from the comparifons of degrees of the meridian. All the comparifons that have been publifhed concur in giving a confiderably fmaller eccentricity to the terraqueous fpheroid than fuits a homogeneous mafs, and which is ufually called Newton's determination. It is indeed his determination, on the fuppofition of homogeneity; but he exprefsly fays that a different denfity in the interior parts will induce a different form, and he points out fome fuppofititious cafes, not indeed very probable, where the form will be different. Newton has not conceived this fubject with his ufual fagacity, and

has

has made fome inferences that are certainly inconfiftent with his law of gravitation.

That the protuberancy of the terreftrial equator is certainly lefs than $\frac{1}{211}$ proves the interior parts to be of a greater mean denfity than the exterior, and even gives us fome means for determining how much they exceed in denfity. For, by making the fraction $\frac{5\,e}{2\,g} \times \frac{4\,n - 3\,f}{5\,n - 3\,f} = \frac{1}{180}$, as indicated by the experiments with pendulums, we can find the value of n.

605. The length of the feconds pendulum is the meafure of the accelerating force of gravity. Therefore let l be this length at the equator, and $l + d$ the length at the pole. We have $\frac{5\,c}{2\,g} \times \frac{4\,n - 3\,f}{5\,n - 3\,f} = \frac{d}{l}$, whence $\frac{4\,n - 3\,f}{5\,n - 3\,f} = \frac{2\,g\,d}{5\,c\,l}$. This equation, when properly treated, gives $\frac{n}{f} = \frac{15\,c\,l - 6\,g\,d}{20\,c\,l - 10\,g\,d}$, &c. &c.*

The fame principles may be applied to any other planet as well as to this Earth. Thus, we can tell what portion of the equatoreal gravity of Jupiter is expended in keeping bodies on his furface, by comparing the time

of

---

* We have information very lately of the meafurement of a degree, by Major Lambton in the Myfore in India, with excellent inftruments. It lies in lat. 12° 32′, and its length is 60494 Britifh fathoms. We are alfo informed by Mr Melanderhielm of the Swedifh academy that the meafure of the degree in Lapland by Maupertuis is found to be 208 toifes too great. This was fufpected.

of his rotation with the period of one of his fatellites. We find that the centrifugal force at his equator is $\frac{2}{94}$ of the whole gravity, and from the equation $\frac{5\,c\,r}{4\,g} = x$, we fhould infer that if Jupiter be a homogeneous fluid or flexible fpheroid, his equatoreal diameter will exceed his polar axis nearly 10 parts in 113, which is not very different from what we obferve ; fo much however as to authorife us to conclude that his denfity is greater near the centre than on his furface.

Thefe obfervations muft fuffice as an account of this fubject. Many circumftances, of great effect, are omitted, that the confideration might be reduced to fuch fimplicity as to be difcuffed without the aid of the higher geometry. The ftudent who wifhes for more complete information muft confult the elaborate performances of Euler, Clairaut, D'Alembert, and La Place. The differtation of Th. Simpfon on the fame fubject is excellent. The differtation of F. Bofcovich will be of great fervice to thofe who are lefs verfant in the fluxionary calculus, that author having every where endeavoured to reduce things to a geometrical conftruction. To thefe I would add the Cofmographia of Frifius, as a very mafterly performance on this part of his fubject.

It were defireable that another element were added to the problem, by fuppofing the planet to confift of coherent flexible matter. It is apprehended that this would give it a form more applicable to the actual ftate of things. If a planet confift of fuch matter, ductile like melted glafs, the fhape which rotation, combined with gravitation

vitation and this kind of cohefion, would induce, will be confiderably different from what we have been confidering; and fufceptible of great variety, according to the thicknefs of the fhell of which it is fuppofed to confift. The form of fuch a fhell will have the chief influence on the form which will be affumed by an ocean or atmofphere which may furround it. If the globe of Mars be as eccentric as the late obfervations indicate it to be, it is very probable that it is hollow, with no great thicknefs. For the centrifugal force muft be exceedingly fmall.

606. The moft fingular example of this phenomenon that is exhibited in the folar fyftem, is the vaft arch or ring which furrounds the planet Saturn, and turns round its axis with moft aftonifhing rapidity. It is above 200000 miles in diameter, and makes a complete rotation in ten hours and thirty-two minutes. A point on its furface moves at the rate of $1000\frac{1}{2}$ miles in a minute, or nearly 17 miles in one beat of the clock, which is 58 times as fwift as the Earth's equator.

M. La Place has made the mechanifm of this motion a fubject of his examination, and has profecuted it with great zeal and much ingenuity. He thinks that the permanent ftate of the ring, in its period of rotation, may be explained, on the fuppofition that its parts are without connexion, revolving round the planet like fo many fatellites, fo that it may be confidered as a vapour. It appears to me that this is not at all probable.

3 T   He

He fays that the obferved inequalities in the circle of the ring are neceffary for keeping it from coalefcing with the planet. Such inequalities feem incompatible with its own conftitution, being inconfiftent with the *equilibrium* of forces among incoherent bodies. Befides, as he fuppofes no cohefion in it, any inequalities in the conftitution of its different parts cannot influence the general motion of the whole *in the manner he fuppofes*, but merely by an inequality of gravitation. The effect of this, it is apprehended, would be to deftroy the permanency of its conftruction, without fecuring, as he imagines, the fteadinefs of its pofition. But this feems to be the point which he is eager to eftablifh; and he finds, in the numerous lift of poffibilities, conditions which bring things within his general equation for the *equilibrium* of revolving fpheroids; but the equation is fo very general, and the conditions are fo many, and fo implicated, that there is reafon to fear that, in fome circumftances, the *equilibrium* is of that kind that has no ftability, but, if difturbed in the fmalleft degree, is deftroyed altogether, being like the *equilibrium* of a needle poifed upright on its point. There is a ftronger objection to M. La Place's explanation. He is certainly miftaken in thinking that the period of the rotation of the ring is that which a fatellite would have at the fame diftance. The fecond Caffinian fatellite revolves in 65^h 44′, and its diftance is 56,2 (the elongation in feconds). Now $\overline{65^h\,44'}|^2 : \overline{10^h\,32\frac{1}{4}}|^2 = 56,2^3 : 16,4^3$. This is the diftance at which a fatellite would revolve in 10^h 32′.

It

It muſt be ſomewhat leſs than this, on account of the oblate figure of the planet. Yet even this is leſs than the radius of the very inmoſt edge of the ring. The radius of the outer edge is not leſs than 22½, and that of its middle is 20.

. It is a much more probable ſuppoſition (for we can only ſuppoſe) that the ring conſiſts of coherent matter. It has been repreſented as ſupporting itſelf like an arch; but this is leſs admiſſible than La Place's opinion. The rapidity of rotation is ſuch as would immediately ſcatter the arch, as water is flirted about from a mop. The ring muſt cohere, and even cohere with conſiderable force, in order to counteract the centrifugal force, which conſiderably exceeds its weight. If this be admitted, and ſurely it is the moſt obvious and natural opinion, there will be no difficulty ariſing from the velocity of rotation or the irregularity of its parts. M. La Place might eaſily pleaſe his fancy by contriving a mechaniſm for its motion. We may ſuppoſe that it is a viſcid ſub-ſtance like melted glaſs. If matter of this conſtitution, covering the equator of a planet, turn round its axis too ſwiftly, the viſcid matter will be thrown off, retaining its velocity of rotation. It will therefore expand into a ring, and will remove from the planet, till the velocity of its equatoreal motion correſpond with its diameter and its curvature. However ſmall we ſuppoſe the co-heſive or viſcid force, it will cauſe this ring to ſtop at a dimenſion ſmaller than the orbit of a planet moving with the ſame velocity.—Theſe ſeem to be legitimate conſe-quences of what we know of coherent matter, and they

3 T 2   greatly

greatly refemble what we fee in Saturn's ring. This conftitution of the ring is alfo well fitted for admitting thofe irregularities which are indicated by the fpots on the ring, and which M. La Place employs with fo much ingenuity for keeping the ring in fuch a pofition that the planet always occupies its centre. This is a very curious circumftance, when confidered attentively, and its importance is far from being obvious. The planet and the ring are quite feparate. The planet is moving in an orbit round the Sun. The ring accompanies the planet in all the irregularities of its motion, and has it always in the middle. This ingenious mathematician gives ftrong reafons for thinking that, if the ring were perfectly circular and uniform, although it is *poffible* to place Saturn exactly in its centre, yet the fmalleft difturbance by a fatellite or paffing comet would be the beginning of a derangement, which would rapidly increafe, and, after a very fhort time, Saturn would be in contact with the inner edge of the ring, never more to feparate from it. But if the ring is not uniform, but more maffive on one fide of the centre than on the other, then the planet and the ring may revolve round a common centre, very near, but not coinciding with the centre of the ring. He alfo maintains that the oblate form of the planet is another circumftance abfolutely neceffary for the ftability of the ring. The redundancy of the equator, and flatnefs of the ring, fit thefe two bodies for acting on each other like two magnets, fo as to adjuft each other's motions.

The

The whole of this analyfis of the mechanifm of Saturn's ring is of the moft intricate kind, and is carried
on by the author by calculus alone, fo as not to be inftructive to any but very learned and expert analyfts.
Several points of it however might have been treated
more familiarly.   But, after all, it muft reft entirely on
the truth of the conjectures or affumptions made for
procuring the poffible application of the fundamental
equations.

607.   The Moon prefents to the reflecting mind a
phenomenon that is curious and interefting.   She always
prefents the fame face to the Earth, and her appearance
juft now perfectly correfponds with the oldeft accounts
we have of the fpots on her difk.   Thefe indeed are not
of very ancient date, as they cannot be anterior to the
telefcope.   But this is enough to fhew that the Moon
turns round her axis in precifely the fame time that fhe
revolves round the Earth.   Such a precife coincidence
is very remarkable, and naturally induces the mind to
fpeculate about the caufe of it.   Newton afcribed it to
an oblong oval figure, more denfe, or at leaft heavier, at
one end than at the other.   This he thought might o-
perate on the Moon fomewhat in the way that gravity
operates on a pendulum.   He defines this figure in Propofition 38. B. III. ; and as the eccentricity, or any deviation of its centre of gravity from that of its figure, is extremely fmall, the *vis difponens*, by which one diameter
is directed towards the Earth, is alfo very minute, and
                                                            its

its operation muft be too flow to keep one face fteadily
turned to the Earth, in oppofition to the momentum of
rotation round the axis, feven or eight days being all the
time that is allowed for producing this effect.   Therefore we obferve what is called the *Libration* of the Moon,
arifing from the uniform rotation of the Moon, combined with her unequable orbital motion.   One diameter of the Moon is always turned to the upper focus of
her orbit, becaufe her angular motion round that focus
is almoft perfectly uniform, and therefore correfponds
with her uniform rotation.   But that diameter which is
towards us when the Moon is in her apogee or perigee,
deviates from the Earth almoft fix degrees when fhe is
in quadrature.   But although, in the fhort fpace of eight
days, the pendulous force of the Moon cannot prevent
this deviation altogether, it undoubtedly leffens it.   It is
faid to produce another effect.   If the original projection of the Moon in the tangent of her orbit did not
precifely, but very nearly, correfpond with the rotation
impreffed at the fame time, this pendulous tendency
would, in the courfe of many ages, gradually leffen the
difference, and at laft make the rotation perfectly com-
menfurate with the orbital revolution.

But we apprehend that this conclufion cannot be admitted.   For, in whatever way we fuppofe this arranging force to operate, if it has been able, in the courfe of
ages, to do away fome fmall primitive difference between
the velocity of rotation and the velocity of revolution,
it muft certainly have been able to annihilate a much
                                                      fmaller

fmaller difference in the pofition of the Moon's figure, namely, the obliquity of the axis to the plane of the orbit. * It deviates about 1 or 2 degrees from the perpendicular, and it firmly retains this obliquity of pofition ; and no obfervation can difcover any deviation from perfect parallelifm of the axis in all fituations. It furely requires much lefs action of the directing force to produce this change in the pofition of the axis, than to overcome even a very fmall difference in angular motion, becaufe this laft difference accumulates, and makes a great difference of longitude.

Thefe confiderations feem to prove that the conftant appearance of one and the fame part of the Moon's furface has not been produced by the caufe fufpected by Newton. The coincidence has more probably been original. We have no reafon to doubt that the fame confummate fkill that is manifeft in every part of the fyftem, in which every thing has an accurate adjuftment, *pondere et menfura*, alfo made the primitive revolution rotation of the Moon that which we now behold and admire.

---

* The axis round which the rotation of the Moon is performed is inclined to the plane of the ecliptic in an angle of 88½°, and it is inclined to the plane of the lunar orbit 82¼. It is always fituated in the plane paffing through the poles of the ecliptic and of the lunar orbit. It therefore deviates about 1½ from the axis of the ecliptic, and 7 from that of the Moon's orbit. The defcending node of the Moon's equator coincides with the afcending node of her orbit.

mire. The manifest fubferviency to great and good purpofes, in every thing that we in fome meafure underftand, leaves us no room to imagine that this adjuftment
of the lunar motions is not equally proper.

608. Philofophers have fpeculated about the nature
of that body of faintly fhining matter in which the Sun
feems immerged, and is called the *zodiacal light*, becaufe
it lies in the zodiac. It is rarely perceptible in this climate, yet may fometimes be feen in a clear night in February and March, appearing in the weft, a little to the
north of where the Sun fet, like a beam of faint yellowifh grey light, flanting toward the north, and extending, in a pointed or leaf fhape, about eight or ten
degrees. The appearance is nearly what would be exhibited by a fhining or reflecting atmofphere furrounding the Sun, and extending, in the plane of the ecliptic,
at leaft as far as the orbit of Mercury, but of fmall thicknefs, the whole being flat like a cake or difk, whofe
breadth is at leaft ten times its thicknefs in the middle.
This has been the fubject of fpeculation to the mechanical philofophers. It is fomething connected with
the Sun. We have no knowledge of any connecting
principle but gravitation. But fimple gravitation would
gather this atmofphere into a globular fhape, whereas it
is a very oblate difk or lens. Gravitation, combined with
a proper revolution of the particles round the Sun, might
throw the vapour into this form ; and the object of the
fpeculation is to affign the rotation that is fuitable to it.

If

If the zodiacal light be produced by the reflection of an atmofphere that is retained by gravity alone, without any mutual adhefion of its particles, it cannot have the form that we obferve. The greateft proportion that the equatoreal diameter can have to the polar is that of 3 to 2 ; for, beyond that, the centrifugal force would more than balance its gravitation, and it would diffipate. A very ftrong adhefion is neceffary for giving fo oblate a form as we obferve in the zodiacal light. Combined with this, it may indeed expand to any degree, by rapidly whirling about, as we fee in the manufacture of crown-glafs. But how is this whirling given to the folar atmofphere ? It may get it by the mere action of the furface of the Sun, in the manner defcribed by Newton in his account of the production of the Cartefian vortices. The furface drags round what is in contact with it. This ftratum acts on the next, and communicates to it part of its own motion. This goes on from ftratum to ftratum, till the outermoft ftratum begins to move alfo. All this while, each interior ftratum is circulating more fwiftly than the one immediately without it. Therefore they are ftill acting on one another. It is very evident that a permanent ftate is not acquired, till all turn round in the fame time with the Sun's body. This circumftance limits the poffible expanfion of an atmofphere that does not cohere. It cannot exceed the orbit of a planet which would revolve round the Sun in that time. But the zodiacal light extends much farther.

The difcoveries of Dr Herfchel on the furface of the

3 U

Sun,

Sun, if confirmed by future obfervation, render this production of the zodiacal light inconceivable.   For motions and changes are obferved there, which fhew a perfect freedom, not conftrained by the adhefion of any fuperior ftrata. This would give a conftant wefterly motion on the furface of the Sun.

The difficulty in accounting for this phenomenon is
greatly increafed by the fact that when a comet paffes
through this atmofphere, the tail of the comet is not per-
ceptibly affected by it.   The comet of 1743 gave a very
good opportunity of obferving this.   It was not attended
to ; but the defcriptions that are given of the appearances
of that comet fhew clearly that the tail was (as ufual)
directed almoft ftraight upward from the Sun, and therefore it mixed with this vapour, or whatever it may be,
without any mutual difturbance.

It appears therefore, on the whole, that we are yet
ignorant of the nature and mechanifm of the zodiacal
light.

609.   Before concluding this fubject, it is not improper to take fome notice of an obfervation to which
great importance has been attached by a certain clafs of
philofophers. We fhall find it demonftrated in its proper place, that when the force which impels a firm body
forward acts in a direction which paffes through its centre
of gravity, it merely impels it forward.   The body moves
in that direction, and every particle moves alike, fo that,
during its progrefs, the body preferves the fame attitude
(fo

(fo to fpeak). Taking any tranfverfe line of the body for a diameter, we exprefs the circumftance by faying that this diameter keeps parallel to itfelf, that is, all its fucceffive pofitions are parallel to its firft pofition. But, when the moving force acts in a line which paffes on one fide of the centre of the body, the body not only advances in the direction of the force, but alfo changes its attitude, by turning round an axis. This is eafily feen and underftood in fome fimple cafes. Thus, if a beam of timber, floating on water, be pufhed or pulled in the middle, at right angles to its length, it will move in that direction, keeping parallel to its firft pofition. But, if it be pufhed or pulled in the fame direction, applying the force to a point fituated at the third of its length, that end is moft affected (as we fhall fee fully demonftrated) and advances fafteft, while the remote end is left a little behind. In this particular cafe, the *initial* motion of all the parts of the beam is the fame as if the remote end were held faft for an inftant. If the impulfe has been nearer to one end than $\frac{1}{3}$ of the length, the remote end will, *in the firft inftant*, even move a little backward. We fhall be able to ftate precifely the relation that will be obferved between the progreffive motion and the rotation, and to fay how far the centre of the body will proceed while it makes one turn round the axis. We fhall demonftrate that this axis, round which the body turns, always paffes through its centre of gravity in a certain determined direction.

It very rarely happens that the direction of the impelling

pelling

pelling force paffes exactly through the centre of a body; and accordingly we very rarely obferve a body moving forward in free fpace without rotation. A ftone thrown from the hand never does. A bomb-fhell, or a cannon bullet, has commonly a very rapid motion of rotation, which greatly deranges its intended direction.

The fpeculative philofophers who wifh to explain all the celeftial motions mechanically, think that they explain the rotation of the planets, and all the phenomena depending on it, by faying that one and the fame force produced the revolution round the Sun, and the rotation round the axis; and produced thofe motions, becaufe the direction of the primitive impulfe did not pafs precifely through the centre of the planet. They even fhew by calculation the diftance between the centre and the line of direction of the impelling force. Thus, they fhew that the point of impulfion on this Earth is diftant from its centre $\frac{1}{157}$ of its diameter.

Having thus accounted, as they imagine, for the Earth's rotation, they fay that this rotation caufes the Earth to fwell out all around the equator, and they affign the precife eccentricity that the fpheroid muft acquire. They then fhew that the action of the Sun and Moon on this equatoreal protuberance deranges the rotation, fo that the axis does not remain parallel to itfelf, and produces the phenomenon called the preceffion of the equinoxes. And thus all is explained mechanically. And on this explanation a conjecture is founded, which leads

to

to very magnificent conceptions of the vifible univerfe. The Sun turns round an axis. Analogy fhould lead us to afcribe this to the fame caufe—to the action of a force whofe direction does not pafs through his centre. If fo, the Sun has alfo a progreffive motion through the boundlefs fpace, carrying all the planets and comets along with him, juft as we obferve Jupiter and Saturn carrying their fatellites round their annual orbits.

This is, for the moft part, perfectly juft. A planet turns round its axis and advances, and therefore the force which refults from the actual compofition *of all the forces* which cooperated in producing both motions, does not pafs through the centre of the planet, but precifely at the diftance affigned by thefe gentlemen. But there is nothing of explanation in all this. From the manner in which the remark and its application are made, we are mifled in our conception of the fact, and the imagination immediately fuggefts a *fingle force*, fuch as we are accuftomed to apply in our operations, acting in one precife line, and therefore on one point of the body. It is this fimplification of conception alone which gives the remark the appearance of explanation. A mathematician may thus give an explanation of a firft rate fhip of war turning to windward, by fhewing how a rope may be attached to the fhip, and how this rope may be pulled, fo as to make her defcribe the very line fhe moves in. But the feaman knows that this is no explanation, and that he produced this motion of the fhip by various manœuvres of the fails and rudder. The only

only explanation that could be given, correfponding to the natural fuggeftion by this remark, would be the fhewing fome general fact in the fyftem, in which this fingle force may be found that muft thus impel the planets eccentrically, and thus urge them into revolution and rotation at once, as they would be urged by a ftroke from fome other planet or comet. With refpect to this Earth, there is not the leaft appearance of the effect which muft have been produced on it, had it been urged into motion by a fingle force applied to one point. The force has been applied alike to every particle; there is no appearance of any fuch general force competent to the production of fuch motions. Nay, did we clearly perceive the exiftence of fuch a force, we fhould be as far from an explanation as ever. It is not enough that Jupiter receives an impulfe which impreffes both the progreffive and rotative motion. His four fatellites muft receive, each feparately, an impulfe of a certain precife intenfity, and in a certain precife direction, very different in each, and which cannot be deduced from any thing that we know of matter and motion. No principle of general influence has been contrived by the zealous patrons of this fyftem (for it is a fyftem) that gives the fmalleft fatisfaction even to themfelves, and they are obliged to reft fatisfied with expreffing their hopes that it may yet be accomplifhed.

But fuppofe that an expert mechanician fhould fhew how the planets, fatellites, and comets may be fo placed that an impulfe may at once be given to them all, precifely

competent

competent to the production of the very motions that we obferve, which motions will now be maintained for ever by the 'univerfal operation of gravity. We fhould certainly admire his fagacity and his knowledge of nature. But we ftill wonder as much as ever at the nice adjuftment of all this to ends which have evidently all the excellence that order and fymmetry can give, while many of them are indifpenfably fubfervient to purpofes which we cannot help thinking good. The fuggeftion of purpofe and final caufes is as ftrong as ever. It is no more eluded than it would be, fhould any man perfectly explain the making of a watch wheel, by fhewing that it was the neceffary refult of the fhape and hardnefs of the files and drills and chizels employed, and the intenfity and direction of the forces by which thofe tools were moved; and having done all this, fhould fay that he had accounted for the nice and fuitable form of the wheel as a part of a watch. And, with refpect to the fubfequent oblate form of the planet fet in rotation, the mechanical explanation of this is incompatible with the fuppofition that the revolution and rotation are the effects of one fimple force. The oblate form, if acquired by rotation, requires primitive fluidity, which is incompatible with the operation of one fimple force as the primitive mover. There is no proof whatever that this Earth was originally fluid; it is not nearly fo oblate as primitive fluidity requires; yet its form is fo nicely adjufted to its rotation, that the thin film of water on it is diftributed with perfect uniformity. We are obliged

to

to grant that a form has been originally given it fuitable to its deftination, and we enjoy the advantages of this exquifite adjuftment.

I acknowledge that the influence of final caufes has been frequently and egregioufly mifapplied, and that thefe ignorant and precipitate attempts to explain phenomena, or to account for them, and even fometimes to authenticate them, have certainly obftructed the progrefs of true fcience. But what gift of God has not been thus abufed ? A true philofopher will never be fo regardlefs of logic as to adduce final caufes as arguments for the reality of any fact ; but neither will he have fuch a horror at the appearances of wifdom, as to fhun looking at them. And we apprehend that unlefs fome

    ‘ *Frigidus obftiterit circum præcordia fanguis,* ’
it is not in any man's power to hinder himfelf from perceiving and wondering at them. Surely

    ‘ *To look thro' nature up to Nature's God,* ’
cannot be an unpleafant tafk to a heart endowed with an ordinary fhare of fenfibility ; and the face of nature, expreffing the Supreme Mind which gives animation to its features, is an object more pleafing than the mere workings of blind matter and motion.

But enough of this.——We fhall clofe this fubject of planetary figures by flightly noticing, for the prefent, a confequence of the oblate form perceptible in all the planets which turn round their axes ; in the explanation of which the penetration of Newton's intellect is eminently confpicuous.

                                 610.

610. In § 584, and feveral following paragraphs, we explained the effects arifing from the inclination of the Moon's orbit round the Earth to the plane of the Earth's orbit round the Sun. We faw, for example, that when the interfection of the two planes is in the line A B (fig. 61.) of quadrature, the Moon is perpetually drawn out of that plane, and her path is continually bent down toward the ecliptic, during her moving along the femi-circle A C B, and fhe defcribes another path A c b, croff-ing the ecliptic in b, nearer to A than B is. In the o-ther half of her orbit, the fame deviation is continued, and the Moon again croffes the ecliptic before fhe come to A, croffes her laft path near to c, and the ecliptic a third time at d, and fo on continually. Hence arifes the retrograde motion of the nodes of the lunar orbit. We fhewed that this obtains, in a greater or lefs degree, in every pofition of the nodes, except when they are in the line of fyzigy.

What is true of one moon, would be true of any number : It would be true, were there a complete ring of moons furrounding the Earth, not adhering to one another. We faw that the inclination of the orbit is continually changing, being greateft when the nodes are in the line of the fyzigies, and fmalleft when they are in quadrature. Now, if we apply this to a ring of moons, we fhall find that it will never be a ring that is all in one plane, except when the nodes are in the fyzigies, and at all other times will be warped, or out of fhape. Now, let the moons all cohere, and the ring become

3 X   ftiff;

ftiff; and let this happen when its nodes are in fyzigy.
It will turn round without difturbance of this fort.
But this pofition of the nodes of the ring foon changes,
by the Sun's change of relative fituation, and now all
the derangements begin again. The ring can no longer
go out of fhape or warp, becaufe we may fuppofe it inflexible. But, as in the courfe of any one revolution of
the Moon round the Earth, the inclination of the orbit would either be increafed, on the whole, or diminifhed, on the whole, and the nodes would, on the
whole, recede, this effect muft be obferved in the ring.
When the nodes are fo fituated that, in the courfe of one
revolution of a fingle Moon, the inclination will be more
increafed in one part than it is diminifhed in another,
the oppofite actions on the different parts of a coherent
and inflexible ring will deftroy each other, as far as they
are equal, and the excefs only will be perceived on the
whole ring. Hence we can infer, with great confidence,
that from the time that the nodes of the ring are in fyzigy to the time they are in quadrature, the inclination
of the ring of moons will be continually diminifhing;
will be leaft of all when the Sun is in quadrature with
the line of the nodes; and will increafe again to a maximum, when the Sun again gets into the line of the nodes,
that is, when the nodes are in the line of the fyzigies.
But the inertia of the ring will caufe it to continue any
motion that is accumulated in it till it be deftroyed by
contrary forces. Hence, the times of the maximum and
minimum of inclination will be confiderably different
from

from what is now ftated. This will be attended to by
and by.

For the fame reafon, the nodes of the ring will continually recede ; and this retrograde motion will be moſt
remarkable when the nodes are in quadrature, or the Sun
in quadrature with the line of the nodes ; and will gradually become lefs remarkable, as the nodes approach
the line of the fyzigies, where the retrograde motion
will be the leaft poſſible, or rather ceafes altogether.

All thefe things may be diſtinctly perceived, by ſtea-
dily confidering the manner of acting of the diſturbing
force. This ſteady contemplation however is neceſſary,
as fome of the effects are very unexpected.

Suppofe now that this ring contracts in its dimenſions. The diſturbing force, and all its effects, muſt diminiſh in the fame proportion as the diameter of the
ring diminiſhes. But they will continue the fame in
kind as before. The inclination will increafe till the Sun
comes into the line of the nodes, and diminiſh till he
gets into quadrature with them. Suppofe the ring to
contract till almoſt in contact with the Earth's furface.
The recefs of the nodes, inſtead of being almoſt three
degrees in a month, will now be only three minutes, and
the change of inclination in three months will now be
only about five feconds.

Suppofe the ring to contract ſtill more, and to cohere
with the Earth. This will make a great change. The tendency of the ring to change its inclination, and to change its
interfection with the ecliptic, ſtill continues. But it can-

not

not now produce the effect, without dragging with it the whole mafs of the Earth. But the Earth is at perfect liberty in empty fpace, and being retained by nothing, yields to every impulfe, and therefore yields to this action of the ring.

Now, there is fuch a ring furrounding the Earth, having precifely this tendency. The Earth may be confidered as a fphere, on which there is fpread a quantity of redundant matter which makes it fpheroidal. The gravitation of this redundant matter to the Sun fuftains all thofe difturbing forces which act on the inflexible ring of moons; and it will be proved, in its proper place, that the effect in changing the pofition of the globe is $\frac{1}{5}$ of what it would be, if all this redundant matter were accumulated on the equator. It will alfo appear that the force by which every particle of it is urged to or from the plane of the ecliptic, is as its diftance from that plane. Indeed, this appears already, becaufe all the difturbing forces acting on the particles of this ring are fimilar, both in direction and proportion, to thofe which we fhewed to influence the Moon in the fimilar fituations of her monthly courfe round the Earth. Similar effects will therefore be produced.

Let us now fee what thofe effects will be.—The lunar nodes continually recede; fo will the nodes of this equatoreal ring, that is, fo will the nodes of the equator, or its interfection with the ecliptic. But the interfections of the equator with the ecliptic are what we call the Equinoctial Points. The plane of the Earth's equator,

equator, being produced to the ftarry heavens, interfects that feemingly concave fphere in a great circle, which may be traced out among the ftars, and marked on a celeftial globe.   Did the Earth's equator always keep the fame pofition, this circle of the heavens would always pafs through the fame ftars, and cut the ecliptic in the fame two oppofite points.   When the Sun comes to one of thofe points, the Earth turning round under him, every point of its equator has him in the zenith in fucceffion ; and all the inhabitants of the Earth fee him rife and fet due eaft and weft, · and have the day and night of the fame length.   But, in the courfe of a year, the action of the Sun on the protuberance of our equator deranges it from its former pofition, in fuch a manner that each of its interfections with the ecliptic is a little to the weftward of its former place in the ecliptic, fo that the Sun comes to the interfection about 20′ before he reaches the interfection of the preceding year.   This anticipation of the equal divifion of day and night is therefore called the PRECESSION OF THE EQUINOXES.

The axis of diurnal revolution is perpendicular to the plane of the equator, and muft therefore change its pofition alfo.   If the inclination of the equator to the ecliptic were always the fame (23½ degrees), the pole of the diurnal revolution of the heavens (that is, the point of the heavens in which the Earth's axis would meet the concave) would keep at the fame diftance of 23½ degrees from the pole of the ecliptic, and would therefore always be found in the circumference of a circle, of which the

pole

pole of the ecliptic is the centre. The meridian which paffes through the poles of the ecliptic and equator muft always be perpendicular to the meridian which paffes through the equinoctial points, and therefore, as thefe fhift to the weftward, the pole of the equator muft alfo fhift to the weftward, on the circumference of the circle above mentioned.

But we have feen that the ring of redundant matter does not preferve the fame inclination to the ecliptic. It is moft inclined to it when the Sun is in the nodes, and fmalleft when he is in quadrature with refpect to them. Therefore the obliquity of the equator and ecliptic fhould be greateft on the days of the equinoxes, and fmalleft when the Sun is in the folftitial points. The Earth's axis fhould twice in the year incline downward toward the ecliptic, and twice, in the intervals, fhould raife itfelf up again to its greateft elevation.

Something greatly refembling this feries of motions may be obferved in a child's humming top, when fet a fpinning on its pivot. An equatoreal circle may be drawn on this top, and a circular hole, a little bigger than the top, may be cut in a bit of ftiff paper. When the top is fpinning very fteadily, let the paper be held fo that half of the top is above it, the equator almoft touching the fides of the hole. When the whirling motion abates, the top begins to ftagger a little. Its equator no longer coincides with the rim of the hole in the paper, but in-terfects it in two oppofite points. Thefe interfections will be obferved to fhift round the whole circumference

of

of the hole, as the axis of the top veers round. The axis becomes continually more oblique, without any periods of recovering its former pofition, and, in this refpect only the phenomena differ from thofe of the precefsion.

It was affirmed that the obliquity of the equator is greateft at the equinoxes, and fmalleft at the folftices. This would be the cafe, did the redundant ring inftantly attain the pofition which makes an *equilibrium* of action. But this cannot be ; chiefly for this reafon, that it muft drag along with it the whole infcribed fphere. During the motion from the equinox to the next folftice, the Earth's equator has been urged toward the ecliptic, and it muft approach it with an accelerated motion. Suppofe, at the inftant of the folftice, all action of the Sun to ceafe ; this motion of the terreftrial globe would not ceafe, but would go on for ever, equably. But the Sun's action continuing, and now tending to raife the equator again from the ecliptic, it checks the contrary motion of the globe, and, at length, annihilates it altogether ; and then the effect of the elevating force begins to appear, and the equator rifes again from the ecliptic. When the Sun is in the equinox, the elevation of the equator fhould be greateft ; but, as it arrived at this pofition with an accelerated motion, it continues to rife (with a retarded motion) till the continuance of the Sun's deprefsing force puts an end to this rifing ; and now the effect of the deprefsing force begins to appear. For thefe reafons, it happens that the greateft obliquity of

the

the equator to the ecliptic is not on the days of the equinoxes, but about fix weeks after, viz. about the firft of May and November; and the fmalleft obliquity is not at midfummer and midwinter, but about the beginning of February and of Auguft.

And thus, we find that the fame principle of univerfal gravitation, which produces the elliptical motion of the planets, the inequalities of their fatellites, and determines the fhape of fuch as turn round their axes, alfo explains this moft remarkable motion, which had baffled all the attempts of philofophers to account for—a motion, which feemed to the ancients to affect the whole hoft of heaven; and when Copernicus fhewed that it was only an appearance in the heavens, and proceeded from a real fmall motion of the Earth's axis, it gave him more trouble to conceive this motion with diftinctnefs, than all the others. All thefe things—*obvia confpicimus, nubem pellente mathefi.*

611. Such is the method which Sir Ifaac Newton, the fagacious difcoverer of this mechanifm, has taken to give us a notion of it. Nothing can be more clear and familiar in general. He has even fubjected his explanation to the fevere teft of calculation. The forces are known, both in quantity and direction. Therefore the effects muft be fuch as legitimately flow from thofe forces. When we confider what a minute portion of the globe is acted upon, and how much inert matter is to be moved by the force which affects fo fmall a

portion,

portion, we muft expect very feeble effects. All the change that the action of the Sun produces on the inclination of the equator amounts only to the fraction of a fecond, and is therefore quite infenfible. The change in the pofition of the equinoxes is more confpicuous, becaufe it accumulates, amounting to about 9″ annually, by Newton's calculation. We fhall take notice of this calculation at another time, and at prefent fhall only obferve that this motion of the equinox is but a fmall part of the preceffion actually obferved. This is about $50\frac{1}{3}″$ annually. It would therefore feem that the theory and obfervation do not agree, and that the preceffion of the equinoxes is by no means explained by it.

612. It muft be remarked that we have only given an account of the effect refulting from the unequal gravitation of the terreftrial matter to the Sun. But it gravitates alfo to the Moon. Moreover, the inequality of this gravitation (on which inequality the difturbance depends) is vaftly greater. The Moon being almoft 400 times nearer than the Sun, the gravitation to a pound of lunar matter is almoft 640,000,000 times greater than to as much folar matter. When the calculation is made from proper data, (in which Newton was confiderably miftaken) the effect of the lunar action muft very confiderably exceed that of the Sun. He was miftaken, in refpect to the quantity of matter in the Sun and in the Moon. The tranfit of Venus, and the obfervations which have been made on the tides, have

brought

brought us much nearer the truth in both thefe refpects.
When the calculation is made on fuch affumptions of the
matter in the Sun and Moon as are beft fupported by
obfervation, we find that the annual preceffion occafioned by the Sun's action on the equatoreal protuberance
is about 14″ or 15″, and that produced by the Moon is
about 35″.   The preceffion really obferved is about
50″, and the agreement is abundantly exact.   It muft
be farther remarked that this agreement is no longer inferred from a due proportioning of the whole obferved
preceffion between the Sun and the Moon, as we were
formerly obliged to do ; but each fhare is an independent
thing, calculated without any reference to the whole
preceffion.   It is thus only that the phenomenon may be
affirmed to be truly explained.

613.   For this demonftration we are indebted to Dr
Bradley.   His difcovery of what is now called the
NUTATION of the Earth's axis, gave us a precife mea-
fure of the lunar action which removed every doubt.
It therefore muft be confidered here.

   The action of the luminaries on the Earth's equator, by
which the pofition of it is deranged, depends on the magnitude of the angle which the equator makes with the line
joining the Earth with the difturbing body.   The Sun is never more than 23½ degrees from the equator.   But when the
Moon's afcending node is in the vernal equinox, fhe may
deviate nearly 29 degrees from it.   And when the node
is in the autumnal equinox, fhe cannot go more than 17
                                                degrees

degrees from it. Thus, the action of the Sun is, from year to year, the fame. But as, in 19 years, the Moon's nodes take all fituations, the action of the Moon is very variable. It was one of the effects of this variation that Bradley difcovered. While the Earth's equator continued to open farther and farther from the line joining the Earth with the Moon, the axis of the Earth was gradually depreffed towards the ecliptic, and the diminution of its inclination at laft amounted to 18 feconds. Dr Bradley faw this by its incieafing the declination of a ftar properly fituated. After nine years, when the Moon was in fuch a fituation that fhe never went more than 17° from the Earth's equator, the fame ftar had 18″ lefs declination.

614. This change in the inclination of the Earth's equator is accompanied with a change in the preceffion of the equinoxes. This muft increafe as the equator is more open when viewed from the Moon. In the year in which the lunar afcending node is in the vicinity of the vernal equinox, the preceffion is more than 58″; and it is but 43″ when the node is near the autumnal equinox. Thefe are very confpicuous changes, and of eafy obfervation, although long unnoticed, while blended with other anomalies equally unknown.

Few difcoveries in aftronomy have been of more fervice to the fcience than this of the nutation, and that of aberration, both by Dr Bradley. For till they were known, there was an anomaly, which might fometimes

3 Y 2   amount

amount to 58″ (the fum of nutation and aberration), and affected every motion and every obfervation. No theory of any planet could be freed from this uncertainty. But now, we can give to every phenomenon its own proper motions, with all the accuracy that modern inftruments can attain. Without thefe two difcoveries, we could not have brought the folution of the great nautical problem of the longitude to any degree of perfection, becaufe we could not render either the folar or lunar tables perfect. The changes in the pofition of the Earth's axis by nutation, and the concomitant equation of the preceffion, by recurring in the moft regular manner, have given us the moft exact meafure of the changes in the Moon's action ; and therefore gave an incontrovertible meafure of her whole action, becaufe the proportion between the variation and the whole action was diftinctly known.

This not only completes the practical folution of the problem, but gives the moft unqueftionable proof of the foundnefs of the theory, fhewing that the oblate form of the Earth is the caufe of this nutation of its axis, and eftablifhing the univerfal and mutual attraction of all matter. It fhews with what confidence we may proceed, in following this law of gravitation into all its confequences, and that we may predict, without any chance of miftake, what will be the effect of any combination of circumftances that can be mentioned. And it furely fhews, in the moft confpicuous manner, the penetration and fagacity of Newton, who gave encouragement to a furmife fo fingular and fo unlike all the ufual queftions of

progreffive

progreffive motion, even in all their varieties. Yet this moft recondite and delicate fpeculation was one of his early thoughts, and is one of the twelve propofitions which he read to the Royal Society.

615. It muft be acknowledged however that this manner of exhibiting the theory of the preceffion of the equinoxes is not complete, or even accurate in the felection of the phyfical circumftances on which the proof proceeds. It is merely a popular way of leading the mind to the view of actions, which are indeed of the fame kind with thofe actually concurring in the production of the effect. But it is not a narration of the real actions. Nor are the effects of thofe that are employed eftimated according to their real manner of acting. The whole is rather a fhrewd guefs, in which Newton's great penetration enabled him to catch at a very remote analogy between the libration of the Moon and the wavering motion of the Earth's axis. We are not in a condition in this part of the courfe to treat this queftion in the proper manner. We muft firft underftand the properties of the lever as a mechanical power, and the operation of the connecting forces of firm or rigid bodies. What we have faid will fuffice however for giving a diftinct enough conception of the general effects of the action of remote bodies on a fpheroidal planet turning round its axis. * It is

---

* To thofe who wifh to ftudy this very curious and difficult problem, I fhould recommend the folution given by Frifius

is fcarcely neceffary to add that the other planets cannot
fenfibly influence the motion of the Earth's axis.   Their
accumulated action may add about $\frac{1}{7}$ of a fecond to the
annual preceffion of the equinoxes.

The planets Mars, Jupiter, and Saturn, being vaftly
more oblate than the Earth, muft be more expofed to
this derangement of the rotative motion.   Jupiter and
Saturn, having fo many fatellites, which take various pofitions round the planet, the problem becomes immenfely
complicated.   But the fmall inclination of the equator,
and the great mafs of the planet, and its very rapid rotation, muft greatly diminifh the effect we are now confidering.   Mars, being fmall, turning flowly, and yet
being very oblate, muft fuftain a greater degree of this
derangement ; and if Mars had a fatellite, we might expect fuch a change in the pofition of his axis as fhould
become very fenfible, even at this diftance.

The ring of Saturn muft be fubject to fimilar difturbances, and muft have a retrogradation of its interfection
with

---

fius in the fecond part of his Cofmographia, as the moft perfpicuous of any that I am acquainted with.   The elaborate
performance of Mr Walmefely, Euler, D'Alembert, and La
Grange, are acceffible only to expert analyfts.   The effay by
T. Simpfon in the Philofophical Tranfactions, Vol. L. is remarkable for its fimplicity, but, by employing the fymbolical
or algebraic analyfis, the ftudent is not fo much aided by the
conftant accompaniment of phyfical ideas, as in the geometrical method of Frifius.

with the plane of the orbit. Had we nothing to confider but the ring itfelf, it would be a very eafy problem to determine the motion of its nodes. But the proximity, and the oblate form, of the planet, and, above all, the complicated action of the fatellites, make it next to unmanageable. It has not been attempted, that I know of. It may (I think) be deduced, from the Greenwich obfervations fince 1750, that the nodes retreat on the orbit of Saturn about 34′ or 36′ in a century, and that their longitude in 1801 was 5ˢ 17° 13′ and 11ˢ 17° 13′. This may be received as more exact than the determination given in art. 380.

I faid, in art. 370, that we have feen too little of the motions of Ceres and Pallas to announce the elements of their theories with any thing like precifion. But, that they may not be altogether omitted, the following may be received as of moft authority.

	Ceres.	*Pallas.*
Mean diftance - - - - -	2767231	2767123
Eccentricity to m. d. 1. - - - -	0,079	0,2463
Long. aphelion - - - - -	4.26.44	4.1.7.—
Period (fydereal) in days - -	1682,25	1681,22
Mean long. Jan. 1804. - - -	10.11.59	9.29.53
Inclin. orbit - - - - - -	—.10.37	—.34.39
Long. node - - - - - -	2.21. 7	5.22.27

Thefe bodies prefent fome very fingular circumftances to our ftudy; their diftances and periods being almoft the fame, and their longitudes at prefent differing very little. They differ confiderably in eccentricity, the place of the

node,

node, and the inclination of their orbits. They muſt be greatly diſturbed by each other, and by Jupiter, and it will be long before we ſhall obtain exact elements.

With theſe obſervations I might conclude the diſ-cuſſion of the mechaniſm of the ſolar ſyſtem. The facts obſerved in the appearances of the comets are too few to authoriſe me to add any thing to what has been al-ready ſaid concerning them. I refer to Newton's Prin-cipia for an account of that great philoſopher's conjec-tures concerning the luminous train which generally at-tends them, acknowledging that I do not think theſe conjectures well ſupported by the eſtabliſhed laws of motion. Dr Winthorp has given, in the 57th volume of the *Phil. Tranſ.* a geometrical explanation of the me-chaniſm of this phenomenon that is ingenious and ele-gant, but founded on a hypotheſis which I think inad-miſſible.

616. No notice has yet been taken of the relations of the ſolar ſyſtem to the reſt of the viſible hoſt of heaven, and we have, hitherto, only conſidered the ſtarry heavens as affording us a number of fixed points, by which we may eſtimate the motions of the bodies which compoſe our ſyſtem. It will not therefore be unaccept-able ſhould I now lay before the reader ſome reflections, which naturally ariſe in the mind of any perſon who has been much occupied in the preceding reſearches and ſpe-culations, and which lead the thoughts into a ſcene of contemplation far exceeding in magnificence any thing yet

yet laid before the reader. As they are of a mifcella-
neous nature; and not fufceptible of much arrangement,
I fhall not pretend to mark them by any diftinctions, but
fhall take them as they naturally offer themfelves.

The fitnefs for almoft eternal duration, fo confpicuous in the conftitution of the folar fyftem, cannot but
fuggeft the higheft ideas of the intelligence of the Great
Artift. No doubt thefe conceptions will be very obfcure, and very inadequate. But we fhall find that the
farther we advance in our knowledge of the phenomena,
we fhall fee the more to admire, and the more numerous
difplays of great wifdom, power, and kind intentions.

It is not therefore fearful fuperftition, but the cheer-
ful anticipation of a good heart, which will make a ftudent of nature even endeavour to form to himfelf ftill
higher notions of the attributes of the Divine Mind.
He cannot do this in a direct manner. All he can do is
to abftract all notions of imperfection, whether in power,
fkill, or benevolent intentions, and he will fuppofe the
Author of the univerfe to be infinitely powerful, wife
and good.

It is impoffible to ftop the flights of a fpeculative
mind, warmed by fuch pleafing notions. Such a mind
will form to itfelf notions of what is moft excellent in
the defigns which a perfect being may form, and it finds
itfelf under a fort of neceffity of believing that the Divine Mind will really form fuch defigns. This romantic
wandering has given rife to many ftrange theological o-
pinions. Not doubting (at leaft in the moment of en-
3 Z   thufiafm)

thufiafm) that we can judge of what is moft excellent, we take it for granted that this creature of our heated imagination muft alfo appear moft excellent to the Supreme Mind.   From this principle, theologians have ventured to lay down the laws by which God himfelf muft regulate his actions.   No wonder that, on fo fanciful a foundation as our capacity to judge of what is moft excellent, have been erected the moft extravagant fabrics, and that, in the exuberance of religious zeal, the Author of all has been defcribed as the moft limited Agent in the univerfe, forced, in every action, to regulate himfelf by our poor and imperfect notions of what is excellent. We, who vanifh from the fight, at the diftance of a neighbouring hill—whofe greateft works are invifible from the Moon—whofe whole habitation is not vifible to a fpectator in Saturn—fhall fuch creatures pretend to judge of what is fupremely excellent ?

Let us not pretend even to guefs at the fpecific laws by which the conduct of the Divinity muft be directed, except in fo far as it has pleafed him to declare them to us.   We fhall purfue the only fafe road in this fpeculation, if we endeavour to difcover the laws by which his vifible and comprehenfible works are actually conducted.   The more we difcover of thefe, the more do we find to fill us with admiration and aftonifhment. The only fpeculations in which we can indulge, without the continual danger of going aftray, are thofe which enlarge our notions of the fcene on which it has pleafed the Almighty to difplay his perfections.   This will be

the

the undoubted effect of enlarging the field of our own obfervation. After examining this lower world, and obferving the nice and infinitely various adjuftments of means to ends here below, we may extend our obfervation beyond this globe. Then fhall we find that, as far as our knowledge can carry us, there is the. fame art, and the fame production of good effects by beautifully contrived means. We have lately difcovered a new planet, far removed beyond the formerly imagined bounds of the planetary world. This difcovery fhews us that if there are thoufands more, they may be for ever hid from our eyes by their immenfe diftance. Yet *there* we find the fame care taken that their condition fhall be permanent. They are influenced by a force directed to the Sun, and inverfely as the fquare of the diftance from him ; and they defcribe ellipfes. This planet is alfo accompanied by fatellites, doubtlefs rendering to the primary and its inhabitants fervices fimilar to what this Earth receives from the Moon. All the comets of whofe motions we have any precife knowledge, are e-equally fecured ; none feems to defcribe a parabola or hyperbola, fo as to quit the Sun for ever.

This mark of an intention that this noble fabric fhall continue for ever to declare itfelf the work of an Almighty and Kind Hand, naturally carries forward the mind into that unbounded fpace, of which our folar fyftem occupies fo inconfiderable a portion. The mind revolts at the thought that this is ftudded with ftars for no other purpofe than to affift the aftronomer in his computations,

3 Z 2

putations,

putations, and to furnish a gay fpectacle to the unthink-
ing multitude. We fee nothing here below, or in our
fyftem, which anfwers but one folitary purpofe, and we
require that a pofitive reafon fhall be given for limiting
the Hoft of Heaven to fo ignoble an office. As fuch has
not been given, we indulge ourfelves in the pleafing
thought that the ftars make a part of the univerfe, no lefs
important in purpofe than great in extent. We are juftifiable, by what we in fome meafure underftand, in fuppofing each ftar a fun, the centre of a planetary fyftem,
full of enjoyment like our own, and fo conftructed as to
laft for ever.

When the philofopher indulges himfelf in thofe amazing, but pleafing thoughts, he muft regulate his fpeculations by analogies and refemblances to things more familiarly known to him. We muft fuppofe thofe fyftems
to refemble our own, and that they are kept together by
a gravitation in the inverfe duplicate ratio of the diftances. For we know that this alone will infure perma-
nancy and good order.

But in fo doing, we extend the influence of gravity
to diftances inconceivably greater than any that we have
yet confidered, and we come at laft to believe that gravitation is the bond of connexion which unites the moft
diftant bodies of the vifible univerfe, rendering the whole
one great machine, for ever operating the moft magnificent purpofes, worthy of its All-Perfect Creator. And,
when we fee that fuch a connexion is neceffary for this
end, we are apt to imagine that gravity is *effential* to or
                                        indifpenfable

indifpenfable in that matter that is to be moulded into a world.

But let not our ignorance miflead us, nor let us meafure every thing by that fmall fcale which God has enabled us to ufe, unlefs we can fee fome circumftances of refemblance in the appearances, which may juftify the application.

* A frame of material nature of any kind cannot be conceived by the mind, without fuppofing that the matter of which it confifts is influenced by fome active powers, conftituting the relations between its different parts. Were there only the mere inert materials of a world, it would hardly be better than a chaos, although moulded into fymmetrical forms, unlefs the fpirit of its author were to animate thofe dead maffes, fo as to bring forth change, and order, and beauty. Our illuftrious Newton

---

* For many of the thoughts in what follows, the reader is indebted to a very ingenious pamphlet, publifhed by Caddel & Davies in 1777, entitled, *Thoughts on General Gravitation*. It is much to be regreted that the author has not availed himfelf of the fuccefsful refearches of aftronomers fince that time, and profecuted his excellent hints. If it be the performance of the perfon whom I fuppofe to be the author, I have fuch an opinion of his acutenefs, and of his juftnefs of thought, that I take this opportunity of requefting him to turn his attention afrefh to the fubject. His advantages, from his prefent fituation and connexions, are precious, and fhould not be loft.

ton therefore fays, with great propriety, that the bufinefs of a true philofophy is to inveftigate thofe active
powers, by which the courfe of natural events, to a very
great extent at leaft, is perpetually governed. Philofo-
phifing with this view, he difcovered the law of univerfal gravitation, and has thus given the brighteft fpecimen of the powers of human underftanding.

The notion of fomething like gravity feems infeparable from our conception of any eftablifhed order of
things. For unlefs fome principle of general union obtain among the parts of matter, we can have no conception of the very firft formation of the individuals of
which a world may be compofed.

But *general* gravitation, or that power by which the
diftant bodies belonging to any fyftem are connected,
and act on one another, does not feem fo indifpenfably
neceffary to the very being of the fyftem, as *particular*
gravity is to the being of any individual in it. We cannot difcern any abfurdity in the fuppofition of bodies,
fuch as the planets, fo fituated with refpect to another
great body, fuch as the Sun, as to receive from it fuitable degrees of light and heat, without their having any
tendency to approach the Sun, or each other. But then,
how far fuch limitation of gravity may be a poffible
thing, or how far its indefinite extenfion in every direction may be involved in its very nature, we cannot
tell, until we are able to confider gravity as an effect,
and to deduce the laws of its operation from our knowledge of its caufe.

That

That the influence of gravity extends into the boundless void, to the greateft affignable diftance, feems to be almoft the hinge of the Newtonian philofophy. At leaft, there is nothing that warrants any limit to its action. Father Bofcovich indeed fhews that all the phenomena may be what they are, without this as a neceffary confequence. But he is plainly induced to bring forward the limitation in order to avoid what has been thought a neceffary confequence of the indefinite extenfion of gravity ; and what he offers is a mere poffibility.

Now, if fuch extenfion of gravitation be infeparable, in fact, from its nature, then, if all the bodies of our fyftem are at reft in abfolute fpace, no fooner does the influence of general gravitation go abroad into the fyftem, than all the planets and comets muft begin to approach the Sun, and, in a very fmall number of days, the whole of the folar fyftem muft fall into the Sun, and be deftroyed.

But, that this fair order may be preferved, and accommodated to this extended influence of gravity, which appears fo effential to the conftitution of the feveral parts of the fyftem, we fee a moft fimple and effectual prevention, by the introduction of *projectile forces*, and *progreffive motion*. For upon thefe being now combined, and properly adjufted with the variation of gravity, the planets are made to revolve round the Sun in ftated courfes, by which their continual approach to the Sun and to one another is prevented, and the adjuftment is made with fuch exquifite propriety, that the perfect order

der

der of things is almoft unchangeable. This adjuftment
is no lefs manifeft in the fubordinate fyftems of a primary planet and its fatellites, which are not only regular in their own orbital motions, but are the conftant
attendants of their primaries in their revolution round
the Sun.

In this view of the fubject, forafmuch as gravity
feems effential to the conftitution of all the great bodies
of the fyftem, and in fo far as its indefinite extenfion
may be infeparable from its nature, it appears that *periodical motion* muft be neceffary for the permanency and
order of every fyftem of worlds whatever.

But here a thought is fuggefted which obvioufly leads
to a new and a very grand conception of the univerfe.
If periodical motion be thus neceffary for the preferva-
tion of a fmall affemblage of bodies, and if Newton's
law prefent to us the whole hoft of heaven as one great
affemblage affected by gravitation, we muft ftill have recourfe to periodical motion, in order to fecure the eftablifhment of this grand univerfal fyftem. For if there be
no bounds to the influence of gravitation, and if all the
ftars be fo many funs, the centres of as many fyftems
(as is moft reafonable to believe) the immenfity of their
diftance cannot fatisfy us for their being long able to
remain in any fettled order. Thofe that are fituated towards the confines of this magnificent creation muft for-
fake their ftations, and, with an approach, continually
accelerated, muft move onwards to the centre of gene-

ral

ral gravitation, and, after a feries of ages, the whole glory of nature muft end in a univerfal wreck.

As the fyftem of Jupiter and his fatellites is but an epitome of the great folar fyftem to which he belongs, may not this, in its turn, be a faint reprefentation of that grand fyftem of the univerfe, round whofe centre this Sun, with his attending planets, and an inconceiveable multitude of like fyftems, do in reality revolve according to the law of gravitation ? Now, will our anticipation of diforder and ruin be changed into the contemplation of a countlefs number of nicely adjufted motions, all proclaiming the fuftaining hand of God.

This is indeed a grand, and almoft overpowering thought ; yet juftified both by reafon and analogy. The grandeur however of this univerfal fyftem only opens upon us by degrees. If it refemble our folar fyftem in conftruction, what an inconceivable difplay of creation is fuggefted, when we turn our thoughts towards that place which the motions of fo many revolving fyftems are made to refpect ! Here may be an unthought of univerfe of itfelf, an example of material creation, which muft individually exceed all the other parts, though added into one amount. As our Sun is almoft four thoufand times bigger than all his attendants put together, it is not unreafonable to fuppofe the fame thing here. It is not neceffary that this central body fhould be vifible. The great ufe of it is not to illuminate, but to govern the motions of all the reft. We know, however, that the exiftence of fuch a central body is not

4 A   neceffary.

neceffary. Two bodies, although not very unequal, may
be projected with fuch velocities, and in fuch directions,
that they will revolve for ever round their common
centre of pofition and gravitation. But fuch a fyftem
could hardly maintain any regularity of motion when a
third body is added. It may indeed be faid that the
fame tranfcendent wifdom, which has fo exquifitely adapted all the circumftances of our fyftem, may fo adjuft the motions of an immenfe number of bodies, that
their difturbing actions fhall accurately compenfate each
other. But ftill, the beautiful fimplicity that is manifeft
in what we fee and underftand, feems to warrant a like
fimplicity in this great fyftem, and therefore renders the
exiftence of fuch a great central Regulator of the movements of all, the moft probable fuppofition.

Sober reafon will not be difpofed to revolt at fo glo-
rious an extenfion of the works of God, however much
it may overpower our feeble conceptions. Nay this analogy acquires additional weight and authority even from
the tranfcendent nature of the univerfe to which it directs our thoughts. Nothing lefs magnificent feems fuitable to a Being of infinite perfections.

But we are not left to mere conjecture in fupport of
this conception of a great univerfe, connected by mutual powers. There are circumftances of analogy which
tend greatly to perfuade us of the reality of our conjecture—circumftances which feem to indicate a connexion
among the moft diftant objects of the creation vifible
from our habitation. The light by which the fixed ftars
                                                         are

are feen is the fame with that by which we behold our
Sun and his attending planets.   It moves with the fame
velocity, as we difcover by comparing the aberration of
the fixed ftars with the eclipfes of Jupiter's fatellites.
It is refracted and reflected according to the fame laws.
It confifts of the fame colours.   No opinion can be formed therefore of the folar light, which muft not alfo be
adopted with refpect to the light of the fixed ftars.   The
medium of vifion muft be acted on in the fame manner
by both, whether we fuppofe it the undulation of an
æther, or the emiffion of matter from the luminous body.
In either cafe, a mechanical connexion obtains between
thofe bodies, however diftant, and our fyftem.   Such a
connexion in mechanical properties induces us to fuppofe
that gravitation, which we know reaches to a diftance
which exceeds all our diftinct conceptions, extends alfo to
the fixed ftars.

If this be really the cafe, motion muft enfue, even in
producing the final ruin of the vifible univerfe ; and periodic motion is indifpenfably neceffary for its permanency.

If all the fixed ftars, and our Sun, were equal, and
placed at equal diftances, in the angles of regular folids, their mutual ruinous approach could hardly be perceived.   For in every moment, they would ftill have the
fame relative pofitions, and an increafe of brightnefs
is all that could enfue after many ages.   But if they
were irregularly placed, and unequal, their relative pofitions would change, with an accelerated motion, and

4 A 2   this

this change might become fenfible after a long courfe of ages. If they have periodical motions, fuited to the permanency of the grand fyftem of the univerfe, the changes of place may be much more fenfible ; and if we fuppofe that their difference in brilliancy is owing to the differences in their diftance from us, we may expect that thefe changes will be moft fenfible in the brighteft ftars.

Facts are not wanting to prove that fuch changes really obtain in the relative pofitions of the fixed ftars. This was firft obferved by that great aftronomer, mathematician and philofopher, Dr Halley. He found, after comparing the obfervations of Ariftillus, Timochares and Ptolemy with thofe of our · days, that feveral of the brighter ftars had changed their fituation remarkably (See Phil. Tranf. N° 355.) Aldebaran has moved to the fouth about 35′. Syrius has moved fouth about 42′, and Arcturus, alfo to the fouth, about 33′. The eaftern fhoulder of Orion has moved northward about 61′. Obfervations in modern times fhew that Arcturus has moved in 78 years about 3′ 3″. This is a very fenfible quantity, and is eafily obferved, by means of the fmall ftar *b* in its immediate neighbourhood. (See Phil. Tranf. LXIII. alfo 1748.; and Mem. Par. 1755.) Syrius in like manner increafes its latitude about 2′ in a century (Mem. Par. 1758.) Aldebaran moves very irregularly. The bright ftar in *Aquila* has changed its latitude 36′ fince the time of Ptolemy, and 3′ fince the time of Tycho. This is eafily feen by its continual feparation from the fmall ftar *ə*.

Thefe

Thefe motions feem to indicate a motion in our fyftem.   Moft of the ftars have moved toward the fouth.
The ftars in the northern quarters feem to widen their
relative pofitions, while thofe in the fouth feem to contract their diftances.   Dr Herfchel thinks that a comparifon of all thefe changes indicates a motion of our Sun
with his attending planets toward the conftellation Her-
cules (Phil. Tranf. 1788.)   A learned and ingenious
friend thinks it not impoffible to difcover this motion by
means of the aberration of the ftars.   Suppofe the Sun
and planets to be moving toward the Pole-ftar, and that his
motion is 100 times greater than that of the Earth in her orbit (a very moderate fuppofition, when we compare the orbital motion of the Earth with that of the Moon), every
equatoreal ftar will appear about 34′ north of its true
place, when viewed through a common telefcope, but
only 23′ when viewed through a telefcope filled with
water.   The declination of every fuch ftar will be 11′
lefs through a water telefcope than through a common
telefcope.   Stars out of the equator will have their declination diminifhed by a water telefcope 11′ × cof. declin.

In 1761, the ingenious Mr Lambert publifhed his
Letters on Cofmology (in the German language), in which
he has confidered this fubject with much attention and
ingenuity.   He treats of the motion of the Sun round
a central body—of fyftems of fyftems, or milky ways, carried round an immenfe body—of fyftems of fuch galaxies
—and of the great central body of the univerfe.   In thefe
fpeculations

fpeculations he infers much from final caufes, and is often ingenioufly romantic.   But Lambert was alfo a true
inductive philofopher, and makes no affertion with confidence that is not fupported by good analogies.   The
rotation of the Sun is a ftrong ground of belief to Mr
Lambert that he has alfo a progreffive motion.

Tobias Mayer of Gottingen fpeaks in the fame manner, in fome of his differtations publifhed after his death
by Lichtenberg.   See alfo *Bailli's Account of Modern
Aftronomy*, Vol. II. 664, 689.   Mayer of Manheim has
alfo publifhed thoughts to this effect.   See *Comment.
Acad. Palatin.* IV.   Prevoft, *Mem. Berlin* 1781.   Mitchel
Phil. Tranf. LVII. 252.   .

The gravitation to the fixed ftars can produce no fenfible difturbances of the motions of our fyftem.   This
gravitation muft be inconceivably minute, by reafon of
the immenfe diftance ; and, as they are in all quarters of
the heavens, they will nearly compenfate each other's
action ; and the extent of our fyftem being but as a
point, in comparifon with the diftance of the neareft
ftar, the gravitation to that ftar in all the parts of our
fyftem muft be fo nearly equal and parallel, that (98.) no
fenfible derangement can be effected, even after ages of
ages.

As a further circumftance of analogy with a periodical motion in the whole vifible univerfe, we may adduce
the remarkable periodical changes of brilliancy that are
obferved in many of the fixed ftars.

This

This was firft obferved (I think) in a ftar of the conftellation Hydra. Montanari had obferved it in 1670,
and left fome account of it in his papers, which Maraldi
took notice of. Maraldi, after long fearching in vain,
found it in 1704, and faw feveral alternations of its
brightnefs and dimnefs, but without being able to afcertain their period. It was long loft again, till Mr Edward
Pigot found it in 1786. He determined its period to be
404 days. Since that time, this gentleman, and his father, with a Mr Goodricke, have given more attention
to this department of aftronomy, and their example has
been followed by other aftronomers. Mr Pigot has given
us, in *Phil. Tranf.* 1786, a lift of a great number of
ftars (above fifty) in which fuch periodical changes have
been obferved, and has given particular determinations
of twelve or thirteen, afcertaining their periods with precifion. The whole is followed by fome very curious reflections.

Of thefe ftars, one of the moft remarkable is χ Cygni, having a period of 415¼ days. See *Phil. Tranf.*
N° 343.; alfo *Mem. Acad. Paris*, 1719, 1759.

Another remarkable ftar is *o* Ceti, having a period of
334 days. (See *Phil. Tranf.* N° 134. 346.; *Mem. Par.*
1719.)

There is another fuch, clofe to γ Cygni.

The double ftar ζ Lyræ exhibits very fingular appearances, the fouthernmoft fometimes appearing double,
and fometimes accompanied by more little ftars. Gri-
fchoff

fchoff of Berlin is pofitive that it has planets moving round it.

Some of thofe ftars have very fhort periods. The moft remarkable is Algól, in the head of Medufa. Its period is 2ᵈ 20ʰ 49′, in which its changes are very irregular, although perfectly alike in every period. Its ordinary appearance is that of a ftar of the fecond magnitude. It fuffers, for about 3¼ hours, a reduction to the appearance of a ftar of the fourth or fifth magnitude.

Mr Goodricke obferved fimilar variations in the ftar δ Cephei. During 5ᵈ 8ʰ 37′ it is a ftar of the fifth magnitude. For 1ᵈ 13ʰ it is of the fecond or third. It diminifhes during 1ᵈ 18ʰ; remains 36 hours in its fainteft ftate, and regains its brilliancy in 13ʰ more (*Phil. Tranf.* 1786.)

Mr Pigot obferved the ftar η Antinoi to maintain its utmoft brilliancy during 44 hours, and then gradually to fade during 62 hours, and, after remaining 30 hours of the fifth magnitude, it regains its greateft brilliancy in 36 hours (*Phil. Tranf.* 1786.)

Whatever may be the caufe of thefe alternations, they are furely very analagous to what we obferve in our fyftem, the individuals of which, by varying their pofitions, and turning their different fides toward us, exhibit alternations of a fimilar kind; as, for example, the apparition and difparition of Saturn's ring. Thefe circumftances, therefore, encourage us to fuppofe a fimilarity of conftitution in our fyftem to the reft of the

heavenly

heavenly Hoft, and render it more probable that all are connected by one general bond, and are regulated by fimilar laws. Nothing is fo likely for conflituting this connexion as gravitation, and its combination with projectile force and periodic motion tends to fecure the permanency of the whole.

But I muft at the fame time obferve that fuch appearances in the heavens make it evident that, notwithflanding the wife provifion made for maintaining that order and utility which we behold in our fyftem, the day may come ' when the heavens fhall pafs away like a ' fcroll that is folded up, when the ftars in heaven fhall ' fail, and the Sun fhall ceafe to give his light. ' The fuftaining hand of God is ftill neceffary, and the prefent order and harmony which he has enabled us to underftand and to admire, is wholly dependent on his will, and its duration is one of the unfearchable meafures of his providence. What is become of that dazzling ftar, furpaffing Venus in brightnefs, which fhone out all at once in November 1572, and determined Tycho Brahé to become an aftronomer? He did not fee it at half an hour paft five, as he was crofling fome fields in going to his laboratory. But, returning about ten, he came to a crowd of country folks who were ftaring at fomething behind him. Looking round, he faw this wonderful object. It was fo bright that his ftaff had a fhadow. It was of a dazzling white, with a little of a bluifh tinge. In this ftate it continued about three weeks, and then be-

came

came yellowifh and lefs brilliant.   Its brilliancy diminifhed faft after this, and it became more ruddy, like glow-
ing embers.   Gradually fading, it was wholly invifible
after fifteen months.

A fimilar phenomenon is faid to have caufed Hipparchus to devote himfelf to aftronomy, and to his
vaft project of a catalogue of the ftars, that pofterity
might know whether any changes happened in the heavens.   And, in 1604, another fuch phenomenon, though
much lefs remarkable, engaged for fome time the attention of aftronomers.   Nor are thefe all the examples of
the perifhable nature of the heavenly bodies.   Several
ftars in the catalogues of Hipparchus, of Ulugh Beigh,
of Tycho Brahé, and even of Flamftead, are no more to
be feen.   They are gone, and have left no trace.

Should we now turn our eyes to objects that are
nearer us, we fhall fee the fame marks of change.   When
the Moon is viewed through a good telefcope, magnify-
ing about 150 times, we fee her whole furface occupied
by volcanic craters ; fome of them of prodigious magnitude.   Some of them give the moft unqueftionable marks
of feveral fucceffive eruptions, each deftroying in part
the crater of a former eruption.   The precipitous and
craggy appearance of the brims of thofe craters is precifely fuch as would be produced by the ejection of rocky
matter.   In fhort, it is impoffible, after fuch a view of
the Moon, to doubt of her being greatly changed from
her primitive ftate.

Even

Even the Sun himfelf, the fource of light, and heat, and life, to the whole fyftem, is not free from fuch changes.

If we now look round us, and examine with judicious attention our own habitation, we fee the moft incontrovertible marks of great and general changes over the whole face of the Earth. Befides the flow degradation by the action of the winds and rains, by which the foil is gradually wafhed away from the high lands, and carried by the rivers into the bed of the ocean, leaving the Alpine fummits ftripped to the very bone, we cannot fee the face of any rock or crag, or any deep gully, which does not point out much more remarkable changes. Thefe are not confined to fuch as are plainly owing to the horrid operations of volcanoes, but are univerfal. Except a few mountains, where we cannot confidently fay that they are factitious, and which for no better reafon we call primitive, there is nothing to be feen but ruins and convulfions. What is now an elevated mountain has moft evidently been at the bottom of the fea, and, previous to its being there, has been habitable furface.

It is very true that all our knowledge on this fubject is merely fuperficial. The higheft mountains, and deepeft excavations, do not bear fo great a proportion to the globe as the thicknefs of paper that covers a terreftrial globe bears to the bulk of that philofophical toy. We have no authority from any thing that we have feen, for forming

4 B 2

any

any judgement concerning the internal conftitution of the Earth. But we fee enough to convince us that it bears no marks of eternal duration, or of exifting as it is, by its own energy. No!—all is perifhable—all requires the fuftaining hand of God, and is fubject to the unfearchable defigns of its Author and Preferver.

There is yet another clafs of objects in the heavens, of which I have taken no notice. They are called NEBULÆ, or NEBULOUS STARS. They have not the fparkling brilliancy that diftinguifhes the ftars, and they are of a fenfible diameter, and a determinate fhape. Many of them, when viewed through telefcopes, are clufters of ftars, which the naked eye cannot diftinguifh. The moft remarkable of thefe is in the conftellation Cancer, and is known by the name *Præfepe*. Ptolemy mentions it, and another in the right eye of Sagittarius. Another may be feen in the head of Orion. Many fmall clufters have been difcovered by the help of glaffes. The whole galaxy is nothing elfe.

But there is another kind, in which the fineft telefcopes have difcovered no cluftering ftars. Moft of them have a ftar in or near the middle, furrounded with a pale light, which is brighteft in the middle, and grows more faint toward the circumference. This circumference is diftinct, or well defined, and is not always round. One or two nebulæ have the form of a luminous difk, with a hole in the middle like a milftone. They are of various colours, white, yellow, rofe-coloured, &c. Dr Herfchel, in feveral of the late volumes of the Philofophical

cal Tranfactions, has given us the places of a vaft number of nebulæ, with curious defcriptions of their peculiar appearances, and a feries of moft ingenious and interefting reflections on their nature and conftitution.
His *Thoughts on the Structure of the Heavens* are full of
moft curious fpeculation, and fhould be read by every
philofopher.

When we reflect that thefe fingular objects are not,
like the fixed ftars, brilliant points, which become fmaller
when feen through finer telefcopes, but have a fenfible,
and meafureable diameter, fometimes exceeding 2′; and
when we alfo recollect that a ball of 200,090,000 miles
in diameter, which would fill the whole orbit of the
Earth round the Sun, would not fubtend an angle of
two feconds when taken to the neareft fixed ftar, what
muft we think of thefe nebulæ? One of them is certainly fome thoufands of times bigger than the Earth's
orbit. Although our fineft telefcopes cannot feparate it
into ftars, it is ftill probable that it is a clufter. It is
not unreafonable to think, with Dr Herfchel, that this
object, which requires a telefcope to find it out, will
appear to a fpectator in its centre much the fame as the
vifible heavens do to us, and that this ftarry heaven,
which, to us, appears fo magnificent, is but a nebulous
ftar to a fpectator placed in that nebula.

The human mind is almoft overpowered by fuch a
thought. When the foul is filled with fuch conceptions
of the extent of created nature, we can fcarcely avoid
exclaiming, ' Lord, what then is man that thou art
           ' mindful

' mindful of *him !* ' Under fuch impreffions, David
fhrunk into nothing, and feared that he fhould be forgotten amongft fo many great objects of the Divine attention.   His comfort, and ground of relief from this
dejecting thought, are remarkable.   ' But, ' fays he,
' thou haft made man but a little lower than the angels,
' and haft crowned him with glory and honour. '   David
corrected himfelf, by calling to mind how high he ftood in
the fcale of God's works.   He recognifed his own divine
original, and his alliance to the Author of all.   Now,
cheered, and delighted, he cries out, ' Lord, how glori-
ous is thy name ! '

THERE remains yet another phenomenon, which is
very evidently connected with the mechanifm of the folar fyftem, and is in itfelf both curious and important.
I mean the tides of our ocean.   Although it appears improper to call this an aftronomical phenomenon, yet, as
it is moft evidently connected with the pofition of the
Sun and Moon, we muft attribute this connexion in fact
to a natural connexion in the way of caufe and effect.

Of the Tides.

617.   It is a very remarkable operation of nature
that we obferve on the fhores of the ocean, when, in the
calmeft weather, and moft ferene fky, the vaft body of
waters that bathe our coafts advances on our fhores, inundating

undating all the flat fands, rifing to a confiderable height, and then as gradually retiring again to the bed of the ocean ; and all this without the appearance of any caufe to impel the waters to our fhores, and again to draw them off. Twice every day is this repeated. In many places, this motion of the waters is even tremendous, the fea advancing, even in the calmeft weather, with a high furge, rolling along the flats with refiftlefs violence, and rifing to the height of many fathoms. In the bay of Fundy, it comes on with a prodigious noife, in one vaft wave, that is feen thirty miles off; and the waters rife 100 and 120 feet in the harbour of Annapolis-Royal. At the mouth of the Severn, the flood alfo comes up in one head, about ten feet high, bringing certain deftruction to any fmall craft that has been unfortunately left by the ebbing waters on the flats ; and as it paffes the mouth of the Avon, it fends up that fmall river a vaft body of water, rifing forty or fifty feet at Briftol.

Such an appearance forcibly calls the attention of thinking men, and excites the greateft curiofity to difcover the caufe. Accordingly, it has been the object of refearch to all who would be thought philofophers. We find very little however on the fubject in the writings of the Greeks. The Greeks indeed had no opportunity of knowing much about the ebbing and flowing of the fea, as this phenomenon is fcarcely perceptible on the fhores of the Mediterranean and its adjoining feas. The Perfian expedition of Alexander gave them the only opportunity they ever had, and his army was aftonifhed at

finding

finding the ships left on the dry flats when the sea retired. Yet Alexander's preceptor Ariftotle, the prince
of Greek philofophers, fhews little curiofity about the
tides, and is contented with barely mentioning them,
and faying that the tides are moft remarkable in great
feas.

618. When we fearch after the caufe of any recurring event, we naturally look about for recurring concomitant circumftances; and when we find any that generally accompany it, we cannot help inferring fome connexion. All nations feem to have remarked that the
flood-tide always comes on our coafts as the Moon moves
acrofs the heavens, and comes to its greateft height when
the Moon is in one particular pofition, generally in the
fouth-weft. They have alfo remarked that the tides are
moft remarkable about the time of new Moon, and become more moderate by degrees every day, as the Moon
draws near the quadrature, after which they gradually
increafe till about the time of full Moon, when they are
nearly of their greateft height. They now leffen every
day as they did before, and are loweft about the laft quadrature, after which they increafe daily, and, at the next
new Moon are a third time at the higheft.

Thefe circumftances of concomitancy have been noticed by all nations, even the moft uncultivated; and all
feem to have concurred in afcribing the ebbing and flowing of the fea to the Moon, as the efficient caufe, or, at
leaft, as the occafion, of this phenomenon, although
                                                    without

without any comprehenfion, and often without any thought, in what manner, or by what powers of nature, this or that pofition of the Moon fhould be accompanied by the tide of flood or of ebb.

Although this accompaniment has been every where remarked, it is liable to fo many and fo great irregularities, by winds, by frefhes, by the change of feafons, and other caufes, that hardly any two fucceeding tides are obferved to correfpond with a precife pofition of the Moon. The only way therefore to acquire a knowledge of the connexion that may be ufeful, either to the philofopher or to the citizen, is to multiply obfervations to fuch a number, that every fource of irregularity may have its period of operation, and be difcovered by the return of the period. The inhabitants of the fea-coafts, and particularly the fifhermen, were moft anxioufly interefted in this refearch.

619. Accordingly, it was not long after the conquefts of the Romans had given them poffeffion of the coafts of the ocean, before they learned the chief circumftances or laws according to which the phenomena of the tides proceed. Pliny fays that they had their fource in the Sun and the Moon. It had been inferred from the gradual change of the tides between new Moon and the quadrature, that the Sun was not unconcerned in the operation. Pytheas, a Greek merchant, and no mean philofopher, refident at Marfeilles, the oldeft Grecian colony, had often been in Britain, at the tin mines in Cornwall and its ad-

4 C   jacent

jacent iflands. He had obferved the phenomena with great fagacity, and had collected the obfervations of the natives. Plutarch and Pliny mention thefe obfervations of Pytheas, fome of them very delicate, and, the whole taken together, containing almoft all that was known of the fubject, till the difcoveries of Sir Ifaac Newton taught the philofophers what to look for in their inquiries into the nature of the tides, and how to clafs the phenomena. Pytheas had not only obferved that the tides gradually abated from the times of new and full Moon to the time of the quadratures, and then increafed again, but had alfo remarked that this vulgar obfervation was not exact, but that the greateft tide was always two days after new or full Moon, and the fmalleft was as long after the quadratures. He alfo corrected the common obfervation of the tides falling later every day, by obferving that this retardation of the tides was much greater when the Moon was in quadrature than when new or full. The tide-day, about the time of new and full Moon, is really fhorter by 50′ than at the time of her quadrature.

620. This variation in the interval of the tides is called the PRIMING or the LAGGING of the tides, according as we refer them to lunar or folar time. Pytheas probably learned much of this nicety of obfervation from the Cornifh fifhermen. By Ælian's accounts, they had nets extended along fhore for feveral miles, and were therefore much interefted in this matter.

621.

621. Many obfervations on the feries of phenomena which completes a period of the tides are to be found in the books of hydrography, and the inftructions for mariners, to whom the exact knowledge of the courfe of the tides is of the utmoft importance. But we never had any good collection of obfervations, from which the laws of their progrefs could be learned, till the Academy of Paris procured an order from government to the officers at the ports of Breft and Rochefort, to keep a regifter of all the phenomena, and report it to the Academy. A regifter of obfervations was accordingly continued for fix years, without interruption, at both ports, and the obfervations were publifhed, forming the moft complete feries that is to be met with in any department of fcience, aftronomy alone excepted. The younger Caffini undertook the examination of thefe regifters, in order to deduce from them the general laws of the tides. This tafk he executed with confiderable fuccefs; and the general rules which he has given contain a much better arrangement of all the phenomena, their periods and changes, than any thing that had yet appeared. Indeed there had fcarcely any thing been added to the vague experience of illiterate pilots and fifhermen, except two differtations by Wallis and Flamftead, publifhed in the Philofophical Tranfactions.

622. It is not likely, notwithftanding this excellent collection of obfervations, that our knowledge would have proceeded much farther, had not Newton demonftrated

that

that a feries of phenomena perfectly refembling the tides refulted from the mutual attraction of all matter. Thefe confequences pointed out to thofe interefted in the knowledge of the tides what viciffitudes or changes to look for—what to look for as the natural or regular feries—what they are to confider as mere anomalies—what periods to expect in the different variations—and whether there are not periods which comprehend the more obvious periods of the tides, diftinguifhing one period from another. As foon as this clue was obtained, every thing was laid open, and without it, the labyrinth was almoft inextricable; for in the variations of the tides there are periods in which the changes are very confiderable; and thefe periods continually crofs each other, fo that a tide which fhould be great, confidered as a certain tide of one period, fhould be fmall, confidered as a certain tide of another period. When it arrives, it is neither a great nor a fmall tide, but it prevents both periods from offering themfelves to the mere obferver. The tides afford a very ftrong example of the great importance of a theory for directing even our obfervations. Aided by the Newtonian theory, we have difcovered many periods, in which the tides fuffer gradual changes, both in their hour and in their height, which commonly are fo implicated with one another, that they never would have been difcovered without this monitor, whereas now, we can predict them all.

623. The phenomena of the tides are, in general, the following.

1. The waters of the ocean rife, from a medium height to that of high water, and again ebb away from the fhores, falling nearly as much below that medium ftate, and then rife again in a fucceeding tide of flood, and again make high water. The interval between two fucceeding high waters is about $12^h\ 25'$, the half of the time of the Moon's daily circuit round the Earth, fo that we have two tides of flood and two ebb tides in every $24^h\ 50'$. This is the fhorteft period of phenomena obferved in the tides. The gradual fubfidence of the waters is fuch that the diminutions of the height are nearly as the fquares of the times from high water. The fame may be faid of the fubfequent rife of the waters in the next flood. The time of low water is nearly half way between the two hours of high water; not indeed exactly, it being obferved at Breft and Rochefort that the flood tide commonly takes ten minutes lefs than the ebb tide.

624. As the different phenomena of the tides are chiefly diftinguifhable by the periods, or intervals of time in which they recur, it will be convenient to mark thofe periods by different names. Therefore, let the time of the apparent diurnal revolution of the Moon, viz. $24^h\ 50'$, be called A LUNAR DAY, and the 24th part of it be called A LUNAR HOUR. To this interval almoft all the viciffitudes of the tides are moft conveniently referred. Let the name TIDE DAY be given to the interval between two high waters, or two low waters, fucceeding each other with the Moon nearly in the fame pofition. This interval

val comprehends two complete tides, one of the full
feas happening when the Moon is above the horizon, and
the next, when fhe is under the horizon. We fhall alfo
find it convenient to diftinguifh thefe tides, by calling the
firft the SUPERIOR TIDE, and the other the INFERIOR
TIDE. At new Moon they may be called the *Morning*
and *Evening* tides.

625. 2. It is not only obferved that we always have
high water when the Moon is on fome particular point
of the compafs (S. W. nearly) but alfo that the height
of full fea from day to day has an evident reference to
the phafes of the Moon. At Breft, the higheft tide is
always about a day and a half after full or change. If
it fhould happen that high water falls at the very time
of new or full Moon, the third full fea after that one
is the higheft of all. This is called the SPRING-TIDE.
Each fucceeding full fea is lefs than the preceding, till
we come to the third full fea after the Moon's quadrature. This is the loweft tide of all, and it is called
NEAP-TIDE. After this, the tides again increafe, till the
next full or new Moon, the third after which is again
the greateft tide.

626. The higher the tide of flood rifes, the lower
does the ebb tide generally fink on that day. The total
magnitude of the tide is eftimated by taking the difference between high and low water. As this is continually varying, the beft way of computing its magnitude
                                          feems

feems to be, to take the half fum of two fucceeding tides. This muft always give us a mean value for the tide whofe full fea was in the middle. The medium fpring-tide at Breft is about nineteen feet, and the neap-tide is about nine.

Here then we have a period of phenomena, the time of which is half of a lunar month. This period comprehends the moft important changes, both in refpect of magnitude, and of the hours of high and low water, and feveral modifications of both of thofe circumftances, fuch as the daily difference in height, or in time.

627. 3. There is another period, of nearly twice the fame duration, which greatly modifies all thofe leading circumftances. This period has a reference to the diftance of the Moon, and therefore depends on the Moon's revolution in her orbit. All the phenomena are increafed when the Moon is nearer to the Earth. Therefore the higheft fpring-tide is obferved when the Moon is *in perigeo,* and the next fpring-tide is the fmalleft, becaufe the Moon is then nearly *in apogeo.* This will make a difference of 2¾ feet from the medium height of fpring tide at Breft, and therefore occafion a difference of 5¼ between the greateft and the leaft. It is evident that as the perigean and apogean fituation of the Moon may happen in every part of a lunation, the equation for the height of tide depending upon this circumftance may often run counter to the equation correfponding to the

regular

regular monthly feries of tides, and will feemingly deftroy their regularity.

628.   4.   The variation in the Sun's diftance alfo affects the tides, but not nearly fo much as thofe in the
diftance of the Moon.   In our winter, the fpring-tides are
greater than in fummer, and the neap-tides are fmaller.

629.   5.   The declination, both of the Sun and
Moon, affects the tides remarkably ; but the effects are
too intricate to be diftinctly feen, till we perceive the
caufes on which they depend.

630.   6.   All the phenomena are alfo modified by
the latitude of the place of obfervation ; and fome phenomena occur in the high latitudes, which are not feen at
all when the place of obfervation is on the equator.   In
particular, when the obferver is in north latitude, and
the Moon has north declination, that tide in which the
Moon is above the horizon is greater than the other tide
of the fame day, when the Moon is below the horizon.
It will be the contrary, if either the obferver or the Moon
(but not both) have fouth declination.   If the polar
diftance of the obferver be equal to the Moon's declination, he will fee but one tide in the day, containing
twelve hours flood and twelve hours ebb.

631.   7.   To all this it muft be added, that local
circumftances of fituation alter all the phenomena remarkably,

markably, fo as frequently to leave fcarcely any circumftances of refemblance, except the order and periods in
which the various phenomena follow one another.

We muft now endeavour to account for thefe remarkable movements and viciffitudes in the waters of the
ocean.

632. Since the phenomena of the planetary motions
demonftrate that every particle of matter in this globe gravitates to the Sun, and fince they are at various diftances
from his centre, it is evident that they gravitate unequally, and that, from this inequality, there muft arife
a difturbance of that equilibrium which terreftrial gravitation alone might produce. If this globe be fuppofed
either perfectly fluid and homogeneous, or to confift of
a fpherical nucleus covered with a fluid, it is clear that
the fluid muft affume a perfectly fpherical form, and that in
this form alone, every particle will be in equilibrio. But
when we add to the forces now acting on the waters
of the ocean their unequal gravitation to the Sun, this
equilibrium is difturbed, and the ocean cannot remain in
this form. We may apply to the particles of the ocean
every thing that we formerly faid of the gravitation of
the Moon to the Sun in the different points of her orbit;
and the fame conftruction in fig. 59, that gave us a reprefentation and meafure of the forces which deranged
the lunar motions, may be employed for giving us a notion of the manner in which the particles of water in
the ocean are affected.   The circle O B C A may re-

4 D   prefent

prefent the watery fphere, and M any particle of the water. The central particle E gravitates to the Sun with a force which may be reprefented by E S. The gravitation of the particle M muft be meafured by M G. This force M G may be conceived as compounded of M F, equal and parallel to E S, and of M H. The force M F occafions no alteration in the gravitation of M to the Earth, and M H is the only difturbing force. We found that this conftruction may be greatly fimplified, and that M I may be fubftituted for M H without any fenfible error, becaufe it never differs from it more than $\frac{1}{391}$. We therefore made E I, in fig. 60, $= 3$ M N, and confidered M I as the difturbing force. This conftruction is applicable to the prefent queftion, with much greater accuracy, becaufe the radius of the Earth is but the fixtieth part of that of the Moon's orbit. This reduces the error to $\frac{1}{23520}$, a quantity altogether infenfible.

633. Therefore let O A C B (fig. 68.) be the terraqueous globe, and C S a line directed to the Sun, and B E A the fection by that circle which feparates the illuminated from the dark hemifphere. Let P be any particle, whether on the furface or within the mafs. Let Q P N be perpendicular to the plane B A. Make E I $= 3$ P N, and join P I. P I is the difturbing force, when the line E S is taken to reprefent the gravitation of the particle E to the Sun. This force P I may be conceived to be compounded of two forces P E and P Q.

P E

P E tends to the centre of the Earth. P Q tends from the plane B A, or toward the Sun.

If this conftruction be made for every particle in the fluid fphere, it is evident that all the forces P E balance one another. Therefore they need not be confidered in the prefent queftion. But the forces P Q evidently diminifh the terreftrial gravitation of every particle. At C the force P Q acts in direct oppofition to the terreftrial gravity of the particle. And, in the fituation P, it diminifhes the gravity of the particle as eftimated in the direction P N. There is therefore a force acting in the direction N P on every particle in the canal P N. And this force is proportional to the diftance of the particle from the plane B A (for P Q is always $= 3$ P N). Therefore the water in this canal cannot remain in its former pofition, its equilibrium being now deftroyed. This may be reftored, by adding to the column N P a fmall portion Pp, whofe weight may compenfate the diminution in the weight of the column N P. A fimilar addition may be made to every fuch column perpendicular to the plane B E A. This being fuppofed, the fpherical figure of the globe will be changed into that of an elliptical fpheroid, having its axis in the line O C, and its poles in O and C (569.)

Without making this addition to every column N P, we may underftand how the *equilibrium* may be reftored by the waters fubfiding all around the circle whofe fection is B A, and rifing on both fides of it. For it was fhewn (564.) that in a fluid elliptical fpheroid of gravi-

4 D 2   tating

tating matter, the gravitation of any particle P to all the
other particles may be refolved into two forces P N and
P M perpendicular to the plane B A and to the axis
O C, and proportional to P N and P M; and that if the
forces be really in this proportion, the whole will be in
equilibrio, provided that the whole forces at the poles and
equator are inverfely as the diameters O C and B A.
Now this may be the cafe here.   For 'the forces fuperadded to the terreftrial gravitation of any particle are,
1/t, A force P E, proportional to P E.   When this is
refolved into the directions P N and P M, the forces
arifing in this refolution are as P N and P M, and therefore in the due proportion :   2d, The force P Q, which
is alfo as P N.   It is evident therefore that this mafs
may acquire fuch a protuberancy at O and C, that the
force at O fhall be to the force at B as B A to O C, or
as E A to E C.   We are alfo taught in § 585. what
this protuberance muft be.   It muft be fuch that four
times the mean gravity of a particle on the furface is to
five times the difturbing force at O or C as the diameter B A is to the excefs of the diameter O C.   This ellipticity is exprefied by the fame formula as in the former

cafe, viz. $\dfrac{x}{r} = \dfrac{4\,c}{5\,g},\ = \dfrac{E\,C - F\,A}{E\,C}$.

634.   Thus we have difcovered that, in confequence
of the unequal gravitation of the matter in the Earth to
the Sun, the waters will affume the form of an oblong elliptical fpheroid, having its axis directed to the Sun, and its

                                                        poles

poles in thofe points of the furface which have the Sun in the zenith and nadir. There the waters are higheft above the furface of a fphere of equal capacity. All around the circumference B E A, the waters are below the natural level. A fpectator placed on this circumference fees the Sun in the horizon.

We can tell exactly what this protuberance E O — E A muft be, becaufe we know the proportions of all the forces. Let W reprefent the terreftrial gravitation, or the weight of the particle C, and G the gravitation of the fame particle to the Sun, and let F be the difturbing force acting on a particle at C or at O, and therefore $= 3\,C\,E$. Let S and E be the quantity of matter in the Sun and in the Earth.

Then (fig. 59.) $F : G = 3\,C\,E : C\,G$

$$G : W = \frac{S}{C\,S^2} : \frac{E}{C\,E^2} \quad (465.)$$

therefore $\quad F : W = \dfrac{3\,C\,E \times S}{C\,S^2} : \dfrac{C\,G \times E}{C\,E^2} =$

$\dfrac{3\,S}{C\,S^2 \times C\,G} : \dfrac{E}{C\,E^3}.$ But, becaufe $C\,S^2 : E\,S^2 = E\,S : C\,G,$ we have $C\,S^2 \times C\,G = E\,S^2 \times E\,S, = E\,S^3.$ Therefore $F : W = \dfrac{3\,S}{E\,S^3} : \dfrac{E}{E\,C^3}.$ Now $E : S = 1 : 338343,$ and $E\,C : E\,S = 1 : 23668.$ This will give $\dfrac{3\,S}{E\,S^3} : \dfrac{E}{E\,C^3}$ $= 1 : 12773541, = F : W.$

Finally, $4\,W : 5\,F = C\,E : C\,E — A\,E.$ We fhall find this to be nearly $24\frac{1}{4}$ inches.

635. Such is the figure that this globe would affume, had it been originally fluid, or a fpherical nucleus covered

with

with a fluid of equal denſity. The two ſummits of the
watery ſpheroid would be raiſed about two feet above
the equator or place of greateſt depreſſion.

But the Earth is an oblate ſpheroid. If we ſuppoſe
it covered, to a moderate depth, with a fluid, the waters
would acquire a certain figure, which has been conſidered
already. Let the diſturbing force of the Sun act on this
figure. A *change* of figure muſt be produced, and the
waters under the Sun, and thoſe in the oppoſite parts,
will be elevated above their natural ſurface, and the
ocean will be depreſſed on the circumference B E A. It
is plain that this *change* of figure will be almoſt the ſame
in every place as if the Earth were a ſphere. For the
difference between the *change* produced by the Sun's diſturbing force on the figure of the fluid ſphere or fluid ſpheroid, ariſes ſolely from the difference in the gravitation of a
particle of water to the ſphere and to the ſpheroid. This
difference, in any part of the ſurface, is exceedingly ſmall,
not being $\frac{1}{300^2}$ of the whole gravitation. The difference therefore in the *change* produced by the Sun cannot be $\frac{1}{300^2}$ of the whole change. Therefore, ſince it
is from the *proportion* of the diſturbing force to the force
of gravity that the ellipticity is determined, it follows
that the *change* of figure is, to all ſenſe, the ſame, whether the Earth be a ſphere or a ſpheroid whoſe eccentricity is leſs than $\frac{1}{233}$.

Let us ſuppoſe, for the preſent, that the watery ſpheroid always has that form which produces an equilibrium
in

in all its particles. This cannot ever be the cafe, becaufe fome time muft elapfe before an accelerating force
can produce any finite change in the difpofition of the
waters. But the contemplation of this figure gives us
the moft diftinct notion of the forces that are in action,
and of their effects; and we can afterwards ftate the
difference that muft obtain becaufe the figure is not completely attained.

Suppofing it really attained, it follows that the ocean
will be moft elevated in thofe places which have the Sun
in the zenith or nadir, and moft depreffed in thofe places
where the Sun is feen in the horizon. While the Earth
turns round its axis, the pole of the fpheroid keeps ftill
toward the Sun, as if the waters ftood ftill, and the folid
nucleus turned round under it. The phenomena may
perhaps be eafier conceived by fuppofing the Earth to remain at reft, and the Sun to revolve round it in 24 hours
from eaft to weft. The pole of the fpheroid follows
him, as the card of a mariner's compafs follows the magnet; and a fpectator attached to one part of the nucleus
will fee all the viciffitudes of the tide. Suppofe the Sun
in the equinox, and the obferver alfo on the Earth's equator, and the Sun juft rifing to him. The obferver is
then in the loweft part of the watery fpheroid. As
the Sun rifes above the horizon, the water alfo rifes; and
when the Sun is in the zenith, the pole of the fpheroid
has now reached the obferver, and the water is two feet
deeper than it was at fun-rife. The Sun now approaching the weftern horizon, and the pole of the ocean going
along

along with him, the obferver fees the water fubfide again,
and at fun-fet, it is at the fame level as at fun-rife.   As
the Sun continues his courfe, though unfeen, the oppofite pole of the ocean now advances from the eaft, and
the obferver fees the water rife again by the fame degrees
as in the morning, and attain the height of two feet at
midnight, and again fubfide to its loweft level at fix
o'clock in the following morning.

Thus, in 24 hours, he has two tides of flood and two
ebb tides ; high water at noon and midnight, and low
water at fix o'clock morning and evening.   An obferver
not in the equator will fee the fame *gradation* of phenomena, at the fame hours ; but the rife and fall of the
water will not be fo confiderable, becaufe the pole of the
fpheroid paffes his meridian at fome diftance from him.
If the fpectator is in the pole of the Earth, he will fee
no change, becaufe he is always in the loweft part of
the watery fpheroid.

From this account of the fimpleft cafe, we may infer
that the depth of the water, or its change of depth, depends entirely on the fhape of the fpheroid, and the place
of it occupied by the obferver.

636.   To judge of this with accuracy, we muft take notice of fome properties of the ellipfe which forms the meridian of the watery fpheroid.   Let A E *a* Q (fig. 69.)
reprefent this elliptical fpheroid, and let B E *b* Q be the
infcribed fphere, and A G *a g* the circumfcribed fphere.
Alfo let D F *d f* be the fphere of equal capacity with the
fpheroid.

spheroid. This will be the natural figure of the ocean, undisturbed by the gravitation to the Sun.

In a spheroid like this, so little different from a sphere, the elevation A D of its summit above the equally capacious sphere is very nearly double of the depression F E of its equator below the surface of that sphere. For spheres and spheroids, being equal to $\frac{2}{3}$ of the circumscribing cylinders, are in the ratio compounded of the ratio of their equators and the ratio of their axes. Therefore, since the sphere D F df is equal to the spheroid A E a Q, we have $C F^2 \times C D = C E^2 \times C A$, and $C E^2 : C F^2 = C D : C A$. Make $C E : C F = C F : C x$, then $C E : C x = C D : C A$, and $C E : E x = C D : D A$, and $C E : C D = E x : D A$. Now C E does not differ sensibly from C D (only eight inches in near 4000 miles), therefore E x may be accounted equal to D A. But E x is not sensibly different from twice E F. Therefore the proposition is manifest.

637. In such an elliptical spheroid, the elevation I L of any point I above the inscribed sphere is proportional to the square of the cosine of its distance from the pole A, and the depression K I of this point below the surface of the circumscribed sphere is as the square of the sine of its distance from the pole A. Draw through the point I, H I M perpendicular to C A, and I p N perpendicular to C E. The triangles C I N and p I L are similar.

4 E   Therefore

Therefore $\qquad p\,I : I\,L = C\,I : I\,N, = $ rad. : cof. $I\,C\,A$

but, by the ellipfe $A\,B : p\,I = A\,C : I\,N, = $ rad. : cof. $I\,C\,A$

therefore $\qquad A\,B : I\,L = $ rad.^{2} : cof.^{2} $I\,C\,A$

and $I\,L$ is always in the proportion of cof.^{2}, $I\,C\,A$, and is $= A\,B \times$ cof.^{2}, $I\,C\,A$, radius being $= 1$.

In like manner $H\,I : I\,K = C\,I : I\,M = $ rad. : fin. $I\,C\,A$.

and $\qquad G\,E : H\,I = E\,C : I\,M = $ rad. : fin. $I\,C\,A$

therefore $\qquad G\,E : K\,I = $ rad.^{2} : fin.^{2} $I\,C\,A$

and $\qquad K\,I$ is $= A\,B \times$ fin.^{2} $I\,C\,A$.

638. We muft alfo know the elevations and depreffions in refpect of the natural level of the undifturbed ocean. This elevation for any point i is evidently $i\,l - m\,l = A\,B \times$ cof.^{2} $i\,C\,A - \frac{1}{3} A\,B, = A\,B \times \overline{\text{cof.}^2\,i\,C\,A - \frac{1}{3}}$, and the depreffion $n\,r$ of a point r is $k\,r - k\,n = A\,B \times$ fin.^{2} $r\,C\,A - \frac{2}{3} A\,B, = A\,B \times \overline{\text{fin.}^2\,r\,C\,A - \frac{2}{3}}$.

It will be convenient to employ a fymbol for expreffing the whole difference $A\,B$ or $G\,E$ between high and low water produced by the action of the Sun. Let it be expreffed by the fymbol S. Alfo let the angular diftance from the fummit, or from the Sun's place, be x.

The elevation $m\,i$ is $= S \times$ cof.^{2} $x - \frac{1}{3} S$.

The depreffion $n\,r$ is $= S \times$ fin.^{2} $x - \frac{2}{3} S$.

639. The fpheroid interfects the equicapacious fphere in a point fo fituated that $S \times$ cof.^{2} $x - \frac{1}{3} S = 0$, that is, where cof.^{2} $x = \frac{1}{3}$. This is $54° 44'$ from the pole

of

Pl. 19

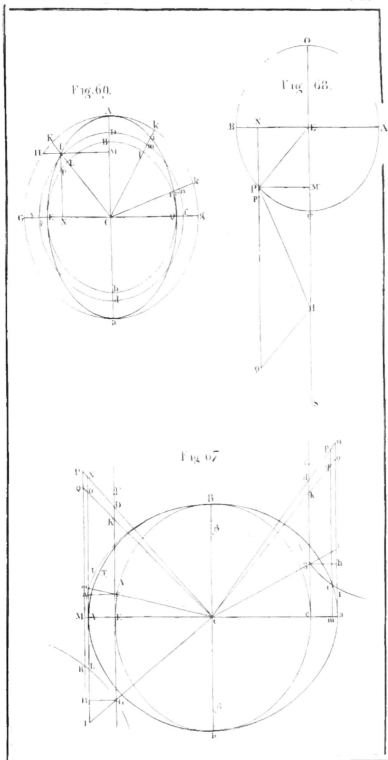

Fig. 66.

Fig. 68.

Fig. 67

of the fpheroid, and 35° 16′ from its equator, a fituation that has feveral remarkable phyfical properties. We have already feen (572.) that on this part of the furface the gravitation is the fame as if it were really a perfect fphere.

640. The ocean is made to affume an eccentric form, not only by the unequal gravitation of its waters to the Sun, but alfo by their much more unequal gravitation to the Moon ; and, although her quantity of matter is very fmall indeed, when compared with the Sun, yet being almoft 400 times nearer, the inequality of gravitation is increafed almoft 400 × 400 × 400 times, and may therefore produce a fenfible effect. * We cannot help prefuming that it does, becaufe the viciffitudes of the tides have a moft diftinct reference to the pofition of the Moon. Without going over the fame ground again, it is plain that the waters will be accumulated under the Moon, and in the oppofite part of the fpheroid, in the fame manner as they are affected by the Sun's action.

Therefore

---

* The diftance of the Sun being about 392 times that of the Moon, and the quantity of matter in the Sun about 338000 times that in the Earth, if the quantity of matter in the Moon were equal to that in the Earth, her accumulating force would be 178 times greater than that of the Sun. We fhall fee that it is nearly 2½ times greater. From which we fhould infer that the quantity of matter in the Moon is nearly $\frac{1}{71}$ of that in the Earth. This feems the beft information that we have on this fubject.

of the fpheroid, and 35° 16' from its equator, a fituation that has feveral remarkable phyfical properties. We have already feen (572.) that on this part of the furface the gravitation is the fame as if it were really a perfect fphere.

640. The ocean is made to affume an eccentric form, not only by the unequal gravitation of its waters to the Sun, but alfo by their much more unequal gravitation to the Moon ; and, although her quantity of matter is very fmall indeed, when compared with the Sun, yet being almoft 400 times nearer, the inequality of gravitation is increafed almoft 400 × 400 × 400 times, and may therefore produce a fenfible effect. * We cannot help prefuming that it does, becaufe the viciffitudes of the tides have a moft diftinct reference to the pofition of the Moon. Without going over the fame ground again, it is plain that the waters will be accumulated under the Moon, and in the oppofite part of the fpheroid, in the fame manner as they are affected by the Sun's action.

Therefore

---

* The diftance of the Sun being about 392 times that of the Moon, and the quantity of matter in the Sun about 338000 times that in the Earth, if the quantity of matter in the Moon were equal to that in the Earth, her accumulating force would be 178 times greater than that of the Sun. We fhall fee that it is nearly $2\frac{1}{2}$ times greater. From which we fhould infer that the quantity of matter in the Moon is nearly $\frac{1}{71}$ of that in the Earth. This feems the beft information that we have on this fubject.

4 E 2

'Therefore let M reprefent the elevation of the pole of
the fpheroid above the equicapacious fphere that is produced by the unequal gravitation to the Moon, and let
y be the angular diftance of any part of this fpheroid
from its pole. We fhall then have

The elevation of any point $= M \times \text{cof.}^2 y - \frac{1}{3} M.$

The depreffion $\qquad\qquad = M \times \text{fin.}^2 y - \frac{2}{3} M.$

641. In confequence of the fimultaneous gravitation
to both luminaries, the ocean muft affume a form differing from both of thefe regular fpheroids. It is a figure
of difficult inveftigation, but all that we are concerned
in may be determined with fufficient accuracy by means
of the following confiderations.

We have feen that the *change* of figure induced on
the fpheroidal ocean of the revolving globe is nearly the
fame as if it were induced on a perfect fphere. Much
more fecurely may we fay that the change of figure, induced on the ocean already difturbed by the Sun, is the
fame that the Moon would have occafioned on the undifturbed revolving fpheroid. We may therefore fuppofe,
without any fenfible error, that the change produced in
any part of the ocean by the joint action of the two luminaries is the fum or the difference of the changes
which they would have produced feparately.

642. Therefore, fince the poles of both fpheroids
are in thofe parts of the ocean which have the Sun and
the Moon in the zenith, it follows that if x be the zenith

nith diftance of the Sun from any place, and y the zenith diftance of the Moon, the elevation of the waters
above the natural furface of the undifturbed ocean will
be $S \times cof.^2 x - \frac{1}{3} S + M \times cof.^2 y - \frac{1}{3} M.$ And the
depreffion in any place will be $S \times fin.^2 x - \frac{2}{3} S +$
$M \times fin.^2 y - \frac{2}{3} M.$ This may be better expreffed as
follows.

$$\text{Elevation} = S \times cof.^2 x + M \times cof.^2 y - \frac{1}{3} \overline{S + M.}$$
$$\text{Depreffion} = S \times fin.^2 x + M \times fin.^2 y - \frac{2}{3} \overline{S + M.}$$

643. Suppofe the Sun and Moon to be in the fame
part of the heavens. The folar and lunar tides will have
the fame axes, poles, and equator, the gravitations to
each confpiring to produce a great elevation at the combined pole, and a great depreffion all round the common
equator. The elevation will be $\frac{2}{3} \overline{S + M}$, and the depreffion will be $\frac{1}{3} \overline{S + M}.$ Therefore the elevation a-
bove the infcribed fphere (or rather the fpheroid fimilar
and fimilarly placed with the natural revolving fpheroid)
will be $\overline{S + M.}$

644. Suppofe the Moon in quadrature in the line
E D M (fig. 70.) It is plain that one luminary tends to
produce an elevation above the equicapacious fphere
A O B C, in the point of the ocean A immediately under it, where the other tends to produce a depreffion,
and therefore their forces counteract each other. Let
the Sun be in the line E S.

The

The elevation at $S = S - \frac{1}{3}\overline{S + M}, = \frac{2}{3}S - \frac{1}{3}M.$

The depreffion at $M = S - \frac{2}{3}\overline{S + M}, = \frac{1}{3}S - \frac{2}{3}M.$

The elevation at S above the infcribed fpheroid $= S - M.$

The elevation at M above the fame $= M - S.$

Hence it is evident that there will be high water at M or at S, when the Moon is in quadrature, according as the accumulating force of the Moon exceeds or falls fhort of that of the Sun. Now, it is a matter of obfervation, that when the Moon is in quadrature, it is high water in the open feas under the Moon, and low water under the Sun, or nearly fo. This obfervation confirms the conclufion drawn from the nutation of the Earth's axis, that the difturbing force of the Moon exceeds that of the Sun. This criterion has fome uncertainty, owing to the operation of local circumftances, by which it happens that the fummit of the water is never fituated either under the Sun or under the Moon. But even in this cafe, we find that the high water is referable to the Moon, and not to the Sun. It is always fix hours of the day later than the high water at full or change. This correfponds with the elongation of the Moon fix hours to the eaftward. The phenomena of the tides fhew further that, at this time, the waters under the Sun are depreffed below the natural furface of the ocean. This fhews that M is more than twice as great as S.

645. When the Moon has any other pofition befides thefe two, the place of high water muft be fome inter-

                                            mediate

mediate pofition. It muft certainly be in the great circle
paffing through the fimultaneous places of the two luminaries. As the place and time of high and low water,
and the magnitude of the elevation and depreffion, are
the moft interefting phenomena of the tides, they fhall
be the principal objects of our attention.

The place of high water is that where the fum of the
elevations produced by both luminaries above the natural furface of the ocean is a maximum. And the
place of low water, in the great circle paffing through
the Sun and Moon, is that where the depreffion below
the natural level of the ocean is a maximum. Therefore, in order to have the place of high water we muft
find where $S \times \text{cof.}^2 x + M \times \text{cof.}^2 y - \frac{1}{3}\overline{S + M}$ is a
maximum. Or, fince $\frac{1}{3}\overline{S + M}$ is a conftant quantity,
we muft find where $S \times \text{cof.}^2 x + M \times \text{cof.}^2 y$ is a
maximum. Now, accounting the tabular fines and co-
fines as fractions of radius, $= 1$, we have

$$\text{Cof.}^2 x = \tfrac{1}{2} + \tfrac{1}{2}\text{cof. } 2 x$$
$$\text{and} \quad \text{Cof.}^2 y = \tfrac{1}{2} + \tfrac{1}{2}\text{cof. } 2 y.$$

For let A B S D (fig. 71.) be a circle, and A S, B D
two diameters croffing each other at .right angles. Defcribe on the femidiameter C S the fmall circle C m S h,
having its centre in d. Let H C make any angle x with
C S, and let it interfect the fmall circle in h. Draw $d h$,
S h, producing S h till it meet the exterior circle in S,
and join A s, C s. Laftly, draw $h o$ and $s r$ perpendicular to C S.

S b is perpendicular to C h, and C S : C $h =$ rad. :
çof.

cof. H C S, and C S : C o = R² : cof.² H C S.   The angle
S C s is evidently = 2 S C H = S d h and A r = 2 C o.
Now if C S be = 1 ; C r = cof.² 2 x ; A r = 1 + cof.
2 x.   Therefore C o = ½ + ¼ cof. 2 x.   In like manner
cof.² y = ½ + ¼ cof. 2 y.

Therefore we muſt have $\dfrac{S}{2}$ + $\dfrac{S \times \text{cof. } 2\,x}{2}$ + $\dfrac{M}{2}$ +
$\dfrac{M \times \text{cof. } 2\,y}{2}$ a maximum, or, neglecting the conſtant
quantities $\dfrac{S}{2}$, $\dfrac{M}{2}$, and the conſtant diviſor 2, we muſt
have S × cof. 2 x + M × cof. 2 y a maximum.

Let A B S D (fig. 71.) be now a great circle of the
Earth, paſſing through thoſe points S and M of its ſurface which have the Sun and the Moon in the zenith.
Draw the diameter S C A, and croſs it at right angles
by B C D.   Let S d be to d a as the accumulating force of
the Moon to the accumulating force of the Sun, that is, as
M to S, which proportion we ſuppoſe known.   Draw
C M in the direction of the Moon's place.   It will cut
the ſmall circle in ſome point m.   Join m a.   Let H be
any point of the ſurface of the ocean.   Draw C H, cutting the ſmall circle in h.   Draw the diameter h d h'.
Draw m t and a x perpendicular to h h', and a y parallel to h h', and join m d.   Alſo draw the chords m h
and m h'.

In this conſtruction, m d and d a repreſent M and
S, the angle M C H = y, and S C H = x.   It is farther
manifeſt that the angle m d h = 2 m C h, = 2 y, and that
d t = M × cof. 2 y.   In like manner h d S = 2 H C S,
                                                        = 2 x,

$= 2x$, and $dx = da \times$ cof. $2x$, $= S \times$ cof. $2x$. There-fore $tx = S \times$ cof. $2x + M \times$ cof. $2y$. Moreover tx $= ay$, and is a maximum when ay is a maximum. This muſt happen when ay coincides with am, that is, when hd is parallel to am.

Hence may be derived the following conſtruction.

Let A M S (fig. 72.) be, as before, a great circle whoſe plane paſſes through the Sun and the Moon. Let S and M be thoſe points which have the Sun and the Moon in the zenith. Deſcribe, as before, the circle CmS, cutting C M in m. Make Sd : $da = $ M : S, and join ma. Then, for the place of high water, draw the diameter hdh' parallel to ma, cutting the circle CmS in h. Draw C h H cutting the ſurface of the ocean in H and H'. Then H and H' are the places of high water. Alſo draw C h', cutting the ſurface of the o-cean in L and L'. L and L' are the places of low water in this circle.

For, drawing mt and ax perpendicular to hh', it is plain that $tx = $ M $\times$ cof. $2y + $ S $\times$ cof. $2x$. And what was juſt now demonſtrated ſhews that tx is in its maximum ſtate. Alſo, if the angle L C S $= u$, and L C M $= z$, it is evident that $dx = $ S $\times$ cof. adx, $= $ S $\times$ cof. $h'd$ S, $= $ S $\times$ cof. $2h'$ C S, $= $ S $\times$ cof. 2 L C S, $= $ S $\times$ cof. $2u$; and in like manner, $td = $ M $\times$ cof. $2z$; and therefore $tx = $ S $\times$ cof. $2u + $ M $\times$ cof. $2z$, and it is a maximum.

It is plain, independent of this conſtruction, that the places of high and low water are 90° aſunder; for the

two

two hemifpheres of the ocean muft be fimilar and equal, and the equator muft be equidiftant from its poles.

648. Draw df perpendicular to ma. Then, if dS be taken to reprefent the whole tide produced by the Moon, that is, the whole difference in the height of high and low water, ma will reprefent the compound tide at H, or the difference between high and low water corresponding to that fituation of the place H with refpect to the Sun and Moon. mf will be the part of it produced by the Moon and af the part produced by the Sun.

For, the elevation at H above the natural level is $S \times \overline{cof.^2 x - \frac{1}{3}} + M \times \overline{cof.^2 y - \frac{1}{3}}$, and the depreffion below it at L is $\overline{S \times fin.^2 u - \frac{2}{3}} + M \times \overline{fin.^2 z - \frac{2}{3}}$. But $fin.^2 u = cof.^2 x$, and $fin.^2 z = cof.^2 y$. Therefore the depreffion at L is $S \times \overline{cof.^2 x - \frac{2}{3}} + M \times \overline{cof.^2 y - \frac{2}{3}}$. The fum of thefe makes the whole difference between high and low water, or the whole tide. Therefore the tide is $= S \times \overline{2 cof.^2 x - 1} + \overline{M \times 2 cof.^2 y - 1}$. But $2 cof.^2 x - 1 = cof. 2x$, and $2 cof.^2 y - 1 = cof. 2y$. Therefore the tide $= S \times cof. 2x + M \times cof. 2y$. Now it is plain that $mf = md \, cof. \, dmf$, and that the angle $dmf = mdh, = 2mCh, = 2y$. Therefore $md \times cof. \, dmf = M \times cof. 2y$. In like manner $af = S \times cof. 2x$.

The point a muft be within or without the circle CmS, according as M is greater or lefs than S, that is, according as the accumulating force of the Moon is greater or lefs than that of the Sun.   It appears alfo that, in the firft cafe, H will be nearer to M, and in the fecond cafe, it will be nearer to S.

Thus have we given a conftruction that feems to ex-prefs all the phenomena of the tides, as they will occur to a fpectator placed in the circle paffing through thofe points which have the Sun and Moon in the zenith.   It marks the diftance of high water from thofe two places, and therefore, if the luminaries are in the equator, it marks the time that will elapfe between the paffage of the Sun or Moon over the meridian and the moment of high water.   It alfo ex-preffes the whole height of the tide of that day.   And, as the point H may be taken without any reference to high water, we fhall then obtain the ftate of the tide for that hour, when it is high water in its proper place H. By confidering this conftruction for the different relative pofitions of the Sun and Moon, we fhall obtain a pretty diftinct notion of the feries of phenomena which proceed in regular order during a lunar month.

649.   To obtain the greater fimplicity in our firft and moft general conclufions, we fhall firft fuppofe both luminaries in the equator.   Alfo, abftracting our atten-tion from the annual motion of the Sun, we fhall confi-der only the relative motion of the Moon in her fynodi-cal revolution, ftating the phenomena as they occur when the Moon has got a certain number of degrees away from the Sun ; and we fhall always fuppofe that the watery fpheroid has attained the form fuited to its equilibrium

4 F 2

in

in that fituation of the two luminaries. The conclufions will frequently differ much from common obfervation. But we fhall afterwards find their agreement very fatisfactory. The reader is therefore expected to go along with the reafoning employed in this difcuffion, although the conclufions may frequently furprife him, being very different from his moft familiar obfervations.

650. · 1. At new and full Moon, we fhall have high water at noon, and at midnight, when the Sun and Moon are on the meridian. For in this cafe C M, $a\,m$, C S, $d\,h$, C H, all coincide.

651. 2. When the Moon is in quadrature in B, the place of high water is alfo in B, under the Moon, and this happens when the Moon is on the meridian. For when M C is perpendicular to C S, the point m coincides with C, $a\,m$ with a C, and $d\,h$ with d C.

652. 3. While the Moon paffes from a fyzigy to the next quadrature, the place of high water follows the Moon's place, keeping to the weftward of it. It overtakes the Moon in the quadrature, gets to the eaftward of the Moon (as it is reprefented at $M^2\,H^2$, by the fame conftruction), preceding her while fhe paffes forward to the next fyzigy, in A, where it is overtaken by the Moon's place. For while M is in the quadrant S B, or A D, the point h is in the arch S m. But when M is in the quadrant B A or D S, h^2 is without or beyond

yond the arch S m^2 (counted *eaſtward* from S). Therefore, during the firſt and third quarters of the lunation,
we have high water after noon or midnight, but before
the Moon's ſouthing. But in the ſecond and fourth
quarters, it happens after the Moon's ſouthing.

653. 4. Since the place of high water coincides
with the Moon's place both in ſyzigy and the following
quadrature, and in the interval is between her and the
Sun, it follows that it muſt, during the firſt and third
quarters, be gradually left behind, for a while, and then
muſt gain on the Moon's place, and overtake her in quadrature. There muſt therefore be a certain greateſt diſtance between the place of the Moon and that of high
water, a certain maximum of the angle M C H. This
happens when H′ C S is exactly 45°. For then $h'dS$ is
90°, $m'a$ is perpendicular to a S, and the angle $a\,m'd$
is a maximum. Now $a\,m'd = m'd\,h', = 2y'$.

654. When things are in this ſtate, the motion of
high water, or its ſeparation from the Sun to the eaſtward, is equal to the Moon's eaſterly motion. Therefore, at new and full Moon, it muſt be ſlower, and at
the quadratures it muſt be ſwifter. Conſequently, when
the Moon is in the octant, 45° from the Sun, the interval between two ſucceſſive ſouthings of the Moon, which
is always 24^h 50′ nearly, muſt be equal to the interval of
the two concomitant or ſuperior high waters, and each
tide muſt occupy 12^h 25′, the half of a lunar day. But

at

at new or full Moon, the interval between the two fucceffive high waters muft be lefs than 12ʰ 25′, and in the
quadratures it muft be more.

655. The tide day muft be equal to the lunar day
only when the high water is in the octants. It muft be
fhorter at new and full Moon, and while the Moon is
paffing from the fecond octant to the third, and from the
fourth to the firft. And it muft exceed a lunar day
while the Moon paffes from the firft octant to the fecond,
and from the third to the fourth. The tide day is always greater than a folar day, or twenty-four hours.
For, while the Sun makes one round of the Earth, and
is again on the meridian, the Moon has got about 13°
eaft of him, or S M is nearly 13°, and S H is nearly
9°, fo that the Sun muft pafs the meridian about 35 or
36 minutes before it is high water. Such is the law of
the daily retardation called the priming or lagging of the
tides. At new and full Moon it is nearly 35′, and at
the quadratures it is 85′, fo that the tide day at new and
full Moon is 24ʰ 35′, and in the quadratures it is 25ʰ 25′
nearly.

Our conftruction gives us the means of afcertaining
this circumftance of the tides, or interval between two
fucceeding full feas, and it may be thus expreffed.

656. The fynodical motion of the Moon is to the fynodical motion of the high water as $m\,a$ to $m\,f$. For,
take a point u very near to m. Draw $u\,a$ and $u\,d$, and
draw

draw $d\,i$ parallel to $a\,u$, and with the centre a, and distance $a\,u$, describe the arch $u\,v$, which may be considered as a straight line perpendicular to $m\,a$. Then $u\,m$ and $i\,b$ are respectively equal to the motions of M and H (though they subtend twice the angles). The angles $a\,u\,v$, $d\,u\,m$ are equal, being right angles. Therefore $m\,u\,v = a\,u\,d$, $= a\,m\,d$, and the triangles $m\,u\,v$, $d\,m\,f$, are similar, and the angles $u\,a\,m$, $i\,d\,b$ are equal, and therefore

$$u\,v : i\,b = m\,a : b\,d, \; = m\,a : m\,d$$
$$u\,m : u\,v = \qquad\qquad m\,d : m\,f$$
$$\text{therefore } u\,m : i\,b = \qquad\quad m\,a : m\,f.$$

When m coincides with S, that is, at new or full Moon, $m\,a$ coincides with S a, and $m\,f$ with S d. But when m coincides with C, that is, in the quadratures, $m\,a$ coincides with C a, and $m\,f$ with C d.

657. Hence it is easy to see that the retardation of the tides at new and full Moon is to the retardation in the quadratures as C a to S a, that is, as M $+$ S to M $-$ S.

When the high water is in the octant, $m\,a$ is perpendicular to S a, and therefore a and f coincide, and the synodical motion of the Moon and of high water are the same, as has been already observed.

Let us now consider the elevations of the water, and the magnitude of the tide, and its gradual variation in the course of a lunation. This is represented by the line $m\,a$.

658.

658. This series of changes is very perceptible in our construction. At new and full Moon, $m\,a$ coincides with $S\,a$, and in the quadratures, it coincides with $C\,a$. Therefore, the spring-tide is to the neap-tide as $S\,a$ to $C\,a$, that is, as $M + S$ to $M - S$. From new or full Moon the tide gradually lessens to the time of the quadrature. We also see that the Sun contributes to the elevation by the part $a\,f$, till the high water is in the octants, for the point f lies between m and a. After this, the action of the Sun diminishes the elevation, the point f then lying beyond a.

659. The momentary change in the height of the whole tide, that is, in the difference between the high and low water, is proportional to the sine of twice the arch M H. It is measured by df in our construction. For, let $m\,u$ be a given arch of the Moon's synodical motion, such as a degree. Then $m\,v$ is the difference between the tides $m\,a$ and $u\,a$, corresponding to the constant arch of the Moon's momentary elongation from the Sun. The similarity of the triangles $m\,u\,v$ and $m\,df$ gives us $m\,u : m\,v = m\,d : df$. Now $m\,u$ and $m\,d$ are constant. Therefore $m\,v$ is proportional to df, and $m\,d : df = $ rad. : sin. $d\,m\,f$, $=$ sin. $m\,d\,h$, $=$ sin. 2 M C H.

Hence it follows that the diminution of the tides is most rapid when the high water is in the octants. This will be found to be the difference between the twelfth and thirteenth tides, counted from new or full Moon, and between the seventh and eighth tides after the quadratures.

dratures. If $m\,u$ be taken $= \frac{1}{2}$ the Moon's daily elongation from the Sun, which is 6° 30′ nearly, the rule will give, with fufficient accuracy, $\frac{1}{2}$ the difference between the two fuperior or the two inferior tides immediately fucceeding. It does not give the difference between the two immediately fucceeding tides, becaufe they are alternately greater and leffer, as will appear afterwards.

660. Having thus given a reprefentation to the eye of the various circumftances of thefe phenomena in this fimple cafe, it would be proper to fhew how all the different quantities fpoken of may be computed arithmetically. The fimpleft method for this, though perhaps not the moft elegant, feems to be the following.

In the triangle $m\,d\,a$, the two fides $m\,d$ and $d\,a$ are given, and the contained angle $m\,d\,a$, when the proportion of the forces M and S, and the Moon's elongation M C S are given. Let this angle $m\,d\,a$ be called a. Then make M $+$ S : M $-$ S $=$ tan., a : tan. b. Then $y = \dfrac{a-b}{2}$, and $x = \dfrac{a+b}{2}$.

For M $+$ S : M $-$ S $= m\,d + d\,a : m\,d - d\,a$, $=$ tan. $\dfrac{m\,a\,d + a\,m\,d}{2}$: tan. $\dfrac{m\,a\,d - a\,m\,d}{2} =$ tan. $\dfrac{2\,x + 2\,y}{2}$: tan. $\dfrac{2\,x - 2\,y}{2}$, $=$ tan. $\overline{x+y}$: tan. $\overline{x-y} =$ tan. a : tan. b. Now $\overline{x+y} + \overline{x-y} = 2\,x$ and $\overline{x+y} - \overline{x-y} = 2\,y$. Therefore $a + b = 2\,x$ and $a - b = 2\,y$, and $x = \dfrac{a+b}{2}$, and $y = \dfrac{a-b}{2}$.

4 G

661. It is of peculiar importance to know the greateſt ſeparation of the high water from the Moon. This happens when the high water is in the octant. In this ſituation it is plain that $m'd : d\,a$, that is, $M : S$, = rad. : ſin. $d\,m'\,a$, = rad. : ſin. $2\,y'$, and therefore ſin. $2\,y' = \dfrac{S}{M}$. Hence $2\,y'$ and y' are found.

662. It is manifeſt that the applicability of this conſtruction to the explanation of the phenomena of the tides depends chiefly on the proportion of $S\,d$ to $d\,a$, that is, the proportion of the accumulating force of the Moon to that of the Sun. This conſtitutes the ſpecies of the triangle $m\,d\,a$, on which every quantity depends. The queſtion now is, What is this proportion? Did we know the quantity of matter in the Moon, it would be decided in a minute. The only obſervation that can give us any information on this ſubject is the nutation of the Earth's axis. This gives at once the proportion of the diſturbing forces. But the quantities obſerved, the deviation of the Earth's axis from its uniform conical motion round the pole of the ecliptic, and the equation of the preceſſion of the equinoctial points, are much too ſmall for giving us any precife knowledge of this ratio.

Fortunately, the tides themſelves, by the modification which their phenomena receive from the comparative magnitude of the forces in queſtion, give us means of diſcovering the ratio of S to M. The moſt obvious circumſtance of this nature is the magnitude of the ſpring and neap-tides. Accordingly, this was employed by

Newton

'Newton in his theory of the tides. He collected a number of obfervations made at Briftol, and at Plymouth, and, ftating the fpring-tide to the neap-tide as M + S to M — S, he faid that the force of the Moon in raifing the tide is to that of the Sun nearly as $4\frac{1}{2}$ to 1. But it was foon perceived that this was a very uncertain method. For there are fcarcely any two places where the proportion between the fpring-tide and the neap-tide is the fame, even though the places be very near each other. This extreme difcrepancy, while the proportion was obferved to be invariable for any individual place, fhewed that it was not the theory that was in fault, but that the local circumftances of fituation were fuch as affected very differently tides of different magnitudes, and thus changed their proportion. It was not till the noble collection of obfervations was made at Breft and Rochefort that the philofopher could affort and combine the immenfe variety of heights and times of the tides, fo as to throw them into claffes to be compared with the afpects of the Sun and Moon according to the Newtonian theory. M. Caffini, and, after him, M. Daniel Bernoulli, made this comparifon with great care and difcernment; and on the authority of this comparifon, M. Bernoulli has founded the theory and explanation contained in his excellent Differtation on the tides, which fhared with M'Laurin and Euler the prize given by the Academy of Paris in 1740.

M. Bernoulli employs feveral circumftances of the tides for afcertaining the ratio of M to S. He employs

the

the law of the retardation of the tides. This has great
advantages over the method employed by Newton. Whatever are the obftructions or modifications of the tides,
they will operate equally, or nearly fo, on two tides that
are equal, or nearly equal. This is the cafe with two fucceeding tides of the fame kind.

, The Moon's mean motion from the Sun, in time, is
about 50½ minutes in a day. The fmalleft retardation,
in the vicinity of new and full Moon, is nearly 35′,
wanting 15½ of the Moon's retardation. Therefore, by
art. 656,

$$M : S = 35 : 15\tfrac{1}{2}, = 5 : 2\tfrac{1}{7} \text{ nearly.}$$

The longeft tide-day about the quadratures is 25^h 25′,
exceeding a folar day 85′, and a lunar day 34½. Therefore

$$M : S = 85 : 34\tfrac{1}{2}, = 5 : 2\tfrac{1}{36} \text{ nearly.}$$

The proportion of M to S may alfo be inferred by a
direct comparifon of the tide-day at new Moon and in
the quadratures.

$$35 : 85 = M - S : M + S. \text{ Therefore}$$

$$M : S = \frac{85 + 35}{2} : \frac{85 - 35}{2}, = 5 : 2\tfrac{1}{12}.$$

It may alfo be difcovered by obferving the greateft
feparation of the place of high water from that of the
Moon, or the elongation of the Moon when the tide-day
and the lunar day are equal. In this cafe y is obferved
to be nearly 12° 30′. Therefore $\dfrac{S}{M} = \text{fin. } 25°$, and
$M : S = 5 : 2\tfrac{1}{3}$ nearly.

Thus it appears that all thefe methods give nearly
the

the fame refult, and that we may adopt 5 to 2 as the ratio of the two difturbing forces. This agrees extremely well with the phenomena of nutation and preceffion.

Inftead of inferring the proportion of M to S from the quantity of matter in the Moon, deduced from the phenomena of nutation, as is affected by D'Alembert and La Place, I am more difpofed to infer the mafs of the Moon from this determination of M : S, confirmed by fo many coincidences of different phenomena. Taking 5 : 2,13 as the mean of thofe determinations, and employing the analogy in § 465, we obtain for the quantity of matter in the Moon nearly $\frac{1}{7\sigma}$, the Earth being 1.

If the forces of the two luminaries were equal, there would be no high and low water in the day of quadrature. There would be an elevation above the infcribed fpheroid of $\frac{1}{3}\overline{M + S}$ all round the circumference of the circle paffing through the Sun and Moon, forming the ocean into an oblate fpheroid.

663. Since the gravitation to the Sun alone produces an elevation of 24½ inches, the gravitation to the Moon will raife the waters 58 inches ; the fpring-tide will be 24½ + 58, or 82½ inches, and the neap-tide 33¾ inches.

664. The proportion now adopted muft be confidered as that correfponding to the mean intenfity of the accumulating forces. But this proportion is by no means conftant, by reafon of the variation in the diftances of

the

the luminaries. Calling the Sun's mean diſtance 1000, it is 983 in January and 1017 in July. The Moon's mean diſtance being 1000, ſhe is at the diſtance 1055 when in apogeo, and 945 when in perigeo. The action of the luminaries in producing a change of figure varies in the inverſe triplicate ratio of their diſtances (519.) Therefore, if 2 and 5 are taken for the mean diſturbing forces of the Sun and Moon, we have the following meaſures of thoſe forces.

	Sun.	*Moon.*
Apogean	1,901	4,258
Mean	2,——	5,——
Perigean	2,105	5,925

Hence we ſee that M : S may vary from 5,925 : 1,901 to 4,258 : 2,105, that is, nearly from 6 : 2 to 4 : 2.

The general expreſſion of the diſturbing force of the Moon will be $M = \frac{5}{2} S \times \frac{D^3}{\Delta^3} \times \frac{d^3}{\delta^3}$ where D and d expreſs the mean diſtances of the Sun and Moon, and Δ and δ any other ſimultaneous diſtances.

The ſolar force does not greatly vary, and need not be much attended to in our computations for the tides. But the change in the lunar action muſt not be neglected, as this greatly affects both the time and the height of the tide.

665. Firſt, as to the times.

1. The tide-day following ſpring-tide is 24ʰ 27½′ when the Moon is in perigeo, and 24ʰ 33′ when ſhe is in apogeo.

2 ꝗ

2. The tide-day following neap-tide is 25ʰ 15′ in the firſt caſe, and 25ʰ 40′ in the ſecond.

3. The greateſt interval between the Moon's ſouthing and high water (which happens in the octants) is 39′ when the Moon is in perigeo, and 61′ when ſhe is in apogeo, *y* being 9° 45′ and 15° 15′.

666. The height of the tide is ſtill more affected by the Moon's change of diſtance.

If the Moon is in perigeo, when new or full, the ſpring-tide will be eight feet, inſtead of the mean ſpring-tide of ſeven feet. The very next ſpring-tide will be no more than ſix feet, becauſe the Moon is then in apogeo. The neap-tides, which happen between theſe very unequal tides, will be regular, the Moon being then in quadrature, at her mean diſtance.

But if the Moon change at her mean diſtance, the ſpring-tide will be regular, but one neap-tide will be four feet, and another only two feet.

We ſee therefore that the regular monthly ſeries of heights and times correſponding to our conſtruction can never be obſerved, becauſe in the very ſame, or nearly the ſame period, the Moon makes all the changes of diſtance which produce the effects above mentioned. As the effect produced by the ſame change of the Moon's diſtance is different according to the ſtate of the tide which it affects, it is by no means eaſy to apply the e-quation ariſing from this cauſe.

667.

667. As a fort of fynopfis of the whole of this defcription of the monthly feries of tides, the following
Table by D. Bernoulli will be of fome ufe. The firft
column contains the Moon's elongation S M (eaftward)
from the Sun, or from the point oppofite to the Sun,
in degrees. The fecond column contains the minutes
of folar time that the moment of high water precedes
or follows the Moon's fouthing. This correfponds to
the arch H M. The third column gives the arch S H,
or nearly the hour and minute of the day at the time
of high water; and the fourth column contains the
height of the tide, as exprefled by the line *m a*, the
fpace S *a* being divided into 1000 parts, as the height
of a fpring-tide. Note that the elongation is fuppofed
to be that of the Moon at the time of her fouthing.

TABLE

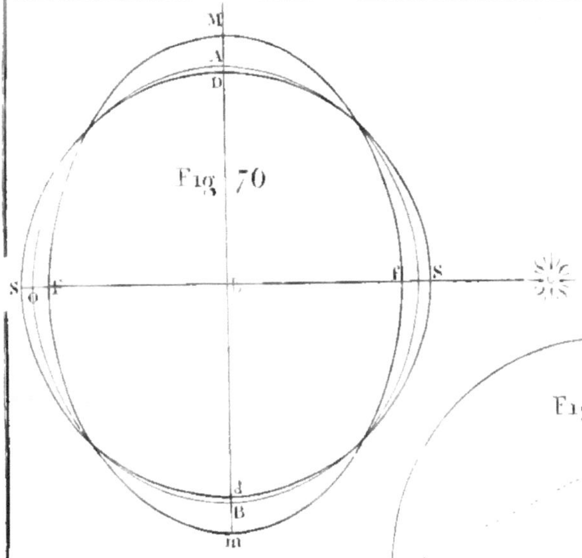

Pl.20

Fig. 70

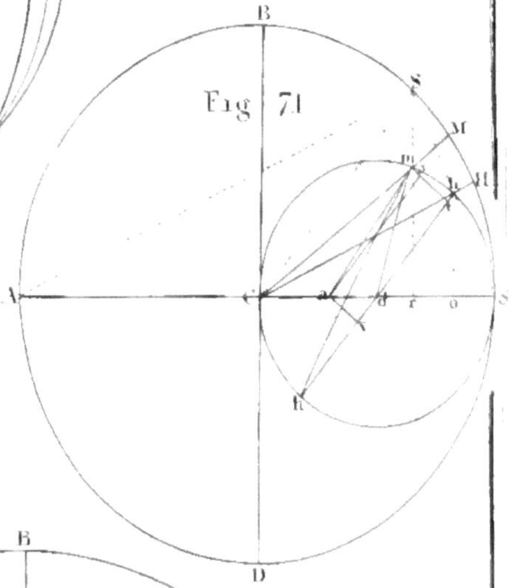

Fig. 71

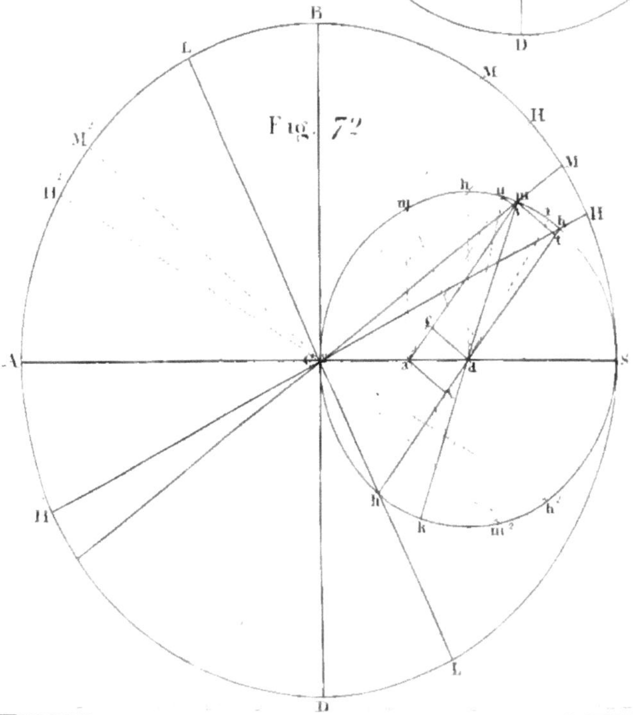

Fig. 72

TABLE I.

S M	H M		Hour.	m a
	Minutes.			
0	—		—.——	1000
10	$11\frac{1}{2}$		—.$28\frac{1}{2}$	987
20	22		—.58	949
30	$31\frac{1}{2}$	Before the Moon's Southing.	1.$28\frac{1}{2}$	887
40	40		2.——	806
50	45		2.35	715
60	$46\frac{1}{2}$		3.$13\frac{1}{2}$	610
70	$40\frac{1}{2}$		3.$59\frac{1}{2}$	518
80	25		4.55	453
90	—		6.——	429
100	25	After the Moon's Southing.	7. 5	453
110	$40\frac{1}{2}$		8. $\frac{1}{2}$	518
120	$46\frac{1}{2}$		8.$46\frac{1}{2}$	610
130	45		9.25	715
140	40		10.——	806
150	$31\frac{1}{2}$		10.31	887
160	22		11.2	949
170	$11\frac{1}{2}$		11.31	987
180	—		12.——	1000

668. It is proper here to notice a circumstance, of very general observation, and which appears inconsistent with our construction, which states the high water of neap-tides to happen when the Moon is on the meridian. This must make the high water of neap-tides six

4 H   hours

TABLE I.

S M	H M		Hour.	m a
	Minutes.			
0	—		—.——	1000
10	$11\frac{1}{2}$		$-.28\frac{1}{2}$	987
20	22		$-.58$	949
30	$31\frac{1}{2}$		$1.28\frac{1}{2}$	887
40	40	Before the Moon's Southing.	2.——	806
50	45		2.35	715
60	$46\frac{1}{2}$		$3.13\frac{1}{2}$	610
70	$40\frac{1}{2}$		$3.59\frac{1}{2}$	518
80	25		4.55	453
90	—		6.—	429
100	25		7. 5	453
110	$40\frac{1}{2}$		8. $\frac{1}{2}$	518
120	$46\frac{1}{2}$	After the Moon's Southing.	$8.46\frac{1}{2}$	610
130	45		9.25	715
140	40		10.—	806
150	$31\frac{1}{2}$		10.31	887
160	22		11.2	949
170	$11\frac{1}{2}$		11.31	987
180	—		12.—	1000

668. It is proper here to notice a circumstance, of very general observation, and which appears inconsistent with our construction, which states the high water of neap-tides to happen when the Moon is on the meridian. This must make the high water of neap-tides six

4 H

hours

hours later than the high water of fpring-tides, fuppofing that to happen when the Sun and Moon are on the meridian. But it is univerfally obferved that the high water of tides in quadrature is only about five hours and ten or twelve minutes later than that of the tides in fyzigy.

This is owing to our not attending to another circumftance, namely, that the high water which happens in fyzigy, and in quadrature, is not the high water of fpring and of neap-tides, but the third before them. They correfpond to a pofition of the Moon 19° weftward of the fyzigy or quadrature, as will be more particularly noticed afterwards. At thefe times, the points of high water are $13\frac{1}{2}$ weft of the fyzigy, and 29 weft of the quadrature, as appears by our conftruction. The lunar hours correfponding to the interval are exactly $5^h 02'$, which is nearly $5° 12'$ folar hours.

669. Hitherto we have confidered the phenomena of the tides in their moft fimple ftate, by ftating the Moon and the Sun in the equator. Yet this can never happen. That is, we can never fee a monthly feries of tides nearly correfponding with this fituation of the luminaries. In the courfe of one month, the Sun may continue within fix degrees of the equator, but the Moon will deviate from it, from 18 to 28 or 30 degrees. This will greatly affect the height of the tides, caufing them to deviate from the feries expreffed by our conftruction. It ftill more affects the time, particularly of low water. The phenomena depend primarily on the zenith diftances

of

of the luminaries, and, when thefe are known, are accurately 'expreffed by the conftruction. But thefe zenith
diftances depend both on the place of the luminaries in
the heavens, and on the latitude of the obferver. It is
difficult to point out the train of phenomena as they occur in any one place, becaufe the figure affumed by the
waters, although its depth be eafily afcertained in any
fingle point, and for any one moment, is too complicated
to be explained by any general defcription. It is not
an oblong elliptical fpheroid, formed by revolution, except in the very moment of new or full Moon. In other
relative fituations of the Sun and Moon, the ocean will
not have any fection that is circular. Its poles, and the
pofition of its equator, are eafily determined. But this
equatoreal fection is not a circle, but approaches to an
elliptical form, and, in fome cafes, is an exact ellipfe.
The longer axis of this oval is in the plane paffing
through the Sun and Moon, and its extremities are in
the points of low water for this circle, as determined by
our conftruction. Its fhorter axis paffes through the
centre of the Earth, at right angles to the other, and its
extremities are the points of the *loweft low water*. In
thefe two points, the depreffion below the natural level
of the ocean is always the fame, namely, the fum of the
greateft depreffion produced by each luminary. It is
fubjected therefore only to the changes arifing from the
changes of diftance of the Sun and Moon.

Thus it appears that the furface of the ocean has generally four poles, two of which are prolate or prutube-

4 H 2   rant,

rant, and two of them are compreſſed. This is moſt remarkably the caſe when the Moon is in quadrature, and
there is then a ridge all round that ſection which has the
Sun and Moon in its plane. The ſection through the
four poles, upper and lower, is the place of high water
all over the Earth, and the ſection perpendicular to the
axis of this is the place of low water in all parts of the
Earth.

Hence it follows that when the luminaries are in the
plane of the Earth's equator, the two depreſſed poles of
the watery ſpheroid coincide with the poles of the Earth;
and what we have ſaid of the times of high and low
water, and the other ſtates of the tide, are exact in their
application. But the heights of the tides are diminiſhed
as we recede from the Earth's equator, in the proportion
of radius to the coſine of the latitude. In all other ſituations of the Sun and Moon, the phenomena vary exceedingly, and cannot eaſily be ſhewn in a regular train.
The poſition of the high water ſection is often much inclined to the terreſtrial meridians, ſo that the interval between the tranſit of the Moon and the tranſit of this ſection acroſs the meridian of places in the ſame meridian is
often very different. Thus, on midſummer day, ſuppoſe
the Moon in her laſt quadrature, and in the node, therefore in the equator. The ridge which forms high water
lies ſo oblique to the meridians, that when the Moon arrives at the meridian of London, the ridge of high water
has paſſed London about two hours, and is now on the
north coaſt of America. Hence it happens that we have

no fatisfactory account of the times of high water in different places, even though we fhould learn it for a particular day. The only way of forming a good guefs of
the ftate of the tides is to have a terreftrial globe before
us, and having marked the places of the luminaries, to
lap a tape round the globe, paffing through thofe points,
and then to mark the place of high water on that line,
and crofs it with an arch at right angles. This is the
line of high water. Or, a circular hoop may be made,
croffed by one femicircle. Place the circle fo as to pafs
through the places of the Sun and Moon, fetting the interfection with the femicircle on the calculated place of
high water. The femicircle is now the line of high water, and if this armilla be held in its prefent pofition,
while the globe turns once round within it, the fucceffion of tide, or the regular hour of high water for every
part of the Earth will then be feen, not very diftant from
the truth.

At prefent, in our endeavour to point out the chief
modifications of the tides which proceed from the declination of the luminaries, or the latitude of the place of
obfervation, we muft content ourfelves with an approximation, which fhall not be very far from the truth. It
will be fufficiently exact, if we attend only to the Moon.
The effects of declination are not much affected by the
Sun, becaufe the difference between the declination of the
Moon and that of the pole of the ocean can never exceed
fix or feven degrees. When the great circle paffing
through the Sun and Moon is much inclined to the equator

tor (it may even be perpendicular to it), the luminaries are very near each other, and the Moon's place hardly deviates from the line of high water. At prefent we fhall confider the lunar tide only.

670. Let N Q S E (fig. 73.) reprefent the terra-queous globe, N S being the axis, E Q the equator, and O the centre. Let the Moon be in the direction O M, having the declination B Q. Let D be any point on the furface of the Earth, and C D L its parallel of latitude, and N D S its meridian. Let B' F b' f be the elliptical furface of the ocean, having its poles B' and b' in the line O M. Let f O F be its equator.

As the point D is carried along the parallel C D L, it will pafs in fucceffion through all the ftates of the tide, having high water when it is in C, and in L, and low water when it gets into the interfection d of its parallel C L with the equator f d F of the watery fpheroid. Draw the meridian N d G through this interfection, cutting the terreftrial equator in G. Then the arch Q G, converted into lunar hours, will give the duration of ebb of the fuperior tide, and G E is the time of the fubfequent flood of the inferior tide. It is evident that thefe are unequal, and that the whole tide G Q G, confifting of a flood-tide G Q and ebb-tide Q G, while the Moon is above the horizon (which we called the *fuperior tide*), exceeds the duration of the whole *inferior tide* G E G by four times G O (reckoned in lunar hours.)

If the fpheroid be fuppofed to touch the fphere

in

in f and F, then C c' is the height of the tide. At L, the height of the tide is L L', and if the concentric circle L'q be defcribed, C'q is the difference between the fuperior and inferior tides.

From this conftruction we learn, in general, that when the Moon has no declination, the duration of the fuperior and inferior tides of one day are equal, over all the Earth.

671. 2. If the Moon has declination, the fuperior tide will be of longer or of fhorter duration than the inferior tide, according as the Moon's declination B Q, and the latitude C Q of the place of obfervation are of the fame or of different denominations.

672. 3. When the Moon's declination is equal to the colatitude of the place of obfervation, or exceeds it, that is, if B Q is equal to N o, or exceeds it, there will be only a fuperior or inferior tide in the courfe of a lunar day. For in this cafe, the parallel of the place of obferva-tion will pafs through f, or between N and f, as k $\bar{m}$.

673. 4. The fine of the arch G O is $=$ tan. lat. $\times$ tan. declin. For rad. : cot. d O G $=$ tan. d G : fin. G O, and fin. G O $=$ tan. d G $\times$ cot. d O G. Now d G is the latitude, and d O G is the codecl.

674. The heights of the tides are affected in the fame way by the declination of the Moon, and by the la-

titude

titude of the place of obfervation. The height of the
fuperior tide exceeds that of the inferior, if the Moon's
declination is of the fame denomination with the latitude
of the place, and *vice verſâ*. It often happens that the
reverfe of this is uniformly obferved. Thus, at the Nore,
in the entry to the river Thames, the inferior tide is
greater than the fuperior, when the Moon has north declination, and *vice verſâ*. But this happens becaufe the
tide at the Nore is only the derivation of the great tide
which comes round the north of Scotland, ranges along
the eaftern coafts of Britain, and the high water of a
fuperior tide arrives at the Nore, while that of an inferior
tide is formed at the Orkney iflands, the Moon being under the horizon.

675. The height of the tide in any place, occafioned
by the action of a fingle luminary, is as the fquare of the
cofine of the zenith or nadir diſtance of that luminary.
Hence we derive the following conſtruction, which will
exprefs all the modifications of the lunar tide produced
by declination or latitude. It will not be far from the
truth, even for the compound tide, and it is perfectly exact in the cafe of fpring or neap-tides.

With a radius C Q (fig. 74.) taken as the meafure
of the whole elevation of a lunar tide, defcribe the circle
E P Q *p*, to reprefent a terreſtrial meridian, where P
and *p* are the poles, and E Q the equator. Bifect C P
in O, and round O defcribe the circle P B C D. Let
M be that point of the meridian which has the Moon in
the

the zenith, and let Z be the place of obfervation. Draw
the diameter Z C N, cutting the fmall circle in B, and
M C *m* cutting it in A.   Draw A I parallel to E Q.
Draw the diameter B O D of the inner circle, and draw
I K, G H, and A F perpendicular to B D. Laftly,
draw I D, I B, A D, A B, and C I M', cutting the meridian in M'.

After half a diurnal revolution, the Moon comes into
the meridian at M', and the angle M' C N is her diftance
from the nadir of the obferver.   The angle I C B is the
fupplement of I C N, and is alfo the fupplement of I D B,
the oppofite angle of a quadrilateral in a circle.   Therefore I D B is equal to the Moon's nadir diftance.   Alfo
A D B, being equal to A C B, is equal to the Moon's
zenith diftance.   Therefore, accounting D B as the radius of the tables, D F and D K are as the fquares of
the cofines of the Moon's zenith and nadir diftances ;
and fince P C, or D B, was taken as the meafure of the
whole lunar tide, D F will be the elevation of high water
at the fituation Z of the obferver, when the Moon is
above his horizon, and D K is the height of the fubfequent tide, when the Moon is under his horizon, or,
more accurately, it is the height of the tide feen at the
fame moment with D F, by a fpectator at *z'* in the fame
meridian and parallel.   (For the *fubfequent* tide, though
only twelve hours after, will be a little greater or lefs,
according as they are on the increafe or decreafe).   D F,
then, and D K, are proportional to the heights of the
fuperior and inferior tides of that day.   Moreover, as A I

4 I   is

is bifected in G, F K is bifected in H, and D H is the arithmetical mean between the heights of the fuperior and inferior tides. Accounting O C as the radius of the tables, A G is the fine of the arch A C, which meafures twice the angle M C Q, the Moon's declination. O G is the cofine of twice the Moon's declination. Alfo the angle B O G is equal to twice the angle B C Q, the latitude of the obferver. Therefore O H = cof. 2 decl. × cof. 2 lat., and D H = D O + O H, = M ×

$$\frac{1 + \text{cof. 2 decl. } \mathfrak{C} \times \text{cof. 2 lat.}}{2}.$$ This value of the medium tide will be found of continual ufe.

This conftruction gives us very diftinct conceptions of all the modifications of the height of a lunar tide, proceeding from the various declinations of the Moon, and the pofition of the obferver ; and the height of the compound tide may be had by repeating the conftruction for the Sun, fubftituting the declination of the Sun for that of the Moon, and S for M in the laft formula. The two elevations being added together, and $\frac{1}{3} \overline{M + S}$ taken from the fum, we have the height required. If it is a fpring-tide that we calculate for, there is fcarcely any occafion for two operations, becaufe the Sun cannot then be more than fix degrees from the Moon, and the pole of the fpheroid will almoft coincide with the Moon's place. We may now draw fome inferences from this reprefentation.

676.   1. The greateft tides happen when the Moon is

is in the zenith or nadir of the place of obfervation. For as M approaches to Z, A and I approach to B and D, and when they coincide, F coincides with B, and the height of the fuperior tide is then $= M$. The medium tide however diminifhes by this change, becaufe G comes nearer to O, and confequently H comes alfo nearer to O, and D H is diminifhed.

If, on the other hand, the place of obfervation be changed, Z approaching to M, the fuperior, inferior and medium tides are all increafed. For in fuch cafe, D feparates from I, and D K, D H, and D F are all enlarged.

677. 2. If the Moon be in the equator, the fuperior and inferior tides are equal, and $= M \times \text{cof.}^2 \text{lat.}$ For then A and I coincide with C; and F and K coalefce in i; and $D i = D B \times \text{cof.}^2 B D C, = D B \times \text{cof.}^2 Z C Q.$

678. 3. If the place of obfervation be in the equator, the fuperior and inferior tides are equal every where, and are $= M \times \text{cof.}^2$, declin. ☾. For B then coincides with C; the points F and K coincide with G; and $P G = P C \times \text{cof.}^2 C P A, = M \times \text{cof.}^2 M C Q.$

679. 4. The fuperior tides are greater or lefs than the inferior tides, according as Z and M are on the fame or on oppofite fides of the equator. For, by taking Q Z' on the other fide of the equator, equal to Q Z, and

4 I 2 drawing

drawing $Z' C z'$, cutting the fmall circle in β, we fee
that the figure is fimply reverfed. The magnitudes and
proportions of the tides are the fame in either cafe, but
the combination is inverted, and what belongs to a fuperior tide in the one cafe belongs to an inferior tide in the
other.

680. 5. If the colatitude be equal to the Moon's
declination, or lefs than it, there will be no inferior
tide, or no fuperior tide, according as the latitude and
Moon's declination are of the fame or of different denominations. For when $P Z = M Q$, D coincides with I,
and K alfo coincides with I. Alfo when P Z is lefs
than M Q, D falls below I, and the point Z never
paffes through the equator of the watery fpheroid. The
low water $m\,m'$ (fig. 73.) obferved in the parallel $k\,m$ is
only a lower part of the fame tide $k\,k'$, of which the
high water is alfo obferved in the fame place. In fuch
fituations, the tides are very fmall, and are fubjected to
fingular varieties which arife from the Moon's change of
declination and diftance. Such tides can be feen only in
the circumpolar regions. The inhabitants of Iceland notice a period of nineteen years, in which their tides gradually increafe and diminifh, and exhibit very fingular
phenomena. This is undoubtedly owing to the revolution of the Moon's nodes, by which her declination is
confiderably affected. That ifland is precifely in the
part of the ocean where the effect of this is moft remarkable. A regifter kept there would be very inftructive;
and

and it is to be hoped that this will be done, as in that fequeſtrated Thulé, there is a zealous aſtronomer, M. Lievog, furniſhed with good inſtruments, to whom this feries of obſervations has been recommended.

681. 6. At the very pole there is no daily tide. But there is a gradual rife and fubfidence of the water twice in a month, by the Moon's declining on both fides of the equator. The water is loweſt at the pole when the Moon is in the equator, and it rifes about twenty-fix inches when the Moon is in the tropics. Alſo, when her afcending node is in the vernal equinox, and ſhe has her greateſt declination, the water will be thirty inches above its loweſt ſtate, by the action of the Moon alone.

682. 7. The medium tide is, as has already been obſerved, $= M \times \dfrac{1 + \text{coſ. } 2 \text{ decl. } ☾ \times \text{coſ. } 2 \text{ lat.}}{2}$.

As the Moon's declination never exceeds 30°, the cofine of twice her declination is always a pofitive quantity, and never leſs than $\frac{1}{2}$. When the latitude is leſs than 45°, the cofine of twice the latitude is alſo pofitive, but negative when the latitude exceeds 45°. Attending to thefe circumſtances, we may infer,

683. 1. That the mean tides are equally affected by the northerly and foutherly declinations of the Moon.

684. 2. If the latitude be exactly 45°, the mean tide is always the fame, and $= \frac{1}{2} M$. For in this cafe

B D

B D is perpendicular to P C, and the point H always coincides with O. This is the reafon why, on the coafts of France and Spain, the tides are fo little affected by the declination of the luminaries.

685. 3. When the latitude is lefs than 45°, the mean-tides increafe as the declination of the Moon diminifhes. For *cofin.* 2 *lat.* being then a pofitive quantity, the formula increafes when the cofine of the declination of the Moon increafes, that is, it diminifhes when the declination of the Moon increafes. As B Q diminifhes, G comes nearer to C, and H feparates from O towards B, and D H increafes.

But if the latitude exceed 45°, the point H muft fall between O and D, and the mean-tide will increafe as the declination increafes.

686. 5. If the latitude be $= 0$, the point H coincides with G, and the effect of the Moon's declination is then the moft fenfible. The mean-tide in this cafe is

$$M \times \frac{1 + \text{cof. 2 declin. } \mathbb{C}}{2}.$$

685. Every thing that has been determined here for the lunar tide may eafily be accommodated to the high and low water of the compound tide, by repeating the computations with S in the place of M, as the conftant coefficient. But, in general, it is almoft as exact as the nature of the queftion will admit, to attend only to the

lunar

Pl 21

Fig 73

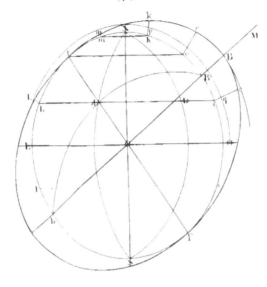

Fig 74

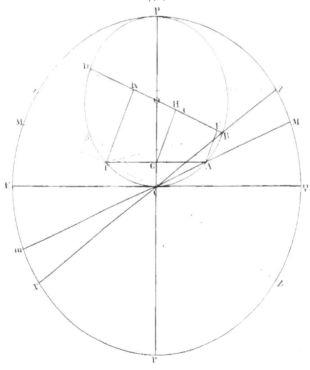

lunar tide. The declination of the real fummit of the fpheroid, in this cafe, never differs from the declination of the fummit of the lunar tide more than two degrees, and the correction may be made at any time by a little reflection on the fimultaneous pofition of the Sun. What has been faid is ftrictly applicable to the fpring-tides.

$\overline{M + S - \text{tide}} \times \text{fin.}^2 d\,O$ (fig. 73.) is the quantity to be added to the tide found by the conftruction. It is exact in fpring-tides and very near the truth in all other cafes. The fin.$^2 d\,O$ is $= \dfrac{S^2 \text{ lat.}}{\text{cof.}^2 \text{ decl. } \mathbb{C}}$. For fin. $d\,O\,G$: fin. $d\,G\,O =$ fin. $d\,G$: fin. $d\,O$.

Such, then, are the more fimple and general confequences of gravitation on the waters of our ocean, on the fuppofition that the whole globe is covered with water, and that the ocean always has the form which produces a perfect equilibrium of force in every particle.

686. But the globe is not fo covered, and it is clear that there muft be a very great extent of open fea, in order to produce that elevation at the fummit of the fpheroid which correfponds with the accumulating force of the luminaries. A quadrant at leaft of the ellipfe is neceffary for giving the whole tide. With lefs than this, there will not be enough of water to make up the fpheroid. And, to produce the full daily viciffitude of high and low water, this extent of fea muft be in longitude. An equal extent in latitude may produce the greateft elevation; but it will not produce the feries of heights that fhould

fhould occur in the courfe of a lunar day. In confined feas of fmall extent, fuch as the Cafpian, the Euxine, the Baltic, and the great lakes in North America, the tides muft be almoft infenfible. For it is evident that the greateft difference of height on the fhore of fuch confined feas can be no more than the deflection from the tangent of the arch of the fpheroid contained in that fea. This, in the Cafpian Sea, cannot exceed feven inches; a quantity fo fmall, that a flight breeze of wind, fetting off fhore, will be fufficient for preventing the accumulation, and even for producing a depreffion. A moderate breeze, blowing along the canal in St James's Park at London, raifes the water two inches at one end, while it depreffes it as much at the other. The only confined feas of confiderable extent are the Mediterranean and the Red Sea. The firft has an extent of 40° in longitude, and the tides there might be very fenfible, were it on the equator, but being in lat. 35 nearly, the effects are leffened in the proportion of five to four. In fuch a fituation, the phenomena are very different, both in regard to time and to kind, from what they would be, if the Mediterranean were part of the open ocean. Its furface will be *parallel* to what it would be in that cafe, but *not the fame*. This will appear by infpection of fig. 75, where *m r p* reprefents the natural level of the ocean, and M *o* Q reprefents the watery fpheroid, having its pole in M, and its equator at Q. S *s* may reprefent a tide poft, fet up on the fhore of Syria, at the eaft end of the Mediterranean, and G *o* a poft fet up at the Gut of Gibraltar, which we

fhall

fhall fuppofe at prefent to be dammed up. When the
Moon is over M, the waters of the Mediterranean affume
the furface *g r s*, parallel to the correfponding portion of
the elliptical furface Q *o* M, croffing the natural furface
at *r*, nearly in the middle of its length. Thus, on the
Syrian coaft, there is a confiderable elevation of the waters, and at Gibraltar, there is a confiderable depreffion.
In the middle of the length, the water is at its mean
height. The water of the Atlantic Ocean, an open and
extenfive fea, affumes the furface of the equilibrated
fpheroid, and it ftands confiderably higher on the outfide
of the dam, as is feen by G *o*, than on the infide, as expreffed by G *g*. It is nearly low water within the Straits,
while it is about $\frac{1}{3}$ or $\frac{1}{4}$ flood without. The water has
been ebbing for fome hours within the Straits, but flow-
ing for great part of the time without. As the Moon
moves weftward, toward Gibraltar, the water will begin
to rife, but flowly, within the Straits, but it is flowing
very faft without. When the Moon gets to P, things
are reverfed. The fummit of the fpheroid (it being fuppofed a fpring-tide) is at P, and it is nearly high water
within the Straits, but has been ebbing for fome hours
without. It is low water on the coaft of Syria. All this
while, the water at *r*, in the middle of the Mediterranean, has not altered its height by any fenfible quantity.
It will be high water at one end of the Mediterranean,
and low water at the other, when the middle is in that
part of the general fpheroid where the furface makes the
moft unequal angles with the vertical. This will be

4 K   nearly

nearly in the octants, and therefore about 1¾ hours before and after the Moon's fouthing (fuppofing it fpring-
tide).

These obfervations greatly contribute to the explanation of the fingular currents in the Straits of Gibraltar,
as they are defcribed by different authors. For although
the Mediterranean is not fhut up, and altogether feparated from the Atlantic Ocean at Gibraltar, the communication is extremely fcanty, and by no means fufficient for
allowing the tide of the ocean to diffufe itfelf into this
bafon in a regular manner. Changes of tide, always different, and frequently quite oppofite, are obferved on the
eaft and weft fide of the narrow neck which connects
the Rock with Spain; and the general tenor of thofe
changes has a very great analogy with what has now
been defcribed. The tides in the Mediterranean are
fmall, and therefore eafily affected by winds. But
they are remarkably regular. This may be expected.
For as the collection or abftraction neceffary for producing the change is but fmall, they are foon accomplifhed. The regifters of the tides at Venice and fome
other ports in the Adriatic are furprifingly conformable
to the theory. See Phil. Tranf. Vol. LXVII.

From this example, it is evident that great deviations
may be expected in the obferved phenomena of the tides
from the immediate refults of the fimple unobftructed
theory, and yet the theory may be fully adequate to the
explanation of them, when the circumftances of local
fituation are properly confidered.

688.

688. The real ftate of things is fuch, that there are very few parts of the ocean where the theory can be applied without very great modifications. Perhaps the great Pacific Ocean is the only part of the terraqueous globe in which all the forces have room to operate. When we confider the terreftrial globe as placed before the acting luminaries, which have a relative motion round it from eaft to weft, and confider the accumulation of the waters as keeping pace with them on the ocean, we muft fee that the tides with which we are moft familiarly acquainted, namely, thofe which vifit the weftern fhores of Europe and Africa, and the eaftern fhores of America, muft alfo be irregular, and be greatly diverfified by the fituation of the coafts. The accumulation on our coafts muft be in a great meafure fupplied by what comes from the Indian and Ethiopic Ocean from the eaftward, and what is brought, or kept back, from the South Sea ; and the accumulation muft be diffufed, as from a collection coming round the Cape of Good Hope, and round Cape Horn. Accordingly, the propagation of high water is entirely confonant with fuch a fuppofition. It is high water at the Cape of Good Hope about three o'clock at new and full moon, and it happens later and later, as we proceed to the northward along the coaft of Africa ; later and later ftill as we follow it along the weft coafts of Spain and France, till we get to the mouth of the Englifh Channel. In fhort, the high water proceeds a-long thofe fhores juft like the top of a wave, and it may be followed, hour after hour, to the different harbours

4 K 2   along

along the coaſt. The ſame wave continues its progreſs northwards (for it ſeems to be the only ſupply), part of it going up St George's Channel, part going northward by the weſt ſide of Ireland, and a branch of it going up the Engliſh Channel, between this iſland and France. What goes up by the eaſt and weſt ſides of Ireland unites, and proceeds ſtill northward, along the weſtern coaſts and iſlands of Scotland, and then diffuſes itſelf to the eaſtward, toward Norway and Denmark, and, circling round the eaſtern coaſts of Britain, comes ſouthward, in what is called the German Ocean, till it reaches Dover, where it meets with the branch which went up the Eng- liſh Channel.

689. It is remarkable that this northern tide, after having made ſuch a circuit, is more powerful than the branch which proceeds up the Engliſh Channel. It reaches Dover about a quarter of an hour before the ſouthern tide, and forces it backwards for half an hour. It muſt alſo be remarked, that the tide which comes up channel is not the ſame with the tide which meets it from the north, but is a whole tide earlier, if not two tides. For the ſpring-tide at Rye is a tide earlier than the ſpring-tide at the Nore. It even ſeems more nearly two tides earlier, appearing the one as often as the other. This may be better ſeen by tracing the hour of high water from the Lizard up St George's Channel and along the weſt coaſts of Scotland. Now it is very clear that the ſuperior tide at the Orkney iſlands is ſimultaneous

with

with the inferior tide at the mouth of the Thames. It is therefore moſt probable that the Orkney tide is at leaſt one tide later than at the Lizard. The whole of this tide is very anomalous, eſpecially after getting to the Orkneys. It is a derivative from the great tide of the open ſea, which being very diſtant, is ſubjected to the influence of hard gales, at a diſtance, and frequently unlike what is going on upon our coaſts. .

690. A ſimilar progreſs of the ſame high water from the ſouthward, is obſerved along the eaſtern ſhores of South America. But, after paſſing Brazil and Surinam, the Atlantic Ocean becomes ſo wide that the effect of this high water, as an adventitious thing ſupplied from the ſouthward, is not ſo ſenſible, becauſe the Atlantic itſelf is now extenſive enough to contribute greatly to the formation of the regular ſpheroid. But it contributes chiefly by abſtraction of the waters from the American ſide, while the accumulation is forming on the European ſide of the Atlantic. By ſtudying the ſucceſſive hours of high water along the weſtern coaſts of Africa and Europe, it appears that it takes nearly two days, or between four and five tides, to come from the Cape of Good Hope to the mouth of the Engliſh Channel. This remark is of peculiar importance.

691. Few obſervations have, as yet, been made public concerning the tides in the Great Pacific Ocean. They muſt exhibit phenomena conſiderably different from

from what are feen in the Atlantic. The vaft ftretch of uninterrupted coaft from Cape Horn to Cook's Straits, prevents all fupply from the eaftward for making up the fpheroid. So far as we have information, it appears that the tides are very unlike the European tides, till we get 40° or 50° weft from the coaft of America. In the neighbourhood of that coaft, there is fcarcely any inferior tide. Even in the middle of the vaft Pacific Ocean the tides are very fmall, but abundantly regular.

692. The fetting of the tides is affected, not only by the form of the fhores, but alfo by the inequalities which undoubtedly obtain in the bottom of the ocean. A deep and long valley there will give a direction to the waters which move along it, even although they far overtop the higher parts on each fide, juft as we obferve the wind follow the courfe of the vallies. This direction of the undermoft waters affects thofe that flow above them, in confequence of the mutual adhefion of the filaments; and thus the whole ftream is deflected from the direction which it would have taken, had the ground been even. By fuch deflections the path is lengthened, and the time of its reaching a certain place is protracted; and this produces other deviations from the calculations by the fimple theory.

693. Thefe peculiarities in the bed or channel alfo greatly affect the height of the tides. When a wave of a certain magnitude enters a channel, it has a certain

quantity

quantity of motion, meafured by the quantity of water and its velocity. If the channel, keeping the fame depth, contract in its width, the water, keeping for a while its momentum, muft increafe its velocity, or its depth, or both. And thus it may happen that, although the greateft elevation produced by the joint action of the Sun and Moon in the open fea does not exceed eight or nine feet, the tide in fome fingular fityations may mount confiderably higher. It feems to be owing to this that the high water of the Atlantic Ocean, which at St Helena does not exceed four or five feet, fetting in obliquely on the coaft of North America, ranges along that coaft, in a channel gradually narrowing, till it is ftopped in the Bay of Fundy as in a hook, and there it heaps up to an aftonifhing degree. It fometimes rifes 120 feet in the harbour of Annapolis-Royal. Were it not that we fee inftances of as ftrange effects of a fudden check given to the motion of water, we fhould be difpofed to think that the theory is not adequate to the explanation of the phenomena. But the extreme difparity that we may obferve in places very near each other, and which derive their tide from the very fame tide in the open fea, muft convince us that fuch anomalies do not impugn the general principle, although we fhould never be able fully to account for the difcrepancy.

694. Nothing caufes fo much irregularity in the tides as the reflection of the tide from fhore to fhore. If a pendulum, while vibrating, receives little impulfes,

at

at intervals that are always the fame, and very nearly equal to its own vibrations, or even to an aliquot
part of them, the vibrations may be increafed to a great
magnitude after fome time, and then will gradually diminifh, and thus have periods of increafe and decreafe.
So it happens in the undulation which conftitutes a tide.
The fituation of the coafts may be fuch, that the time
in which this undulation would, of itfelf, play backward
and forward from fhore to fhore, may be fo exactly fitted
to the recurring action of the Moon, that the fucceeding
impulfes, always added to the natural undulation, may
raife it to a height altogether difproportioned to what the
action of the Moon can produce in open fea, where
the undulation diffufes itfelf to a vaft diftance. What
we fee in this way fhould fuffice for accounting for the
great height of the tides on the coafts of continents.
Dan. Bernoulli, juftly thinking that the obftructions of
various kinds to the movements of the ocean fhould make
the tides lefs than what the unobftructed forces are able
to produce, concluded, from the great tides actually obferved, and compared with the tides producible by the
Newtonian theory, that this theory was erroneous. He
thought it all derived from Newton's erroneous idea of
the proportion of the two axes of the terraqueous globe ;
which miftake refults from the fuppofition of primitive fluidity, and uniform denfity. He inveftigates the
form of the Earth, accommodated to a nucleus of great
denfity, covered with a rarer fluid, and he thinks that
he has demonftrated that the height of the tide will be
in

in proportion to the comparative denfity of this nucleus, or the rarity of the fluid. This, fays he, alone can account for the tides that we really obferve ; and which, great as they are, are certainly only a part of what they would be, were they not fo much obftructed. This is extremely fpecious, and, coming from an eminent mathematician, has confiderable authority. But the problem of the figure of the Earth has been examined with the moft fcrupulous attention, fince the days of M. Bernoulli, by the firft mathematicians of Europe, who are all perfectly agreed in their deductions, and confirm that of Sir Ifaac Newton. They have alfo proved, and we apprehend that it is fufficiently eftablifhed in art. 603, that a denfer nucleus, inftead of making a greater tide, will make it fmaller than if the whole globe be of one denfity. The ground of Bernoulli's miftake has alfo been clearly pointed out. There remains no other way of accounting for the great tides but by caufes fuch as have now been mentioned. When the tides in the open Pacific Ocean never exceed three or four feet, we muft be convinced that the extravagant tides obferved on the coafts of great continents are anomalies ; for there, the obftructions are certainly greater than in the open fea. We muft therefore look for an explanation in the motions and collifions of difturbed tides. Thefe anomalies therefore bring no valid objection againft the general theory.

695. There are fome fituations where it is eafy to explain the deviations, and the explanation is inftructive.

4 I. Suppofe

Suppofe a great navigable river, running nearly in a meridional direction, and falling into the fea in a fouthern
coaft.   The high water of the ocean reaches the mouth
of this river (we may fuppofe) when the Sun and Moon
are together in the meridian.   It is therefore a fpring-
tide high water at the mouth of the river at noon.   This
checks the ftream at the mouth of the river, and caufes
it to deepen.   This again checks the current farther up
the river, and it deepens there alfo, becaufe there is always the fame quantity of land water pouring into it.
The ftream is not perhaps ftopped, but only retarded.
But this cannot happen without its growing deeper.   This
is propagated farther and farther up the ftream, and it
is perceived at a great diftance up the river.   But this
requires a confiderable time.   Our knowledge in hydraulics is too imperfect as yet to enable us to fay in what
number of hours this fenfible check, indicated by the
fmaller velocity, and greater depth, will be propagated to a certain diftance.   We may fuppofe it juft a
lunar day before it arrive at a certain wharf up the
river.   The Moon, at the end of the day, is again on
the meridian, as it was when it was a fpring-tide at the
mouth of the river the day before.   But, in this interval, there has been another high water at the mouth of
the river, at the preceding midnight, and there has juft
been a third high water, about fifteen minutes before
the Moon came to the meridian, and thirty-five minutes
after the Sun has paffed it.   There muft have been two
low waters in the interval, at the mouth of the river.
                                                      Now,

Now, in the fame way that the tide of yeſterday noon is propagated up the ſtream, the tide of midnight has alfo proceeded upwards. And thus, there are three coexiſtent high waters in the river. One of them is a ſpring-tide, and it is far up, at the wharf above mentioned. The fecond, or the midnight tide, muſt be half way up the river, and the third is at the mouth of the river. And there muſt be two low waters intervening. The low water, that is, a ſtate of the river below its natural level, is produced by the paſſing low water of the ocean, in the fame way that the high water was. For when the ocean falls below its natural level at the mouth of the river, it occaſions a greater declivity of the iſſuing ſtream of the river. This muſt augment its velocity— this abſtracts more water from the ſtream above, and that part alfo ſinks below its natural level, and gives a greater declivity to the waters behind it, &c. And thus the ſtream is accelerated, and the depth is leſſened, in fucceſſion, in the fame way as the oppoſite effects were produced. We have a low water at different wharfs in fucceſſion, juſt as we had the high waters.

696. This ſtate of things, which muſt be familiarly known to all who have paid any attention to thefe matters, being feen in almoſt every river which opens into a tide way, gives us the moſt diſtinct notion of the mechaniſm of the tides. The daily returning tide is nothing but an undulation or wave, excited and maintained by the action of the Sun and Moon. It is a great miſtake

to

to imagine that we cannot have high water at London
Bridge (for example) unlefs the water be raifed to that
level all the way from the mouth of the Thames.   In
many places that are far from the fea, the ftream, at the
moment of high water, is down the river, and fometimes
it is confiderable.   At Quebec, it runs downward at leaft
three miles per hour.   Therefore the water is not heaped
up to the level ; for there is no ftream without a declivity.   The harbour at Alloa in the river Forth is dry at
low water, and the bottom is about fix feet higher than
the higheft water mark on the ftone pier at Leith.   Yet
there are at Alloa tides of twenty, and even twenty-two
feet.   All Leith would then be under water, if it ftood
level from Alloa at the time of high water there.

After confidering a tide in this way, any perfon who
has remarked the very ftrange motions of a tide river, in
its various bendings and creeks, and the currents that
are frequently obferved in a direction, oppofite to the
general ftream, will no longer expect that the phenomena
of the tides will be fuch as immediately refult from the
regular operation of the folar and lunar forces.

697.   There is yet another caufe of deviation, which
is perhaps more diffimilating than any local circumftances,
and the operation of which it is very difficult to ftate familiarly, and yet precifely.   This is the inertia, as it is
called, of the waters.   No finite change of place or of
velocity can be produced in an inftant by any accelerating force.   Time muft elapfe before a ftone can acquire any meafurable velocity by falling.

Suppofe

Suppofe the Earth fluid to the centre, and at reft, without any external difturbing force. The ocean will form a perfect fphere. Let the Moon now act on it. The waters will gradually rife immediately under the Moon and in the oppofite part of the Earth, finking all around the equator of the fpheroid. Each particle proceeds to its ultimate fituation with an accelerated motion, becaufe, till then, the difturbing force exceeds the tendency of the water to fubfide. Therefore, when the form is attained which balances thofe forces, the motion does not ftop, juft as a pendulum does not ftop when it reaches the loweft point of its arch of vibration. Suppofe that the Moon ceafes to act at this inftant. The motion will ftill go on, and the ocean will overpafs the balanced figure, but with a retarded motion, as the pendulum rifes on the other fide of the perpendicular. It will ftop at a certain form, when all the former acceleration is done away by the tendency of the water to fubfide. It now begins to fubfide at the poles of the fpheroid, and to rife at the equator, and after a certain time, it becomes a perfect fphere, that is, the ocean has its natural figure. But it paffes this figure as far on the other fide, and makes a flood where there was formerly an ebb; and it would now ofcillate for ever, alternately fwelling and contracting at the points of fyzigy and quadrature. If the Moon do not ceafe to act, as was juft now fuppofed, there will ftill be ofcillations, but fomewhat different from thofe now mentioned. The middle form, on both fides of which it ofcillates in this cafe, is not the perfect fphere, but the balanced fpheroid.

698.

698. All this is on the fuppofition that there is no obftruction. But the mutual adhefion of the filaments of water will greatly check all thefe motions. The figure will not be fo foon formed ; it will not be fo far over-paffed in the firft ofcillation ; the fecond ofcillation will be lefs than the firft, the third will be lefs than the fecond, and they will foon become infenfible.

But if it were poffible to provide a recurring force, which fhould tend to raife the waters where they are already rifing, and deprefs them where they are fubfiding, and that would always renew thofe actions in the proper time, it is plain that this force may be fuch as will juft balance the obftructions competent to any particular degree of ofcillation. Such a recurring force would juft maintain this degree of ofcillation. Or the recurring force may be greater than this. It will therefore increafe the ofcillations, till the obftructions are alfo fo much increafed that the force is balanced by them. Or it may be lefs than what will balance the obftructions to the degree of ofcillation excited. In this cafe the ofcillation will decreafe, till its obftructions are no more than what this force will balance. Or this recurring force may come at improper intervals, fometimes tending to raife the waters when they are fubfiding in the courfe of an ofcillation, and depreffing them when they are rifing. Such a force muft check and greatly derange the ofcillations ; deftroying them altogether, and creating new ones, which it will increafe for fome time, and then check and deftroy them ; and will do this again and again.

Now

Now there is fuch a recurring force. As the Earth turns round its axis, fuppofe the form of the balanced fpheroid attained in the place immediately under the Moon. This elevation or pole is carried to the eaftward by the Earth, fuppofe into the pofition D O B (fig. 76.), the Moon being in the line O M. The pole of the watery fpheroid is no longer under the Moon. The Moon will therefore act on it fo as to change its figure, making it fubfide in the remote quadrant B *b* C, and rife a little in the quadrant B *a* A. Thus its pole will come a little nearer to the line O M. It is plain that if B is carried farther eaftward, but within certain limits, the fituation of the particles will be ftill more unfuitable to the lunar difturbing force, and its action on each to change its pofition will be greater. The action upon them all will therefore make a more rapid change in the pofition of the pole of the difplaced fpheroid. It feems not impoffible that this pole may be juft fo far eaft, that the changing forces may be able to caufe its pole to fhift its pofition fifteen miles in one minute. If this be the cafe, the pole of the fpheroid will keep precifely at its prefent diftance from the line O M. For, fince it would fhift to the weftward fifteen miles in one minute by the action of the Moon, and is carried fifteen miles to the eaftward in that time by the rotation of the Earth, the one motion juft undoes the effect of the other. The pole of the watery fpheroid is really made to fhift fifteen miles to the weftward on the furface of the Earth, and arrives at a place fifteen miles weft of its former place

on

the globe ; but this place of arrival is carried fifteen miles to the eaftward ; it is therefore as far from the line O M as before.

This may be illuftrated by a very fimple experiment, where the operation of the acting forces is really very like that of the lunar difturbing force. Suppofe a chain or flexible rope A B C E D F laid over a pulley, and hanging down in a bight, which is a catenarean curve, having the vertical line O D for its axis, and D for its loweft point, which the geometers call its vertex. Let the pulley be turned very flowly round its axis, in the direction A B C. The fide C E will defcend, and F A will be taken up, every link of the chain moving in the curve C E D F A. Every link is in the vertex D in its turn, juft as every portion of the ocean is in the vertex or pole of the fpheroid in its turn. Now let the pulley turn round very brifkly. The chain will be obferved to alter its figure and pofition. O D will no longer be its axis, nor D its vertex. It will now form a curve C e d f A, lying to the left hand of C E D F A. O d will be its new axis, and d will be its vertex. Gravity acts in lines parallel to O D. The motions in the direction C E and F A nearly balance each other. But there is a general motion of every link of the hanging chain, by which it is carried from E towards F. Did the chain continue in the former catenarea, this force could not be balanced. It therefore keeps fo much awry, in the form C e d f A, that its tendency by gravity to return to its former pofition is juft equal to the fum of all the motions in the links from E towards F. And it will fhew this tendency by returning to that pofition, the moment that the pulley gives over turning. The more rapidly we turn the pulley round, the farther will the chain go afide before its attitude become permanent.

700. It furpaffes our mathematical knowledge to fay with precifion how far eaftward the pole of the tide muft be from the line of the Moon's direction, even in the fimple cafe which we have been confidering. The real ftate of things is far more complicated. The Earth is not fluid to the centre, but is a folid nucleus, on which flows an ocean of very fmall depth. In the former cafe, a very moderate motion of each particle of water is fufficient for making the accumulation in one place and the depreffion in another. The particles do little more than rife or fubfide vertically. But, in the cafe of a nucleus covered with an ocean of fmall depth, a confiderable horizontal motion is required for bringing together the quantity of water wanted to make up the balanced fpheroid. The obftructions to fuch motion muft be great, both fuch as arife from the mutual adhefion of the filaments of water, and many that muft arife from friction and the inequalities of the bottom, and the configuration of the fhores. In fome places, the force of the acting luminaries may be able to caufe the pole of the fpheroid to fhift its fituation as faft as the furface moves away, when the angle M O B is 20 degrees. In other places, this may not be till it is 25°, and in another, 15° may be e-

4 M   nough.

nough. But, in every fituation, there will be an arrangement that will produce this permanent pofition of the
fummit. For when the obftructions are great, the balanced form will not be nearly attained ; and when this is
the cafe, the change producible on the pofition of a particle is more rapidly effected, the forces being great,
or rather the refiftance arifing from gravity alone being
fmall.

701. The confequence of all this muft be, in the
firft place, that that form which the ocean would ultimately affume, did the Earth not turn round its axis,
will never be attained. As the waters approach to that
form, they are carried eaftward, into fituations where
the difturbing forces tend to deprefs them on one fide,
while they raife them on the other, caufing a wefterly
undulation, which keeps its fummit at nearly the fame
diftance from the line of the acting luminary's direction.
This wefterly motion of the fummit of the undulation
does not neceffarily fuppofe a real transference of the
water to the weftward at the fame rate. It is more
like the motion of ordinary waves, in which we fee a
bit of wood or other light body merely rife and fall without any fenfible motion in the direction of the wave.
In no cafe whatever is the horizontal motion of the water
nearly equal to the motion of the fummit of the wave.
It refembles an ordinary wave alfo in this, that the rate
at which the fummit of the undulation advances in any
direction is very little affected by the height of the wave.
Our

Our knowledge however in hydraulics has not yet enabled us to fay with precifion what is the relation between the height of the undulation and the rate of its advance.

702. Thus then it appears, in general, that the fummit of the tide muft always be to the eaftward of the place affigned to it by our fimple theory, and that experience alone can tell us how much. Experience is more uniform in this refpect than one fhould expect. For it is a matter of almoft univerfal experience that it is very nearly 19 or 20 degrees. In a few places it is lefs, and in many it is 5 or 6, or 7 degrees more. This is inferred from obferving that the greateft and the fmalleft of all the tides do not happen on the very time of the fyzigies and quadratures, but the third, and in fome places, the fourth tide after. Subfequent obfervation has fhewn that this is not peculiar to the fpring and neaptides, but obtains in all. At Breft (for example) the tide which bears the mark of the augmentation arifing from the Moon's proximity is not the tide feen while the Moon is in perigeo, but the third after. In fhort, the whole feries of monthly tides difagree with the fimultaneous pofition of the luminaries, but correfpond moft regularly with their pofitions 37 or 38 hours before.

703. Another obfervation proper for this place is, that as different extent of fea, and different depth of water, will and do occafion a difference in the time in which a great undulation may be propagated along it, it

4 M 2   may

may happen that this time may fo correfpond with the
repetition of all the agitating forces, that the action of
to-day may fo confpire with the remaining undulation
of yefterday, as to increafe it by its reiterated impulfes,
to a degree vaftly greater than its original quantity.   By
giving gentle impulfes in this way to a pendulum, in the
direction of its motion, its vibrations may be increafed
to fifty times their firft fize.   It is not neceffary, for this
effect, that the return of the luminary into the favourable fituation be juft at the interval of the undulation.
It will do if it confpire with every fecond or third or
fourth undulation ; or, in general, if the amount of its
confpiring actions exceeds confiderably, and at no great
diftance of time, the amount of its oppofing actions.
In many cafes this cooperation will produce periods of
augmentation and diminution, and many feeming anomalies, which may greatly vary the phenomena.

704.   A third obfervation that fhould be made here
is, that as the obftructions to the motion of the ocean
arifing from the mutual adhefion and action of the filaments are known to be fo very great, we have reafon to
believe that the change of form actually produced is but
a moderate part of what the force can ultimately produce, and that none of the ofcillations are often repeated.
It is not probable that the repetitions of the great undulations can much exceed four or five.   When experiments are made on ftill water, we rarely fee a pure undulation repeated fo often.   Even in a fyphon of glafs,

where

where all diffusions of the undulating power is prevented, they are rarely fenfible after the fifth or fixth. A gentle fmooth undulation on the furface of a very fhallow bafon, in the view of agitating the whole depth, will feldom be repeated thrice. This is the form which moft refembles a tide.

705. After this account of the many caufes of deviation from the motions affigned by our theory, many of which are local, and reducible to no rule, it would feem that this theory, which we have taken fo much pains to eftablifh, is of no ufe, except that of giving us a general and moft powerful argument for the univerfal gravitation of matter. But this would be too hafty a conclufion. We fhall find that a judicious confideration of the different claffes of the phenomena of the tides will fuggeft fuch relations among them, that by properly combining them, we fhall not only perceive a very fatisfactory agreement with the theory, but fhall alfo be able to deduce fome important practical inferences from it.

706. Each of the different modifications of a tide has its own period, and its peculiar magnitude. Where the change made by the acting force is but fmall, and the time in which it is effected is confiderable, we may look for a confiderable conformity with the theory ; but, on the other hand, if the change to be produced on the tide is very great, and the time allowed to the forces for effecting it is fmall, it is equally reafonable to expect fenfible

fenfible deviations. If this confideration be judicioufly
applied, we fhall find a very fatisfactory conformity.

707. Of all the modifications of a tide, the greateſt,
and the moſt rapidly effected, is the difference between
the fuperior and inferior tides of the fame day. When
the Moon has great declination, the fuperior tide at Breſt
may be three times greater than the fucceeding or inferior tide. But the fact is, that they differ very little.
M. de la Place fays that they do not differ at all. We
cannot find out his authority. Having examined with
the moſt fcrupulous attention more than 200 of the obfervations at Breſt and Rochefort and Port l'Orient, and
made the proper allowance for the diſtances of the luminaries, we can fay with confidence that this general affertion of M. de la Place is not founded on the obfervations that have been publiſhed, and it does not agree
with what is obferved in the other ports of Europe.
There is always obferved a difference, agreeing with
theory in the proportions, and in the order of their fucceffion, although much fmaller. A very flight confideration will give us the reafon of the obferved difcrepancy.
It is not poffible to make two immediately fucceeding undulations of inert water remarkably different from each
other. The great undulation, in retiring, caufes the water to heap up to a greater height in the offing ; and
this, in diffufing itfelf, muſt make the next undulation
greater on the fhore. That this is the true account of
the matter is fully proved by obferving that when the
theoretic

theoretic difference between thofe two tides is very fmall, it is as diftinctly obferved in the harbours as when it is great. This is clearly feen in the Breft obfervations.

708. The abfolute magnitudes of the tides are greatly modified by local circumftances. In fome harbours there is but a fmall difference between the fpring and neap-tides, and in other harbours it is very great. But, in either cafe, the fmall daily changes are obferved to follow the proportion required by the theory with abundant precifion. Counted half way from the fpring to the neap-tides, the hourly fall of the tide is as the fquare of the time from fpring-tide, except fo far as this may be changed by the pofition of the Moon's perigee. In like manner, the hourly increafe of the tides after neap-tide is obferved to be as the fquares of the time from neap-tide.

709. The priming and lagging of the tides correfponds with the theory with fuch accuracy, that they feem to be calculated from it, independent of obfervation. There is nothing that feems lefs likely to be deranged than this. Tides which differ very little from each other, either as to magnitude or time, fhould be expected to follow one another juft as the forces require. There is indeed a deviation, very general, and eafily accounted for. There is a fmall acceleration of the tides from fpring-tide to neap-tide. This is un-

doubtedly

doubtedly owing to the obſtructions. A ſmaller tide being leſs able to overcome them, is ſooner brought to its
maximum. The deviation however is very ſmall, not
exceeding ¼ of an hour, by which the neap-tide antici-
pates the theoretical time of its accompliſhment. It
would rather appear at firſt ſight that a ſmall tide would
take a longer time of going up a river than a great one.
And it may be ſo, although it be ſooner high water, becauſe the defalcation from its height may ſooner terminate its riſing. There is no difference obſerved in this
reſpect, when we compare the times of high water at
London Bridge and at the Buoy of the Nore. They
happen at the very ſame time in both places, and therefore the ſpring-tides and the neap-tides employ the ſame
time in going up the river Thames.

710. This agreement of obſervation with theory is
moſt fortunate ; and indeed without it, it would ſcarcely
have been poſſible to make any practical uſe of the theory.
But now, if we note the exact time of the high water
of ſpring-tide for any harbour, and the exact poſition of
the Sun and Moon at that time, we can eaſily make a
table of the monthly ſeries for that port, by noticing
the difference of that time from our table, and making
the ſame difference for every ſucceeding phaſis of the
tide.

711. But, in thus accommodating the theoretical
ſeries to any particular place, we muſt avoid a miſtake
                                                    commonly

commonly made by the compofers of tide tables. They give the hour of high water at full and change of the Moon, and this is confidered as fpring-tide. But perhaps there is no part in the world where that is the cafe. It is ufually the third tide after full or change that is the greateft of all, and the third tide after quadrature is, in moft places, the fmalleft tide. Now it is with the greateft tide that our monthly feries commences. Therefore, it is the hour of *this* tide that is to be taken for the hour of the harbour. But, as winds, frefhes, and other caufes, may affect any individual tide, we muft take the medium of many obfervations; and we muft take care that we do not confider as a fpring-tide one which is indeed the greateft, but chances to be enlarged by being a perigean tide.

When thefe precautions are taken, and the tides of one monthly feries marked, by applying the fame correction to the hours in the third column of Bernoulli's table (I.), it will be found to correfpond with obfervation with fufficient accuracy for all purpofes. In making the comparifon, it will be proper to take the medium between the fuperior and inferior tides of each day, both with refpect to time and height, becaufe the difference in thefe refpects between thofe two tides never entirely difappears.

712. The feries of changes which depend on the change of the Moon's declination are of more intricate comparifon, becaufe they are fo much implicated with

4 N

the

the changes depending on her diftance. But when freed
as much as poffible from this complication, and then eftimated by the medium between the fuperior and inferior
tide of the fame day, they agree extremely well with
the theoretical feries.

This, by the way, enables us to account for an obfervation which would otherwife appear inconfiftent with
the theory, which affirms that the fuperior tide is greateft
when the Moon is in the zenith (676.) The obfervation
is, that on the coafts of France and Spain the tides increafe as the Moon is nearer to the equator. But it was
fhewn in the fame article, that in latitudes below 45°,
the medium tide increafes as the Moon's declination diminifhes. Bernoulli juftly obferves that the tides with which
we are moft familiarly acquainted, and from which we
form all our rules, muft be confidered as derived from the
more perfect and regular tide formed in the wideft part
of the Atlantic ocean. Extenfive however as this may
be, it is too narrow for a complete quadrant of the fpheroid. Therefore it will grow more and more perfect as
its pole advances to the middle of the ocean ; and the
changes which happen on the bounding coafts, from
which the waters are drawn on all fides to make it up,
muft be vaftly more irregular, and will have but a partial refemblance to it. They will however refemble it
in its chief features. This tide being formed in a confiderably fouthern latitude, it becomes the more certain
that the medium tide will diminifh as the Moon's declination increafes. But although this feeming objection
                                        occurs

occurs on the French coafts, it is by no means the cafe on ours, or more to the north. We always obferve the fuperior tide to exceed the inferior, if the Moon have north declination.

The fame agreement with theory is obfervable in the folar tides, or in the effect of the Sun's declination. This indeed is much fmaller, but is obferved by reafon of its regularity. For although it is alfo complicated with the effects of the Sun's change of diftance, this effect having the fame period with his declination, one equation may comprehend them both. M. Bernoulli's obfervation, juft mentioned, tends to account for a very general opinion, that the greateft tides are in the equinoxes. I obferve, however, that this opinion is far from being well eftablifhed. Both Sturmy and Coleprefs fpeak of it as quite uncertain, and Wallis and Flamftead reject it. It is agreed on all hands that our winter tides exceed the fummer tides. This is thought to confirm that point of the theory which makes the Sun's accumulating force greater as his diftance diminifhes. I am doubtful of the applicability of this principle, becaufe the approach of the Sun caufes the Moon to recede, and her recefs is in the triplicate ratio of the Sun's approach. Her accumulating force is therefore diminifhed in the fefquiplicate ratio of the Sun's approach, and her influence on the phenomena of the tides exceeds the Sun's.

713. The changes arifing from the Moon's change of diftance are more confiderable than thofe arifing from

her

her change of declination. By reafon of their implica-
tion with thofe changes, the comparifon becomes more
difficult. M. Bernoulli did not find it fo fatisfactory.
They are, in general, much lefs than theory requires.
This is probably owing to the mutual effects of undulations which fhould differ very confiderably, but follow
each other too clofely. In M. de la Place's way of confidering the phenomena (to be mentioned afterwards) the
diminution in magnitude is very accountable, and, in
other refpects, the correfpondence is greatly improved.
When the Moon changes either in perigeo or apogeo,
the feries is confiderably deranged, becaufe the next
fpring-tide is formed in oppofite circumftances. The derangement is ftill greater, when the Moon is in perigee
or apogee in the quadratures. The two adjoining fpring-
tides fhould be regular, and the two neap-tides extremely
unequal.

714. We fhall firft confider the changes produced
on the times of full fea, and then the changes in the
height. M. Bernoulli has computed a table for both the
perigean and apogean diftance of the Moon, from which
it will appear what correction muft be made on the regular feries. It is computed precifely in the fame way
as the former, the only difference being in the magnitude of M and S, and we may imitate it by a conftruction fimilar to fig. 72. To make this table of eafier ufe,
M. Bernoulli introduces the important obfervation, that
the greateft tide is not, in any part of the world, the
                                                    tide

tide which happens on the day of new or full Moon, nor even the firft or the fecond tide after ; and that with refpect to the Atlantic Ocean, and all its coafts, it is very precifely the third tide. So that fhould we have high water in any port precifely at noon on the full or change of the Moon, and on the firft day of the month, the greateft tide happens at midnight on the fecond day of the month, or, expreffing it in the common way, it is the tide which happens when the Moon is a day and a half old. The fummit of the fpheroid is therefore 19 or 20 degrees to the eaftward of the Sun and Moon. At this diftance, the tendency of the accumulating forces of the Sun and Moon to complete the fpheroid, and to bring its pole precifely under them, is juft balanced by the tendency of the waters to fubfide. Therefore it is raifed no higher, nor can it come nearer to the Sun and Moon, becaufe then the obliquity of the force is diminifhed, on which the changing power depends. That this is the true caufe, appears from this, that it is, in like manner, on the third tide that all the changes are perceived which correfpond to the declination of the Moon, or her diftance from the Earth. Every thing falls out therefore as if the luminaries were 19 or 20 degrees eaftward of where they are, having the pole of the fpheroid in its theoretical fituation with refpect to this fictitious fituation of the luminaries. But, in fuch a cafe, were the Sun and Moon 20° farther eaftward, they would pafs the meridian 80 minutes, or one hour and 20 minutes later. Therefore $1^h 20'$ is added to the hours

of

of high water of the former table, calculated for the mean diftance of the Moon from the Earth. Thus, on the day of new Moon, we have not the fpring-tide, but the third tide before it, that is, the tide which fhould happen when the Moon is 20° weft of the Sun, or has the elongation 160°. This tide, in our former table, happens at 11^h 02'. Therefore add to this 1^h 20', and we have 0^h 22' for the hour of high water on the day of full and change for a harbour which would other-wife have high water when the Sun and Moon are on the meridian. In this way, by adding 1^h 20' to the hours of high water in the former table for a pofition of the luminaries 20° farther weft, it is accommodated to the obferved elongation of the Moon, this elongation being always fuppofed to be that of the Moon when fhe is on the meridian. Such then is the following table of M. Bernoulli. The firft column gives the Moon's elongation from the Sun, or from the oppofite point of the heavens, the Moon being then on the meridian. The fecond column gives the hour of high water when the Moon is in perigeo. The third column (which is the fame with the former table, with the addition of 1^h 20') gives the hour of high water when the Moon is at her mean diftance. And the fourth column gives the hour when fhe is in apogeo.

TABLE

TABLE II.

☾ α' ☉	☾ in Perigeo.	☾ in M. Dist.	☾ in Apogeo	☾ in Perigeo.	☾ in M. Dist.	☾ in Apogeo
0	−.18	−.22	−.27½	After. 18	After. 22	After. 27
10	−.49½	−.51½	−.54	9½	11½	14
20	1.20	1.20	1.20	—	—	—
30	1.50½	1.48½	1.46	9½	11½	14
40	2.22	2.18	2.12½	18	22	27½
50	2.54	2.48½	2.40½	26	31½	39½
60	3.27	3.20	3.10	33	40	50
70	4. 2½	3.55	3.44	37	45	56
80	4.41½	4.33½	4.22	38½	46½	58
90	5.26½	5.19½	5. 9½	33½	40½	50½
100	6.19	6.15	6. 9	22	25	31
110	7.20	7.20	7.20	—	—	—
120	8.21	8.25	8.31	21	25	31
130	9.13½	9.20½	9.30½	33	40	50
140	9.58½	10. 6½	10.18	38	46	58
150	10.37½	10.45	10.56	37	45	56
160	11.13	11.20	11.30	33	40	50
170	11.46	11.51½	11.59½	26	31	39
180	—.18	—.22	—.27½	18	22	27

(Columns 4–6 rotated labels: *Before the Moon's Southing.* and *After the M's Southing.*)

715. This table, though of confiderable fervice, be
g far preferable to the ufual tide tables, may fometime
:viate a few minutes from the truth, becaufe it is cal
ilated on the fuppofition of the luminaries being in th
ĮuĮator. But when they have confiderable declination
th

the horary arch of the equator may differ two or three
degrees from the elongation. But all this error will be
avoided by reckoning the high water from the time of
the Moon's fouthing, which is always given in our al-
manacks. This interval being always very fmall (never 12°) the error will be infenfible. For this reafon,
the three other columns are added, expreffing the priming of the tides on the Moon's fouthing.

To accommodate this table to all the changes of the
Moon's declination would require more calculation than
all the reft. We fhall come near enough to the truth, if
we leffen the minutes in the three hour-columns $\frac{1}{10}$ when
the Moon is in the equator, and increafe them as much
when fhe is in the tropic, and if we ufe them as they
ftand when fhe is in a middle fituation.

716. All that remains now, is to adjuft this general
table to the peculiar fituation of the port. Therefore,
collect a great number of obfervations of the hour of
high water at full or change of the Moon. In making
this collection, note particularly the hour on thofe days
where the Moon is new or full precifely at noon; for
this is the circumftance neceffary for the truth of the
elongations in the firft column of the table. A fmall
equation is neceffary in correcting the obferved hour of
high water, when the fyzigy is not at noon, becaufe in
this fituation of the luminaries, the tide lags 35' behind
the Sun in a day, as has been already fhewn. Suppofe
the lagging to be 36', this will make the equation 1½ minute

nute for every hour that the full or change has happened before or after the noon of that day. This correction muft be added to the obferved hour of high water, if the fyzigy was before noon, and fubtracted, if it happened after noon. Or, if we choofe to refer the time of high water to the Moon's fouthing, which, in general, is the beft method, we muft add a minute to the time between high fea and the Moon's fouthing for every hour and half that the fyzigy is before noon, and fubtract it if the fyzigy has happened after noon. For the tides prime 15′ in 24 hours.

717. Having thus obtained the medium hour of high water at full and change of the Moon, note the difference of it from 0ʰ 22′, and then make a table peculiar to that port, by adding that difference to all the numbers of the columns. The numbers of this table will give the hour of high water correfponding to the Moon's elongation for any other time. It will, however, always be more exact to refer the time to the Moon's fouthing, for the reafons already given.

By means of a table fo conftructed, the time of high water for the port, in any day of the lunation, may be depended on to lefs than a quarter of an hour, except the courfe of the tides be difturbed by winds or frefhes, which admit of no calculation. It might be brought nearer by a much more intricate calculation; but this is altogether unneceffary, on account of the irregularities arifing from thofe caufes.

4 O   It

It is not fo eafy to ftate in a feries the variations which happen in the *height* of the tides by the Moon's change of diftance, although they are greater than the variations in the *times* of high water. This is partly owing to the great differences which obtain in different ports between the greateft and fmalleft tides, and partly from the difficulty of expreffing the variations in fuch a manner as to be eafily underftood by thofe not familiar with mathematical computations. M. Bernoulli, whom we have followed in all the practical inferences from the phyfical theory, imagines that, notwithftanding the great difproportion between the fpring and neap-tides in different places, and the differences in the abfolute magnitudes of both, the middle between the higheft and loweft daily variations will proceed in very nearly the fame way as in theory. Inftead therefore of taking the values of M and S as already eftablifhed, he takes the height of fpring and neap-tides in any port as indicative of $M + S$ and $M - S$ for that port. Calling the fpring-tide A and the neap-tide B, this principle will give us $M = \dfrac{A + B}{2}$, and $S = \dfrac{A - B}{2}$. From thefe values of M and S he computes their apogean and perigean values, and then conftructs columns of the height of the tides, apogean and perigean, in the fame manner as the column already computed for the mean diftance of the Moon, that is, computing the parts mf and af (fig. 72.) of the whole tide ma feparately. The fame may be done with incomparably lefs trouble by our conftruction (fig. 72.) and the values $M = \dfrac{A + B}{2}$, and $S = \dfrac{A - B}{2}$.

Although

Although this is undoubtedly an approximation, and perhaps all the accuracy that is attainable, it is not founded on exact phyfical principles. The local proportion of A to B depends on circumftances peculiar to the place ; and we have no affurance that the changes of the lunar force will operate in the fame manner and proportion on thefe two quantities, however different. We are certain that it will not ; otherwife the proportion of fpring and neap-tides would be the fame in all harbours, however much the fprings may differ in different harbours. I compared Bernoulli's apogean and perigean tides, in about twenty inftances, felected from the obfervations at Breft and St Malo, where the abfolute quantities differ very widely. I was furprifed, but not convinced, by the agreement. I am however perfuaded that the table is of great ufe, and have therefore inferted it, as a model by which a table may eafily be computed for any harbour, employing the fpring-tide and neaptide heights obferved in that harbour as the A and B for that place. The table is, like the laft, accommodated to the eafterly deviation of the pole of the fpheroid from its theoretical place.

It appears from this table, and alfo from the laft, that the neap-tides are much more affected by the inequalities of the forces than the fpring-tides are. The neap-tides vary from 70 to 128, and the fprings from 90 to 114. The firft is almoft doubled, the laft is augmented but $\frac{1}{4}$.

TABLE

TABLE III.

Elongation ☽ ☉	HEIGHT OF THE TIDE.		
	☽ in Perigeo.	☽ in M. Dist.	☽ in Apogeo.
0	0,99A+0,15B	0,88A+0,12B	0,79A+0,08B
10	1,10A+0,04B	0,97A+0,03B	0,87A+0,02B
20	1,14A+0,00B	1,00A+0,00B	0,90A+0,00B
30	1,10A+0,04B	0,97A+0,03B	0,87A+0,02B
40	0,99A+0,15B	0,88A+0,12B	0,79A+0,08B
50	0,85A+0,32B	0,75A+0,25B	0,68A+0,18B
60	0,67A+0,53B	0,59A+0,41B	0,53A+0,29B
70	0,46A+0,75B	0,41A+0,59B	0,37A+0,41B
80	0,28A+0,96B	0,25A+0,75B	0,23A+0,53B
90	0,13A+1,13B	0,12A+0,88B	0,11A+0,62B
100	0,03A+1,24B	0,03A+0,97B	0,03A+0,68B
110	0,00A+1,28B	0,00A+1,00B	0,00A+0,70B
120	0,03A+1,24B	0,03A+0,97B	0,03A+0,68B
130	0,13A+1,13B	0,12A+0,88B	0,11A+0,62B
140	0,28A+0,96B	0,25A+0,75B	0,23A+0,53B
150	0,46A+0,75B	0,41A+0,59B	0,37A+0,41B
160	0,67A+0,53B	0,59A+0,41B	0,53A+0,29B
170	0,85A+0,32B	0,75A+0,25B	0,68A+0,18B
180	0,99A+0,15B	0,88A+0,12B	0,79A+0,08B

719. The attentive reader cannot but observe that all the tables of this monthly conftruction muft be very imperfect, although their numbers are perfectly accurate, becaufe, in the courfe of a month, the declination and diftance of the Moon vary, independently of each other,

other, through all their poffible magnitudes. The laft table is the only one that is immediately applicable, by interpolation. It would require feveral tables of the fame extent, to give us a fet of equations, to be applied to the original table of art. 667.; and the computation would become as troublefome for this approximation as the calculation of the exact value, taking in every circumftance that can affect the queftion. For that calculation requires only the computation of two right-angled fpherical triangles, preparatory to the calculation of the place of high water. But, with all thefe imperfections, M. Bernoulli's fecond table is much more exact than any tide table yet publifhed,

———

Such, on the whole, is the information furnifhed by the doctrine of univerfal gravitation concerning this curious and important phenomenon. It is undoubtedly the moft irrefragable argument that we have for the truth and univerfality of this doctrine, and at the fame time for the fimplicity of the whole conftitution of the folar fyftem, fo far as it can be confidered mechanically. No new principle is required for an operation of nature fo unlike all the other phenomena in the fyftem.

720. The method which I have followed in the inveftigation is nearly the fame with that of its illuftrious difcoverer. We have contented ourfelves with fhewing various feriefes of phenomena, which tally fo well with the legitimate confequences of the theory, that the real

· fource

fource of them can no longer be doubted. And, notwithftanding the various deviations from thofe confequences, arifing from other circumftances, we have obtained practical rules, which make the mariner pretty
well acquainted with the general courfe of the tides ;
fufficiently to put him on his guard againft the dangers
he runs by grofsly miftaking them, and even enabling
him to take advantage of the courfe of the tide for profecuting his voyage.   Still, however, a great ftore of local information is neceffary.   For there are fome parts of
the ocean, where the tides follow an order extremely unlike what we have defcribed.   The bar of Tonquin in
China is one of the moft remarkable ; and its chief peculiarity confifts in its having but one tide in each lunar
day.   It has been traced to the cooperation of two great
tides, coming from oppofite quarters, with almoft fix
hours of difference in the time of high water.   The refult of which is, that the compound tide is the excefs of
the one above the other, forming a high water when the
fum of both their elevations is a maximum.   Dr Halley
has given a very diftinct explanation of this tide in N° 162
of the Philofophical Tranfactions.

721.   A very different method of inveftigating this
and a fimilar phenomenon has been employed by the eminent mathematicians D'Alembert and La Place, in which
M. La Place, who makes this a chief article of his Mechanique Celefte, deduces the whole directly from the
interior mechanifm of hydroftatical undulations.   His
main inferences perfectly agree with thofe already delivered.

vered. The method of Newton and Bernoulli has been preferred here, becaufe by this means the connexion with the operation of univerfal gravitation is much better kept in fight. At the fame time La Place's method allows us, in fome cafes, to ftate the individual fact more nearly as it occurs, without confidering it as the modification of another fact that is more general. But it may be doubted, whether La Place has explained all the variety of phenomena. His whole application is limited by the data which furnifh the arbitrary quantities in his equations. Thefe being wholly taken from the obfervations in the ports of France and Spain, it may be queftioned whether the famenefs, arifing from the latitude being fo near 45°, may not have made the ingenious author fimplify too much his theory. He confiders every clafs of phenomena as operations completely accomplifhed, and the ocean at the end of the action of any one of the forces as in a ftate of indifference, ready for the free operation of the next. For example, the equality of the fuperior and inferior tides of one day is deduced by La Place immediately from the circumftance of the ocean being of nearly an uniform depth, faying that the fmall inferior tide is not affected by the greatnefs of the preceding fuperior tide, becaufe the obftructions are fuch that all motions ceafe very foon, almoft immediately after the force has ceafed to act. We doubt the truth of the near uniformity of the fea's depth. The unequal tides are confeffedly moft remarkable on the coafts, where the depth is the moft unequal. The other

principle,

principle, that the effects of primitive motions are all
obliterated, and therefore every tide is the completed
operation of the prefent force, is ftill more queftionable.
It is well known that the roll of a great ftorm in the
Bay of Bifcay is very fenfible indeed for three days. Of
this we have had repeated experience. The *fuperficial*
agitation of a ftorm (for it is no more) is nothing in
comparifon with the huge uniform momentum of a tide ;
and the greateft ftorm, even while it blows, cannot raife
the tide three feet ; nor does it even then change what
we have called the tide, the difference between high and
low water ; it raifes or keeps down both nearly alike.
Befides, how will M. La Place account for the undeniable duration of every tide wave on the coafts of Europe and America for a day and a half ? There can be
no queftion about this, becaufe the courfe of the tides
during a month is precifely conformable to it. The tide
which bears the mark of the perigean tide is not the
tide which happens when the Moon is in perigeo, but
the third following that tide, juft as in the fprings and
neaps. In like manner, it is obferved at Breft, without
one exception for fix years, that the morning or fuperior
tide at new Moon is fmaller than the înferior tide in
fummer. In winter it is the contrary, not, however,
with fuch conftant accuracy. Now, it fhould be juft the
contrary, if the tides obferved were the tides correfponding with the then ftate of the forces. But they are not.
They are tides correfponding with the ftate of the forces
thirty-fix hours before. (See Mem. Acad. Par. 1720,
                                                          P.

p. 206, duodecimo). It is the fame at full Moon, that is, the morning tide in fummer is lefs than the evening tide. The morning tide correfponding to the then ftate of the forces is what we have called an inferior tide, the Moon being then under the horizon, with fouth declination. The tide therefore fhould be greater than the fubfequent or evening, or fuperior tide. But, like the laft example, it is the tide correfponding to the forces in action thirty-fix hours before. Can we now deny that the prefent ftate of the waters is affected by the action of forces which have ceafed thirty-fix hours ago? and if this be granted, it is impoffible that two tides immediately fucceeding can be very unequal. The contrary can be fhewn in an experiment perfectly refembling the great tides of the ocean. An apparatus, made for exhibiting the appearance of a reciprocating fpring, was fo conftructed that one of its runnings was very fudden and copious, and the next was moderate and flow. It emptied into a fmall bafon, which communicated with a long and narrow horizontal channel, fhut at the far end, the bafon emptying itfelf by a fmall fpout on the oppofite fide. Thus, two very unequal floods and ebbs prefented themfelves at the mouth of this channel, and fent a wave along it, which, at the firft, was very unequal. But, when it was mixed with the returning wave from the far end, they were foon brought to an apparent equality. The experiment appearing curious, it was profecuted, by various changes of the apparatus; and feveral effects tended very much to explain fome of the more

4 P   fingular

fingular appearances of the tides.   There is an example
of the continuance of former impreffions in the tides
among the weftern iflands of Scotland, that confiderably
refembles the tide on the bar of Tonquin.   The general
courfe of the flood round the little ifland of Berneray is
N. E. and that of the ebb is S W.   But at a certain
time in the fpring, both flood and ebb run N. E. during
twelve hours, and the next flood and ebb run S. W.
The contrary happens in autumn.   Yet in the offing,
the flood and ebb hold their regular courfes.   This greatly
refembles the tide at Tonquin, and alfo the Grecian
Euripus.

722.   The reader will recollect that we ftated as our
opinion that, in confequence of the inertia of the waters, the pole of the ocean is always to the eaftward of
its theoretical place.   For which reafon, the figure actually attained by the ocean is not a figure of equilibra-
tion.   Did the Earth ftand ftill, it would foon be brought
to its proper pofition, and completed to its due form.
Therefore, there is always a motion *towards* this com-
pletion : *And this motion is obftructed.*   Hence we apprehend that there muft be a perpetual current of the waters, efpecially in the tropical regions, from eaft to weft.
We cannot fee how this can be avoided ; and we think
that it is eftablifhed as a matter of nautical obfervation.
In regard to the Atlantic, this feems to be a general opinion of the navigators.   There are two very excellent
journals of voyages from Stockholm to China, by Cap-
tain

tain Eckhart, in which there is a very frequent comparifon of the fhip's reckoning with lunar obfervations and
the arrivals on known coafts, from which we cannot help
inferring the fame general current in the Indian and Ethiopic feas. It feems ther▼ore to obtain over the whole.
The part of this current which diffufes itfelf into the Atlantic is but fmall, it having a freer paffage ftraight forward. But the part thus diffufed produces the gulf
ftream, in its way along the American coafts, and efcapes
round the north capes of Europe and America. In all
probability, a foutherly current may be obferved in the
ftraits which feparate America from the Afiatic continent. The whole amount of this motion cannot be confiderable, but there muft be fome, if there be two circumpolar communications between the great eaftern and
weftern divifions of the ocean. Without this, it muft
be reduced to a reciprocating motion too intricate for inveftigation.

723. There is another circumftance which feems to
ftrengthen our confidence in the reality of this wefterly
current of the ocean. The gravity of the waters being
more diminifhed in conjunction and oppofition than it is
augmented in quadrature with the acting luminary, each
particle tends to recede from the centre, and to defcribe
a larger circle, employing a longer time. Here is a tendency or *nifus* to a relative motion wefterly. Water,
being almoft perfectly fluid, will obey this tendency, and
in time acquire fuch a motion, were it not obftructed by

4 P 2   folid

folid obſtacles.   But ſome effeƈt muſt remain, too intricate to admit any calculation, and perhaps not ultimately
ſenſible.

724.   If the height of the atmoſphere be equal to the
radius of the Earth, we ſhall have a tide in the air double
of that in the ocean.   When all the affeƈting circumſtances are conſidered, it appears that an ebb and flood
of the atmoſphere may differ in elevation about 120 feet.
This might be ſenſible by affeƈting the barometer.   True,
the gravity of the mercury is alſo diminiſhed, but not ſo
much as that of the more diſtant air.   But the height of
the atmoſphere is too ſmall to give riſe to any ſuch tides.
They cannot ſenſibly exceed thoſe of the ocean, and this
cannot change the height of the mercury in the barometer $\frac{1}{100}$ of an inch.   Profeſſor Toaldo at Padua kept a
regiſter of the barometer for more than thirty years.   He
has added into one ſum all the mercurial heights obſerved
at new Moon.   Another ſum was made of all the heights
obſerved in the quadratures ; another of the perigean ;
and another of the apogean heights, &c. &c.   He thinks
that differences were obſerved in thoſe ſums ſufficient for
proving the accumulation and compreſſion of the air by
its unequal gravitation to the Moon.   Thus, the apogean
heights exceeded the perigean by 14 inches.   The heights
in ſyzigy exceeded thoſe in quadrature by 11 inches.
(See Mem. Berlin 1777, and a book expreſsly on the ſub-
jeƈt).

     But there is another effeƈt of this diſturbing force
                              .   which

which may be much more fenfible, namely, the general
wefterly current of the air. M. D'Alembert has inveftigated this with great care, and fingular addrefs, and has
proved that there muft be a wefterly current in the tropical regions, at the rate of eight feet nearly in a fecond.
This is a very adequate caufe of the trade winds which
are obferved between the tropics. It is indeed increafed
by the rarefaction of the air occafioned by the heat of the
Sun, which expands the air heated by the ground, and
it is both raifed and diffufed laterally. When the Sun
has paffed the meridian a proper number of degrees, the
air muft now cool, and in cooling contract behind the
Sun. Air from the eaft comes in greater abundance
than from any other quarter to fupply the vacancy.

725. The difk of Jupiter, when viewed through a
good telefcope, is diftinguifhable into zones, like a bit of
ftriped fatin. Thefe zones, or belts, are of changeable
breadth and pofition, but all parallel to his equator.
Therefore they are not attached to his furface, but float
on it, as clouds float in our atmofphere. This Earth
will have fomewhat of this appearance, if viewed from the
Moon. For each climate has a ftate of the fky peculiar
in fome degree to itfelf in this refpect, and there muft
be a fort of famenefs in one climate all round the globe.
A feries of obfervations on a particular fpot of Jupiter's
furface demonftrate his rotation in $9^h 56'$. Spots have
been obferved in the belts, which have lafted fo long as
to make feveral revolutions before they were effaced.
They

They appear to require a minute or two more for their rotation, and therefore have a wefterly motion relative to the firm furface of the planet. This however cannot be depended on from the time of their rotation. But a few obfervations have been had of fpots in the vicinity of the fixed fpot of his furface, and here the relative motion weftward was diftinctly obferved. M. Schroeter at Manheim has obferved the atmofphere of Jupiter with great care, and finds it exceedingly variable ; and fpots are obferved to change their fituations with amazing rapidity, with great irregularity, but moft commonly eaftward. The motions and changes are fo rapid, and fo extenfive, that we can fcarcely confider them as the transference of matter from one place to another. They more refemble the changes which happen in our atmofphere, which are fometimes progreffive, over a great tract of the country. The ftorm in 1772 was felt from Siberia to America in fucceffion. The gale blew from the weft, but the chemical operation which produced it was in the oppofite direction, being firft obferved in Siberia ; three days afterward, it was felt at St Peterfburg ; two days after this, at Berlin ; two days more, it was in Britain ; and feven days after, it was felt in North America. Here then, while a fpectator on the Earth faw the clouds moving to the eaftward, a fpectator in the Moon would fee the change of appearance proceed from eaft to weft. The motions in the atmofphere of Jupiter muft be very complicated, becaufe they are the joint operation of four fatellites. The inequality of gravitation to the

firft

firft fatellite muft be very great. And as each fatellite produces a peculiar tide, the combination of all their actions muft be very intricate. We can draw no conclufions from the variable fpots, becaufe their change of place is no proof of the actual transference of matter.

Such a relative motion in our atmofphere and in the ocean may affect the rotation, retarding it, by its action on the eaftern furface of every obftacle. Yet no change is obferved. The year, and the periods of the planets, in the time of Ptolemy are the fame with the prefent, that is, contain the fame number of rotations of the Earth. Perhaps a compenfation is maintained by this means for the acceleration that fhould arife from the transference of foil from the high land to the bottom of the fea, where it is moving round the axis with diminifhed velocity.

726. With this we conclude our account of phyfical aftronomy, a department of natural philofophy which fhould ever be cherifhed with peculiar affection by all who think well of human nature. There is none in which the accefs to well founded knowledge feems fo effectally barred againft us, and yet there is none in which we have made fuch unqueftionable progrefs ; none in which we have acquired knowledge fo uncontrovertibly fupported, or fo complete. How much therefore are we indebted to the man who laid the magnificent fcene open to our view, and who gave us the optics by which we can examine its moft extenfive, and its moft minute

parts !

parts ! For Newton not only taught us all that we know of the celeſtial mechaniſm, but alſo gave us the mathematics, without which it would have remained unſeen.

    ‘ *Tu Pater et rerum Inventor.   Tu patria nobis*
    ‘ *Suppeditas præcepta, tuiſque ex inclyte chartis*
    ‘ *Floriferis ut apes in ſaltibus omnia libant,*
    ‘ *Omnia nos itidem depaſcimur aurea dicta*
    ‘ *Aurea, perpetua ſemper digniſſima vitâ.* ’

                                  LUCRETIUS.

For ſurely, the leſſons are precious by which we are taught a ſyſtem of doctrine which cannot be ſhaken, or ſhare that fluctuation which has attached to all other ſpeculations of curious man. But this cannot fail us, becauſe it is nothing but a well ordered narration of facts, preſenting the events of nature to us in a way that at once points out their ſubordination, and moſt of their relations. While the magnificence of the objects commands reſpect, and perhaps raiſes our opinion of the excellence of human reaſon as high as is juſtifiable, we ſhould ever keep in mind that Newton's ſucceſs was owing to the modeſty of his procedure. He peremptorily refiſted all diſpoſition to ſpeculate beyond the province of human intellect, conſcious that all attainable ſcience conſiſted in carefully aſcertaining nature's own laws, and that every attempt to explain an ultimate law of nature by aſſigning its cauſe is abſurd in itſelf, againſt the acknowledged laws of judgement, and will moſt certainly lead to error. It is only by following his example that we can hope for his ſucceſs.

                                         It

It is furely another great recommendation of this branch of natural philofophy, that it is fo fimple. One fingle agent, a force decreafing as the fquare of the diftance increafes, is, of itfelf, adequate to the production of all the movements of the folar fyftem. If the direction of the projection do not pafs through the centre of gravity, the body will not only defcribe an ellipfe round the central body, but will alfo turn round its axis. By this rotation, the body will alter its form. But the fame power enables it to affume a new form, which is perfectly fymmetrical, and is permanent. This new form, however, in confequence of the univerfality of gravitation, induces a new motion in the body, by which the pofition of the axis is flowly changed, and the whole hoft of heaven appears to the inhabitants of this Earth to change its motions. Laftly, if the revolving planet have a covering of fluid matter, this fluid is thrown into certain regular undulations, which are produced and modified by the fame power.

Thus we fee that, by following this fimple fact of gravitation of every particle of matter to every other particle, through all its complications, we find an explanation of almoft every phenomenon of the folar fyftem that has engaged the attention of the philofopher, and that nothing more is needed for the explanation. Till we were put on this track of inveftigation, thefe different movements were folitary facts ; and, being fo extremely unlike, the wit of man would certainly have attempted to explain them by caufes equally diffi-

4 Q   milar.

milar. The happy detection of this simple and easily observed principle, by a genius qualified for following it into its various consequences, has freed us from numberless errors, into which we must have continually run while pertinaciously proceeding in an improper path. But this detection has not merely saved us from errors, but, which is most remarkable, it has brought into view many circumstances in the phenomena themselves, many peculiarities of motion, which would never have been observed by us, had we not gotten this monitor, pointing out to us where to look for peculiarities. We should never have been able to predict, with such wonderful precision, the complicated motions of some of the planets, had we not had this key to all the equations by which every deviation from regular elliptical motion is expressed.

On all these accounts, physical astronomy, or the mechanism of the celestial motions, is a beautiful department of science. I do not know any body of doctrine so comprehensive, and yet so exceedingly simple ; and this consideration made me the more readily accede to those reasons of scientific propriety which point it out as the first article of a course of mechanical philosophy. Its simplicity makes it easy, and the exquisite agreement with observation makes it a fine example of the truth and competency of our dynamical doctrines.

727. But it has other recommendations, of a far greater value. Nothing surely so much engages a heart possessed
of

of a proper fenfibility, as the contemplation of order and harmony. No philofophy is requifite for being fufceptible of this impreffion. We fee it influence the conduct of the moft uncultivated. What elfe does man aim at in all the buftle of cultivated fociety? Nay, even the favage makes fome rude aim at order and ornament.

But what we contemplate in the folar fyftem is fomething more than mere order and fymmetry, fuch as may be obferved in a fine fpecimen of cryftallization. The order of the folar fyftem is made up of many palpable *fubferviences*, where we fee one thing plainly done for the fake of another thing. And, to render this ftill more interefting, a manifeft *utility* appears in every circumftance of the conftitution of the fyftem, as far as we underftand its applicability to what we conceive to be ufeful purpofes. We can mean nothing by utility but the fubferviency to the enjoyments of fentient beings. Our opportunities for obfervations of this kind are no doubt very limited, confined to our own fublunary habitation. But this circumfcribed fcene of obfervation is even crowded with examples of utility. Surely it is unneceffary to recal our attention to the numberlefs adaptations of the fyftematic connexion with the Sun and Moon to the continuance and the diffufion of the means of animal life and enjoyment. As our knowledge of the celeftial phenomena is enlarged, the probability becomes ftronger that other planets are alfo ftored with inhabitants who fhare with

4 Q 2.   us

us the Creator's bounty. Their rotation, and the evident changes that we fee going on in their atmofpheres, fo much refemble what we experience here, that I imagine that no man, who clearly conceives them, can fhut out the thought that thefe planets are inhabited by fentient beings. And there is nothing to forbid us from fuppofing that there is the fame inexhauftible ftore of fubordinate contrivance for their accommodation that we fee here for living creatures in every fituation, with appropriate forms, defires, and abilities. I fear not to appeal to the heart of every man who has learned fo much of the celeftial phenomena, even the man who fcouts this opinion, whether he does not feel the difpofition to entertain it. And I infift on it, that fome good reafon is required for rejecting it.

728. When beholding all this, it is impoffible to prevent the furmife, at leaft, of purpofe, defign, and contrivance, from arifing in the mind. We may try to fhut it out—We may be convinced, that to allege any purpofe as an argument for the reality of any difputed fact, is againft the rules of good reafoning, 'and that final caufes are improper topics of argument. But we cannot hinder the anatomift, who obferves the exquifite adaptation of every circumftance in the eye to the forming and rendering vivid and diftinct a picture of external objects, from believing that the eye was made for feeing— or the hand for handling. Neither can we prevent our
heart

heart from fuggefting the thought of tranfcendent wifdom, when we contemplate the exquifite fitnefs and adjuftment which the mechanifm of the folar fyftem exhibits
in all its parts.

729. Newton was certainly thus affected, when he
took a confiderate view of all his own difcoveries, and
perceived the almoft eternal order and harmony which refults from the fimple and unmixed operation of univerfal gravitation. This fingle fact produces all this fair
order and utility. Newton was a mathematician, and
faw that the law of gravitation obferved in the fyftem is
the only one that can fecure the continuance of order.
He was a philofopher, and faw that it was a contingent
law of gravitation, and might have been otherwife. It
therefore appeared to Newton, as it would to any unpre-
judiced mind, a law of gravitation felected as the moft
proper, out of many that were equally poffible; it appeared to be a choice, the act of a mind, which comprehended the extent of its influence, and intended the
advantages of its operation, being prompted by the defire of giving happinefs to the works of almighty power.

Impreffed with fuch thoughts, Newton breaks out into
the following exclamation. ‘ *Elegantiffima hæcce compages*
‘ *Solis Planetarum et Cometarum, non nifi confilio et dominio*
‘ *Entis cujufdam potentis et intelligentis oriri potuit. Hæc*
‘ *omnia regit, non ut anima mundi, fed ut univerforum*
‘ *Dominus mundorum. Et propter dominium Dominus*
‘ *Deus,*

' *Deus,* Παντοκρατωρ, *dici folet. Deitas eſt dominatio Dei,*
' *non in corpus proprium, uti fentiunt quibus Deus eſt ani-*
' *ma mundi, fed in fervos,*' &c.

Thefe were the effufions of an affectionate heart,
fympathifing with the enjoyment of thofe who fhared
with him the advantages of their fituation. Yet Newton
did not know the full extent of the harmony that he had
difcovered. He thought that, in the courfe of ages, things
would go into diforder, and need the reftoring hand of
God. But, as has been already obferved (543.), De la
Grange has demonftrated that no fuch diforder will happen. The greateft deviations from the moſt regular motions will be almoft infenfible, and they are all periodical,
waneing to nothing, and again rifing to their fmall maximum.

730. Thefe are furely pleafing thoughts to a cultivated mind. It is not furprifing therefore that men of
affectionate hearts fhould too fondly indulge them, and
that they fhould fometimes be miftaken in their notions
of the purpofes anfwered by fome of the infinitely varied and complicated phenomena of the univerfe. ' And
it would be nothing but what we have met with in other
paths of fpeculation, fhould we fee them confider a fubferviency to this fancied purpofe as an argument that an
operation of nature is effected in one way, and not in
another. In this way, the employment of final caufes
has fometimes obftructed the progrefs of knowledge,
and

and has been productive of error. But the impropriety of this kind of argumentation proceeds chiefly from the great chance of our being miftaken with refpect to the aim of nature on the occasion. Could this be properly eftablifhed as a fact, and could the fubferviency of a precife mode of accomplifhing a particular operation be as clearly made out, I apprehend that, however unwilling the logician may be to admit this as a good reafon, he cannot help feeling its great force. That this is true, is plain from the rules of evidence that are admitted in all courts; where a purpofe being proved, the fubferviency of a certain deed to that purpofe is allowed to be evidence that this was the intention in the commiffion of that deed. It is, however, very rarely indeed that fuch argument can be ufed, or that it is wanted, and it never fuperfedes the inveftigation of the efficient caufe.

731. But fpeculative men have of late years fhewn a wonderful hoftility to final caufes. Lord Bacon had faid, more wittily than juftly, that all ufe of final caufes fhould be banifhed from philofophy, becaufe, ' like Veftals, ' they produce nothing. ' This is not hiftorically true; for much has been difcovered by refearches conducted *entirely* by notions of final caufes. What other evidence have we for all that we know concerning the nature of man? Is not this a part of the book of Nature, and fome of its moft beautiful pages? We know them only by the

the appearances of defign, that is, by the adaptations of things in evident fubferviency to certain refults. Are there no fuch adaptations to be feen, except in the works of man? Nature is crowded with them on every hand, and fome of her moft important operations have been afcertained by attending to them. Dr Harvey difcovered the circulation of the blood in this very way. He faw that the valves in the arteries and veins were conftructed precifely like thofe of a double forcing pump, and that the mufcles of the heart were alfo fitted for an alternate fyftole and diaftole, fo correfponding to the ftructure of thofe valves, that the whole was fit for performing fuch an office. With boldnefs therefore he afferted that the beatings of the heart were the ftrokes of this pump; and, laying the heart of a living animal open to the view, he had the pleafure of feeing the alternate expanfion and contractions of its auricles and ventricles, exactly as he had expected. Here was a difcovery, as curious, as great, as important, as univerfal gravitation. In precifely the fame way have all the difcoveries in anatomy and phyfiology been made. A new object is feen. The difcoverer immediately examines its ftructure—why? To fee what it can perform; and if he fees a number of coadaptations to a particular purpofe, he does not hefitate to fay, ' this is its purpofe.' He has often been miftaken; but the miftakes have been gradually corrected— how? By difcovering what is the real ftructure, and what the thing is really fit for performing. The anato-
                                                          mift

mift never imagines that what he has difcovered is of no
ufe. *

732. So far therefore from banifhing the confideration of final caufes from our difcuffions, it would look
more like philofophy, more like the love of true wifdom,
and it would tafte lefs of an idle curiofity, were we to
multiply our refearches in thofe departments of nature
where final caufes are the chief objects of our attention—the ftructure and œconomy of organifed bodies
in the animal and vegetable kingdoms. I cannot help
remarking, with regret, that of late years, the tafte
of naturalifts has greatly changed, and, in my hum-
ble opinion, for the worfe. The ftudy of inert matter has fupplanted that of animal life. Chemiftry and
mineralogy are almoft the fole objects of attention. Nay,
the *ruins* of nature, the fhattered relicks of a former
world, feems a more engaging object than the numberlefs beauties that now adorn the prefent furface of our
globe. I acknowledge that, even in thofe inanimate
works, God has not left himfelf without a witnefs. Yet
furely

* I would earneftly recommend to my young readers fome
excellent remarks on the argument of final caufes (without
which Cicero thought that there is no philofophy) in the
preface by the editor of Derham's Phyfico-Theology, publifhed at London in 1798. He there confiders the proper
province of this argument, its ufe, and incautious abufe, with
the greateft perfpicuity and judgement.

4 R

furely we do not, in the bowels of the Earth, nor even in the curious operations of chemical affinity, fee fo palpably, or fo pleafantly, the incomprehenfible wifdom and the providential beneficence of the Father of all, as in the animated objects. *

It is not eafy to account for it, and perhaps the explanation would not be very agreeable, why many naturalifts fo faftidioufly avoid fuch views of nature as tend to lead the mind to the thoughts of its Author. We fee them even anxious to weaken every argument for the appearance of defign in the conftruction and operations of nature. One fhould think, that, on the contrary, fuch appearances would be moft welcome, and that nothing would be more dreary and comfortlefs than the belief that chance or fate rules all the events of nature.

733. I have been led into thefe reflections by reading a paffage in M. de la Place's beautiful Synopfis of the Newtonian Philofophy, publifhed by him in 1796, under

---

* A naturalift repeats a faying of his own to the celebrated cryftallographer Haüy, ' That, in future, the name of God ' would be as diftinctly written on a cryftal as it had hitherto ' been feen in the heavens. ' This feems to me little better than declamation, if it be not irony. Haüy is the difcoverer of the *neceffity* of the cryftalline forms ; and this philofopher thinks himfelf the difcoverer of a fimilar neceffity in the celeftial mechanifm. (See *Nicholfon's Journal, October* 1804, *p.* 87.)

under the title of *Syſtême du Monde*. In the whole of this work, the author miſſes no opportunity of leſſening the impreſſion that might be made by the peculiar ſuitableneſs of any circumſtance in the conſtitution of the ſolar ſyſtem to render it a ſcene of habitation and enjoyment to ſentient beings, or which might lead the mind to the notion of the ſyſtem's being contrived for any purpoſe whatever. He ſometimes, on the contrary, endeavours to ſhew how the alleged purpoſe may be much better accompliſhed in ſome other way. He labours to leave a general impreſſion on the mind, that the whole frame is the neceſſary reſult of the primitive and eſſential properties of matter, and that it could not be any thing but what it is. He indeed concludes, like the illuſtrious Newton, with a ſurvey of all that has been done and diſcovered, followed by ſome reflections, ſuggeſted (as he ſays) by this ſurvey.

' Aſtronomy,' ſays M. de la Place, ' in its preſent ſtate, ' is unqueſtionably the moſt brilliant ſpecimen of the pow- ' ers of the human underſtanding. ' He does not however tell us how this is ſo manifeſt. He does not ſay that this object, which has engaged, and ſo properly occupied this fine underſtanding, has any thing to juſtify the choice, either on account of its beautiful ſymmetry, or exquiſite contrivance, or multifarious utility ; or, in ſhort, that is an object that is worth looking at. But he gives us to underſtand that aſtronomy has now taught us how much we were miſtaken, in thinking ourſelves an important part of the univerſe, for whoſe accommo-

4 R 2

dation

dation much has been done, as if we were objects of peculiar care.   But we have been punifhed, fays he, for
thefe miftaken notions of felf-importance, by the foolifh
anxieties to which they have given rife, and by the fub-
jugation to which we have fubmitted, while under the
influence of thefe fuperftitious terrors.   Miftaking our
relations to the reft of the univerfe, focial order has
been fuppofed to have other foundations than juftice and
truth, and an abominable maxim has been admitted, that
it was fometimes ufeful to deceive and to fubdue mankind, in order to fecure the happinefs of fociety.   But
nature refumes her rights, and cruel experience has fhewn
that fhe will not allow thofe facred laws to be broken
with impunity.

734.   I think it will require fome inveftigation before
we can find out what connexion there is between the
difcoveries of Sir Ifaac Newton and this myfterious detection that M. de la Place has at laft deduced from the
furvey.   It is communicated in the dark words of an
oracle, and we are left to interpret for ourfelves.   I can
affix no meaning but this, that ignorance and felf-conceit
have made us imagine that this Earth is the centre, and
the principal object of the univerfe, and that all that we
fee derives its value from its fubferviency to this Earth,
and to man its chief inhabitant.   We fondly imagined
that we are the objects of peculiar care,—that it is for
us that the magnificent fpectacle is difplayed,—and that
our fortunes are to be read in the ftarry heavens.   But it
is

is now demonſtrated that this Earth, when compared, even with ſome ſingle objeĉts of our ſyſtem, is but like a peppercorn. The whole ſyſtem is but as a point in the univerſe. How inſignificant then are we! But we have been juſtly puniſhed for our ſelf-conceit, by imagining that the ſtars influence our fortunes, and have made ourſelves the willing dupes of aſtrologers and footh-ſayers.

Thus far I think that M. de la Place's words have ſome meaning, but, ſurely, very little importance ; nor did it call for any congratulatory addreſs to his contemporaries on their emancipation from ſuch fears. It is more than a century ſince all thoughts of the central ſituation and great bulk of the Earth, and of the influence of the ſtars on human affairs, have been exploded and forgotten.

But the remaining part of the remarks, about ſocial order, and truth, and juſtice, and about deceiving and enſlaving mankind, in order to ſecure their happineſs, is more myſterious. ' More is meant than meets the ear. ' M. de la Place carefully abſtains, through the whole of this performance, from all reference to a Contriver, Creator, or Governor of the univerſe, particularly in the preſent refleĉtions, *which are ſo pointedly contraſted* with the concluding refleĉtions of the great Newton. The oppoſition is ſo remarkable, that it ſtartles every reader who has peruſed the Principia. I cannot but ſuſpeĉt that M. de la Place would here inſinuate that the doĉtrine of a Deity, the Maker and Governor of this World, and of

his

his peculiar attention to the conduct of men, is not
confiftent with truth ; and that the fanctions of religion,
which have long been venerated as the great fecurity of
fociety, are as little confiftent with juftice. The duties
which we are faid to owe to this Deity, and the terrors
of punifhment in a future ftate of exiftence for the neglect of them, have enabled wicked men to enflave the
world, fubjecting mankind to an oppreffive hierarchy, or
to fome temporal tyrant. The priefthood has, in all ages
and nations, been the great fupport of the defpot's
throne. But now, man has refumed his natural rights.
The throne and the altar are overturned, and truth and
juftice are the order of the day.

735. This is by no means a groundlefs interpretation of De la Place's words. He has given abundant
proofs of thefe being his fentiments. It accords completely with his anxious endeavours, on all occafions, to
flatten or deprefs every thing that has the appearance of
order, beauty, or fubferviency, and to refolve all into the
irrefiftible operation of the effential properties of matter.

736. Of all the marks of purpofe and of wife contrivance in the folar fyftem, the moft confpicuous is the
felection of a gravitation in the inverfe duplicate ratio of
the diftances. Till within thefe few eventful years, it
has been the profeffed admiration of philofophers of all
fects. Even the materialifts have not always been on
their guard, nor taken care to fupprefs their wonder at
                                                    the

the almoft eternal duration and order which it fecures to the folar fyftem.   But M. de la Place annihilates at once all the wifdom of this fele£tion, by faying that this law of gravitation is effential to all qualities that are diffufed from a centre.   It is the law of action inherent in an atom of matter in virtue of its mere exiftence.   Therefore it is no indication of purpofe, or mark of choice, or example of wifdom.   It cannot be otherwife.   Matter is what it is.

M. de la Place was aware that this affertion, fo contrary to a notion long and fondly entertained, would not be admitted without fome unwillingnefs.   He therefore gives a demonftration of his propofition.   He compares the action of gravity at different diftances with the illumination of a furface placed at different diftances from the radiant point.   Thus, let light, diffufed from the point A (fig. 77.) fhine through the hole B C D E, which we fhall fuppofe an inch fquare, and let this light be received on a furface $b\,c\,d\,e$ parallel to the hole, and twice as far from A.   We know that it will illuminate a furface of four fquare inches.   Therefore, fince all the light which covers thefe four inches came through a hole of one inch, the light in any part of the illuminated furface is four times weaker than in the hole, where it is four times denfer.   In like manner, the intenfity, and efficiency of any quality diffufed from A, and operating at twice the diftance, muft be four times lefs or weaker; and at thrice the diftance it muft be nine times weaker, &c. &c.

737. But there is not the leaft fhadow of proof here, nor any fimilarity, on which an argument may be founded. We have no conception of any degrees or magnitude in the intenfity of any fuch quality as gravitation, attraction, or repulfion, nor any meafure of them, except the very effect which we conceive them to produce. At a double diftance, gravity will generate one fourth of the velocity in the fame time. But this meafure of its ftrength or weaknefs has no connexion whatever with denfity, or figured magnitude, on which connexion the whole argument is founded. What can be meant by a double denfity of gravity ? What is this denfity ? It is purely a geometrical notion, and in our endeavour to conceive it with fome diftinctnefs, we find our thoughts employed upon a *certain determined number* of lines fpreading every way from the radiant point, and paffing through the hole B C D E at equal diftances among themfelves. It is very true that *the number* of thofe lines which will be intercepted by a given furface at twice the diftance will be only one fourth of the number intercepted by the fame furface at the fimple diftance. But I do not fee how this can apply to the intenfity of a mechanical force, unlefs we can confider this force as an effect, and can fhew the influence of each line in producing the effect which we call the force, and which we confider as the caufe of the phenomenon called gravitation. But if we take this view of it, it is no longer an example of his propofition—a force diffufed from a centre. For, in order to have the efficiency inverfely as the fquare of the diftance,

Pl 22.

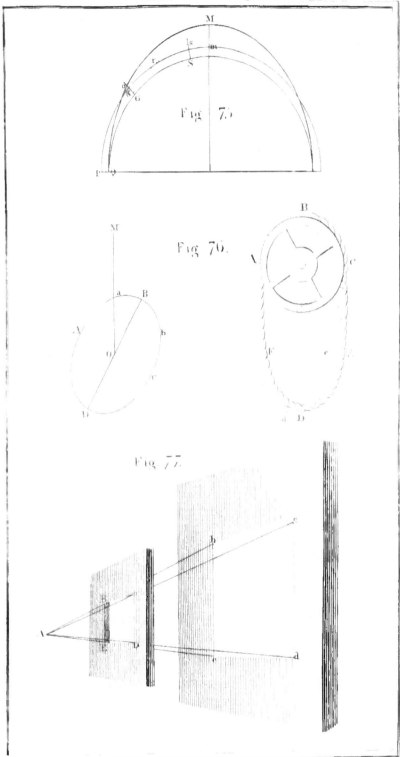

Fig. 75.

Fig. 76.

Fig. 77.

diftance, it is meafured by the number of efficient lines intercepted. Here it is plain that the efficiency of one of thofe lines is held to be equal at every diftance from the centre. Such incongruity is mere nonfenfe.

This conception of a bundle of lines is the fole foundation for any argument in the prefent cafe. La Place indeed tries to avoid this by a different way of expreffing his example. A certain quantity of light, fays he, goes through the hole. This is uniformly fpread over four times the furface, and muft be four times thinner fpread. But this, befides employing a gratuitous notion of light, which may be refufed, involves the fame notion of *difcrete* numerical quantity. If light be not conceived to confift of atoms, there can be no difference of denfity; and if we confider gravity in this way, we get into the hypothefis of mechanical impulfion, and are no longer confidering gravity as a primordial force or quality.

738. But this pretended demonftration is ftill more deficient in metaphyfical accuracy. The propofition to be demonftrated is, that the gravitation towards an atom of matter is in the inverfe duplicate ratio of the diftance, *in whatever point of fpace the gravitating atom is placed.* But, if we take our proof of the ratio from the conception of thefe lines, and their denfity, we at once admit that there are an infinity of fituations in which there is no gravitation at all, namely, in the intervals of thefe lines. The number of fituations in which the atom gra-

4 S

4 S   vitates

vitates is a mere nothing in comparifon with thofe in which it does not. We muft either fuppofe that both the quality and the furface influenced by it are continuous, uninterrupted,—or both muft be conceived as *difcrete* numerical quantities, the quality operating along a *certain number* of lines, and the furface confifting of a *certain number* of points. We muft take one of thefe views. But neither of them gives us any conception of a different energy at different diftances. If the furface be *continuous*, and the quality *every where* operative, there can be no difference of effect, unlefs we at once admit that the energy itfelf changes with the diftance. But this change can have no relation to a change of denfity, a thing altogether inconceivable in a continuous fubftance ; —where every place is full, there can be no more. On the other hand, if the quality be exerted only along certain lines, and the furface only contain a certain number of points, we can find no ground for eftablifhing any proportion.

739. The fimple and true ftate of the queftion is this. Suppofe only two indivifible atoms, or two mathematical points of fuch atoms, in the univerfe. If thefe atoms be fuppofed to attract each other, *wherever they are placed*, do we perceive any thing in our conception of this force that can enable us to fay that the attraction is equal or unequal, at different diftances ? For my own part, I know nothing. The gravitation, and its law of action, are mere phenomena, like the thing which

I call matter. This is equally unknown to me. I merely obferve certain relations, which have hitherto been conftant, and I am led by the conftitution of my mind to expect the continuation of thefe relations. My collection of fuch obfervations is my knowledge of its nature. This gravitation is one of them, and this is all that I know about it.

740. The obferved relations may be fuch that they involve certain confequences. This, in particular, has confequences that cannot be difputed. If gravitation in the ratio of $\frac{1}{x^2}$ be the primordial relation of all matter, and the fource of all others (which is a part of La Place's fyftem), it is impoffible that a particle compofed of fuch atoms can act with a force which decreafes more rapidly by an increafe of diftance. But there are many phenomena which indicate a much more rapid decreafe of force. Simple cohefion of folid bodies is one of thefe. The expanfion of fome exploding compofitions fhew the fame thing. We may add, that no compofition of fuch atoms can form repelling particles, nor give rife to many expanfive fluids, or indeed to any of the ordinary phenomena of elaftic bodies. But thefe things are not immediately before us, and we fhall have another and a better opportunity of confidering many things connected with this great queftion.

741. De la Place is not the firft perfon who has attempted a demonftration of this propofition. Dr David

4 S 2

vid

vid Gregory, in his valuable work on aftronomy, has done the fame thing, and nearly in the fame way with La Place. Leibnitz, in that ftrange letter to the editors of the Leipzig Review, in which he anfwers fome of Gregory's objections to his own theory of the celeftial motions, mentions an Italian profeffor who gave the fame argument, and affected to confider this ratio of planetary force as known to him before Newton's difcovery. Leibnitz thinks the argument a very good one, becaufe, mathematically fpeaking, it is the fame thing whether the rays be illuminative or attractive. If this be not nonfenfe, I do not know what is.—Several compilers of elements employ the fame argument. But nothing can be lefs to the purpofe. Nothing can be more illogical than to fpeak of demonftrating any primordial quality. Newton was furely more interefted in this queftion than any other perfon, and we may be certain that if he could have fupported his difcovery of this law of gravitation by any argument from higher principles, he moft certainly would have done it. But there is no trace of any attempt of the kind among his writings; doubtlefs becaufe he faw the folly of the attempt.

742. I truft that the reader will forgive me for taking up fo much of his time with this queftion. It feems to me of primary importance. Charged as I am with the inftruction of youth—the future hopes of our country—it is my bounden duty to guard their minds from every thing that I think hazardous. This is the more

incumbent

incumbent on me, when I fee natural philofophy calum-
niated, and accufed of lending her fupport to doctrines
which are the abhorrence of all the wife and good. I
cannot better difcharge this duty than by wiping off this
ftain, with which carelefs ignorance, or atheiftical perver-
fion, has disfigured the fair features of philofophy. I
was grieved when I firft faw M. de la Place, after having fo beautifully epitomifed the philofophy of Sir Ifaac
Newton, conclude his performance with fuch a marked
and ungraceful parody on the clofing reflections of our
illuftrious mafter ; and, as I warmly recommend this epitome to my pupils, it became the more neceffary to take
notice of the reprehenfible peculiarities which occur in
different parts of the work ; and particularly of this propofition, from which the materialifts feem to entertain
fuch hopes. Nor am I yet done with it. A demonftration has been recently offered, in a work which profeffes
to explain *the intimate conflitution of matter*, and to account for *all* the phenomena of the univerfe. This will
come in my way when we fhall be employed in confidering the force of cohefion. Till then, *requiefcat in pace.*

It is fomewhat amufing to remark how the authority
of Sir Ifaac Newton has been eagerly catched at by the
atheiftical fophifts to fupport their abject doctrines. While
fome hankering remained in France for the Atomiftic
philofophy, and there was any chance of bewildering the
imaginations, and mifleading the underftandings, of fuch
as wifhed to acquire a confident faith in the reveries of
Democritus and Epicurus, M. Diderot worked into a
better

better fhape the flovenly performance of Robinet, the *Syſléme de la Nature*, and affeded to deduce all his vibrations and vibratiuncles from the elaſtic æther of Sir Ifaac Newton, dreffing up the fcheme with mathematical theorems and corollaries. And thus, Newton, one of the moſt pious of mankind, was fet at the head of the atheiſtical feð.

But this mode, having had its day, is now paſſed, and is become obfolete—the tide has completely turned, and the æther is no longer wanted. But the fed would not quit their hold of Sir Ifaac Newton. The doðrine of univerfal fate is now founded on Newton's great difcovery of gravitation in the inverfe duplicate ratio of the diſtances. It is ſtill called the difcovery of the illuſtrious Engliſhman, and is paſſed from hand to hand with all the authority of his name.

743. But furely to us, the fcholars of Newton, the futility of this attempt is abundantly manifeſt. As the worthy pupils of our accompliſhed teacher, we will join with him in confidering univerfal gravitation as a noble proof of the exiſtence and fuperintendance of a SUPREME MIND, and a confpicuous mark of ITS tranfcendent wifdom. The difcovery of this relation between the particles of that matter of which the folar fyſtem confiſts is acknowledged, even by the materialiſts, to have fet Newton at the head of philofophers. They muſt therefore grant that it has fomething in it of peculiar excellence. Indeed whoever is able to follow the ſteps of Newton

over

over the magnificent fcene, muft be affected as he was, and muft pronounce ' all very good.' M. de la Place feems to think the lefs of man on account of the fmallnefs of his habitation. Is ABBA THULE, King of Pelew, a lefs noble creature than M. de la Place's CORSICAN MASTER ? Or, does the fmallnefs of this globe fhew that little has been done for man ?—It is peculiarly deferving of remark, that we fee many contrivances in this fyftem, which are of manifeft fubferviency to the enjoyments of man, and which do not appear to have any farther importance. Man is unqueftionably the lord of this lower world, and all things are placed under his feet. But we fee nothing to which man is exclufively fubfervient—nothing that is fuperior to man in excellence, fo far as we can judge of what is excellent—nothing but that wifdom, that power, and that beneficence, which feem to indicate and to characterife the Author and Conductor of the whole;—and, I may add, that it is not one of our fmalleft obligations to the Author of Nature, that He has given us thofe powers of mind which enable us to perceive and to be delighted with the fight of this bright emanation of all his perfections.

' *Sanctius his animal, mentifque capacius altæ,*
' *Finxit in effigiem moderantûm cuncta Deorum,*
' *Pronaque cum fpectent animalia cætera terram,*
' *Os homini fublime dedit, cœlumque tueri*
' *Juffit, et erectos ad fidera tollere vultus.*'

OVID.

Allow

Allow me to conclude in the words of Dr Halley.

' *Talia monſtrantem mecum celebrate Camœnis,*
' *Vos, ó cœlicolûm gaudentes neƈtare veſci,*
' NEWTONUM, *clauſi reſerantem ſcrinia Veri,*
' NEWTONUM, *Muſis charum, cui peƈtore puro*
' *Phœbus adeſt, totoque inceſſit Numine mentem,*
' *Nec fas eſt propiùs mortali attingere divos.* '

HALLEY.

END OF VOLUME FIRST.

Printed by D. Willifon, Craig's Clofe, Edinburgh.

RETURN TO ➡ CIRCULATION DEPARTMENT
202 Main Library

LOAN PERIOD 1 HOME USE	2	3
4	5	6

ALL BOOKS MAY BE RECALLED AFTER 7 DAYS
1-month loans may be renewed by calling 642-3405
6-month loans may be recharged by bringing books to Circulati
Renewals and recharges may be made 4 days prior to due date

DUE AS STAMPED BELOW

ET'D DEC 2 1981		
REC CIRC FEB 1 6 1986		
JUN 5 1987		
MAY 1 1 1987		

WS - #0070 - 301023 - C0 - 229/152/45 - PB - 9781313977876 - Gloss Lamination